Critical Acclaim for
FODOR'S AFFORDABLES

"The Fodor's series puts a premium on showing its readers a good time."

—*Philadelphia Inquirer*

"Concentrates on life's basics...without skimping on literary luxuries."

—*New York Daily News*

"Good helpmates for the cost-conscious traveler."

—*Detroit Free Press*

"These books succeed admirably; easy to follow and use, full of cost related information, practical advice and recommendations...maps are clear and easy to use."

—*Travel Books Worldwide*

"The books can help you fill the gap between deprivation and ostentation when you travel."

—*Dawson Sentinel*

W9-CHM-479

Fodor's Affordable Italy

SECOND
New
EDITION

Portions of this book appear in *Fodor's Italy*.

Fodor's Travel Publications, Inc.
New York • Toronto • London • Sydney • Auckland

Fodor's Affordable Italy

Editor: Kristin Moehlmann
Editorial Contributors: Robert Andrews, Barbara Walsh Angelillo, Roderick Conway Morris, Amy Hunter, Caroline Liou, Marcy Pritchard, George Sullivan, Phoebe Tait, Robert Tine
Creative Director: Fabrizio La Rocca
Cartographer: David Lindroth
Illustrator: Karl Tanner
Cover Photograph: Michel Gotin/Scope

Design: Vignelli Associates

Special Sales

Contents

Maps

How These Guides Will Save You Money

We would like to express our gratitude to Rob Andrews, Barbara Walsh Angelillo, and Roderick Conway Morris, for their patience, enthusiasm, and hard work in preparing this new edition.

The Affordables are aimed at people like you and me—people with discriminating tastes and limited budgets.

This is a new series that combines essential budget travel information with all the great editorial features of a Fodor's gold guide: quality writing, authoritative hotel and restaurant reviews, detailed exploring tours, and wonderful maps.

The idea behind these guides is that you, the budget traveler, have the same curiosity, good taste, and high expectations as those who travel first class, and you need information with the same depth and detail as readers of Fodor's gold guides. But as a budget traveler you also need to know about low-cost activities, meals, and lodging, and especially how to get around by train or bus.

Some of you, of course, will spend a bit more on a hotel with full service and amenities but will eat simply; others will be willing to go the hostel route in order to splurge on meals; yet others will save by sticking to public transportation and picnic lunches in order to do some serious shopping. We've tried to include enough options so that each of you can spend your money in the way you most enjoy spending it.

The Affordables, therefore, tell you about activities you can enjoy for free—or close to it. They also place a special emphasis on bargain shopping—what to buy and where to find it.

These are not guides for the hotdog-on-the-run-it's-okay-to-sleep-on-a-park-bench crowd, but for those of you who insist on at least two good, healthy meals a day and a safe, comfortable place to put your head at night. The hotels we recommend offer good value, and there are no dives, thank you—only clean, friendly places with an acceptable level of comfort, convenience, and charm. There's also a wide range of inexpensive and moderately priced dining options, mostly small, family-run restaurants offering healthy, home-cooked, regional cuisine.

Equally important, the Affordables organize all travel according to convenient train and bus routes, and include point-to-point directions that get you to each town and attraction. No matter how you're traveling—by car, train, or bus—your Fodor's Affordable will tell you exactly how to get there. We even locate train routes on maps—a feature every cost-conscious traveler will appreciate, but which (if we may wave our own flag) you won't find in any other budget guide.

Fodor's has made every effort to provide you with accurate, up-to-date information, but time always brings change, and consequently the publisher cannot accept responsibility for errors that may occur. Hours and admission fees in particular may change, so, when it matters to you, we encourage you to call ahead.

We also encourage you to write and share your travel experiences with us—pleasant and unpleasant. When a hotel or restaurant fails to live up to its billing, please let us know, and we'll investigate the complaint and revise our entries when the facts warrant it. Send your letters to The Editor, Fodor's Affordables, 201 East 50th Street, New York, NY 10022.

Have a great trip!

Michael Spring
Editorial Director

Fodor's Choice for Budget Travelers

No two people will agree on what makes a perfect vacation, but it's fun and helpful to know what others think. We hope you'll have a chance to experience some of Fodor's Choices yourself while visiting Italy. For detailed information about each entry, refer to the appropriate chapters (given in parentheses) within this guidebook.

Picturesque Villages and Towns

Alberobello (Apulia)

Asolo (Excursions from Venice)

Assisi (Umbria and the Marches)

Cinque Terre (The Italian Riviera)

San Gimignano (Tuscany)

Positano (Campania)

Taormina (Sicily)

Classical Sites

Agrigento (Sicily)

Aosta (Piedmont/Valle d'Aosta)

Herculaneum (Campania)

Ostia Antica (Rome)

Paestum (Campania)

Pompeii (Campania)

Roman Forum (Rome)

Siracusa (Sicily)

Works of Art

Byzantine mosaics in Ravenna (Emilia-Romagna)

Giotto's paintings in the Cappella Scrovegni, Padua (Excursions from Venice)

Leonardo's *Last Supper*, Milan (Milan, Lombardy, and the Lakes)

Michelangelo's *David* and *Slaves* (Florence)

Michelangelo's Sistine Chapel ceiling (Rome)

Raphael's Vatican *Stanze* (Rome)

Veronese's *Feast at the House of Levi* (Venice)

Churches

Basilica di Santa Croce, Lecce (Apulia)

Basilica di San Francesco, Assisi (Umbria and the Marches)

Basilica di San Marco (Venice)

Cathedral of Monreale (Sicily)

Duomo, Milan (Milan, Lombardy, and the Lakes)

Duomo, Orvieto (Umbria and the Marches)

Il Gesù (Rome)

San Miniato al Monte (Florence)

San Vitale, Ravenna (Emilia-Romagna)

Santa Maria Maggiore (Rome)

Museums

Accademia (Venice)

Galleria degli Uffizi (Florence)

Museo Archeologico, Naples (Campania)

Museo Egizio, Turin (Piedmont/Valle d'Aosta)

Museo Nazionale, Taranto (Apulia)

Museo Nazionale, Urbino (Umbria and the Marches)

Vatican Museums (Rome)

Architectural Gems

Baptistery (Florence)

Castel del Monte (Apulia)

Castello Sforzesco, Milan (Milan, Lombardy, and the Lakes)

Duomo, Siena (Tuscany)

Pantheon (Rome)

Palazzo Ducale (Venice)

Villa Rotonda, Vicenza (Excursions from Venice)

Bargain Dining

Beccherie, Treviso (Excursions from Venice) *Moderate*

La Caravella, Amalfi (Campania) *Moderate*

Da Gigio, (Venice) *Moderate*

Trattoria di Re Enzo, Bologna (Emilia-Romagna) *Moderate*

Zio, Rimini (Emilia-Romagna) *Moderate*

Angiolino (Florence) *Inexpensive*

Vecchia Roma da Severino (Rome) *Inexpensive*

Birreria Tempera (Rome) *Budget*

Shangai, Palermo (Sicily) *Budget*

Cafés

Baratti e Milano, Turin (Piedmont)

Caflisch, Naples (Campania)

Florian (Venice)

Pedrocchi, Padua (Excursions from Venice)

Tre Scalini (Rome)

Bargain Lodging

Agnello d'Oro, Bergamo (Milan, Lombardy, and the Lakes) *Moderate*

Bellettini (Florence) *Moderate*

Fasce, Santa Margherita Ligure (The Italian Riviera) *Moderate*

Locanda Fiorita (Venice) *Moderate*

Margutta (Rome) *Moderate*

Stella Maris, Levanto (The Italian Riviera) *Moderate*

Villa Giusy, Castellaneta Marina (Apulia) *Moderate*

Il Marzocco, Montepulciano (Tuscany) *Inexpensive*

Al Pescatore, Gallipoli (Apulia) *Inexpensive*

San Paolo, Ferrara (Emilia-Romagna) *Budget*

Villa Eva, Capri (Campania) *Budget*

Times to Treasure

Attending the open-air opera performances in Verona's Roman Arena (Excursions from Venice)

Cheering for the boats in Venice's Historic Regatta (Venice)

Experiencing the pageantry and excitement of Siena's Palio (Tuscany)

Looking down on the Bay of Naples from Villa Jovis, Capri (Campania)

Peeping through the Knights of Malta keyhole to see St. Peter's dome (Rome)

Rose-color walls in Assisi catching the autumn sun (Umbria and the Marches)

The sleepy view of Florence and the Arno valley from Via San Francesco, Fiesole (Florence)

Italy by Road

SWITZERLAND

AUSTRIA

HUNGARY

SLOVENIA

CROATIA

BOSNIA AND HERZEGOVINA

MONTENEGRO

FRANCE

Adriatic Sea

Ligurian Sea

Golfo di Venezia

Corsica

Elba

VALLE D'AOSTA

PIEMONTE

LOMBARDIA

TRENTINO-ALTO ADIGE/SÜDTIROL

FRIULI VENEZIA GIULIA

VENETO

LIGURIA

EMILIA-ROMAGNA

TOSCANA

UMBRIA

MARCHE

A L P S

THE DOLOMITES

Lago Maggiore

Lago di Como

Lago di Garda

Lugano

Mt. Blanc

Aosta

Turin

Asti

Novara

Pavia

Milan

Como

Bergamo

Brescia

San Remo

Genoa

Rapallo

La Spezia

Livorno

Pisa

Lucca

Pistoia

Florence

Siena

Arezzo

Perugia

Assisi

Orvieto

Viterbo

Civitavecchia

Ancona

Pescara

Rimini

Ravenna

Bologna

Ferrara

Modena

Parma

Mantua

Verona

Vicenza

Padua

Venice

Treviso

Trento

Bolzano

Cortina d'Ampezzo

Udine

SAN MARINO

Po

Adige

Arno

Tiber

A5

A4

A21

A26

A10

A12

A11

A1

A13

A14

A15

A22

A23

A24

A25

A6

A7

N

Italy by Rail

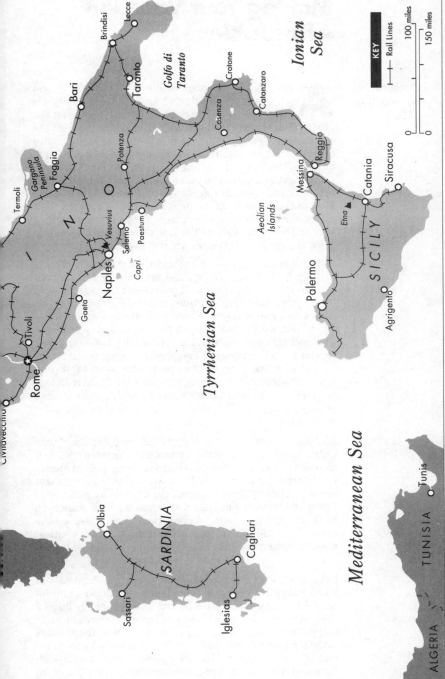

Making Your Vacation Affordable

*By Barbara
Walsh Angelillo*

Although the exchange rate between the dollar and the lira seesawed during 1993, it is generally expected to remain favorable for travelers from the United States and Canada. This will take the edge off the cost of touring Italy, still one of Europe's most expensive countries. After a painful economic slump in 1992 continued into 1993 and taxes rose even higher, Italians cut their spending drastically, a fact that made it more important for hoteliers and restaurateurs to attract tourist business. Most of them have seen the light and have abandoned their policy of continual price increases. They declare that they will do their best to hold the line as much as they can in 1994, though some increases are inevitable.

As a rule of thumb, you can expect to pay about a third more in Italy for lodging, dining, and museums/entertainment than in the United States. If businesses manage to keep prices at present levels, a tourist traveling at the equivalent of Fodor's Inexpensive level will have to spend an average of 180,000 lire per day per person for a stay in Rome. This includes one night and breakfast at a two-star hotel, two meals in trattorias or inexpensive eating places, a 24-hour tourist ticket for city transport, admissions to two museums or sites, and an evening at a disco or pub. Remember, you may get a discount on hotel rates simply for the asking, mainly during the off-season or when business is slack. It's worth a try.

By 1994, Italians should be forging the "new Republic" they called for after corruption scandals and a vigorous political shakeup in 1993 sent the Old Guard packing and set electoral reforms in motion. Under a more stable government made possible by these changes, the day-to-day business of living and traveling in Italy may become a little easier. In 1993, for instance, second-class cars were added to the crack ETR-450 trains that connect major Italian cities, making them more affordable for budget-conscious travelers.

Other good news for 1994 is the promised implementation of a new policy regarding opening hours for state-run museums. Up to now, national museums have generally limited their hours to a 9 to 2 schedule, closing on Monday. Tourists and residents alike have long complained that these hours make it extremely difficult for them to plan visits to museums of their choice. Of Rome's 20-or-so museums and galleries, only a few are open at other times. By 1994, state museums nationwide should be staying open longer, in many cases seven days a week. Such amenities as museum cafés, cafeterias, and shops have been promised, too.

Rome is also making it cheaper to visit city museums with the Museidoncard. Issued for periods of two, four, or seven days, and costing from 13,000 to 48,000 lire, the card is valid for such city museums as the Museo Capitolino, the Museo Baracco, Museo della Civiltà Romana, and monuments such as the Ara Pacis and Trajan's Market. Since entrance fees to national museums and to the Vatican Museums are not covered, prospective purchasers should make sure that they will get their money's worth by adding up the fees of the museums they want to visit. Card-holders can also book visits to more than 30 ancient sites in Rome, including temples, tombs, and circuses, that are normally closed to the public (tel. 1678/61248 toll-free). The Museidoncard can be purchased at any of the participating museums, at hotels, at Italian Touring Club offices in Rome, at INA-Banca offices, and at many tobacconists. Inquire about similar cards in Turin and Milan.

One of Rome's most important museums, the Museo Nazionale Romano, which has a stunning collection of Roman antiquities, is finally getting its act together, after decades of dithering about how to organize the works in three separate buildings, including the museum's original home in the former monastery of Santa Maria degli Angeli (on the site of the ancient Roman Baths of Diocletian). Nearby Palazzo Massimo has been restored to house part of the collection and the grand opening was scheduled for autumn 1993. A third historic building, Palazzo Altemps, near Piazza Navona, will hold the remainder, but will probably not open until late 1994.

After a long battle with the ministry in charge of preserving Italy's ancient monuments, the Rome Opera has won permission to continue staging spectacular outdoor productions among the towering ruins of the Baths of Caracalla. The performances, a highlight of the Roman summer and a major tourist attraction, will take place on a new site within the grounds, only slightly removed from the imposing 3rd-century AD structures.

Sorrento, Taormina, and Rimini are among the Italian cities that have applied for licenses to open gambling casinos; if authorization comes through, there may be a casino in almost every one of Italy's 20 regions in 1994.

Art lovers should look for important exhibitions in connection with the centenaries of some of Italy's celebrated artists. The year 1994 is the 500th anniversary of the death of Florentine painter Domenico Ghirlandaio and of the birth of Jacopo Caracci, known as Pontormo. Both were active in Florence, where anniversary exhibitions will be held. It is unlikely that the Bolognese will let the 500th anniversary of the death of sculptor Niccolo dell'Arca go unnoticed; although he was a southerner, he worked mainly in Bologna. A quincentenary is coming up for Melozzo da Forlì, who was active chiefly in Urbino, Loreto, and Rome. And Perugia, Siena, and Rome will surely mark the 550th anniversary of the birth of Pinturicchio, painter of sumptuous fresco cycles.

Some rebuilding in 1994 and continued restorations will remind visitors of the tragic car bomb that damaged the Galleria degli Uffizi in Florence in May 1993, though the museum reopened in record time. Florentines mourned the death of five people and lamented damage (from flying glass) to many works, even as they rejoiced that the museum's most precious masterpieces escaped harm.

At press time, telephone numbers in Rome are in the process of changing from seven or fewer digits to eight. If you dial an affected number, you will hear a recorded message giving you the new number. If you don't speak Italian and are calling from the United States, ask the international operator for assistance. If you're in Italy, a hotel staff, bilingual friend, or even a bystander may be able to help.

Money-saving Tips

- **Choose when to travel.** European tourism peaks over the summer, and prices are accordingly high. If you're at all flexible, plan to travel during the low season—between November and March—or else the shoulder season—April, May, and mid-September through October. Since many people begin their vacations on Friday or Saturday, airfares are usually more expensive on weekends, so try to travel midweek. Also, since city hotels are often filled with business travelers during the week, you may save money by arranging to stop in big cities over the weekend when the rates may be less expensive. (*See* When to Go in Chapter 1.)

- **Consult discount travel clubs and agencies.** Before going away, you may want to look into organizations that specialize in discounted hotel and airfares. Some travel clubs are especially good at arranging cut-rate deals with suppliers. Other clubs and agencies offer smaller discounts through partial rebates of commissions. (*See* From North America by Plane in Chapter 1.)

- **Stay in cheaper regions.** You can save money by spending more time off-the-beaten track, in regions that tend to accommodate fewer tourists. This means less time in Venice and on the Riviera, but vacations in the countryside can be equally rewarding.

- **Avoid the single supplement fee.** Solo travelers looking to reduce their expenses can join the **Travel Companion Exchange** (Box 833, Amityville, NY 11701, tel. 516/454–0880), a well-established organization that helps singles find traveling companions, largely by means of a newsletter (six times yearly, 30-plus pages per issue) devoted to travel tips and "Travel Personals," in which prospective travelers describe themselves, their travel plans, and travel style (budget or deluxe, compulsive museum-going or dedicated window-shopping, smoking or nonsmoking). A six-month membership costs $36 if you're looking for a same-sex match, or $66 for an opposite-sex match, and includes six back issues by return mail; yearly rates are $60 and $120. A sample copy of the newsletter, with a full explanation of services, is available for $4. If you're traveling alone on a group tour, note that **Cosmos** is one of only a few tour operators that attempts to match singles willing to share. (*See* Tours and Packages in Chapter 1.)

- **Think about buying the *Half Price Europe* book.** This includes discount coupons for hotels, restaurants, rental cars, shops, tours, and special events. However, it's fairly expensive—$39 at the time of writing, plus postage and handling—and some travel experts feel that the hotel coupons are the only worthwhile deals in the book. Even so, if you have your heart set on a specific hotel at a particular time, you may be disappointed; many hotels offer a limited number of rooms at discount prices. Send $39 (plus $2.95 for shipping and handling) to **Entertainment Publications** (Box 1014, Trumbull, CT 06611, tel. 800/477–3234), or order by phone; MasterCard and Visa accepted.

- **Make a budget.** Allow yourself a certain amount of spending money each day and try not to exceed that limit. There's no reason to set the same limit every day; you may want to live the spartan life for a while, then indulge yourself later. But make a habit of adhering to your daily allowances, so the cost of your trip can be kept below a predetermined sum.

- **Categorize expenses.** Travel expenses generally fall into these categories: accommodation, food, transportation, cultural and recreational activities, and gifts and souvenirs. Use these headings as guidelines for setting your priorities when you're deciding where you want to cut back. Eating sandwiches and staying at a youth hostel, for example, may save enough for a concert or a night at the theater.

- **Ask about discounts.** Not all discounts are advertised, so make an effort to ask about discounts before paying. Watch for weekend rates, student and age-related reductions, and special promotions.

- **Be creative about accommodations.** Though Italy offers an abundance of inexpensive hotels, they are *not* your only budget-wise option. Other possibilities include licensed rooming houses (*affittacamere*), hostels, and religious institutions.

  Hotel rooms with shower or bath cost more than rooms with neither. But opting to go without facilities in your room isn't always the least expensive way to go: You may have to pay extra to bathe or shower down the hall—so inquire about charges in advance. (*See* Lodging in Chapter 1.)

- **Go camping.** If you enjoy the outdoors, try spending some or all of your nights at the very affordable campsites located throughout Italy. Equipment is likely to be less expensive at home, so buy what you need before you go.

- **Save money on food.** Trattorias and pizzerias offer hearty food and drink at affordable prices. You're likely to find less expensive restaurants in the countryside, or on the outskirts of town, away from the heavily populated areas. You can also buy your food at a store, and find an attractive park or roadside spot and have a picnic lunch or an early dinner. In big cities especially, this is the best way to lower dining expenses without resorting to fast food. (*See* Dining in Chapter 1.)

- **Save on money exchange.** Inquire with someone at your hotel or at a tourist office about banks that specialize in changing money. Whatever you do, don't cash your traveler's checks at shops, hotels, or tourist attractions. (*See* Taking Money Abroad in Chapter 1.)

- **Don't make phone calls from your hotel.** If you make a call from your hotel room, you'll have to pay a surcharge. When calling home, prepare yourself with lots of change, *gettoni* (tokens), or a phone card, then find a pay phone and dial your call directly. This may be inconvenient, but it's cheaper than an operator-assisted call. Better yet, to call home, use an AT&T or similar card.

- **Shop wisely.** Some of the best bargains can be found at street markets. Cities, with their high prices and attractive items, are often frustrating for budget travelers, but ask at your hotel or at the tourist office about the flea markets around town.

- **Consider your rail-travel needs.** Individual tickets aren't always more expensive than the pass you may be considering. If you don't plan to cover a lot of ground, it can be cheaper to pay for your trips individually. (*See* Rail Passes *and* Student and Youth Travel in Chapter 1.)

- **Travel at night.** Keep in mind that overnight rail travel saves money on accommodations. But if you decide to spend the night on a train, take the necessary precautions against thieves, such as locking your bag to the rack and sleeping on top of your wallet or valuables.

- **Consider a public-transportation pass.** In some cities you can buy passes for unlimited travel, good for a certain number of days on city buses and trains; in others, you can save money by purchasing several tickets at a time. If you plan to rely at all on public transportation in urban areas, passes or multiple purchases will save you money.

- **Compare car-rental companies.** The multinational American companies don't always offer the best deals. You may do better with North American tour operators and wholesalers that arrange for cars from European rental companies. Weekly touring packages offer unlimited mileage and a much better rate than day-to-day rentals. To qualify for most of these touring rates, you need to keep the car for a set number of days, so plan your itinerary accordingly. (*See* Getting Around in Chapter 1.)

- **Find out about the arts for free.** Before spending your money on high-priced culture and entertainment, find out what's being offered for free. Local newspapers and magazines are good sources. While theater and concert tickets are expensive, performances in churches are often free, as are the festas and fireworks extravaganzas staged outdoors at tourist venues in summer.

1 Essential Information

Before You Go

Government Tourist Offices

In the U.S. Contact the Italian Government Travel Office at 630 5th Ave., Suite 1565, New York, NY 10111, tel. 212/245–4822; 500 N. Michigan Ave., Chicago, IL 60611, tel. 312/644–0990; 12400 Wilshire Blvd., Suite 550, Los Angeles, CA 90025, tel. 310/820–0098.

The Department of State's **Citizens Emergency Center** issues Consular Information Sheets, which cover any crime, security, and health risks that may exist in a country, as well as embassy locations, entry requirements, currency regulations, and other routine matters. For the latest information, stop at any passport office, consulate, or embassy; call the interactive hotline (tel. 202/647–5225); or, with your PC's modem, tap into the Bureau of Consular Affairs' computer bulletin board (tel. 202/647–9225).

In Canada 1 Place Ville Marie, Montréal, Québec H3B 3M9, tel. 514/866–7667.

In the U.K. 1 Princes St., London W1R 8AY England, tel. 071/408–1254.

Tours and Packages

Should you buy your travel arrangements to Italy packaged or do it yourself? There are advantages either way. Buying packaged arrangements saves you money, particularly if you find a program that includes exactly the features you want. You also get a pretty good idea of what your trip will cost from the outset. Generally, there are two options: escorted tours and independent packages.

Escorted tours are most often via motorcoach, with a tour director in charge. Your baggage is handled, your time rigorously scheduled, amd most meals planned. Escorted tours are therefore the most hassle-free way to see a destination, as well as generally the least expensive. Independent packages allow flexibility. They generally include airline travel and hotels, with other options available, such as sightseeing, car rental, and excursions. Independent packages are usually more expensive than escorted tours, but your time is your own.

Travel agents are the best source of information for both tours and independent packages. They should have a large selection available, and the cost to you is the same as buying direct. Whatever program you ultimately choose, be sure to find out exactly what is included: taxes, tips, transfers, meals, baggage handling, ground transportation, entertainment, excursions, sports or recreation (and rental equipment if necessary). Ask about the level of hotel used, its location, the size of its rooms, the kind of beds, and such amenities as pool, room service, or programs for children, if they're important to you. Find out the operator's cancellation penalties. Nearly everyone charges them and the only way to avoid them is to buy trip-cancellation insurance (*see* Trip Insurance, *below*). Also ask about the single supplement, a surcharge assessed to solo travelers. Some operators do not make you pay it if you agree to be matched with a roommate of the same sex, even if one is not found by departure time. Remember that a program that has features you won't use, whether for rented sporting equipment or discounted museum admissions, may not be the most cost-wise choice for you. Don't buy a Rolls-Royce, even at a reduced price, if all you want is a Chevy!

Fully Escorted Tours Escorted tours are usually sold in three categories: deluxe, first-class, and tourist or budget class. The most important differences are the price, of course, and the level of accommodations. Some operators specialize in one category, while others offer a range.

Even deluxe tours can be affordable in that they give you the best available accommodations at the best available price; contact **American Express Vacations** (300 Pinnacle Way, Norcross, GA 30093, tel. 800/241–1700), **Central Holiday Tours** (206 Central Ave., Jersey City, NJ 07307, tel. 201/798–5777 or 800/935–5000), **Donna Franca Tours** (470 Commonwealth Ave., Boston, MA 02215, tel. 617/227–3111 or 800/225–6290), **Globus-Gateway** (95-25 Queens Blvd., Rego Park, NY 11374, tel. 800/221–0090), **Maupintour** (Box 807, Lawrence, KS 66044, tel. 913/843–1211 or 800/255–4266), **Perillo Tours** (577 Chestnut Ridge Rd., Woodcliff Lake, NJ 07675, tel. 201/307–1234 and 800/431–1515), **Tauck Tours** (11 Wilton Rd., Westport, CT 06881, tel. 203/226–6911 or 800/468–2825), and **Trafalgar Tours** (21 E. 26th St., New York, NY 10010, tel. 212/689–8977 or 800/854–0103). For tourist-class programs, try **Cosmos**, a sister company of Globus (*see above*), and the "Cost Savers" of **Trafalgar** Tours (*see above*).

Most itineraries are jam-packed with sightseeing, so you see a lot in a short amount of time (usually one place per day). To judge just how fast-paced the tour is, review the itinerary carefully. If you are in a different hotel each night, you will be getting up early each day to head out, travel to your next destination, do some sightseeing, have dinner, and go to bed; then you'll start all over again. If you want some free time, make sure it's mentioned in the tour brochure; if you want to be escorted to every meal, confirm that any tour you consider does that. Also, when comparing programs, be sure to find out if the motorcoach is air-conditioned and has a restroom on board. Make your choice based on price and stops on the itinerary.

Independent Packages Independent packages, which travel agents call FITs (for foreign independent travel), are offered by airlines, tour operators who may also do escorted programs, and any number of other companies from large, established firms to small, new entrepreneurs. Contact **American Airlines Fly AAway Vacations** (tel. 800/321–2121), **American Express Vacations** (*see above*), **CIT Tours** (tel. 800/248–8687), **Continental's Grand Destinations** (tel. 800/634–5555), **DER Tours** (11933 Wilshire Blvd., Los Angeles, CA 90025, tel. 800/782–2424 or 310/479–4140), **Italiatour** (tel. 800/237–0517), and **United Airlines' Vacation Planning Center** (tel. 800/328–6877).

These programs come in a wide range of prices based on levels of luxury and options—in addition to hotel and airfare, sightseeing, car rental, transfers, admission to local attractions, and other extras may be offered. Again, base your choice on what's available at your budget for the destinations you want to visit.

Special-Interest Travel Special-interest programs may be fully escorted or independent. Some require a certain amount of expertise, but most are for the average traveler with an interest in the subject, and they are usually hosted by experts. When the program is escorted, it enjoys the advantages and disadvantages of all escorted programs; because your fellow travelers are apt to be passionate or knowledgeable about the subject, they can prove as enjoyable a part of your travel experience as the destination itself. The price range is wide, but the cost is usually higher—sometimes a lot higher—than for ordinary escorted tours and packages, because of the expert guiding and special activities.

Art/Architecture **Esplanade Tours** (581 Boylston St., Boston, MA 02116, tel. 617/266–7465 or 800/628–4893) offers tours that focus on Italy's rich artistic heritage.

Biking **Backroads** (1516 5th St., Suite Q333, Berkeley, CA 94710–1740, tel. 510/527–1555 or 800/BIKE–TRIP) has trips for all levels of ability, with inn accommodations and a sag wagon just in case the hills are too much for you.

Wine/Cuisine **Donna Franca Tours** (*see above*) has an Italian cooking program in Venice.

When to Go

The main tourist season in Italy, when hotel rates are highest and discounted airfares are hard to come by, begins in late spring, includes the summer months, and ends in early fall. Hotel rates are usually lower from mid-October through early April, except in such cities as Milan or Bologna, where business activities and trade fairs keep hotel rooms occupied for part of or most of the year (even in those cities, however, you can sometimes get lower rates on weekends). During the low season, particularly in November, February, and March, special discount programs are offered by most U.S. airlines with European destinations. Often the airfares offered are only a little more than half the cost of normal high season rates.

Be aware that foreign tourists crowd the major art cities at Easter, when Italians flock to resorts and to the country. From March through May, busloads of eager schoolchildren on excursions take cities of artistic and historical interest by storm.

Traveling in August can sometimes bring you savings, since nearly all Italians desert their cities for the beach or mountains during this month, and some hoteliers offer lower rates to tourists in an attempt to keep business up. When making hotel reservations, especially in such cities as Rome and Milan, ask specifically if there are special bargain rates. But August in Italy has its drawbacks: The heat can be oppressive, and vacationing Italians cram roads, trains, and planes on their way to shore and mountain resorts. All this is especially true around the August 15 national holiday, when cities are deserted and many restaurants and shops are closed.

Except for a few year-round resorts, such as Taormina and some towns on the Italian Riviera, coastal resorts usually close up tight from October or November to April; they're at their best in June and September, when everything is open but uncrowded.

The best months for sightseeing are April, May, June, September, and October, when the weather is usually pleasant and not too hot. In general, the northern half of the peninsula and the entire Adriatic Coast, with the exception of Apulia, are rainier than the rest of Italy.

The hottest months are July and August, when brief afternoon thunderstorms are common in inland areas. Winters are relatively mild in most places on the main tourist circuit but always include some rainy spells.

Climate The following are average daily maximum and minimum temperatures for major cities in Italy.

Milan	Jan.	40F	5C	May	74F	23C	Sept.	75F	24C
		32	0		57	14		61	16
	Feb.	46F	8C	June	80F	27C	Oct.	63F	17C
		35	2		63	17		52	11
	Mar.	56F	13C	July	84F	29C	Nov.	51F	10C
		43	6		67	20		43	6
	Apr.	65F	18C	Aug.	82F	28C	Dec.	43F	6C
		49	10		66	19		35	2

Rome	Jan.	52F	11C	May	74F	23C	Sept.	79F	26C
		40	5		56	13		62	17
	Feb.	55F	13C	June	82F	28C	Oct.	71F	22C
		42	6		63	17		55	13
	Mar.	59F	15C	July	87F	30C	Nov.	61F	16C
		45	7		67	20		49	10
	Apr.	66F	19C	Aug.	86F	30C	Dec.	55F	13C
		50	10		67	20		44	6

Venice	Jan.	42F	6C	May	70F	21C	Sept.	75F	24C
		33	1		56	13		61	16
	Feb.	46F	8C	June	76F	25C	Oct.	65F	19C
		35	2		63	17		53	12
	Mar.	53F	12C	July	81F	27C	Nov.	53F	12C
		41	5		66	19		44	7
	Apr.	62F	17C	Aug.	80F	27C	Dec.	46F	8C
		49	10		65	19		37	3

Information Sources For current weather conditions for cities in the United States and abroad, plus the local time and helpful travel tips, call the **Weather Channel Connection** (tel. 900/WEATHER; 95¢ per minute) from a touch-tone phone.

Festivals and Seasonal Events

Contact the **Italian Government Travel Office** for exact dates and further information.

January 5–6 **Epiphany Celebrations.** Roman Catholic Epiphany celebrations and decorations are evident throughout Italy. Notable is the Epiphany Fair at Piazza Navona in Rome.

Late January **Festival of Italian Popular Song.** A three-day festival in San Remo, this is actually a competition, with the latest Italian songs performed by leading artists.

February **Carnival in Viareggio.** Masked pageants, fireworks, a flower show, and parades are among the festivities along the Tuscan Riviera.

Early February   **Almond Blossom Festival** in Agrigento. A week of folk music and dancing, with groups from many countries, in the Valley of the Temples.
Carnival in Venice. A big do in the 18th century, revived in the last half of the 20th century, this includes plays, masked balls, fireworks, and indoor and outdoor happenings of every sort.

Good Friday   In Rome, a torchlit nighttime **Good Friday Procession** led by
(April 1, 1994)   the Pope winds from the Colosseum past the Forum and up the Palatine Hill.

Easter Sunday   The **Scoppio del Carro,** or "Explosion of the Cart," in Florence,
(April 3, 1994)   is a cartful of fireworks in the Cathedral Square, set off by a mechanical dove released from the altar during High Mass.

Late April–   The **Florence May Music Festival** is the oldest and most pres-
Early July   tigious Italian festival of the performing arts.

Mid-May   **Race of the Candles.** This procession, in local costume, leads to the top of Mount Ingino in Gubbio.

Late May   The **Palio of the Archers** is a medieval crossbow contest in Gubbio.

Early June   The **Battle of the Bridge,** in Pisa, is a medieval parade and contest.
The **Regatta of the Great Maritime Republics** sees keen competition among the four former maritime republics—Amalfi, Genoa, Pisa, and Venice.

Late June   **Soccer Games in 16th-Century Costume,** in Florence, commemorate a match played in 1530. Festivities include fireworks.

Late June–   The **Festival of Two Worlds,** in Spoleto, is a famous performing-
Early July   arts festival.

Early July and   The **Palio Horse Race,** in Siena, is a colorful bareback horse race
Mid-August   with participants competing for the *palio* (banner).

Early July–   The **Arena of Verona Outdoor Opera Season** heralds spectacular
Late August   productions in the 22,000-seat Roman amphitheater of Verona.

Mid-July   The **Feast of the Redeemer** is a procession of gondolas and other craft, commemorating the end of the epidemic of 1575 in Venice. The fireworks over the lagoon are spectacular.

Early August   The **Joust of the Quintana** is a historical pageant in Ascoli Piceno.

Late August–   The **Siena Music Week** features opera, concerts, and chamber
Early September   music.
The **Venice Film Festival,** oldest of the international film festivals, takes place mostly on the Lido.

Late August–   The **Stresa Musical Weeks** comprise a series of concerts and
Mid-September   recitals in Stresa.

Early September   The **Historic Regatta** includes a traditional competition between two-oar gondolas in Venice.
The **Joust of the Saracen** is a tilting contest with knights in 13th-century armor in Arezzo.

Early October   Alba's **100 Towers Tournament** features costumes and races and is held simultaneously with the **Truffle Fair,** a food fair centered on the white truffle.

October 4   The **Feast of St. Francis** is celebrated in Assisi, his birthplace.

Early December The **Feast of St. Ambrose,** in Milan, officially opens La Scala Opera House.

December–June The **Opera Season** is in full swing at La Scala in Milan and elsewhere, notably in Turin, Rome, Naples, Parma, and Genoa.

What to Pack

Clothing The weather is considerably milder in Italy all year round than it is in the north and central United States or Great Britain. In summer, stick with clothing that's as light as possible, although a sweater or woolen stole may be necessary in the cool of the evening, even during the hot months. Brief summer afternoon thunderstorms are common in Rome and inland cities, so carry a folding umbrella. And if you go into the mountains, you will find the evenings there quite chilly. During the winter a medium-weight coat and a raincoat will stand you in good stead in Rome and farther south. Northern Italy calls for heavier clothes, gloves, hats, and boots. Even in Rome and other milder areas, central heating may not be up to your standards and interiors can be cold and damp; take wools rather than sheer fabrics, flannel rather than flimsy nightwear, and boots or shoes that can accommodate socks rather than dainty pumps. As a matter of fact, pack sturdy walking shoes, preferably with crepe or rubber soles, at any time of the year, because cobblestone streets and gravel paths are common and can be murder on both feet and footwear.

In general, Italians dress well and are not sloppy. They do not usually wear shorts in the city, unless longish bermudas happen to be in fashion. Even when dressed casually or informally, they are careful about the way they look, which is why so few restaurants establish dress codes. Men aren't required to wear ties or jackets anywhere, except in some of the grander hotel dining rooms and top-level restaurants. Formal wear is the exception rather than the rule at the opera nowadays, though people in expensive seats usually do get dressed up.

Dress codes are strict for visits to churches–especially St. Peter's in Rome and St. Mark's in Venice–and to the Vatican Museums. Women must cover bare shoulders and arms–a shawl will do—but no longer need cover their heads. Shorts are taboo for both men and women. For the huge general papal audiences, no rules of dress apply other than those of common sense. For other types of audience, the Vatican Information Office will give requirements.

Miscellaneous To protect yourself against purse snatchers and pickpockets, wear a money belt or a pouch around the neck. If you carry a handbag (or camera bag), make it a handbag with long straps that you can sling across your body bandolier-style. Take your own soap, because many budget hotels do not provide soap or else give guests only one tiny bar per room. Also, travel with a wash cloth, or face flannel, if you use one; Italian hotels generally supply only towels. If you have a health problem that requires you to take a prescription drug, pack enough to last the duration of the trip, or have your doctor write a prescription using the drug's generic name, since the brand name may not be the same. Also bring extra pairs of eyeglasses, sunglasses, and contact lenses. And don't forget to pack a list of the addresses of offices that supply refunds for lost or stolen traveler's checks.

Electricity The electrical current in most of Italy is 220 volts, 50 cycles alternating current (AC); the United States runs on 110-volt, 60-cycle AC current. Unlike wall outlets in the United States, which accept plugs that have two flat prongs, Italian outlets take continental-type plugs, with two round prongs.

Adapters, To plug in U.S.-made appliances abroad, you'll need an adapter
Converters, plug. To reduce the voltage entering the appliance from 220 to
Transformers 110 volts, you'll also need a converter, unless it is a dual-voltage appliance, made for travel. There are converters for high-wattage appliances (such as hair dryers), low-wattage items (such as electric toothbrushes and razors), and combination models. Hotels sometimes have outlets marked "For Shavers Only" near the sink; these are 110-volt outlets for low-wattage appliances: don't use them for a high-wattage appliance. For more information, get a copy of the free brochure "Foreign Electricity is No Deep Dark Secret," published by adapter-converter manufacturer Franzus (Murtha Industrial Park, Box 142, Beacon Falls, CT 06403, tel. 203/723–6664; send a stamped, self-addressed envelope when ordering).

Luggage Free baggage allowances on an airline depend on the airline,
Regulations the route, and the class of your ticket. In general, on domestic flights and on international flights between the United States and foreign destinations, you are entitled to check two bags—neither exceeding 62 inches, or 158 centimeters (length + width + height), or weighing more than 70 pounds (32 kilograms). A third piece may be taken aboard as a carryon; its total dimensions are generally limited to less than 45 inches (114 centimeters), so it will fit easily under the seat in front of you or in the overhead compartment. There are variations, so ask in advance. The only rule, a Federal Aviation Administration safety regulation that pertains to carry-on baggage on U.S. airlines, requires only that carryons be properly stowed and allows the airline to limit allowances and tailor them to different aircraft and operational conditions. Charges for excess, oversize, or overweight pieces vary, so inquire before you pack.

If you are flying between two foreign destinations, note that baggage allowances may be determined not by the piece method but by the weight method, which generally allows 88 pounds (40 kilograms) of luggage in first class, 66 pounds (30 kilograms) in business class, and 44 pounds (20 kilograms) in economy. If your flight between two cities abroad *connects* with your transatlantic flight, the piece method still applies.

Safeguarding Your Before leaving home, itemize your bags' contents and their
Luggage worth; this list will help you estimate the extent of your loss if your bags go astray. To minimize that risk, tag them inside and out with your name, address, and phone number. (If you use your home address, cover it so that potential thieves can't see it.) At check-in, make sure that the tag attached by baggage handlers bears the correct three-letter code for your destination. If your bags do not arrive with you, or if you detect damage, do not leave the airport until you've filed a written report with the airline.

Taking Money Abroad

Traveler's Checks Although you will want plenty of cash when visiting small cities or rural areas, traveler's checks are usually preferable. The most widely recognized are **American Express, Barclay's,**

Thomas Cook, and those issued by major commercial banks such as **Citibank** and **Bank of America.** American Express also issues *Traveler's Cheques for Two*, which can be signed and used by you or your traveling companion. Some checks are free: usually the issuing company or the bank at which you make your purchase charges 1% of the checks' face value as a fee. Be sure to buy a few checks in small denominations to cash toward the end of your trip, when you don't want to be left with more foreign currency than you can spend. Always record the numbers of checks as you spend them, and keep this list separate from the checks.

Currency Exchange Before any foreign trip, pay attention to how the dollar is doing vis-à-vis the local currency. If it is losing strength, try to pay as many travel bills as possible in advance, especially the big ones. If it is getting stronger, pay for costly items overseas, and use your credit card whenever possible—you'll come out ahead, whether the exchange rate at which your purchase is calculated is the one in effect the day the vendor's bank abroad processes the charge or the one prevailing on the day the charge company's service center processes it at home.

Banks and bank-operated exchange booths, including those at airports and railroad stations, tend to be the best places to change money. Hotels, stores, and privately run exchange firms typically offer less favorable rates or tack on excessive commissions. (Not all banks exchange currency: Look for the *Cambio* sign on the window and go directly to the Cambio teller inside.) Even so, it's not a good idea to change a large amount at the first currency-exchange booth you see upon arrival; wait until you're familiar with the going exchange. Also, to avoid lines at airport exchange booths, arrive with a small amount of Italian currency already in your pocket. **Thomas Cook Currency Services** (630 5th Ave., New York, NY 10111, tel. 212/757–6915) supplies foreign currency by mail.

Getting Money from Home

Cash Machines Automated-teller machines (ATMs) are proliferating; many are tied to international networks such as **Cirrus** and **Plus.** You can use your bank card at ATMs away from home to withdraw money from an account and get cash advances on a credit-card account (providing your card has been programmed with a personal identification number, or PIN). Check in advance on limits on withdrawals and cash advances within specified periods. Ask whether your bank-card or credit-card PIN number will need to be reprogrammed for use in the area you'll be visiting—a possibility if the number has more than four digits. Remember that on cash advances you are charged interest from the day you get the money from ATMs as well as from tellers. And note that, although transaction fees for ATM withdrawals abroad will probably be higher than fees for withdrawals at home, Cirrus and Plus exchange rates tend to be good.

Be sure to plan ahead: Obtain ATM locations and the names of affiliated cash-machine networks before departure. For specific foreign Cirrus locations, call 800/4–CIRRUS; for foreign Plus locations, consult the Plus directory at your local bank.

American Express Cardholder Services The company's **Express Cash** system lets you withdraw cash and/or traveler's checks from a worldwide network of 57,000 American Express dispensers and participating bank ATMs.

You must *enroll first* (call 800/CASH–NOW for a form and allow two weeks for processing). Withdrawals are charged not to your card but to a designated bank account. You can withdraw up to $1,000 per seven-day period on the basic card, more if your card is gold or platinum. There is a 2% fee (minimum $2.50, maximum $10) for each cash transaction, and a 1% fee for traveler's checks (except for the platinum card), which are available only from American Express dispensers.

At AmEx offices, cardholders can also cash up to $1,000 worth of personal checks in any seven-day period (21 days abroad); of this, $200 (more if available) can be claimed in cash, with the balance paid in traveler's checks (subject to the 1% fee). Higher limits apply to gold and platinum cards.

Wiring Money You don't have to be a cardholder to send or receive an **American Express MoneyGram** for up to $10,000. To send one, go to an American Express MoneyGram agent, pay up to $1,000 with a credit card and anything over that in cash, and phone a transaction reference number to your intended recipient, who needs only present identification and the reference number to the nearest MoneyGram agent to pick up the cash. There are MoneyGram agents in more than 60 countries (call 800/926–9400 for locations). Fees range from 5% to 10%, depending on the amount and how you pay. You can't use American Express, which is really a convenience card—only Discover, Master-Card, and Visa credit cards.

You can also use **Western Union.** To wire money, take either cash or a check to the nearest office. (Or you can order the money sent by phone, using a credit card.) Money sent from the United States or Canada will be available for pickup at agent locations in Italy within minutes; fees are roughly 5%–10%. Note that once the money is in the system it can be picked up at *any* location. You don't have to miss your train waiting for it to arrive in City A, because if there's an agent in City B, where you're headed, you can pick it up there, too. There are approximately 20,000 agents worldwide, including locations in Rome, Florence, Venice, Naples, Palermo, and other major Italian cities (call 800/325–6000 for specific locations).

Currency

The unit of currency in Italy is the lira. There are bills of 500,000, 100,000, 10,000, 5,000, 2,000, and 1,000 lire. Coins are 1,000, 500, 100, 50, 20, and 10, but the last two are rarely found, and prices are often rounded out to the nearest 50 lire. At press time (July 1993) the exchange rate was about 1,530 lire to the U.S. dollar, 1,290 to the Canadian dollar, and 2,330 to the pound sterling.

What It Will Cost

Italy is no longer the travel bargain it was years ago. The country has been hit in recent years by a rising cost of living, high taxes on goods and services, and an unfavorable exchange rate vis à vis the dollar, all of which increased restaurant prices, hotel rates, and museum admission fees. But in 1993, improvement in the rate of exchange motivated many travelers who had been biding their time to seize the moment, making summer 1993 a healthy one for Italian tourism Nevertheless, Rome is still among the most expensive European capitals to visit. Italy can be affordable, but only with careful planning.

Package tours, group or individual, remain the best way to beat costs. Off-season travel (*see* When To Go, *above*) can bring costs down, and traveling by train within Italy continues to be relatively cheap. Don't count on doing much shopping: Clothing is still much too pricey, and even leather shoes and wallets may be cheaper at home.

Sample Costs These sample prices are meant only as a general guide.

Admission to the Vatican Museums or the Uffizi Gallery: 12,000 and 10,000 lire, respectively

Budget hotel room for two in Rome: 60,000 lire (Zurigo)

Budget Rome dinner: 23,000 lire (Vecchia Roma da Severino)

Cheapest seat at Rome's Opera House: 20,000 lire

Cup of coffee: 1,000 lire

Bowl of pasta: 10,000 lire

Cover charge in an inexpensive restaurant: 2,000 lire

½ liter carafe of house wine: 4,000 lire

Rome taxi ride (1 mile): 8,000 lire

McDonald's Big Mac in Rome: 4,500 lire

Metro ride in Rome: 800 lire (probably 1,000 by 1994)

Entrance to a Milan disco: 30,000 lire

Movie ticket: 10,000 lire

Daily English-language newspaper: 2,400 lire

Pint of beer in a pub: 6,000 lire

Rosticceria lunch: 12,000 lire (Il Delfino, Rome)

Round-trip IC train ride from Rome to Florence: 62,000 lire

Taxes Both U.S. and Italian airport departure taxes are charged on a U.S.-Italy round-trip by air; these and other fees, such as a U.S. Customs users fee, are added to the total you pay when you buy the ticket. The Value-Added Tax (VAT, or IVA in Italy) is a sales tax levied in European Community countries; the amount varies from country to country, and also within a country depending on the nature of the goods or services. In Italy, the tax is 12% on most clothing and shoes, 19% on leather clothing and bags, jewelry, and furs. On most consumer goods, it is already included in the amount shown on the price tag, whereas on services, it may not be. The 9% IVA is generally included in the price quoted for hotel rooms, but the 19% IVA on car rentals is usually an extra charge, added when you settle the bill (luxury hotels also quote rates *exclusive* of 19% IVA). The IVA paid on consumer goods can be refunded to travelers in some cases (*see* Shopping in Staying in Italy, *below*).

A service charge of approximately 15% is added to all restaurant bills; in some cases the menu may state that the service charge is included in the menu prices. A similar service charge also applies to hotels and is included in the rates quoted. In restaurants, an additional *coperto* (cover charge) of 2,000 lire or so will be the first item on the check.

FYI: By law, everyone in Italy, including foreign tourists, is obliged to obtain a cash-register receipt for any purchase or service rendered. This means that whether you are paying the pizzeria check or picking up the laundry, you are required to get the receipt and take it with you. Officers of the Guardia della Finanza may ask individuals to produce the receipts, not to make sure that you've paid the bill but to make sure that vendors are in compliance with tax laws. You can throw out the day's accumulation when you return to your hotel.

Passports and Visas

If your passport is lost or stolen abroad, report it immediately to the nearest embassy or consulate and to the local police. If you can provide the consular officer with the information contained in the passport, they will usually be able to issue you a new passport. For this reason, it is a good idea to keep a copy of the data page of your passport in a separate place, or to leave the passport number, date, and place of issuance with a relative or friend at home.

U.S. Citizens   All U.S. citizens, even infants, need a valid passport to enter Italy; no visa is necessary for stays up to three months. Check with the Italian Embassy, 1601 Fuller St., N.W., Washington, DC 20009, tel. 202/328–5500, or with the nearest consulate concerning requirements for longer stays. You can pick up new and renewal application forms at any of the 13 U.S. Passport Agency offices and at some post offices and courthouses. Although passports are usually mailed within two weeks of your application's receipt, it's best to allow three weeks for delivery in low season, five weeks or more from April through summer. Call the Department of State Office of Passport Services' information line (1425 K St. NW, Washington, DC 20522, tel. 202/647–0518) for fees, documentation requirements, and other details.

Canadian Citizens   Canadian citizens need a valid passport to enter Italy for stays of up to three months; check with the nearest Italian consulate regarding longer stays. Application forms are available at 23 regional passport offices as well as post offices and travel agencies. Whether applying for a first or subsequent passport, you must apply in person. Children under 16 may be included on a parent's passport but must have their own passport to travel alone. Passports are valid for five years and are usually mailed within two weeks of an application's receipt. For fees, documentation requirements, and other information in English or French, call the passport office (tel. 514/283–2152).

U.K. Citizens   Citizens of the United Kingdom need a valid passport to enter Italy; no visa is necessary for stays up to three months. Applications for new and renewal passports are available from main post offices as well as at the six passport offices, located in Belfast, Glasgow, Liverpool, London, Newport, and Peterborough. You may apply in person at all passport offices, or by mail to all except the London office. Children under 16 may travel on a parent's passport when accompanying them. All passports are valid for 10 years. Allow a month for processing.

A British Visitor's Passport is valid for holidays and some business trips of up to three months to Italy. It can include both partners of a married couple. Valid for one year, it will be issued on the same day that you apply. You must apply in person at a main post office.

Customs and Duties

On Arrival There are two levels of duty-free allowances for visitors to Italy.

For goods obtained anywhere outside the EC or for goods purchased in a duty-free shop within an EC country, the allowances are: (1) 200 cigarettes or 100 cigarillos or 50 cigars or 250 grams of tobacco (these are doubled if you live outside Europe); (2) 2 liters of still table wine plus (3) 1 liter of spirits over 22% volume or 2 liters of spirits under 22% volume (fortified and sparkling wines) or 1 more liter of table wine; and (4) 50 milliliters of perfume and 250 milliliters of toilet water.

For goods obtained (duty and tax paid) within another EC country, the allowances are: (1) 300 cigarettes or 150 cigarillos or 75 cigars or 400 grams of tobacco; (2) 5 liters of still table wine plus (3) 1.5 liters of spirits over 22% volume or 5 liters of spirits under 22% volume (fortified or sparkling wines) or 3 more liters of table wine; and (4) 75 milliliters of perfume and 375 milliliters of toilet water.

Officially, two still cameras with 10 rolls of film each and one movie camera with 10 rolls of film may be brought in duty-free. Other items intended for personal use are generally admitted, as long as the quantities are reasonable.

Returning Home
U.S. Customs Provided you've been out of the U.S. for at least 48 hours and haven't already used the exemption, or any part of it, in the past 30 days, you may bring home $400 worth of foreign goods duty-free. So can each member of your family, regardless of age; and your exemptions may be pooled, so that one of you can bring in more if another brings in less. A flat 10% duty applies to the next $1,000 of goods; above $1,400, the rate varies with the merchandise. (If the 48-hour or 30-day limits apply, your duty-free allowance drops to $25, which may *not* be pooled.)

Travelers 21 or older may bring back one liter of alcohol duty-free, provided the beverage laws of the state through which they reenter the U.S. allow it. In addition, 100 non-Cuban cigars and 200 cigarettes are allowed, regardless of age. Antiques and works of art over 100 years old are duty-free.

Gifts under $50 may be mailed duty-free to stateside friends and relatives, with a limit of one package per day per addressee (do not send alcohol or tobacco products, nor perfume valued at over $5). These gifts do not count as part of your exemption, although if you bring them home with you, they do. Mark the package "Unsolicited Gift" and include the nature of the gift and its retail value.

For a copy of "Know Before You Go," a free brochure detailing what you may and may not bring back to the United States, rates of duty, and other pointers, contact the **U.S. Customs Service** (Box 7407, Washington, DC 20044, tel. 202/927–6724).

Canadian Customs Once per calendar year, when you've been out of Canada for at least seven days, you may bring in $300 worth of goods duty-free. If you've been away less than seven days but more than 48 hours, the duty-free exemption drops to $100 but can be claimed any number of times (as can a $20 duty-free exemption for absences of 24 hours or more). You cannot combine the yearly and 48-hour exemptions, use the $300 exemption only partially (to save the balance for a later trip), or pool exemptions with family members. Goods claimed under the $300 exemption may follow you by mail; those claimed under the lesser exemptions must accompany you on your return.

Alcohol and tobacco products may be included in the yearly and 48-hour exemptions but not in the 24-hour exemption. If you meet the age requirements of the province through which you reenter Canada, you may bring in, duty-free, 1.14 liters (40 imperial ounces) of wine or liquor *or* two dozen 12-ounce cans or bottles of beer or ale. If you are 16 or older, you may bring in, duty-free, 200 cigarettes, 50 cigars or cigarillos, and 400 tobacco sticks or 400 grams of manufactured tobacco. Alcohol and tobacco must accompany you on your return.

Gifts may be mailed to friends in Canada duty-free. These do not count as part of your exemption. Each gift may be worth up to $60—label the package "Unsolicited Gift—Value under $60." There are no limits on the number of gifts that may be sent per day or per addressee, but you can't mail alcohol or tobacco.

For more information, including details of duties on items that exceed your duty-free limit, ask the Revenue Canada Customs and Excise Department (Connaught Bldg., MacKenzie Ave., Ottawa, Ont. K1A OL5, tel. 613/957–0275) for a copy of the free brochure "I Declare/Je Déclare."

U.K. Customs If your journey was wholly within EC countries, you no longer need to pass through customs when you return to the United Kingdom. According to EC guidelines, you may bring in 800 cigarettes, 400 cigarillos, 200 cigars, and 1 kilogram of smoking tobacco, plus 10 liters of spirits, 20 liters of fortified wine, 90 liters of wine, and 110 liters of beer. If you exceed these limits, you may be required to prove that the goods are for your personal use or are gifts.

No animals or pets of any kind can be brought into the United Kingdom without a lengthy quarantine. The law is strictly enforced, with severe penalties.

For further information or a copy of "A Guide for Travellers," which details standard customs procedures as well as what you may bring into the United Kingdom from abroad, contact HM Customs and Excise (New King's Beam House, 22 Upper Ground, London SE1 9PJ, tel. 071/620–1313).

Traveling with Cameras, Camcorders, and Laptops

About Film and Cameras If your camera is new or if you haven't used it for a while, shoot and develop a few rolls of film before leaving home. Pack some lens tissue and an extra battery for the built-in light meter, and invest in an inexpensive skylight filter, to both protect the lens and provide some definition in hazy shots. Store film in a cool, dry place—never in the car's glove compartment or on the shelf under the rear window.

Films above ISO 400 are more sensitive to damage from airport security X-rays than others; very high speed films, ISO 1,000 and above, are exceedingly vulnerable. To protect your film, don't put it in checked luggage; carry it with you in a plastic bag and ask for a hand inspection. Such requests are honored at American airports, but are up to the inspector abroad. Don't depend on a lead-lined bag to protect film in checked luggage—

the airline may very well turn up the dosage of radiation to see what you've got in there. Airport metal detectors do not harm film, although you'll set off the alarm if you walk through one with a roll in your pocket. Call the Kodak Information Center (tel. 800/242–2424) for details.

About Camcorders Before your trip, put new or long-unused camcorders through their paces, and practice panning and zooming. Invest in a skylight filter to protect the lens, and check the lithium battery that lights up the LCD (liquid crystal display) modes. As for the rechargeable nickel-cadmium batteries that are the camera's power source, take along an extra pair, so while you're using your camcorder you'll have one battery ready and another recharging. Most newer camcorders come equipped with the battery (which generally slides or clicks onto the camera body) and, to recharge it, with what's known as a universal or worldwide AC adapter charger (or multivoltage converter) that can be used whether the voltage is 110 or 220. All that's needed is the appropriate plug.

About Videotape Unlike still-camera film, videotape is not damaged by X-rays. However, it may well be harmed by the magnetic field of walk-through metal detectors. Note that although the United States, Canada, and some other countries operate on the National Television System Committee video standard (NTSC), Italy uses PAL technology. You will not be able to view your tapes through the local TV set or view movies bought there in your home VCR. Blank tapes bought in Italy can be used for NTSC camcorder taping, however—although you'll probably find they cost more there and wish you'd brought an adequate supply with you.

Language

In the main tourist cities, language is no problem. You can always find someone who speaks at least a little English, albeit with a heavy accent; remember that the Italian language is pronounced exactly as it is written (many Italians try to speak English as it is written, with disconcerting results). You may run into a language barrier in the countryside, but a phrase book and close attention to the Italians' astonishing use of pantomime and expressive gestures will go a long way.

Try to master a few phrases for daily use, and familiarize yourself with the terms you'll need to decipher signs and museum labels. You'll find the basics in the Vocabulary and Menu Guide in the back of this book. The exhortation "Va via!" (Go away!) is useful in warding off beggars.

Staying Healthy

There are no serious health risks associated with travel to Italy and no inoculations are needed to enter the country. However, the Centers for Disease Control (CDC) in Atlanta caution that most of Southern Europe is in the "intermediate" range for risk of contacting traveler's diarrhea. Part of this risk may be attributed to an increased consumption of olive oil and wine, which can have a laxative effect on stomachs used to a different diet. (Pepto Bismol is recommended for minor cases of traveler's diarrhea.) The CDC also advises all international travelers to swim only in chlorinated swimming pools, unless they are absolutely certain the local beaches and fresh-water lakes are not contaminated.

Finding a Doctor The **International Association for Medical Assistance to Travelers** (IAMAT, 417 Center St., Lewiston, NY 14092, tel. 716/754–4883; 40 Regal Rd., Guelph, Ont. N1K 1B5; 57 Voirets, 1212 Grand-Lancy, Geneva, Switzerland) publishes a worldwide directory of English-speaking physicians whose qualifications meet IAMAT standards and who have agreed to treat members for a set fee. Membership is free.

Assistance Pretrip medical referrals, emergency evacuation or repatria-
Companies tion, 24-hour telephone hot lines for medical consultation, dispatch of medical personnel, relay of medical records, up-front cash for emergencies, and other personal and legal assistance are among the services provided by several membership organizations specializing in medical assistance to travelers. Among them are **International SOS Assistance** (Box 11568, Philadelphia, PA 19116, tel. 215/244–1500 or 800/523–8930; Box 466, pl. Bonaventure, Montréal, Qué. H5A 1C1, tel. 514/874–7674 or 800/363–0263), **Near Services** (450 Prairie Ave., Suite 101, Calumet City, IL 60409, tel. 708/868–6700 or 800/654–6700), and **Travel Assistance International** (1133 15th St. NW, Suite 400, Washington, DC 20005, tel. 202/331–1609 or 800/821–2828), part of Europ Assistance Worldwide Services, Inc. Because these companies will also sell you death-and-dismemberment, trip-cancellation, and other insurance coverage, there is some overlap with the travel-insurance policies discussed below, which may include the services of an assistance company among the insurance options or reimburse travelers for such services without providing them.

Insurance

U.S. Residents Most tour operators, travel agents, and insurance agents sell specialized health-and-accident, flight, trip-cancellation, and luggage insurance as well as comprehensive policies with some or all of these features. But before you make any purchase, review your existing health and home-owner policies to find out whether they cover expenses incurred while traveling.

Health-and-Accident Supplemental health-and-accident insurance for travelers is
Insurance usually a part of comprehensive policies. Specific policy provisions vary, but they tend to address three general areas, beginning with reimbursement for medical expenses caused by illness or an accident during a trip. Such policies may reimburse anywhere from $1,000 to $150,000 worth of medical expenses; dental benefits may also be included. A second common feature is the personal-accident, or death-and-dismemberment, provision, which pays a lump sum to your beneficiaries if you die or to you if you lose one or both limbs or your eyesight. This is similar to the flight insurance described below, although it is not necessarily limited to accidents involving airplanes or even other "common carriers" (buses, trains, and ships) and can be in effect 24 hours a day. The lump sum awarded can range from $15,000 to $500,000. A third area generally addressed by these policies is medical assistance (referrals, evacuation, or repatriation, and other services). Some policies reimburse travelers for the cost of such services; others may automatically enroll you as a member of a particular medical-assistance company.

Flight Insurance This insurance, often bought as a last-minute impulse at the airport, pays a lump sum to a beneficiary when a plane crashes and the insured dies (and sometimes to a surviving passenger who loses eyesight or a limb); thus, it supplements the airlines' own coverage as described in the limits-of-liability paragraphs on the ticket (up to $75,000 on international flights, $20,000 on domestic ones—and that is generally subject to litigation). Charging an airline ticket to a major credit card often automatically signs you up for flight insurance; in this case, the coverage may also embrace travel by bus, train, and ship.

Baggage Insurance In the event of loss, damage, or theft on international flights, airlines limit their liability to $20 per kilo for checked baggage (roughly $640 per 70-pound bag) and to $400 per passenger for unchecked baggage. On domestic flights, most airlines limit liability to $1,250 per passenger. Excess-valuation insurance can be bought directly from the airline at check-in, but it still leaves your bags vulnerable on the ground. Broader protection may be available (or automatic) if you charge your tickets to a credit card. Alternatively, you can buy baggage insurance from travel agents and insurance companies, either separately or in conjunction with comprehensive coverage.

Trip Insurance There are two sides to this coin. **Trip-cancellation-and-interruption insurance** protects you in the event you are unable to undertake or finish your trip. **Default** or **bankruptcy insurance** protects you against a supplier's failure to deliver. Consider the former if your airline ticket, cruise, or package tour does not allow changes or cancellations. The amount of coverage to buy should equal the cost of your trip should you, a traveling companion, or a family member get sick, forcing you to stay home, plus the nondiscounted one-way airline ticket you would need to buy if you had to return home early. Read the fine print carefully; pay attention to sections defining "family member" and "preexisting medical conditions." A characteristic quirk of default policies is that they often do not cover default by travel agencies, or default by a tour operator, airline, or cruise line if you bought your tour and the coverage directly from the firm in question. To reduce your need for default insurance, give preference to tours packaged by members of the United States Tour Operators Association (USTOA), which maintains a fund to reimburse clients in the event of member defaults. Even better, pay for travel arrangements with a major credit card, so that you can refuse to pay the bill if services have not been rendered—and let the card company fight your battles.

Comprehensive Policies Companies supplying comprehensive policies with some or all of the above features include **Access America, Inc.** (Box 11188, Richmond, VA 23230, tel. 800/284–8300), underwritten by BCS Insurance Company; **Carefree Travel Insurance** (Box 310, 120 Mineola Blvd., Mineola, NY 11501, tel. 516/294–0220 or 800/323–3149), underwritten by The Hartford; **Tele-Trip** (Mutual of Omaha Plaza, Box 31762, Omaha, NE 68131, tel. 800/228–9792), a subsidiary of Mutual of Omaha; **The Travelers Companies** (1 Tower Sq., Hartford, CT 06183, tel. 203/277–0111 or 800/243–3174); **Travel Guard International** (1145 Clark St., Stevens Point, WI 54481, tel. 715/345–0505 or 800/782–5151), underwritten by Transamerica Occidental Life Companies; and **Wallach and Company, Inc.** (107 W. Federal St., Box 480, Middleburg, VA 22117, tel. 703/687–3166 or 800/237–6615), underwritten by Lloyds, London. These companies may also offer the above types of insurance separately.

U.K. Residents Most tour operators, travel agents, and insurance agents sell specialized policies covering accident, medical expenses, personal liability, trip cancellation, and loss or theft of personal property. Some policies include coverage for delayed departure and legal expenses, winter-sports accidents, or motoring abroad. You can also purchase an annual travel-insurance policy valid for every trip you make during the year in which it's purchased (usually only trips of less than 90 days). Before you leave, make sure you will be covered if you have a preexisting medical condition or are pregnant; your insurers may not pay for routine or continuing treatment, or may require a note from your doctor certifying your fitness to travel.

For advice by phone or a free booklet, "Holiday Insurance," that sets out what to expect from holiday-insurance policies and gives price guidelines, contact the Association of British Insurers (51 Gresham St., London EC2V 7HQ, tel. 071/600–3333; 30 Gordon St., Glasgow G1 3PU, tel. 041/226–3905; Scottish Provincial Bldg., Donegall Sq. W, Belfast BT1 6JE, tel. 0232/249176; call for other locations), a trade association representing 450 insurance companies.

Car Rentals

Most major car-rental companies are represented in Italy, including **Avis** (tel. 800/331–1212, 800/879–2847 in Canada); **Budget** (tel. 800/527–0700); **Dollar** (tel. 800/800–4000); **Hertz** (tel. 800/654–3131, 800/263–0600 in Canada); **National** (tel. 800/227–7368), known internationally as InterRent and Europcar. In addition, a rate of VAT tax on car rentals in Italy is 19%. In cities, unlimited-mileage rates range from about $40 per day for an economy car to about $61 for a mid-size car; weekly unlimited-mileage rates range from about $180 to $309. This does not include VAT tax, which in Italy is 19% on car rentals. Theft protection is also mandatory, and ranges from about $10 to $15 per day depending on the vehicle you rent.

Requirements In Italy, you must usually be 21 (sometimes 25 to rent the more expensive cars). Your own U.S., Canadian, or British driver's license is acceptable, provided you have had it at least a year. It is supposed to be accompanied by a translation, so it may be useful to take out an International Driver's Permit before you leave, to smooth out difficulties or as additional identification. Permits are available ($10, two passport photos required) through local offices of the American Automobile Association (AAA) or from the main office (AAA, 1000 AAA Dr., Heathrow, FL 32746, tel. 800/336–4357); in Canada, from the Canadian Automobile Association, (CAA, 2 Carlton St., Toronto, Ont. M5B 1K4, tel. 416/964–3002). Alternatively, upon presentation of a foreign license, **ACI** (Automobile Club of Italy) will issue a declaration at frontier points for a small fee.

Extra Charges Automatic transmissions and air-conditioning are not universally available abroad; ask for them when you book if you want them and check the cost before you commit yourself to the rental. Picking up the car in one city or country and leaving it in another may also raise prices in the form of drop-off charges or one-way service fees, which can be substantial. The same goes for the cost of collision or loss damage waiver (CDW or LDW, *see below*).

Cutting Costs If you know you will want a car for more than a day or two, you can do much better than the above rates by arranging the rental before you leave home. Major international companies such as Avis, Budget, Dollar, Hertz, and National have programs that discount their standard rates by 15%–30% if you make the reservation before departure (anywhere from 2 to 14 days), rent for a minimum number of days (typically three or four), and prepay the rental. Ask about these advance-purchase schemes when you call for information. More economical rentals are those that come as part of fly/drive or other packages, even those as bare-bones as the rental plus an airline ticket (*see* Tours and Packages, *above*).

Other sources of savings are a number of companies that operate as wholesalers—companies that do not own their own fleets but rent in bulk from those that do and are thus able to pass on advantageous rates to their retail customers. Rentals through such companies must be arranged and paid for before you leave the United States. Among them are **Auto Europe** (Box 1097, Camden, ME 04843, tel. 207/236–8235 or 800/223–5555, 800/458–9503 in Canada); **Connex International** (23 N. Division St., Peekskill, NY 10566, tel. 914/739–0066; 800/333–3949; 800/843–5416 in Canada); **Europe by Car** (mailing address, 1 Rockefeller Plaza, New York, NY 10020; walk-in address, 14 W. 49th St., New York, NY 10020, tel. 212/581–3040 or 212/245–1713; 9000 Sunset Blvd., Los Angeles, CA 90069, tel. 213/252–9401 or 800/223–1516 in CA); **Foremost Euro-Car** (5430 Van Nuys Blvd., Suite 306, Van Nuys, CA 91401, tel. 818/786–1960 or 800/272–3299); and **Kemwel** (106 Calvert St., Harrison, NY 10528, tel. 914/835–5555 or 800/678–0678). Find out whether there are cancellation penalties, whether the prices quoted are guaranteed in U.S. dollars or foreign currency, are for unlimited mileage, include any expected drop-off charges, and include the VAT tax. Also, confirm the cost of the CDW and make sure you understand what you are liable for if you refuse it.

Insurance and The standard rental contract includes liability coverage (for
Collision Damage damage to public property, injury to pedestrians, etc.) and cov-
Waiver erage for the car against fire and collision damage with a deductible—most commonly $2,000–$3,000, occasionally more. In the case of an accident, you are responsible for the deductible amount unless you've purchased the collision damage waiver (CDW), which varies according to what you've rented, where, and from whom ($12 a day is a rough average).

Because this adds up quickly, you may be inclined to say "no thanks"—and that's certainly your option, although the rental agent may not tell you so. Planning ahead will help you make the right decision. Find out if your own auto insurance covers damage to a rental car while traveling (not simply a car rented to drive at home when yours is in for repairs). And check with your credit card company, which may automatically include CDW for car rentals charged to the card. Note before you decline that deductibles are occasionally high enough that totaling a car would make you responsible for its full value.

One last tip: remember to fill the tank when you turn in a rented vehicle, to avoid being charged for refueling at what you'll swear is the most expensive pump in town.

Rail Passes

Italy is one of 17 countries in which you can use **EurailPasses,** which provide unlimited first-class rail travel during their period of validity. If you plan to rack up the miles, they can be an excellent value. Standard passes are available for 15 days ($460), 21 days ($598), one month ($728), two months ($998), and three months ($1,260). **Eurail Saverpasses,** valid for 15 days, cost $390 per person; you must do all your traveling with at least one companion (two companions others from April through September). **Eurail Youthpasses,** which cover second-class travel, cost $508 for one month, $698 for two; you must be under 26 on the first day you travel. Flexipasses allow you to travel for five, 10, or 15 days within any two-month period. You pay $298, $496, and $676 for the **Eurail Flexipass,** sold for first-class travel; and $220, $348, $474 for the **Eurail Youth Flexipass,** available to those under 26 on their first travel day, sold for second-class travel. Ask also about the **EurailDrive** Pass, which lets you combine four days of train travel with three days of car rental (through Hertz or Avis) at any time within a two-month period. Charges vary according to size of car, but two people traveling together can get the basic package for $289 per person. Apply through your travel agent, **Rail Europe** (226–230 Westchester Ave., White Plains, NY 10604, tel. 914/682–5172 or 800/848–7245 from the East and 800/438–7245 from the West), or **CIT Tours Corp.** (342 Madison Ave., Room 207, New York, NY 10173, tel. 212/697–2100 or 800/248–8687 for orders).

Italy has three rail passes, which can be bought at main train stations in Italy or in the U.S. through travel agents or the official representative for **Italian State Railways, CIT Tours Corp.** *(see above).* In the past, you saved money buying the passes in the United States, but at press time, with an improved rate of exchange for the dollar, it was more economical to buy them in Italy. A few lire prices are given for purposes of comparison.

The **Italian Tourist Ticket** (BTLC)—the country's basic unlimited-travel rail pass—is an excellent value because it covers the entire system, including Sicily. The pass is available in a first-class version for periods of 8 days ($236 in U.S./269,000 lire in Italy), 15 days ($294), 21 days ($340), and 30 days ($406). For second-class travel, the prices for the same periods are $162 (or 179,000 lire), $200, $230, and $274.

A variation on the BTLC is the **Italy Flexi Railcard,** which entitles purchasers to four days of travel within nine days of validity; eight days of travel within 21 days; and 12 days of travel within 30 days. Rates for the three types for first-class travel are $180 in the United States (220,000 lire in Italy), $260, and $324; for second-class travel, $126 (148,000 lire), $174, and $220.

The third Italian rail pass is the **Italian Kilometric Ticket,** which is a good bet for families. It is valid for 20 train trips, up to a total of 3,000 kilometers (1,875 miles) of train travel, within a two-month period, and it can be used by up to five people (related or not). Children under 12 are counted for only half the distance, those under 4 travel free. A first-class ticket costs $274 and a second-class ticket $166 if bought in the United States, or 312,000 lire and 183,000 lire if bought at main train stations and CIT offices in Italy.

Don't make the mistake of assuming that your rail pass guarantees you seats on the trains you want to ride. Seat reservations are required on some trains, particularly high-speed trains, and are a good idea on trains that may be crowded. you will also need reservations for overnight sleeping accommodations. Rail Europe can help you determine if you need reservations and can make them for you (about $10 each, less if you purchase them in Europe at the time of travel). (*See also* Staying in Italy: Getting Around by Train, *below*).

Student and Youth Travel

Travel Agencies The **Centro Turistico Studentesco** (CTS) is a student and youth travel agency with offices in major Italian cities; CTS helps its clients find low-cost accommodations and bargain fares for travel in Italy and elsewhere and also serves as a meeting place for young people of all nations. The main Rome office is at Via Genova 16, near the railroad station (tel. 06/467–9271). CTS is also the Rome representative for **EuroTrain International.**

The foremost U.S. student travel agency is **Council Travel,** a subsidiary of the nonprofit Council on International Educational Exchange (CIEE). It specializes in low-cost travel arrangements, is the exclusive U.S. agent for several discount cards, and, with its sister CIEE subsidiary, **Council Charter,** is a source of airfare bargains. The Council Charter brochure and CIEE's twice-yearly *Student Travels* magazine, which details its programs, are available at the Council Travel office at CIEE headquarters (205 E. 42nd Street, New York, NY 10017, tel. 212/661–1450) and at 37 branches in college towns nationwide (free in person, $1 by mail). The **Educational Travel Center** (ETC, 438 N. Francis St., Madison, WI 53703, tel. 608/256–5551) also offers low-cost rail passes, domestic and international airline tickets (mostly for flights departing from Chicago), and other budgetwise travel arrangements. Other travel agencies catering to students include **Travel Management International** (TMI, 18 Prescott St., Suite 4, Cambridge, MA 02138, tel. 617/661–8187) and **Travel Cuts** (187 College St., Toronto, Ont. M5T 1P7, tel. 416/979–2406).

Discount Cards For discounts on transportation and on museum and attractions admissions, buy the **International Student Identity Card** (ISIC) if you're a bona fide student, or the **International Youth Card** (IYC) if you're under 26. In the United States the ISIC and IYC cards cost $15 each and include basic travel accident and sickness coverage. Apply to **CIEE** (*see above*, tel. 212/661–1414; the application is in *Student Travels*). In Canada the cards are available for $15 each from **Travel Cuts** (*see above*). In the United Kingdom they cost £5 and £4 respectively at student unions and student travel companies, including Council Travel's London office (28A Poland St., London W1V 3DB, tel. 071/437–7767).

Hosteling An **International Youth Hostel Federation** (IYHF) membership card is the key to more than 5,300 hostel locations in 59 countries. Contrary to what might be assumed, given the names of the organizations running them, IYHF-affiliated hostels are open to guests of all ages (an exception is some German hostels, for those up to 26 years of age only). Sleeping quarters are sex-segregated, largely dormitory-style, but there are some rooms for families; rates are from $7 to $20 a night per person. Membership is available in the United States through **American Youth Hostels** (AYH, 733 15th St. NW, Washington, DC 20005, tel. 202/783–6161), the American link in the worldwide chain, and costs $25 for adults 18–54, $10 for those under 18, $15 for those 55 and over, and $35 for families. Volume 1 of the two-volume *Guide to Budget Accommodation* lists hostels in Europe and the Mediterranean, including Italy ($13.95, including postage). IYHF membership is available in Canada through the **Canadian Hostelling Association** (CHA, 1600 James Naismith Dr., Suite 608, Gloucester, Ont. K1B 5N4, tel. 613/748–5638) for $26.75, and in the United Kingdom through the **Youth Hostel Association of England and Wales** (Trevelyan House, 8 St. Stephen's Hill, St. Albans, Herts. AL1 2DY, tel. 0727/55215) for £9. (For more information on hostels in Italy, *see* Lodging in Staying in Italy, *below*.)

Traveling with Children

Although Italians love children and are generally very tolerant and patient with them, they provide few amenities for them. In restaurants and trattorias you may find a high chair or a cushion for the child to sit on, but there is no such thing as a children's menu. Order a half-portion (*mezza porzione*) of any dish, or ask the waiter for a child's portion (*porzione da bambino*).

Discounts do exist. Always ask about a *sconto-bambino* before purchasing tickets. Children under 6 or under a certain height ride free on municipal buses and trams. Children under 18 are admitted free to state-run museums and galleries, and there are similar privileges in many municipal or private museums.

Publications
Newsletter

Family Travel Times, published 10 times a year by **Travel With Your Children** (TWYCH, 45 W. 18th St., 7th Floor Tower, New York, NY 10011, tel. 212/206–0688; annual subscription $55), covers destinations, types of vacations, and modes of travel.

Books

Great Vacations with Your Kids, fby Dorothy Jordon and Marjorie Cohen ($13; Penguin USA, 120 Woodbine St., Bergenfield, NJ 07621, tel. 800/253–6476) and *Traveling with Children—And Enjoying It,* by Arlene K. Butler ($11.95 plus $3 shipping per book; Globe Pequot Press, Box 833, Old Saybrook, CT 06475, tel. 800/243–0495, or 800/962–0973 in CT) help plan your trip with children, from toddlers to teens. *Innocents Abroad: Traveling with Kids in Europe,* by Valerie Wolf Deutsch and Laura Sutherland ($15.95 or $4.95 paperback, Penguin USA, *see above*), covers child- and teen-friendly activities, food, and transportation.

Tour Operators

GrandTravel (6900 Wisconsin Ave., Suite 706, Chevy Chase, MD 20815, tel. 301/986–0790 or 800/247–7651) offers international and domestic tours for grandparents traveling with their grandchildren. The catalogue, as charmingly written and illustrated as a children's book, positively invites armchair traveling with lap-sitters aboard. **Families Welcome!** (21 W. Colony Pl., Suite 140, Durham, NC 27705, tel. 919/489–2555 or 800/326–0724) packages and sells family tours to Europe. **Rascals in Paradise** (650 5th St., Suite 505, San Francisco, CA 94107, tel. 415/978–9800, or 800/872–7225) specializes in programs for families.

Getting There
Air Fares On international flights, the fare for infants under 2 not occupying a seat is generally 10% of the accompanying adult's fare; children ages 2 through 11 usually pay half to two-thirds of the adult fare. On domestic flights, children under 2 not occupying a seat travel free, and older children currently travel on the "lowest applicable" adult fare.

Baggage In general, infants paying 10% of the adult fare are allowed one carry-on bag, not to exceed 70 pounds or 45 inches (length + width + height). The adult baggage allowance applies for children paying half or more of the adult fare. Check with the airline for particulars, especially regarding flights between two foreign destinations, where allowances for infants may be less generous than those above.

Safety Seats A certain amount of confusion surrounds children's car seats aloft. The FAA recommends their use and details approved models in the free leaflet "**Child/Infant Safety Seats Recommended for Use in Aircraft**" (available from the Federal Aviation Administration, APA–200, 800 Independence Ave. SW, Washington, DC 20591, tel. 202/267–3479). Airline policy varies. U.S. carriers must allow FAA-approved models, but because these seats are strapped into a regular passenger seat they may require that parents buy a ticket even for an infant under two who would otherwise ride free. Foreign carriers may not allow infant seats, may charge the child's rather than the infant's fare for their use, or may require you to hold your baby during takeoff and landing, thus defeating the seat's purpose.

Facilities Aloft Airlines do provide other facilities and services for children, such as children's meals and freestanding bassinets (to those sitting in bulkhead seats, where there's enough legroom to accommodate them). Make your request when reserving. The annual February/March issue of *Family Travel Times* gives details of the children's services of dozens of airlines. "Kids and Teens in Flight" (free from the U.S. Department of Transportation, tel. 202/366–2220) offers tips for children flying alone.

Lodging Children are generally welcome in Italian hotels, which will set up extra beds in the parents' room or give families adjoining rooms. The charge for an extra bed added to a double room can be no more than 35% of the normal price of the room. If you are traveling with an infant, it is best to bring along your own folding crib.

Club Med (40 W. 57th St., New York, NY 10019, tel. 800/CLUB–MED) has a Mini Club (for ages 4–9) and Kids Club (for ages 10 and 11) at its ski village in Sestriere; there are also Baby Clubs, Mini Clubs, and Kids Clubs (the applicable ages vary) at summer resort villages in Metaponto (Basilicata) and on the islands of Sicily and Sardinia, marketed mainly to Europeans. Some of the Valtur vacation villages (Via Milano 42, Rome, tel. 06/482–1000, fax 06/470–6334) also have special facilities and activities for children in various age groups.

(For information on alternative lodgings, *see* Home Exchange and Apartment and Villa Rentals in Staying in Italy, *below*).

Baby-sitting Services You can usually arrange for a baby-sitter through your hotel; it may cost 10,000–20,000 lire per hour.

Hints for Disabled Travelers

Italy has only recently begun to provide for handicapped travelers, and facilities such as ramps, telephones, and toilets for the disabled are still the exception, not the rule. ENIT (Italian Government Travel Office) can provide disabled travelers with a list of accessible hotels and with the addresses of Italian associations for the disabled. Travelers' wheelchairs must be transported free of charge, according to Italian law, and seats are reserved for the disabled on public transportation, but the high, narrow steps on trains, and the lack of lifts on buses can make these requirements irrelevant. In many monuments and museums, even in some hotels and restaurants, architectural barriers make it difficult, if not impossible, for the handicapped to gain access. In Rome, however, St. Peter's, the Sistine Chapel, and the Vatican Museums are all accessible by wheelchair.

To bring a Seeing Eye dog into Italy requires an import license, a current certificate detailing the dog's inoculations, and a letter from your veterinarian certifying the dog's health. Contact the nearest Italian consulate.

Organizations Several organizations provide travel information for people with disabilities, usually for a membership fee, and some publish newsletters and bulletins. Among them are the **Information Center for Individuals with Disabilities** (Fort Point Pl., 27–43 Wormwood St., Boston, MA 02210, tel. 617/727–5540 or 800/462–5015 in MA between 11 and 4, or leave message; TDD/TTY tel. 617/345–9743); **Mobility International USA** (Box 3551, Eugene, OR 97403, voice and TDD tel. 503/343–1284), the U.S. branch of an international organization based in Britain *(see below)* and present in 30 countries; **MossRehab Hospital Travel Information Service** (1200 W. Tabor Rd., Philadelphia, PA 19141, tel. 215/456–9603, TDD tel. 215/456–9602); the **Society for the Advancement of Travel for the Handicapped** (SATH, 347 5th Ave., Suite 610, New York, NY 10016, tel. 212/447–7284, fax 212/725–8253); the **Travel Industry and Disabled Exchange** (TIDE, 5435 Donna Ave., Tarzana, CA 91356, tel. 818/368–5648); and **Travelin' Talk** (Box 3534, Clarksville, TN 37043, tel. 615/552–6670).

In the United Kingdom Main sources include the **Royal Association for Disability and Rehabilitation** (RADAR, 25 Mortimer St., London W1N 8AB, tel. 071/637–5400), which publishes travel information for the disabled in Britain, and **Mobility International** (228 Borough High St., London SE1 1JX, tel. 071/403–5688), the headquarters of an international membership organization that serves as a clearinghouse of travel information for people with disabilities.

Travel Agencies and Tour Operators **Directions Unlimited** (720 N. Bedford Rd., Bedford Hills, NY 10507, tel. 914/241–1700), a travel agency, has expertise in individual and group tours and cruises for the disabled. **Evergreen Travel Service** (4114 198th St. SW, Suite 13, Lynnwood, WA 98036, tel. 206/776–1184 or 800/435–2288) operates Wings on Wheels Tours for those in wheelchairs, White Cane Tours for the blind, tours for the deaf, and makes group and independent arrangements for travelers with any disability. **Flying Wheels Travel** (143 W. Bridge St., Box 382, Owatonna, MN 55060, tel. 800/535–6790 or 800/722–9351 in MN), a tour operator and travel agency, arranges international tours, cruises, and independent travel itineraries for people with mobility disabilities. **Nautilus,** at the same address as TIDE (*see above*), packages tours for the disabled internationally.

Publications Several free publications are available from the Consumer Information Center (Pueblo, CO 81009): "New Horizons for the Air Traveler with a Disability," a U.S. Department of Transportation booklet describing changes resulting from the 1986 Air Carrier Access Act and those still to come from the 1990 Americans with Disabilities Act (include Department 608Y in the address), and the Airport Operators Council's *Access Travel: Airports* (Dept. 5804), which describes facilities and services for the disabled at more than 500 airports worldwide.

Twin Peaks Press (Box 129, Vancouver, WA 98666, tel. 206/694-2462 or 800/637-2256) publishes the *Directory of Travel Agencies for the Disabled* ($19.95), listing more than 370 agencies worldwide; *Travel for the Disabled* ($19.95), listing some 500 access guides and accessible places worldwide; the *Directory of Accessible Van Rentals* ($9.95) for campers and RV travelers worldwide; and *Wheelchair Vagabond* ($14.95), a collection of personal travel tips. Add $2 per book for shipping.

Hints for Older Travelers

In Italy, travelers over 60 can purchase the **Carta d' Argento,** a rail pass good for a 30% discount on the Italian State railway system. It costs 40,000 lire and is valid for one year, except for June 26–August 14 and December 18–28. Travelers over 60 are also entitled to free admission to state museums, as well as to many other museums—always ask at the ticket office. Older travelers planning to visit Italy during the hottest months should be aware that few public buildings, restaurants, and shops are air-conditioned. Public toilets are few and far between, other than those in coffee bars, restaurants, and hotels. Older travelers may find it difficult to board trains and some buses and trams with very high steps and narrow treads.

Organizations The **American Association of Retired Persons** (AARP, 601 E St. NW, Washington, DC 20049, tel. 202/434-2277) offers independent travelers the Purchase Privilege Program, which provides discounts on hotels, car rentals, and sightseeing. AARP also arranges group tours, cruises, and apartment living through AARP Travel Experience from American Express (400 Pinnacle Way, Suite 450, Norcross, GA 30071, tel. 800/927-0111); these can be booked through travel agents, except for the cruises, which must be booked directly (tel. 800/745-4567). AARP membership is open to those 50 and over; annual dues are $8 per person or couple.

Two other membership organizations offer discounts on lodgings, car rentals, and other travel products, along with such nontravel perks as magazines and newsletters. The **National Council of Senior Citizens** (1331 F St. NW, Washington, DC 20004, tel. 202/347-8800) is a nonprofit advocacy group with some 5,000 local clubs across the United States; membership costs $12 per person or couple annually. **Mature Outlook** (6001 N. Clark St., Chicago, IL 60660, tel. 800/336-6330), a Sears Roebuck & Co. subsidiary with 800,000 members, charges $9.95 for an annual membership.

Note: When using any senior-citizen identification card for reduced hotel rates, mention it when booking, not when checking out. At restaurants, show your card before you're seated; discounts may be limited to certain menus, days, or hours. If you are renting a car, ask about promotional rates that might improve on your senior-citizen discount.

Educational Travel   **Elderhostel** (75 Federal St., 3rd Floor, Boston, MA 02110, tel. 617/426–7788) is a nonprofit organization that has offered inexpensive study programs for people 60 and older since 1975. Programs take place at more than 1,800 educational institutions in the United States, Canada, and 45 countries overseas, and courses cover everything from marine science to Greek myths and cowboy poetry. Participants generally attend lectures in the morning and spend the afternoon sightseeing or on field trips; they live in dorms on the host campuses. Fees for the two-to three-week international trips—including room, board, tuition, and transportation from the United States—range from $1,800 to $4,500.

Interhostel (University of New Hampshire, 6 Garrison Ave., Durham, NH 03824, tel. 800/733–9753), a slightly younger enterprise than Elderhostel, caters to a slightly younger clientele—that is, 50 and over—and runs programs overseas in some 25 countries. But the idea is similar: Lectures and field trips mix with sightseeing, and participants stay in dormitories at cooperating educational institutions or in modest hotels. Programs are usually two weeks in length and cost $1,500–$2,100, not including airfare from the United States.

Tour Operators   **Saga International Holidays** (222 Berkeley St., Boston, MA 02116, tel. 800/343–0273), which specializes in group travel for people over 60, offers a selection of variously priced tours and cruises covering five continents, as well as a Road Scholar program of educational tours, mostly to European destinations.

Further Reading

The Italians, by Luigi Barzini, is a comprehensive and lively analysis of the Italian national character, still worthy reading although published in 1964 (Atheneum). More recent musings on Italian life include *Italian Days*, by Barbara Grizzuti Harrison (Ticknor & Fields) and *That Fine Italian Hand*, by Paul Hofmann (Henry Holt), for many years *New York Times* bureau chief in Rome. Matthew Spender's *Within Tuscany* (Viking) and Tim Parks' *Italian Neighbors* (Grove) are accounts of life in rural Tuscany and Verona by British expatriates.

Classics of the travel essay genre include James Morris's *The World of Venice* (Harcourt Brace Jovanovich), Mary McCarthy's *Venice Observed* and *The Stones of Florence* (both HBJ also), and Lawrence Durrell's *Sicilian Carousel* (out of print).

For historical background, Edward Gibbon's *Decline and Fall of the Roman Empire* is available in three volumes (Modern Library). Consult Giorgio Vasari's *Lives of the Artists*, *The Autobiography of Benvenuto Cellini*, and Machiavelli's *The Prince* (all available in Penguin Classics) for eyewitness accounts of the 16th century. Otherwise, many still consider *The Civilization of the Renaissance in Italy*, by 19th-century Swiss historian Jacob Burckhardt (Modern Library), must reading.

Christopher Hibbert's *The House of Medici* (Quill/William Morrow) details the family's rise and fall. For a good, all-round history of the country, consult Denis Mack Smith's *Italy: A Modern History* (University of Michigan Press) or *Italy and Its Monarchy* (Yale University Press).

For lively historical fiction, pick up Irving Stone's *Agony and the Ecstasy* (NAL) based on the life of Michelangelo. Susan Sontag's *The Volcano Lover* (Farrar Straus Giroux), set in 18th-century Naples, is about Sir William Hamilton, his wife Emma, and Lord Nelson. *The Leopard*, by Giuseppe di Lampedusa (Pantheon) is a compelling portrait of Sicily during the political upheavals of the 1860s. Historical fiction set in World War II includes *History: A Novel*, by Elsa Morante (Vintage Aventura), about the fate of inhabitants of Rome's Jewish ghetto, and *Bread and Wine* by Ignazio Silone (Signet Classics), about Italian peasants under the control of the Fascists. Anne Cornelison's *Women of the Shadows*, non-fiction, portrays the life of peasant women in early post-WWI southern Italy (Vintage).

Waverley Root's *The Food of Italy* (Vintage), published in 1977, is not a cookbook but an unsurpassed region-by-region exploration of the subject. Marcella Hazan's new *Essentials of Classic Italian Cooking* (Knopf) is an update, with modern sensibilities and lowfat diets in mind, of her earlier cookbooks. It goes well with *Italian Wine* (Knopf), by her husband, Victor Hazan, or with *Vino* by Burton Anderson (Little Brown). *Made in Italy*, a shopper's guide by Annie Brody and Patricia Schultz (1988, Workman) is unrevised but still valuable for its knowledge of Italian products and producers.

What about a video? The delightful "Roman Holiday" (1953), in which a young princess plays hooky from her royal entourage to go "slumming" with Gregory Peck, won Audrey Hepburn an Oscar. In "Summertime" (1955), a visiting American (Katharine Hepburn) falls in love with Venice and a handsome Venetian shopkeeper (Rossano Brazzi). Federico Fellini's "La Dolce Vita" (1961), with Marcello Mastroianni discovering the decadence of high society in Rome, gave its name to an era. "Fellini's Roma" (1972) is the director's paean to the city; "Amarcord" (1974), his paean to the small Adriatic town of his childhood. Merchant/Ivory's "Room with a View" (1986), a period piece based on the E. M. Forster novel of the same name (recommended), is good cinema with good views of Florence.

A magazine for Italophiles, *Italy Italy*, published in Italy in English, is available in the United States (Italian American Multimedia Corporation, 138 Wooster St., New York, NY 10012, tel. 212/674–4132, fax 212/674–4933; $30 for six yearly issues).

Arriving and Departing

From North America by Plane

Flights are either nonstop, direct, or connecting. A **nonstop** flight requires no change of plane and makes no stops. A **direct** flight stops at least once and can involve a change of plane, although the flight number remains the same; if the first leg is late, the second waits. This is not the case with a **connecting** flight, which involves a different plane and a different flight number.

Airports and Airlines Airlines serving Italy nonstop from the United States are **Alitalia** (tel. 800/223–5730), **Delta** (tel. 800/241–4141), and **TWA** (tel. 800/892–4141), which all fly to Rome and Milan; and **American** (800/624–6262), which flies to Milan only. These flights land at Rome's **Leonardo da Vinci Airport,** better known as Fiumicino (from its location outside the city) and at Milan's **Malpensa Airport.**

Flying Time The flying time to Rome from New York is 8½ hours; from Chicago, 10–11 hours; from Los Angeles, 12–13 hours.

Cutting Flight Costs The Sunday travel section of most newspapers is a good source of deals. When booking, particularly through an unfamiliar company, call the Better Business Bureau to find out whether any complaints have been registered against the company, pay with a credit card if you can, and consider trip-cancellation and default insurance (*see* Insurance, *above*). *The Airline Passenger's Guerrilla Handbook,* by George Albert Brown ($14.95; distributed by Slawson Communications, Inc., 165 Vallecitos de Oro, San Marcos, CA 92069, tel. 619/744–2299 or 800/752–9766), may be out of date in a few areas but remains a solid source of information on every aspect of air travel, including finding the cheapest fares.

Promotional Airfares Most scheduled airlines offer three classes of service: first class, business class, and economy or coach. To ride in the first-class or business-class sections, you pay a first-class or business-class fare. To ride in the economy or coach section—the remainder of the plane—you pay a confusing variety of fares. Most expensive is full-fare economy or unrestricted coach, which can be bought one-way or round-trip and can be changed and turned in for a refund.

All the less expensive fares, called promotional or discount fares, are round-trip and involve restrictions. The exact nature of the restrictions depends on the airline, the route, and the season and on whether travel is domestic or international, but you must usually buy the ticket—commonly called an APEX (advance purchase excursion) when it's for international travel—in advance (7, 14, or 21 days are usual). You must also respect certain minimum- and maximum-stay requirements (for instance, over a Saturday night or at least seven and no more than 30, 45, or 90 days), and you must be willing to pay penalties for changes. Airlines generally allow changes in the dates of the outbound or return leg of the trip for a fee. But the cheaper the fare, the more likely the ticket is nonrefundable–it would take a death in the family for the airline to give you any of your money back if you had to cancel. The cheapest fares are also subject to availability; because only a certain percentage of the plane's total seats will be sold at that price, they may go quickly.

Consolidators Consolidators or bulk-fare operators—also known as bucket shops—buy blocks of seats that scheduled airlines anticipate they won't be able to sell. They pay wholesale prices, add a markup, and resell the seats to travel agents or directly to the public at prices that still undercut the airline's promotional or discount fares. Consolidator fares are not as low as charter fares but they tend to be lower than APEX fares, and even when there is not much of a price difference, the consolidator ticket may be available without the advance-purchase restriction. Moreover, although tickets are marked nonrefundable so you can't turn them in to the airline for a full-fare refund, some consolidators sometimes give you your money back. Read the fine print detailing penalties for changes and cancellations carefully. If you doubt the reliability of a company, call the airline once you've made your booking and confirm that you do, indeed, have a reservation on the flight.

The biggest U.S. consolidator, C.L. Thomson Express, sells only to travel agents. Well-established consolidators selling to the public include **UniTravel** (Box 12485, St. Louis, MO 63132, tel. 314/569–0900 or 800/325–2222); **Council Charter** (205 E. 42nd St., New York, NY 10017, tel. 212/661–0311 or 800/800–8222), a division of the Council on International Educational Exchange and a longtime charter operator now functioning more as a consolidator; and **Travac** (989 6th Ave., New York, NY 10018, tel. 212/563–3303 or 800/872–8800), also a former charterer.

Charter Flights Charters usually have the lowest fares and the most restrictions. Departures are limited and seldom on time, and you can lose all or most of your money if you cancel. (Generally, the closer to departure you cancel, the more you lose, although sometimes you will be charged only a small fee if you supply a substitute passenger.) The charterer, on the other hand, may legally cancel the flight for any reason up to 10 days before departure; within 10 days of departure, the flight may be canceled only if it becomes physically impossible to operate it. The charterer may also revise the itinerary or increase the price after you have bought the ticket, but if the new arrangement constitutes a "major change," you have the right to a refund. Before buying a charter ticket, read the fine print for the company's refund policy and details on major changes. Money for charter flights is usually paid into a bank escrow account, the name of which should be on the contract. If you don't pay by credit card, make your check payable to the escrow account (unless you're dealing with a travel agent, in which case, his or her check should be payable to the escrow account). The Department of Transportation's Consumer Affairs Office (I–25, Washington, DC 20590, tel. 202/366-2220) can answer questions on charters and send you its "Plane Talk: Public Charter Flights" information sheet.

Charter operators may offer flights alone or with ground arrangements that constitute a charter package. Well-established charter operators include **Council Charter** (205 E. 42nd St., New York, NY 10017, tel. 212/661–0311 or 800/800–8222), now largely a consolidator, despite its name, and **Travel Charter** (1120 E. Long Lake Rd., Troy, MI 48098, tel. 313/528–3570 or 800/521–5267), with Midwestern departures. **DER Tours** (Box 1606, Des Plains, IL 60017, tel. 800/782–2424), a charterer and consolidator, sells through travel agents.

Discount Travel Travel clubs offer their members unsold space on airplanes, *Clubs* cruise ships, and package tours at nearly the last minute and at well below the original cost. Suppliers thus receive some revenue for their "leftovers," and members get a bargain. Membership generally includes a regular bulletin or access to a toll-free telephone hot line giving details of available trips departing anywhere from three or four days to several months in the future. Packages tend to be more common than flights alone, so if airfares are your only interest, read the literature before joining. Reductions on hotels are also available. Clubs include **Discount Travel International** (114 Forrest Ave., Suite 203, Narberth, PA 19072, tel. 215/668–7184; $45 annually, single or family), **Moment's Notice** (425 Madison Ave., New York, NY 10017, tel. 212/486–0503; $45 annually, single or family), **Travelers Advantage** (CUC Travel Service, 49 Music Sq. W, Nashville, TN 37203, tel. 800/548–1116; $49 annually, single or family); and **Worldwide Discount Travel Club** (1674 Meridian Ave., Miami Beach, FL 33139, tel. 305/534–2082; $50 annually for family, $40 single).

Flying as a Courier A courier is someone who accompanies a shipment between designated points so it can clear customs quickly as personal baggage. Because the courier company actually purchases a seat for the package, which uses the seat's checked-baggage allowance, it can allow you to occupy the paid seat at a vastly reduced rate. You must have a flexible schedule, however, as well as the ability to travel light, because you usually must make do with only carry-on baggage. *The Insiders Guide to Air Courier Bargains*, by Kelly Monaghan, gives more information ($16.95, including postage; Intrepid Traveler, Box 438, New York, NY 10034, tel. 800/356–9315), including sections on flying from Canada and England as well as the United States. If you're really serious, you might want to join a membership organization such as the **International Association of Air Travel Couriers** (Box 1349, Lake Worth, FL 33460, tel. 407/582–8320), which publishes six newsletters and six bulletters yearly listing courier opportunities worldwide. In general, couriers get their assignments from a booking agent, not directly from the courier company. One such agent is **Now Voyager** (74 Varick St., Suite 307, New York, NY 10013, tel. 212/431–1616), which places couriers on flights to various destinations.

Enjoying the Flight Fly at night if you're able to sleep on a plane. Because the air aloft is dry, drink plenty of beverages while on board; remember that drinking alcohol contributes to jet lag, as do heavy meals. Sleepers usually prefer window seats to curl up against; restless passengers ask to be on the aisle. Bulkhead seats, in the front row of each cabin, have more legroom, but since there's no seat ahead, trays attach awkwardly to the arms of your seat, and you must stow all possessions overhead. Bulkhead seats are usually reserved for the disabled, the elderly, and people traveling with babies.

Smoking Since February 1990, smoking has been banned on all domestic flights of less than six hours duration; the ban also applies to domestic segments of international flights aboard U.S. and foreign carriers. On U.S. carriers flying overseas, a seat in a no-smoking section must be provided for every passenger who requests one, and the section must be enlarged to accommodate such passengers if necessary as long as they have complied with the airline's deadline for check-in and seat assignment. If smoking bothers you, request a seat far from the smoking section.

Foreign airlines are exempt from these rules but do provide no-smoking sections, and some nations, including Canada as of July 1, 1993, have gone as far as to ban smoking on all domestic flights; other countries may ban smoking on flights of less than a specified duration. The International Civil Aviation Organization has set July 1, 1996, as the date to ban smoking aboard airlines worldwide, but the body has no power to enforce its decisions.

From the U.K. by Plane, Car, Train, and Bus

By Plane   **Alitalia** (tel. 081/745–8400) and **British Airways** (tel. 081/897–4000) operate direct flights from London (Heathrow) to Rome, Milan, Venice, Pisa, and Naples. Flying time is 2½ to 3 hours. There's also one direct flight a day from Manchester to Rome. Standard fares are extremely high, but several less expensive tickets are available. Both airlines offer APEX tickets (usual booking restrictions apply) and PEX tickets (which don't have to be bought in advance). The Eurobudget ticket (no length-of-stay or advance-purchase restrictions) is another option.

Less expensive flights are available: It pays to look in the classified advertisements of reputable newspapers and magazines such as *Time Out*. But remember to check the *full* price, inclusive of airport taxes and surcharges. Some of the bargains are not as inexpensive as they seem at first glance.

By Car   The distance from London to Rome is 1,810 kilometers (1,125 miles) via Calais/Boulogne/Dunkirk and 1,745 kilometers (1,085 miles) via Oostende/Zeebrugge (excluding sea crossings). Milan is about 645 kilometers (400 miles) closer. The drive from the Continental ports takes about 24 hours; the trip in total takes about three days. The shortest and quickest channel crossings are via Dover or Folkestone to one of the French ports (Calais or Boulogne); the ferry takes around 75 minutes and the Hovercraft just 35 minutes. Crossings from Dover to the Belgian ports take about four hours, but Oostende and Zeebrugge have good road connections. The longer crossing from Hull to Zeebrugge is useful for travelers from the north of England. The ferry from Sheerness, at the mouth of the Thames, to Vlissingen in Holland makes a comfortable overnight crossing; it takes about nine hours.

Fares on the cross-channel ferries vary considerably from season to season. Until the end of June and from early September onward, savings can be made by traveling midweek. Don't forget to budget for the cost of gas and road tolls, plus a couple of nights' accommodations.

Roads from the channel ports to Italy are mostly toll-free. The exceptions are the road crossing the Ardennes, the Swiss superhighway network (for which a special tax sticker must be bought at the frontier or in advance), the St. Gotthard Tunnel, and the road between the tunnel and the Italian superhighway system. The reduced-price petrol coupons once offered by the Italian government have been discontinued, but it won't hurt to check with the AA or RAC before departure to be sure they haven't become available again.

If these distances seem too great to drive, there's always the Motorail from the channel ports. However, no car/sleeper expresses run beyond Milan, 630 kilometers (390 miles) north of the capital.

By Train   Visitors traveling to Italy by train have several options. You can leave London's Victoria train station at 9:15 AM or 12:15 PM for the Folkestone–Boulogne Seacat catamaran service; from Boulogne Maritime, you take the train to Gare du Nord in Paris and then a taxi or metro across town to Gare de Lyons. From

there, you pick up the 8:56 PM "Napoli Express" for Rome.
There are first- and second-class sleeping cars and second-class
couchettes for the overnight run into Italy. From Paris to Dijon
there's a refreshment service, and a buffet car is attached in the
morning. The train reaches Turin at 6:10 AM the next day and
Rome at 2:19 PM.

Alternatively, the 9 AM Victoria service catches the Dover–
Calais ferry crossing; arrival time in Paris is 5:20 PM. The "Pal-
atino" leaves Paris at Gare de Lyons and travels via Chambéry
and the Mont Cenis tunnel to Turin, arriving about 2:50 AM.
You reach Rome by 9:35 AM. The train has first- and second-
class sleepers and second-class couchettes, but no ordinary day
cars for sitting up overnight. There's a buffet car from Paris to
Chambéry and from Genoa to Rome.

A year-round service leaves Victoria at 1:30 PM, catching the
Jetfoil for Oostende in plenty of time to take the 8:53 PM train to
Brig, Switzerland, arriving at about 9 AM. Change there for the
10:31 AM Milan train. At Milan there's a 12:55 PM departure for
Bologna, Florence, and Rome, arriving at Rome at 5:50 PM.

Train, ferry, and hovercraft schedules are subject to change, so
consult with **French Railways** (tel. 071/491–1573) and **British
Rail** (tel. 071/928–5151) before you leave.

By Bus   **Eurolines** (52 Grosvenor Gdns., London SW1W 0AU, tel. 071/
730–8235 or 071/730–3499, or any National Express agent)
runs a weekly bus service to Rome that increases to three times
a week between June and September. Buses leave on Monday,
Wednesday, and Friday over the summer, and on Saturday the
rest of the year. The trip takes about 30 hours. Buses travel via
Dover, Calais, Paris, and Lyon. Have a few French francs for
spending en route. Fares are quite high, especially when you
consider the long and tiring overnight journey and compare the
price with that of a charter flight.

Staying in Italy

Getting Around

By Train   Among transportation options in Italy, the train is still the best
bargain. The **Ferrovie dello Stato** (FS), the Italian state railway, has an extensive network providing relatively inexpensive service. There are two classes on trains; second-class
travel is inexpensive and comfortable, and, for a small fee, you
can reserve a seat in advance.

The fastest trains are the high-speed ETR 450 trains, operating on a few main lines; seat reservations are required, and
you must pay an extra charge for the airline-type meals and
service. The next fastest trains are the Intercity (IC) and
rapido (nonstop express) trains, some of which are first-class
only. You must pay a *supplemento* (extra charge) for IC and
Rapido service, although the supplement is waived for
EurailPass holders. The IC *supplemento* includes seat reservations, for which you ordinarily have to pay a small fee. IC trains
are often crowded, so try to purchase your tickets and make
reservations well in advance.

Espresso trains usually make more stops and are a little slower.
Diretto and *locale* are the slowest. If you study train schedules

carefully, you can often find an espresso train that will get you
to your destination almost as fast as an IC.

To avoid long lines at station windows, buy tickets and make
seat reservations at least a day in advance at travel agencies
displaying the FS emblem. If you have to reserve at the last
minute, reservation offices at the station accept reservations
up to three hours before departure. You can also get a seat assignment just before boarding the train; look for the conductor
on the platform near the train. If you don't want to pay for a
seat reservation, and know that the train originates in the station where you're boarding, get there at least 20 minutes prior
to departure time to board the empty train and find an unre-
served seat. (A card just outside the compartment or over the
seat indicates whether it has been reserved.) If the train is just
stopping en route at your station, you'll have to push your way
on and elbow through the corridors in hopes of finding a seat.
Read the reservation cards; you can use a seat from Rome to
Florence if the card says that it is reserved from Florence on to
another destination.

Taking an overnight train helps to cut down on hotel costs. On
overnight trips, a small extra fee (normally about 20,000 lire)
pays for a *cuccetta*—a fold-down bunk, usually arranged six to
a compartment. Passengers traveling on overnight trains
should secure their bags to the luggage rack with a small pad-
lock and keep all valuables on their person in a money belt while
sleeping.

Note that some Italian cities (including Milan, Turin, Genoa,
Naples, and Rome) have two or more main-line stations, although one is usually the principal terminus or through-
station. Be sure of the name of the station at which your train
will arrive, or from which it will depart.

There is refreshment service on all long-distance trains, with
mobile carts and a cafeteria or dining car. Tap water on trains is
not drinkable.

Rail Passes For those planning on doing a lot of traveling by train, the Italian Tourist Ticket (BTLC) is an excellent value. The Ticket
may be purchased before you leave, or in Italy at main train stations. For more information on discount rail passes, *see* Rail
Passes in Before You Go, *above.*

Travelers under 26 who have not invested in any of the above
passes should inquire about the **Carta Verde,** or Green Card,
which entitles the holder to a 20% discount on all first- and second-class tickets. Travelers over 60 are entitled to similar discounts with the **Carta d'Argento** (*see* Hints for Older Travelers,
above). Those under 26 should also inquire about discount travel fares under the Billet International Jeune (BIJ) scheme. The
special one-trip tickets are sold by **EuroTrain International** (no
connection with EurailPass) at its offices in various European
cities, including Rome, and by travel agents, mainline rail stations, and youth travel specialists (*see* Student and Youth Travel, *above*).

By Bus Italy's bus network is extensive, although not as attractive as
those in other European countries, partly because of the low
cost of train travel. Italian buses, however, are usually even
cheaper than trains, and buses are often the only way to reach
smaller towns or regions not served by a main train route.

Moreover, buses in Italy are in many cases more reliable and more direct than local trains. For example, Siena, which is difficult to reach by train, is easily accessible by bus from Florence or Rome; the fare from Florence to Siena is about 7,200 lire one way. You can reach Sorrento from Rome in about five effortless hours by Cital bus from Rome, avoiding a change from train to local bus in Naples; the fare is about 22,000 lire. To find out about buses to nearby destinations, go to CTS offices or local tourist information offices, especially those in train stations; they can supply schedules, tell you where to buy tickets (or sell them to you), and direct you to where the buses depart.

Local bus companies operate in many regions (*see* Getting Around by Bus in most chapters). In the hillier parts of Italy, particularly in the Alpine north, they take over when the gradients become too steep for train travel. A village shop or café will sometimes double as the ticket office and bus stop for these services. You should have your ticket before you board.

Most of the major cities have urban bus services, usually operating on a system involving the prepurchase of tickets (from a machine, a newsstand, or a tobacco store). These buses are inexpensive, but they can become unbearably jammed at rush hours. Remember that there are also lunchtime rush hours in the hotter periods, particularly in the south, when people go home for a siesta.

By Car If you plan to concentrate on Italy's major cities, such as Rome, Florence, and Milan, you'll find it easier and more economical to get around by public transportation. Automobile traffic is severely restricted in downtown areas of most cities and towns, and parking is scarce. In Venice, you can't use a car anywhere within the city, so you'll have to pay for a parking garage for the duration of your stay.

There is an extensive network of *autostrade* (toll highways), complemented by equally well-maintained but free *superstrade* (expressways). All are clearly signposted and numbered. The ticket you are issued upon entering an autostrada must be returned when you exit and pay the toll. On some shorter autostrade, mainly connecting highways, you pay the toll upon entering. A *raccordo* is a connecting expressway. *Strade statali* (state highways, denoted by S or SS numbers) may be single-lane roads, as are all secondary roads; directions and turnoffs are not always clearly marked. Information is obtainable from ACI (Automobile Club of Italy, Via Marsala 8, 00185 Rome, tel. 06/499–8389) and from ACI offices throughout Italy.

Rules of the Road Driving is on the right, as in the United States. Regulations are largely as in Britain and the United States, except that the police have the power to levy on-the-spot fines. In most Italian towns the use of the horn is forbidden in certain, if not all, areas; a large sign, *Zona di Silenzio*, indicates where. Speed limits are 130 kmh (80 mph) on autostrade and 110 kmh (70 mph) on state and provincial roads, unless otherwise marked. Fines for driving after drinking are heavy, with the additional possibility of six months' imprisonment, but there is no fixed blood-alcohol regulation and no official test.

Parking In most cities, parking space is at a premium; historic town centers are closed to most traffic, and peripheral parking areas are usually full. Parking in a *Zona Disco* is allowed for limited periods (30 minutes to 2 hours or more—the limit is posted); if you don't have the cardboard disk to show what time you parked, you can use a piece of paper. It's advisable to leave your car in a guarded parking area; many are run by ACI. Unofficial parking attendants can help you find a space but offer no guarantees. In major cities your car may be towed away if illegally parked.

Gas Gas ranges from 1,450 lire to 1,550 lire per liter, the equivalent of about $4 a U.S. gallon. Only a few gas stations are open on Sunday, and most close for a couple of hours at lunchtime and at 7 PM for the night. Self-service pumps may be few and far between outside major cities. Gas stations on autostrade are open 24 hours.

Breakdowns **ACI Emergency Service** (Servizio Soccorso Stradale, Via Solferino 32, 00185 Rome, tel. 06/44595) offers 24-hour road service. Dial 116 to reach the nearest ACI service station.

By Plane Fares are high on Italy's three domestic airlines, **ATI, Alitalia,** and **Alisarda,** but these airlines offer many discounts, such as same-day and weekend fares. Italy is a long, narrow country, and the fastest way to travel north–south is by air; depending on your interests and your time schedule, it may be worth it for you to spend the extra money in order to see places you wouldn't otherwise be able to include in your itinerary. Otherwise, it's best to stick to train and bus travel. Apart from the major international airports, you can find frequent flights between airports serving smaller cities, such as Bologna, Genoa, Naples, Palermo, Turin, and Verona. Flight times are never much more than an hour (long flights usually are those going from the extreme north to Naples or Sicily), and most of these smaller airports are close to the cities and linked by good bus services. Italian travel agents will inform you of the discounts available, some of which include a 50% family reduction for a spouse and/or children traveling with you, or up to 30% for certain night flights.

By Bike Cycling is a good way to see the flatter parts of the country, but remember that Italy is made up mainly of mountains and their foothills. You can rent bicycles and mopeds in most major tourist cities at a reasonable daily fee. In Rome, for example, a bike rents for about 12,000 lire per day, 35,000 lire per week, 55,000 lire for up to 30 days; a moped costs 35,000–55,000 lire per day.

To transport your own bike by train within Italy, label it and take it to the baggage window, the *ufficio bagagli*, at the train station; it should arrive at its destination within three days.

By Foot Hiking through the Chianti district, the Dolomites, or many other parts of the country gives you a close look at Italy and its people. Local tourist information offices can provide information on trails. The national organization is the **Club Alpino Italiano** (CAI), Piazza Sant'Andrea della Valle 3, Rome, tel. 06/686–1011. CTS also can provide information on hiking.

Telephones

To call Italy from the United States dial 011-39, plus the area code and number.

Local Calls Pay phones in Italy take either a 200-lire coin, two 100-lire coins, a *gettone* (token), or a *scheda* (prepaid calling card). The gettone-only phones are the oldsters; if you happen upon one, buy tokens from the nearest cashier or the token machine near the phone. Insert the token (which doesn't drop right away), dial the number, wait for an answer, then complete the connection by pushing the knob at the token slot. When the token drops, the other party is able to hear you. Scheda phones are becoming common everywhere. You buy the card at Telefoni offices or tobacconists for 5,000 or 10,000 lire. Insert the card as indicated by the arrow on it, and you will see the value of the card in the window. After the call, hang up, and the card will be returned, usable until its value runs out. The card makes long-distance direct dialing *(teleselezione)* much easier than it used to be. Without it, insert at least five 100 lire coins and have more handy; unused coins will be returned.

International Calls Since hotels tend to overcharge, sometimes exorbitantly, for long-distance and international calls, it's best to make such calls from Telefoni offices, where operators will assign you a booth, help you place your call, and collect payment when you have finished, at no extra charge. There are Telefoni offices, designated *SIP* (sometimes also *ASST*), in all cities and towns. You can make collect calls from any phone by dialing 170, which will get you an English-speaking operator. Rates to the United States are lowest round the clock on Sunday and 11 PM–8 AM, Italian time, on weekdays.

Another way to avoid high hotel phone charges is to make your international call from any public phone, using AT&T or MCI international operators;. you can use a long-distance calling card or make a collect call. To call the United States from Italy, dial 172–1011 for AT&T; 172–1022 for MCI.

A three-minute call from Rome to New York or Los Angeles should cost about 10,000 lire.

Operators and Information For general information in English on calling in Europe and the Mediterranean area, dial 176. For operator-assisted service in those areas, dial 15. For operator-assisted service and information regarding intercontinental calls, dial 170.

Mail

Postal Rates Airmail letters (lightweight stationery) to the United States and Canada cost 1,200 lire for the first 19 grams and an additional 1,800 lire for up to 50 grams. Airmail postcards cost 1,000 lire if the message is limited to a few words and a signature; otherwise, you pay the letter rate. Airmail letters to the United Kingdom cost 750 lire; postcards, 650 lire. You can buy stamps at tobacconists.

Receiving Mail Mail service is generally slow; allow up to 14 days for mail from Britain, 21 days from North America. Correspondence can be addressed to you care of the Italian post office. Letters should be addressed to your name, "c/o Ufficio Postale Centrale," followed by "FERMO POSTA" on the next line, and the name of the city (preceded by its postal code) on the next. You can collect it at the central post office by showing your passport or photo-bearing ID and paying a small fee. American Express also has a general-delivery service for clients. There's no charge for cardholders, holders of American Express Traveler's checks, or anyone who booked a vacation with American Express.

Tipping

Tipping practices vary, depending on where you are. The following guidelines apply in major cities, but Italians tip smaller amounts in smaller cities and towns. Tips may not be expected in cafés and taxis north of Rome.

In restaurants a service charge of about 15% usually appears as a separate item on your check. A few restaurants state on the menu that the service charge is included in the menu prices. Either way, it's customary to leave an additional 5%–10% tip for the waiter, depending on the service. Restroom attendants are given about 200 lire in public restrooms. Tip 100 lire for whatever you drink standing up at a coffee bar, 500 lire or more for table service in a smart café, and less in neighborhood cafés.

Taxi drivers are usually happy with 5%–10% of the meter amount. Railway and airport porters charge a fixed rate per bag. Tip an additional 500 lire per person, but more if the porter is very helpful. Theater ushers expect 500 lire per person, but more for very expensive seats. Give a barber 2,000 lire and a hairdresser's assistant 3,000 lire for a cut or shampoo in a moderate establishment.

On sight-seeing tours, tip guides about 2,000 lire per person for a half-day group tour, more if they're especially good. In museums and other places of interest where admission is free but an offering is expected, give anything from 500 to 1,000 lire for one or two persons, more if the guardian has been especially helpful. Service station attendants are tipped only for special services.

In hotels, give the porter 5,000–10,000 lire if he or she has been generally helpful. For two people in a double room, leave the room attendant about 1,000 lire per day, or about 4,000–5,000 a week; tip a minimum of 1,000 lire for room service.

Opening and Closing Times

Banks Branches are open weekdays 8:30–1:30 and 2:45–3:45.

Churches Most are open from early morning until noon or 12:30, when they close for two hours or more; they open again in the afternoon, closing about 7 PM or later. Major cathedrals and basilicas, such as St. Peter's, are open all day. Sight-seeing in churches during religious rites is usually discouraged. Be sure to have a fistful of 100-lire coins handy for the *luce* (light) machines that illuminate the works of art in the perpetual dusk of ecclesiastical interiors. A pair of binoculars will help you get a good look at painted ceilings and domes.

Museums Hours vary and may change with the seasons. Many important national museums have short hours and are closed one day a week, often on Monday. They're open on some holidays, closed on others. Check individual listings in the individual chapters, and always check locally. Remember that ticket offices close from 30 minutes to one hour before official closing time.

Shops There are individual variations, depending on climate and season, but most are open 9:30–1 and 3:30 or 4–7 or 7:30. Food shops open earlier in the morning and later in the afternoon. In all but resorts and small towns, shops close on Sunday and one half-day during the week. Some tourist-oriented shops in such places as Rome and Venice are open all day, as are some department stores and supermarkets. Post offices are open 8–2; central and main district post offices stay open until 8 or 9 PM for some services. Barbers and hairdressers, with some exceptions, are closed Sunday and Monday.

National Holidays January 1 (New Year's Day); January 6 (Epiphany); April 3, 4, 1994 (Easter Sunday and Monday); April 25 (Liberation Day); May 1 (Labor Day or May Day); August 15 (Assumption of Mary, also known as Ferragosto); November 1 (All Saints Day); December 8 (Immaculate Conception); December 25, 26 (Christmas Day and Boxing Day).

The feast days of patron saints are also holidays, observed locally. Many businesses and shops may be closed in Florence, Genoa, and Turin on June 24 (St. John the Baptist); in Rome on June 29 (Sts. Peter and Paul); in Palermo on July 15 (Santa Rosalia); in Naples on September 19 (San Gennaro); in Bologna on October 4 (San Petronio); and in Milan on December 7 (St. Ambrose). Venice's feast of St. Mark is April 25, the same as Liberation Day.

Shopping

Don't expect to find bargains on Italian designer clothes or luxury items: The high Italian cost of living makes such goods just as expensive in Italy as they are abroad, although recent changes in the exchange rate have favored the dollar and improved the picture for tourists somewhat. One thing to bear in mind when traveling around the country is that good buys may be found in goods that are regional specialties, since lots of local competition can keep prices reasonable.

Venice is known for glassware, lace, and velvet; Milan and Como for silk; the Dolomites and the mountainous regions of Calabria and Sicily for hand-carved wooden objects; Florence for straw goods, gold jewelry, and leather; Naples for coral and cameos; Assisi for embroidery; and Deruta, Vietri, and many towns in Apulia and Sicily for ceramics.

In Milan and Venice, you may want to limit yourself to window shopping, since goods tend to be more expensive there than anywhere else. The one exception in Venice is the superb glassware, which, although not necessarily cheap, can be bought at lower prices than anywhere else in the world. Only buy what you can carry away with you, however, since it's risky to ship such fragile articles.

Bargain shopping is generally best in Rome and Florence; investigate the outdoor markets especially, such as Porta Portese in Rome and San Lorenzo in Florence. If you buy from a market stall, go over your choice with a fine eye for defects. If you find a fault that doesn't really bother you too much, point it out to the dealer, and bargain the price down as much as you can. You can sometimes find splendid second-hand art books and old prints in the bookshops and stalls of Rome and Florence.

Always shop around before you buy, since prices for the same item can vary dramatically from store to store. Remember that shops in Italy do not refund money and may not always exchange goods, since their stocks are often limited, so make sure your choice is exactly what you want before you leave the store.

Unless your purchases are too bulky, avoid having them shipped home; if the shop seems extremely reliable about shipping, get a written statement of what will be sent, when, and how. (*See* Shopping in individual chapters for details.)

IVA (VAT) Refunds   Italy's IVA-refund system, once applicable only to really big spenders, has recently been made more "user-friendly." Now a non-EC resident can obtain a refund after spending a total of 300,000 lire in one store (before tax—and note that price tags and prices quoted, unless stated otherwise, are inclusive of IVA). At the time of purchase, with passport or ID in hand, ask the store for an invoice itemizing the price of the article(s) and the amount of tax. When you leave the EC, take the still-unused goods and the invoice to the customs office at the airport (or other point) of departure and have the invoice stamped. For example, if your itinerary is USA–Italy–England–USA, you would take goods purchased in Italy, with the invoice, to the customs office at the airport in England before boarding your flight home. If you depart directly from Italy, go through the procedure at the Italian airport. Once back home—and within 90 days of the date of purchase—send the stamped invoice back to the store, which will then forward the IVA rebate to you. A growing number of stores in Italy (and Europe) are members of the Tax-Free Shopping System, which expedites things by providing an invoice that is actually a Tax-free Cheque in the amount of the tax refund. Once it has been stamped at customs, it can be cashed at the Tax-Free Cash Refund window in the transit area of major airports and border crossings.

Bargaining   The notice *Prezzi fissi* (fixed prices) means just that; in shops displaying this sign it's a waste of time to bargain unless you're buying a sizable quantity of goods or a particularly costly object. Always bargain, instead, at outdoor markets and when buying from street vendors.

Beaches

Italy isn't the place for an exclusively "beach" holiday; you'll find cleaner water and better beaches at lower prices in other parts of the world. The waters that are least polluted and best for swimming are off portions of the coasts of Calabria and Apulia; and off the islands of Elba, Capri, Ischia, Ustica, the Aeolians, and western Sicily. Topless bathing is widespread, except for a few staid family-type beaches near large cities. Nudism is discreetly practiced on out-of-the-way beaches, mainly on the islands and on deserted stretches of the mainland coast. Singles will find the liveliest resorts on the Adriatic Coast and on the coasts of Tuscany and Calabria. Certain expensive resorts—the Costa Smeralda in Sardinia, Forte dei Marmi in Tuscany, and the Lido in Venice—are beyond the scope of a budget traveler, but elsewhere, even in Capri, Positano, Taormina, and on the Italian Riviera, you can find inexpensive accommodations and eating places. To avoid high admission fees at beach concessions, walk or take a bus to more out-of-the-way beaches. The resorts strung out along the Adriatic coast of Emilia-Romagna (and, farther south, Abruzzo) offer very good value, especially in the shoulder seasons (May to June and September to October). During the winter, the few hotels and restaurants that remain open in beach resorts can be real bargains.

Dining

Unfortunately, high prices are the norm in Italian restaurants. For the traveler with a budget it takes a bit of looking to find a good meal that won't empty the wallet. But don't despair—it's not impossible. One rule of thumb is to avoid establishments near tourist attractions, where the food is usually mediocre, the service rushed, and the prices high. Instead, search out places farther away from the busy sights. Ask the desk clerk at your hotel for suggestions.

It's also possible to keep meal costs down by not ordering a full three-course meal. The *primi piatti*—first courses, usually pastas and risottos—are so delicious and filling, you may not necessarily need to order the more expensive meat course (or, even more expensive, seafood), even though that's what waiters expect of you. Green salads are normally inexpensive, as are side orders of vegetables. Bread is included in the cover charge. Bottled water ranges in price from 2,000 to 3,000 lire in a restaurant; if you don't want it, ask instead for *acqua naturale*, or *acqua semplice* (from the tap), which is, of course, free. Bottled wine could double your bill, so stay with the house red or white, which is usually good. The price of desserts, cappuccino, and after-dinner drinks may rudely surprise you. It is always cheaper to go to a bar or a gelateria for dessert and coffee.

Visitors have a choice of eating places, ranging from a *ristorante* (restaurant) to a *trattoria*, *tavola calda*, or *rosticceria*. A trattoria is usually a family-run place, simpler in decor, menu, and service than a ristorante, and slightly less expensive. Some rustic-looking spots call themselves *osterie* but are really restaurants. (A true osteria is a wineshop, a very basic and down-to-earth tavern.) The countless fast-food places opening up everywhere are variations of the older Italian institutions of the *tavola calda* or *rosticceria*, which offer a selection of hot and cold dishes that you may take out or eat on the premises. (A tavola calda is more likely to have seating.) At either a tavola calda or rosticceria, some items are priced by the portion, others by weight. You usually select your food, find out how much it costs, then pay the cashier and get a stub that you must give to the counterman when you pick up the food.

A sit-down meal in a *pizzeria* is a good option if you want to save money. Pizzerias and trattorias serving pizza usually offer other quick dishes at reasonable prices as well. Pizzas, which range in price from 7,000 to 10,000 lire, normally come in one size (medium to large) and can, depending on how hungry you are, feed one or two people. Harder to find up north, but situated on practically every street corner from Rome southward, *pizza rustica* shops offer take-out pizza *a taglia* (by the slice) from morning till night. You won't find American-style pepperoni on the pizza, but there are many other interesting toppings.

None of the above serves breakfast; in the morning, if you don't eat at your hotel, you can go to a coffee bar. Later in the day, the same bars are good spots for quick, inexpensive lunches of *panini* and *tramezzini*, little ready-made sandwiches costing about 2,000 lire. Eat standing up; it costs less than sitting down at a table, for which you will pay an extra charge, not to mention higher per-item prices (a cappuccino could cost you 5,000 lire instead of 1,800 lire). A glass of wine usually costs less than a Coca-Cola or beer. Some bars in larger cities also have a selection of hot dishes, such as pasta and roast meat, at reasonable prices.

In fair weather, picnics are another money-saving lunch option. Buy the ingredients—cheeses, cold meats, bread, fruit—at *alimentari* stores or supermarkets such as Standa. Some grocery stores will make up a sandwich for you if they're not busy.

Unlike fast-food chains in the United States, Italian equivalents are not necessarily cheaper than trattorias and aren't half as appealing. And although you'll see the golden arches of McDonald's in many locations in Italy, don't be tempted—it'll cost you nearly 12,000 lire for a Big Mac, fries, and a soda. The same applies to the plethora of Chinese restaurants that have opened all over Italy; the Italian version of Chinese food is usually disappointing, and not cheap.

In eating places of all kinds, the menu is posted in the window or just inside the door so you can see what you're getting into (in a snack bar or tavola calda the price list is usually displayed near the cashier). In all but the simplest places there's a *coperto* (cover charge) and usually also a *servizio* (service charge) of 10%–15%, only part of which goes to the waiter. Look at these items first: If the restaurant charges 3,000 lire for *coperto* plus 15% for *servizio*, think twice about entering; another place around the corner may charge less for cover and service and have proportionately lower prices for food, too. A *menù turistico* (tourist menu) includes taxes and service, but beverages are usually extra. In some trattorias, menus are not printed, and the waiter simply rattles off the specials. If you're concerned about price, ask how much the dish you're interested in costs. As a general rule, meat and seafood dishes cost much more than pasta and pizza.

Beware of menu items marked "SQ" (according to quantity), which means you'll be charged according to the weight of the item ordered, or "L. 18,000 hg," which means the charge will be 18,000 lire per hectogram (3½ ounces). Pricing by weight usually refers to items such as fresh fish or Florentine steaks and fillets.

Mealtimes Lunch is served in Rome from 1 to 3, dinner from 8 to 10, or later in some restaurants. Service begins and ends a half-hour earlier in Florence and Venice, an hour earlier in smaller towns in the north, a half-hour to one hour later in the south. Almost all eating places close one day a week and for vacations in summer and/or winter.

Precautions Tap water is safe almost everywhere unless labeled "*Non Potabile.*" Most people order bottled *acqua minerale* (mineral water), either *gassata* (bubbles) or *naturale*, or *non gassata* (without). In a restaurant you order it by the *litro* (liter) or *mezzo litro* (half-liter); often the waiter will bring it without being asked, so if you want to keep your check down, make a point of ordering *acqua semplice* (tap water). You can also order *un bicchiere di acqua minerale* (a glass of mineral water) at any bar. If you are on a low-sodium diet, ask for everything (within reason) *senza sale* (without salt).

Ratings Restaurants in our listings are divided by price into three categories:

Category	Cost: Rome, Venice, Milan	Cost: Elsewhere
Moderate	under 45,000 lire	under 30,000 lire
Inexpensive	under 35,000 lire	under 24,000 lire
Budget	under 25,000 lire	under 20,000 lire

Prices are quoted for a two-course meal without wine, service, or taxes. Unless otherwise noted, reservations are not needed and dress is casual. Highly recommended restaurants are indicated by a star ★.

Lodging

The official government rating system in Italy—from five stars down to one star—provides comparative guidelines for prices, but they are not necessarily an indication of the quality of the establishment. Hotels in Italy, generally speaking, offer lower levels of comfort for higher prices than hotels in the United States. This is especially true of affordable hotels.

Hotels in the affordable category include a few three-star establishments in some towns, but are mainly two- and one-star hotels, including what used to be called pensions. Small, family-run hotels in these categories are often friendly and hospitable, but few have dining rooms. Their guest rooms generally have no radio or TV, and furnishings are usually simple—often, frankly, drab.

Downright budget-level hotels are plentiful in the main tourist cities, but be selective when you book: In Rome or Milan, for instance, many cheap hotels near the train stations are undesirable, though there are some good choices (*see* our listings).

Although by law, breakfast is supposed to be optional, most hotels quote room rates including breakfast. When you book a room, ask specifically whether the rate includes breakfast (*colazione*). You are under no obligation to take breakfast at your hotel, but in practice most hotels expect you to do so. Considering that Italian hotel breakfasts usually are very simple, even skimpy, this is not good value for the money; you can eat better for less at the nearest coffee bar. If you don't mind bucking the system, specify when you make your reservation—*and* when you check in—that you don't want breakfast at the hotel and do not expect to pay for it. The hotel may not be happy about it, and a few will not accept reservations without breakfast, but you are entirely within your rights. If more guests oppose this practice of padding the bill, hotel owners may see the light. Report any overcharging to the local tourist information office.

In all hotels you will find a rate card inside the door of your room, or inside the closet door; it tells you exactly what you will pay for that particular room (room rates in the same hotel may vary according to the location and type of room), with breakfast and any other optionals listed separately. Any discrepancy between the basic room rate and that charged on your bill is cause for complaint to the manager and to the local tourist office.

To stay within the price categories for affordable hotels, you may have to take a room without private bath. Many rooms are equipped with sinks, however. In one-star hotels, you may have to pay extra to use the shower or tub down the hall. If you do pay extra for a private bathroom, don't expect luxury; it may only be a shower, often with a drain in the floor, rarely with a shower curtain.

Even in expensive hotels in Italy, good reading lights are a rarity. Consider carrying your own small battery-run reading light. If you are traveling in the summer, you may want to pay extra for air-conditioning, if it is available at all. Ask how much it costs—it's usually 7,000–15,000 lire per day, and that adds up fast.

People traveling alone are always penalized by rates for single rooms, which cost more per person than doubles and are usually less attractive. If you're traveling in a group, however, many affordable hotels will allow you to add one, two, or even three beds to a double room, charging no more than 35% of the normal room rate for each extra bed.

Reservations are vital during the main tourist season and advisable even off-season, since the better affordable hotels are small and are booked way ahead by regulars. Expect to pay a deposit to hold your reservation. International mails are slow, so write to the hotel of your choice as early as possible—or, even better, use the telephone or fax. If you arrive without a reservation, look for a hotel association desk or booth in the train station or airport; the staff will help you book a room, and if a deposit is charged, it will be subtracted from your hotel bill. Local tourist information offices also will help you find a hotel room.

In many small towns rooms are available in private homes. The local tourist office provides a list of those it has licensed; the cost is usually a little less than what you would pay in a budget hotel. Another way to keep your lodging costs to a bare minimum is to stay in certain religious institutions that offer hospitality to pilgrims at low prices. Most will accept guests of all faiths, though some are only for men, others only for women. Some accept couples and families. There is usually a curfew at night, and meals may be offered, sometimes even required. Local tourist offices can provide information; in Rome, the Vatican information office in Piazza San Pietro has a list of accommodations of this type. There are several in Venice as well.

Camping Camping is becoming a popular choice for Italians themselves, who take to the road and can avail themselves of some 1,700 official campsites. Apart from cost considerations, camping is a good way to find accommodations in otherwise overcrowded resorts. Make sure you stay only on authorized campsites (camping on private land is frowned upon). You must also have an international camping *carnet* (permit), which you can obtain from your local camping association before you leave home. You can obtain a directory of campgrounds in Italy by writing to the **Federazione Italiana del Campeggio e del Caravanning** (Federcampeggio, Casella Postale 23, 50041 Calenzano, Florence, fax 055/882–5918) and requesting *Campeggiare in Italia;* send three international reply coupons to cover mailing. (This directory is also available through the Italian Government Travel Office in the United States or at tourist information offices in Italy, until supplies run out.) The Touring Club Italiano publishes a multilingual *Guida Camping d'Italia* (campsite directory), available in bookstores in Italy for about 30,000 lire, with more detailed information on the sites. Camp rates for two persons, with tent, average about 20,000 lire a day.

Camper rental agencies operate throughout Italy: Contact your travel agency for details. One package, for example, allows you to fly to Sicily, pick up a fully equipped camper on arrival, and explore the island as you please.

Hostels The Italian Youth Hostels Association operates about 50 hostels in Italy, some in such beautiful settings as the 14th-century castle of Rocca degli Alberi at Montagnana, near Padua, and the Castello di Scilla, on the Straits of Messina. Hostel rates are about 18,000 lire per person per night, including breakfast, but it's not easy to find accommodations, especially in tourist centers, unless you have reservations. Access to international hostels comes with membership in the International Youth Hostel Federation, which, in turn, is provided by membership in any national association; guidebooks listing the hostels worldwide are available through these same associations. (*See* Hosteling in Student and Youth Travel, *above* for particulars.) In Italy, contact the **Associazione Italiana Alberghi per la Gioventù** (Via Cavour 44, Rome, tel. 06/487–1152), the Italian member of the International Youth Hostel Federation.

Home Exchange This is obviously an inexpensive solution to the lodging problem, because house-swapping means living rent-free. You find a house, apartment, or other vacation property to exchange for your own by becoming a member of a home-exchange organization, which then sends you its annual directories listing available exchanges and includes your own listing in at least one of them. Arrangements for the actual exchange are made by the two parties to it, not by the organization. Principal clearinghouses include **Intervac U.S./International Home Exchange** (Box 590504, San Francisco, CA 94159, tel. 415/435–3497), the oldest, with thousands of foreign and domestic homes for exchange in its three annual directories; membership is $62, or $72 if you want to receive the directories but remain unlisted. The **Vacation Exchange Club** (Box 650, Key West, FL 33041, tel. 800/638–3841), also with thousands of foreign and domestic listings, publishes four annual directories plus updates; the $50 membership includes your listing in one book. **Loan-a-Home** (2 Park La., Apt. 6E, Mount Vernon, NY 10552, tel. 914/664–7640) specializes in long-term exchanges; there is no charge to list your home, but the directories cost $35 or $45 depending on the number you receive.

Apartment and Villa Rentals If you want a home base that's roomy enough for a family and comes with cooking facilities, a furnished rental may be the solution. It can be a cost-wise solution, too, although not always—many rentals are luxury properties, economical only when your party is large. Home-exchange directories do list rentals—often second homes owned by prospective house swappers—but there are services that look for a house or apartment for you and also handle the paperwork. Some send an illustrated catalogue and others send photographs of specific properties, sometimes at a charge; up-front registration fees may apply. In Italy, the possibilities include rustic, converted stone farmhouses, seaside villas, city apartments, and even quarters in a 16th-century Renaissance palace or two.

Among the companies are **At Home Abroad** (405 East 56th St., Suite 6H, New York, NY 10022, tel. 212/421–9165); **Interhome Inc.** (124 Little Falls Rd., Fairfield, NJ 07004, tel. 201/882–6864); **Overseas Connection** (31 North Harbor Dr., Sag Harbor, NY 11963, tel. 516/725–9308); **Rent a Home International** (7200 34th Ave. NW, Seattle, WA 98117, tel. 206/789–9377 or 800/488–7368); **Vacation Home Rentals Worldwide** (235 Kensington Ave., Norwood, NJ 07648, tel. 201/767–9393 or 800/633–3284); **Villa Leisure** (Box 209, Westport, CT 06881, tel. 407/624–9000 or 800/526–4244); **Villas and Apartments Abroad** (420 Madison Ave., Suite 1105, New York, NY 10017, tel. 212/759–1025 or 800/433–3020); and **Villas International** (605 Market St., Suite 510, San Francisco, CA 94105, tel. 415/281–0910 or 800/221–2260). **Hideaways International** (767 Islington St., Box 4433, Portsmouth, NH 03802, tel. 603/430–4433 or 800/843–4433) functions as a travel club. Membership ($79 yearly per person or family at the same address) includes receipt of two annual guides plus quarterly newsletters; rentals are arranged directly between members, not by the club staff.

All of the above represent properties in Italy along with other locations worldwide. Two companies that focus on Italy nearly exclusively are **Cuendet USA** (165 Chestnut St., Allendale, NJ 07401, tel. 201/327–2333), the U.S. representative of Cuendet of Italy, and **Vacanze in Italia** (Box 297, Falls Village, CT 06031, tel. 413/528–6610 or 800/533–5405).

Also of interest is **Italy Farm Holidays** (547 Martling Ave., Tarrytown, NY 10591, tel. 914/631–7880, fax 914/631–8831), which specializes in Agriturismo properties. These are working farms that supplement their income by renting out furnished bed-and-breakfast rooms or apartments or separate houses with kitchens. The accommodations, which range from $366 to $630 per couple per week in a B&B (more for larger quarters holding more people), can be too rustic for some or unreliable in quality, but IFH represents fewer than 50 properties (Umbria, Toscany, with Piedmont and the Veneto to come), all of which they have inspected personally.

Two London-based companies with a good selection of rentals on their books are **Villas Italia Ltd.** (Astral Towers, Betts Way, Crawley, West Sussex RH10 29X, tel. 0293/599988) and **CV Travel** (43 Cadogan St., London SW3 2PR, tel. 071/581–0851).

Ratings   Hotels in our listings are divided by price into three categories:

Category	Cost: Rome, Venice, Milan	Cost: Elsewhere
Moderate	under 125,000 lire	under 115,000 lire
Inexpensive	under 100,000 lire	under 85,000 lire
Budget	under 65,000 lire	under 60,000 lire

The prices indicated are for a double room, double occupancy. Obviously, within hotels there are variations in room prices: If you ask for a private bath in a Budget hotel, the extra charge may push your rate up into the Inexpensive category; on the other hand, you may be able to get the comforts of a Moderate hotel for Inexpensive rates if you choose a room without private bath. *See* our warning about breakfast charges, *above.* Hotels in some regions, particularly the northern mountainous areas, offer attractive half- and full-board packages (in which some or all meals are included in the price) and usually require that you stay a certain number of days. These deals can often "lower" an establishment into a less expensive classification in real terms because the inclusive rates are a bargain.

Highly recommended lodgings are indicated by a star ★.

Credit Cards

The following credit card abbreviations are used: AE, American Express; DC, Diners Club; MC, MasterCard; V, Visa.

Popular Itineraries

Rome to Florence

This itinerary offers a chance to experience a wide range of scenery and historical influences in a relatively short distance. The route and terrain would be equally familiar to an Etruscan nobleman, Roman centurion, or medieval cardinal because the main lines of communication in central Italy have always run along, or parallel to, the Apennines.

Heading north from Rome along the coast, you pass the Etruscan city of Tarquinia before reaching Viterbo, which is still guarded by its medieval walls and is full of crafts shops. The next stop is Orvieto, perched on the top of a rocky peak and living up to its reputation as a romantic medieval city. The area boasts one of Italy's most famous white wines, and the surrounding countryside, made up of jagged outcrops of volcanic rock, is as dramatic as Orvieto itself.

A few miles north and you're in Tuscany, with its rolling countryside of olive groves and cypresses that captivated the Renaissance painters. The next stop is welcoming Siena, the beautiful art city famous for its motto on the city gates: *Cor Magis tibi Sena pandit* (Siena opens its heart to you). Siena's medieval past comes alive twice a year when the colorful riders in the Palio horse race charge round the fan-shape Piazza del Campo.

The last stop is Florence, the cradle of the Renaissance and the highlight of many trips to Italy. Birthplace of artistic and literary giants, Renaissance Florence nurtured its native talents and attracted others from all over Italy and Europe. The result is one of the world's greatest concentrations of art and architecture, crammed into what is really a compact city along the banks of the river Arno. Just northeast of Florence is Fiesole, a hilltop village that dates as far back as the Etruscans and provides some of the best views of the Arno Valley and Florence itself.

Length of Trip Seven days.

Getting Around The most direct route from Rome to Florence is about 275 ki-
By Car lometers (170 miles), but to appreciate the scenery you should add to that figure by keeping off the direct superhighway (A1). Instead, take S2 almost all the way, leaving it only to head east to Orvieto along S71.

By Public
Transportation

Take an express bus to Viterbo and then another bus from Viterbo to Orte, where you can get a fast train to Orvieto. A slower train makes the scenic trip to Siena, passing through Montepulciano. Take the local train north from Siena, changing at Empoli for Florence.

The Main Route

One Night: Viterbo. Either stop in Tarquinia en route (taking S1 from Rome to Tarquinia) or make a side trip to the Etruscan settlement from Viterbo. In Viterbo explore Piazza San Lorenzo and the San Pellegrino quarter, one of the best preserved and most hauntingly medieval cores in any Italian city.

One Night: Orvieto. Stop a few miles west of Orvieto, on S71, to appreciate the best view of the cliff-top city. In Orvieto, visit the Duomo, one of Italy's most dramatically sited cathedrals, noted for its stunning, intricately multicolored facade. Walk to St. Patrick's Well. Make sure to sample some of the local white wine.

Two Nights: Siena. You could spend a whole day relaxing in the beguiling Piazza del Campo, which is bathed in a warm and ever-changing light. Visit the Palazzo Pubblico, the Pinacoteca Gallery, and the Duomo (Cathedral). Try to be on hand for one of the two runnings of the Palio.

Three Nights: Florence. This is the minimum stay in one of the world's great cities. If you do nothing else, visit the Duomo, Baptistery, Piazza della Signoria, Uffizi Gallery, Palazzo Pitti, Galleria dell'Accademia, and the charming church of San Miniato al Monte. If all the art is overwhelming, make a side trip to Fiesole and relax while overlooking the entire valley of the Arno.

Information

See Chapters 2, 3, 4, and 11.

From the Ligurian Sea to the Adriatic

Italy's sea trade in the Middle Ages was dominated by two maritime republics—Genoa, on the Ligurian Sea, and Venice, on the Adriatic. It was inevitable that these two powers would eventually clash over supremacy in the eastern Mediterranean: The Venetian victory at the Battle of Chioggia, in 1381, settled more than 100 years of conflict.

The development of the two cities since the decisive battle in the 14th century would have been hard to predict at the time. Genoa, defeated militarily, developed economically into one of the world's great ports. Powerful Venice remained in ascendancy for more than a century, amassing colonies along the eastern Adriatic Coast and as far east as Cyprus before sinking into a languid decline.

This west–east itinerary offers a chance to explore these contrasting cities—one a busy, modern port and the other the caretaker of a gilded past. In between you'll pass spectacular scenery along the Ligurian coastline, culminating in the remote fishing villages of the Cinque Terre. After turning inland across mountains, you'll reach Parma, known as much for its harmonious medieval cathedral and majestic baptistry as for its famous ham and cheese. Farther east, along the banks of the fast-flowing Adige River, is Verona, with its Roman arena and attractive medieval quarter—the setting for Shakespeare's *Romeo and Juliet*. Between Verona and Venice is Padua, noted for its famous university and the Scrovegni Chapel, decorated with magnificent wall paintings by Giotto. Finally there is glorious Venice, a city that has learned to cope with the tides of visitors and of the waters of its lagoon in equal measure.

Length of Trip Eight to 11 days.

Getting Around The total distance is about 450 kilometers (270 miles). The *By Car* coastal S1 route is the most scenic way to get to La Spezia from Genoa, although you'll need to hike or take a train if you want to visit the Cinque Terre. From there to Parma, Verona, Padua, and Venice, you have the choice of fast superhighways or good secondary roads the entire way.

By Public Good trains connect all the destinations on the tour. The slow-*Transportation* est, but most scenic, are from Genoa to La Spezia (the route follows the coast, winding along cliffs and through mountains); between La Spezia and Parma the train crosses some dramatic Apennine passes.

The Main Route **Two Nights: Genoa.** Visit the port, with its 16th-century lighthouse (La Lanterna), and admire the view from above the city at Monte Righi. Visit Genoa's well-preserved medieval quarter around Piazza San Matteo; see Via Garibaldi and the Palazzo Bianco.

Two Nights: La Spezia. Leave your city concerns behind as you hike or take the train along Italy's most imposing coastline, with the fishing villages of the Cinque Terre as your aim. Visit the coastal towns of Lerici and Portovenere.

One Night: Parma. Sample the excellent Parma ham and cheeses and meander through the old streets around Piazza del Duomo. Satisfy your artistic yearnings with visits to the Galleria Nazionale and the medieval baptistry. See Correggio's frescoes in the cathedral and the church of San Giovanni Evangelista.

Two Nights: Verona. Visit the Roman Arena and the spacious Piazza Brà that abuts it. Wander through the medieval quarter and see the Castelvecchio and the church of San Zeno.

One Night: Padua. See the famous university and Giotto's masterpiece, the Cappella Scrovegni. Join the pilgrimage to the Basilica di San Antonio, patron saint of Padua, and stop for coffee at the grand Caffè Pedrocchi.

Three Nights: Venice. This is the minimum stay for the world's most romantic city. Not-to-be-missed sights include St. Mark's Basilica and all the rest of Piazza San Marco, the Doge's Palace, the church of the Frari, the Accademia, and the entire length of the Grand Canal, seen from the decks of a *vaporetto* (water bus).

Information *See* Chapters 5, 6, 7, and 10.

Lake Route to the Dolomites

This itinerary takes you into the lakes and mountains north of Milan, the busy financial and fashion capital of northern Italy. Starting on the Lombard plain, you begin to climb as you head north toward Bergamo in the foothills of the Alps. From there take the bus (there is frequent service throughout the day) to Gardone Riviera, on the western shore of Lake Garda, Italy's largest lake, and then up to Riva del Garda at the northern end of the lake.

From Riva del Garda, proceed to Trento, an important trading post on the north–south trade route to Germany and Austria and famous for the Council of Trent, which formulated the Catholic response to the Reformation. From Trento, head almost due north to Bolzano, also known as Bozen because of the large German-speaking population in this region. Bolzano has some intriguing medieval architectural gems, but its main attraction is its handy location, on the doorstep of the dramatic Dolomite mountain range.

Length of Trip Five days.

Getting Around The total distance to Bolzano is 380 kilometers (210 miles).
By Car Take Autostrada A4 to Bergamo. From there, S42 runs up the west coast of Lake Iseo, and S510 goes down the east to Brescia. Join S45bis along Lake Garda and continue into Trento. From there you can take either S12 or A22 north to Bolzano.

By Public Good train service takes you as far as Brescia (east of Berga-
Transportation mo), from where there is frequent bus service to Gardone Riviera, and about six buses a day on up to Riva del Garda. From Riva del Garda, direct buses to Trento run about eight times a day, or you can take a 20-minute bus ride to the Rovereto train station and catch a train to Trento. From Trento to Bolzano is a 45-minute train trip; trains run hourly.

The Main Route **One Night: Bergamo.** Visit the Colleoni chapel and Piazza Vecchia in the Città Alta (Upper Town) and the Carrara Academy in the lower. Make an early start the next day to wind your way past Lake Iseo. Stop at Gardone Riviera along Lake Garda to see Il Vittoriale, the imaginatively designed mansion built by the poet Gabriele D'Annunzio.

One Night: Riva del Garda. Relax in this attractive town, which is one of Europe's best windsurfing centers. Visit the Torre Apponale, in the town center overlooking the lake.

One Night: Trento. Wander through the medieval quarter of town before climbing one of the narrow streets to the Castello del Buonconsiglio, which commands an excellent view of the city and surrounding valley.

Two Nights: Bolzano (Bozen). Savor the German-Italian atmosphere of the capital of the Alto Adige part of Italy's autonomous Trentino-Alto Adige region. Make the best of the dramatic scenery and the hiking and skiing options of the nearby Dolomites. Savor the view from the plateau of the Renon.

Information *See* Chapters 6 and 9.

Classical Highlights

Well colonized by the ancient Greeks, then epicenter of the Roman Empire, Italy has a wealth of classical sites, many of them quite well-preserved, thanks in part to the Italian appreciation for history and heritage. Rome was, of course, the glorious capital of the Roman Empire, and a number of ancient sites remain there today, seemingly plunked down in the middle of the bustling modern metropolis. It is quite an experience to turn a corner and see a famous building, such as the Colosseum, across the street, with Fiats and Vespas buzzing blithely past its crumbling arches. Campania, too, has a number of important classical landmarks, from both the Roman and the Greek eras. Below the volcanic cone of Mount Vesuvius, the buried ruins of Pompeii are the most famous, but even better-preserved relics are still being unearthed from the lava at nearby Herculaneum. Farther down the coast is Paestum, the remains of an ancient town with both Greek and Roman buildings; some classicists enjoy uncrowded Paestum more than either Pompeii or Herculaneum.

Length of Trip   Five to eight days.

Getting Around   On the A2 autostrada, it takes about three hours to drive from
By Car   Rome to Naples. Most of the classical sites in Campania can be seen on day trips from Naples; the farthest away is Paestum, 99 kilometers (60 miles) down the coast on S18.

By Public   Train service between Rome and Naples is fast and frequent,
Transportation   taking less than two hours on express trains. The Circumvesuviana train line can take you conveniently from Naples to Pompeii and Herculaneum, and there is a train station right in Paestum.

The Main Route   **Two–Three Nights: Rome.** Spend at least a day exploring Ancient Rome—the Capitoline Hill, the Roman Forum, the Circus Maximus, the Colosseum, the Pantheon—and on subsequent days, venture out to the Catacombs and the Appian Way, or study classical sculptures in the Vatican museums and antiquities in the Museo Nazionale.

Three–Five Nights: Naples. After arriving from Rome, spend the afternoon at the Museo Archeologico Nazionale. Herculaneum and Pompeii can be visited in one day from Naples, though it is a full day—some travelers may want to break it into two separate excursions. On another day, enjoy an excursion down the Amalfi coast to Paestum, with its well-preserved Greek temples. An optional day can be spent touring the area just south and west of Naples, taking in the Roman amphitheater at Pozzuoli, spooky Lake Avernus, the Roman resort town at Baia with its excavated baths, and the Sibyl's Cave at Cumae, perhaps the oldest Greek colony in Italy.

Information   *See* Chapters 2 and 12.

Italy at a Glance: A Chronology

c. 1000 BC   Etruscans arrive in central Italy.

c. 800   Rise of Etruscan city-states.

753   Traditional date for the founding of Rome.

750   Greek city-states begin to colonize Sicily and southern Italy.

600   Latin language becomes dominant in Etruscan League; Rome becomes established urban center.

510   Foundation of the Roman republic; expulsion of Etruscans from Roman territory.

410   Rome adopts the 12 Tables of Law, based on Greek models.

343   Roman conquest of Greek colonies in Campania.

312 Completion of Appian Way to the south of Rome; an extensive Roman road system begins to develop.

264–241 First Punic War (with Carthage): Increased naval power helps Rome gain control of southern Italy and then Sicily.

218–200 Second Punic War: Hannibal's attempted conquest of Italy, using elephants, is eventually crushed.

176 Roman Forum begins to take shape as the principal civic center in Italy.

146 Third Punic War: Rome razes city of Carthage and emerges as the dominant Mediterranean force.

133 Rome rules entire Mediterranean Basin except Egypt.

49 Julius Caesar conquers Gaul.

45 Civil War leaves Julius Caesar as sole ruler (dictator); Caesar's Forum is established.

44 Julius Caesar is assassinated.

31 The Battle of Actium resolves the power struggle that continued after Caesar's death; Octavian becomes sole ruler.

27 Rome's Imperial Age begins; Octavian (now named Augustus) becomes the first emperor and is later deified. The Augustan Age is celebrated in the works of Virgil (70 BC–AD 19), Ovid (43 BC–AD 17), Livy (59 BC–AD 17), and Horace (65 BC–AD 27).

AD 14 Augustus dies.

29 Jesus Christ crucified in the Roman colony of Judea.

43 Rome invades Britain.

50 Rome is now the largest city in the world, with a population of a million.

65 Emperor Nero begins the persecution of Christians in the empire; saints Peter and Paul are executed.

70–80 Vespasian builds the Colosseum.

98–117 Trajan's Imperial military successes are celebrated with his Baths (98), Forum (110), and Column (113); the Roman Empire reaches its apogee.

165 A smallpox epidemic ravages the Empire.

c 200–150 Christianity gains a foothold within the Empire, with the theological writings of Clement, Tertullian, and Origen.

212 Roman citizenship is conferred on all nonslaves in the Empire.

238 The first wave of Germanic invasions penetrates Italy.

293 Diocletian reorganizes the Empire into West and East.

313 The Edict of Milan grants toleration of Christianity within the Empire.

330 Constantine founds a new Imperial capital in the East (Constantinople).

410 Rome is sacked by Visigoths.

476 The last Roman Emperor, Romulus Augustus, is deposed.

552 Eastern Emperor Justinian (527–565) recovers control of Italy.

570 Lombards gain control of much of Italy, including Rome.

590 Papal power expands under Gregory the Great.

610 Heraldius revives the Eastern Empire, thereafter known as the Byzantine Empire.

774 Frankish ruler Charlemagne invades Italy under papal authority and is crowned Holy Roman Emperor by Pope Leo III (800).

c 800–900 The breakup of Charlemagne's (Carolingian) realm leads to the rise of Italian city-states.

811 Venice founded by mainlanders escaping Barbarian invasions.

1054 The Schism develops between Greek (Orthodox) and Latin churches.

c 1060 Europe's first university founded in Bologna.

1077 Pope Gregory VII leads the Holy See into conflict with the Germanic Holy Roman Empire.

1152–1190 Frederick I (Barbarossa) is crowned Holy Roman Emperor (1155); punitive expeditions by his forces (Ghibellines) are countered by the Guelphs, creators of the powerful Papal States in central Italy. Guelph-Ghibelline conflict becomes a feature of medieval life.

1204 Crusaders, led by Venetian Doge Dandolo, capture Constantinople.

1257 The first of four wars is declared between Genoa and Venice; at stake is the maritime control of the eastern Mediterranean.

1262 Florentine bankers issue Europe's first bills of exchange.

1264 Charles I of Anjou invades Italy, intervening in the continuing Guelph-Ghibelline conflict.

1275 Marco Polo reaches the Orient.

1290–1375 Tuscan literary giants Dante Alighieri (1265–1321), Francesco Petrarch (1304–74), and Giovanni Boccaccio (1313–75) form the basis of literature in the modern Italian language.

1309 The pope moves to Avignon in France, under the protection of French kings.

1355 Venetian Doge Marino Falier is executed for treason.

1376 The pope returns to Rome, but rival Avignonese popes stand in opposition, creating the Great Schism until 1417.

1380 Venice finally disposes of the Genoese threat in the Battle of Chioggia.

1402 The last German intervention into Italy is repulsed by the Lombards.

1443 Brunelleschi's dome is completed on Florence's Duomo (Cathedral).

1447 Nicholas V founds the Vatican Library. This begins an era of nepotistic popes who devalue the status of the papacy but greatly enrich the artistic and architectural patronage of the Holy City.

1469–92 Lorenzo "Il Magnifico," the Medici patron of the arts, rules in Florence.

1498 Girolamo Savonarola, the austere Dominican friar, is executed for heresy after leading Florence into a drive for moral purification, typified by his burning of books and decorations in the "Bonfire of Vanities."

1499 Leonardo da Vinci's *Last Supper* is completed in Milan.

1508 Michelangelo begins work on the Sistine Chapel.

1509 Raphael begins work on his *Stanze* in the Vatican.

1513 Machiavelli's *The Prince* is published.

1521 The Pope excommunicates Martin Luther of Germany, precipitating the Protestant Reformation.

1545–63 The Council of Trent formulates the Catholic response to the Reformation.

1546 Andrea del Palladio, architectural genius, wins his first commission in Vicenza.

1571 The combined navies of Venice, Spain, and the Papacy defeat the Turks in the Battle of Lepanto.

1626 St. Peter's is completed in Rome.

1633 Galileo Galilei faces the Inquisition.

1652 The church of Sant'Agnese, Borromini's Baroque masterpiece, is completed in Rome.

1667 St. Peter's Square, designed by Bernini, is completed.

---

c 1700 Opera develops as an art form in Italy.

1720–90 The Great Age of the Grand Tour. Northern Europeans visit Italy and start the vogue for classical studies. Among the famous visitors are Edward Gibbon (1758), Jacques-Louis David (1775), and Johann Wolfgang von Goethe (1786).

1778 Teatro alla Scala is completed in Milan.

1796 Napoleon begins his Italian campaigns, annexing Rome and imprisoning Pope Pius VI four years later.

1809 Napoleon annexes papal states to France.

1815 Austria controls much of Italy after Napoleon's downfall.

1848 Revolutionary troops under Risorgimento (Unification) leaders Giuseppe Mazzini (1805–72) and Giuseppe Garibaldi (1807–82) establish a republic in Rome.

1849 French troops crush rebellion and restore Pope Pius IX.

1860 Garibaldi and his "Thousand" defeat the Bourbon rulers in Sicily and Naples.

1870 Rome finally captured by Risorgimento troops and declared capital of Italy by King Victor Emmanuel II.

1900 King Umberto I is assassinated by an anarchist; he is succeeded by King Victor Emmanuel III.

1915 Italy enters World War I on the side of the Allies.

1922 Fascist "black shirts" under Benito Mussolini march on Rome; Mussolini becomes prime minister and later "Duce" (head of Italy).

1929 The Lateran Treaty: Mussolini recognizes Vatican City as a sovereign state, and the Church recognizes Rome as the capital of Italy.

1940–44 In World War II Italy fights with the Axis powers until its capitulation (1943), when Mussolini flees Rome. Italian partisans and Allied troops from the landings at Anzio (January 1944) win victory at Cassino (March 1944) and force the eventual withdrawal of German troops from Italy.

1957 The Treaty of Rome is signed, and Italy becomes a founding member of the European Economic Community.

1966 November flood damages much of Florence's artistic treasure.

1968–1979 The growth of left-wing activities leads to the formation of the Red Brigade and provokes right-wing reactions. Bombings and kidnappings culminate in the abduction and murder of Prime Minister Aldo Moro in 1980.

1980 Southern Italy is hit by a severe earthquake.

1991 Waves of refugees from neighboring Albania flood southern ports on the Adriatic. Mount Etna erupts, spewing forth a stream of lava that eventually threatens the Sicilian town of Zafferana.

1992 The Christian Democrat Party loses its hold on a relative majority in Parliament in elections that underscore voters' desire for institutional reforms.

1993 Italians vote for sweeping reforms after Tangentopoli (Bribe City) scandal exposes widespread political corruption, including politicians' collusion with organized crime. Following the arrest or interrogation of some 2,500 political and business elite, voters opt to scrap an electoral system that was devised after World War II to prevent the rise of another Fascist dictatorship but that also led to weak coalitions and easy abuse. Bomb outside Uffizi Gallery in Florence kills five, spares most precious artworks; authorities blame Mafia, flexing its muscle in the face of crackdown.

2 Rome

In a city where antiquity is taken for granted and the pope is a next-door neighbor, there are plenty of things to see and do without blowing your travel budget. After all, since the days of free circuses for the plebs of ancient Rome and public entertainment staged by Roman aristocrats in the city's Baroque piazzas, much of what goes on in Rome has cost little or nothing to enjoy.

People-watching is a favorite pastime here, whether from a sidewalk café or a perch on the Spanish Steps. Although not all of them are inexpensive, the museums of Rome and the Vatican are among the world's richest, and the city's churches are treasure houses of art and architecture. From ancient times, Romans have been piling the present on top of the past, blithely building, layering, and overlapping the evidence of almost 3,000 years of history to create the variegated fabric of modern Rome.

You may choose to see the grandiose remains of classical Rome—the Colosseum and the Pantheon are certainly two of the greatest buildings of all time—or the sumptuous churches, palaces, and squares of later eras, when Rome's powerful families vied with one another for recognition as supreme patrons of the arts. And there are the pleasures of modern Rome— window-shopping, irresistibly good food and wine, the fun of watching the Romans go about their business, the special quality of light on a late Roman afternoon when warm ocher and pink buildings glow against a clear sky. Don't be self-conscious in your wanderings about the city. Poke and pry under the surface of things. Walk boldly through gates that are ajar to peek into the hidden world of Roman courtyards; step from the dusky depths of historic churches into the little gardens of adjacent cloisters.

Although walking in the center of Rome is more pleasant now that traffic is limited in many downtown areas, air and noise pollution are still problems. You may find several of the monuments that you wanted to see covered with scaffolding or shrouded in green netting while work proceeds on cleaning and restoring them.

Keep your sightseeing flexible. You'll have to plan your day to take into account a wide range of opening hours, and you'll find yourself mixing classical sites with 17th-century piazzas, museums with parks, and churches with cafés. However you do it, take time out for simply sitting and observing the passing pageant, even more varied now that immigration is bringing people of many lands to work and settle in Rome, just as in the days of the Roman Empire.

Essential Information

Important Addresses and Numbers

Tourist Information
The main **EPT** (Rome Provincial Tourist Office) is at Via Parigi 5, tel. 06/488–3748. Open Mon.–Fri. 8:15–7:15, Sat. 8:15–1:15. There are also EPT booths at Termini Station and Leonardo da Vinci airport.

For information on places other than Rome, there's a booth at **ENIT** (National Tourist Board), Via Marghera 2, tel. 06/497–1293. Open Mon., Wed., Fri. 9–1 and 4–6; Tues., Thurs. 9–1.

Consulates
U.S. Consulate (Via Veneto 121, tel. 06/46741). **Canadian Consulate** (Via Zara 30, tel. 06/440–3028). **U.K. Consulate** (Via Venti Settembre 80A, tel. 06/482–5441).

Emergencies
Police, tel. 06/4686.

Ambulance (Red Cross), tel. 06/5100.

Doctors and Dentists: Call your consulate or the private Rome American Hospital (tel. 06/22551), which has English-speaking staff, for recommendations.

Late-Night Pharmacies
You will find American and British products—or their equivalents—and English-speaking staff at **Farmacia Internazionale Capranica** (Piazza Capranica 96, tel. 056/679–4680), **Farmacia Internazionale Barberini** (Piazza Barberini 49, tel. 06/482–5456), and **Farmacia Doricchi** (Via Venti Settembre 47, tel. 06/487–3880), among others. Most are open 8:30–1 and 4–8; some are open all night. Pharmacies take turns opening on Sunday. A schedule is posted in each pharmacy.

English-Language Bookstores
English-language paperback books and magazines are available at newsstands in the center of Rome, especially on Via Veneto. For all types of books in English, visit the **Economy Book and Video Center** (Via Torino 136, tel. 06/474–6877), the **Anglo-American Bookstore** (Via della Vite 27, tel. 06/679–5222), or the **Lion Bookshop** (Via del Babuino 181, tel. 06/322–5837).

Travel Agencies
American Express (Piazza di Spagna 38, tel. 06/67641), **CIT** (Piazza della Repubblica 64, tel. 06/47941), **Wagons Lits** (Via

Boncompagni 25, tel. 06/481–7655), **CTS** (information, tel. 06/
467–9241, offices at Via Genova 16, tel. 06/46791; Corso
Vittorio Emanuele 297, tel. 06/687–2672; Via Appia Nuova 434,
tel. 06/780–8449; Via degli Ausoni 5, tel. 06/445–0141; Ostiense
Air Terminal, tel. 06/574–7950).

Where to Change Money   There are exchange windows and automatic exchange machines on the arrivals level of the international terminal at
Fiumicino airport. Downtown there are exchange windows at
the Ostiense Air Terminal and at Termini train station. Remember, though, that you can get the best exchange rates at
banks. In the Termini Station area, go to the **Banca Nazionale
del Lavoro,** Via Marsala 6, tel. 06/446–3251.

There are several exchange bureaus near the station, among
them **Frama** (Via Torino 21/b, tel. 06/474–6870) and **Casa del
Turista** (Via del Viminale 2/e, tel. 06/485–713; Via Giolitti 97,
tel. 06/446–3347), open Mon.–Fri. 9–7, Sat. 9–1:30. Frama also
has an office near Piazza Navona (Corso Vittorio Emanuele
106, tel. 06/683–08406), open Mon.–Fri. 9–1:30 and 3–5:30,
Sat. 9–1:30. **Eurocambio** (Via Francesco Crispi 92, tel. 06/488–
0135) is between Piazza di Spagna and Via Veneto and is open
Mon.–Fri. 8:30–12:45 and 3:30–6. **American Express** (Piazza di
Spagna 38, tel. 06/67641) usually has long lines but is open
Mon.–Fri. 9–5:30, Sat. 9–12:30.

Arriving and Departing by Plane

Airports and Airlines   Most international flights and all domestic flights arrive at **Leonardo da Vinci** airport, also known as **Fiumicino,** 30 kilome-
ters (18 miles) outside the city. Some international charter
flights land at **Ciampino,** a military airport on the Via Appia
Nuova, 15 kilometers (9 miles) from the center of Rome.

Between Leonardo da Vinci Airport and Downtown
By Train   An express train service of the state-owned railway (FS) connects Fiumicino airport and the Air Terminal at Ostiense Station in Rome, with departures every 20 minutes 6:30 AM–12:45
AM. The trip takes 30 minutes. At Fiumicino, tickets can be
purchased (6,000 lire) from ticket machines on the arrivals level
or at a ticket window near the track. After intermediate stops
(Muratella, Trastevere), the train arrives at the Ostiense Air
Terminal. Depending on where your hotel is located, you can
take either a taxi, bus, or Metro from here. If you have to go to
Rome's main Termini train station, take a shuttle bus from the
Air Terminal's main entrance or walk the considerable distance
(only partly served by moving sidewalks) to the Piramide
Metro station, where you can get Metro Line B. Between 1 AM
and 5 AM, buses run every hour or so between the airport and
Piazza Partigiani, in front of the Ostiense Air Terminal.

Between Ciampino Airport and Downtown
By Bus   An ACOTRAL bus connects the airport with the Anagnina station of Metro Line A. Both bus and metro fares were 800 lire at
press time but may be 1,000 lire by 1994.

Arriving and Departing by Train and Bus

By Train   Termini Station is Rome's main train terminal; the Tiburtina
and Ostiense stations serve a few long-distance trains. Some
trains for Pisa and Genoa leave Rome from, or pass through,
the Trastevere Station. For train information, call 06/4775,
7 AM–10:40 PM. You can find English-speaking staff at the infor-

mation office at Termini Station, or ask for information at travel agencies. If you purchase tickets and book seat reservations in advance, either at the main stations or at travel agencies bearing the FS (Ferrovie dello Stato) emblem, you'll avoid long lines at ticket windows. At a ticket office on the lower level you can buy both train and subway tickets. Tickets for train rides within a radius of 100 kilometers (62 miles) of Rome can also be purchased at tobacco shops.

By Bus There is no central bus terminal in Rome. Long-distance and suburban buses terminate either near Termini Station or near Metro stops. For ACOTRAL bus information, call 06/591–5551, Mon.–Fri. 7 AM–6 PM, Sat. 7 AM–2 PM.

Getting Around

Although most of Rome's sights are in a relatively circumscribed area, the city is too large to be seen solely on foot. Take the Metro (subway) or a bus to the area you plan to visit, and expect to do a lot of walking once you're there. Wear a comfortable, sturdy pair of shoes, preferably with rubber or crepe soles to cushion the impact of the cobblestones. Heed our advice on security and get away from the noise and polluted air of heavily trafficked streets by taking parallel streets whenever possible. You can buy transportation-route maps at newsstands and at ATAC (Rome's public transit authority) information and ticket booths. The free city map distributed by Rome EPT offices is good; it also shows metro and bus routes, although bus routes are not always marked clearly.

By Metro This is the easiest and fastest way to get around, but it's limited in extent. The Metro opens at 5:30 AM, and the last trains leave the farthest station at 11:30 PM. The two lines—A and B—intersect at Termini Station (*see* Metro map, *below*). The fare is presently 800 lire but may be raised to 1,000 lire by 1994. There are ticket booths at major stations, but elsewhere you must use ticket machines. It's best to buy single tickets or books of 5 or 10 at newsstands and tobacconists. The "BIG" daily tourist ticket, good on buses as well, costs 2,800 lire at present and is sold at Metro and ATAC ticket booths. Metro information (ACOTRAL), tel. 06/591–5551.

By Bus Orange ATAC city buses and two tram lines run from about 6 AM to midnight, with skeleton (*notturno*) services on main lines through the night. Remember to board at the back and exit at the middle. The ticket, 800 lire at present, is valid on all ATAC bus lines for a total of 90 minutes. Buy it before boarding and time-stamp it in the machine on the first bus you board. Tickets are sold at tobacconists and newsstands. A weekly tourist ticket costs 10,000 lire and is sold at ATAC booths. The BIG tourist ticket is also valid on the Metro for one day (*see above*). For ATAC bus and tram information, call 06/469–54444.

By Taxi Taxis wait at stands and can also be called by phone, in which case you're charged a small supplement. The meter starts at 6,400 lire, a fixed rate for the first 3 kilometers (1.8 miles); there are supplements for service after 10 PM and on Sundays or holidays, as well as for each piece of baggage. Use only metered yellow or white cabs. To call a cab, dial 06/3875, 06/3570, 06/4994, or 06/8433. **Radio Taxi** (tel. 06/3875) accepts American Express and Diners Club credit cards, but you must specify when calling that you will pay that way.

Rome Metro

By Bicycle Pedaling through Villa Borghese, along the Tiber, and through the center of the city when traffic is light is a pleasant way to see the sights, but remember: Rome is hilly. You can rent a bike at **St. Peter's Moto** (Via di Porta Castello 43, tel. 06/687–5714, between St. Peter's and Castel Sant'Angelo), and at Piazza Navona 69, next to Bar Navona. There are bike-rental concessions at the Metro stop at Piazza di Spagna and at Piazza del Popolo, Largo San Silvestro, and Largo Argentina, as well as in Villa Borghese at three locations: Viale della Pineta, Viale del Bambino on the Pincio, and the underground parking lot (Via Veneto), tel. 06/322–5240. **CTS** (Via Genova 16, tel. 06/46791), organizes guided bike tours of Rome.

By Scooter You can rent a moped or scooter and mandatory helmet at **Scoot-a-Long** (Via Cavour 302, tel. 06/678–0206) or **St. Peter's Moto** (Via di Porta Castello 43, tel. 06/687–5714).

Opening and Closing Times

Rome's churches have erratic and unpredictable opening times; they are *not* open all the time. Most are open from about 7 to noon and 3 to 7, but don't be surprised if the church you were especially keen on seeing is closed even during these times. Many churches that are shut during the week can, however, be visited on Sunday. Appropriate dress—no shorts—is required.

Banks are open weekdays 8:30–1:30 and 3 or 3:30–4 or 4:30. Shops are open Monday through Saturday 9:30–1 and 3:30 or 4–7 or 7:30. Some shops, department stores, and supermarkets in downtown Rome stay open all day. Food shops close on Thursday afternoon, or Saturday afternoon in July and August. Most other types of shops are closed Monday mornings from September through June and Saturday afternoons from July through August.

Lodging

Rome has scores of hotels in the inexpensive and budget range, but relatively few of them offer accommodations that are more than merely adequate. Proprietors and managers of lower-priced hotels, on the other hand, may make up for sagging beds and dingy hallways by taking a warm and friendly interest in their guests. There is a plethora of budget hotels in the Termini Station area, but some are fleabags. The best bets are in the Via Palestro–Via Montebello section. Here, as elsewhere in Rome, one big turn-of-the-century building may house several small hotels, each on a different floor.

It's wise to reserve a room before you arrive, but in case you haven't done so, or in case the hotel does not honor your reservation (as is sometimes the case when a remunerative group booking turns up), you have a few options. Try one of the **EPT information offices:** The main office, at Via Parigi 5 (tel. 06/488–3748), is the most helpful; the bureau at Termini Station (tel. 06/487–1270 or 06/482–4078) has longer lines. The EPT desk at Leonardo da Vinci airport (tel. 06/601–1255) also can make same-day bookings for a room. The **CTS student and youth travel agency** (tel. 06/46791), a few blocks from Termini Station, at Via Genova 16, off Via Nazionale, is open Monday–Friday 9–1 and 4–7, Saturday 9–1; you can get help there booking a room. CTS also has a bureau at the Ostiense Air Terminal (tel. 06/574–7950; open 9–1 and 2–6). Young women can also try the **Protezione Giovani** office on the lower level of Termini Station; it specializes in finding low-cost accommodations for women. Don't listen to the official-looking men who approach tourists at Termini Station; they tout for the less desirable hotels around the station.

You can save time and car fare if you stay at a hotel that's within easy walking distance of at least some of the main sights; however, many of the better budget hotels are on the fringes of downtown Rome, in semiresidential areas where you can find good neighborhood eating places and food stores.

Wherever you stay, take a look at your room before you check in and try to determine whether it gets a lot of street noise and whether the plumbing works. The hot-water supply may be erratic, too. Remember that breakfast is an option, and also that you may be able to get a lower room rate depending on the time of year and the length of your stay. Highly recommended lodgings are indicated by a star ★.

Under 125,000 lire

Termini Station area **Montreal.** This is a compact hotel on a central avenue across the square from Santa Maria Maggiore, only three blocks from Termini Station, with bus and subway lines close by. On one floor of an older building, it has been totally renovated and offers fresh-looking rooms. The owner-managers are pleasant and helpful, and the neighborhood has plenty of reasonably priced eating places, plus one of Rome's largest outdoor markets. *Via Carlo Alberto 4, tel. 06/446–5522, fax 06/445–7797. 16 rooms with bath or shower. MC, V.*

★ **Romae.** It has the advantages of a strategic location, handy to bus and subway lines and within walking distance of many sights, and a friendly, helpful management. The white walls, light wood furniture in the airy bedrooms, and bright little baths all have a clean, fresh look. Such amenities as satellite TV and hair dryers in every room make this hotel a very good value. The English-speaking management offers special rates and services for families. *Via Palestro 49, tel. 06/446–3554, fax 06/446–3914, 20 rooms with bath. AE, MC, V.*

Spanish Steps area **Erdarelli.** Run by the Erdarelli family since 1935, with some furnishings that appear to be that old, it has comfortable beds and clean rooms, most of which are on a side street or the quiet inner courtyard. You have to take a room without bath here to remain within the affordable range, but the location is worth any inconvenience. *Via Due Macelli 28, tel. 06/679–1265, fax 06/679–0705. 28 rooms, 12 with bath. AE, MC, V.*

★ **Margutta.** This small hotel is centrally located on a quiet side street between the Spanish Steps and Piazza del Popolo. Lobby and halls are unassuming, but rooms are a pleasant surprise, with light walls, a clean and airy look, attractive wrought-iron bedsteads, and modern baths. Three rooms on the roof terrace are much in demand for their views of the city's domes, bell towers, and the pines of the Pincian hill, but their rates nudge a higher price category. Though it's in an old building, there is an elevator. *Via Laurina 34, tel. 06/322–3674. 21 rooms with bath or shower. AE, DC, MC, V.*

Pierina. Run by the Erdarelli family, this hotel is smaller, quieter, and sunnier than their other property a few doors away (*see above*). Simply furnished, it is in the same price category, so reserve a room without bath. If you want to spend about 20,000 lire extra for a private bath, then ask for one of the three double rooms with terrace overlooking a quiet side street. *Via Due Macelli 47, tel. 06/678–4010, for reservations tel. 06/679–1265, fax 06/679–0705. 9 rooms, 3 with bath. AE, MC, V.*

Piazza Navona area **Lunetta.** Around the corner from the colorful street market at Campo dei Fiori in the heart of Old Rome, this hotel has a drab entrance but spacious, attractive rooms. Handy for sightseeing, it's in a lively neighborhood of economical trattorias and shops. *Piazza del Paradiso 68, tel. 06/686–1080. 34 rooms, 18 with bath or shower. No credit cards.*

Smeraldo. Near Largo Argentina and Campo dei Fiori, Smeraldo is on a narrow street typical of Old Rome. A fully renovated lobby, breakfast room, and bar make the public areas of this hotel inviting. Rooms are small, clean, and functional, with telephones and air-conditioning. About half of them have small private bathrooms. *Vicolo dei Chiodaroli 9, tel, 06/687–5929, fax 06/654–5495. 35 rooms, 18 with bath or shower. AE, MC, V.*

Aventine–Testaccio area **Santa Prisca.** In a large brick building that looks something like a school, this hostelry is run by nuns, who make sure everything is clean and orderly. Meals are available, but the hotel is handy to the Testaccio neighborhood's workaday trattorias and trendy nightlife. Tram Nos. 13 and 30, several bus lines, and Metro Line B are close by. *Largo Manlio Gelsomini 25, tel. 06/575–0009. 45 rooms with shower. Facilities: restaurant, garden. No credit cards.*

Rome Lodging

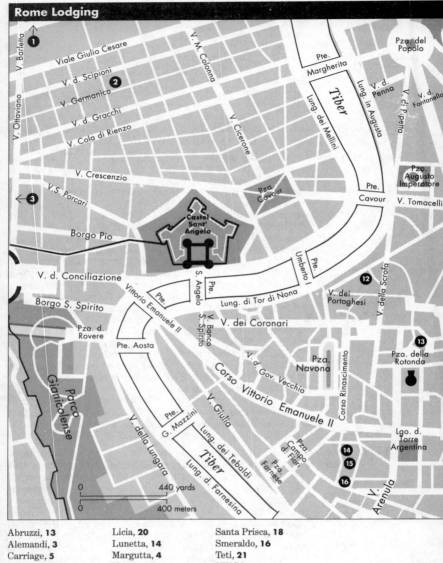

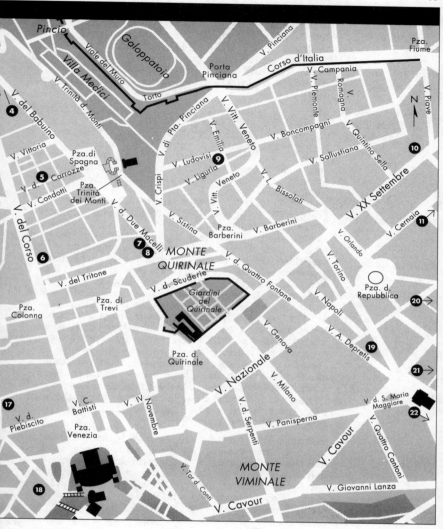

Under 100,000 lire

Termini Station area

Teti. Between the train station and Santa Maria Maggiore, this small hotel is clean and fresh-looking, though austere. Rooms have firm beds and ample closet space. Sinks are standard in all rooms; some have compact wc/shower units, too. *Via Principe Amedeo 76, tel. 06/482–5240. 11 rooms, 8 with bath. No credit cards.*

Pantheon–Via del Corso–Piazza Venezia area

Abruzzi. You choose this hotel located on the same square as the Pantheon to be in the thick of things, day and night. Rooms are tiny and dark, but 21 of them have a view of the Pantheon and the cafés on the square, a Roman rendezvous in all seasons. The party noise continues well past midnight in summer, but the view is worth the aggravation. Bring earplugs. *Piazza della Rotonda 69, tel. 06/679–2021. 25 rooms, no private baths. No credit cards.*

Coronet. This small hotel gives you the feel of what it's like to live in an 18th-century palace. The palace belongs to the aristocratic Doria-Pamphili family, and their fabulous picture gallery is in another wing. Large, high-ceilinged rooms have space for extra beds; some look onto the Doria's garden court, and all have sinks. The courteous owner-manager speaks English. *Piazza Grazioli 5, tel. 06/679–2341. 3 with bath, 10 rooms share 4 baths. Facilities: small TV lounge. AE, MC, V.*

Parlamento. This small, well-kept hotel is conveniently located in the heart of the shopping district, between Piazza Colonna and the Spanish Steps. Some of the rooms here were refurbished in 1992. Parlamento has a rooftop terrace and a friendly management. *Via delle Convertite 5, tel. 06/678–7880. 22 rooms, 14 with shower. No credit cards.*

Pomezia. On a side street near Campo dei Fiori, Pomezia occupies two floors of an old building. Ask for rooms on the first floor; they were renovated in 1991 and have new baths and good lighting but cost the same as the drearier ones on the other floors. *Via dei Chiavari 12, tel. 06/686–1371. 22 rooms, 12 with bath. No credit cards.*

St. Peter's area ★

Alemandi. A few yards from the entrance to the Vatican Museums, this family-run hotel has a homey atmosphere, comfortable public rooms, and a rooftop terrace. Rooms are furnished in functional modern style. You can reach the hotel by taking bus No. 490, 990, or 494. *Via Tunisi 8, tel. 06/314–457. 29 rooms, 22 with shower. Facilities: reading and TV rooms, bar, dining room, rooftop terrace. AE, MC, V.*

Under 65,000 lire

Foro Italico Youth Hostel (Ostello). Only those with AIG or IYHF cards are accepted at this big, barnlike hostel in the city's northern district, but you can buy an IYHF card on the spot. Take Metro A to the Via Ottaviano stop, then the No. 32 bus to the Foro Italico, Mussolini's sports complex. There is a three-day maximum stay, and it's advisable to reserve well in advance. Open 7–9 AM, 2–11 PM. *Viale delle Olimpiadi 61, tel. 06/396–4709. 350 beds. No credit cards.*

Fraterna Domus. This religious-run establishment is recommended by the Vatican Information Office, and it has a very central location, between Piazza Navona and the Tiber. It offers good value; all rooms have private bath and the 32,000-lire-per-person rate includes breakfast. Full- or halfboard terms are also offered. There is, however, an 11 PM curfew. *Via di Monte Brianzo 62, tel. 06/654–2727. 20 rooms with bath. No credit cards.*

Licia. Although the area around the train station is rundown, this little hotel is a safe bet. It's managed by the mother of the owner of the Teti, and it's clean, with basic furnishings. It's located halfway between the station and Santa Maria Maggiore. *Via Principe Amedeo 76, tel. 06/482–5293. 10 rooms, none with bath. No credit cards.*

Monaco. Centrally located between the train station and Villa Borghese, this small hotel is simply furnished and is kept scrupulously clean by Signora Maria, the owner. Although she doesn't speak English, others in the family do. There's a small lounge where guests—mainly students—can fraternize and there's a midnight curfew. *Via Flavia 84, tel. 06/474–4335. 12 rooms, none with bath. No credit cards.*

YWCA. Near Termini Station, but in a fairly safe part of the neighborhood, this facility is used as a dorm by many Italian students, so your chances of finding a room are better during school vacations, around holidays, and in August and September. Only women are admitted. Accommodations are spartan, and there is a midnight curfew. *Via Cesare Balbo 4, tel. 06/460–460. 80 beds. No credit cards.*

Zurigo. Part of a double-barrelled operation that includes the Nautilus hotel, this clean, well-run hotel is in a solid residential building near the Vatican, in a neighborhood that offers a good range of eating places and shops. The desk staff speaks English. *Via Germanico 198, tel. 06/372–0139. 13 rooms, 5 with shower. No credit cards.*

Splurges

★ **Carriage.** Stay here for the location (by the Spanish Steps), the Old World elegance, and the reasonable rates. Totally renovated over the past few years, the hotel is decorated in soothing tones of blue and pale gold, with subdued Baroque accents adding a touch of luxury. The rooms have antique-looking closets and porcelain telephones. Double room 402 and single room 305 have small balconies; elegant room 302 is spacious, with an oversize bathroom. Alternatively, try for one of the two rooms adjoining the roof terrace. Doubles go for 245,000 lire, including breakfast. *Via delle Carrozze 36, tel. 06/699–0124, fax 06/678–8279. 27 rooms and suites with bath. AE, DC, MC, V.*

★ **La Residenza.** In a converted town house near Via Veneto, this hotel is a good value, offering first-class comfort and atmosphere at reasonable rates. The canopied entrance, spacious, well-furnished lounges, and the bar and terrace are of the type you would expect to find in a deluxe category. Rooms have large closets, color TV, fridge-bar, and air-conditioning; bathrooms have heated towel racks. The decor includes a color scheme of aquamarine and beige, combined with bentwood furniture. The clientele is mostly American. Rates are 230,000 lire for a double and include a generous American-style buffet breakfast. *Via Emilia 22, tel. 06/488–0789. 27 rooms with bath or shower. Facilities: bar, rooftop terrace, parking. MC, V.*

Exploring Rome

Guided Tours

Orientation Tours American Express (tel. 06/67641), CIT (tel. 06/47941), Appian Line (tel. 06/488–4151), and other operators offer three-hour tours in air-conditioned, 60-passenger buses with English-speaking guides. There are four standard itineraries: "Ancient Rome" (including the Roman Forum and the Colosseum), "Classic Rome" (including St. Peter's Basilica, the Trevi Fountain, and the Janiculum Hill), "Christian Rome" (some major churches and the Catacombs), and "The Vatican Museums and Sistine Chapel." Most cost about 36,000 lire, but the Vatican Museums tour costs about 46,000 lire. American Express tours depart from Piazza di Spagna, and CIT from Piazza della Repubblica; Appian Line picks you up at or near your hotel.

The least expensive organized sightseeing tour of Rome is run by **ATAC,** the municipal bus company. Tours leave from Piazza dei Cinquecento, in front of Termini Station, last about two hours, and cost about 6,000 lire. There's no running commentary, but you're given an illustrated guide with which you can easily identify the sights. Buy tickets at the ATAC information booth in front of Termini Station. The least expensive sightseeing of all are the routes of bus No. 119 downtown, bus No. 56 across Rome to Trastevere, or the circle route of the No. 19 tram. For each, the cost is 800 lire one-way (may be 1,000 lire by 1994).

Special-Interest Tours If the **Acquabus** boat service is operating, you can take a ride between Trastevere (near Ponte Garibaldi) and the Foro Italico landing upstream, every 20 minutes 8 AM–8 PM, Tuesday–Sunday (Consorzio Servizi Tevere, Corso Vittorio Emanuele 326, tel. 06/686–9068).

Walking Tours If you have a reasonable knowledge of Italian, you can take advantage of the free guided visits and walking tours organized by Rome's cultural associations and the city council for museums and monuments. These usually take place on Sunday mornings. Programs are announced in the daily newspapers.

Rome for Free—or Almost

Thanks to its balmy climate and wealth of eye-filling architecture, Rome is a city that you can enjoy outdoors, without spending a lira on admission fees or worrying about opening hours. In fact, you could construct several memorable itineraries—taking in dozens of piazzas, churches, streets, and fountains—all free of charge.

Views You might start by taking in the marvelous views of the city from some of its hills. Walk up to the **Aventine Hill,** stopping at the Roseto, the municipal rose garden, in May and June to see the roses in bloom. Stroll through **Parco Savello,** known for its orange trees and view of the Tiber, the Janiculum Hill across the river, and the dome of St. Peter's. You get a surprising perspective on St. Peter's dome from the keyhole in the old gate to the gardens of the Knights of Malta (on Piazza Cavalieri di Malta, at the end of Via di Santa Sabina).

Another view—one of the most panoramic in Rome—is the main feature of the **Janiculum Hill** (*see* Tour 9, *below*), which also offers an itinerant Punch and Judy show in good weather and the unfailing boom of the noontime cannon from a position right below the belvedere. The view from the top of the **Spanish Steps** (*see* Tour 5, *below*) is only slightly less impressive than that from the **Pincio** (*see* Tour 8, *below*), which is perhaps the most panoramic of all.

Parks and Gardens **Villa Borghese** (*see* Tour 8, *below*) offers a range of sights and activities from jogging or walking under centuries-old pines to strolling through the botanical garden (entrance on Viale Canonica), where there is a little lake. The park of **Villa Pamphili** is Rome's largest; it has Italian gardens and an extensive natural park that, like Villa Borghese, is ideal for jogging, walking, and picnicking. To get to Villa Pamphili, take bus No. 144 to Piazza San Pancrazio.

The gardens of **Castel Sant'Angelo** (*see* Tour 2, *below*), in what was once the castle's moat, afford interesting vistas of the massive brick fortress that was built over a Roman emperor's tomb. The gardens are often the scene of festivals and book fairs, where there are plenty of free exhibits.

Concerts On Sunday mornings military bands often play at the Pincio; look for posters or inquire at Rome EPT offices.

People-watching This is a favorite Roman pastime—that's why the city has so many sidewalk cafés and restaurants. Some of the best spots for indulging in this sport are Piazza Navona (*see* Tour 4, *below*), the Spanish Steps (*see* Tour 5, *below*), Piazza Santa Maria in Trastevere (*see* Tour 9, *below*) and Piazza della Rotonda, in front of the Pantheon (*see* Tour 4, *below*).

Monuments Admission to many of Rome's classical monuments is free. You can visit the **Pantheon** (*see* Tour 4, *below*), the ground level of the **Colosseum** (*see* Tour 1, *below*), and the temples at **Largo Argentina,** a major traffic hub in Old Rome (on the route of Tour 4, *below*), free of charge. On the **Quirinal Hill** (*see* Tour 7, *below*), where the former palace of the pope is now the official residence of the president of Italy, the monthly changing of the guard is a rousing affair. It takes place on the second Sunday of the month, except in June and November, when it is held on the first Sunday of the month. At 3:45 the honor guard marches from the barracks on Via XX Settembre in full panoply and accompanied by a military band. At 4 o'clock, the changing of the guard takes place, and the band plays several pieces.

Markets Enjoy the vivacity and color of Rome's street markets, especially the one held in Campo dei Fiori (*see* Tour 4, *below*) every morning Monday–Saturday, or go to Rome's original Sunday morning flea market at **Porta Portese.** (A newer, even larger market is open every Sunday on the extreme eastern periphery of the city.) Once a happy hunting ground for antiques, Porta Portese now offers mainly new and secondhand clothing; bargaining is the rule here, and visitors should beware of pickpockets. Take bus No. 44 or 75, or any of the many buses that run along Viale Trastevere, and get off at Via Ippolito Nievo.

Walks Explore the **Isola Tiberina,** the little island in the Tiber between the ghetto and Trastevere (*see* Tour 9, *below*). Descend the stone steps to the embankment if the river is not running too high. The rapids here mark the navigable downstream limit of the river within the city. Walk around the embankment to see the remains of the marble wall that the ancient Romans built around the island and embellished with a rostrum to make it look like a ship with its prow pointed downstream.

Orientation

Our exploration of Rome is divided into 10 tours. We begin where Rome itself began, amid the ancient ruins, and follow with a look at the Vatican and its museums—two separate tours. The next six tours explore places of interest in various sections of central Rome, while Tour 10 takes you on a short trip outside the city walls. With the exception of Tours 2 and 3, which concentrate on the Vatican; Tour 8, which explores Villa Borghese; Tour 9, which crosses the Tiber to the Trastevere district; and Tour 10, out the Appian Way to the Catacombs, these Rome tours begin in or around Piazza Venezia.

A word of caution: Gypsy children, present around sites popular with tourists throughout Europe, are rife in Rome and are adept pickpockets. One modus operandi is to approach a tourist and proffer a piece of cardboard with writing on it. While the unsuspecting victim attempts to read the message on the cardboard, the children's hands are busy under it, making like piranhas with the contents of a purse. If you see such a group (recognizable by their unkempt appearance, often with cigarettes hanging from prepubescent lips), do not even allow them near you—they are quick and know more tricks than you do. Also be aware of the indigenous Italian perpetrators who ride by on motorbikes, grab the shoulder strap of your bag, and step on the gas. Keep your bag tucked well under your arm, especially if you're walking on the street edge of the sidewalk, or wear a money belt.

Highlights for First-time Visitors

Campidoglio (Tour 1: Ancient Rome)
Castel Sant'Angelo (Tour 2: The Vatican)
Colosseum (Tour 1: Ancient Rome)
Fountain of Trevi (Tour 5: The Spanish Steps and the Trevi Fountain)
Piazza Navona (Tour 4: Old Rome)
Roman Forum (Tour 1: Ancient Rome)
Saint Peter's (Tour 2: The Vatican)
Santa Maria Maggiore (Tour 6: Historic Churches)
Spanish Steps (Tour 5: The Spanish Steps and the Trevi Fountain)
Sistine Chapel (Tour 3: The Vatican Museums)

Tour 1: Ancient Rome

Numbers in the margin correspond to points of interest on the Rome map.

Rome, as is common knowledge, was built on seven hills. Its legendary founders, the twins Romulus and Remus, were abandoned as infants but were suckled by a she-wolf on the banks of the Tiber and adopted by a shepherd. Encouraged by the gods to build a city, the twins chose a site in 735 BC, fortifying it with a wall that has been identified by archaeologists digging on the Palatine, the first hill of Rome to be inhabited.

During the building of the city the brothers quarreled, and in a fit of anger Romulus killed Remus. Excavations on the Palatine and in the Forum area have revealed hard evidence of at least some aspects of the city's legendary beginnings.

The monuments and ruins of the two most historic hills—the Capitoline and the Palatine—mark the center of ancient Rome, capital of the classical world and seat of a vast empire. The former hill held the seat of government, the Capitol, whose name lives on in every "capital" city in the world, as well as in government buildings, such as the Capitol in Washington, D.C.

If you stand on the Capitoline and gaze out over the ruins of the Forum to the Palatine, with the Colosseum looming in the background, you can picture how Rome looked when it was the center of the known world. Imagine the Forum filled with immense, brightly painted temples. Picture the faint glow from the temple of Vesta, where the Vestal Virgins tended their sacred fire, and the glistening marble palace complex on the Palatine, its roof studded with statues, where the emperors and their retinues lived in incredible luxury. Then think of how the area looked in the Dark Ages, when Rome had sunk into malaria-ridden squalor.

The **Capitoline Hill** is a good place to begin exploring the city. Rome's first and most sacred temples stood here. The city's archives were kept in the Tabularium (hall of records), the tall, gray stone structure that forms the foundations of today's city hall, the **Palazzo Senatorio.** By the Middle Ages, the Campidoglio, as the hill was then known, had fallen into ruin. In 1537 Pope Paul III called on Michelangelo to restore it to grandeur, and the artist designed the ramp, the buildings on three sides of the **Campidoglio** Square, the slightly convex pavement and its decoration, and the pedestal for the bronze equestrian statue of Marcus Aurelius. A work of the 2nd century AD, the statue stood here from the 16th century until just recently, when it was removed for restoration and reinstallation at a more environmentally friendly location inside the Palazzo dei Conservatori (*see below*). A copy of the original statue occupies the pedestal outdoors.

The palaces flanking the Palazzo Senatorio contain two museums, the **Museo Capitolino** and the **Palazzo dei Conservatori,** whose collections were assembled in the 15th century by Pope Sixtus V, one of the earliest of the great papal patrons of the arts. Those with a taste for Roman and Greek sculpture will appreciate both museums; others may find the collections dull but the setting impressive. Many of the statues were restored by overconscientious 18th- and 19th-century collectors, who added heads and limbs with considerable abandon. Originally almost all of these works were brilliantly colored and gilded. Remember that many of the works here and in Rome's other museums are copies of Greek originals. For hundreds of years, craftsmen of ancient Rome prospered by producing copies of Greek statues on order; they used a process called "pointing," by which exact copies could be made.

Portraiture, however, was one area in which the Romans outstripped the Greeks. The hundreds of Roman portrait busts in the **Museo Capitolino** are the highlight of a visit here. In the courtyard, the reclining river god is one of the "talking statues" to which citizens of ancient Rome affixed anonymous polit-

Rome

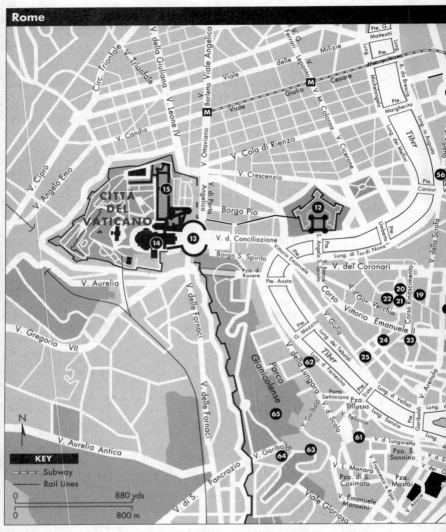

Acqua Paola
Fountain, **64**
Aracoeli, **4**
Ara Pacis, **56**
Arch of Constantine, **9**
Campo dei Fiori, **24**
Castel Sant'Angelo, **12**
Circus Maximus, **8**
Colosseum, **10**
Column of Marcus
Aurelius, **29**

Domus Aurea, **11**
Fountain of the
Barcaccia, **31**
Fountain of the Four
Rivers, **21**
Fountain of the
Naiads, **46**
Fountain of Trevi, **32**
Fountain of the
Turtles, **58**
Galleria Borghese, **50**
Galleria Nazionale
(Palazzo Barberini), **41**

Galleria Nazionale
d'Arte Moderna, **51**
Il Gesù, **16**
Janiculum Park, **65**
Mamertine Prison, **6**
Museo Capitolino, **2**
Museo di
Villa Giulia, **52**
Museo Nazionale, **48**
Palazzo dei
Conservatori, **3**

Palazzo del
Quirinale, **38**
Palazzo Farnese, **25**
Palazzo Senatorio, **1**
Palazzo Venezia, **27**
Pantheon, **18**
Piazza del Popolo, **54**
Piazza Navona, **20**
Piazza San Pietro, **13**
Piazza Santa Maria in
Trastevere, **61**
Pincio, **53**
Porta Pinciana, **49**
Roman Forum, **7**

ical protests and satirical barbs. The most interesting pieces, on display upstairs, include the poignant *Dying Gaul* and the delicate *Marble Faun*, which inspired novelist Nathaniel Hawthorne's tale of the same name. Then you'll come upon the rows of portrait busts, a kind of ancient *Who's Who*, though rather haphazardly labeled. Look for cruel Caracalla, vicious Nero, and haughty Marcus Aurelius.

❸ Across the square is the **Palazzo dei Conservatori,** which contains similar treasures. The huge head and hand in the courtyard are fragments of a colossal statue of the emperor Constantine; these immense effigies were much in vogue during the later days of the Roman Empire. The resplendent Salone dei Orazi e Curiazi upstairs is a ceremonial hall with a magnificent gilt ceiling, carved wooden doors, and 16th-century frescoes. Farther on, you'll see the famous *Capitoline Wolf,* a 6th-century BC Etruscan bronze; the twins were added during the Renaissance to adapt the statue to the legend of Romulus and Remus. *Museo Capitolino and Palazzo dei Conservatori, Piazza del Campidoglio, tel. 06/671–02071. Admission: 10,000 lire. Open May–Sept., Tues. 9–1:30 and 5–8, Wed.–Fri. 9–1:30, Sat. 9–1:30 and 7:30–11:30, Sun. 9–1; Oct.–Apr., Tues. and Sat. 9–1:30 and 5–8, Wed.–Fri. 9–1:30, Sun. 9–1.*

❹ The Capitoline's church of **Aracoeli** was one of the first churches in the city built by the emerging Christians. It's known for Pinturicchio's 16th-century frescoes in the first chapel on the right and for a much-revered wooden figure of the Christ Child, kept in a small chapel in the sacristy.

The Campidoglio gardens offer the best view of the sprawling ruins of ancient Rome. **Caesar's Forum** lies below the garden, to the left of Palazzo Senatorio. It is the oldest of the Imperial Fora, those built by the emperors, as opposed to those built during the earlier, Republican period (6th–1st centuries BC), as part of the original Roman Forum.

Across Via dei Fori Imperiali, the broad avenue created by Premier Benito Mussolini for his triumphal parades, are, from **❺** the left, **Trajan's Column,** in the base of which the emperor Trajan's ashes were buried, **Trajan's Forum,** with its huge, semicircular market building, and the ruins of the **Forum of Augustus.**

Now turn your attention to the Roman Forum, in what was once a marshy valley between the Capitoline and Palatine hills. The shortest way down is Via San Pietro in Carcere—actually a flight of stairs descending to the church that stands over the **❻** **Mamertine Prison,** a series of gloomy, subterranean cells where Rome's vanquished enemies were finished off. Legend has it that St. Peter was held prisoner here and that he miraculously brought forth a spring of water in order to baptize his jailers. *Donation requested. Open daily 9–12:30 and 2–7:30.*

From the main entrance on Via dei Fori Imperiali, descend into **❼** the extraordinary archaeological complex that is the **Roman Forum.** This was the civic heart of Republican Rome, the austere Rome that preceded the hedonistic society that grew up under the emperors between the 1st and 4th centuries AD. Today it seems no more than a baffling series of ruins, marble fragments, isolated columns, a few worn arches, and occasional paving stones. Yet it once was filled with stately and extravagant buildings—temples, palaces, shops—and crowded with people from all corners of the world. What you see are the ruins not of one period but of almost 900 years, from about 500 BC to AD 400. As the original buildings became too small or old-fashioned, they were pulled down and replaced by more lavish structures. Making sense of these scarred and pitted stones is not easy; you may want to just wander along, letting your imagination dwell on Julius Caesar, Cicero, and Mark Antony, who delivered the funeral address in Caesar's honor from the rostrum just left of the Arch of Septimius Severus. *Entrances on Via dei Fori Imperiali, Piazza Santa Maria Nova, and Via di San Gregorio, tel. 06/699–0110. Admission: 10,000 lire. Open Apr.–Sept., Mon., Wed.–Sat. 9–6, Tues. and Sun. 9–1; Oct.–Mar., Mon., Wed.–Sat, 9–4, Sun. 9–1.*

Leave the Forum by the exit at the Arco di Tito (Arch of Titus), which is at the end of the Forum away from the Capitoline. From here, the Clivus Palatinus, an ancient path, leads up the Palatine Hill, where the emperors built their palaces. From the belvedere you can see the **Circus Maximus,** where more than 300,000 spectators could watch chariot and horse races while the emperors looked on from this very spot. The Italian garden on the Palatine was laid out during the Renaissance. Leaving the Palatine by way of the Via di San Gregorio exit, you'll come upon the imposing **Arch of Constantine,** erected in AD 315 to commemorate Constantine's victory over Maxentius at the Milvian Bridge.

Just beyond is the **Colosseum,** the most famous monument of ancient Rome. Begun by the Flavian emperor Vespasian in AD 72, it was inaugurated by Titus eight years later with a program of games and shows lasting 100 days. On the opening day alone, 5,000 wild beasts perished in the arena. Its 573-yard circumference could contain more than 50,000 spectators. It was faced with marble and boasted an ingenious system of awnings to shade spectators from the sun. Originally known as the Flavian Amphitheater, in later centuries it came to be called the Colosseum, after a colossal gilded bronze statue of Nero that stood nearby. It served as a fortress during the 13th century and then as a quarry from which materials were filched to build sumptuous Renaissance churches and palaces. Finally it was declared sacred by the popes, in memory of the many Christians believed to have been martyred there. If you pay admission to the upper levels, you can see a scale model of the Colosseum as it was in its heyday. *Piazza del Colosseo, tel. 06/700–4261. Admission free; admission to upper levels: 6,000 lire. Open Mon., Tues., Thurs.–Sat. 9–one hour before sunset, Wed. and Sun. 9–1.*

Behind the Colosseum at the Colle Oppio (Oppian Hill) on the Esquiline Hill is what's left of Nero's fabulous **Domus Aurea,** a sumptuous palace later buried under Trajan's Baths. Returning back toward Piazza Venezia on Via dei Fori Imperiale, you can get a good look at the Imperial Fora and Trajan's Market.

Tour 2: The Vatican

While the ancient Roman emperors presided over the decline of their empire, a vibrant new force emerged. Christianity came to Rome, the seat of the pope was established over the tomb of St. Peter, and the Vatican became the spiritual focus of the Roman Catholic Church. There are two principal reasons for seeing the Vatican. One is to visit St. Peter's, the largest church in the world and the most overwhelming architectural achievement of the Renaissance. The other is to visit the Vatican Museums, which contain collections of staggering richness and diversity—including, of course, the Sistine Chapel. There's little point in trying to take it all in on just one visit. See St. Peter's first, and come back later to see the Vatican Museums.

12 Start at **Castel Sant'Angelo,** the fortress that guarded the Vatican for hundreds of years. One of Rome's most beautiful bridges, **Ponte Sant'Angelo** spans the Tiber in front of the fortress and is studded with graceful angels designed by Giovanni Lorenzo Bernini (1598–1680). The distinctive silhouette of Castel Sant'Angelo is a throwback to its original function; it was built as a mausoleum, or tomb, for the emperor Hadrian in AD 135. By the 6th century it had been transformed into a fortress, and it remained the military stronghold of Rome and a refuge for popes for almost 1,000 years.

According to legend, the castle got its name during the plague of 590, when Pope Gregory the Great, passing by in a religious procession, had a vision of an angel sheathing its sword atop the stone ramparts. He interpreted this as a sign that the plague would end immediately, and, after it did, he had a chapel built on the highest level of the fortress, where he had seen the angel. Visit the lower levels, the base of Hadrian's mausoleum, and then climb ancient ramps and narrow staircases to explore the castle's courtyards and frescoed halls, the collection of antique arms and armor, and the open loggia, where there's a café. Climb to the upper terraces for views of the city's rooftops and the lower bastions of the castle, as well as of the Passetto, the fortified corridor connecting Castel Sant'Angelo with the Vatican. *Lungotevere Castello 50, tel. 06/687–5036. Admission: 8,000 lire. Open Apr.–Sept., usually Mon.–Sat. 9–7, though hours vary from year to year; Oct.–Mar., Mon. 2–6:30, Tues.–Sat. 9–1, Sun. 9–noon.*

From Castel Sant'Angelo, turn right onto Via della Conciliazione, a broad, rather soulless avenue conceived by Mussolini in the 1930s to celebrate the "conciliation" between the Vatican and the Italian government under the Lateran Pact of 1929. The pact ended 60 years of papal protest against the state, which the Vatican had refused to recognize. Indeed, after Italian troops wrested control of Rome from the pope in 1870 to make it the capital of a newly united Italy, popes refused to leave the Vatican.

The Via della Conciliazione approach to St. Peter's gives your eyes time to adjust to the enormous dimensions of the square and the church, although the intent of Baroque artist Bernini, who designed the square, was to surprise the visitor emerging suddenly from shadowy alleys into the square's immense space and full light. **13** **Piazza San Pietro** (St. Peter's Square) is one of Bernini's masterpieces, completed after 11 years' work—a relatively short time in those days, considering the vastness of the job. The square can hold as many as 400,000 people and is surrounded by a pair of quadruple colonnades, which are topped by a balustrade and 140 statues of saints. Look for the two stone disks set into the pavement on each side of the obelisk, between the obelisk and the fountains. If you stand on one disk, a trick of perspective makes the colonnades seem to consist of a single row of columns.

14 The history of **St. Peter's** goes back to the year AD 319, when the emperor Constantine built a basilica here over the site of the tomb of St. Peter. The original church stood for more than 1,000 years, undergoing a number of restorations, until it threatened to collapse. Reconstruction began in 1452 but was soon abandoned due to a lack of funds. In 1506 Pope Julius II instructed the architect Donato Bramante (1444–1514) to raze the existing structure and build a new and greater basilica, but it wasn't until 1626 that the new church was completed and dedicated. Five of Italy's greatest Renaissance artists died while working on it—Bramante, Raphael, Peruzzi, Antonio Sangallo the Younger, and Michelangelo. Bramante outlined a basic plan for the church and built the massive pillars that were to support the dome. After his death in 1514, his successors made little progress with the work and altered his master plan. In 1546 Pope Paul III more or less forced the aging Michelangelo to take on the job of completing the building. Michelangelo returned to Bramante's ground plan and designed the dome to cover the crossing, but his plans, too, were modified after his death. The result is nevertheless breathtaking. As you approach the church, look at the people going in and out of the portico, and note the contrast between their size and the immense scale of the building. (Persons wearing shorts, miniskirts, sleeveless T-shirts, or other revealing clothing are not allowed entrance to St. Peter's or the Vatican Museums. Women should carry scarves to cover their bare upper arms.)

Now climb the broad steps yourself and enter the portico. Notice Filarete's 15th-century bronze doors, salvaged from the old basilica. Once inside, pause a moment to consider the size of this immense temple. Look at the massive pillars, the holy-water stoups borne by colossal cherubs, the distance to the main altar. Look for the brass inscriptions in the marble pavement along the center of the nave (the long central section), indicating the approximate length of the world's principal Christian churches, all of which fall far short of St. Peter's. The chapel immediately to your right holds Michelangelo's *Pietà*, one of the world's most famous statues. It is now screened behind shatterproof glass, after a serious incident of vandalism (and a masterful restoration in the Vatican workshops). This is the only sculpture Michelangelo ever signed, although the signature—on the sash across the Virgin's chest—is too high up behind glass to be seen. The story goes that he completed the work unsigned but stole back to sign it when he was told that others might take credit for it.

Four massive piers support the dome at the crossing, where the mighty Bernini *baldacchino* (canopy), made of bronze stripped from the Pantheon by order of the Barberini pope Urban VIII, rises high above the papal altar. The pope celebrates mass here, over the crypt holding the tombs of many of his predecessors. Deep in the earth under the foundations of the original basilica is what is believed to be the tomb of St. Peter. A very old bronze statue of the saint stands at the last pillar on the right before the crossing, its foot worn and burnished by the kisses of the faithful throughout the centuries. Beautiful bronze vigil lights flicker around the ceremonial entrance to the crypt in front of the papal altar. In the niche below is an antique casket containing the *pallia* (bands of white wool conferred by the Pope on archbishops as a sign of authority). The splendid gilt-bronze throne above the altar in the apse was designed by Bernini and contains a wood-and-ivory chair that St. Peter was supposed to have used, though in fact it dates back no farther than the Middle Ages. You can see a copy of the chair in the Treasury.

Stop in to see the small collection of Vatican treasures in the little **museum** in the sacristy, among them priceless antique chalices and the massive 15th-century bronze tomb of Pope Sixtus V by Antonio Pollaiuolo (1429–98). *Admission: 3,000 lire. Open Apr.–Sept., daily 9–6:30; Oct.–Mar., daily 9–5:30.*

Visit the **crypt** to see the tombs of the popes. The only exit from the crypt leads outside St. Peter's, near the entrance to the roof and dome. *Entrance at St. Longinus Pier but alternatively at one of the other piers. Admission free. Open Apr.–Sept., daily 7–6; Oct.–Mar., daily 7–5.*

Take the elevator or climb the stairs to the **roof** of the church, an interesting landscape of domes and towers. From here, climb a short interior staircase to the base of the dome for a dove's-eye view of the interior of the church. It's a taxing climb to the lantern—the architectural term for the delicate structure crowning the dome; the stairs are steep and narrow and one-way only, so there's no turning back. Those who make it are rewarded with views embracing the Vatican gardens and all of Rome. *Entrance to roof and dome in courtyard on the left as you leave the church. Admission: 5,000 lire if you use the elevator to the roof, 4,000 if you use the stairs. Open Apr.–Sept., daily 8–6; Oct.–Mar., daily 8–5.*

Visit the excavations under St. Peter's for a fascinating glimpse of the underpinnings of the great basilica, which was built over the cemetery where archaeologists say they have found **St. Peter's tomb**. *Apply (a few days in advance, if possible, though there may be places open on the guided tours the same day you apply) to the Ufficio Scavi (Excavations Office), to the right beyond the Arco delle Campane entrance to the Vatican, which is left of the basilica. Just tell the Swiss guard you want the Ufficio Scavi, and he will let you enter the confines of Vatican City. Tel. 06/698–5318. Admission: 8,000 lire with guide, 5,000 lire with taped guide. Ufficio Scavi open Mon.–Sat. 9–5.*

For many, a **papal audience** is the highlight of a trip to Rome. The pope holds mass audiences on Wednesday mornings at about 11, and at 10 during the hottest months. During winter and summer, audiences take place in a modern audience hall. In spring and fall they may be held in St. Peter's Square, and in summer, sometimes at the papal residence at Castel Gandolfo. You must apply for tickets in advance, and it may be it easier to arrange for them through a travel agency, but expect to pay about 36,000 lire for the service, which includes a bus tour of the city. Of course, you can avoid the formalities by seeing the pope when he makes his weekly appearance at the window of the Vatican Palace, every Sunday at noon when he is in Rome, to address the crowd and give a blessing. *For audience tickets, apply in writing well in advance, to the Papal Prefecture (Prefettura), 00120 Città del Vaticano, Italy, tel. 06/6982, indicating the date you prefer, the language you speak, and the hotel where you will be staying. For same-day tickets (which may not be available) go directly to the Prefettura, through the bronze door in the right-hand colonnade, open Mon. and Tues. 9–1 for the Wed. audience, also open Wed. 9 until shortly before* *the audience commences. You can also pick up free tickets at the North American College, Via dell'Umiltà 30, tel. 06/678-9184, or through Santa Susanna American Church, Piazza San Bernardo, tel. 06/482-7510.*

Tour 3: The Vatican Museums

The Vatican Palace, which has been the residence of popes on and off since 1377, is made up of several interlocking buildings containing 1,400 rooms, chapels, and galleries. The pope and his household occupy only a small part of the palace, most of which is given over to the Vatican Library and Museums. The main entrance to the museums, on Viale Vaticano, is a long walk from Piazza San Pietro, but there is bus service between the square and a secondary museum entrance. It takes a route through the Vatican gardens and costs 2,000 lire, and although it deposits you at a side entrance, it saves a lot of walking and allows a glimpse of some of Vatican City that would otherwise be off-limits. *Service 8:45–12:45 on the half hour, except Sun. and Wed. Bus tours of the Vatican gardens available Mon., Tues., and Thurs.–Sat. Cost: 16,000 lire. Tickets at the Vatican Information Office in Piazza San Pietro.*

15 The collections of the **Vatican Museums** are immense, covering about 4½ miles of displays. Special posters at the entrance and throughout the museum plot a choice of four color-coded itineraries, the shortest taking approximately 90 minutes and the longest five hours. You can rent a taped commentary in English that describes the Sistine Chapel and the Raphael Rooms. You're free to photograph what you like, although if you want to use a flash, tripod, or other special equipment, you must get permission. The main entrance is on Viale Vaticano and can be reached by the No. 49 bus from Piazza Cavour, which stops right in front; on foot from bus No. 81 or tram No. 19, which stop at Piazza Risorgimento; or from the Ottaviano stop on Metro line A. Pick up a leaflet at the entrance in order to see the overall layout. The Sistine Chapel, the main attraction for most visitors, is at the far end of the complex, and the leaflet charts two abbreviated itineraries through other collections to reach it. It would be a shame to miss the collections en route to the Sistine Chapel, and below we give some of the highlights, whether or not you follow the itineraries suggested by the curators. *Viale Vaticano, tel. 06/698–3333. Admission: 12,000 lire; free on last Sun. of month. Open Easter week and July–Sept., weekdays 8:45–5 (no admission after 4), Sat. 8:45–2; Oct.–June (except Easter), Mon.–Sat. 9–2 (no admission after 1). Closed Sun. year-round, except last Sun. of month (open 9–2, admission free), and on religious holidays: Jan. 1, Jan. 6, Feb. 11, Mar. 19, Easter Sun. and Mon., May 1, Ascension Thurs., Corpus Christi, June 29, Aug. 15–16, Nov. 1, Dec. 8, Dec. 25–26.*

Among Vatican City's many riches, probably the single most important is the Sistine Chapel. However, unless you're following one of the two abbreviated itineraries, you'll begin your visit at the **Egyptian Museum** and go on to the **Chiaramonti** and **Pio Clementino Museums**, which are given over to classical sculptures (among them some of the best-known statues in the world—the *Laocoön*, the *Belvedere Torso*, and the *Apollo Belvedere*—works that, with their vibrant humanism, had a tremendous impact on Renaissance art). Next come the **Etruscan**

Museum and three other sections of limited interest. All itineraries merge in the **Candelabra Gallery** and proceed through the **Tapestry Gallery,** which is hung with magnificent tapestries executed from Raphael's designs.

The **Gallery of Maps** is intriguing; the **Apartment of Pius V,** a little less so. After them you'll enter the **Raphael Rooms,** second only to the Sistine Chapel in artistic interest. In 1508 Pope Julius II employed Raphael Sanzio, on the recommendation of Bramante, to decorate the rooms with biblical scenes. The result was a Renaissance masterpiece. Of the four rooms, the second and third were decorated mainly by Raphael; the others, by Giulio Romano and other assistants of Raphael. The lovely Loggia (covered balcony) was designed and frescoed by the master himself. Next you'll pass through the Chiaroscuro Room to the tiny **Chapel of Nicholas V,** aglow with frescoes by Fra Angelico (1387–1455), the Florentine monk whose sensitive paintings were guiding lights for the Renaissance. If your itinerary takes you to the **Borgia Apartments,** you'll see their elaborately painted ceilings, designed and partially executed by Pinturicchio (1454–1513). The Borgia Apartments have been given over to the Vatican's large but not particularly interesting collection of modern religious art, which continues at a lower level. Once you've seen the Borgia Rooms you can skip the rest in good conscience and get on to the Sistine Chapel.

In 1508, while Raphael was put to work on his series of rooms, Pope Julius II commissioned Michelangelo to fresco the more than 10,000 square feet of the **Sistine Chapel** ceiling single-handedly. The task took four years of mental and physical anguish. It's said that for years afterward Michelangelo couldn't read anything without holding it up over his head. The result, however, was the masterpiece you now see, its colors cool and brilliant after recent restoration. Bring a pair of binoculars to get a better look at this incredible work, and if you want to have some leisure to study it, try to beat the tour groups by getting there early in the day. Some 20 years after completing the ceiling, Michelangelo was commissioned to paint the *Last Judgment* on the wall above the altar. The aged and embittered artist painted his own face on the wrinkled human skin in the hand of St. Bartholomew, below and to the right of the figure of Christ, which he clearly modeled on the *Apollo Belvedere.*

After this experience, which can be marred by the crowds of tourists, you'll pass through some of the exhibition halls of the **Vatican Library.** Look in on Room X, Room of the Aldobrandini Marriage, to see its beautiful Roman frescoes of a nuptial rite. You can see more classical statues in the new wing and then, perhaps after taking a break at the cafeteria, go on to the **Pinacoteca** (Picture Gallery). It displays mainly religious paintings by such artists as Giotto, Fra Angelico, and Filippo Lippi. The **Raphael Room** holds his exceptional *Transfiguration, Coronation,* and *Foligno Madonna.*

In the **Pagan Antiquities Museum,** modern display techniques enhance another collection of Greek and Roman sculptures. The **Christian Antiquities Museum** has early Christian and medieval art, while the **Ethnological Museum** shows art and artifacts from exotic places throughout the world. The complete itinerary ends with the **Historical Museum**'s collection of carriages, uniforms, and arms.

In all, the Vatican Museums offer a staggering excursion into the realms of art and history. It's foolhardy to try to see all the collections in one day, and it's doubtful that anyone could be interested in everything on display. Simply aim for an overall impression of the collections' artistic and cultural riches. If you want to delve deeper, you can come back another day.

Tour 4: Old Rome

A district of narrow streets with curious names, airy Baroque piazzas, and picturesque courtyards, Old Rome *(Vecchia Roma)* occupies the horn of land that pushes the Tiber westward toward the Vatican. It has been an integral part of the city since ancient times, and its position between the Vatican and the Lateran palaces, both seats of papal rule, placed it in the mainstream of Rome's development from the Middle Ages onward. Today it's full of old artisans' workshops, trendy cafés and eating places, and offbeat boutiques. On weekends and summer evenings Old Rome is a magnet for crowds of young people.

16 Start at Piazza Venezia and take Via del Plebiscito to the huge Baroque **Il Gesù,** comparable only to St. Peter's for sheer grandeur. Inside it's encrusted with gold and precious marbles and topped by a fantastically painted ceiling that flows down over the pillars to become three-dimensional, merging with painted stucco figures in a swirling composition glorifying the Jesuit **17** order. Then head for nearby Piazza della Minerva to see **Santa Maria Sopra Minerva,** a Gothic church with some beautiful frescoes, in a side chapel, by Filippo Lippi (1406–69), the monk who taught Botticelli. The tomb of another great artist-monk, Fra Angelico (c. 1400–1455), stands to the left of the altar. Bernini's charming elephant bearing an obelisk stands in the center of the piazza.

18 The huge brick building opposite is the **Pantheon,** one of the most harmonious and best-preserved monuments of antiquity. It was first erected in 27 BC by Augustus's general Agrippa and completely redesigned and rebuilt by Hadrian, who deserves the credit for this fantastic feat of construction. At its apex, the dome is exactly as tall as the walls, so that you could imagine it as the upper half of a sphere resting on the floor; this balance gives the building a serene majesty. The bronze doors are the original ones; most of the other decorations of gilt bronze and marble that covered the dome and walls were plundered by later Roman emperors and by the popes. The Pantheon gets light and air from the apex of the dome—another impressive feature of this remarkable edifice. *Piazza della Rotonda, tel. 06/654–3311. Admission free. Open Oct.–June, Mon.–Sat. 9–5, Sun. 9–1; July–Sept., daily 9–6.*

The areas around the Pantheon and Piazza Navona have more *gelaterie* (ice-cream parlors) than can be found anywhere else in Rome. Romans consider **Giolitti** (Via Uffizi del Vicario 40, closed Mon.) to be superlative and take the counter by storm. Remember to pay the cashier first and hand the stub to the man at the counter when you order your cone. Giolitti has good snacks, too.

19 From Piazza della Rotonda in front of the Pantheon, take Via Giustiniani onto Via della Dogana Vecchia to the church of **San Luigi dei Francesi.** In the last chapel on the left are three stunning works by Caravaggio (1571–1610), the master of the heightened approach to light and dark. A light machine (operated with a couple of 100-lire coins) provides illumination to view the paintings. *Open Fri.–Wed. 7:30–12:30 and 3:30–7, Thurs. 7:30–12:30.*

In the church of **Sant'Agostino,** close by (Piazza di Sant'-Agostino), there is another Caravaggio above the first altar on the left. Just beyond these churches is **Piazza Navona,** a beautiful Baroque piazza that traces the oval of Emperor Domitian's stadium. It still has the carefree air of the days when it was the scene of Roman circus games, medieval jousts, and 17th-century carnivals. Bernini's splashing **Fountain of the Four Rivers,** with an enormous rock squared off by statues representing the four corners of the world, makes a fitting centerpiece. Behind it stands the church of **Sant' Agnese in Agone.** Its Baroque facade is by Francesco Borromini (1599–1667), a contemporary and sometime rival of Bernini. One story has it that the Bernini statue nearest the church is hiding its head because it can't bear to look upon the inferior Borromini facade; in fact, the facade was built after the fountain, and the statue hides its head because it represents the Nile River, whose source was unknown until relatively recently. The sidewalk tables of the **Tre Scalini** café, where the luscious chocolate ice cream *tartufo* (truffle) was invented, offer a grandstand view of the piazza, but at a splurge price.

Leaving Piazza Navona by way of the Corsia Agonalis, the street opposite Tre Scalini, you'll see the 17th-century **Palazzo Madama,** now the Senate, on Corso Rinascimento. To the right, at the end of the street, the huge church of **Sant'Andrea della Valle** looms mightily over a busy intersection. Puccini set the first act of his opera *Tosca* here.

Now make your way through side streets to **Campo dei Fiori.** Once the scene of public executions (including that of philosopher-monk Giordano Bruno, whose statue broods in the center), it now holds one of Rome's busiest, most colorful food markets, in full swing Monday through Saturday from 8 to 2.

Continue on to Piazza Farnese, where Michelangelo had a hand in building **Palazzo Farnese,** now the French Embassy and perhaps the most beautiful of the Renaissance palaces in Rome. (Puccini set the second act of *Tosca* here.) The twin fountains in the piazza are made with basins of Egyptian granite from the Baths of Caracalla. Behind Palazzo Farnese, turn onto Via Giulia, where you'll see some elegant palaces (step inside the portals to take a look at the courtyards), old churches, and a number of antiques shops.

Tour 5: The Spanish Steps and the Trevi Fountain

The walk up Via del Corso from Piazza Venezia takes you to Rome's classiest shopping streets and to two visual extravaganzas: the Spanish Steps and the Fountain of Trevi.

Start at the **Vittorio Emanuele Monument** in Piazza Venezia. Rome's most flamboyant landmark, this structure was erected in the late 19th century to honor Italy's first king, Vittorio Emanuele II, and the unification of Italy. This vast marble monument, said to resemble a wedding cake or a Victorian typewriter, houses the **Tomb of the Unknown Soldier,** with its eternal flame. Although the monument has been closed to the public for many years, plans are in the works to reopen it; the views from the top of the steps are among Rome's best.

㉗ On the left, as you look up the Corso, is **Palazzo Venezia,** a blend of medieval solidity and Renaissance grace. It contains a good collection of paintings, sculptures, and objets d'art in handsome salons, some of which Mussolini used as his offices. Notice the balcony over the main portal, from which Il Duce addressed huge crowds in the square below. *Via del Plebiscito 118, tel. 06/ 679–8865. Admission: 8,000 lire. Open Mon.–Sat. 9–2, Sun. 9–1.*

Along the Corso are some fine old palaces and a church or two.
㉘ Detour to the left to see the church of **Sant'Ignazio,** where what seems to be the dome is really an illusionist canvas. Put some coins in the light machine to illuminate the dazzling frescoes on the vault of the nave. Next you'll come to Piazza Colonna,
㉙ named for the ancient **Column of Marcus Aurelius,** with its extraordinarily detailed reliefs spiraling up to the top.

From Largo Goldoni, on Via del Corso, you'll get a head-on view of the Spanish Steps and the church of Trinità dei Monti as you start up Via Condotti, an elegant and expensive shopping street. Look for the historic **Caffè Greco** on the left. More than 200 years old, it was the haunt of Goethe, Byron, and Liszt; now it's a hangout for well-dressed ladies carrying Gucci shopping bags.

㉚ Piazza di Spagna and the **Spanish Steps** get their names from the Spanish Embassy to the Holy See (the Vatican), opposite the American Express office, though they were built with French funds. This was once the core of Rome's bohemian quarter, especially favored by American and British artists and writers in the 18th and 19th centuries. At the center of the
㉛ square is Bernini's **Fountain of the Barcaccia** (Old Boat), and just to the right of the steps is the house where Keats and Shelley lived. Sloping upward in broad curves, the Spanish Steps are perfect for socializing, and they draw huge crowds on weekend and holiday afternoons. From mid-April to early May, the steps are blanketed with azaleas in bloom.

From the narrow end of the piazza, take Via Propaganda Fide to Sant'Andrea delle Fratte, swerving left on Via del Nazareno, then crossing busy Via del Tritone to Via della
㉜ Stamperia. This street leads to the **Fountain of Trevi,** one of Rome's most spectacular fountains when it's gushing. It was featured in the 1954 film *Three Coins in the Fountain.* And legend has it that you can ensure your return to Rome by tossing a coin in the fountain. Unfortunately, legend doesn't tell you how to cope with the souvenir vendors and aggressive beggars who are looking for a share of your change.

Tour 6: Historic Churches

Three churches are the highlights of this walk, two of them major basilicas with roots in the early centuries of Christianity. Not far from Piazza Venezia and the Roman Forum, off Via Cavour, is the church of **San Pietro in Vincoli.** Look for Via San
㉝ Francesco da Paola, a street staircase that passes under the old Borgia palace and leads to the square in front of the church. Inside are St. Peter's chains (under the altar) and Michelangelo's

Moses, a powerful statue almost as famed as his frescoes in the Sistine Chapel. The *Moses* was destined for the tomb of Julius II, but Michelangelo was driven to distraction by the interference of Pope Julius and his successors, and the tomb was never finished. The statue, intended as part of the tomb, is a remarkable sculpture and a big tourist attraction, but crass commercialism has ruined the starkly majestic effect of this memorial. The church is usually jammed with tour groups, and the monument itself is a front for a large and ugly souvenir shop.

34 Continue along Via Cavour to **Santa Maria Maggiore,** one of the oldest and most beautiful churches in Rome. Built on the spot where a 3rd-century pope witnessed a miraculous midsummer snowfall, it is resplendent with gleaming mosaics—those on the arch in front of the main altar date from the 5th century; the apse mosaic dates from the 13th century—and an opulent carved-wood ceiling supposed to have been gilded with the first gold brought from the New World. Urgently needed restoration may continue into 1994, hiding some of the interior from view.

35 Via Merulana runs straight as an arrow from Santa Maria Maggiore to the immense cathedral of Rome, **San Giovanni in Laterano,** where the early popes once lived and where the present pope still officiates in his capacity as Rome's bishop. The towering facade and Borromini's cool Baroque interior emphasize the majesty of its proportions.

The adjoining **Lateran Palace,** once the popes' official residence and still technically part of the Vatican, now houses the offices of the Rome Diocese and the **Vatican Historical Museum** (admission 6,000 lire; open first Sun. of each month, 8:45–1). Across the street, opposite the Lateran Palace, a small build-
36 ing houses the **Scala Santa** (Holy Stairs), claimed to be the staircase from Pilate's palace in Jerusalem. Circle the palace to see the 6th-century octagonal **Baptistery of San Giovanni,** forerunner of many similar buildings throughout Italy, and Rome's oldest and tallest obelisk, brought from Thebes and dating from the 15th century BC.

37 One more church awaits you just down Via Carlo Felice. **Santa Croce in Gerusalemme,** with a pretty Rococo facade and Baroque interior, shelters what are believed to be relics of the True Cross found by St. Helena, mother of the emperor Constantine and a tireless collector of holy objects.

Tour 7: The Quirinale and Piazza della Repubblica

Although this tour takes you from ancient Roman sculptures to early Christian churches, it's mainly an excursion into the 16th and 17th centuries, when Baroque art—and Bernini—triumphed in Rome. The **Quirinale** is the highest of Rome's seven original hills (the others are the Capitoline, Palatine, Esquiline, Viminal, Celian, and Aventine) and the one where ancient Romans and later the popes built their residences in order to escape the deadly miasmas and the malaria of the low-lying
38 area around the Forum. **Palazzo del Quirinale,** the largest on the square, belonged first to the popes, then to Italy's kings, and is now the official residence of the nation's president. The fountain in the square boasts ancient statues of Castor and Pollux reining in their unruly steeds and a basin salvaged from the Roman Forum.

Along Via del Quirinale (which becomes Via XX Settembre) are two interesting little churches, each an architectural gem. The first you'll come upon is **Sant'Andrea,** a small but imposing Baroque church designed and decorated by Bernini, who considered it one of his finest works and liked to come here occasionally just to sit and enjoy it. The second is the church of **San Carlo alle Quattro Fontane** (Four Fountains), at the intersection. It was designed by Bernini's rival, Borromini, who created a building that is an intricate exercise in geometric perfection, all curves and movement.

Turn left down Via delle Quattro Fontane to a splendid 17th-century palace, **Palazzo Barberini.** Inside, the **Galleria Nazionale** offers some fine works by Raphael (the *Fornarina*) and Caravaggio and a salon with gorgeous ceiling frescoes by Pietro da Cortona. Upstairs, don't miss the charming suite of rooms decorated in 18th-century fashion. *Via delle Quattro Fontane 13, tel. 06/481–4591. Admission: 6,000 lire. Open Tues.–Sat. 9–2, Sun. 9–1.*

Down the hill, Piazza Barberini has Bernini's graceful **Tritone Fountain,** designed in 1637 for the sculptor's munificent patron, Pope Urban VIII, whose Barberini coat of arms, featuring bees, is at the base of the large shell.

Via Veneto winds its way upward from Piazza Barberini past **Santa Maria della Concezione,** a Capuchin church famous for its crypt, where the skeletons and assorted bones of 4,000 dead monks are artistically arranged in four macabre chapels. *Via Veneto 27, tel. 06/462850. Donations requested. Open daily 9–noon, 3–6.*

The avenue curves past the American Embassy and Consulate; the luxurious Excelsior Hotel; and Doney's and the Café de Paris, famous from the days of *la dolce vita* in the 1950s. At the U.S. Embassy, take Via Bissolati to Piazza San Bernardo. The church of **Santa Maria della Vittoria,** on the corner, is known for Bernini's sumptuous Baroque decoration of the Cornaro Chapel, an exceptional fusion of architecture, painting, and sculpture, in which the *Ecstasy of St. Theresa* is the focal point. The statue represents a mystical experience in what some regard as very earthly terms.

Art buffs may want to take a side trip from Piazza San Bernardo to the early Christian churches of **Sant'Agnese** and **Santa Costanza,** about a mile beyond the old city walls. Take bus No. 36, 37, 60, or 136 along Via Nomentana to get there. Santa Costanza, a church-in-the-round, has vaults decorated with bright 4th-century mosaics. The custodian of the catacomb of Sant'Agnese accompanies you up the hill to see it. *Via di Sant'Agnese, tel. 06/832–0743. Admission to Sant'Agnese catacombs: 6,000 lire. Admission to Santa Costanza is free, but a tip is in order if you do not buy a ticket to Sant'Agnese. Open Mon., Wed., Thurs.–Sat. 9–noon and 4–6, Tues. 9–noon, Sun. 4–6.*

From Piazza San Bernardo, it's not far to Piazza della Repubblica, where the pretty **Fountain of the Naiads,** a turn-of-the-century addition, features voluptuous bronze ladies wrestling happily with marine monsters. On one side of the square is an ancient Roman brick facade, which marks the church of **Santa Maria degli Angeli,** adapted by Michelangelo from the vast central chamber of the colossal Baths of Diocletian, built in the 4th century AD, the largest and most impressive of the ancient baths. The baths were on such a grandiose scale that the church and its former monastery, which now houses one section of the Museo Nazionale Romano around the corner to the right, account for only part of the bath area. Inside the church, take a good look at the eight enormous columns of red granite; these are the original columns of the baths' central chamber and are 45 feet high and more than 5 feet in diameter.

48 The collections of ancient Roman art of the **Museo Nazionale Romano** are now divided between the old museum, in the former monastery of Santa Maria degli Angeli, and a new museum in Palazzo Massimo, across the square on the other side of the gardens (and an annex near Piazza Navona is also planned). In an upstairs gallery in the former monastery, frescoes from Empress Livia's villa outside Rome are delightful depictions of a garden in bloom. Palazzo Massimo, which should be open by 1994, will house most of the sculpture collections. *Museo Nazionale Romano: Monastery of Santa Maria degli Angeli, Viale E. De Nicola 79, tel. 06/488–0530. Admission: 3,000 lire. Open Tues.–Sat., 9–2, Sun. 9–1. Palazzo Massimo, Piazza dei Cinquecento. Admission: 6,000.*

Tour 8: The Villa Borghese to the Ara Pacis

49 A half-mile walk northwest from Piazza della Repubblica up Via Orlando and Via Vittorio Veneto leads you to **Porta Pinciana** (Pincian Gate), one of the historic city gates in the Aurelian Walls surrounding Rome. The Porta itself was built in the 6th century AD, about three centuries after the walls were built to keep out the barbarians. These days it is one of the entrances to the **Villa Borghese,** which is in fact the name of Rome's large 17th-century park, built as the pleasure gardens of the powerful Borghese family.

50 Once inside the park, turn right up Viale del Museo Borghese and make for the **Galleria Borghese,** which was built as a venue for entertaining and to hold the family's art collection. At the time of this writing, the gallery was undergoing extensive renovations, and its important picture collection had been moved to the large San Michele a Ripa complex in Trastevere, where the paintings will be on view at least through 1994. *(Via di San Michele, tel. 06/58431. Admission: 4,000 lire. Open Mon.–Fri. 9:30–1:30 and 4–8, Sat. 9:30–1:30).* At the Villa Borghese location there's a sculpture collection on the first floor, including Canova's famous statue of Pauline Borghese, wife of Camillo Borghese and sister of Napoleon. Officially known as *Venus Vincitrix,* it is really a depiction of a haughty (and very seductive) Pauline lying provocatively on a Roman sofa. The next two rooms hold two important Baroque sculptures by Bernini: *David* and *Apollo and Daphne.* In each you can see the vibrant attention to movement that marked the first departure from the Renaissance preoccupation with the idealized human form. Daphne is being transformed into a laurel tree while fleeing from a lecherous Apollo: Twigs sprout from her fingertips while her pursuer recoils in amazement. *During renovations the Galleria Borghese entrance is off Via Raimondi, tel. 06/ 858577. Admission free for duration of renovation. Open Mon.–Sat. 9–1:30, Sun. 9–1.*

From the Galleria Borghese you can cross the park, taking Viale dell'Uccelleria and then a left on Viale del Giardino
⑤ Zoologico to the **Galleria Nazionale d'Arte Moderna** (National Gallery of Modern Art), a large white building boasting Italy's leading collection of 20th-century works. *Viale delle Belle Arti 131, tel. 06/322-4151. Admission: 8,000 lire. Open Tues.-Sat. 9-2, Sun. 9-1.*

⑤ Close by is the **Museo di Villa Giulia,** housing one of the world's great Etruscan collections. The villa is a former papal summer palace set in lovely gardens. This is the place to study the strange, half-understood Etruscan civilization, for here are magnificent terra-cotta statues, figurines, jewelry, household implements, sarcophagi—a way of life on display. Among the most precious gems are the *Apollo of Veio* and the *Sarcophagus of the Sposi.* When you have had your fill of these treasures, step out into the nymphaeum (the architectural term for this place of cool recesses and fern-softened fountains) and take a close look at the full-scale reconstruction of an Etruscan temple in the garden. *Piazza di Villa Giulia 9, tel. 06/320-1951. Admission: 8,000 lire. Open Wed. 9-7, Tues. and Thurs.-Sat. 9-2, Sun. 9-1.*

⑤ The **Pincio** is an extension of Villa Borghese, with gardens on a terrace overlooking much of Rome. It was laid out by the early-19th-century architect Valadier as part of his overall plan for Piazza del Popolo. The Pincio offers a superb view, absolutely spectacular when there is a fine sunset, and it's also a vantage point from which you can study Valadier's arrangement of
⑤ **Piazza del Popolo.**

This is one of Rome's largest squares and a traditional place for mass meetings and rallies. At the center, four dignified stone lions guard an obelisk relating the life and times of Ramses II in the 13th century BC. Next to the 400-year-old **Porta del Popolo,**
⑤ Rome's northern city gate, stop in at the church of **Santa Maria del Popolo** to see a pair of Caravaggios and some Bernini sculptures in a rich Baroque setting.

From here it's a short walk down Via Ripetta to the large **Augusteum,** the mausoleum Augustus built for himself and his family. Next to it is an unattractive modern edifice that shel-
⑤ ters the **Ara Pacis** (Altar of Augustan Peace), erected in 13 BC to celebrate the era of peace ushered in by Augustus's military victories. The reliefs on the marble enclosure are magnificent. *Via Ripetta, tel. 06/671-0271. Admission: 3,750 lire. Open Wed.-Fri. 9-1:30, Tues. and Sat. 9-1:30 and 3:30-7:30, Sun. 9-1.*

Tour 9: The Jewish Ghetto and Trastevere

For the authentic atmosphere of Old Rome, explore the old Jewish ghetto and the narrow streets of Trastevere, two tightly knit communities whose inhabitants proudly claim descent—whether real or imagined—from the ancient Romans. Then climb the Janiculum, a hill with views overlooking the entire city, a vantage point beloved of all Romans.

The shadowy area bounded by Piazza Campitelli and Lungotevere Cenci constituted Rome's old Jewish ghetto. Within this cramped quarter, from the 16th century until 1870, all Rome's Jews (and they were many, tracing their presence in the city to

ancient Roman times) were confined under a rigid all-night curfew. At the little church opposite Quattro Capi Bridge, they
were forced to attend sermons that aimed to convert them to
Catholicism, and to pay for the privilege.

Many Jews have remained here, close to the bronze-roofed
⑤⑦ synagogue on Lungotevere Cenci and to the roots of their community. Among the most interesting sights in the ghetto are
⑤⑧ the pretty **Fontana delle Tartarughe** (Turtle Fountain) on Piazza Mattei; the old houses on Via Portico d'Ottavia, where medieval inscriptions and ancient friezes testify to the venerable
⑤⑨ age of these buildings; and the **Teatro di Marcello,** hardly recognizable as a theater now, but built at the end of the 1st century
BC by Julius Caesar to hold 20,000 spectators.

⑥⓪ Cross the Tiber over the ancient Ponte Fabricio to the **Tiberina
Island,** where a city hospital stands on a site that has been dedicated to healing ever since a temple to Aesculapius was erected
here in 291 BC. If you have time, and if the river's not too high,
go down the stairs for a different perspective on the island and
the Tiber.

Then continue across Ponte Cestio into **Trastevere,** a maze of
narrow streets that despite creeping gentrification is still one
of the city's most authentically Roman neighborhoods (another
is the jumble of streets between the Roman Forum, Santa Maria Maggiore, and the Colosseum). Among self-consciously picturesque trattorias and trendy tearooms, you'll also find old
shops in alleys festooned with washing hung out to dry and
dusty artisans' workshops. Trastevere's population has become
increasingly diverse, and it has acquired a reputation for
purse-snatching and petty thievery, much to the chagrin of the
authentic *trasteverini,* so keep your purses and cameras out of
⑥① sight as you stroll these byways. Be sure to see **Piazza Santa
Maria in Trastevere,** the heart of the quarter, with one of
Rome's oldest churches, decorated inside and out with
12th- and 13th-century mosaics.

Follow Via della Scala to Via della Lungara, where Raphael
⑥② decorated the garden loggia of **Villa Farnesina** for extravagant
host Agostino Chigi, who delighted in impressing guests by
having his servants clear the table by casting precious gold and
silver dinnerware into the Tiber. Naturally, the guests did not
know of the nets he had stretched under the waterline to catch
everything. *Via della Lungara 230, tel. 06/654–0565. Admission free. Open Mon.–Sat. 9–1.*

From Porta Settimiana you can follow Via Garibaldi as it curves
⑥③ up to the Janiculum, past the church of **San Pietro in Montorio,**
known for its views and for the Tempietto, Bramante's little
⑥④ temple in the cloister. Beyond the impressive **Acqua Paola
⑥⑤ Fountain,** you'll come upon the **Janiculum Park,** which offers
splendid views of Rome.

Tour 10: The Catacombs and the Appian Way

This tour offers a respite from museums, though it's no easier
on the feet. Do it on a sunny day and take along a picnic. The
Rome EPT office distributes a free, informative pamphlet on
this itinerary. Take the No. 118 bus from San Giovanni in
⑥⑥ Laterano to the catacombs on the **Via Appia Antica** ("the Queen
of Roads"), completed in 312 BC by Appius Claudius, who also

built Rome's first aqueduct. You pass Porta San Sebastiano, which gives you a good idea of what the city's 5th-century fortifications looked like, and farther along you'll see the little church of **Domine Quo Vadis,** where tradition says that Christ appeared to St. Peter, inspiring him to return to Rome to face martyrdom.

There are two important **catacombs** on the Via Appia Antica. The first you'll come upon is that of **San Callisto,** one of the best-preserved of these underground cemeteries. A friar will guide you through its crypts and galleries. *Via Appia Antica 110, tel. 06/513–6725. Admission: 6,000 lire. Open Apr.–Sept., Thurs.–Tues. 8:30–noon and 2:30–6; Oct.–Mar., Thurs.–Tues. 8:30–noon and 2:30–5.*

The 4th-century catacomb of **San Sebastiano,** a little farther on, which was named for the saint who was buried here, burrows underground on four levels. The only one of the catacombs to remain accessible during the Middle Ages, it is the origin of the term "catacomb," for it was located in a spot where the road dips into a hollow, a place the Romans called *catacumbas* (near the hollow). Eventually the Christian cemetery that had existed here since the 2nd century came to be known by the same name, which was applied to all underground cemeteries discovered in Rome in later centuries. *Via Appia Antica 136, tel. 06/788–7035. Admission: 6,000 lire. Open Fri.–Wed. 8:30–noon and 2:30–5.*

On the other side of Via Appia Antica are the ruins of the **Circus of Maxentius,** where the obelisk now in Piazza Navona once stood. Farther along the ancient road is the circular **Tomb of Cecilia Metella,** the mausoleum of a Roman noblewoman who lived at the time of Julius Caesar. It was transformed into a fortress in the 14th century.

The Tomb of Cecilia Metella marks the beginning of the most interesting and evocative stretch of the Via Appia Antica, lined with tombs and fragments of statuary. Cypresses and umbrella pines stand guard over the ruined sepulchers, and the occasional tracts of ancient paving stones are the same ones trod by triumphant Roman legions.

Day Trips from Rome

Naples. The riches of the museums of Naples and a glimpse of this rundown but once glorious city and its vivacious street life make this a rewarding day out of Rome. Fast trains get you there in two hours, but you have to start out early in order to get into the Museo Archeologico Nazionale, which closes at 2. *See* Chapter 12, Campania.

Pompeii. You don't have to take an organized excursion to visit Pompeii from Rome in a day. A nonstop, public, air-conditioned CITAL coach leaves from Piazza della Repubblica every morning at about 6:45, arriving in Pompeii at about 10:30; there is a return trip to Rome in the late afternoon. The bus stops right in front of one of the entrances to the excavated city. For information and tickets (ticket window opens 6 AM), call Marozzi, c/o Eurojet Travel Agency, Piazza della Repubblica 54, tel 06/474–2801. *See* Chapter 12, Campania.

Shopping

Shopping in Rome is part of the fun, no matter what your budget. You're sure to find something that suits your fancy *and* your pocketbook, but don't expect to get bargains on Italian brands, such as Benetton, that are exported to the United States; prices are about the same on both sides of the Atlantic.

Shops are open from 9 or 9:30 to 1 and from 3:30 or 4 to 7 or 7:30. There's a tendency in Rome for shops in central districts to stay open all day, but for many this is still in the experimental stage. Department stores and centrally located UPIM and Standa stores are open all day. Remember that most stores are closed on Sunday and, with the exception of food and technical-supply stores, also on Monday mornings from September to June and on Saturday afternoons in July and August. Italian sizes are not uniform, so always try on clothing before you buy or measure gift items. Glove sizes are universal. In any case, remember that Italian stores generally will *not* refund your purchases and that they often cannot exchange goods because of limited stock. *Always* take your purchases with you; having them shipped home from the shop can cause hassles. If circumstances are such that you can't take your goods with you and if the shop seems reliable about shipping, get a firm statement of *when* and *how* your purchase will be sent.

Prezzi fissi means that prices are fixed and bargaining is a waste of time unless you're buying a sizable quantity of goods or a particularly costly object. Most stores have a fixed-price policy, and most honor a variety of credit cards. They will also accept foreign money at the current exchange rate, give or take a few lire. Ask for a receipt for your purchases; you may need it at customs on your return home. Bargaining is still an art at Porta Portese flea market and is routine when purchasing anything from a street vendor.

Shopping Districts The most elegant and expensive shops are concentrated in the **Piazza di Spagna** area, especially along **Via Condotti** and **Via Borgognona**. **Via Margutta** is known for art galleries and **Via del Babuino** for antiques. There are several high-fashion outlets on **Via Gregoriana** and **Via Sistina**. Bordering this top-price shopping district is **Via del Corso**, which—along with **Via Frattina** and **Via del Gambero**—is lined with shops and boutiques of all kinds where prices and goods are competitive.

Via del Tritone, leading up from Piazza Colonna off Via del Corso, has some medium-priced as well a few expensive shops that sell everything from fashion fabrics to trendy furniture. Still farther up, on **Via Veneto,** you'll find more high-priced boutiques and shoe stores, as well as newsstands selling English-language newspapers, magazines, and paperback books. **Via Nazionale** features shoe stores, moderately priced boutiques, and shops selling men's and women's fashions. **Via Cola di Rienzo** offers high-quality goods of all types; it's a good alternative to the Piazza di Spagna area.

In Old Rome, **Via dei Coronari** is lined with antiques shops and some new stores selling designer home accessories. **Via Giulia** and **Via Monserrato** also feature antiques dealers galore, plus a few art galleries. In the **Pantheon** area there are many shops selling liturgical objects and vestments. But the place to go for religious souvenirs is, obviously, the area around St. Peter's, especially **Via della Conciliazione** and **Via di Porta Angelica.**

Department Stores Rome has only a handful of department stores. **Rinascente,** at Piazza Colonna, sells clothing and accessories only. Another Rinascente, at Piazza Fiume, has the same stock. **Coin,** on Piazzale Appio, near San Giovanni in Laterano, has fashions for men and women. There is another Coin store in the U.S.-style shopping mall at CinecittàDue (Subaugusta Metro stop). The **UPIM** and **Standa** chains offer low to moderately priced goods. They're the place to go if you need a pair of slippers, a sweater, a bathing suit, or the like to see you through until you get home. In addition, they carry all kinds of toiletries and first-aid needs. Most Standa and UPIM stores have invaluable while-you-wait shoe-repair service counters.

Discount Stores Fashions with designer labels at big discounts can be found at **Discount System** (Via del Viminale 35) and **Discount dell'Alta Moda** (Via Gesù e Maria 16/A), branches of the same operation. Another discount store for men's and women's quality fashions is **Vesti-a-Stock** (Via Germanico 170).

Food and Flea Markets Rome's biggest and most colorful outdoor food markets are at **Campo dei Fiori** (just south of Piazza Navona), **Via Andrea Doria** (Trionfale district, about a quarter mile north of the entrance to the Vatican Museums), and **Piazza Vittorio** (just down Via Carlo Alberto from the church of Santa Maria Maggiore). There's a flea market on Sunday morning at **Porta Portese;** it now offers mainly new or secondhand clothing, but there are still a few dealers in old furniture and intriguing junk. Bargaining is the rule here, as are pickpockets, so beware. To reach Porta Portese, take Via Ippolito Nievo, off Viale Trastevere. All outdoor markets are open from early morning to about 2, except Saturday, when they may stay open all day.

Specialty Stores *Antiques and Prints* For old prints and antiques, the **Tanca** shop (Salita dei Crescenzi 10, near the Pantheon) is a good hunting ground. Early photographs of Rome and views of Italy from the archives of **Alinari** (Via Aliberti 16/a) make interesting souvenirs. **Nardecchia** (Piazza Navona 25) is reliable for prints.

Handicrafts and Souvenirs For pottery, handwoven textiles, and other handicrafts, **Myricae** (Via Frattina 36, with another store at Piazza del Parlamento 38) has a good selection. **La Galleria** (Via della Pelliccia 29) in Trastevere is off the beaten track but well worth a visit; it has a wealth of handicrafts, beautifully displayed in a rustic setting. A bottle of liqueur, jar of marmalade, or bar of chocolate handmade by Cistercian monks in several monasteries in Italy makes an unusual gift to take home; they are all on sale at **Ai Monasteri** (Piazza Cinque Lune 2). Among the inexpensive souvenirs you can buy in Rome are art calendars from the Vatican. These are on sale at the big newsstand under the colonnade off Piazza San Pietro, at the end of Via di Porta Angelica, and in the Vatican bookshop and the souvenir stores along Via di Porta Angelica.

Knitwear **Luisa Spagnoli** (Via del Corso 382, with other shops at Via Frattina 116 and Via Veneto 130) is always reliable for good quality at the right price and styles to suit American tastes. **Miranda** (Via Bocca di Leone 28) is a treasure trove of warm jackets, skirts, and shawls, handwoven in gorgeous colors of wool or mohair, or in lighter yarns for summer.

Leather Goods   **Ceresa** (Via del Tritone 118) has reasonably priced fine-leather goods, including many handbags and leather fashions. **Volterra** (Via Barberini 102) is well stocked and offers a wide selection of handbags at moderate prices. **Sermoneta** (Piazza di Spagna 61) shows a varied range of gloves in its windows, and there are many more inside. **Di Cori,** a few steps away, also has a good selection of gloves; there's another Di Cori store at Via Nazionale 183.

Nickol's (Via Barberini 21) is in the moderate price range and is one of the few stores in Rome that stock shoes in American widths. **Ferragamo** (Via Condotti 73) is one of Rome's best stores for fine shoes and leather accessories, and its silk scarves are splendid; you pay for quality here, but you can get great buys during the periodic sales. **Magli** (Via del Gambero 1 and Via Veneto 70) is known for well-made shoes and matching handbags at high to moderate prices. **Campanile** (Via Condotti 58) has four floors of shoes in the latest as well as classic styles, and other leather goods.

Dining

Lunch hour in Rome lasts from about 1 to 3, and dinner is served from 8 or 8:30 to about 10:30 and even later in summer. Romans love to eat out, so most restaurants, especially the inexpensive and budget ones, are jammed on weekend evenings. To get a table you have to arrive 15 minutes or so before normal dining hours. Service may be very informal, and the waiters may recite the menu. You can ask to see a menu if you don't understand, or if you're doubtful of the prices. The waiter should be able to produce a written one, but the day's specials probably won't be on it. The house wine in Rome *trattorie* is generally a dry white wine from the Castelli Romani district. Rome's drinking water is pure and good; order acqua semplice to save lire.

There are plenty of places where you can eat inexpensively, especially in the Trastevere, Testaccio, and San Lorenzo quarters, and around Santa Maria Maggiore. Italy's answer to McDonald's (the Big M is here, too, in Piazza di Spagna, Piazza della Repubblica, and Piazza Sonnino) is Italy & Italy, serving Italian fast food. The *tavola calda* (literally "hot table," a more traditional sort of fast-food place) provides local specialties: *supplì* (rice croquettes with a tidbit of mozzarella at their core); *filetti di baccalà* (cod fillets fried in batter); and fried zucchini or artichokes.

Picnic in Rome's parks; the amphitheater of Piazza di Siena in Villa Borghese and the far reaches of the Via Appia Antica are pleasant settings. Avoid the trattorias (with some exceptions) around Termini Station.

Unless otherwise noted, reservations are not needed and dress is casual. Highly recommended restaurants are indicated by a star ★.

Under 45,000 lire

Old Rome   **Le Maschere.** This cellar restaurant between Largo Argentina and Piazza Campo dei Fiori has lots of atmosphere and features a lavish antipasto buffet. The decor is rustic, and the menu offers such southern Italian specialties as pasta with tomato and eggplant sauce, in addition to pizza. There is a pianist most evenings. *Via Monte della Farina 29, tel. 06/697–9444. Reservations advised. AE, DC, MC, V. Open evenings only. Closed Mon. and mid-Aug.–mid-Sept.*

★ **La Rampa.** A haven for exhausted shoppers and sightseers, La Rampa is right behind the American Express office on Piazza Mignanelli, off Piazza di Spagna. The attractive decor evokes a colorful old Roman marketplace, and there are a few tables for outdoor dining on the piazza. The specialties of the house are a lavish antipasto, *gnocchetti al gorgonzola* (small pasta dumplings with cheese), fillet of beef with speck (smoked prosciutto), and *frittura alla Rampa* (deep-fried vegetables and mozzarella). La Rampa is popular and busy, and you may have to wait for a table. Get there early (or late). *Piazza Mignanelli 18, tel. 06/678–2621. No credit cards. Closed Sun., Mon. lunch, and Aug.*

Orso 80. This bright and bustling trattoria is located in Old Rome, on a street famed for artisans' workshops. It has both a Roman and an international following, and is known, above all, for a fabulous antipasto table. If you have room for more, try the homemade egg pasta or the *bucatini all'amatriciana* (thin, hollow pasta with a tomato and bacon sauce); there's plenty of seafood on the menu, too. For dessert, the ricotta cake, a genuine Roman specialty, is always good. *Via dell'Orso 33, tel. 06/686–4904. Reservations advised. AE, DC, MC, V. Closed Mon. and Aug. 10–20.*

Colosseum area **Osteria da Nerone.** Between the Colosseum and the church of San Pietro in Vincoli, this family-run trattoria features a tempting antipasto table and fresh pastas. The specialty is *fettuccine al Nerone* (noodles with peas, salami, and mushrooms), but homemade ravioli are good, too. In fair weather you eat outdoors with a view of the Colosseum. *Via Terme di Tito 96, tel. 06/474–5207. Dinner reservations advised. No credit cards. Closed Sun. and mid-Aug.*

Termini Station area **La Lupa.** This is a tiny trattoria that serves the best food in the area and is consequently crowded all the time. Get there early to feast on Roman dishes such as the specialty, *petto alla Fornara* (roast veal with potatoes). *Via Marghera 39, tel. 06/491–230. MC, V. Closed Sun. and July 20–Aug. 20.*

Testaccio area **Da Bucatino.** A popular trattoria with wood-paneled dining rooms, Da Bucatino serves good Roman food and pizza. Don't let the waiter tempt you with pricey seafood dishes. Instead, order *pasta alla carbonara* (with egg and bacon) or *abbacchio al forno* (roast lamb). *Via Luca della Robbia 84, tel. 06/574–6886. Reservations advised on weekends. No credit cards. Closed Mon.*

San Lorenzo area **Da Pommidoro.** One of the best and noisiest of the many trattorias in this neighborhood near the university and behind Termini Station, Da Pommidoro offers such pasta dishes as *pasta e ceci* (pasta and chick-peas) and game in season. *Piazza Sanniti 44, tel. 06/445–2692. No credit cards. Closed Sun.*

Under 35,000 lire

Old Rome **Abruzzi.** This simple trattoria off Piazza Santi Apostoli, near Piazza Venezia, specializes in country cooking and is a lunchtime favorite with students and local politicians. *Pasta alla* *chitarra* (square-cut noodles) is served with peas and ham in a creamy sauce, and the *abbacchio* (baby lamb) is recommended. *Via del Vaccaro 1, tel. 06/679–3897. Lunch reservations advised. V. Closed Sat. and Aug.*

Hostaria Farnese. This is a tiny trattoria between Campo dei Fiori and Piazza Farnese, in the heart of Old Rome. Mamma cooks, Papa serves, and, depending on what they've picked up at the Campo dei Fiori market, you may find rigatoni with tuna and basil, spaghetti with vegetable sauce, *spezzatino* (stew), and other homey specialties. *Via dei Baullari 109, tel. 06/654–1595. Reservations advised. AE, V. Closed Thurs.*

Polese. It's best to come here in good weather, when you can sit outdoors under trees and look out on the charming square off Corso Vittorio Emanuele in Old Rome. Like most centrally located, inexpensive eateries in Rome, it is crowded on weekends and weekday evenings in the summer. Straightforward Roman dishes are featured; specialties include *fettuccine alla Polese* (with cream and mushrooms) and *vitello alla fornara* (roast brisket of veal with potatoes). *Piazza Sforza Cesarini 40, tel. 06/686–1709. Reservations advised on weekends. AE, DC, MC, V. Closed Tues., 15 days in Aug., 15 days in Dec.*

Pollarola. Close to Campo dei Fiori, this popular trattoria has an ancient column, a remnant of Pompey's theater, embedded in the rear wall of the dining room. The antipasto is varied, and the pasta dishes are offered with some unusual sauces, such as *carciofi* (artichokes). *Piazza della Pollarola (Campo dei Fiori), tel. 06/654–1654. Reservations advised for four or more. AE, V. Closed Sun.*

Tavernetta. The central location—between the Trevi Fountain and the Spanish Steps—and the good-value tourist menu make this a reliable bet for a simple but filling meal. The menu features Sicilian and Abruzzi specialties; try the pasta with eggplant or the *porchetta* (roast suckling pig). Both the red and the white house wines are good. *Via del Nazareno 3, tel. 06/679–3124. Reservations required for dinner. AE, DC, MC, V. Closed Mon. and Aug.*

Piazza del Popolo area **Fratelli Menghi.** At this neighborhood trattoria you can get the Roman standbys: hearty soups—minestrone or *pasta e ceci* (with chick-peas)—stews, and roulades. *Via Flaminia 57, tel. 06/320–0803. No credit cards. Closed Sun.*

St. Peter's area **Armando.** One of many trattorias in Borgo, the blue-collar neighborhood in the shadow of the Vatican, Armando has been spruced up with new curtains, but it's still a family-run favorite of neighborhood regulars and knowledgeable tourists. The cooking is strictly Roman. *Pasta e ceci* (pasta with chick-peas and rosemary) and *petto alla fornara* (roast veal breast) with potatoes are often on the menu. *Via degli Ombrellari 41 (corner Borgo Vittorio), tel. 06/686–1602. Reservations advised in evening. Dress: casual. AE, DC, MC, V. Closed Wed.*

Viale Manzoni area (Termini Station) ★ **Vecchia Roma da Severino.** This is a family-run trattoria specializing in the hearty food of the Puglia region, including some homemade pastas. The antipasto includes everything from vegetables to meat and seafood. Portions are abundant, and the service is very informal. *Viale Manzoni 52, tel. 06/735–344. Reservations necessary in evening. No credit cards. Closed Sun.*

Under 25,000 lire

Old Rome   **Alfio.** Near Piazza Colonna, this busy tavola calda on street level will provide good sandwiches and snacks to eat standing up. The restaurant upstairs is moderately priced but out of budget range. *Via della Colonna Antonina 33, no telephone. No credit cards. Closed Sun.*

Baffetto. Rome's best-known pizzeria is ultraplain and very popular; you may have to wait for seating at paper-covered tables. *Bruschetta* (toast with olive oil) and *crostini* (mozzarella toast) are the only variations on the pizza theme. *Via del Governo Vecchio 114, tel. 06/686–1617. No credit cards. Closed lunch. Closed Sun. and Aug.*

★ **Birreria Tempera.** This old-fashioned beer hall is very busy at lunchtime, when it's invaded by businesspeople and students from the Piazza Venezia area. There's a good selection of salads and cold cuts, as well as pasta and daily specials. Bavarian-style specialties such as goulash and wurst and sauerkraut prevail in the evening, when light or dark Italian beer flows freely. *Via San Marcello 19, tel. 06/678–6203. No credit cards. Closed Sun. and Aug.*

Delfino. This tavola calda on Largo Argentina offers *supplì* and sandwiches at all times of day and a choice of hot and cold dishes—including *lasagne,* roast meat, fresh mozzarella cheese, and salads—at mealtimes. *Corso Vittorio Emanuele 67, tel. 06/654–3521. V. Closed Mon.*

L'Insalata Ricca. At this informal place near Piazza Navona, the specialties are salads and basic pastas. The decor is rustic, with beamed ceilings and copper utensils on the walls. This is one of the few Italian restaurants with a no-smoking policy. A sister restaurant is at Piazza Pasquino 72 (closed Mon.). *Largo dei Chiavari 85, tel. 06/654–3656. Reservations advised in evening. No credit cards. Closed Wed.*

Al Leoncino. An inexpensive pizzeria off Piazza San Lorenzo in Lucina, Al Leoncino offers a range of pizzas from the standard *margherita* (tomato and cheese) to the more sumptuous *capricciosa* (with prosciutto, artichokes and other toppings). *Via del Leoncino 28, tel. 06/687–6306. Closed Mon., Tues., and Aug. No credit cards.*

Palladini. This alimentari (food shop) is famous for pizza-to-go and sandwiches made to order at the marble-topped counter. Try *pizza bianca* (brushed with olive oil) plain or filled with mortadella, prosciutto, or cheese. *Via del Governo Vecchio 102, no telephone. No credit cards. Closed Sun.*

St. Peter's area   **Hostaria Tonino.** A short walk from the Vatican Museums, this is a typical neighborhood wineshop; it serves plain but hearty food, such as *pasta e fagioli* (pasta and bean soup) and spezzatino. *Via Leone IV 60, no telephone. No credit cards. Closed Sun.*

Via Veneto area   **Savoy.** A glass door off the street next to the entrance of the four-star Savoy Hotel opens onto a stairway that leads down to one of the best-kept secrets in the area: the Savoy luncheon buffet, an elegant cafeteria where you choose what you want and pay the cashier. It operates at lunchtime only and is a lifesaver for workers from offices nearby. *Via Ludovisi 15, no telephone. No credit cards. Closed Sun.*

Santa Maria Maggiore area   **Cottini.** On the corner of Piazza Santa Maria Maggiore, this is a reliable cafeteria annexed to a large coffee bar. It offers salads, main courses, and tempting desserts, including chocolate cake and crème caramel, from the in-house bakery. *Via Merulana 287, tel. 06/474–0768. No credit cards. Closed Mon.*

Splurges

★ **Romolo.** Generations of Romans and tourists have enjoyed the romantic garden courtyard and historic dining room of this charming Trastevere haunt, reputedly the onetime home of Raphael's lady love, the Fornarina. In the evening, strolling musicians serenade diners. The cuisine is appropriately Roman; specialties include *mozzarella alla fornarina* (deep-fried mozzarella with ham and anchovies) and *braciolette d'abbacchio scottadito* (grilled baby lamb chops). Alternatively, try one of the new vegetarian pastas featuring carciofi or radicchio. Meats are charcoal-grilled; there's also a wood-burning oven. *Via di Porta Settimiana 8, tel. 06/581–8284. Reservations advised. AE, DC, V. Closed Mon. and Aug. 2–23.*

The Arts and Nightlife

The Arts

Rome offers a vast selection of music, dance, opera, and film. For information, consult Rome EPT offices or its free monthly publication, *Carnet.* Listings can also be found in *Wanted in Rome,* a biweekly newsletter in English, on sale for 1,000 lire at English-language bookstores and downtown newsstands; *Metropolitan,* a biweekly news and features publication in English, free at key bookstores and newsstands; and "Trovaroma," the Thursday supplement of the daily newspaper *La Repubblica.*

Concerts Rome has long been a center for a wide variety of classical music concerts, although it is a common complaint that the city does not have adequate concert halls or a suitable auditorium. Depending on the location, tickets can cost from 10,000 to 45,000 lire. The principal concert series are those of the **Accademia di Santa Cecilia** (offices at Via dei Greci, box office tel. 06/654–1044), the **Accademia Filarmonica Romana** (Teatro Olimpico, Via Gentile da Fabriano 17, tel. 06/320–1752), the **Istituzione Universitaria dei Concerti** (San Leone Magno auditorium, Via Bolzano 38, tel. 06/361–0051), and the **RAI** Italian Radio-TV series at Foro Italico (tel. 06/368–65625). There is also the internationally respected **Gonfalone** (Via del Gonfalone 32, tel. 06/687–5952) series, which concentrates on Baroque music. The **Associazione Musicale Romana** (tel. 06/656–8441) and **Il Tempietto** (tel. 06/481–4800) organize music festivals and concerts throughout the year. There are also many small concert groups. Many concerts are free, including all those performed in Catholic churches, where a special ruling permits only religious music. Look for posters outside churches announcing these; the church of Sant'Ignazio, on Piazza Sant'Ignazio off Via del Corso, hosts many. The Rome EPT tourist board sponsors a free concert series at Christmas and Easter, usually in the church of Sant'Ignazio and in Palazzo della Cancelleria. From early spring through July, band concerts may be held on the Pincio on Sunday mornings.

Rock, pop, and jazz concerts are frequent, especially in summer, although even performances by big-name stars may not be well advertised. Tickets for these performances are usually handled by **Orbis** (Piazza Esquilino 37, tel. 06/482–7403) and **Babilonia** (Via del Corso 185, tel. 06/678–6641).

Opera The opera season runs from November to May, and performances are staged in the **Teatro dell'Opera** (Via del Viminale, information in English: tel. 06/675–95725; ticket reservations in English: tel. 06/675–95721). Tickets go on sale two days before a performance, and the box office is open 10–1 and 5–7. Prices range from 20,000 to 60,000 lire for regular performances; they can go much higher for an opening night or an appearance by an internationally acclaimed guest singer. Standards may not always measure up to those set by Milan's fabled La Scala, but despite strikes and shortages of funds, most performances are respectable.

By 1994 it is likely that the spectacular summer opera season staged outdoors in the ruins of the Baths of Caracalla will be held elsewhere. Authorities are under pressure to prevent further wear on Caracalla's massive structures and foundations. Information and tickets are available at the Teatro dell'Opera box office (*see above*). Wherever performances are being held outdoors, take a jacket or sweater; despite the daytime heat of a Roman summer, nights can be cool and damp.

Dance The **Rome Opera Ballet** gives regular performances at the Teatro dell'Opera (*see above*), often with leading international guest stars. Rome is regularly visited by classical ballet companies from Russia, the United States, and Europe; performances are at Teatro dell'Opera, Teatro Olimpico, or at one of the open-air venues in summer. Small classical and modern dance companies from Italy and abroad also visit.

Film Rome has dozens of movie houses, but the only one to show exclusively English-language films is the **Pasquino** (Vicolo del Piede, just off Piazza Santa Maria in Trastevere, tel. 06/580–3622). Films here are not dubbed, but are shown in English with Italian subtitles. Pick up a weekly schedule at the theater or consult the daily papers.

Festivals In addition to performances of various types held in connection with folklore events, such as the Festival of Noantri in Trastevere in mid-July and the feast of San Giovanni on June 23–24, there is a festival of the arts on the Tiberina Island from July through mid-September. The Estate Romana program of arts and entertainment offers performances and exhibitions (admission is charged for many) in several venues, from Foro Italico to EUR.

Nightlife

Although Rome is not one of the world's most exciting cities for nightlife (despite the popular image of the city as the birthplace of *la dolce vita*), discos, live-music spots, and quiet late-night bars have proliferated in recent years. This has been true in the streets of the old city and in far-flung parts of town. The "flavor of the month" factor works here, too, and many places fade into oblivion after a brief moment of popularity. The best source for an up-to-date list of late-night spots is the weekly entertainment guide "Trovaroma," published every Thursday in the Italian daily newspaper *La Repubblica*.

Bars Rome has a range of bars offering drinks and background music. Informal wine bars are popular with Romans who like to stay up late but don't dig disco music. Near the Pantheon is **Spiriti** (Via Sant'Eustachio 5, tel. 06/689–2499), which also serves light lunches at midday and is open until 1:30 AM. The same atmosphere prevails at **Cavour 313** (Via Cavour 313, tel. 06/678–5496), near the Roman Forum. Both are closed on Sunday. Trendy types gather at the **Antico Caffè della Pace** (Via della Pace 3, tel. 06/686–1216) near Piazza Navona.

Beer halls and pubs are popular with young Italians. **Birreria Marconi** (Via di Santa Prassede 9c, tel. 06/486636), near Santa Maria Maggiore, is also a pizzeria; it is closed on Sunday. **Birreria Santi Apostoli** (Piazza Santi Apostoli 52, tel. 06/678–8285) is open every day until 2 AM. Among the pubs, **Fiddler's Elbow** (Via dell'Olmata 43, no phone) is open 5 PM–midnight but is closed on Monday. **Four Green Fields** (Via Costantino Morin 42, off Via della Giuliana, tel. 06/359–5091) features live music and is open daily 8:30 PM–1 AM.

Music Clubs Jazz, folk, pop, and Latin music clubs are flourishing in Rome, particularly in the picturesque Trastevere neighborhood. Jazz clubs are especially popular, and talented local groups may be joined by visiting musicians from other countries. As admission, many clubs require that you buy a membership card for about 10,000–20,000 lire.

In the Trionfale district near the Vatican, **Alexanderplatz** (Via Ostia 9, tel. 06/372–9398) has both a bar and a restaurant, and features nightly live programs of jazz and blues played by Italian and foreign musicians. For the best live music, including jazz, blues, rhythm and blues, African, and rock, go to **Big Mama** (Vicolo San Francesco a Ripa 18, tel. 06/581–2551). There is also a bar and snack food. Latin rhythms are the specialty at **El Charango** (Via di Sant'Onofrio 28, tel. 06/687–9908), near Ponte Amedeo d'Aosta, a live music club.

In the trendy Testaccio neighborhood, **Caffè Latino** (Via di Monte Testaccio 96, tel. 06/574–4020) attracts a thirtysomething crowd with concerts (mainly jazz) in one room and a separate video room and bar for socializing. **Music Inn** (Largo dei Fiorentini 3, tel. 06/654–4934) is Rome's top jazz club and features some of the biggest names on the international scene. It's open Thursday through Sunday evenings.

Live performances of jazz, soul, and funk by leading musicians draw celebrities to **St. Louis Music City** (Via del Cardello 13a, tel. 06/474–5076). There is also a restaurant. It's closed on Thursday.

Fonclea (Via Crescenzio 82a, tel. 06/689–6302), near Castel Sant'Angelo, has a pub atmosphere and live music ranging from jazz to Latin American to rhythm-and-blues, depending on who's in town. The kitchen serves Mexican and Italian food.

Discos and Nightclubs Most discos open at about 10:30 PM and charge an entrance fee of around 25,000–30,000 lire, which sometimes includes the first drink. Subsequent drinks cost about 10,000–15,000 lire. Some discos also open on Saturday and Sunday afternoons for those under 16.

There's deafening disco music at **Frankie Go** (Via Schiaparelli 29–30, tel. 06/322–1251) for the under-30 crowd, which sometimes includes young actors. Special events, such as beauty pageants, fashion shows, and theme parties, are featured, and there's a restaurant. Despite the address, the entrance is actually on Via Luciani 52. It's closed Monday.

Alien (Via Velletri 17, tel. 06/841–2212), near Piazza Fiume, is a very large, informal American-style disco favored by the under-28 crowd. It has two dance floors and two bars, where barmaids with shaved pates do their best to look like Sigourney Weaver.

Hysteria (Via Giovanelli 12, tel. 06/855–4587) attracts a very young crowd who come to enjoy the variety of music: disco, funk, soul, and hard rock. It's located off Via Salaria near the Galleria Borghese. It's closed on Monday.

One of Rome's first discos, **The Piper** (Via Tagliamento 9, tel. 06/841–4459), is an "in" spot for teenagers. It has disco music, live groups, and pop videos. Occasionally there's ballroom dancing for an older crowd. It opens weekends at 4 PM and is closed on Monday and Tuesday. Funky music and huge video screens make **Scarabocchio** (Piazza Ponziani 8, tel. 06/580–0495) another popular spot. It's closed on Monday.

Veleno (Via Sardegna 27, tel. 06/493583) is one of the few places in Rome to offer black dance music, including disco, rap, funk, and soul. It attracts sports personalities and other celebrities.

For singles Locals and foreigners of all nations and ages gather at Rome's cafés on **Piazza della Rotonda** in front of the Pantheon, at **Piazza Navona,** or **Piazza Santa Maria in Trastevere.** The cafés on **Via Veneto** and the bars of the big hotels draw mainly tourists and are good places for meeting other travelers in the over-30 age group. In fair weather, under-30s will find crowds of contemporaries on the **Spanish Steps,** where it's easy to strike up a conversation.

Excursions from Rome

Ostia Antica

There is a regular train from Ostiense train station, near Porta San Paolo, which is connected with the Piramide stop on Metro Line B. Trains leave every half hour, and the ride takes about 30 minutes. The train fare is about 1,000 lire. (If trackwork is under way, the train for Ostia Scavi does not leave from Ostiense Station but from Magliana Station on Metro Line B; inquire at Metro stations.)

One of the easiest excursions from the capital takes you west to the sea, where tall pines stand among the well-preserved ruins of Ostia Antica, the main port of ancient Rome. Founded around the 4th century BC, Ostia Antica conveys the same impression as Pompeii, but on a smaller scale and in a prettier, parklike setting. The city was inhabited by a cosmopolitan population of rich businessmen, wily merchants, sailors, and slaves. The great *horrea* (warehouses) were built in the 2nd century AD to handle huge shipments of grain from Africa; the *insulae*, forerunners of the modern apartment building, provided housing for the growing population. Under the combined assaults of the barbarians and the anopheles mosquito, the port was eventually abandoned, and it silted up. Tidal mud and windblown sand covered the city, and it lay buried until the

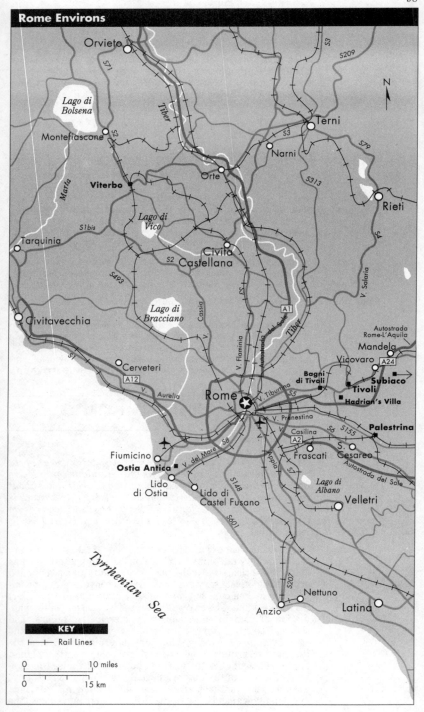

Rome Environs

Orvieto

Lago di Bolsena

Montefiascone

Terni

Narni

Viterbo

Orte

Rieti

Maria

Tiber

S71

S2

S3

S3

S209

S79

S313

S4

Lago di Vico

Tarquinia

Civita Castellana

S1bis

S2

S493

Cassia

Lago di Bracciano

Civitavecchia

Cerveteri

A12

V. Aurelia

V.

Cassia

V. Flaminia

Autostrada del Sole

A1

Tiber

V. Salaria

Mandela

Vicovaro

A24

Autostrada Rome-L'Aquila

Bagni di Tivoli

Subiaco

Tivoli

Hadrian's Villa

Rome

V. Tiburtina

S5

V. Prenestina

Palestrina

S6

S155

Fiumicino

Ostia Antica

Lido di Ostia

Lido di Castel Fusano

V. del Mare

S8

V. Appia

Casilina

A2

Frascati

S. Cesareo

Autostrada del Sole

S7

Lago di Albano

Velletri

S148

S601

S207

Anzio

Nettuno

Latina

Tyrrhenian Sea

N

KEY
⊢—⊣ Rail Lines

0   10 miles

0   15 km

beginning of this century. Now extensively excavated and excellently maintained, it makes for a fascinating visit on a sunny day.

Near the entrance to the *Scavi* (excavations) is a fortress built in the 15th century for Pope Julius II. The hamlet that grew up around it is charming. However, your visit to Ostia Antica itself starts at **Via delle Tombe,** lined with sepulchers from various periods. From here, passing through the **Porta Romana,** one of the city's three gates, you'll come to the **Decumanus Maximus,** the main thoroughfare crossing the city from end to end.

About 300 yards up on the right are the **Terme di Nettuno** (Baths of Neptune), decorated with black-and-white mosaics representing Neptune and Amphitrite. Directly behind the baths is the barracks of the fire department, which played an important role in a town with warehouses full of valuable goods and foodstuffs.

Just ahead, and also on the right side of the Decumanus Maximus, is the beautiful **Theater,** built by Augustus and completely restored by Septimius Severus in the 2nd century AD. Behind it, in the vast Piazzale delle Corporazioni, where trade organizations similar to guilds had their offices, is the **Temple of Ceres:** This is appropriate for a town that deals in grain imports, since Ceres, who gave her name to cereal, was the goddess of agriculture. Next to the theater, where there is a coffee bar, you can visit the **House of Apuleius,** built in Pompeiian style—containing fewer windows and built lower than those in Ostia. Next to it is the **Mithraeum,** with balconies and a hall decorated with symbols of the cult of Mithras. This men-only religion, imported from Persia, was especially popular with legionnaires.

On Via dei Molini, 200 yards beyond the theater, there is a mill where grain for the warehouses next door was ground with the stones you see there. Along Via di Diana, a left turn 50 yards up Via dei Molini, you'll come upon a **thermopolium** (bar) with a marble counter and a fresco depicting the fruit and foodstuffs that were sold here. Turn right at the end of Via di Diana onto Via dei Dipinti; at the end is the **Museo Ostiense,** which displays some of the ancient sculptures and mosaics found among the ruins.

Retrace your steps along Via dei Dipinti and turn right just before Via di Diana for the **Forum,** with monumental remains of the city's most important temple, dedicated to Jupiter, Juno, and Minerva; other ruins of baths; a basilica (in Roman times a basilica served the secular purpose of a hall of justice); and smaller temples.

A continuation of the Decumanus Maximus leads from the Forum. From the crossroads, about 100 yards on, Via Epagathiana, on the right, leads down toward the Tiber, where there are large warehouses, erected in the 2nd century AD to deal with enormous amounts of grain imported into Rome during that period, the height of the empire.

Take the street opposite the entrance to the warehouses to the **House of Cupid and Psyche,** a residential house named for a statue found there; you can see what remains of a large pool in an enclosed garden decorated with marble and mosaic motifs. It takes little imagination to notice that even then, a premium was placed on water views: The house faces the shore, which would have been only about a quarter-mile away. Take Via del Tempio di Ercole left and then go right on Via della Foce to see (on the left) the **House of Serapis,** a 2nd-century multi-level dwelling, and the **Baths of the Seven Wise Men,** named for a fresco found there.

Take Via del Tempio di Serapide away from Via della Foce and then the Cardo Degli Aurighi, where you'll pass—just on the left—another apartment building. The road leads back to the Decumanus Maximus, which continues to the **Porta Marina.** Off to the left, on what used to be the seashore, are the ruins of the **Synagogue,** one of the oldest in the Western world. This is where you'll begin your return; Porta Marina is the farthest point in the tour. Go right at the **Bivio del Castrum,** past the slaughterhouse and the large round temple. You'll come to the **Cardine Massimo,** a road lined with ruined buildings. From here, turn left onto Via Semita dei Cippi to see the **House of Fortuna Annonaria,** the richly decorated house of a wealthy Ostian. Here, too, you'll marvel at the skill of the mosaic artists and realize, with awe, that this really was someone's home. One of the rooms opens onto a secluded garden.

Continue on Via Semita dei Cippi for about 150 yards until you turn right onto the Decumanus Maximus to retrace the last leg of the tour back to the entrance.

The admission fee for the **Scavi di Ostia Antica** excavation complex includes entrance to the Ostiense Museum, which is on the grounds and observes the same opening hours. *Via dei Romagnoli, tel. 06/565–1405. Admission: 8,000 lire. Open daily 9–one hour before sunset.*

Dining **Monumento.** Handily located near the entrance to the excava-
Under 35,000 tions, this attractive trattoria serves Roman specialties and seafood. *Piazza Umberto I, tel. 06/565–0021. Reservations advised in the evening. AE, DC, MC, V. Closed Mon. and Aug. 20–Sept. 7.*

Tivoli, Palestrina, Subiaco

ACOTRAL buses for Tivoli leave Rome every 15 minutes from the terminal at the Rebibbia stop on Metro Line B, but not all take the route that passes near Hadrian's Villa. Inquire which bus passes closest to Villa Adriana and tell the driver to let you off there. The ride takes about 60 minutes and costs about 2,300 lire. The FS train from Rome's Termini Station to Palestrina takes about 40 minutes and costs about 2,500 lire; you can then board a bus from the train station to the center of town. You can also take the ACOTRAL bus from the Anagnina stop on Metro Line A to Palestrina. The fare is about 2,300 lire. There is local bus service between Tivoli and Palestrina, but check schedules locally. From Rome to Subiaco, take the ACOTRAL bus from the Rebibbia stop on Metro Line B; buses leave every 40 minutes, and those that take the autostrada make the trip in 70 minutes, as opposed to an hour and 45 minutes by another route. The fare is about 4,800 lire. Tourist information: **Tivoli** *(Largo Garibaldi, tel. 0774/293522) and* **Subiaco** *(Via Cadorna 59, tel. 0774/85397).*

Tivoli The road east from Rome to **Tivoli** passes through some unattractive industrial areas and burgeoning suburbs. You'll know

you're close when you see vast quarries of travertine marble
and smell the sulfurous vapors of the little spa, Bagni di Tivoli.
This was once green countryside; now it's ugly and overbuilt.
But don't despair, because this tour takes you to two of the
Rome area's most attractive sights: Hadrian's Villa and the Villa d'Este. The Villa d'Este is a popular destination; fewer people go to Hadrian's Villa. Both are outdoor sights, which entail
a lot of walking, and in the case of the Villa D'Este, stair climbing. That also means that good weather is a virtual prerequisite
for enjoying the itinerary. Hadrian's Villa, or Villa Adriana, is
the perfect place for a picnic. There's a café at the entrance
where you can pick up something to drink, but it's a good idea to
bring your own foodstuffs from Rome, as there are no food
stores near the site. In the town of Tivoli there are several
pizza-to-go stores and cafés around the main square.

Visit **Hadrian's Villa** first, especially in the summer, to take advantage of the cooler morning sun: There's little shade. Hadrian, who succeeded Trajan as emperor in AD 117, was a man of
genius and intellectual curiosity. Fascinated by the accomplishments of the Hellenistic world, he decided to re-create it
for his own enjoyment by building this villa over a vast tract of
land below the ancient settlement of Tibur. From AD 118 to 130,
architects, laborers, and artists worked on the villa, periodically spurred on by the emperor himself, as he returned from another voyage full of ideas for even more daring constructions.
After Hadrian's death in AD 138, the fortunes of his villa declined. The villa was sacked by barbarians and Romans alike;
by the Renaissance, many of his statues and decorations had
ended up in the Villa d'Este. Still, it is an impressive complex.

Study the exhibits in the visitor center at the entrance and the
scale model in the building adjacent to the bar, close by, to help
you make sense of what can otherwise be a maze of ruins. It's
not the single elements but the peaceful and harmonious effects
of the whole that make Hadrian's Villa such a treat. Oleanders,
pines, and cypresses growing among the ruins heighten the
visual impact. *Villa Adriana. Admission: 8,000 lire. Open daily 9–90 minutes before sunset.*

From Hadrian's Villa, catch the local bus up to Tivoli's main
square, Largo Garibaldi. Take a left onto Via Boselli and cross
Piazza Trento, with the church of Santa Maria Maggiore on
your left, to reach the entrance to the **Villa d'Este.** Ippolito
d'Este was an active figure in the political intrigues of mid-
16th-century Italy. He was also a cardinal, thanks to his grand-
father, Alexander VI, the infamous Borgia pope. To console
himself at a time when he saw his political star in decline,
Ippolito tore down part of a Franciscan monastery that occupied the site he had chosen for his villa. Then the determined
prelate diverted the Aniene River into a channel to run under
the town and provide water for the Villa d'Este's fountains.
Big, small, noisy, quiet, rushing, and running, the fountains
create a late-Renaissance playground, now run-down, with
fountains spouting polluted water. *Villa d'Este. Admission:
5,000 lire. Open daily 9–90 minutes before sunset.*

Tivoli Dining
Under 35,000 lire

Del Falcone. A central location—on the main street leading off
Largo Garibaldi—means that this restaurant is popular and often crowded. In the ample and rustic dining rooms, you can try
homemade fettuccine and cannelloni. Country-style grilled

meats are excellent. *Via Trevio 34, tel. 0774/22358. Reservations not necessary. No credit cards. Closed Mon.*

Palestrina Only 27 kilometers (17 miles) south of Tivoli and 37 kilometers (23 miles) outside Rome along Via Prenestina, **Palestrina** is set on the slopes of Mount Ginestro, from which it commands a sweeping view of the green plain and the distant mountains. It is surprisingly little known outside Italy, except to students of ancient history and music lovers. Its most famous native son, Giovanni Pierluigi da Palestrina, born here in 1525, was the renowned composer of 105 masses, as well as madrigals, magnificats, and motets. But the town was celebrated long before the composer's lifetime.

Ancient Praeneste, modern Palestrina, was founded much earlier than Rome. It was the site of the Temple of Fortuna Primigenia, which dates from the beginning of the 2nd century BC. This was one of the biggest, richest, and most frequented temple complexes in all antiquity. People came from far and wide to consult its famous oracle, yet in modern times no one had any idea of the extent of the complex until World War II bombings exposed ancient foundations that stretched way out into the plain below the town. It has since become clear that the temple area was larger than the town of Palestrina is today. Now you can make out the four superimposed terraces that formed the main part of the temple; they were built up on great arches and were linked by broad flights of stairs. The entire town sits on top of what was once the main part of the temple.

Large arches and terraces scale the hillside up to the **Palazzo Barberini,** built in the 17th century along the semicircular lines of the original temple. It's now a museum containing a wealth of material found on the site, some dating from the 4th century BC. The collection of splendid engraved bronze urns was plundered by art thieves in 1991, but they couldn't carry off the chief attraction, a 1st-century-BC mosaic representing the Nile in flood. This delightful work—a large-scale composition in which form, color, and innumerable details captivate the eye— is alone worth the trip to Palestrina. But there's more: a perfect scale model of the temple as it was in ancient times, which will help you appreciate the immensity of the original construction. *Museo Nazionale Archeologico, Palazzo Barberini. Admission: 6,000 lire. Open Tues.–Sun., spring and fall 9–6, summer 9–7:30, winter 9–4.*

Palestrina Dining **Coccia.** In this dining room of a small, centrally located hotel in
Under 35,000 lire Palestrina's public garden, you'll find simple decor, a cordial welcome, and local dishes with a few interesting variations. The fettuccine, light and freshly made, is served with a choice of sauces. A more unusual item on the menu is the *pasta e fagioli con frutti di mare* (thick bean and pasta soup with shellfish). *Piazzale Liberazione, tel. 06/953–8172. AE, DC, MC, V.*

Subiaco If you don't mind setting out on a roundabout route by local bus, you could continue on to **Subiaco,** tucked away in the mountains above Tivoli and Palestrina. It's about 65 kilometers (40 miles) from Palestrina, and its inaccessibility was undoubtedly a point in its favor for St. Benedict: The 6th-century monastery that he founded here became a landmark of Western monasticism. A visit to Subiaco and the site on which St. Benedict founded the hermitage that gave rise to Western monasticism requires some effort, mainly strenuous walking, but you are rewarded by the aura of medieval mysticism that permeates the monasteries dedicated to the saint and his sister Scolastica. It's nearly a 3-kilometer (2-mile) walk from Subiaco to the convent of Santa Scolastica, and another half hour by footpath up to San Benedetto. Inquire at Subiaco about a local bus to take you at least part of the way.

The first monastery you'll come upon is that of **Santa Scolastica,** actually a convent, and the only one of the hermitages founded by St. Benedict and his sister Scolastica to have survived the Lombard invasion of Italy in the 9th century. It has three cloisters, the oldest dating from the 13th century. The library, which is not open to visitors, contains some precious volumes; this was the site of the first print shop in Italy, set up in 1474. *Admission free. Open daily 9–12:30 and 4–7.*

Drive up to the **monastery of St. Benedict,** or take the footpath that climbs the hill. The monastery was built over the grotto where St. Benedict lived and meditated. Clinging to the cliff on nine great arches, the monastery has resisted the assaults of man and nature for almost 800 years. To reach the monastery you'll climb a broad, sloping avenue and enter through a little wooden veranda, where a Latin inscription augurs "peace to those who enter." You'll then find yourself in the colorful world of the upper church, every inch of it covered with frescoes by Umbrian and Sienese artists of the 14th century. In front of the main altar a stairway leads down to the lower church, carved out of the rock, with yet another stairway down to the grotto, or cave, where Benedict lived as a hermit for three years. The frescoes here are even earlier than those above; look for the portrait of St. Francis of Assisi, painted from life in 1210, in the Chapel of St. Gregory, and for the oldest fresco in the monastery, in the Shepherd's Grotto. *Admission free. Open daily 9–12:30 and 3–6.*

Back in town, if you've got the time, stop at the 14th-century **Church of San Francesco** to see the frescoes by Il Sodoma. *Ring for admission.*

Subiaco Dining
Under 35,000 lire

Belvedere. This small hotel on the road between the town and the monasteries is equipped to serve crowds of skiers from the slopes of nearby Mount Livata, as well as pilgrims on their way to St. Benedict's hermitage. The atmosphere is homey and cordial. Specialties include homemade fettuccine with a tasty *ragù* sauce and grilled meats and sausages. *Via dei Monasteri 33, tel. 0774/85531. No credit cards.*

Viterbo

Take the Ferrovia Roma Nord train (6,300 lire) to the Saxa Rubra stop, where you can get the ACOTRAL bus to Viterbo (4,500 lire). There are a few direct (diretta) bus departures between 7 and 9 AM. Slower buses leave every hour or so during the day. The ride takes from 60 to 90 minutes. You can also take a train directly to Viterbo from the Ferrovia Roma Nord station at Piazzale Flaminio, but this service is infrequent and takes about 2 hours. Tourist Offices: Piazzale dei Caduti 14, tel. 0761/234–795, open Mon.–Sat. 9–2; and Loggia di San Tommaso, Piazza della Morte, near the cathedral, open Mon.–Sat. 9–7.

Viterbo is about 80 kilometers (50 miles) from Rome in the heart of Tuscia, the modern name for the Etruscan domain of Etruria, a landscape of dramatic beauty punctuated by thickly forested hills and deep, rocky gorges. Viterbo's chief attractions are its 12th-century walls and towers, the historic palace of the popes who held court here, and the perfectly preserved medieval quarter of San Pellegrino. Viterbo is the perfect place to get the feel of the Middle Ages, to see a town where daily life is carried on in a setting that has remained practically unchanged over the centuries.

Both train station and bus terminal are just outside the old town walls. Walk to Piazza San Lorenzo, where the Gothic Palazzo Papale was built in the 13th century as a residence for the popes who chose to sojourn here. A conclave held here in 1271 to elect a new pope provided the people of Viterbo with a glorious moment of fame. The meeting had dragged on for months, apparently making no progress. Fed up with paying for the cardinals' board and lodging, the inhabitants tore the roof off the great hall in which the meeting was held and put the churchmen on bread and water. Sure enough, a new pope— Gregory X—was elected in short order. The fine Romanesque cathedral on the piazza has a Renaissance facade, but its interior has been restored to its original medieval look. Inside you can see the chips that an exploding bomb took out of the ancient columns during World War II. To the left of the cathedral is a fine 15th-century town house.

Now walk down Via San Lorenzo and follow Via San Pellegrino through the medieval quarter, one of the best-preserved in Italy. It's a charming vista of dark stone arches, vaults, towers, exterior staircases, worn wooden doors on great iron hinges, and tiny hanging gardens. At the end of Via San Pellegrino, turn left toward Via delle Fabbriche and Piazza della Fontana Grande, where the largest and most original of Viterbo's quaint Gothic fountains spouts steady streams of water.

Dining **Da Ciro.** In the heart of the medieval quarter, Da Ciro has a
Under 35,000 lire huge stone hearth where meat and sausages are grilled. The decor is a highly unlikely mélange of rustic and contemporary kitsch, but the effect is warm and inviting. In summer you eat outdoors. *Via Cardinale La Fontaine 74, tel 0761/234-722. Reservations advised on Sun. AE, DC, MC, V. Closed Fri.*

3 Florence

Florence is a prime destination for art lovers. This is where the Renaissance began, and this is where you can see an incredible number of the great art works of that period. In Florence you get the feel of a city made to man's measure centuries before the invasion of automobiles; with most of the center of Florence free of traffic, it's easier to imagine it as it was when a new vision of politics and learning gave rise to a golden age. Because it attracts so many tourists, Florence is best off-season—that is, from October through March. Since nearly everything you'll want to see there is within walking distance, you won't be spending much on getting around. Your main expense, other than bed and board, will almost certainly be entrance fees for the museums.

As a city, Firenze (as it is known in Italian) can be surprisingly forbidding to the first-time visitor. Its architecture is predominantly early Renaissance and retains many of the harsh, implacable, fortresslike features of pre-Renaissance palazzi, whose facades were mostly meant to keep intruders out rather than to invite sightseers in. With the exception of a very few buildings, the stately dignity of the High Renaissance and the exuberant invention of the Baroque are not to be found here. The typical Florentine exterior gives nothing away, as if obsessively guarding secret treasures within.

Prior to the 15th century, Florence was a medieval city not much different from its Tuscan neighbors. It began as a Roman settlement, laid out in the 1st century BC, and served as a provincial capital when the Roman Empire was at its height. Its rise to real power, however, did not begin until the era of the medieval Italian city-states, beginning in the 11th century.

From the 11th to the 14th century, northern Italy was ruled by feudal lords, and by the 13th century Florence was a leading contender in the complicated struggle between the Guelphs and the Ghibellines. Florence was mostly Guelph, and its Ghibelline contingent ruled the city only sporadically (which did not, however, keep the Florentine Guelphs from squabbling among themselves). In those bloody days, Florence was filled with tall defensive towers built by the city's leading families on a competitive anything-you-can-build-I-can-build-bigger basis; the towers (and the houses below them) were connected by overhead bridges and catwalks, constructed to allow the members of allied families access to one another's houses without venturing into the dangerous streets below. The era gave rise, possibly for the first time in history, to the concept of turf, and its urban conflicts were at times just as vicious and irrational as the gang warfare within cities today.

The Guelph-Ghibelline conflict ended, finally, with the victory of the Guelphs and the rise of the Medici in the 15th century. The famous dynasty (which ruled Florence, and later all Tuscany, for more than three centuries) began with Giovanni di Bicci de' Medici and his son Cosimo, who transformed themselves from bankers into rulers. The dynasty reached its zenith with Cosimo's grandson Lorenzo the Magnificent (1449–92), patron and friend of some of Florence's most famous Renaissance artists. The towers were torn down, and the city assumed a slightly softer aspect. Today it still looks much the way it did then.

Essential Information

Important Addresses and Numbers

Tourist Information The city information office is at Via Cavour 1/r (next to the Palazzo Medici Riccardi), tel. 055/276–0382. Open 8:30–7.

The **APT** (tourist office) is just off Piazza Beccaria, at Via Manzoni 16, tel. 055/234–6284. Open Mon.–Sat. 8:30–1:30. There is an information office next to the train station and another near Piazza della Signoria, at Chiasso dei Baroncelli 17/r (tel. 055/230–2124).

Consulates **U.S.** Lungarno Vespucci 38, tel. 055/239–8276. Open weekdays 8:30–noon and 2–4.

British. Lungarno Corsini 2, tel. 055/284133. Open weekdays 9:30–12:30 and 2:30–4:30.

Canadians should contact their embassy in Rome.

Emergencies **Police.** Tel. 113. The main police station is located at Via Zara 2, near Piazza della Libertà.

Doctors and Dentists For English-speaking doctors and dentists, get a list from the U.S. consulate, or contact **Tourist Medical Service** (Viale Lorenzo Il Magnifico, tel. 055/475411). **Ambulance.** Misericordia (Piazza del Duomo 20, tel. 055/212222). If you need hospital treatment and an interpreter to help you communicate with the hospital staff, call AVO, a group of volunteer interpreters who offer their services free (tel. 055/403126; Mon., Wed., and Fri. 4–6 PM, tel. 055/324–4567).

Late-Night The following drugstores are open 24 hours a day, seven days a
Pharmacies week. For others, call 055/110.

Comunale No. 13 (train station, tel. 055/289435).

Molteni (Via Calzaiuoli 7/r, tel. 055/289490).

Taverna (Piazza San Giovanni 20/r, tel. 055/284013).

English-Language **Paperback Exchange** (Via Fiesolana 31/r, tel. 055/247-8154)
Bookstores will do just that, besides selling books outright. **BM Bookshop**
(Borgo Ognissanti 4/r, tel. 055/294575) has a fine selection of
books on Florence. **Seeber** (Via Tornabuoni 68, tel. 055/215697)
has English-language books alongside the other titles. *All are
open 9–1 and 3:30–7:30. Closed Mon. morning, Sun.*

Travel Agencies **American Express** (Via Guicciardini 49/r, near Piazza Pitti, tel.
055/288751) is also represented by **Universalturismo** (Via
Speziali 7/r, off Piazza della Repubblica, tel. 055/217241). **CIT**
has a main office (Via Cavour 56 tel. 055/294306) and a branch
near the train station (Piazza Stazione 51, tel. 055/239-6963).
Thomas Cook is represented by **World Vision** (Via Cavour
154/r, tel. 055/579294). *All agencies are open weekdays 9–12:30
and 3:30–7:30, Sat. 9–noon.*

Where to Change The **Cassa di Risparmio di Firenze** bank has 24-hour automatic
Money exchange machines at Via dei Servi 38/r and Via degli Speziali
16/r, near the cathedral, and at Via Tornabuoni 23/r and Via dei
Bardi 73/r, near the Ponte Vecchio. The **American Express** office is across the Ponte Vecchio, at Via Guicciardini 49/r, tel.
055/288751, but the Universalturismo branch at Via Speziali
7/r, off Piazza della Repubblica, tel. 055/217241, is more convenient. The **Banca Nazionale di Comunicazione** has an exchange
window in the Santa Maria Novella train station. It's open
Mon.–Sat. 8:20–6:20.

Arriving and Departing by Plane

Airports and The A. Vespucci airport, called **Peretola** (tel. 055/373498), is 10
Airlines kilometers (6 miles) northwest of Florence. Although it accommodates flights from Milan, Rome, and some European cities,
it is still a relatively minor airport. **Galileo Galilei** airport in
Pisa (tel. 050/44325) is 80 kilometers (50 miles) west of Florence
and is used by most international carriers. For flight information call the Florence Air Terminal at Santa Maria Novella train
station (tel. 055/216073) or Galilei airport information (tel. 050/
500707).

International travelers flying Alitalia to Rome's **Leonardo da
Vinci** airport can go directly nonstop to Florence's Santa Maria
Novella station via Alitalia's twice-daily Airport Train. Luggage is checked through to Florence, and meals and extras are
available on the train. Airport Train arrangements must be
made when you buy your plane ticket. The service also operates
in the other direction, returning from Florence to the da Vinci
airport.

Between the A scheduled service connects the station at Pisa airport with
Airports and the Santa Maria Novella station in Florence, roughly a one-
Downtown hour trip. Trains start running about 7 AM from the airport, 6
By Train AM from Florence, and continue service every hour until about
11:30 PM from the airport, 8 PM from Florence. You can check in
for departing flights at the air terminal at Track 5 of the train
station (tel. 055/216073).

By Bus There is no direct bus from **Pisa** airport to Florence. Buses do go to Pisa itself, but then you have to change to a slow train. There is a local bus service from Peretola to Florence (*see* Getting Around By Bus, *below*).

Arriving and Departing by Train and Bus

By Train Florence is on the principal Italian train route between most European capitals and Rome, and is served quite frequently from Milan, Venice, and Rome by nonstop Intercity (IC) trains. The **Santa Maria Novella** station is near the downtown area; avoid trains that stop only at the Campo di Marte station in an inconvenient location on the east side of the city. For train information in Florence, call 055/288785.

By Bus Long-distance buses run by **SITA** (Via Santa Caterina da Siena 15/r, tel. 055/483651 on weekdays, 055/211487 on weekends) and **Lazzi Eurolines** (Via Mercadante 2, tel. 055/215154) offer inexpensive if somewhat claustrophobic service between Florence and other cities in Italy and Europe.

Getting Around

By Bus Maps and timetables are available for a small fee at the ATAF booth next to the train station or at the office at Piazza del Duomo 57r, or for free at tourist information offices (*see* Important Addresses and Numbers, *above*). Tickets must be bought in advance, at tobacco stores, newsstands, from automatic ticket machines near main stops, or at ATAF booths (next to the station and at strategic locations throughout the city). They must then be canceled in the small validation machines immediately upon boarding. Two types of tickets are available, and they are both valid for one or more rides on all lines. One costs 1,100 lire and is valid for 60 minutes from the time it is first canceled; the other costs 1,500 lire for 120 minutes. A multiple ticket—eight tickets, each valid for 60 minutes—costs 8,000 lire. A 24-hour tourist ticket costs 5,000 lire. Long-term visitors or frequent users of the bus should look into the monthly passes sold at the ATAF office.

By Taxi Taxis usually wait at stands throughout the city (such as in front of the train station and ·in Piazza della Repubblica), or they can be called by dialing 055/4390 or 055/4798.

By Moped Those who want to go native and rent a noisy Vespa (Italian for wasp) or other make of motorcycle or moped may do so at **Motorent** (Via San Zanobi 9/r, tel. 055/490113) or **Alinari** (Via Guelfa 85/r, tel. 055/280500). Helmets are mandatory and can be rented here.

By Bicycle Brave souls may also rent bicycles at easy-to-spot locations at Fortezza da Basso, Santa Maria Novella train station, and Piazza Pitti; from Alinari or Motorent (*see above*); or from **Ciao e Basta** (Lungarno Pecori Girardi 1, tel. 055/234–2726).

By Foot This is definitely the best way to see the major sights of Florence, since practically everything of interest is within walking distance along the city's crowded, narrow streets or is otherwise accessible by bus.

Lodging

There are many small one- and two-star hotels in Florence, but
since the city is a magnet for not only tourists and students but
also trade fairs and conventions, reservations are a must at all
times of the year. If you arrive without reservations, go to the
Consorzio ITA (hotel association) office in the train station. It's
open daily from 8:20 AM to 9 PM and charges 3,000–6,000 lire,
depending on the category of the hotel, to make a reservation.
If you arrive late or want to avoid the reservations fee, try the
many small hotels on Via Nazionale and Via Faenza, both near
the station. Be aware that many hotels listed here under one
category have rooms without private baths that can be had for
rates that fall under a lower category. Although the hotel may
quote a rate inclusive of breakfast that is higher than the official room rate posted on the door of each room, you are not
obliged to take breakfast; if you don't want it, make that clear
when checking in.

Highly recommended lodgings are indicated by a star ★.

Under 115,000 lire

★ **Bellettini.** You couldn't ask for anything more central; this
small hotel occupies three floors (the top floor has two nice
rooms with a view) of an old but well-kept building near the cathedral. The cordial family management takes good care of
guests, providing a friendly atmosphere and homemade cakes
for breakfast, which is included in the low room rate, as is air-
conditioning. Halls and lounges are furnished with a smatter-
ing of antiques. The good-size rooms have Venetian or Tuscan
provincial decor; bathrooms are bright and modern. *Via dei
Conti 7, tel. 055/213561, fax 055/283551. 28 rooms with bath.
Facilities: bar, lounge. AE, DC, MC, V.*

Liana. This small hotel, located near the English Cemetery, is
in a quiet 19th-century villa that formerly housed the British
Embassy. Its clean and pleasant rooms all face a stately garden. *Via Vittorio Alfieri 18, tel. 055/245303, fax 055/234–4596.
23 rooms with bath or shower. AE, MC, V.*

Monica. Close to the train station but very quiet, the Monica
offers upscale elegance at low rates. Tastefully decorated, with
white walls, terra-cotta floors, old prints, and charming reproductions of 19th-century iron bedsteads, it has good-size rooms
and large terraces. The abundant breakfast is an extra charge,
but room and breakfast do not exceed the price level of this category. *Via Faenza 66, tel. 055/281706, fax 055/283804. 15
rooms, 13 with bath. AE, MC, V.*

Nuova Italia. Near the train station and within walking
distance of the sights, this hotel is run by a cordial, English-
speaking family. It has a homey atmosphere; rooms are clean,
simply furnished, and bright, with pictures and posters; all
have private baths. Some rooms can accommodate extra beds.
Low, bargain rates include breakfast. *Via Faenza 26, tel. 055/
268430, fax 055/210941. 20 rooms with bath. AE, DC, MC, V.*

Rigatti. Occupying the top two floors of the 19th-century Palazzo Alberti, between the Palazzo Vecchio and Santa Croce, this
elegantly furnished hotel has wonderful views of the Arno from
its tiny front terrace, as well as five quiet rooms overlooking a
garden in back. The rooms are spacious and tastefully fur-

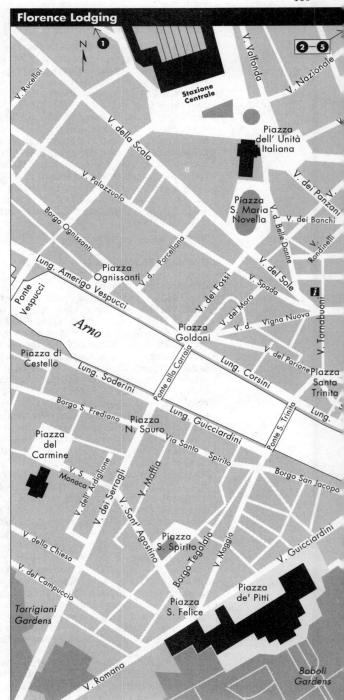

Florence Lodging

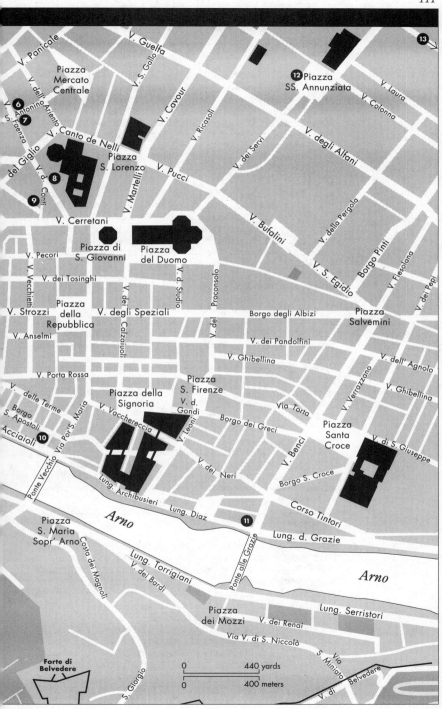

nished, with modern bathrooms. *Lungarno Diaz 2, tel. 055/213022. 28 rooms, 14 with bath. No credit cards.*

Under 85,000 lire

Alessandra. Only a block from the Ponte Vecchio, the Alessandra is clean and well kept, with large rooms and a friendly, English-speaking staff. *Borgo Santi Apostoli 17, tel. 055/283438, fax 055/210619. 25 rooms, 18 with bath. MC, V.*

Ausonia. A helpful young management and simple modern decor characterize this small hotel near the train station. Many rooms have private bath; those without are budget values. Special winter rates make it even more affordable. *Via Nazionale 24, tel. 055/495547, fax 055/496324. 20 rooms, 11 with bath. AE, MC, V.*

Azzi. Billed as "the inn of artists," the Azzi has whimsically eccentric, old-fashioned, frayed-around-the-edges decor. Rooms are very clean and can accommodate several beds, and there is a large living room and a charming terrace where guests can have breakfast. It is a favorite with musicians, performers, and students. *Via Faenza 56, tel. 055/213806. 12 rooms, 5 with bath. MC, V.*

Under 60,000 lire

Accademia. Near the train station and within walking distance of most sights, this is a simply furnished but comfortable family-run hotel. Guests mingle in the homey living room and large breakfast room. *Via Faenza 7, tel. 055/293451. 16 rooms, 9 with bath. V.*

★ **Globus.** The Globus has a handy location between the train station and the San Lorenzo market, where there are plenty of inexpensive eating places. There is a small, homey lounge. The hotel was renovated in 1992. *Via Sant'Antonino 24, tel. 055/211062. 21 rooms with bath. No credit cards.*

Mary. Located on a parklike square, the Mary is near the station and the San Marco museum. Rooms are simply furnished, and there are three flights of stairs to climb, but the proprietor couldn't be nicer (regulars say staying here is like staying at a friend's home). Rates are low, even for rooms with private baths. *Piazza Indipendenza 5, tel. 055/496310. 12 rooms, 9 with bath. No credit cards.*

Splurges

Villa Azalee. In a residential area about five minutes from the train station, this century-old mansion is set in a large garden. It has the atmosphere of a private home and comfortable living rooms. Bedrooms are individually furnished and air-conditioned. A double with bath costs about 170,000 lire with breakfast. *Viale Fratelli Rosselli 44, tel. 055/214242, fax 055/268264. 24 rooms with bath. AE, DC, MC, V.*

★ **Loggiato dei Serviti.** A relatively new and charming hotel, the Loggiato dei Serviti is tucked away under a historic loggia in one of the city's quietest and loveliest squares. Vaulted ceilings and tasteful furnishings, some of them antiques, make this a hotel for those who want to get the feel of Florence in a spare Renaissance building while enjoying modern creature comforts. The hotel has no restaurant. A double room with bath costs about 190,000 lire. *Piazza Santissima Annunziata 3, tel. 055/289592, fax 055/289595. 29 rooms with bath. AE, DC, MC, V.*

Exploring Florence

Guided Tours

Because its historic center is so compact, with most sights and museums in a relatively small area, Florence is a city you can easily see on your own. But if you have a limited amount of time, you may find a guided tour to be the most efficient way of covering the city's major sights. Tours offered by the major operators follow essentially the same itinerary. Morning and afternoon tours last about three hours each. One includes Michelangelo's *David* and the Palatine Gallery in the Pitti Palace; the other takes in the Uffizi and includes a brief excursion to Fiesole. A tour costs about 45,000 lire, including entrance fees. Book tours at **American Express** (tel. 055/288751), **CIT** (tel. 055/294306), and **SITA** (tel. 055/214721).

Florence for Free — or Almost

Gardens
Take a break from masterpieces, museums, and churches, and stroll through the **Boboli Gardens** (*see* Tour 1, *below*), making your way uphill to the neo-Gothic coffeehouse. Then go through the little gate nearby onto the grounds of the Belvedere Fortress. There you can get a superlative view of Florence (if it's clear) and either have refreshments at the café tucked into the ramparts or enjoy a picnic lunch if you've had the foresight to purchase provisions in the food shops off Via Guicciardini.

You might also visit one of the oldest **botanical gardens** in the world, founded by Cosimo de' Medici in 1545. *Via Micheli 3, behind San Marco. Admission: 5,000 lire. Open Mon., Wed., and Fri. 9–noon., Sun. in April and first 2 Sun. in May 9–1.*

Markets
Take in the sights and aromas of the **Mercato Centrale**, Florence's principal food market, on Piazza del Mercato Centrale, between San Lorenzo and Via Nazionale. *Open June–Sept., Mon.–Sat. 8–1; Oct.–May, Mon.–Sat. 8–1 and 4–8:30.*

Art in Churches
Much of Florence's most glorious art is in its churches, which charge no admission fees. Besides the **Duomo** and the **Battistero** (Tour 1, *below*), you can see several masterpieces in **Santa Maria Novella** (Tour 2, *below*), the Ghirlandaio frescoes in **Santa Trinita** (Tour 2, *below*), and the Giotto frescoes, along with several other masterpieces, in **Santa Croce** (Tour 3, *below*).

You can also stop in to see 15th-century artist Andrea del Castagno's solemn fresco of the Last Supper covering a wall of the former refectory of **Sant'Apollonia**. *Via XXVII Aprile 1. Open Tues.–Sat. 9–2, Sun. 9–1. Admission free.*

Another fresco of the Last Supper—this one by Ghirlandaio—can be seen at no cost in the refectory of the monastery adjacent to the Ognissanti Church. *Borgo Ognissanti 42. Open Mon., Tues., and Sat. 9–noon.*

You can also admire Perugino's Crucifixion in the chapter room of the monastery of **Santa Maria Maddalena dei Pazzi** free of charge. *Borgo Pinti 58. Open daily 9 –noon and 5–7.*

Stop to see the staircase that Michelangelo designed for the **Biblioteca Laurenziana,** at the church of San Lorenzo (*see* Tour 3, *below*).

Window Shopping Browse at the newsstand at the corner of Via dei Calzaiuoli and Piazza della Signoria, which is a treasure trove of quirky postcards and classic Florentine views.

Streetlife Pause to watch the street performers in Piazza della Signoria (many of them are quite accomplished).

Orientation

No city in Italy can match Florence's astounding artistic wealth. Celebrated paintings and sculptures are everywhere, and art scholars and connoisseurs have been investigating the subtleties and complexities of these works for hundreds of years. But what makes the art of Florence a revelation to the ordinary sightseer is a simple fact that scholarship often ignores: An astonishing percentage of Florence's art is just plain beautiful. Nowhere in Italy—perhaps in all Europe—is the act of looking at art more rewarding.

But a word of warning is in order here. For some years now, Florentine psychiatrists have recognized a peculiar local malady to which foreign tourists are particularly susceptible. It's called "Stendhal's syndrome," after the 19th-century French novelist, who was the first to describe it in print. The symptoms can be severe: confusion, dizziness, disorientation, depression, and sometimes persecution anxiety and loss of a sense of identity. Some victims immediately suspect food poisoning, but the true diagnosis is far more outlandish. They are suffering from art poisoning, brought on by overexposure to so-called Important Works of High Culture. Consciously or unconsciously, they seem to view Florentine art as an exam (Aesthetics 101, 10 hours per day, self-taught, pass/fail), and they are terrified of flunking.

Obviously the art of Florence should not be a test. So if you are not an inveterate museum goer or church collector with established habits and methods, take it easy. Don't try to absorb every painting or fresco that comes into view. There is second-rate art even in the Uffizi and the Pitti (*especially* the Pitti), so find some favorites and enjoy them at your leisure. Getting to know a few paintings well will be far more enjoyable than breezing by a vast number.

And when fatigue begins to set in, stop. Take time off, and pay some attention to the city itself. Too many first-time visitors trudge dutifully from one museum to the next without really seeing what is in between. They fail to notice that Florence the city (as opposed to Florence the museum) is a remarkable phenomenon: a bustling metropolis that has managed to preserve its predominantly medieval street plan and predominantly Renaissance infrastructure while successfully adapting to the insistent demands of 20th-century life. The resulting marriage between the very old and the very new is not always tranquil, but it is always fascinating. Florence the city can be chaotic, frenetic, and full of uniquely Italian noise, but it is alive in a way that Florence the museum, however beautiful, is not. Do not miss the forest for the trees.

The three walking tours outlined in the following pages are best taken a day at a time. Attempts to complete them in fewer than three days will prove frustrating, for many (if not most) Florentine museums and churches close sometime between noon and 2, and only the churches reopen in the late afternoon.

Highlights for First-time Visitors

Duomo (Cathedral of Santa Maria del Fiore) (Tour 1: From the Duomo to the Boboli Gardens).

Battistero (Baptistery) (Tour 1: From the Duomo to the Boboli Gardens).

Museo dell'Opera del Duomo (Tour 1: From the Duomo to the Boboli Gardens).

Bargello (Museo Nazionale) (Tour 1: From the Duomo to the Boboli Gardens).

Piazza della Signoria (Tour 1: From the Duomo to the Boboli Gardens).

Galleria degli Uffizi (Tour 1: From the Duomo to the Boboli Gardens).

Galleria dell'Accademia (Tour 3: From the Duomo to Santa Croce and Beyond).

Ponte Vecchio (Tour 1: From the Duomo to the Boboli Gardens).

Santa Croce (Tour 3: From the Duomo to Santa Croce and Beyond).

Tour 1: From the Duomo to the Boboli Gardens

Numbers in the margin correspond to points of interest on the Florence map.

The first tour begins with the Cathedral of Santa Maria del Fiore, more familiarly known as the **Duomo,** located in Piazza del Duomo, with its adjacent **Battistero** (Baptistery), the octagonal building that faces the Duomo facade. The Baptistery is one of the oldest buildings in Florence, and local legend has it that it was once a Roman temple of Mars; modern excavations, however, suggest that its foundation was laid during the 6th or 7th century AD, well after the collapse of the Roman Empire. The round-arched Romanesque decoration on the exterior probably dates from the 11th or 12th century. The interior ceiling mosaics (finished in 1297) are justly famous, but—glitteringly beautiful as they are—they could never outshine the building's most renowned feature: its bronze Renaissance doors decorated with panels crafted by Lorenzo Ghiberti (1378–1455). The doors, on which Ghiberti spent most of his adult life (from 1403 to 1452), are on the north and east sides of the Baptistery—at least copies of them are—while the south door panels, in the Gothic style, were designed by Andrea Pisano in 1330. The originals of the Ghiberti doors were removed to protect them from the effects of pollution and acid rain and have been beautifully restored; they are now on display in the Cathedral Museum (*see below*). *Admission to Baptistery interior free. Open Mon.–Sat. 1–6, Sun. 9–1.*

Ghiberti's north doors depict scenes from the life of Christ; his later east doors, facing the Duomo facade, depict scenes from the Old Testament. The doors are worth a close examination,

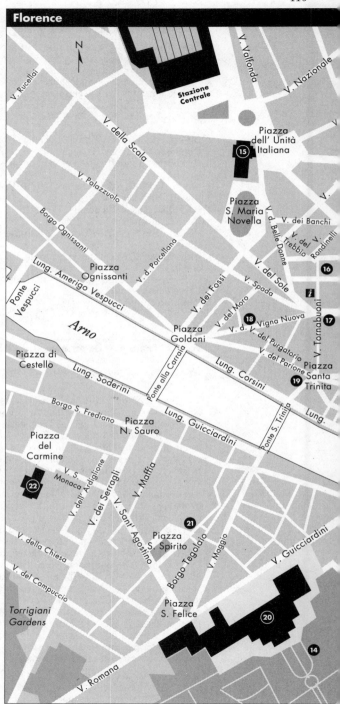

Florence

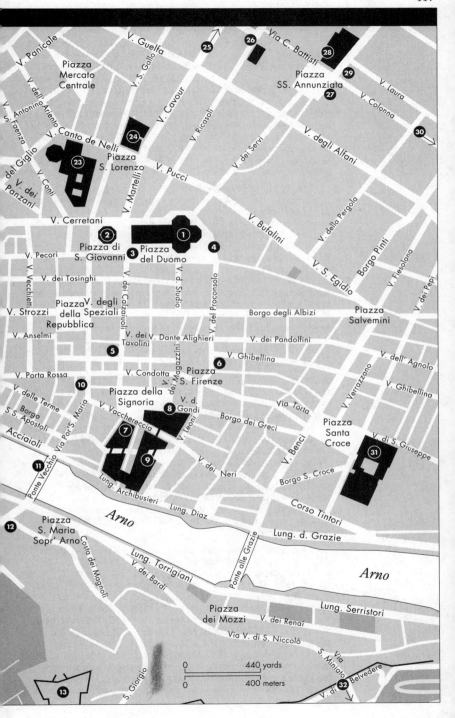

for they are very different in style and illustrate with great clarity the artistic changes that marked the beginning of the Renaissance. Look, for instance, at the far right panel of the middle row on the earlier north doors *(Jesus Calming the Waters)*. Here Ghiberti captured the chaos of a storm at sea with great skill and economy, but the artistic conventions he used are basically pre-Renaissance: Jesus is the most important figure, so he is the largest; the disciples are next in size, being next in importance; the ship on which they founder is a mere toy. But you can sense Ghiberti's impatience with these artificial spatial conventions. The Cathedral Works Committee made him retain the decorative quatrefoil borders of the south doors for his panels here, and in this scene Ghiberti's storm seems to want to burst the bounds of its frame.

On the east doors, the decorative borders are gone. The panels are larger, more expansive, more sweeping, and more convincing. Look, for example, at the middle panel on the left-hand door. It tells the story of Jacob and Esau, and the various episodes of the story (the selling of the birthright, Isaac ordering Esau to go hunting, the blessing of Jacob, and so forth) have been merged into a single beautifully realized street scene. A perspective grid is employed to suggest depth, the background architecture looks far more convincing than that of the north door panels, the figures in the foreground are grouped realistically, and the naturalism and grace of the poses (look at Esau's left leg) have nothing to do with the sacred message being conveyed. Although the religious content remains, man and his place in the natural world are given new prominence and are portrayed with a realism not seen in art since the fall of the Roman Empire, more than a thousand years earlier.

When Ghiberti was working on these panels, three of his artist friends were bringing the same new humanistic focus to their own very different work. In sculpture, Donato di Niccolò Betto Bardi, known as Donatello, was creating statuary for churches all over town; in painting, Tommaso di Ser Giovanni, known as Masaccio, was executing frescoes at the churches of Santa Maria del Carmine and Santa Maria Novella; in architecture, Filippo Brunelleschi was building the Duomo dome, the Ospedale degli Innocenti, and the church interiors of San Lorenzo and Santo Spirito. They are the fathers of the Renaissance in art and architecture—the four great geniuses who created a new artistic vision—and among them they began a revolution that was to make Florence the artistic capital of Italy for more than a hundred years.

As a footnote to Ghiberti's panels, one small detail of the east doors is worth a special look. Just to the lower left of the Jacob and Esau panel, Ghiberti placed a tiny self-portrait bust. From either side, the portrait is extremely appealing—Ghiberti looks like everyone's favorite uncle—but the bust is carefully placed so that there is a single spot in front of the doors from which you can make direct eye contact with the tiny head. When that contact is made, the impression of intelligent life— of *modern* intelligent life—is astonishing. It is no wonder that when these doors were completed, they received one of the most famous compliments in the history of art from a competitor known to be notoriously stingy with praise: Michelangelo himself declared them so beautiful that they could serve as the gates to Paradise.

The immense Duomo—the fourth-largest church in the world—was designed by Arnolfo di Cambio in 1296 but was not consecrated until 1436. The imposing facade dates only from the 19th century; it was built in the neo-Gothic style to comple-
❸ ment Giotto's genuine 14th-century Gothic **Campanile** (Bell Tower), which stands to the right of the church's facade. The real glory of the Duomo, however, is Filippo Brunelleschi's dome, herald of the new Renaissance in architecture, which hovers over the cathedral (and the entire city when seen from afar) with a dignity and grace that few domes, even to this day, can match. It was the first of its kind in the world, and for many people it is still the best.

Brunelleschi's dome was epoch-making as an engineering feat as well. The space to be enclosed by the dome was so large and so high above the ground that traditional methods of dome con-struction—wooden centering and scaffolding—were of no use whatever. So Brunelleschi developed entirely new building methods, which he implemented with equipment of his own de-vising (including the modern crane). Beginning work in 1420, he built not one dome but two, one inside the other, and con-nected them with common ribbing that stretched across the in-tervening empty space, thereby considerably lessening the crushing weight of the structure. He also employed a new method of bricklaying, based on an ancient Roman herring-bone pattern, interlocking each new course of bricks with the course below in a way that made the growing structure self-supporting. The result was one of the great engineering break-throughs of all time: Most of Europe's great domes, including St. Peter's in Rome, were built employing Brunelleschi's meth-ods, and today the Duomo has come to symbolize Florence in the same way that the Eiffel Tower symbolizes Paris. The Flor-entines are justly proud, and to this day the Florentine phrase for "homesick" is *nostalgia del cupolone* (homesick for the dome).

The interior is a fine example of Italian Gothic, although any-one who has seen the Gothic cathedrals of France will be disap-pointed by its lack of dramatic verticality. Italian architecture, even at the height of the Gothic era, never broke entirely free of the influence of Classical Rome, and its architects never learned (perhaps never wanted to learn) how to make their in-teriors soar like the cathedrals in the cities around Paris.

Most of the cathedral's best-known artworks have now been moved to the nearby cathedral museum. Notable among the works that remain, however, are two equestrian frescoes hon-oring famous soldiers: Andrea del Castagno's *Niccolò da Tolentino*, painted in 1456, and Paolo Uccello's *Sir John Hawkwood*, painted 20 years earlier; both are on the left-hand wall of the nave. *Niccolò da Tolentino* is particularly impres-sive: He rides his fine horse with military pride and wears his even finer hat—surely the best in town—with panache.

If time permits, you may want to explore the upper and lower reaches of the cathedral as well. Ancient remains have been ex-cavated beneath the nave; the stairway down is near the first pier on the right. The climb to the top of the dome (463 steps) is not for the fainthearted, but the view is superb; the entrance is on the left wall just before the crossing. *Piazza del Duomo, tel. 055/230–2885. Excavation admission: 3,000 lire. Ascent ad-*

mission: 5,000 lire. Duomo open daily 7:30 AM–6:30 PM; open for nonreligious purposes 10–5.

Leave the Duomo by the right-aisle exit and turn left; at the east end of the piazza, opposite the rear of the cathedral, is the ❹ **Museo dell'Opera del Duomo** (Cathedral Museum). Its major attractions—other than the Ghiberti door panels mentioned earlier and the sculptured marble choir lofts by Donatello and Luca della Robbia—are Donatello's *Mary Magdalen* and Michelangelo's *Pietà* (not to be confused with the more famous *Pietà* in St. Peter's, in Rome). The High Renaissance in sculpture is in part defined by revolutionary realism, but Donatello's *Magdalen* goes beyond realism: It is suffering incarnate. Michelangelo's heart-wrenching *Pietà* was unfinished at his death; the female figure supporting the body of Christ on the left was added by one Tiberio Calcagni, and never has the difference between competence and genius been manifested so clearly. *Piazza del Duomo 9, tel. 055/230–2885. Admission: 5,000 lire. Open Mar.–Oct., Mon.–Sat. 9–7:30; Nov.–Feb., Mon.–Sat. 9–6.*

Return to the Duomo facade and turn left onto **Via dei Calzaiuoli.** This unusually wide street dates from the 14th century and probably represents Florence's first effort at modern city planning. The street received special attention because it ran directly from the city's main religious square to its main civic square, Piazza della Signoria, where the medieval city hall was located. Both the axis and the city hall remain intact to this day.

A short detour to the west (down Via degli Speziali) leads to **Piazza della Repubblica.** The piazza's location, if not its architecture, is historically important: The ancient forum around which lay the original Roman settlement was located here. The street plan in the area around the piazza still reflects the carefully plotted orthogonal grid of the Roman military encampment. The Mercato Vecchio (Old Market), located here since the Middle Ages, was demolished at the end of the past century, and the current piazza was constructed between 1890 and 1917 as a neoclassical showpiece. Nominally the center of town, it has yet to earn the love of most Florentines.

Return to Via dei Calzaiuoli and turn right. Just down the ❺ street is the rectangular church of **Orsanmichele,** containing a beautifully detailed 14th-century Gothic tabernacle by Andrea Orcagna. Of particular note here, however, is the building's exterior. Originally a granary, it was transformed in 1336 into a church with 14 exterior niches. Each of the major Florentine trade guilds was assigned its own niche and paid for the sculpture the niche contains. All of the statues are worth examining, though many are copies, and one that is particularly deserving of scrutiny—Andrea del Verrocchio's *Doubting Thomas* (ca. 1470), which stood in the middle niche on Via dei Calzaiuoli—has been removed for restoration (it was on view in New York City in summer 1993 and eventually will be placed in a museum, perhaps even in Orsanmichele, along with the other originals). In it, the viewer sees Christ, like the building's other figures, entirely framed within the niche but St. Thomas standing on its bottom ledge, with his right foot outside the niche frame. This detail alone, the positioning of a single foot, brings the entire composition to life. It is particularly appropriate that this was the only niche to be topped with a Renaissance pediment, for it is the revolutionary vitality of sculpture like this that gave the Renaissance its name.

From Via dei Calzaiuoli, follow Via dei Tavolini (which turns into Via Dante Alighieri after one block and passes the fraudulently named Casa di Dante on the left) to the intersection of Via del Proconsolo. The church on the southwest corner is the ancient **Badia Fiorentina,** built in 1285; its graceful bell tower (best seen from the interior courtyard) is one of the most beautiful in Florence. The interior of the church proper was half-heartedly remodeled in the Baroque style during the 17th century; its best-known work of art is Filippino Lippi's delicate *Apparition of the Virgin to St. Bernard* (1486), on the left as you enter. The painting—one of Lippi's finest—is in superb condition and is worth exploring in detail. The Virgin's hands are perhaps the most beautiful in the city. (For illumination, drop a coin in the box near the floor to the painting's right.)

❻ On the opposite side of Via del Proconsolo from the Badia is the **Bargello.** During the Renaissance the building was used as a prison, and the exterior served as a "most-wanted" billboard: Effigies of notorious criminals and Medici enemies were painted on its walls. Today the building is the **Museo Nazionale** and houses what is probably the finest collection of Renaissance sculpture in Italy. Michelangelo, Donatello, and Benvenuto Cellini are the preeminent masters here, and the concentration of masterworks displayed in this imposing setting is remarkable despite the fact that they are interspersed with eclectic collections of arms, ceramics, and enamels. For Renaissance art lovers, the Bargello is to sculpture what the Uffizi is to painting.

One particular display—easily overlooked—should not be missed. In 1402 Filippo Brunelleschi and Lorenzo Ghiberti competed to earn the most prestigious commission of the day: the decoration of the north doors of the Baptistery in Piazza del Duomo. For the competition, each designed a bronze bas-relief panel on the theme of the Sacrifice of Isaac; both panels are on display, side by side, in the room devoted to the sculpture of Donatello on the upper floor. The judges chose Ghiberti for the commission; you can decide for yourself whether or not they were right. *Via del Proconsolo 4, tel. 055/210801. Admission: 6,000 lire. Open Tues.–Sat. 9–2, Sun. 9–1.*

Leaving the Bargello, continue south along Via del Proconsolo to the small Piazza San Firenze. The church of San Firenze, on the left, is one of Florence's few Baroque structures; its steps offer a fine view of the Badia bell tower. From the north end of the piazza, go west on Via Condotta, then left onto Via dei Magazzini, which leads into **Piazza della Signoria,** recently excavated and then repaved, the most striking square in Florence. It was here, in 1497, that the famous "bonfire of the vanities" took place, when the fanatical monk Savonarola induced his followers to hurl their worldly goods into the flames; it was also here, a year later, that he was hanged as a heretic and, ironically, burned. A bronze plaque in the piazza pavement marks the exact spot of his execution.

❼ The statues in the square and in the 14th-century **Loggia dei Lanzi** on the south side are variable in quality. Benvenuto Cellini's famous bronze *Perseus Holding the Head of Medusa* is his masterpiece; even the pedestal is superbly executed (the statuettes in its niches are recent copies of the originals). Other works in the Loggia include *The Rape of the Sabine Women* and *Hercules and the Centaur,* both late-16th-century works by Giambologna, and, in the back, a row of sober matrons dating from Roman times. The Loggia recently underwent lengthy structural restorations; many of the statues have been replaced by copies.

In the square, Bartolomeo Ammannati's Neptune Fountain, dating from 1565, takes something of a booby prize. Ammannati himself considered it to be a failure, and the Florentines call it *Il Biancone,* which can be translated as "the big white man" or "the big white lump," depending on your point of view. Giambologna's equestrian statue, to the left of the fountain, pays tribute to the Medici grand duke. Occupying the steps of the Palazzo Vecchio are a copy of Donatello's proud heraldic lion of Florence, known as the *Marzocco* (the original is now in the Bargello); a copy of Donatello's *Judith and Holofernes* (the original is inside the Palazzo Vecchio); a copy of Michelangelo's *David* (the original is now in the Accademia); and Baccio Bandinelli's *Hercules* (1534).

⑧ The **Palazzo Vecchio** itself is far from beautiful, but it possesses a more than acceptable substitute: character. The palazzo was begun in 1299 and designed (probably) by Arnolfo di Cambio, and its massive bulk and towering campanile dominate the piazza masterfully. It was built as a meeting place for the heads of the seven major guilds that governed the city at the time; over the centuries it has served lesser purposes, but today it is once again the city hall of Florence. The interior courtyard is a good deal less severe, having been remodeled by Michelozzo in 1453; Verrocchio's bronze *puttino* (little cherub, or child) topping the central fountain softens the effect considerably.

Although most of the interior public rooms are well worth exploring, the main attraction is on the second floor: two adjoining rooms that supply one of the most startling contrasts in Florence. The first is the vast **Sala dei Cinquecento** (Room of the Five Hundred), named for 500 deputies who debated here from 1865 to 1871, when Florence served as the capital of the kingdom of Italy. The Sala was decorated by Giorgio Vasari, around 1570, with huge frescoes celebrating Florentine history; depictions of battles with neighboring cities predominate. Continuing the martial theme, the Sala also contains Michelangelo's *Victory* group, intended for the never-completed tomb of Pope Julius II, plus miscellaneous sculptures of decidedly lesser quality.

The second room is the little **Studiolo,** entered to the right of the Sala's entrance. This was the study of Cosimo de' Medici's son, the melancholy Francesco I, designed by Vasari and decorated by Vasari and Agnolo Bronzino. It is intimate, civilized, and filled with complex, questioning, allegorical art. It makes the vainglorious proclamations next door ring more than a little hollow. *Piazza della Signoria, tel. 055/276–8465. Admission: 8,000 lire. Open weekdays 9–7, Sun. 8–1.*

⑨ Just south of the Palazzo Vecchio is the **Palazzo degli Uffizi,** a U-shape building fronting on the Arno, designed by Vasari in 1559. Built as an office building—*uffizi* means "offices" in Italian—the palazzo now houses the finest collection of paintings in Italy. Hard-core museum goers will want to purchase the English guide sold outside the entrance.

The collection's highlights include Paolo Uccello's *Battle of San Romano* (its brutal chaos of lances is one of the finest visual metaphors for warfare ever committed to paint); Fra Filippo Lippi's *Madonna and Child with Two Angels* (the foreground angel's bold, impudent eye contact would have been unthinkable prior to the Renaissance); Sandro Botticelli's *Primavera* (its nonrealistic fairy-tale charm exhibits the painter's idiosyncratic genius at its zenith); Leonardo da Vinci's *Adoration of the Magi* (unfinished and perhaps the best opportunity in Europe to investigate the methods of a great artist at work); Raphael's *Madonna of the Goldfinch* (darkened by time, but the tenderness with which the figures in the painting touch each other is undimmed); Michelangelo's *Holy Family* (one of the very few easel works in oil he ever painted, clearly reflecting his stated belief that draftsmanship is a necessary ingredient of great painting); Rembrandt's *Self-Portrait as an Old Man* (which proves that even Michelangelo could, on occasion, be wrong); Titian's *Venus of Urbino* and Caravaggio's *Bacchus* (two very great paintings whose attitudes toward myth and sexuality are—to put it mildly—diametrically opposed); and many, many more. If panic sets in at the prospect of absorbing all this art at one go, bear in mind that the three tours outlined here are structured to offer late-afternoon free time, and the Uffizi is open late every day except Sunday. Also there's a coffee bar inside; its terrace offers a fine, close-up view of the Palazzo Vecchio. Note: A car bomb that exploded in the vicinity of the Uffizi on May 27, 1993, killing five, damaged a Sebastiano del Piombo painting, among others, but spared more precious works. By June 20, the gallery's first 24 rooms had already reopened, but at press time it was not known when the entire collection would again be on view. *Piazzale degli Uffizi 6, tel. 055/ 218341. Admission: 10,000 lire. Open Tues.–Sat. 9–7, Sun. 9–1.*

Leave Piazza della Signoria at the southwest corner and follow Via Vaccereccia one block west to Via Por Santa Maria. Just north of the intersection is an open-air loggia known as the **⑩** **Mercato Nuovo** (New Market). It was new in 1551. Today it harbors mostly souvenir stands; its main attraction is Pietro Tacca's bronze *Porcellino* (Piglet) fountain on the south side, dating from around 1612 and copied from an earlier Roman work now in the Uffizi. Rubbing its drooling snout is a Florentine tradition—it is said to bring good luck.

Follow Via Por Santa Maria toward the river and you'll arrive at **⑪** the **Ponte Vecchio** (the Old Bridge), which is to Florence what Tower Bridge is to London. It was built in 1345 to replace an earlier bridge that was swept away by flood, and its shops housed first butchers, then grocers, blacksmiths, and other merchants. But in 1593 the Medici grand duke Ferdinando I, whose private corridor linking the Medici palace (the Palazzo Pitti) with the Medici offices (the Uffizi) crossed the bridge atop the shops, decided that all this plebeian commerce under his feet was unseemly. So he threw out all the butchers and blacksmiths and installed 41 goldsmiths and eight jewelers. The bridge has been devoted solely to these two trades ever since.

In the middle of the bridge, take a moment to study the **Ponte Santa Trinita,** the next bridge downriver. It was designed by Bartolomeo Ammannati in 1567 (possibly from sketches by Michelangelo), blown up by the retreating Germans during World War II, and painstakingly reconstructed after the war ended. Florentines like to claim it as the most beautiful bridge in the world. Given its simplicity, this may sound like idle Tuscan boasting; but if you commit its graceful arc and delicate curves to memory and then begin to compare these characteristics with those of other bridges encountered in your travels, you may well conclude that the boast is justified. The Ponte Santa Trinita is a beautiful piece of architecture.

Once you've crossed the bridge, you are in Florence's Oltrarno—beyond, or across the Arno—district. A few yards past the south end of the Ponte Vecchio (on the left side of Via dei Guicciardini) is the church of **Santa Felicita,** in the tiny piazza of the same name. Rarely visited by sightseers, the church contains one of Florence's finest Mannerist masterpieces: Jacopo da Pontormo's *Deposition*, painted around 1526, above the altar in the Capponi Chapel, just to the right of the entrance. The painting's swirling design and contorted figures are quintessentially Mannerist. The palette, however, transcends Mannerism: Despite being ill lit (the lights must be turned on by the sacristan), the altarpiece's luminous colors are among the most striking in Florence.

After leaving Santa Felicita, walk along Costa di San Giorgio, which starts as a tiny alley to the left of the church, passes a house once occupied by Galileo (No. 11), and continues on to the Porta San Giorgio entrance in the old city walls. The walk up this narrow street is one of Florence's least-known pleasures. The climb is steep, but just as you begin to wonder when it's going to end, a remarkable transformation takes place: The city falls away, the parked cars disappear, vine-covered walls screening olive trees appear on both sides, birds begin to chirp, and Florence becomes—of all things—tranquil. A narrow Florentine street has suddenly turned into a picturesque Tuscan country lane.

Just before the costa ends at Porta San Giorgio, turn onto the short lane on the right (Via del Forte di San Giorgio), which leads to the main entrance of the **Belvedere Fortress** (down the steps and through the arch). The fortress, where temporary art exhibitions are sometimes held, was built in 1429 to help defend the city against siege. But time has effected an ironic transformation, and what was once a first-rate fortification is now a first-rate picnic ground. Buses carry view-seeking tourists farther up the hill to the Piazzale Michelangelo, but, as the natives know, the best views of Florence are right here. To the north, all the city's monuments are spread out in a breathtaking cinemascopic panorama, framed by the rolling Tuscan hills beyond: the squat dome of Santa Maria Novella, Giotto's proud campanile, the soaring dome of the Duomo, the forbidding medieval tower of the Palazzo Vecchio, the delicate Gothic spire of the Badia, and the crenellated tower of the Bargello. It is one of the best city views in Italy. To the south the nearby hills furnish a complementary rural view that is in its way equally memorable. If time and weather permit, a picnic lunch here on the last day of your stay is the perfect way to review the city's splendors and fix them forever in your memory. *Admission free. Open daily 9–sunset.*

(14) Leave the Belvedere Fortress by the north exit, turn left, and you will come to the rear entrance of the **Boboli Gardens,** adjacent to the Pitti Palace. Once inside the entrance, follow the path at the far left. The gardens began to take shape in 1549, when the Pitti family sold the palazzo to Eleanor of Toledo, wife of the Medici grand duke Cosimo I. The initial landscaping plans were laid out by Niccolò Pericoli Tribolo. After his death in 1550, development was continued by Bernardo Buontalenti, Giulio and Alfonso Parigi, and, over the years, many others, who produced the most spectacular backyard in Florence. The Italian gift for landscaping—less formal than the French but still full of sweeping drama—is displayed here at its best. A description of the gardens' beauties would fill a page but would be self-defeating, for the best way to enjoy a pleasure garden is to wander about, discovering its pleasures for yourself. But one small fountain deserves special note: the famous *Bacchino*, next to the garden exit at the extreme north end of the palace, nearest the river. It is a copy of the original, showing Pietro Barbino, Cosimo's favorite dwarf, astride a particularly unhappy tortoise. It seems to be illustrating—very graphically, indeed—the perils of too much pasta. *Admission: 5,000 lire. Open Tues.–Sun. 9–one hour before sunset.*

Tour 2: From the Duomo to the Cascine

Tour 2 also begins at the Duomo. From the north side of the Baptistery, walk west along the mostly modern Via dei Cerretani; after three blocks it forks. Take the middle fork (Via dei Banchi), which leads into Piazza Santa Maria Novella, domi-
(15) nated by the church of **Santa Maria Novella** on the north side.

The facade of the church looks distinctly clumsy by later Renaissance standards, and with good reason: It is an architectural hybrid. The lower half of the facade was completed mostly in the 14th century; its pointed-arch niches and decorative marble patterns reflect the Gothic style of the day. About a hundred years later (around 1456), architect Leon Battista Alberti was called in to complete the job. The marble decoration of his upper story clearly defers to the already existing work below, but the architectural features he added evince an entirely different style. The central doorway, the four ground-floor half-columns with Corinthian capitals, the triangular pediment atop the second story, the inscribed frieze immediately below the pediment—these are classical features borrowed from antiquity, and they reflect the new Renaissance era in architecture, born some 35 years earlier at the Ospedale degli Innocenti (*see* Tour 3: From the Duomo to Santa Croce and Beyond, *below*). Alberti's most important addition, however, the S-curve scrolls that surmount the decorative circles on either side of the upper story, had no precedent whatever in antiquity. The problem was to soften the abrupt transition between wide ground floor and narrow upper story. Alberti's solution turned out to be definitive. Once you start to look for them, you'll find scrolls such as these (or sculptural variations of them) on churches all over Italy, and every one of them derives from Alberti's example here.

The architecture of the interior is (like the Duomo) a dignified but somber example of Italian Gothic. Exploration is essential, however, because the church's store of art treasures is remarkable. Highlights include the 14th-century stained-glass rose window depicting *The Coronation of the Virgin* (above the central entrance door); the Filippo Strozzi Chapel (to the right of the altar), containing late-15th-century frescoes and stained glass by Filippino Lippi; the chancel (the area around the altar), containing frescoes by Domenico Ghirlandaio (1485); and the Gondi Chapel (to the left of the altar), containing Filippo Brunelleschi's famous wooden crucifix, carved around 1410 and said to have so stunned the great Donatello when he first saw it that he dropped a basket of eggs.

One other work in the church is worth special attention, for it possesses great historical importance as well as beauty. It is Masaccio's *Holy Trinity with Two Donors*, on the left-hand wall, almost halfway down the nave. Painted around 1425 (at the same time Masaccio was working on his frescoes in Santa Maria del Carmine, described later in this tour), it unequivocally announced the arrival of the Renaissance era. The realism of the figure of Christ was revolutionary in itself, but what was probably even more startling to the contemporary Florentines was the coffered ceiling in the background. The mathematical rules for employing perspective in painting had just been discovered (probably by Brunelleschi), and this was one of the first paintings to employ them with utterly convincing success. As art historian E. H. Gombrich expressed it, "We can imagine how amazed the Florentines must have been when this wall painting was unveiled and seemed to have made a hole in the wall through which they could look into a new burial chapel in Brunelleschi's modern style."

Leave Piazza Santa Maria Novella by Via delle Belle Donne, which angles off to the south, where you entered the square from Via dei Banchi, and leads to a tiny piazza. In the center is a curious column topped by a roofed crucifix, known as the **Croce al Trebbio.** The cross was erected in 1308 by the Dominican Order (Santa Maria Novella was a Dominican church) to commemorate a famous victory: It was here that the Dominican friars defeated their avowed enemies, the Patarene heretics, in a bloody street brawl.

Beyond the piazza, bear left onto the short Via del Trebbio, then turn right onto Via Tornabuoni. On the left side of the street is the church of **San Gaetano,** with a rather staid Baroque facade (and Albertian scrolls), finished in 1645. Florence never fully embraced the Baroque movement—by the 17th century the city's artistic heyday was long over—but the decorative statuary here does manage to muster some genuine Baroque exuberance. The cherubs on the upper story, setting the coat of arms in place, are a typical (if not very original) Baroque motif.

Via Tornabuoni is probably Florence's finest shopping street, and it supplies an interesting contrast to the nearby Piazza della Repubblica. There, at the turn of the century, the old was leveled to make way for the new; here, past and present cohabit easily and efficiently, with the oldest buildings housing the newest shops. Ironically, the "modern" Piazza della Repubblica now looks dated and more than a little dowdy, and it is the unrenewed Via Tornabuoni, bustling with activity, that seems up to the minute.

Via Tornabuoni is lined with Renaissance buildings. But its ⑰ most imposing palazzo is the **Palazzo Strozzi,** a block south, at the intersection of Via Strozzi. Designed (probably) by Giuliano da Sangallo around 1489 and modeled after Michelozzo's earlier Palazzo Medici-Riccardi (*see* Tour 3: From the Duomo to Santa Croce and Beyond, *below*), the exterior of the palazzo is simple and severe; it is not the use of classical detail but the regularity of its features, the stately march of its windows, that marks it as a product of the early Renaissance. The interior courtyard (entered from the rear of the palazzo) is another matter altogether. It is here that the classical vocabulary—columns, capitals, pilasters, arches, and cornices—is given uninhibited and powerful expression. Unfortunately, the courtyard's effectiveness is all but destroyed by its outlandish modern centerpiece: a brutal metal fire escape. Its introduction here is one of the most disgraceful acts of 20th-century "progress" in the entire city.

One block west, down Via della Vigna Nuova, in Piazza ⑱ Rucellai, is Alberti's **Palazzo Rucellai,** which goes a step farther than the Palazzo Strozzi and possesses a more representative Renaissance facade. A comparison between the two is illuminating. Evident on the facade of the Palazzo Rucellai is the ordered arrangement of windows and rusticated stonework seen on the Palazzo Strozzi, but Alberti's facade is far less forbidding. Alberti devoted a much larger proportion of his wall space to windows (which soften the facade's appearance) and filled in the remainder with rigorously ordered classical elements borrowed from antiquity. The end result, though still severe, is far less fortresslike, and Alberti strove for this effect purposely (he is on record as stating that only tyrants need fortresses). Ironically, the Palazzo Rucellai was built some 30 years *before* the Palazzo Strozzi. Alberti's civilizing ideas here, it turned out, had little influence on the Florentine palazzi that followed. To the Renaissance Florentines, power—in architecture, as in life—was just as impressive as beauty.

If proof of this dictum is needed, it can be found several short blocks away. Follow the narrow street opposite the Palazzo Rucellai (Via del Purgatorio) almost to its end, then zigzag right and left to reach Piazza di Santa Trinita. In the center of the piazza is a column from the Baths of Caracalla, in Rome, given to the Medici grand duke Cosimo I by Pope Pius IV in 1560. The column was raised here by Cosimo in 1565 to mark the spot where he heard the news, in 1537, that his exiled Ghibelline enemies had been defeated at Montemurlo, near Prato; the victory made his power in Florence unchallengeable and all but absolute. The column is called, with typical Medici self-assurance, the **Colonna della Giustizia,** the Column of Justice.

Halfway down the block to the right (toward the Arno) is the ⑲ church of **Santa Trinita.** Originally built in the Romanesque style, the church underwent a Gothic remodeling during the 14th century (remains of the Romanesque construction are visible on the interior front wall). Its major artistic attractions are the cycle of frescoes and the altarpiece in the Sassetti Chapel, the second to the altar's right, painted by Domenico Ghirlandaio around 1485. Ghirlandaio was a conservative painter for his day, and generally his paintings exhibit little interest in the investigations into the laws of perspective that had been going on in Florentine painting for more than 50 years. But his work here possesses such graceful decorative appeal that his lack of interest in rigorous perspective hardly seems to matter. The wall frescoes illustrate the life of St. Francis, and the altarpiece, *The Adoration of the Shepherds*, seems to stop just short of glowing.

From Santa Trinita, cross the Arno over the Ponte Santa Trinita and continue down Via Maggio until you reach the crossroads of Sdrucciolo dei Pitti (on the left) and the short Via dei Michelozzi (on the right). Here you have a choice. If the noon hour approaches, you may want to postpone the next stop temporarily in order to see the churches of Santo Spirito and Santa Maria del Carmine before they close for the afternoon. If this is the case, follow the directions given below and return here after seeing the churches. Otherwise, turn left onto the Sdrucciolo dei Pitti.

As you emerge from the Sdrucciolo into Piazza dei Pitti, you will see one of Florence's largest (if not one of its best) architectural set pieces unfold before you: the famous **Pitti Palace.** The original palazzo, built for the Pitti family around 1460, comprised only the middle cube (on the upper floors, the middle seven windows) of the present building. In 1549 the property was sold to the Medici, and Bartolomeo Ammannati was called in to make substantial additions. Although he apparently operated on the principle that more is better, he succeeded only in producing proof that enough is enough.

Today the immense building houses four separate museums: the former **Royal Apartments,** containing furnishings from a remodeling done in the 19th century; the **Museo degli Argenti,** containing a vast collection of Medici household treasures; the **Galleria d'Arte Moderna,** containing a collection of 19th- and 20th-century paintings, mostly Tuscan; and, most famous, the **Galleria Palatina,** containing a broad collection of 16th- and 17th-century paintings. The rooms of the latter remain much as the Medici family left them, but, as Mary McCarthy pointed out, the Florentines invented modern bad taste, and many art lovers view the floor-to-ceiling painting displays here as Italy's most egregious exercise in conspicuous consumption, aesthetic overkill, and trumpery. Still, the collection possesses high points that are very high indeed, including a number of portraits by Titian and an unparalleled collection of paintings by Raphael, among them the famous *Madonna of the Chair. Piazza Pitti, tel. 055/210323. Admission: Galleria Palatina, 8,000 lire; Museo degli Argenti, 6,000 lire; Royal Apartments, by appointment (tel. 055/287096, open Sat. 10:30–11:30; 6,000 lire, valid also for the Galleria d'Arte Moderna); Galleria d'Arte Moderna: 6,000 lire. Open Tues.–Sat. 9–2, Sun. 9–1.*

Return to Via Maggio from the Pitti and take Via dei Michelozzi, a short street that leads into Piazza Santo Spirito; at the north end rises the church of **Santo Spirito.** Its unfinished facade gives nothing away, but, in fact, the interior, although it appears chilly (or even cold) compared with later churches, is one of the most important pieces of architecture in all Italy. One of a pair of Florentine church interiors designed by Filippo Brunelleschi in the early 15th century (the other, San Lorenzo, is described in Tour 3: From the Duomo to Santa Croce and Beyond, *below*) it was here that Brunelleschi supplied definitive solutions to the two main problems of interior Renaissance church design: how to build a cross-shape interior using classical architectural elements borrowed from antiquity and how to reflect in that interior the order and regularity that Renaissance scientists (of which Brunelleschi was one) were at the time discovering in the natural world around them.

Brunelleschi's solution to the first problem was brilliantly simple: Turn a Greek temple inside out. To see this clearly, look at one of the stately arch-topped arcades that separate the side aisles from the central nave. Whereas the ancient Greek temples were walled buildings surrounded by classical colonnades, Brunelleschi's churches were classical arcades surrounded by walled buildings. This was perhaps the single most brilliant architectural idea of the early Renaissance, and its brilliance overthrew the previous era's religious taboo against pagan architecture once and for all, triumphantly reclaiming that architecture for Christian use.

Brunelleschi's solution to the second problem—making the entire interior orderly and regular—was mathematically precise: He designed the ground plan of the church so that all its parts are proportionally related. The transepts and nave have exactly the same width; the side aisles are exactly half as wide as the nave; the little chapels off the side aisles are exactly half as deep as the side aisles; the chancel and transepts are exactly one-eighth the depth of the nave; and so on, with dizzying exactitude. For Brunelleschi, such a design technique would have been far more than a convenience; it would have been a matter of passionate conviction. Like most theoreticians of his day, he believed that mathematical regularity and aesthetic beauty were opposite sides of the same coin, that one was not possible without the other. The conviction stood unchallenged for a hundred years, until Michelangelo turned his hand to architecture and designed the Medici Chapel and the Biblioteca Laurenziana in San Lorenzo across town (*see* Tour 3: From the Duomo to Santa Croce and Beyond, *below*), and thereby unleashed a revolution of his own that spelled the end of the Renaissance in architecture and the beginning of the Baroque.

Leave Piazza Santo Spirito by Via Sant'Agostino, diagonally across the square from the church entrance, and follow it to Via dei Serragli. You are now in the heart of the working-class Oltrarno neighborhood, which is to Florence what Trastevere is to Rome: unpretentious, independent, and proud. Cross Via dei Serragli and follow Via Santa Monaca to Piazza del Carmine. The church of **Santa Maria del Carmine** at the south end contains, in the Brancacci Chapel, at the end of the right transept, a masterpiece of Renaissance painting, a fresco cycle that changed art forever. Fire almost destroyed the church in the 18th century, but miraculously the Brancacci Chapel survived almost intact.

The cycle is the work of three artists: Masaccio and Masolino, who began it in 1423, and Filippino Lippi, who finished it after a long interruption during which the sponsoring Brancacci family was exiled, some 50 years later. It was Masaccio's work that opened a new frontier for painting; tragically, he did not live to experience the revolution his innovations caused, for he was killed in 1428 at the age of 27.

Masaccio collaborated with Masolino on several of the paintings, but by himself he painted *The Tribute Money* on the upper-left wall; *Peter Baptizing the Neophytes* on the upper altar wall; *The Distribution of the Goods of the Church* on the lower altar wall; and, most famous, *The Expulsion of Adam and Eve* on the chapel's upper-left entrance pier. If you look closely at the latter painting and compare it with some of the chapel's other works, you'll see a pronounced difference. The figures of Adam and Eve possess a startling presence, a presence primarily due to the dramatic way in which their bodies seem to reflect light. Masaccio here shaded his figures consistently, in order to suggest emphatically a single, strong source of light within the world of the painting but outside its frame. In so doing, he succeeded in imitating with paint the real-world effect of light on mass, and he thereby imparted to his figures a sculptural reality unprecedented in its day. To contemporary Florentines his Adam and Eve must have seemed surrounded by light and air in a way that was almost magical. All the painters of Florence came to look.

These matters have to do with technique, but with *The Expulsion of Adam and Eve*, Masaccio's skill went beyond technical innovation, and if you look hard at the faces of Adam and Eve you'll see more than just finely modeled figures. You'll see terrible shame and terrible suffering, and you'll see them depicted with a humanity rarely achieved in art. *Admission to Brancacci Chapel: 6,000 lire. Open Mon. and Wed.–Sat. 10–5, Sun. 1–5.*

From Piazza del Carmine, return to Via dei Serragli and walk back across the river over the Ponte alla Carraia (with a fine view of the Ponte Santa Trinita, to the right) to Piazza Carlo Goldoni, named for the 18th-century Italian dramatist. Here you again have a choice: You can turn left to explore the Cascine, a vast (2-mile-long) park laid out in the 18th century on the site of the Medici dairy farms (it begins some 10 blocks downriver, at Piazza Vittorio Veneto), or, if you haven't overdosed on art, you can turn right and return to the Uffizi, which is open all day on most days and is usually far less crowded in the late afternoon than in the morning.

Tour 3: From the Duomo to Santa Croce and Beyond

Like the other two tours, Tour 3 begins at the Duomo. From the west side of the Baptistery, follow Borgo San Lorenzo north one block to Piazza San Lorenzo, in which stands a bustling outdoor clothing market overlooked by the unfinished facade of the **㉓** church of **San Lorenzo.** Like Santo Spirito on the other side of the Arno, the interior of San Lorenzo was designed by Filippo Brunelleschi in the early 15th century. The two church interiors are similar in design and effect and proclaim with ringing clarity the beginning of the Renaissance in architecture. (If you have not yet taken Tour 2, you might want to read its entry on Santo Spirito now; it describes the nature of Brunelleschi's architectural breakthrough, and its main points apply equally well here. *See* Tour 2: From the Duomo to the Cascine, *above.*) San Lorenzo possesses one feature that Santo Spirito lacks, however, which considerably heightens the dramatic effect of the interior: the grid of dark, inlaid marble lines on the floor. The grid makes the rigorous regularity with which the interior was designed immediately visible and offers an illuminating lesson on the laws of perspective. If you stand in the middle of the nave at the church entrance, on the line that stretches to the high altar, every element in the church—the grid, the nave columns, the side aisles, the coffered nave ceiling—seems to march inexorably toward a hypothetical vanishing point beyond the high altar, exactly as in a single-point-perspective painting.

The church complex contains two other important interiors, designed by Michelangelo, which contrast markedly with the interior of the church proper and in their day marked the end of Brunelleschi's powerful influence and of the High Renaissance in architecture. The first is the **Biblioteca Laurenziana,** the Laurentian Library and its famous anteroom, entered from the church cloister (exit the church through the door at the left side of the nave just before the crossing, take an immediate right, climb the stairs to the cloister balcony, and enter the first door to the right). Michelangelo the architect was every bit as original as Michelangelo the sculptor. Unlike Brunelleschi, however, he was not interested in expressing the ordered harmony of the spheres in his architecture. He was interested in experimentation and invention and in expressing a personal vision that was at times highly idiosyncratic.

It was never more idiosyncratic than here. This strangely shaped anteroom has had scholars scratching their heads for centuries. In a space more than two stories high, why did Michelangelo limit his use of columns and pilasters to the upper two-thirds of the wall? Why didn't he rest them on strong pedestals instead of on huge, decorative curlicued scrolls, which rob them of all visual support? Why did he recess them into the wall, which makes them look weaker still? The architectural elements here do not stand firm and strong and tall, as inside the church next door; instead, they seem to be pressed into the wall as if into putty, giving the room a soft, rubbery look that is one of the strangest effects ever achieved by classical architecture. It is almost as if Michelangelo purposely set out to defy his predecessors, intentionally flouting the conventions of the High Renaissance in order to see what kind of bizarre, mannered effect might result. His innovations were tremendously influential and produced a period of architectural experimentation—the Mannerist era in architecture—that eventually evolved into the Baroque. As his contemporary Giorgio Vasari (the first art historian) put it, "Artisans have been infinitely and perpetually indebted to him because he broke the bonds and chains of a way of working that had become habitual by common usage."

Many critics have thought that the anteroom is a failure and have complained that Michelangelo's experiment here was willful and perverse. But nobody has ever complained about the room's staircase (best viewed head-on), which emerges from the library with the visual force of an unstoppable flow of lava. In its highly sculptural conception and execution, it is quite simply one of the most original and beautiful staircases in the world. *Admission free. Open Mon.–Sat. 10–1.*

The other Michelangelo interior is San Lorenzo's **New Sacristy,** so called to distinguish it from Brunelleschi's **Old Sacristy** (which can be entered from inside the church at the end of the left transept). The New Sacristy is reached from outside the rear of the church, through the imposing **Cappella dei Principi**, the Medici mausoleum that was begun in 1605 and kept marble workers busy for several hundred years.

Michelangelo received the commission for the New Sacristy in 1520 from Cardinal Giulio de' Medici, who later became Pope Clement VII and wanted a new burial chapel for his father, Giuliano, his uncle Lorenzo the Magnificent, and two recently deceased cousins. The result was a tour de force of architecture and sculpture. Architecturally, Michelangelo was as original and inventive here as ever, but it is—quite properly—the powerful sculptural compositions of the side-wall tombs that dominate the room. The scheme is allegorical: On the wall tomb to the right are figures representing day and night, and on the wall tomb to the left are figures representing dawn and dusk; above them are idealized portraits of the two cousins, usually interpreted to represent the active life and the contemplative life. But the allegorical meanings are secondary; what is most important is the intense presence of the sculptural figures, the force with which they hit the viewer. Michelangelo's contemporaries were so awed by the impact of this force (in his sculpture here and elsewhere) that they invented an entirely new word to describe the phenomenon: *terribilità* (dreadfulness). To this day the word is used only when describing his work, and it is in evidence here at the peak of its power. *Piazza di Madonna degli Aldobrandini, tel. 055/213206. Admission: 9,000 lire. Open Tues.–Sat. 9–2, Sun. 9–1.*

Just north of the Medici Chapel (a block up Via dell'Ariento) is Florence's busy main food market, the **Mercato Centrale.** If a reminder that Florence is more than just a museum is needed, this is the perfect place for it. There is food everywhere, some of it remarkably exotic, and many of the displays verge on the magnificent. At the Mercato Nuovo, near Ponte Vecchio, you will see tourists petting the snout of the bronze boar for good luck; here you will see Florentines petting the snout of a real one, very recently deceased and available for tonight's dinner.

Return to the clothing market in front of San Lorenzo, and from the north end of the piazza follow Via dei Gori east one block and turn left onto Via Cavour. As you turn the corner, you will (24) pass **Palazzo Medici-Riccardi** (entrance on Via Cavour). Begun in 1444 by Michelozzo for Cosimo de' Medici, the main attraction here is the interior chapel on the upper floor. Painted on its walls is Benozzo Gozzoli's famous *Procession of the Magi,* finished in 1460 and celebrating both the birth of Christ and the greatness of the Medici family, whose portraits it contains. Like his contemporary Ghirlandaio, Gozzoli was not a revolutionary painter and is today considered less than first-rate because of his old-fashioned (even for his day) technique. Gozzoli's gift, however, was for entrancing the eye, not challenging the mind, and on those terms his success here is beyond question. The paintings are full of activity yet somehow frozen in time in a way that fails utterly as realism but succeeds triumphantly as soon as the demand for realism is set aside. Entering the chapel is like walking into the middle of a magnificently illustrated child's storybook, and the beauty of the illustrations makes this one of the most unpretentiously enjoyable rooms in the entire city. *Via Cavour 1, tel. 055/276–0340. Admission: 5,000 lire. Open Mon., Tues., Thurs.–Sat. 10–6, Sun. 10–noon.*

From the Palazzo Medici-Riccardi, follow Via Cavour two blocks north to Piazza San Marco. At the north end of the square is the church of San Marco; attached to the church (entrance just to the right of the church facade) is a former Dominican monastery that now houses the **Museo San Marco.** The museum—in fact, the entire monastery—is a memorial to Fra Angelico, the Dominican monk who, when he was alive, was as famous for his piety as for his paintings. When the monastery was built in 1437 he decorated it with his frescoes, which were meant to spur religious contemplation; when the building was turned into a museum, other works of his from all over the city were brought here for display. His paintings are simple and direct and furnish a compelling contrast to the Palazzo Medici-Riccardi Chapel (Fra Angelico probably would have considered the glitter of Gozzoli's work there worldly and blasphemous). The entire monastery is worth exploring, for Fra Angelico's paintings are everywhere, including the Chapter House, at the top of the stairs leading to the upper floor (the famous *Annunciation)*, in the upper-floor monks' cells (each monk was given a different religious subject for contemplation), and in the gallery just off the cloister as you enter. The latter room contains, among many other works, his beautiful *Last Judgment;* as usual with Last Judgments, the tortures of the damned are far more inventive than the pleasures of the redeemed. *Piazza San Marco 1, tel. 055/210741. Admission: 6,000 lire. Open Tues.-Sat. 9–2, Sun. 9–1.*

From Piazza San Marco, take a short detour a half block down Via Ricasoli (which runs back toward the Duomo from the square's east side) to the **Galleria dell'Accademia.** The museum contains a notable collection of Florentine paintings dating from the 13th to the 18th centuries, but it is most famous for its collection of statues by Michelangelo—including the unfinished *Slaves*—which were meant for the tomb of Michelangelo's patron and nemesis Pope Julius II (and which seem to be fighting their way out of the marble), and the original *David*, which was moved here from Piazza della Signoria in 1873. The *David* was commissioned in 1501 by the Opera del Duomo (Cathedral Works Committee), which gave the 26-year-old sculptor a leftover block of marble that had been ruined by another artist. Michelangelo's success with the defective block was so dramatic that the city showered him with honors, and the Opera del Duomo voted to build him a house and a studio in which to live and work.

Today the *David* is beset not by Goliath but by tourists, and seeing the statue at all—much less really studying it—can be a trial. After a 1991 attack upon it by a hammer-wielding frustrated artist (luckily, the only damage was a few minor nicks on the toes), the sculpture was surrounded by a plexiglass barrier. But a close look is worth the effort it takes to combat the crowd. The statue is not quite what it seems. It is so poised and graceful and alert—so miraculously *alive*—that it is often considered to be the definitive embodiment of the ideals of the High Renaissance in sculpture. But its true place in the history of art is a bit more complicated.

As Michelangelo well knew, the Renaissance painting and sculpture that preceded his work were deeply concerned with ideal form. Perfection of proportion was the ever-sought Holy Grail; during the Renaissance, ideal proportion was equated with ideal beauty, and ideal beauty was equated with spiritual perfection. In painting, Raphael's tender Madonnas are perhaps the preeminent expression of this philosophy: They are meant to embody a perfect beauty that is at once physical and spiritual.

But Michelangelo's *David,* despite its supremely calm and dignified pose, departs from these ideals. As a moment's study will show, Michelangelo did not give the statue ideal proportions. The head is slightly too large for the body, the arms are slightly too large for the torso, and the hands are dramatically too large for the arms. By High Renaissance standards these are defects, but the impact and beauty of the *David* are such that it is the *standards* that must be called into question, not the statue. Michelangelo was a revolutionary artist (and the first Mannerist) because he brought a new expressiveness to art: He created the "defects" of the *David* intentionally. He knew exactly what he was doing, and he did it in order to express and embody, as powerfully as possible in a single figure, an entire biblical story. David's hands *are* too big, but so was Goliath, and these are the hands that slew him. *Via Ricasoli 60, tel. 055/214375. Admission: 10,000 lire. Open Tues.–Sat. 9–2, Sun. 9–1.*

From the Accademia, return to Piazza San Marco and turn right onto Via Battisti, which leads into Piazza della Santissima Annunziata. The building directly across the square as you enter is the **Ospedale degli Innocenti,** or Foundling Hospital, built by Brunelleschi in 1419. He designed the building's portico with his usual rigor, building it out of the two shapes he considered mathematically (and therefore philosophically and aesthetically) perfect: the square and the circle. Below the level of the arches, the portico encloses a row of perfect cubes; above the level of the arches, the portico encloses a row of intersecting hemispheres. The whole geometric scheme is articulated with Corinthian columns, capitals, and arches borrowed directly from antiquity. At the time he designed the portico, Brunelleschi was also designing the interior of San Lorenzo, using the same basic ideas. But since the portico was finished before San Lorenzo, the Ospedale degli Innocenti takes the historical prize: It is the very first Renaissance building. The 10 ceramic medallions of swaddled infants that decorate it are by Andrea della Robbia, done in approximately 1487.

The church at the north end of the square is **Santissima Annunziata;** it was designed in 1447 by Michelozzo, who gave it an uncommon (and lovely) entrance cloister. The interior is an extreme rarity for Florence: a sumptuous example of the Baroque. But it is not really a fair example, since it is merely 17th-century Baroque decoration applied willy-nilly to an earlier structure—exactly the sort of violent remodeling exercise that has given the Baroque a bad name ever since. The **Tabernacle of the Annunziata,** immediately inside the entrance to the left, illustrates the point. The lower half, with its stately Corinthian columns and carved frieze bearing the Medici arms, was built at the same time as the church; the upper half, with its erupting curves and impish sculpted cherubs (badly in need of a bath), was added 200 years later. Each is effective in its own way, but together they serve only to prove that dignity is rarely comfortable wearing a party hat.

One block east of the entrance to Santissima Annunziata (on the left side of Via della Colonna) is the **Museo Archeologico.** If time and interest permit, a visit here is unquestionably worthwhile. The collection contains Etruscan, Egyptian, and Greco-Roman antiquities; guidebooks in English are available. The Etruscan collection is particularly notable—the largest in northern Italy—and includes the famous bronze *Chimera*, which was discovered (without the tail, which is a reconstruction) in the 16th century. *Via della Colonna 36, tel. 055/247-8641. Admission: 6,000 lire. Open Tues.–Sat. 9–2, Sun. 9–1.*

Follow Via della Colonna east to Borgo Pinti and turn right, following Borgo Pinti through the arch of San Piero to the small Piazza San Pier Maggiore. The tower at the south end is the **Torre dei Corbizi,** dating from the Middle Ages. During the Guelph-Ghibelline conflict of the 13th and 14th centuries, Florence was a forest of such towers—more than 200 of them, if the smaller three- and four-story towers are included. Today only a handful survive.

From Piazza San Pier Maggiore, Via Palmieri (which becomes Via Isola delle Stinche) leads to Via Torta, which curves around to the left—it takes its shape from the outline of a Roman amphitheater once located here—and opens out onto Piazza Santa Croce.

Like the Duomo, the church of **Santa Croce** is Gothic, but (also like the Duomo) its facade dates only from the 19th century. The interior is most famous for its art and its tombs. As a burial place, the church is a Florentine pantheon and probably contains a larger number of important skeletons than any church in Italy. Among others, the tomb of Michelangelo is immediately to the right as you enter (he is said to have chosen this spot so that the first thing he would see on Judgment Day, when the graves of the dead fly open, would be Brunelleschi's Duomo dome through Santa Croce's open doors); the tomb of Galileo Galilei, who produced evidence that the earth is not the center of the universe (and who was not granted a Christian burial until 100 years after his death because of it), is on the left wall, opposite Michelangelo; the tomb of Niccolò Machiavelli, the Renaissance political theoretician whose brutally pragmatic philosophy so influenced the Medici, is halfway down the nave on the right; the grave of Lorenzo Ghiberti, creator of the Gates of Paradise doors to the Baptistery, is halfway down the nave on the left; the tomb of composer Gioacchino Rossini, of "William Tell Overture" fame, is at the end of the nave on the right. The monument to Dante Alighieri, the greatest Italian poet, is a memorial rather than a tomb (he is actually buried in Ravenna); it is located on the right wall near the tomb of Michelangelo.

The collection of art within the church and the church complex is by far the most important of that in any church in Florence. Historically, the most significant works are probably the Giotto frescoes in the two adjacent chapels immediately to the right of the altar, which illustrate scenes from the lives of St. John the Evangelist and St. John the Baptist (in the right-hand chapel) and scenes from the life of St. Francis (in the left-hand chapel). Time has not been kind to them; over the centuries wall tombs were introduced into the middle of them, whitewash and plaster covered them, and in the 19th century they underwent a clumsy restoration. But the reality that Giotto introduced into painting can still be seen. He did not paint beautifully stylized symbols of religion, as the Byzantine style that preceded him prescribed; instead he painted drama—St. Francis surrounded by grieving monks at the very moment of his death. This was a radical shift in emphasis, and it changed the course of art. Before him, the role of painting was to symbolize the attributes of God; after him, it was to imitate life. The style of his work is indeed primitive, compared with later painting, but in its day (the Proto-Renaissance of the early 14th century), it caused a sensation that was not equaled for another 100 years. He was for his time the equal of both Masaccio and Michelangelo.

Among the church's other highlights are Donatello's *Annunciation,* one of the most tender and eloquent expressions of surprise ever sculpted (located on the right wall two-thirds of the way down the nave); Taddeo Gaddi's 14th-century frescoes illustrating the life of the Virgin, clearly showing the influence of Giotto (in the chapel at the end of the right transept); and Donatello's *Crucifix,* criticized by Brunelleschi for making Christ look like a peasant (in the chapel at the end of the left transept). Outside the church proper, in the church museum off the cloister, is Giovanni Cimabue's 13th-century *Triumphal Cross,* which was badly damaged by the flood of 1966. The **Pazzi Chapel,** yet another of Brunelleschi's crisp exercises in architectural geometry, is at the end of the cloister. *Piazza Santa Croce 16, tel. 055/244619. Church Cloister and Museum admission: 4,000 lire. Open Mar.–Sept., Thurs.–Tues. 10–12:30 and 2:30–6:30; Oct.–Feb., Thurs.–Tues. 10–12:30 and 3–5.*

After leaving Santa Croce you have a choice. If you have a fair amount of stamina left, you can cross the river at the Ponte alle Grazie (west of the church complex) and climb the Monte alle Croci above it to investigate the view from **Piazzale Michelangelo** and the church of **San Miniato al Monte;** the latter is a famous example of Romanesque architecture dating from the 11th century and contains a fine 13th-century apse mosaic. If the climb seems too arduous, you can take bus No. 12 from the Lungarno to Piazzale Michelangelo, or you can (as always) return to the Uffizi.

Day Trips from Florence

Fiesole. The closest destination for a day or half-day trip from Florence is Fiesole, a lovely—and hilly—town only 20 minutes away from downtown Florence by bus (No. 7). Fiesole has wonderful views of Florence and the countryside, an ancient Roman amphitheater, a medieval cathedral, and a pleasantly relaxed atmosphere. This is a good place for a picnic, a walk, or a longer hike through the surrounding countryside. For more information, contact the tourist office at Piazza Mino da Fiesole 37, tel. 055/598–720. It's open Apr.–Oct., weekdays 9–1 and 3–6; Nov.–Mar., weekdays 9–1 and 2:30–5:30, and Sat. 9–1.

Siena. This perfectly preserved medieval city has what is considered one of the world's most beautiful squares. SITA buses from Florence take about 90 minutes and run frequently throughout the day; trains take 75 minutes, requiring a change at Empoli. *See* Chapter 4, Tuscany.

Lucca. Puccini's hometown is a gracious and civilized city, with decorative churches, medieval streets, and a parklike promenade on 16th-century ramparts. Lucca is about 90 minutes from Florence by train and half an hour from Pisa by train. *See* Chapter 4, Tuscany.

Pisa. You visit Pisa to see the magnificent Romanesque-Gothic architecture of the cathedral, baptistery, and the famous bell tower. Pisa is about half an hour from Lucca by train and an hour from Florence by train. *See* Chapter 4, Tuscany.

Arezzo. Though rather plain, Arezzo has a well-preserved medieval-Renaissance center, a picturesque square where an open-air antiques fair and flea market is held on the first weekend of every month, and the seminal frescoes of Piero della Francesca in the church of San Francesco. Arezzo is an hour from Florence by train, 90 minutes by SITA bus. *See* Chapter 4, Tuscany.

Bologna. This easygoing but well-organized city is known for its rich cuisine, porticoed streets, and fine art collections; it is also the site of Italy's oldest university. Bologna is only one hour from Florence by fast train, and train service is frequent. *See* Chapter 10, Emilia-Romagna.

Shopping

Since the days of the medieval guilds, Florence has been synonymous with fine craftsmanship and good business. Such time-honored Florentine specialties as antiques (and reproductions), bookbinding, jewelry, lace, leather goods, silk, and straw attest to that. More recently, the Pitti fashion shows and the burgeoning textile industry in nearby Prato have added fine clothing to the merchandise available in the shops of Florence.

Another medieval feature is the distinct feel of the different shopping areas, a throwback to the days when each district supplied a different product. Florence's most elegant shops are concentrated in the center of town, with Via Tornabuoni leading the list for designer clothing and the Ponte Vecchio housing the city's jewelers, as it has since the 16th century.

Those with a tight budget or a sense of adventure may want to take a look at the souvenir stands under the loggia of the Mercato Nuovo, or at the stalls that line the streets between the church of San Lorenzo and the Mercato Centrale, or the open-air market that takes place in the Cascine Park every Tuesday morning. You might also browse through the bric-a-brac and old postcards at the flea market at Piazza Ciompi, off Via Pietrapiana near Santa Croce (open Mon.–Sat. 9–1 and 4–7, last Sun. of the month 9–7). In addition, an outdoor crafts fair is held in Piazza Santo Spirito on the second Sunday of every month.

Among the affordable souvenirs to be found in Florence are straw and leather goods, antiqued wooden trays and boxes, and Florentine stationery and desk accessories. Although the Mercato Nuovo is well stocked with souvenirs, you may be able to get a better price at the San Lorenzo street market. In either place, be sure to bargain.

Shops in Florence are generally open from 9 to 1 and 3:30 to 7:30 and closed on Sundays and Monday mornings most of the year. During the summer the hours are usually 9–1 and 4–8, with closings on Saturday afternoons but not Monday mornings. When locating the stores, remember that the addresses with "r" in them, which stands for "rosso," or red, and indicates a commercial address, follow a separate numbering system from the black residential addresses. Most shops take major credit cards and will ship purchases, though it's wiser to take your purchases with you.

Alinari (Via della Vigna Nuova 46/r). This is one of Florence's oldest and most prestigious photography shops. Prints of its historic photographs are sold along with books and posters. A museum next door chronicles the renowned Alinari family's involvement in photography.

Calamai (Via Cavour 78/r). One of Florence's largest gift shops, Calamai carries everything from inexpensive stationery to housewares in bright, bold colors and designs in its largest of three stores.

Salimbeni (Via Matteo Palmieri 14/r). Long one of Florence's best art bookshops, Salimbeni specializes in publications on Tuscany; it publishes many itself.

Sbigoli Terrecotte (Via Sant'Egidio 4/r). This crafts shop carries a wide selection of terra-cotta and ceramic vases, pots, cups, and saucers.

Leather Guild (Piazza Santa Croce 20/r). This is one of many such shops throughout the area that produce inexpensive, antique-looking leather goods of mass appeal, but here you can see the craftspersons at work.

Cimabue. (Piazza Santa Croce 9/r). An extensive selection of leather goods—wallets, bags, briefcases, and gloves among them—with free initialing done on the spot and discounts for the asking, make this shop worth a visit.

Giannini (Piazza Pitti 37/r). One of Florence's oldest paper-goods stores, Giannini is *the* place to buy the marbleized version, which comes in a variety of forms ranging from flat sheets to boxes and even pencils.

Soluzioni (Via Maggio 82/r). This offbeat store displays some of the most unusual items on this staid street, ranging from clocks to compacts, all selected with an eye for the eccentric.

Dining

Florentines are justifiably proud of their robust food, claiming that it became the basis for French cuisine when Catherine de' Medici took a battery of Florentine chefs with her when she reluctantly relocated to become queen of France in the 16th century.

A typical Tuscan repast starts with an antipasto of *crostini* (toasted bread spread with a chicken-liver pâté) or cured meats such as *prosciutto crudo* (a salty prosciutto), *finocchiona* (salami seasoned with fennel), and *salsiccia di cinghiale* (sausage made from wild boar). This is the time to start right in on the local wine—Chianti, *naturalmente*. Don't be surprised if the waiter brings an entire straw-covered flask to the table. Customers are charged only for what they consume (*al consumo*, the arrangement is called), but it's wise to ask for a flask or bottle to be opened then and there, since leftover wines are often mixed together.

Peculiar to Florence are the vegetable-and-bread soups such as *pappa al pomodoro* (tomatoes, bread, olive oil, onions, and basil), *ribollita* (white beans, bread, cabbage, and onions), or, in the summer, *panzanella* (tomatoes, onions, vinegar, oil, and bread).

Second to none among the *secondi piatti* (main courses) is *bistecca alla fiorentina*—a thick slab of local Chianina beef, grilled over charcoal, seasoned with olive oil, salt, and pepper, and served rare—but save this for a splurge, since it's not exactly a budget item. *Trippa alla fiorentina* (tripe stewed with tomatoes in a meat sauce) and *arista* (roast loin of pork seasoned with rosemary) are also regional specialties, as are many other roasted meats that go especially well with the Chianti.

Tuscan desserts are typically Spartan. The cheese is the hard *pecorino*, and locals like to go for the even tougher *biscottini di Prato*, which provide an excuse for dunking in the potent, sweet dessert wine called *vin santo*, made of dried grapes, which they say will bring the dead back to life! Strange to say, cheesecake has become a popular dessert in Florence, even in otherwise traditional trattorias.

Remember that dining hours are earlier here than in Rome, starting at 12:30 for the midday meal and from 7:30 on in the evening. Many of Florence's restaurants are small, so go early to be sure you get a table. Be prepared to share a table if you go to an informal trattoria, usually downstairs, called a *buca* (literally, "hole in the wall"). Reservations are a must. When going to the restaurants, note that the "r" in some of the following addresses indicates the red numbering system used for Florentine businesses, which differs from the black numbers used for residences.

Unless otherwise noted, reservations are not needed and dress is casual. Highly recommended restaurants are indicated by a star ★.

Under 30,000 lire

Acqua al Due. You'll find this tiny restaurant near the Bargello. It serves an array of Florentine specialties in a lively, very casual setting. Acqua al Due is popular with young Florentines, partly because it's air-conditioned in the summer and always open late. *Via dell'Acqua 2/r, tel. 055/284170. AE, DC, MC, V. Closed Mon. and Aug.*

Buca dell'Orafo. One of the best of the Florentine buca restaurants, Buca dell'Orafo is set in the cellar of a former goldsmith's shop near the Ponte Vecchio. It offers all the Florentine specialties and could be the place to splurge on a bistecca alla fiorentina or to enjoy *fagioli al fiasco* (beans). *Via dei Girolami 28, tel. 055/213619. Reservations advised. No credit cards. Closed Sun., Mon., and Aug.*

Buca Mario. Expect to share a table at this characteristically unadorned buca near Santa Maria Novella, with typical Florentine whitewashed walls and dark wood fittings. The menu includes down-to-earth Tuscan food such as *stracotto* (beef stew) with beans. *Piazza Ottaviani 15/r, tel. 055/214–179. Reservations advised in the evening. AE, DC, MC, V. Closed Wed., Thurs. lunch, and Aug.*

Enzo e Piero. This rustic trattoria is a neighborhood favorite and a change from more touristy restaurants. The day's specials may include veal stew; roasted or grilled meat is always on the menu. A large wine barrel divides two of the three dining rooms, which have wood paneling and rough white stucco walls. The fixed-price menu, at about 17,000 lire, is a bargain. *Via Faenza 105, tel. 055/214901. Reservations advised in the evening. AE, DC, MC, V. Closed Sun.*

Il Fagioli. This typical Florentine trattoria near Santa Croce has simple decor and a menu of local dishes, including *ribollita* (vegetable soup) and *polpettine* (meatballs). *Corso Tintori 47/r, tel. 055/244–285. Reservations advised. No credit cards. Closed weekends, Aug., and Christmas Day.*

Mario da Ganino. On a side street between the Duomo and the Palazzo Vecchio, this tiny trattoria is informal, rustic, and cheerful; in warm months you can eat outdoors under market umbrellas. You are offered a taste of mortadella (at no charge) to start off your meal, which might include some of the home-made pasta on the menu. *Gnudoni* (ravioli filling without the pasta casing) are a specialty, as is cheesecake for dessert. Main courses uphold Florentine tradition, with grilled steak and chops and bean dishes. Get there early; it seats only about 35, and double that number in good weather at outside tables. *Piazza dei Cimatori 4/r, tel. 055/214125. Reservations advised. AE, DC. Closed Sun. and Aug. 15–25.*

Under 24,000 lire

★ **Angiolino.** This bustling little trattoria in the Oltrarno district is popular with locals and visitors. It has a real charcoal grill and an old wood-burning stove to keep customers warm on nippy days. The menu offers such Tuscan specialties as ribollita and a classic bistecca alla fiorentina. The bistecca can push the check up into a higher price category. *Via Santo Spirito 36/r, 055/239–8976. Reservations advised in the evening. No credit cards. Closed Sun. dinner, Mon., and last 3 weeks in July.*

La Maremmana. A display of market-fresh victuals at the entrance hints at what's on the menu here. This is an authentic Florentine trattoria near Santa Croce, and you will probably have to share a table in the wood-paneled dining room. The fixed-price menu offers generous servings and good value; it may include *zuppa di verdura* (green vegetable soup) and *arista* (roast pork). *Via dei Macci 77/r, tel. 055/241226. No credit cards. Closed Sun.*

Mossacce. You share a table here and watch the cook in the glassed-in kitchen prepare your order, chosen from a menu of Florentine classics. *Via del Proconsolo 55/r, tel. 055/294361. AE, MC, V. Closed weekends and Aug.*

Cantinone del Gallo Nero. This is a wine cellar in the Oltrarno district, with vaulted brick ceilings, excellent Chianti wines, and such simple but filling Tuscan food as *ribollita* (vegetable soup) and crostini. *Via Santo Spirito 6/r, tel. 055/218–898. No credit cards. Closed Mon.*

Del Carmine. A typical neighborhood trattoria, Del Carmine has been discovered by tourists out to see the Masaccio frescoes in the Carmine church across the square. It serves simple Florentine fare, including *fagioli al fiasco* (beans) and arista. *Piaz-*

za del Carmine 18/r, tel. 055/218–601. *Reservations advised.*
AE, DC, MC, V. Closed Sun.
Za-Za. Slightly more upscale than neighboring trattorias, Za-
Za attracts white-collar workers and theater people. Posters of
movie stars hang on wood-paneled walls, and classic Florentine
cuisine is served at communal tables. *Piazza Mercato Centrale*
16/r, tel. 055/215411. Reservations advised. AE, DC, MC, V.
Closed Sun. and Aug.

Under 20,000 lire

Casalinga. Loitering is discouraged in this bustling trattoria
near the church of Santo Spirito, where there is always someone waiting for a seat at one of the communal tables. In a typically spare, wood-paneled setting under high vaulted ceilings
you'll have a choice of such pastas as *pappardelle* (broad noodles), soups, and roasted meat. *Via dei Michelozzi 9, tel. 055/*
218624. No reservations. No credit cards. Closed Sat., Sun.
Fiaschetteria. Between the Palazzo Vecchio and Santa Croce,
this is a typical Florentine wineshop with a counter where
wine, salami, and cheese are sold. You can have a sandwich
made to order or have the pasta or soup of the day. *Via dei Neri*
17/r, no telephone. No credit cards. Closed Sun.
Ginone. Located in the Santo Spirito neighborhood, this is not
a traditional trattoria in that food is prepared ahead and served
from a counter cafeteria style. But it has atmosphere, rustic
chairs, and old photos of Florence. Different types of *zuppa di*
fagioli (bean soup) and *stracotto* (braised beef) may be among
the day's offerings. *Via dei Serragli 35, tel. 055/218758. No res-*
ervations. No credit cards. Closed Sun.
Mario. Clean and classic, this family-run trattoria on the corner of Piazza del Mercato near San Lorenzo offers a genuine
Florentine atmosphere, with oilcloth on the tables, and a
glassed-in kitchen. Thick ribollita, pappardelle, or market-
fresh *verdure* (vegetables) are good choices. Open for lunch
only. It's just around the corner from Za-Za (*see above*). *Via*
Rosina 2/r (Piazza del Mercato Centrale) tel. 055/218550. No
credit cards. Closed evenings and Sun.
Nuti. On a central street near San Lorenzo, where there are a
number of budget eating places, Nuti is an old favorite with
minimal decor and good pizza, soups, and pasta. It's open all
day until 1 AM. *Via Borgo San Lorenzo 22, tel. 055/210–145. No*
credit cards. Closed Mon.

Wineshops In addition, there are many wineshops where you can have a
snack or sandwich. Of these, **Le Cantine** (Via dei Pucci) is stylish and popular; more modest are **Borgioli** (Piazza dell'Olio),
Fratellini (Via dei Cimatori), **Nicolino** (Volta dei Mercanti), and
Piccolo Vinaio (Via Castellani).

Splurge

★ **Le Fonticine.** Owner Silvano Bruci is from Tuscany, wife
Gianna from Emilia-Romagna, and the restaurant combines
the best of both worlds in a trattoria-type setting liberally
hung with Silvano's extensive collection of paintings. Emilia-
Romagna specialties such as tortellini ready the taste buds for
Tuscan grilled *porcini* (a type of mushrooms) so meaty they
provide serious competition for the bistecca alla fiorentina. *Via*

Nazionale 79/r, tel. 055/282106. Reservations advised. AE, DC, MC, V. Closed Sun., Mon, and July 25–Aug. 25.

The Arts and Nightlife

The Arts

For information on performances, exhibitions, sports events, and festivals, pick up a free copy of the **Comune Aperto** monthly bulletin at the city or APT tourist information offices (*see* Important Addresses and Numbers, *above*). The **Universalturismo Agency**, Via degli Speziali 7/r (tel. 055/217241), handles tickets to some events, including the Estate Fiesolana. Concerts in churches are often free, but venues change; check with tourist information offices.

Theater **Estate Fiesolana.** From June through August, this festival of theater, music, dance, and film takes place in the churches and the archaeological area of Fiesole (Teatro Romano, Fiesole, tel. 055/599931).

Concerts **Maggio Musicale Fiorentina.** This series of internationally acclaimed concerts and recitals is held in the **Teatro Comunale** (Corso Italia 16, tel. 055/277–9236) from late April through June. From December to early June, there is a concert season of the Orchestra Regionale Toscana, in the church of **Santo Stefano al Ponte Vecchio** (tel. 055/242767). Amici della Musica organizes concerts at the **Teatro della Pergola** (box office Via della Pergola 10/r, tel. 055/247–9652).

Opera Operas are performed in the Teatro Comunale from December through February.

Nightlife

Unlike the Romans and the Milanese, the frugal and reserved Florentines do not have a reputation for an active nightlife; however, the following places attract a mixed crowd of Florentines and visitors.

Piano Bars Many of the more expensive hotels have their own piano bars, where nonguests are welcome to come for an *aperitivo* or an after-dinner drink. The best view is from the bar at the **Excelsior** (Piazza Ognissanti 3, tel. 055/264201), on a rooftop garden overlooking the Arno. **Caffè Pitti** (Piazza Pitti 9, tel. 055/239–6241), an informal bar, is a popular afternoon and evening gathering place for Florence's international colony. The accent is on Brazil at **Caffè Voltaire** (Via della Scala 9/r, tel. 055/218255), where there's Latin food and music.

Jazz Clubs The generically named **Jazz Club** (Via Nuova dei Caccini 3, tel.
and Bars 055/247–9700) has live music and closes only on Monday. **BeeBop** (Via dei Servi) is a popular spot for beer-drinking students, despite the cover charge.

Discos The two largest discos, with the youngest crowds, are **Yab Yum** (Via Sassetti 5/r, tel. 055/282018) and **Space Electronic** (Via Palazzuolo 37, tel. 055/239–3082). Less frenetic alternatives are **Jackie O'** (Via Erta Canina 24, tel. 055/234–2442) and **Full Up** (Via della Vigna Vecchia 21/r, tel. 055/293006).

4 Tuscany

Lucca, Siena, and the Hill Towns

A region best known for its landscape, art, wines, and language—the language of Dante, Petrarch, and Boccaccio, whose Tuscan dialect became Italy's national tongue—Tuscany remains magically untouched. The region's hill towns and art cities allow the aesthetic eye to zoom in for a closer focus on a particular artist or school and quietly complement the artistic riches of Florence. And with its restful pace and orderly landscape of cultivated fields and vast vineyards, rural Tuscany offers a rejuvenating alternative to the fatiguing round of sightseeing that Florence too often demands. It's relatively easy to get around the region by train and bus, and you'll find reasonably priced lodging and dining in most small cities and towns.

For a long time the Tuscan hill towns were notorious. Even their earliest civilized settlers, the Etruscans, chose their city sites for defensive purposes (the fortress town of Fiesole, above Florence, is a fine surviving example). With the end of the Roman Empire, the region fell into disunity, and by the 11th century Tuscany had evolved into a collection of independent city-states, each city seeking to dominate, and sometimes forcibly overpower, its neighbors. The region then became embroiled in an apparently endless international quarrel between a long succession of popes and Holy Roman Emperors. By the 13th century, Tuscany had become a battleground: The infamous conflict between the Guelphs and the Ghibellines had begun. Today the hill towns are no longer fierce, although they retain a uniquely medieval air, and in most of them the citizens walk the same narrow streets and inhabit the same houses that their ancestors did 600 years ago.

Essential Information

Lodging Although affordable accommodations in Florence are abundant, there are generally few choices in the smaller towns in Tuscany, for the simple reason that there are few hotels. However, there is at least one reasonably priced commercial hotel in every town, a haven for traveling salesmen. Budget hotels tend to be small and are furnished with the bare necessities; on the other hand, they may offer a homey atmosphere and views of medieval streets and clay-tile roofs from their bedrooms. It is always advisable to book a room before arriving, even if it's just a day ahead or in the morning before your arrival. Hotels in Tuscany's smaller towns are less likely than those in Florence to insist that you take a pricey breakfast, but it's a good idea to make sure of this when you check in. Agriturismo (accommodations on farms and country estates) is highly developed in Tuscany, but prices are usually out of the affordable range; clients are mainly Italians who are willing to spend for the pleasures of "roughing it" in an elegantly restored Chianti farmhouse.

Highly recommended lodgings are indicated by a star ★.

Dining Though Florentine cuisine now predominates throughout Tuscany, the Etruscan influence on regional food still persists after more than three millennia. As the ancient Etruscans were responsible for the introduction of the cypress to the Tuscan landscape, they are also credited with the use of herbs in cooking. Such basic ingredients as tarragon, sage, rosemary, and thyme appear frequently, happily coupled with game, Chianina beef, or even seafood. Each region has its own specialties, usually based on simple ingredients, and Tuscans are disparagingly called *mangiafagioli*, or bean eaters, by other Italians. However, Tuscan chefs have recently discovered the rest of the world, and for better or worse, an "international cuisine" has gradually been making its appearance throughout the region.

Fortunately, Tuscany's wines remain unaltered. Grapes have been cultivated here since Etruscan times, and Chianti still rules the roost (the *Gallo Nero*, or Black Rooster, label, is a symbol of one of the region's most powerful wine-growing consortiums; the other is a *putto*, or cherub). A bottle of the robust red wine is still a staple on most tables, and the discerning can select from a multitude of other varieties, including such reds as Brunello di Montalcino and Vino Nobile di Montepulciano, and such whites as Valdinievole and Vergine della Valdichiana. The dessert wine *vin santo* is produced throughout the region and is often enjoyed with hard, dry almond cookies called *biscottini di Prato*, which are perfect for dunking.

Unless otherwise noted, reservations are not needed and dress is casual. Highly recommended restaurants are indicated by a star ★.

Shopping The prize products of Tuscany are its robust wines and dark, flavorful olive oils—both fairly affordable, though buying more than a couple of bottles will weigh down your luggage. The best places to buy them are the small towns of the Chianti country, between Florence and Siena. Another typically Tuscan souvenir is chunky, brightly painted pottery, available in gift stores in most inland towns.

Bicycling Although the Tuscan landscape is hilly, it's a popular area for cycling tours. Rent bikes in Florence at Fortezza da Basso, Santa Maria Novella train station, or Piazza Pitti, or from Alinari (Via Guelfa 85/r, tel. 055/280500, and other locations in Florence). Alinari also has a branch in Pisa (Via Lavagna 10).

Hiking Networks of footpaths thread through the hills and valleys of central Tuscany. For information on hiking routes, inquire at the Florence city and provincial information office, Via Cavour 1/r (next to Palazzo Medici Riccardi), tel. 055/276–0382.

The Arts and From June to September, music festivals abound in the Tuscan **Nightlife** hills. They include the Estate Musicale Lucchese in Lucca; the Festival of Marlia, near Lucca; opera festivals in Barga and Torre del Lago, both near Lucca; the Estate Fiesolana in Fiesole, near Florence; and the Settimana Musicale Chigiana in Siena. In addition, there are summer arts festivals in smaller towns, such as Montepulciano and Volterra.

Highlights for First-time Visitors

Lucca (Tour 1: West to Pisa)
Piazza del Duomo, in Pisa, including the Leaning Tower (Tour 1: West to Pisa)
San Gimignano (Tour 2: South to Siena)
Piazza del Campo, in Siena (Tour 2: South to Siena)
Duomo, in Siena (Tour 2: South to Siena)
Pinacoteca Nazionale, in Siena (Tour 2: South to Siena)
San Francesco, in Arezzo (Tour 2: South to Siena)
Piazza Grande, in Montepulciano (Tour 3: Southern Tuscany)

Tour 1: West to Pisa

This tour is organized as a train trip from Florence to Lucca and Pisa, with optional stops along the way in Prato and Pistoia. If you're coming from Rome, the best route is to go to Pisa first and follow this tour in reverse order. Lucca is probably the most sensible choice of the four for an overnight stay. The black-and-white striped marble of Pisa's buildings are as noteworthy as the famous Leaning Tower; Lucca's ornamental churches and piazzas gracefully embody the refined tastes of the medieval and Renaissance eras. In all of these cities, you can either walk from the train station to the main sights or take a city bus.

From Florence All four cities on this tour are on the same main train route from **By Train** Florence, with trains running approximately every hour. From Florence, travel times by train are: 30 minutes to Prato, 50 minutes to Pistoia, 90 minutes to Lucca, 1 hour to Pisa.

By Bus The **SITA** (tel. 055/211487) bus terminal in Florence is at Via Santa Caterina da Siena 15/A, around the corner from the Santa Maria Novella train station, to the right. SITA buses go to Prato (a 30-minute trip) and Pistoia (a one-hour trip). The **Lazzi** (tel. 055/215–154) bus terminal is at Piazza Stazione, in front of the train station. Lazzi buses travel from Florence to Lucca in about 1¾ hours.

146

Tuscany

Ligurian Sea

TO CORSICA

La Spezia
Carrara
Seravezza
Pietrasanta
Forte dei Marmi
Viareggio
Livorno

GARFAGNANA
ALPI APUANE

Abetone
S. Marcello
Pist
Marlia
Lucca
Montecatini Terme
Altopascio
Pistoia
Prato
Pisa
Florence
Arno
Pontassieve
Stia
Strada
Greve

A15
A12
A11
A1
A12
S1
S12
S435
S439
S206
S2
S429
S222
S65
S67
S71
S302
S303
S62
S64
S12
S324
S445
S63
Elsa
Rhano
Panaro
Arno

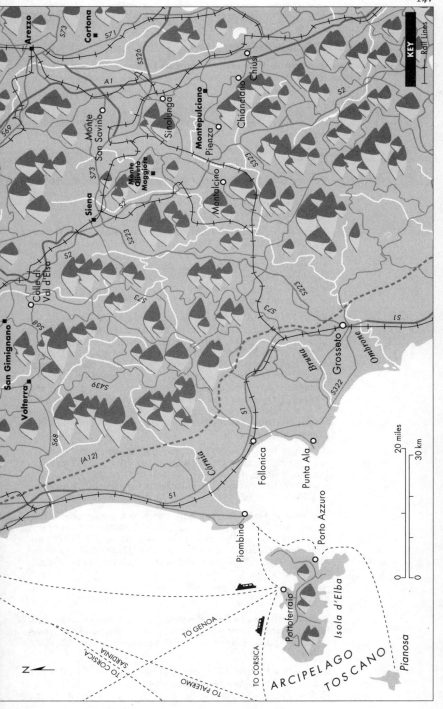

KEY

Rail Lines

N

Arezzo
Cortona
S73
S71
S326
A1
Chiusi
Chianciano
Sinalunga
Monte San Savino
Montepulciano
Pienza
S2
S73
Monte Oliveto Maggiore
Montalcino
S223
Siena
S2
S223
Colle di Val d'Elba
S73
S2
San Gimignano
S68
S439
Volterra
S68
(A12)
S223
S73
Bruna
S322
Grosseto
Ombrone
S1
Cecina
S1
Follonica
Punta Ala
20 miles
30 km
Piombino
Porto Azzuro
Portoferraio
Isola d'Elba
ARCIPELAGO
TOSCANO
Pianosa
TO GENOA
TO CORSICA, SARDINIA
TO PALERMO
TO CORSICA

By Car	The Firenze-Mare autostrada (A11) leads from Florence through Prato, Pistoia, and Lucca to the coast; to drive to Pisa, take S12 south from Lucca. The drive to Lucca from Florence takes about 1½ hours.
From Rome *By Train*	The trip to Pisa takes about two hours on the main Rome–Genoa line.
By Car	The drive from Rome to Pisa takes about four hours along the A12 Aurelia coastal highway.
By Plane	**Galileo Galilei** airport at Pisa handles domestic and some charter flights.

Prato

Prato is only 21 kilometers (13 miles) northwest of Florence, a 30-minute ride by bus or local train. If you take the train, get off at the Porta al Serraglio station. Service is frequent. Tourist office: Via Cairoli 48, tel. 0574/24112.

A textile center since its early medieval days, Prato was known for its wool throughout Europe during the 13th century. During the 14th century, a local cloth merchant, Francesco di Marco Datini, who built his business, according to one of his surviving ledgers, "in the name of God and of profit," further stimulated the local industry. To this day the city remains one of the world's largest manufacturers of cloth.

From the Porta al Serraglio train station, walk down Via Magnolfi to Piazza del Duomo. Prato's main attraction is its 11th-century **Duomo**. Romanesque in style, it is famous for its Chapel of the Holy Girdle (to the left of the entrance), which enshrines the sash of the Virgin; it is said that the girdle was given to the apostle Thomas by the Virgin herself when she miraculously appeared after her Assumption. The Duomo also contains 16th-century frescoes by Prato's most famous son, the libertine monk Fra Filippo Lippi; the best-known depict Herod's banquet and Salome's dance. *Piazza del Duomo. Open 7–noon and 4–7.*

Sculpture by Donatello that originally adorned the Duomo's exterior pulpit is now on display in the **Museo dell'Opera del Duomo**. *Piazza del Duomo 49, tel. 0574/29339. Admission: 5,000 lire (ticket also valid for Galleria Comunale). Open Mon. and Wed.–Sat. 9:30–12:30 and 3–6:30, Sun. 9:30–12:30.*

The nearby **Galleria Comunale** contains a good collection of Tuscan and Sienese paintings, mainly from the 14th century. *Palazzo Pretorio, Piazza del Comune, tel. 0574/452302. Admission: 5,000 lire (ticket also valid for Museo dell' Opera del Duomo). Open Mon. and Wed.–Sat. 9:30–12:30 and 3–6:30, Sun. 9:30–12:30.*

Pistoia

A local train or bus from Prato to Pistoia takes about 30 minutes. The train direct from Florence takes about an hour. Tourist office: Palazzo dei Vescovi, Piazza del Duomo, tel. 0573/21622.

The town of Pistoia, 15 kilometers (9 miles) west of Prato, saw the beginning of the bitter Guelph-Ghibelline conflict of the Middle Ages. Reconstructed after heavy bombing during

World War II, the town contains some fine Romanesque architecture.

From the train station, several city buses go to the Duomo area. Alternatively, walk straight ahead on Via XX Settembre and continue straight to Via Cavour, turning right to get to Via Roma, where you'll take a left to Piazza del Duomo. Here you'll see the **Cathedral of San Zeno,** which houses the **Dossale di San Jacopo,** a magnificent silver altarpiece. The two half figures on its left side are by Filippo Brunelleschi (1377–1446), better known as the first Renaissance architect (and designer of Florence's magnificent Duomo dome). *Illumination of altarpiece: 2,000 lire.*

Other attractions include the **Ospedale del Ceppo** (Piazza Ospedale, a short way down Via Pacini from Piazza del Duomo), a hospital founded during the 14th century, with a superb early 16th-century terra-cotta frieze by Giovanni della Robbia; the church of **Sant'Andrea** (down Via Pappe to Via Sant'Andrea), with a fine early 14th-century pulpit by Giovanni Pisano that depicts the life of Christ; and, back in Piazza del Duomo, an unusual Gothic baptistery and the 14th-century **Palazzo del Comune,** which now houses two museums: the **Museo Civico,** containing medieval art, and the **Centro Marino Marini,** containing contemporary art. *Palazzo del Comune, Piazza del Duomo, tel. 0573/367871 (Museo Civico) or 0573/368182 (Centro Marino Marini). Admission: 5,000 lire. Open Tues.–Sat. 9–1 and 3–7, Sun. 9–1.*

Dining
Under 24,000 lire

Lapo. This trattoria is one of several on a large square between the Duomo and the main train station. Decor and menu are simple; the latter features thick vegetable soup and a pasta or two. *Piazza Mercatale 141, tel. 0574/23745. No reservations. No credit cards. Closed Sun.*

Under 20,000 lire

Frisco. Near the church of Sant'Andrea, this refreshment stand is a favorite local rendezvous. Under the trees in a large piazza, you can make a meal of cold cuts and homemade pastries. *Piazza San Francesco 58/a. No telephone. No credit cards. Closed Tues.*

Festivals

In late July, a week-long festival culminates in the Joust of the Bear, a medieval contest held in Pistoia's Piazza del Duomo on July 25.

Lucca

Lucca is about 90 minutes from Florence by train, about 1¾ hours by Lazzi bus. From Pistoia, the train takes about 40 minutes. Tourist office: Via Vittorio Veneto 40, off Piazza Napoleone, tel. 0583/493639; Piazza Guidiccione 2, tel. 0583/491205.

In Lucca, Caesar, Pompey, and Crassus agreed to rule Rome as a triumvirate in 56 BC; later it became the first town in Tuscany to accept Christianity. Today it still has a mind of its own, and when most of Tuscany was voting Communist recently, its citizens rarely followed suit. For a fine overview of the town, take a walk or a drive along its 16th-century ramparts, which are shaded by stately trees.

Lucca is one of the most picturesque fortress towns in Tuscany and is worth exploring at length on foot. As usual, the main attraction is the **Duomo** (Piazza del Duomo, on the southern side of town). Its round-arched facade is a fine example of the rigorously ordered Pisan Romanesque style, in this case happily enlivened by an extremely disordered collection of carved columns. The decoration of the facade and of the porch below are worth a close look; they make this one of the most entertaining church fronts in Tuscany. The Gothic interior contains a moving Byzantine crucifix (called the **Volto Santo,** or Holy Face), brought here in the 8th century, and the masterpiece of the Sienese sculptor Jacopo della Quercia, the marble *Tomb of Ilaria del Caretto* (1406).

Slightly west of the center of town is the church of **San Michele** (Piazza San Michele), whose facade is even more fanciful than the Duomo's. It was heavily restored during the 19th century, however, and somewhat jarringly displays busts of such modern Italian patriots as Garibaldi and Cavour.

The church of **San Frediano** (Piazza San Frediano) is just inside the middle of the north town wall; it contains more works by Jacopo della Quercia, and, bizarrely, the lace-clad mummy of the patron saint of domestic servants, Santa Zita. Near it, to the southeast, is **Piazza del Mercato,** where the ancient **Anfiteatro Romano,** or Roman amphitheater, once stood. The piazza takes its oval shape from the theater, but the seats disappeared when medieval houses were built on top of them.

Near the west walls of the old city, the **Pinacoteca Nazionale** is worth a visit to see the Mannerist, Baroque, and Rococo art on display. *Palazzo Mansi, Via Galli Tassi 43, tel. 0583/55570. Admission: 6,000 lire. Open Tues.–Sat. 9–7, Sun. 9–2.*

On the eastern end of the historic center, the **Museo Nazionale** houses an extensive collection of local Romanesque and Renaissance art. *Villa Guinigi, Via della Quarquonia, tel. 0583/ 46033. Admission: 5,000 lire. Open May–Sept., Tues.–Sat. 9–7, Sun. 9–1; Oct.–Apr., Tues.–Sat. 9–4:30, Sun. 9–1.*

Finally, for a fine view of the surrounding countryside, climb the tree-topped tower of the medieval **Palazzo Guinigi,** near the center of town. *Admission: 3,000 lire. Open 10–4, summer 9–7.*

Lodging
Under 85,000 lire

Ilaria. This small, family-run hotel enjoys a pretty location on a canal near Porta Elisa, within walking distance of the main sights. Guest rooms are small but clean and attractively furnished. *Via del Fosso 20, tel. 0583/47558. 17 rooms, 12 with bath or shower. AE, DC, MC, V.*

Under 60,000 lire

Cinzia. On the upper floor of a centuries-old building, this small hotel is a favorite of budget-conscious Italians and foreigners. It offers basic rooms in a central location, a quiet street near the cathedral. There are no rooms with private bath. *Via della Dogana 9, tel. 0583/41323. 12 rooms without bath. No credit cards.*

Dining
Under 30,000 lire

Canuleia. A small, popular trattoria between Via Mordini and Piazza Anfiteatro, the Canuleia serves typical Lucca fare, emphasizing vegetables in its minestrone and vegetarian lasagna. *Via Canuleia 14, tel. 0583/47470. Reservations advised. MC, V. Closed Sat., Sun., and Aug. 10–20.*

Giulio. Near Bastione Santa Croce, the Giulio has recently been renovated but remains a classic old trattoria. The menu features local specialties, including *farro* (wheat) soup with beans. *Via delle Conce 47, tel. 0583/55948. Reservations advised. No credit cards. Closed Sun. and Mon.*

Under 20,000 lire **Margherita.** Near the Palazzo Guinigi, this establishment couldn't be simpler, or more popular with locals, for hearty, homestyle dishes and satisfying portions. One specialty: local salami and cheese from the Altopascio highlands. *Via Sant'Andrea 8, tel. 0583/44146. No credit cards. Closed Sun.*

Splurge **Buca di Sant'Antonio.** A favorite with locals, this was once a rustic tavern. It is still one of Lucca's best restaurants, and it specializes in traditional local dishes, some unfamiliar but well worth trying—among them *ravioli di ricotta alle zucchine* (cheese ravioli with zucchini) and kid or lamb roasted with herbs. A three- or four-course dinner with house wine costs about 60,000 lire per person. It is located near the church of San Michele. *Via della Cervia 3, tel. 0583/55881. Dinner reservations advised. AE, DC, MC, V. Closed Sun. evening, Mon., and last 3 weeks in July.*

Shopping There is an open-air market in Lucca's Piazza del Mercato every Wednesday and Saturday morning, and a flea market is held in Piazza San Martino on the second Sunday of every month.

The Arts The **Estate Musicale Lucchese,** a music festival, is held in Lucca from July through September, followed by a September series of folklore and artistic events.

In **Marlia,** 8 kilometers (5 miles) north of Lucca, the gardens of the Villa Reale are the venue of another music festival, this one mainly operatic. It is held from July to September; dates vary from year to year. Inquire at the Lucca tourist office about special bus schedules during the festival.

Pisa

From Lucca, Pisa is only 30 minutes away by train or bus. Tourist offices: Piazza della Stazione 11, tel. 050/42291; Piazza Duomo 8, tel. 050/560–464.

The town of Pisa reached its glory as a maritime republic during the 12th century; its architects and artists strongly influenced the development of the Romanesque and Gothic styles in Tuscany. Defeated by its archrival, Genoa (also a seaport trading center), in 1284, Pisa went into a gradual decline, its harbor filling with silt from the Arno; in the 15th century it became a satellite to Florence, when the Medici gained full control of Tuscany. During World War II, the city was virtually destroyed by Axis and Allied bombing, which miraculously spared its main attraction.

That, of course, is **Piazza del Duomo,** at the northwestern edge of town, also known, appropriately, as the **Campo dei Miracoli** (Field of Miracles). On it stand the **Duomo,** the **Baptistery,** and the famous **Leaning Tower.** Take city bus No. 1 from the station to Campo dei Miracoli, or walk (about 1 mile) through the center of town: take Viale Gramsci and Corso Italia straight ahead from the station, cross the Arno, and follow the signs to Piazza dei Cavalieri and beyond to the tower. The Leaning Tower was begun in 1174, the last of the three structures to be built, and the lopsided settling began when construction reached the third story. The tower's architects attempted to compensate by making the remaining floors slightly taller on the leaning side, but the extra weight only made the problem worse. The settling continues to this day, as do efforts to prop the structure up. Legend holds that Galileo conducted an experiment on the nature of gravity by dropping metal balls from the top of the 187-foot-high tower; historians say this legend has no basis in fact (which is not quite to say that it is false). The tower is now closed for structural reinforcement and will probably remain closed permanently, but this hardly detracts from its allure. Just the sight of it, and of the resplendent marble monuments that accompany it on the bright green lawn, is a treat.

The **Duomo** was the first building to use the horizontal marble striping pattern (borrowed from Moorish architecture in the 11th century) so common to Tuscan cathedrals. It is famous for the Romanesque panels on the transept door facing the tower, which depict the life of Christ, and for its beautifully carved 13th-century pulpit, by Giovanni Pisano. The lovely Gothic **Baptistery,** which stands across from the Duomo's facade, is best known for the pulpit carved by Giovanni's father, Nicola, in 1260. *Duomo open Apr.–Sept., daily 7:45–1 and 3–7; Oct.–Mar., daily 7:45–1 and 3–5. Baptistery admission: 5,000 lire* (see below). *Open Apr.–Sept., daily 9–7; Oct.–Mar., daily 9–5.*

The walled area on the northern side of the Campo dei Miracoli is the **Camposanto,** or cemetery, which is filled, according to legend, with earth brought back from the Holy Land during the Crusades. Its galleries contain numerous frescoes, notably *The Drunkenness of Noah,* by Renaissance artist Benozzo Gozzoli, and the disturbing 14th-century *Triumph of Death,* whose authorship is disputed but whose subject matter shows what was on people's minds in a century that saw the ravages of the Black Death. At the southeast corner of the Campo dei Miracoli, the **Museo dell'Opera del Duomo** holds a wealth of medieval sculptures and the ancient Roman sarcophagi that inspired Nicola Pisano's figures. The well-arranged **Museo delle Sinopie** across the street, on the south side of the square, holds the *sinopie,* or preparatory drawings, for the Camposanto frescoes and is of limited interest to most tourists. *Camposanto, tel. 050/560547. Admission: 5,000 lire. Open Apr.–Sept., daily 9–7; Oct.–Mar., daily 9–5. Museo dell'Opera del Duomo, Via Arcivescovado, tel. 050/560547. Admission: 5,000 lire. Open Apr.–Sept., daily 9–7; Oct.–Mar., daily 9–5. Museo delle Sinopie, Piazza del Duomo, tel. 050/560547. Admission: 5,000 lire. Open daily 9–1 and 3–5. Special ticket valid for admission to Baptistery, Camposanto, and the 2 museums: 12,000 lire.*

In the center of town, **Piazza dei Cavalieri** possesses some fine Renaissance buildings: the **Palazzo dei Cavalieri,** the **Palazzo dell'Orologio,** and the church of **Santo Stefano dei Cavalieri.** The square was laid out around 1560 by Giorgio Vasari, better known for his chronicles of the lives of Renaissance artists that made him the first art historian. Along the Arno, the tiny Gothic church of **Santa Maria della Spina** on Lungarno Sonnino, south of the river, merits a visit. The **Museo di San Matteo,** on the northern side of the Arno, contains some touching examples of local Romanesque and Gothic art. *Lungarno Mediceo, tel. 050/541865. Admission: 6,000 lire. Open Tues.–Sat. 9–7, Sun. 9–1.*

Lodging
Under 115,000 lire

Royal Victoria. In a pleasant palazzo facing the Arno, a 10-minute walk from the Campo dei Miracoli, this hotel is about as close as Pisa comes to Old World ambience. It's comfortably furnished, featuring antiques and reproductions in the lobby and in some rooms, in which the decor varies from functional modern to turn-of-the-century. There's a large restaurant that is open daily for hotel guests. *Lungarno Pacinotti 12, tel. 050/502130. 67 rooms, 46 with bath. AE, DC, MC, V.*

Dining
Under 30,000 lire

Bruno. A pleasant restaurant, with beamed ceilings and the look of a country inn, Bruno is located just outside the old city walls, a short walk from the bell tower and cathedral. Dine on classic Tuscan dishes, from *zuppa alla pisana* (thick vegetable soup) to *baccalà con porri* (cod with leeks). *Via Luigi Bianchi 12, tel. 050/560818. Reservations advised in the evening. AE, DC, MC, V. Closed Mon. eve., Tues., and August 5–15.*

Under 20,000 lire

Matteo. Between Piazza dei Cavalieri and the Arno, this trattoria near Piazza Dante is popular with locals and unknown to many—but not all—tourists. The food is standard Italian. Try the spaghetti *al ragù* (with meat sauce) and *scaloppine al vino* (escallopes of veal sautéed in white wine). *Via l'Aroncio 46. No telephone. No credit cards. Closed Sun.*

Tour 2: South to Siena

The hills and valleys south of Florence are strewn with vineyards, olive groves, meadows full of sunflowers, and medieval towns rich in history and art. Our starting point, and the most logical touring base, is Siena, a perfect medieval time capsule with a wealth of art, architecture, and history. Picturesque San Gimignano bristles with ancient defensive towers. Volterra preserves its past as a hilltop stronghold of the ancient Etruscans. Arezzo, a busy little city with one of those charming piazzas that are at the heart of many Tuscan hill towns, jealously guards one of the seminal art works of the Renaissance, Piero della Francesca's fresco cycle in the church of San Francesco. And nearby Cortona has Luca Signorelli paintings, its own picturesque piazza, and beautiful views. For those with time to spare, a visit to southern Tuscany can also take in Montepulciano and Pienza, two small towns where Renaissance architects brought their skills to bear on a medieval urban core.

From Florence
By Train

The Florence–Siena train takes 75 minutes and involves a change of trains at Empoli; the fare is 7,300 lire. In Siena, you must take a bus from the station up to the town (800 lire). There are about 12 trains daily, with service hourly during the daytime.

By Bus

This is the most convenient way to get to Siena from Florence, because the bus station is within walking distance of most sights. Bus service from Florence to Siena is hourly and even more frequent during the peak tourist season (April to September). SITA buses leave from the bus terminal at Via Santa Caterina da Siena 15/r, on the right of Santa Maria Novella train station, and take about two hours (express buses take 75 minutes). The bus fare is 7,200 lire.

By Car

The modern S2 highway is the fast route from Florence to Siena; if you really want to see the countryside, take the narrower and more meandering S222, also known as the Strada

Chiantigiana because it runs through the heart of Chianti wine country.

From Rome Take the SITA bus that leaves early in the morning, usually
By Bus about 7:30 AM from Piazza della Repubblica (buy tickets in advance at CIT office, Piazza della Repubblica). The bus trip takes about 3½ hours and costs about 16,500 lire.

By Car Take the A1 north from Rome, exiting at the Valdichiana exit to get on E78 west to Siena, about 50 kilometers (31 miles).

Siena

Tourist offices: Piazza del Campo 55, tel. 0577/280551; Via di Città 43, between Piazza del Campo and the Duomo, tel. 0577/ 42209.

Florence's great historical rival, Siena, was founded by Augustus around the time of the birth of Christ, but according to legend it was founded much earlier by Remus, brother of Romulus, the legendary founder of Rome. During the late Middle Ages, the city was both wealthy and powerful: It saw the birth of the world's oldest bank, the Monte dei Paschi, still very much in business. It was bitterly envied by Florence, which in 1254 sent forces that besieged the city for over a year, reducing its population by half and laying waste to the countryside. The city was finally absorbed by the Grand Duchy of Tuscany, ruled by Florence, in 1559.

The train station is below the town; you can get a city bus in front of the station to **Piazza Matteotti**, where long-distance buses arrive, in the northeast corner of the historic center. Here you'll find the public gardens, fortress, stadium, and the church of **San Domenico.** Its **Cappella di Santa Caterina** displays frescoes by Il Sodoma portraying scenes from the life of Saint Catherine and houses a reliquary containing her head.

From there, follow the winding downhill route along Via della Sapienza and Via Banchi di Sopra to Piazza del Campo. Unlike Renaissance Florence, Siena is a Gothic city, laid out over the slopes of three steep hills and practically unchanged since medieval times. Its main square, **Piazza del Campo,** is one of the finest in Italy. Fan-shaped, its nine sections of paving represent the 13th-century government of Nine Good Men, and, at the top, like an ornament, is the Fonte Gaia, so called because it was inaugurated to great jubilation. The bas-reliefs on it are reproductions of the originals by Jacopo della Quercia. Twice a year, on July 2 and August 16, the square is the site of the famous **Palio,** a horse race in which the city's 17 neighborhoods compete to possess the cloth banner that gives the contest its name. Unlike many other such events in Italy, the Palio is deeply revered by the townspeople, and the rivalries it generates are taken very seriously.

Dominating the piazza is the **Palazzo Pubblico,** which has served as Siena's town hall since the 1300s. It now also contains the **Museo Civico,** its walls covered with pre-Renaissance frescoes, including Simone Martini's early 14th-century *Maestà* and *Portrait of Guidoriccio da Fogliano*, and Ambrogio Lorenzetti's famous *Allegory of Good and Bad Government*, painted from 1327 to 1329 to demonstrate the dangers of tyranny. The original bas-reliefs of the Jacopo della Quercia fountain, moved under cover to protect them from the elements, are also on display. The climb up the palazzo's bell tower—the Toree del Mangia—is long and steep, but the superb view makes it worth every step. *Piazza del Campo, tel. 0577/292263. Bell Tower admission: 4,000 lire. Open Mar. 15–Nov. 15, daily 10–one hour before sunset; Nov. 16–Mar. 14, daily 1–10:30. Museo Civico admission: 6,000 lire. Open Mar. 15–Nov. 15, Mon.–Sat 9:30–7:30, Sun. 9:30–1:30; Nov. 16–Mar. 14, daily 9:30–1:30.*

Siena's **Duomo,** several blocks west of Piazza del Campo, is beyond question one of the finest Gothic cathedrals in Italy. Its facade, with its multicolored marbles and painted decoration, is typical of the Italian approach to Gothic architecture, lighter and much less austere than the French. The cathedral, as it now stands, was completed during the 14th century, but at the time, the Sienese had even bigger plans. They decided to enlarge the building, using the current church as the transepts of the new church, which would have a new nave running toward the southeast. But in 1348 the Black Death decimated Siena's population, the city began to decline, funds dried up, and the plans were never carried out. The beginnings of construction of the new nave still stand and may be seen from the steps outside the Duomo's right transept.

The Duomo's interior is one of the most striking in Italy and possesses a fine coffered and gilded dome. It is most famous for its unique and magnificent inlaid marble floors, which took almost 200 years to complete (beginning around 1370); more than 40 artists contributed to the work, made up of 56 separate compositions depicting biblical scenes, allegories, religious symbols, and civic emblems. The Duomo's carousel pulpit, which is almost as famous as the floors, was carved by Nicola Pisano around 1265 and depicts the life of Christ on its rostrum frieze (the staircase is a later addition). Finally, a door in the left-hand aisle just before the crossing leads into the **Biblioteca Piccolomini,** a room painted by Pinturicchio in 1509; its frescoes depict events from the life of native son Aeneas Sylvius Piccolomini, who became Pope Pius II in 1458. The frescoes are in fine repair and have a freshness rarely seen in work so old. *Biblioteca Piccolomini, tel. 0577/283048. Admission: 2,000 lire. Open mid-Mar.–Sept. 30, daily 9–7:30; Oct. 1–Nov. 3, daily 9–6:30; Nov. 4–Mar. 13, daily 10–1 and 2:30–5.*

Next to the Duomo is its museum, the **Museo dell'Opera del Duomo,** occupying part of the unfinished new cathedral's nave and containing a small collection of Sienese art and the cathedral treasury. Its masterpiece is unquestionably Duccio's *Maestà,* painted around 1310 and magnificently displayed in a room devoted entirely to Duccio's work. *Piazza del Duomo, tel. 0577/283048. Admission: 5,000 lire. Open Mar. 14–Sept. 30, daily 9–7:30; Oct. 1–Nov. 3, daily 9–6:30; Nov. 4–Dec. 31, daily 9–1:30, Jan. 2–Mar. 13, daily, 9–1.*

Steps between the cathedral and its museum lead to the **Battistero,** or Baptistery, painted with 15th-century frescoes. Its large bronze baptismal font (also 15th-century) was designed by Jacopo della Quercia and is adorned with bas-reliefs by various artists, including two by Renaissance masters: Lorenzo Ghiberti *(The Baptism of Christ)* and Donatello *(Herod Presented with the Head of St. John).*

Chief among Siena's other attractions is the **Pinacoteca Nazionale,** several blocks southeast of the entrance to the Duomo; it contains a superb collection of Sienese art, including Ambrogio Lorenzetti's 14th-century depiction of a castle that is generally considered the first nonreligious painting—the first pure landscape—of the Christian era. *Via San Pietro 29, tel. 0577/281161. Admission: 8,000 lire. Open Apr.–Sept., Tues.–Sat. 8:30–7; Oct.–Mar., Tues.–Sat. 8:30–2, Sun. 8:30–1.*

Lodging

Under 115,000 lire

Continentale. A block or so from Piazza del Campo, this old-fashioned hotel has public rooms in the grand style of the early 1900s, when a visit from Italian royalty was not an uncommon occurrence. Rooms are clean and quiet, and the location can't be beat. *Via Banchi di Sopra 85, tel. 0577/41451. 42 rooms, 27 with bath. AE, MC, V.*

Under 85,000 lire

Centrale. Recently renovated, this small hotel is only a block from Piazza del Campo. Rooms are simply furnished but large; all are doubles. *Via Cecco Angiolieri 26, tel. 0577/280379. 7 rooms with bath. MC, V.*

Chiusarelli. Located on a main road and close to the intercity bus terminal, the Chiusarelli is near the church of San Domenico and within walking distance of Piazza del Campo. The hotel is in an early 1900s building that mimics Renaissance style, with columns and a loggia on the upper floor, and a small garden. The downstairs restaurant caters to tour groups. *Viale Curtatone 9, tel. 0577/280562, fax 0577/271177. 50 rooms with bath. MC, V.*

Lea. In a residential neighborhood separated by a ravine from the medieval center, this is an 18th-century villa with garden that has been transformed into an intimate, family-run hotel. *Viale XXIV Maggio 10, tel. 0577/283207. 13 rooms with bath. No credit cards.*

Under 60,000 lire

Santuario Santa Caterina-Casa del Pellegrino. This religious-run establishment is located in a historic but totally renovated palazzo behind San Domenico, making it easily accessible to transportation and sights. Some rooms have views of the cathedral; all are spotless, and many can accommodate an extra bed. There is an 11 PM curfew and a distinctly sedate though friendly atmosphere. *Via di Camporegio 31, tel. 0577/44177. 30 rooms, 28 with bath. No credit cards. (No reservations accepted more than 3 or 4 days in advance.)*

Tre Donzelle. In the heart of Siena, off Piazza del Campo, the Tre Donzelle has an unbeatable location and basic modern furnishings; rooms without bath are a real bargain. *Via delle Donzelle 5, tel. 0577/280358. 27 rooms, 7 with bath. No credit cards.*

Dining

Splurge

La Tellina. This trattoria is centrally located and simply decorated with bright ceramic plates on the walls. The menu offers simple soups and such pastas as *penne alla boscaiola* (with tomato and mushroom sauce), with grilled steaks and chops as main courses. *Via delle Terme 52, tel. 0577/283133. No reservations. No credit cards. Closed Fri.*

Under 30,000 lire

Le Logge. Near Piazza del Campo, this typically Sienese trattoria has rustic dining rooms on two levels and tables outdoors from June to October. The menu features Tuscan dishes, such as *pennette all'osteria* (pasta with creamy herbed sauce) and *coniglio con pignoli* (rabbit with pine nuts). *Via del*

Porrione 33, tel. 0577/48013. Reservations advised. DC, MC, V. Closed Sun. and June 1–15, Nov. 1–15.

Under 24,000 lire **La Grotta del Gallo Nero.** Off Piazza del Campo, this is a wine cellar where Chianti is king. You can make a meal of *crostini* (toast with liver paté) and local cheeses, or order one of the hot dishes on the small menu. *Via del Porrione 65, tel. 0577/220446. No credit cards. Closed Sun.*

La Torre. On the narrow street next to the Mangia tower, this family-run trattoria serves local dishes, such as *lasagne* and *arista* (roast pork), in a single room with the kitchen in the corner. Portions are generous. *Via Salicotto 7, tel. 0577/287548. No credit cards. Closed Thurs. and Aug. 14–31.*

Splurge **Ai Marsili.** Located between Piazza del Campo and the cathedral, this 900-year-old wine cellar, with its brick-vaulted ceilings, is an elegant place in which to dine. The menu offers Tuscan and Italian specialties, among them homemade pastas such as *tortelloni burro e salvia* (large cheese-filled ravioli with butter and sage). Some meat dishes are cooked in wine; and the wine list features the finest Tuscan and Italian labels, including many from nearby Chianti country. A full meal, with a medium-priced bottle of Chianti, costs about 60,000 lire. *Via del Castoro 3, tel. 0577/47154. Reservations advised. AE, DC, MC, V. Closed Mon.*

San Gimignano

TRAIN express buses take about 60 minutes from Siena to San Gimignano; you must change buses in Poggibonsi. There are about 15 buses a day; fare is about 4,800 lire. Buses arrive at Porta San Giovanni, just outside the city gate and a 5-minute walk from Piazza del Duomo. Tourist office: Piazza del Duomo, tel. 0577/940008.

San Gimignano's high walls and narrow streets are typical of Tuscan hill towns, but it is the surviving medieval towers that set the town apart from its neighbors. Only a handful remain today, but at the height of the Guelph-Ghibelline conflict, a forest of more than 70 such towers dominated the city, which the locals like to call a mini-Manhattan. The towers were built partly for defensive purposes—they were a safe refuge, and quite useful for pouring boiling oil on attacking enemies—and partly to bolster the egos of their owners, who competed with deadly seriousness to build the highest tower in town.

Many of the town's most important medieval buildings are clustered around the central Piazza del Duomo. They include the **Palazzo del Podestà,** with its imposing tower; the **Palazzo del Popolo,** now the municipal museum, displaying Sienese and Renaissance paintings; and the Romanesque **Collegiata** (which lost its status as a Duomo when San Gimignano lost its bishop), containing fine 15th-century frescoes by Domenico Ghirlandaio in the Chapel of Santa Fina. *Admission to palazzo and chapel: 5,000 lire. Open daily 9:30–12:30 and 2:30–5:30, June–Aug. to 6:30.*

Before leaving San Gimignano, be sure to see its most famous work of art, at the northern end of town, in the church of **Sant' Agostino:** Benozzo Gozzoli's beautiful 15th-century fresco cycle depicting the life of St. Augustine. Also try a taste of Vernaccia, the local white wine, available at the many locations marked *degustazione*.

Lodging
Under 115,000 lire

L'Antico Pozzo. This tiny hotel enjoys a quiet location near Porta San Matteo. Rooms are smallish—though an extra bed can be squeezed into some—and decor is in spare Tuscan style. *Via San Matteo 87, tel. 0577/942041. 18 rooms, 14 with bath. AE, DC, MC, V.*

Under 60,000 lire

Ostello della Gioventù. Highly recommended by youthful travelers, this modern hostel near Porta delle Fonti is very well run. It's open for registration 7:30–9:30 AM and 5–11:30 PM; the cost is about 17,000 lire, and that includes breakfast and a shower. The 11:30 PM curfew is no problem; there's nothing to do in this little burgh at that time of night anyway. It is open for groups only from November 15 to February 28. *Via delle Fonti 1, tel. 0577/941991, fax 0577/941982. 76 beds. No credit cards.*

Dining
Under 30,000 lire

La Mangiatoia. One of the small trattorias hidden in the town's little byways off the main street, La Mangiatoia offers typical Tuscan soups and grilled meat. *Via Mainardi 5, tel. 0577/ 941528. AE, DC, MC, V. Closed Tues.*

Under 24,000 lire

Stella. Farm-fresh vegetables and the owner's own olive oil are offered at this simple trattoria. *Via San Matteo 77, tel. 0577/ 940444. AE, DC, MC, V. Closed Wed.*

Under 20,000 lire

Chiribiri. Near Porta San Giovanni, where you enter the town, Chiribiri is a hole-in-the-wall pizza-by-the-slice place that has good pizza. You can either take out food or eat on the spot. *Off Via San Giovanni, tel. 0577/941948. No credit cards. Closed Wed.*

Lodging and Dining
Under 115,000 lire

Bel Soggiorno. Located on the town's main street, this attractive little inn has small bedrooms, many with views of the countryside. The restaurant, with rustic decor and fine views, serves such Tuscan specialties as *pappardelle alla lepre* (broad noodles with hare sauce) and *risotto del Bel Soggiorno* (with saffron and nutmeg). A half-board plan (room, breakfast, and another meal) costs about 100,000 lire per person). *Via San Giovanni 91, tel. 0577/940375. 27 rooms with bath. Reservations advised for restaurant (closed Mon. and Jan. 7–Feb. 7). AE, DC, MC, V.*

Volterra

From San Gimignano, four SITA buses a day make the 1-hour trip to Volterra. There are also several TRAIN buses daily from Pisa, about 2 hours away; by SITA bus, Florence is about 2½ hours away, Siena 2 hours. Tourist Office: Via Turazza 2, on the left of Palazzo dei Priori, tel. 0588/86150.

D. H. Lawrence, in his *Etruscan Places*, sang the praises of Volterra, "standing somber and chilly alone on her rock." The town has long been known for its alabaster, which has been mined since Etruscan times; today the Volterrans use it to make ornaments and souvenirs sold all over town. A magnificent collection of small alabaster funerary urns that once held the ashes of deceased Etruscans can be seen at the **Museo Etrusco Guarnacci** (Via Don Minzoni), along with many other Etruscan artifacts. Later art can be found in the **Duomo,** at the **Pinacoteca** (Palazzo Minucci-Solaini, Via dei Sarti 1), and at the **Museo di Arte Sacra** (Via Roma). The town's best-known Renaissance works are the 15th-century frescoes in the Duomo by Benozzo Gozzoli and the 16th-century *Deposition* by Rosso Fiorentino in the Pinacoteca. *Combined admission to Museo Etrusco Guarnacci, Pinacoteca, and Museo di Arte Sacra: 8,000 lire. Open Mar. 16–Oct. 14, daily 9:30–6:30 (Museo Etrusco Guarnacci closes 1–3); Oct. 15–Mar.15, daily 9:30–1 (Museo Etrusco Guarnacci 9–2).*

The walls of Volterra also harbor one of the few pieces of Etruscan architecture that escaped Roman destruction: the **Arco Etrusco,** with its weather-worn Etruscan heads, at the Porta all'Arco.

Lodging
Inder 115,000 lire

Nazionale. In the very heart of this little town, on the square where the intercity buses stop, the Nazionale is big enough to handle tour groups and students on class trips in functionally furnished rooms. *Via dei Marchesi 11, tel. 0588/86284. 36 rooms, 24 with bath. Facilities: restaurant. DC, MC, V.*

Under 60,000 lire

Ostella della Gioventù. Just outside the town, across from the massive walls of the Medici fortress (now a prison), this hostel has great views. It is open from 6 PM to 11:30 PM, which means you can't rest there during the day, and you must be inside the doors at curfew. *Via del Poggetto, tel. 0588/85577. 56 beds. No credit cards.*

Splurge

San Lino. Located in a former convent, this hotel has modern comforts, a swimming pool, and its own regional restaurant. On top of that, it's centrally located. A double room will cost you less than 200,000 lire. *Via San Lino 26, tel. 0588/85250. 43 rooms with bath. Facilities: restaurant (closed lunch and Wed.), pool. AE, DC, MC, V.*

Dining
Under 30,000 lire

Da Beppino. One of a number of trattorias on Via delle Prigioni, near the Palazzo dei Priori, catering to the many tourists who find their way to Volterra, Da Beppino serves homemade pasta and local game. *Via delle Prigioni 15, tel. 0588/86051. AE, DC, MC, V. Closed Wed.*

Under 20,000 lire

Sans Souci. Near the Romanesque church of San Michele, this pizzeria serves pizza-by-the-slice and is always crowded with students. *Via Guarnacci 16, no phone. No credit cards. Closed Thurs.*

Arezzo

Arezzo is about 2 hours from Siena by SITA bus (4 buses daily). By train, it's about an hour from Florence and 2 hours from Rome. Buses stop in front of the train station; from there, walk straight up Via Guido Monaco to the church of San Francesco. Tourist office: Piazza Risorgimento 116, tel. 0575/20839.

The town of Arezzo is unfairly snubbed by many; it does have its commercial and industrial side (it is one of the world's major producers of gold jewelry), but the historic medieval and Renaissance district in the center of town, and Piazza Grande, which in its own quiet way rivals Siena's Piazza del Campo, are worth seeing. Arezzo doesn't have Siena's aloof Gothic perfection, but it does give you more of a sense of real life in the easy-going Tuscan manner.

Arezzo was the birthplace of the poet Petrarch; the Renaissance artist and art historian Giorgio Vasari; and Guido d'Arezzo, the inventor of musical notation. Today the town is best known for the magnificent, but very faint, Piero della Francesca frescoes in the church of **San Francesco,** on Via Cavour in the center of town. Painted between 1452 and 1466, they depict *The Legend of the True Cross* on three walls of the choir. What Sir Kenneth Clark called "the most perfect morning light in all Renaissance painting" may be seen in the lowest section of the right wall, where the troops of the emperor Maxentius flee before the sign of the cross.

Other attractions in Arezzo include the church of **San Domenico,** at Piazza Fossombroni, to the north of Piazza Grande, which houses a 13th-century crucifix by Cimabue; the **house** that Giorgio Vasari designed and decorated for himself in 1540, just west of San Domenico; and the **Museo Archeologico,** with a fine collection of Etruscan bronzes. *Vasari house: Via XX Settembre. Open Tues.–Sat. 9–2, Sun. 9–1. Museo Archeologico: Via Margaritone 10, tel. 0575/20882. Admission: 6,000 lire. Open Tues.–Sat. 9–2, Sun. 9–1.*

Lodging
Under 115,000 lire

Continental. Centrally located near the train station and within walking distance of all major sights, the Continental has been a reliable and convenient lodging place since it opened during the 1950s. Recently refurbished, it now has bright-white furnishings with yellow accents, gleaming new bathrooms complete with hair dryers, and a pleasant roof garden. *Piazza Guido Monaco 7, tel. 0575/20251, fax 0575/340485. 74 rooms with bath or shower. Facilities: restaurant (closed Sun. eve. and Mon.), rooftop garden. AE, DC, MC, V.*

Under 60,000 lire

Milano. Centrally located on a quiet street near Piazza Guido Monaco, the Milano is in a modern 1950s building. Rooms are small and sparsely furnished; many are dark, but they are clean. *Via Madonna del Prato 83, tel. 0575/26836. 26 rooms, 8 with bath or shower. V.*

Dining
Under 30,000 lire

Spiedo d'Oro. Cheery red-and-white tablecloths add a bright note to this large, reliable trattoria near the Archaeological Museum. This is your chance to try authentic Tuscan home-style specialties, such as *zuppa di pane* (bread soup), *pappardelle all'ocio* (noodles with duck sauce), and *ossobuco all'aretina* (sautéed veal shank). *Via Crispi 12, tel. 0575/22873. V. Closed Thurs. and July 1–18.*

Splurge

Buca di San Francesco. A frescoed cellar restaurant in a historic building next to the church of San Francesco, this *buca* (literally "hole," figuratively "cellar") has a medieval atmosphere and serves straightforward local specialties. Vegetarians will like the *ribollita* (vegetable soup thickened with bread) and the *sformato di verdure* (spinach or chard pie), though it may be served *con cibreo* (with a giblet sauce). Meat eaters will find the lean Chianina beef a succulent treat. A three-course dinner will set you back about 50,000–55,000 lire. *Piazza San Francesco 1, tel. 0575/23271. Reservations advised. AE, DC, MC, V. Closed Mon. evening, Tues., and July.*

Shopping

On the first Sunday of the month an extensive antiques fair and flea market takes over Piazza Grande and adjacent streets.

Festivals

The Joust of the Saracen, a rousing medieval pageant and contest on horseback, is held in Piazza Grande on the first Sunday in September.

Cortona

By bus, Cortona is about 90 minutes from Arezzo. Tourist office: Via Nazionale 72, near Piazza Garibaldi, where the buses arrive, tel. 0575/630352.

The medieval town of Cortona is known for its excellent small art gallery and a number of fine antiques shops, as well as for its colony of foreign residents. The heart of Cortona is formed by **Piazza della Repubblica** and the adjacent **Piazza Signorelli.** Wander into the courtyard of the picturesque **Palazzo Pretorio,** and, if you want to see a representative collection of Etruscan bronzes, climb its centuries-old stone staircase to the **Museo dell'Accademia Etrusca** (Gallery of Etruscan Art). *Piazza Signorelli 9, tel. 0575/630415. Admission: 5,000 lire. Open Apr.–Sept., Tues.–Sun. 10–1 and 4–7; Oct.–Mar., Tues.–Sun. 9–1 and 3–5.*

The nearby **Museo Diocesano** (Diocesan Museum) houses an impressive number of large and splendid paintings by native son Luca Signorelli, as well as a beautiful *Annunciation* by Fra Angelico, a delightful surprise to find in this small, eclectic town. *Piazza del Duomo 1, tel. 0575/62830. Admission: 5,000 lire. Open Apr.–Sept., Tues.–Sun. 9–1 and 3–6:30; Oct.–Mar., Tues.–Sun. 9–1 and 3–5.*

Lodging
Under 60,000 lire

Italia. Located on one of Cortona's medieval streets, this small hotel offers basic comforts. From guest-room windows, you can look out onto everyday life in a Tuscan hill town. The staff is friendly and helpful. *Via Ghibellina 5, tel. 0575/603264. 12 rooms, none with bath. No credit cards.*

Ostello della Gioventù. Conveniently located in the heart of town, this hotel offers dormitory-style accommodations. Registration is 6–11:30 PM; there's an 11:30 PM curfew. *Via Maffei 57, tel. 0575/601392. No credit cards.*

Dining
Under 30,000 lire

La Grotta. This family-run trattoria off Piazza della Repubblica, in an ancient wine cellar with vaulted ceilings, features classic Italian dishes and a few local specialties. Try the *gnocchi verdi* (tiny ricotta dumplings flavored with spinach and served with tomato sauce) or grilled *lombata di vitello* (veal chops). *Piazza Baldelli 3, tel. 0575/604–834. No credit cards. Closed Tues.*

Montepulciano

From Arezzo or Cortona there is frequent train service to Chiusi, about 20 minutes away; from Chiusi, buses go on to Montepulciano (via Chianciano), taking about 40 minutes for the 20-kilometer (12-mile) ride. On weekdays only, there are several buses a day between Siena and Montepulciano; the trip takes about 75 minutes. There is weekday bus service between Montepulciano and Pienza, approximately a 20-minute trip. Tourist information: c/o Cooperativa Il Sasso, Via Opio nel Corso 3, tel. 0578/758311.

Montepulciano sits high on a hilltop in the rolling green countryside that is the core of southern Tuscany. The town is a pyramid of redbrick buildings set within a circle of cypress trees. At an altitude of almost 2,000 feet, it is cool in summer and chilled in winter by the winds that sweep its spiraling streets. The town has an unusually harmonious look, a result of the work of three architects—Sangallo il Vecchio, Vignola, and Michelozzo—who endowed it with a large number of fine palaces and churches. Their work began under the aegis of Cosimo I de' Medici, who financed the rebuilding of the town after it opted for an alliance with Florence during the early 1500s. The 16th-century Renaissance buildings blend in well with earlier medieval edifices lining the stone streets that curve upward to **Piazza Grande.**

Montepulciano's numerous wine cellars and antiques dealers, and a few trendy shops and cafés hint that this otherwise sleepy town gets its share of tourists, especially during the international arts festival held here in July and August. On the hillside below the town walls is architect Sangallo's church of **San Biagio,** a paragon of Renaissance architectural perfection that is considered his masterpiece.

Another Florentine architect, Bernardo Rossellino, had his turn at achieving perfection when he was commissioned by the vainglorious Pope Pius II, the subject of Pinturicchio's frescoes in the Piccolomini Library in Siena, to design an entire town. A year after his election, the pope decided to transform his native village of Corsignano into a monument to himself. **Pienza,** 12 kilometers (7 miles) west of Montepulciano, is not only a curiosity—as an imperious pope's personal utopia—but also an exquisite example of early Renaissance architectural canons. Today the cool grandeur of Pienza's center seems almost surreal in this otherwise unpretentious village, known locally for *pienzino* (also called *cacio*), a smooth goat's-milk cheese.

Other interesting towns in this part of Tuscany can be reached by bus from Montepulciano or Siena, among them Montalcino, where one of Italy's finest wines, Brunello di Montalcino, is produced; San Quirico d'Orcia, a quiet, walled village with a beautiful Romanesque church; and Castelnuovo dell'Abate, on the bus line between Montalcino and Monte Amiata, with the Abbey of Sant'Antimo, a medieval gem. Monte Oliveto Maggiore, a Benedictine abbey with frescoes by Signorelli and Il Sodoma, is easily reached by car, or with some difficulty by bus from Siena to Chiusure, the nearest town.

Dining and Lodging

Under 85,000 lire

★

Il Marzocco. A 16th-century town house within the city walls has become a dignified, family-run hotel furnished in 19th-century style, with old-fashioned parlors and even a billiard room. Bedrooms are ample (many can accommodate extra beds) and are done up either in turn-of-the-century style or with spindly white wood, and many have large terraces overlooking the countryside. The restaurant serves home-style Tuscan fare; a full meal with house wine costs about 35,000 lire per person. *Piazza Savonarola 18, tel. 0578/757262. 18 rooms, 13 with bath or shower. Restaurant closed Wed. AE, DC, MC, V.*

Under 60,000 lire

Cittino. The bare essentials are what you get in the Cittino's few tiny bedrooms, but the signora-owner is cordial and the windows look onto the countryside. The rooms are located above the signora's trattoria, off one of the town's main streets. *Pici* (homemade spaghetti) with meat sauce and local *pecorino* (sheep's-milk) cheese are good here, as is the house wine. A full meal costs less than 20,000 lire per person. *Vicolo Via Nuovo (Via Voltaia), tel. 0578/757335. 3 rooms. No credit cards. Restaurant closed Wed.*

5   Venice

Venice is one of those cities you either love or hate. Some people are repelled by its maze of narrow, snaking streets, the faint smell of decay rising from its canals, and the hordes of pigeons and tourists in Piazza San Marco; they feel claustrophobic, longing for more grand vistas crowned with monumental architecture. But the far greater number of travelers are simply bowled over by this incredible treasure of a city. No matter how many times you have seen it in pictures or movies or TV commercials, the real thing is stranger and more lovely than you ever imagined. Its landmarks, the Basilica of San Marco and the Palazzo Ducale, are delightfully idiosyncratic, exotic mishmashes of Byzantine, Gothic, and Renaissance styles. Piazza San Marco is a true public gathering space, full of music and laughter and joy, yet only a minute's walk away are streets so quiet that your footsteps echo on the stone pavements and shuttered, crumbling facades. Sunlight shimmers here, and silvery mist softens every perspective. It is a city full of secrets, ineffably romantic, and given over entirely to pleasure.

The labyrinthine complexity of Venice and its detachment from the ways of the rest of the world can be disorienting at first. You have to get used to the idea that water is the city's element. Water forms Venice's main thoroughfares and defines its horizons. It softly laps the foundations of seemingly dilapidated palaces with tall Gothic windows, behind which you can spy the contradictory signs of conspicuous prosperity. Narrow streets twist, turn, and dive under shadowy porticoes only to emerge in vast, airy squares. You stride confidently along other streets to find that they end at a canal, with nary a bridge to take you to the other side. You have to backtrack, and you must consult your map repeatedly to find your way.

There are no cars in Venice; you must walk everywhere. Where you cannot walk you must take some kind of a boat and go by water. Occasionally, from fall to spring, you have to walk *in* the water, when the extraordinarily high tides known as *acque alte* flood the lower parts of the city. Raised walkways made of planks are provided by the city to help keep your feet dry, but a pair of rubber boots—and a sense of humor—come in handy.

From spring to fall another kind of flood flows through Piazza San Marco: Droves of tourists from all over the world eddy wide-eyed around stern guides imparting succinct history lessons in a babble of tongues. Like the Venetians, you will have to adapt to the crowds, visiting the major sights at odd hours, when the tour groups are still at breakfast or have boarded buses for their return to the mainland (most of them are daytrippers). Get away from Piazza San Marco when it's crowded; you'll be surprised to find many parts of Venice practically deserted. Explore the districts of Cannaregio or Castello, quiet areas where you can find the time and space to sit and contemplate the watercolor pages of Venetian history.

In recent years, Venice's municipal Youth Department has been running a special scheme to help young visitors. "Rolling Venice," as it is somewhat oddly titled, is open to everyone ages 14 to 29, operates between June and September inclusive, and costs 5,000 lire to join (at Rolling Venice's office at the Santa Lucia railway station or the APT office at Piazza San Marco). Benefits include a handy guidebook to the city and (sometimes substantial) discounts in hotels, restaurants, and shops. The Youth Department has also produced two useful leaflets, *"Dormire Giovani"* ("Accommodation for Young People," *see* Lodging, *below*) and *"Notturno Veneziano"* ("Venetian Nightlife," *see* Nightlife in The Arts and Nightlife, *below*).

Essential Information

Important Addresses and Numbers

Tourist Information
The main APT tourist office is at Calle dell'Ascensione 71C (tel. 041/522–6356), just off Piazza San Marco, under the arcade in the far left corner opposite the basilica. *Open Apr.–Oct., Mon.–Sat. 8:30–7:30; Nov.–Mar., Mon.–Sat. 8:30–1:30.*

Other information booths are at the Santa Lucia train station (tel. 041/719078) and on the Lido (Gran Viale S. Maria Elisabetta 6A, tel. 041/526–5721, fax 041/529–8720).

Consulates
U.K. (Campo della Carità 1051, Dorsoduro, tel. 041/522–7207). There is no U.S. or Canadian consular service.

Emergencies
Police, tel. 113.
Ambulance, tel. 041/523–0000.

Doctors and Dentists
Dial the number for ambulances (*see above*) and ask the **Croce Azzurra** (Blue Cross) to recommend a doctor or dentist convenient to your location. The British consulate can also recommend doctors and dentists.

Late-Night Pharmacies
Venetian pharmacies take turns opening late or on Sunday; dial 192 for information on which are open. Alternatively, the daily

list of late-night pharmacies is posted on the front of every pharmacy. Two with English-speaking staff are **Farmacia Italo-Inglese** (Calle della Mandola 3717, in San Marco district, tel. 041/522–4837) and **Farmacia Internazionale** (Calle Larga XXII Marzo 2067, in the San Marco district, tel. 041/522–2311).

English-Language Bookstores
Venice's centuries of experience in dealing with foreign visitors mean that bookstores and newsstands throughout the city are well stocked with publications in English. **Fantoni,** on Salizzada San Luca, specializes in art books. **Il Libraio di San Barnaba,** on Fondamenta Gherardini, near Campo San Barnaba, has shelves full of paperbacks and books on Venice in English.

Good general-interest bookstores include **Serenissima** (Salizzada San Zulian), near San Marco; **Emiliana Editrice** (Calle Goldoni), between Piazza San Marco and Rialto; and **Studium** (Calle de la Canonica), off Piazzetta dei Leoncini. Enrico Dorio's newspaper shop on the Frezzaria shopping street, close to the post office off Piazza San Marco, has a good selection of English-language newspapers and magazines and is open from early in the morning until late at night.

Travel Agencies
American Express (Salizzada San Moise 1471, tel. 041/520–0844); **Sattis Viaggi** (Calle Larga dell'Ascensione 1261, tel. 041/528–5101, 041/528–5102, or 041/528–5103); and **Wagons Lits/Turismo** (Piazzetta dei Leoncini 289, tel. 041/522–3405).

Where to Change Money
There is an exchange window at the train station (open 8–6), but you will get slightly better rates at the banks in the vicinity of Piazza San Marco. There are also a number of private exchange bureaus and travel agents that change money. Their rates are invariably lower than those at the banks, however, and they sometimes charge exorbitant commissions, so beware!

Arriving and Departing by Plane

Airports and Airlines
Marco Polo airport at Tessera, about 10 kilometers (6 miles) north of the city on the mainland, is served by domestic and international Alitalia flights, including service from London, Amsterdam, Brussels, Frankfurt, Munich, Paris, Vienna, and Zurich. For information, call 041/661262.

Between the Airport and Downtown
By Bus
Blue **ATVO** buses make the 25-minute nonstop trip from the airport to Piazzale Roma, which is where the road ends at the entrance to Venice; from Piazzale Roma you can get a waterbus to the landing nearest your hotel. ATVO fare is 5,000 lire. There are local **ACTV** buses from the airport, but you need a ticket (fare 1,000 lire) before boarding the bus, and there is no ticket office at the airport. You can buy a ticket at the tobacconist stand in the airport, but this is not always open. Also, luggage can be a problem on the ACTV bus, which is usually crowded with local commuters.

By Boat
Depending on where your hotel is, this may be the best way to get to Venice from the airport. The most direct way is by the **Cooperativa San Marco** launch, with regular scheduled service throughout the day, until midnight; it takes about an hour to get to the landing just off Piazza San Marco, stopping at the Lido on the way, and the fare is 15,000 lire per person, including bags.

Arriving and Departing by Train and Bus

By Train Venice has rail connections with every major city in Italy and the rest of Europe.

The **Santa Lucia** station is on the Grand Canal in the northwest corner of the city. Some through trains do not terminate at Santa Lucia, stopping only at the Venezia–Mestre station on the mainland. All trains traveling to and from Santa Lucia stop at Mestre, so to get from Venezia–Mestre to Santa Lucia, or vice versa (a journey of about 10 minutes), take the first available train. For train information, call 041/715555.

By Bus The bus terminal is at Piazzale Roma, near the vaporetto stop of that name. Express buses operated by SITA connect Venice with major cities and towns in the region.

Porters Because there are no cars in Venice, people sometimes need porters to help carry their luggage and negotiate the footbridges. Porters wear badges and blue shirts or smocks. You will find them at the airport and train stations and also at some of the principal vaporetto landings. They charge about 15,000 lire for one bag and about 5,000 lire for each additional piece of luggage, and there is an extra charge at night and on holidays. Porters will accompany you all the way on the vaporetto between your hotel and the Santa Lucia station or Piazzale Roma; for this service they charge about 50,000 lire inclusive. Since you can't always count on finding a porter when you need one, a folding luggage cart will prove invaluable (suitcases with wheels are not the answer on uneven paving stones and over bridges).

However you arrive in Venice, find out the location of your hotel beforehand and exactly how to get there. Depending on its location, you may have to walk some distance from the landing to reach it, with or without the help and guidance of a porter. Be prepared to find your way on your own or to call the hotel for instructions upon arrival.

Getting Around

First-time visitors find that getting around Venice presents some unusual problems: The layout is complex; the waterborne transportation can be bewildering; the house-numbering system is baffling; street names in the six districts are duplicated; and often you must walk, whether you want to or not. It's essential that you have a good map showing all street names and vaporetto routes; buy one at a newsstand. In the areas where you're most likely to wander, signs are posted on many corners pointing you in the right direction for the nearest major landmark—San Marco, the Rialto, the Accademia, etc.—but don't count on finding such signs once you're deep into residential neighborhoods. Count on getting lost at least once—it's an essential part of the Venice experience.

By Vaporetto ACTV vaporetti run the length of the Grand Canal and circle the city. There are about 20 lines, some of which connect Venice with the major and minor islands in the lagoon. Line 1 is the Grand Canal local. Line 5 takes a circular route skirting Venice, taking in the islands of Murano and the Giudecca. Timetables are posted on all landing stages where ticket booths are located (open early morning–9 PM). Buy single tickets or books of 10, and in the latter case stamp your ticket in the machine at the landing. The fare is 2,200 lire on most lines; 3,300 lire for the Line 2 express connecting the train station to Rialto and to San Marco and the Lido. A 24-hour tourist ticket costs 12,000 lire, while a three-day tourist ticket costs 18,000 lire, but these are not valid on Line 2. Vaporetti run every 10–20 minutes or so during the day and more frequently during the summer; Lines 1 and 2 run more or less every hour between midnight and dawn. Landing stages are clearly marked with name and line number. Check before boarding to make sure the boat is going in your direction.

If you are going to be in Venice for more than a week, or plan to return in the future, it is well worth getting a Cartavenezia, which allows you to travel on vaporetti for at least half the normal fare. The card costs 10,000 lire and is valid for three years. Take your passport and a passport-size photo to one of the ACTV offices: near the Sant'Angelo landing on the Grand Canal (open Mon.–Sat. 8:30–1), at Fondamente Nuove, or at the S. Maria Elisabetta landing on the Lido (both open Mon.–Sat. 8:30–7). You must carry the Cartavenezia with you and show it with your stamped half-price ticket if asked.

By Traghetto Few tourists know about the two-man gondolas that ferry people across the Grand Canal at various fixed points. They are the cheapest and shortest gondola ride in Venice and can save a lot of walking. The fare is 500 lire, which you hand to the gondolier when you get on. Look for *traghetto* signs.

By Gondola No visit to Venice is complete without a gondola ride, and the way to beat the expense of the fare is to form a group of five people so that you can share the cost. The best time is in the late afternoon or early evening hours, when the Grand Canal isn't so heavily trafficked, and it's best to start from a station on the Grand Canal because the lagoon is usually choppy. Make it clear that you want to see the smaller canals and come to terms on the cost and duration of the ride before you start. Gondoliers are supposed to charge a fixed minimum of about 70,000 lire for up to five passengers for 50 minutes. After 8 PM the rate goes up. The official tariffs are quoted in the "Guest in Venice" booklet (*see* The Arts in The Arts and Nightlife, *below*). Bargaining may get you a better price.

On Foot This is the only way to reach many parts of Venice, so wear comfortable shoes. Invest in a good map that names all streets, and count on getting lost more than once. Look for the yellow directional signs on buildings on the main routes, as between Ferrovia (the train station) and San Marco.

Opening and Closing Times

Many tourist-oriented shops in Venice stay open all day. Others observe a midday closing from 12:30 or 1 to 3:30 or 4. Banks are open 8:30–1:30 and 2:30–4.

Lodging

Venice is made up almost entirely of time-worn buildings, and most of its hotels are in renovated palaces. Affordable rooms tend to be small and dowdy, and rarely do affordable hotels have much lounge space. Because of preservation laws, many cannot install elevators, so you will probably have to climb stairs. Air-conditioning can be an important option in the oppressive heat of summer; if available, it is worth the extra charge. Although there are no cars in Venice, there are boats plying the canals and pedestrians chattering in the steets, even late at night. Don't be surprised if your room is noisy (earplugs help).

The busiest seasons for hotels are from spring to autumn, but they are also busy from December 20 to January 2 and during the two-week Carnival period leading up to Ash Wednesday, usually in February. Book well in advance. If you don't have reservations, you can almost always get a room in any category by going upon arrival to the AVA (Venetian Hoteliers Association) booths at the train station (open Apr.–Oct., 8 AM–10 PM; Nov.–Mar., 8 AM–9:30 PM), airport (open Apr.–Oct., 10 AM–9 PM; Nov.–Mar., 10:30 AM–6:30 PM), and at the municipal parking garage at Piazzale Roma (open: Apr.–Oct., 9 AM–10 PM; Nov.–Mar., 9 AM–9 PM). The 15,000- to 60,000-lire deposit (depending on the category of the hotel) is rebated on your bill.

Italian hotels are officially rated with one to five stars. Those listed here as Under 100,000 lire are one-star properties where you can sometimes get a room with a private bath (usually only a shower); those listed as Under 65,000 lire are also one-star hotels, but at these you will certainly have to forgo the private bath. Most hotels quote rates inclusive of breakfast.

To save money you can also stay in the budget accommodations offered by various religious institutions in Venice (*see* Under 65,000 lire). These are most often dormitory-style and may be limited to either men or women, but some take both sexes, as well as families. There is usually a curfew. The Youth Department's *"Dormire Giovani"* leaflet ("Accommodation for Young People"), available from APT information offices, contains an up-to-date list of all the hostels in Venice and details of which hotels offer discounts to card holders in the "Rolling Venice" program (*see* Introduction to Venice, *above*). Remember that it is essential to know how to get to your hotel when you arrive in Venice.

Highly recommended lodgings are indicated by a star ★.

Under 125,000 lire

Bucintoro. A small, family-run hotel overlooking the lagoon, Bucintoro is near the Arsenale. Every room has a view of the water, and rooms without a private bath are a bargain. *Riva San Biagio 2135, Castello, tel. 041/522–3240, fax 041/523–5224. 28 rooms, 18 with bath. No credit cards. Closed Jan.–mid-Feb.*

★ **Locanda Fiorita.** This welcoming, small hotel is tucked away in a sunny little square (where breakfast is served in the summer), just off Campo Santo Stefano, near the Accademia Bridge, and is very central for sightseeing. The rooms have beamed ceilings and are simply and unfussily furnished. *Campiello Novo 3457, San Marco, tel. 041/523–4754. 10 rooms, 7 with shower. AE, MC, V. Closed 2 weeks Nov.–Dec.*

Riva. This small hotel, close to San Marco, stands in a picturesque spot at the junction of three canals, much used by all manner of Venetian watercraft, which are endlessly fascinating to watch but can be a little noisy early in the morning. It has recently been refurbished by its enthusiastic new owner. *Ponte dell'Angelo 5310, Castello, tel. 041/522–7034. 12 rooms, 10 with bath. No credit cards. Closed mid-Nov.–Feb. 1, except 2 weeks at Christmas.*

Under 100,000 lire

Caneva. One of the larger inexpensive hotels, Caneva has its own quiet courtyard, and rooms on one side overlook a canal. It is located between San Marco and the Rialto. *Calle Drio della Fava 5515 (on the calle to the right of the church of the Fava), Castello, tel. 041/522–8118. 23 rooms, 10 with bath. No credit cards.*

Al Piave. You'll find clean, basic accommodations at this hotel, which is centrally located, near San Marco and Santa Maria Formosa. *Ruga Giuffa 4840, Castello, tel. 041/528–5174. 12 rooms without bath. AE, MC, V.*

★ **Silva.** Off Campo Santa Maria Formosa, close to San Marco, this attractive small hotel is on a quiet canal. Low rates include breakfast, and some rooms can accommodate an extra bed. *Fondamenta del Remedio 4423, Castello, tel. 041/522–7643, fax 041/528–6817. 25 rooms, 7 with bath. No credit cards.*

Tintoretto. This is a popular little hotel off Strada Nuova, near the church of Santa Fosca and near the Ca' d'Oro landing stage. *Campiello della Chiesa 2316, Cannaregio, tel. 041/721–522. 20 rooms, 11 with bath. MC, V. Closed Jan.*

Under 65,000 lire

Bernardi Semenzato. This is a welcoming, sympathetic, small hotel just off Strada Nuova and near Rialto. *Calle dell'Oca 4366, Cannaregio, tel. 041/522–7857. 18 rooms, 10 with bath or shower. No credit cards. Closed 3 weeks Jan.–Feb.*

Ca' Foscari. This pleasant little hotel is located between the University of Venice and the San Toma landing on the Grand Canal. *Calle della Frescada 3888, Dorsoduro, tel. 041/522–5817. 10 rooms, 2 with shower. No credit cards. Closed Dec.–Jan.*

Da Pino. This is another pleasant hotel near the university, and one that, unusual for this category, accepts credit cards. *Crosera (San Pantalon) 3891/2, Dorsoduro, tel. 041/522–3646. 16 rooms. DC, MC, V. Closed 1 week during Christmas.*

San Samuele. Very centrally located (near Palazzo Grassi), this friendly, family-run hotel has attractive, sunny rooms. *Salizzada San Samuele 3358, San Marco, tel. 041/522–8045. 10 rooms, 2 with bath. No credit cards. Open all year.*

Istituto Suore Canossiane. This hostel run by nuns is very close to the main Giudecca vaporetto stop (Line 8) and near the Sant'Eufemia and Redentore landings (Line 5). The hostel is primarily for girls, but women are also accepted. It is open all day, but there is a 10:30 PM curfew. *Ponte Piccolo 428, Giudecca, tel. 041/522–2157. No credit cards. Open all year.*

Ostello (Youth Hostel). Located on the Giudecca (at the Zitelle

Venice Lodging

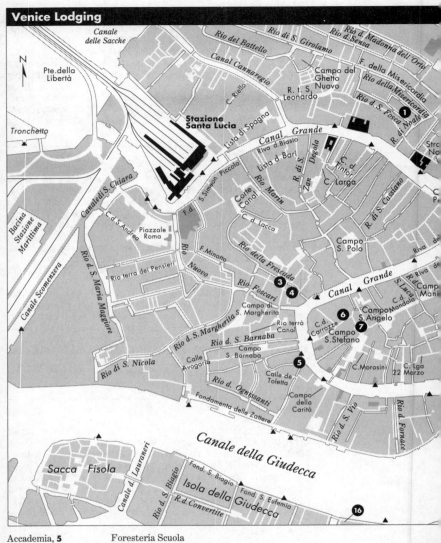

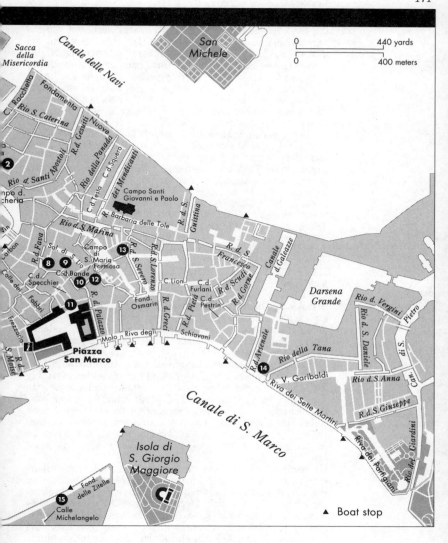

Sacca
della
Misericordia

Canale delle Navi

San
Michele

0 | 440 yards
0 | 400 meters

Rachetta

Fondamenta

Rio S. Caterina

R. d. Gesuiti Nuove

Rio della Panada

C. d. Squero

C. d. Mendicanti

2

Rio d. Santi Apostoli

C. d. Tesla

Campo Santi
Giovanni e Paolo

R. d. S.
Giustina

Rio d. S. Marina

R.t. Barbaria delle Tole

Canale d. Galeazze

Fava

R. d. S.
Francesco

R. d. S.
Marina

Sot. di S. Lio

Campo
di
S. Maria
Formosa

13

R. d. S. Severo

R. d. S. Lorenzo

8 9

C. d. Bande

R. d. Scudi

R. d. Corne

Darsena
Grande

Rio d. Vergini

C. d.
Specchier

10   12

C. Lion

C. d.
Furlani

di S.
Pietro

Fond.
Osmarin

R. d. Pietà

C. d.
Pestrin

R. d. S. Daniele

Calle dei
Fabbri

11

R. d. Greci

Schiavoni

R. d. Palazzo

Frezzaria

i

Molo

Riva degli

Piazza
San Marco

R. d.
S. Moisè

Rio dell'Arsenale

Rio della Tana

14

Cannaregio

Rio d. S. Anna

R. d. S. Giuseppe

Rio dei Giardini

V. Garibaldi

Riva dei Sette Martiri

Canale di S. Marco

Isola di
S. Giorgio
Maggiore

Fond.
delle Zitelle

Riva dei Partigiani

15

Calle
Michelangelo

i

▲ Boat stop

vaporetto stop on Line 5), this hostel has a wonderful view of the city. You'll need an IYHA card to stay here, but you can purchase one on the spot. There's an 11:30 PM curfew, and you have to be out by 9 in the morning. It costs 15,000 lire per night, including breakfast and sheets. Good and generous meals are available for about 11,000 lire. *Fondamenta delle Zitelle 86, Giudecca, tel. 041/523–8211. 385 beds in 16 dormitories. Opens at noon in summer and 4 PM in winter for 6 PM registration. Phone reservations accepted from October to May. No credit cards.*

Foresteria Scuola Valdese. Conveniently located off Campo Santa Maria Formosa, this hostel is run by the Waldesian church and offers dormitory accommodations (20,000 lire per night, including breakfast). You must reserve far in advance for the two big bedrooms, which sleep up to four, or for the two apartments with kitchens, for up to six people. *Calle Lunga Santa Maria Formosa 5170, Castello, tel. 041/528–6797. 42 beds. Telephone reservations accepted 9:30–1 and 6–8. No credit cards.*

There are several additional summer-only hostels, all listed in the *"Dormire Giovani"* ("Accommodation for Young People") leaflet, available free from the APT office (*see* Introduction to Venice, *above*).

Splurge

★ **Accademia.** One of Venice's most charming hotels, the Accademia is also one of its most popular, so early reservations are a must. It's located in a 17th-century villa near the Accademia Gallery and the Grand Canal. The lounges, bar, and wood-paneled breakfast room are cheery, and there are fresh flowers everywhere. You can even have breakfast outside on the garden terrace in good weather. Bedrooms are ample and comfortably furnished, whether in the traditional, wood-paneled style or in the bright, contemporary look of the air-conditioned top floor. A gracious, private-home atmosphere makes this one a gem. Rates run from 130,000 to 170,000 lire. *Fondamenta Bollani 1058, Dorsoduro, tel. 041/523–7846, fax 041/523–9152. 28 rooms, most with bath or shower. Facilities: bar, 2 gardens, landing on canal. AE, DC, MC, V.*

Concordia. Twenty rooms in this stylish, comfortable, four-star hotel overlook the Basilica of San Marco. The rooftop *mansarda* (garret) room even has its own terrace, with a panoramic view of the square. During the hotel's low season (mid-November to mid-March, excluding the weeks of Christmas and Carnival) and mid-season (July and August), the Concordia offers a 25% discount if you stay four to five nights between Sunday and Thursday, which works out to about 180,000 lire per night in low season and about 195,000 lire per night in mid-season—an exceptionally good deal, given the hotel's position and quality. (To be eligible for the discount you must request it when booking.) *Calle Larga San Marco 367, San Marco, tel. 041/520–6866, fax 041/520–6775. 55 rooms with bath. AE, DC, MC, V.*

Exploring Venice

Guided Tours

Orientation Two-hour walking tours of the San Marco area, taking in the basilica and the Doge's Palace, can be booked through **American Express** (tel. 041/520–0844) and other travel agencies. The American Express "Jewels of the Venetian Republic" tour (about 30,000 lire) ends with a glassblowing demonstration. From March 15 to November 15, American Express offers an afternoon walking tour that ends with a gondola ride (about 35,000 lire).

Special-Interest American Express and other operators offer group gondola rides with serenades, daily from May through October in the evening (about 35,000 lire).

During the summer, free guided tours (some in English, including one at 11 AM) of the **Basilica di San Marco** are offered by the Patriarchate of Venice; information is available in the atrium of the church. *Tel. 041/520–0333. No tours Sun.*

Excursions Don't take organized tours to the islands of Murano, Burano, or Torcello. They are annoyingly commercial and emphasize glass-factory showrooms, pressuring you to buy. You can easily visit these islands on your own (*see* Tour 5: Islands of the Lagoon in Exploring Venice, *below*).

Venice for Free—or Almost

People-watching You could spend hours watching the people and pigeons in Piazza San Marco or relaxing on a bench in Campo San Giacomo dell'Orio, where you'll feel that you're part of Venice.

Views Buy an ice-cream cone on the Zattere and sit on a bench while you watch the big ships sail right through Venice on the Giudecca canal.

Take a vaporetto tour of the Grand Canal, for the price of a ticket, but do your best to get one of the few seats at the prow, where you'll have an unobstructed view.

Markets Wander through the food and vegetable market at Rialto any morning except Sunday, and be sure to take in the fish market (closed on Sunday and Monday), where the variety of sea creatures for sale is staggering.

Walks Stroll through the **Ghetto,** the small island in Cannaregio to which the Jews of Venice were confined for more than two centuries beginning in 1516. The Ghetto eventually expanded to include the Ghetto Vecchio, Ghetto Nuovo, and Ghetto Nuovissimo. In 1797, when the Venetian republic fell, Napoleon's troops pulled down the Ghetto's gates, but by then Jewish homes and synagogues were rooted in these neighborhoods and the word *ghetto*—which perhaps derived from foundries for the casting, or "getto," of metal that had existed there—passed into the language as a place for the isolation of Jews or other minorities. The **Museo Ebraico** is in one corner of Campo Ghetto Nuovo, a pretty square with a fountain and a few trees. From the museum, you can join a guided tour of the synagogues; tours are in English and are given several times a day. *Campo del Ghetto Nuovo, tel. 041/715359. Admission: 4,000*

lire; 10,000 lire with tour. Open June–Sept., weekdays and
Sun. 10–7; Oct.–May, weekdays and Sun. 10–4. Closed Sat.
and Jewish holidays.

Art   Stop in to see the **house of playwright Carlo Goldoni,** on Calle
dei Nomboli, near San Tomà, which still contains some original
costumes and manuscripts. *Mon.–Sat. 8:30–1:30. Admission
free.*

See the fabulous Tintorettos in the artist's parish church, **Madonna dell'Orto,** where he was buried to the right of the main
altar. On each side of the altar are his paintings *The Last Judgment* and *Adoration of the Golden Calf,* in which he supposedly
painted his own face (with a black beard) on one of the pagans
holding the calf. There are several more of his paintings here.
Cannaregio district, Fondamenta Madonna dell'Orto.

Visit the **Guggenheim Collection** of modern art in Palazzo
Venier dei Leoni on the Grand Canal on Saturday evening
(6–9), when admission is free. *Calle San Cristoforo,
Dorsoduro, tel. 041/520–6288. Open Wed.–Mon. 11–6, extended until 9 on Sat.*

Orientation

The church of San Marco is unquestionably the heart of Venice,
but venturing even 50 yards from it can sometimes lead to confusion. Although the smaller canals (a canal is called a *rio*) are
spanned by many bridges, the Grand Canal can only be crossed
on foot at three points—near the train station, at the Rialto
bridge, and at the Accademia bridge—which decidedly complicates matters. It's supremely maddening to find yourself on the
wrong bank of a canal with no bridge in sight.

A street is called a *calle,* but a street that runs alongside a canal
is called either a *riva* or a *fondamenta.* The closed-in streetscapes of Venice make it hard to see any reference point, such as
the spire of the Campanile, above the rooftops, and the narrow
back streets often take unpredictable turnings that confound
your sense of direction. Streets and canals may look deceptively familiar only to make sudden dead ends. Keep a map of
vaporetto lines with you at all times because the best way back
to Piazza San Marco or your hotel may well be along one of these
routes.

Our first two tours should help you get your bearings. Tour 1
takes in the sights around the San Marco district, the geographic and spiritual center of the city. Tour 2 takes to the water along the Grand Canal, the main artery of Venice, linking
many of its major sights. Tours 3 and 4 take you east and west,
respectively, giving you the chance to explore some of the more
offbeat sights and areas, as well as the less central churches and
art collections. The last two tours take you to the other major
islands of the Venetian lagoon, places where the pace of life is
slower and such crafts as glassblowing and lace-making are still
practiced.

Highlights for First-time Visitors

Accademia Gallery (Tour 4: The Western and Northern Districts)
Basilica di San Marco (Tour 1: The San Marco District)

Campo Santi Giovanni e Paolo (Tour 3: To the Arsenal and Beyond)
Frari Church (Tour 4: The Western and Northern Districts)
Murano, Burano, and Torcello (Tour 5: Islands of the Lagoon)
Palazzo Ducale (Tour 1: The San Marco District)
Piazza San Marco (Tour 1: The San Marco District)
Ponte di Rialto (Tour 2: The Grand Canal)
San Giorgio Maggiore (Tour 6: San Maggiore and the Giudecca)
Scuola di San Rocco (Tour 4: The Western and Northern Districts)

Tour 1: The San Marco District

Numbers in the margin correspond to points of interest on the Venice map.

❶ **Piazza San Marco** (St. Mark's Square) is the heart of Venice, perpetually animated during the day, when it's filled with people and crowds of fluttering pigeons. It can be magical at night, especially in the winter, when melancholy mists swirl around the lampposts and bell tower. Historically and geographically, it's the logical place to start exploring the city. If you stand at the piazza's far end, facing the basilica, you'll notice that rather than being a strict rectangle, it opens wider at the basilica end, enhancing the perspective and creating the illusion of being even larger than it is. On your left, the long, arcaded building is the **Procuratie Vecchie,** built in the early 16th century as offices and residences for the powerful Procurators of San Marco, administrators of the basilica. Across the piazza, on your right, is the **Procuratie Nuove,** built almost a century later in a more grandiose classical style. The Procuratie Nuove has impeccable architectural lineage: It was originally planned by perhaps Venice's greatest Renaissance architect, Jacopo Sansovino (1486–1570) of Florence, to carry on the look of his **Libreria Vecchia,** where the Marciana National Library is now housed, around the corner to the right, across from the Palazzo Ducale, though Sansovino died before the building was begun. The actual designer was Vincenzo Scamozzi (ca. 1552–1616), a pupil of Palladio and a devout neoclassicist; later sections were completed by Baldassare Longhena (1598–1682), Venice's other great architect, who belonged firmly to the Baroque tradition.

When Napoleon entered Venice with his troops in 1797, he called Piazza San Marco "the world's most beautiful drawing room"—and promptly gave orders to redecorate it. His architects demolished an old church that stood at the end of the square farthest from the basilica and put up the **Ala Napoleonica** (Napoleonic Wing), or Fabbrica Nuova (New Building), to unite the two 16th-century buildings on either side.

Today the arcades of these three grand buildings shelter shops and cafés. Several of the cafés have their own small orchestras that play outdoors in fair weather; though patrons of the cafés must pay an additional charge for the entertainment, passersby in the piazza can enjoy it for free. On warm summer nights, the orchestras compete to see which can draw the biggest crowd, and the fun is infectious.

On the Procuratie Vecchie side is the historic **Café Quadri,** which was shunned by Venetians during the 19th century when the occupying Austrians made it their gathering place; loyal Venetians preferred the venerable **Café Florian,** on the

Venice

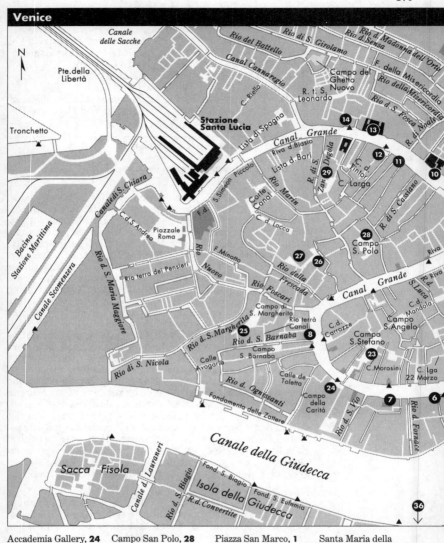

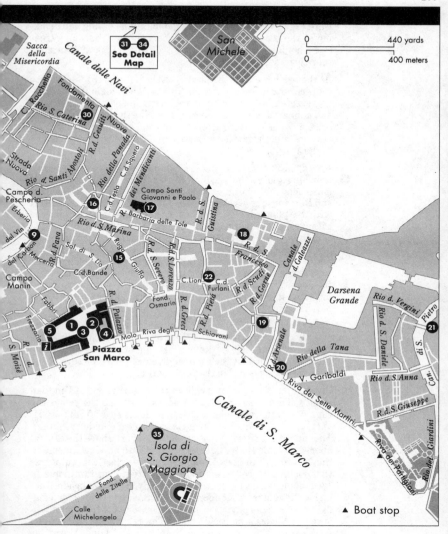

31 – 34
See Detail Map

Sacca della Misericordia

San Michele

0 ____ 440 yards
0 ____ 400 meters

Canale delle Navi

Fondamenta Nuove

Rio S. Caterina

30

Racchetta

Strada Nuova

Rio d. Santi Apostoli

R. d. Gesuiti

Rio della Panada

C. d. Squero

C. d. Tetta

C. d. Mendicanti

Campo Santi Giovanni e Paolo

16

17

R. Barbaria delle Tole

Rio d. S. Marina

Campo d. Pescheria

Erberia

del Vin

9

del Ca' Mison

Merceria

R. d. Fava

Sal. di S. Lio

Ruga Giuffa

15

C. d. Bande

Campo Manin

Fabbri

R. d. S. Severo

R. d. S. Lorenzo

Fond. Osmarin

Frezzaria

R. d. Palazzo

Molo

R. d. Pietà

R. d. Greci

C. Lion

22

C. d. Furlani

R. d. Scudi

R. d. Corte

Fond.

19

Riva degli Schiavoni

1 2 3 4 5

i

Piazza San Marco

R. d. S. Moise

Cristina

R. d. S. Francesco

18

Canale d. Galeazze

Darsena Grande

Rio d. Vergini

Rio d. S. Daniele

21

Pietro

S. ip.

Con.

R. d. Arsenale

20

V. Garibaldi

Rio della Tana

Rio d. S. Anna

Riva dei Sette Martiri

R. d. S. Giuseppe

Canale di S. Marco

35

Isola di S. Giorgio Maggiore

ci

Fond. delle Zitelle

Calle Michelangelo

Rio dei Giardini

Riva dei Partigiani

▲ Boat stop

Procuratie Nuove side, where Casanova, Wagner, and Proust were regular customers. Like a gondola ride, eating and drinking at these expensive cafés may be a splurge, but it's a treat that shouldn't be missed. (If you sit at the bar at Florian's, there is no service charge.)

At the basilica end of the piazza, on the left (north) side next to the Procuratie Vecchie, is the **Torre dell'Orologio** (Clock Tower), erected in 1496 and endowed with an enameled timepiece and animated figures of Moors that strike the hour. During Ascension Week (40 days after Easter) and on Epiphany (Jan. 6), an angel and three wise men go in and out of the doors and bow to the Virgin.

Now it is finally time to turn your attention to the piazza's crowning glory, the **Basilica di San Marco,** one of Europe's most beautiful churches. An opulent synthesis of Byzantine and Romanesque styles, it is laid out in a Greek cross topped off with five plump domes. The basilica did not actually become the cathedral of Venice until as late as 1807, but its role as the church of the doge (the elected head of the Venetian republic) gave it immense power and wealth. It was begun in 1063 to house the remains of St. Mark the Evangelist, which had been filched from Alexandria two centuries earlier by two agents of the doge. The story goes that they stole the saint's remains and hid them in a barrel under layers of pickled pork to get them past Islamic guards.

That escapade is illustrated in a mosaic in the lunette (semicircular decoration) over the farthest left of the front doors. This 13th-century mosaic is the earliest one on this heavily decorated facade; look at it closely and you can see a picture of the church as it appeared in the 13th century.

Throughout the years this church stood as a symbol of Venetian wealth and power, and it was endowed with all the riches the republic's admirals and merchants could carry off from the Orient, earning it the nickname *Chiesa D'Oro* (Golden Church). The four bronze horses that prance and snort above the central doorway (copies only, but the originals are on view indoors in the Museo di San Marco, *see below*) were classical sculptures that victorious Venetians took away from Constantinople in 1204, along with a lot of other loot that you can see inside. Just inside the central front doors in the church porch, look for a medallion of red porphyry set in the floor to mark the spot of another of Venice's political coups: The reconciliation between Barbarossa, the Holy Roman Emperor, and Pope Alexander III was brought about by Doge Sebastiano Ziani in 1177.

Entrance to the church is free, but be warned: Guards at the door turn away any visitors, male or female, wearing shorts or inappropriate attire. If you want to take a free guided tour in English (offered Mon.–Sat. at 11 AM in summer, and with less certainty in winter, since the guides are volunteers), wait on the left in the porch for a group to form. *Church open Mon.– Sat. 9:30–5:30, Sun. 2:30–5:30.*

One of the innovations of this church was a roof of brick vaulting, rather than wood, enabling the ceiling to be decorated with mosaics. As you enter the basilica, you'll find it surprisingly dark inside, compared with the soaring, light-filled Gothic cathedrals of northern Europe. This is because many of the original windows were filled in and covered with even more mosaics. In the mysterious dusk, candles flicker and the gold tiles of mosaics glitter softly, sensuously. (The tiles were laid on at slight angles to achieve precisely this effect.) The earliest mosaics are from the 11th and 12th centuries; later ones, such as the Last Judgment on the arch between the porch and the nave, said to be based on drawings by Tintoretto, were done as late as the 16th century. Go into the Zen Chapel (to the right just off the porch, and named after a local cardinal rather than any form of Buddhism) to see some earlier (13th-century) mosaics, telling the story of the life of St. Mark. Next to it, the **Baptistery** contains a bronze font cover by Jacopo Sansovino and the tomb of Doge Andrea Dandolo (1307–1354), a friend of Petrarch and a writer in his own right. Several of the earlier doges were buried here, while later ones were interred in the church of Santi Giovanni e Paolo (*see* Tour 3, *below*).

Two more chapels, both in the left transept, are worth a special look: the **Chapel of the Madonna of Nicopeia,** which holds a precious icon (part of the loot from Constantinople) that many consider to be Venice's most powerful protector; and next to it, on the left, a small chapel dedicated to the Virgin Mary, with fine 15th-century mosaics depicting her life, possibly based on drawings by Andrea Mantegna.

If you stand in the central aisle facing the main altar, notice the polygonal pulpit to the right, at the intersection of the nave and right transept. After the coronation ceremony, each new doge stood here for the people to behold him in the glory of his new office.

To enter the **sanctuary,** you must pay an admission fee (2,000 lire), but it's well worth it. (Open Mon.–Sat. 10–4, Sun. 1:45–4.) The main altar, with its green marble canopy lifted high on carved alabaster columns, covers the tomb of St. Mark. Behind this is the real attraction: the **Pala d'Oro** (Golden Altarpiece), a dazzling gold-and-silver screen encrusted with precious gems and enameled panels. Originally made in Constantinople in the 10th century, it was continually embellished during the next few centuries by master craftsmen in Venice and elsewhere. Invest a few 100-lire coins to listen to a recorded description—otherwise you'll miss some of the incredible detail. The bronze door leading from the sanctuary back into the sacristy is another Sansovino work; check out the top-left corner, where the artist included a self-portrait and, above that, a picture of his friend and fellow artist Titian.

The same ticket admits you to the **Treasury,** which is entered from the right transept. It contains some exquisite pieces, many of them exotic treasures borne away from Constantinople and other vanquished places.

From the atrium, climb the steep stairway to the **Museo di San Marco** (St. Mark's Museum) for a look at the interior of the church from the organ gallery and a sweeping view of Piazza San Marco and the Piazzetta dei Leoncini from the outdoor gallery. The highlight of the museum is the close-up of the four magnificent gilded bronze horses that once stood outside on the gallery. The originals, they were probably cast in Constantinople in the 4th century AD, but some believe they are Greek works of the 3rd century BC. Napoleon hauled them off to Paris after he conquered Venice in 1797, but they were returned after the fall of the French Empire. *Admission: 2,000 lire. Open Apr.–Sept., daily 9:30–5:30; Oct.–Mar., daily 10–4.*

❸ Just outside the basilica is the tall brick **Campanile** (Bell Tower), a reconstruction of the original, which stood for 1,000 years before it collapsed one morning in 1912, practically without warning. In the 15th century, clerics found guilty of immoral behavior were suspended in wooden cages from the tower, sometimes to subsist on bread and water for as long as a year, sometimes to starve to death. The pretty marble loggia (covered gallery) at its base was built in the early 16th century by Jacopo Sansovino; it, too, has been carefully restored. The view from the tower on a clear day is worth the price of admission. You get a pigeon's-eye view of the city, the Lido, the lagoon, and the mainland as far as the distant Alps. Oddly, you can't see the myriad canals that snake through the 117 islets on which Venice is built. *Piazza San Marco, tel. 041/522–4064. Admission: 4,000 lire. Open Easter–Oct., daily 10–8; Nov.–Easter, daily 10–4. Closed for maintenance most of Jan.*

The square that leads from Piazza San Marco down to the waters of St. Mark's Basin is called **Piazzetta San Marco.** This landing stage, now crowded with excursion boats, was once the grand entrance to the republic. Two tall columns rise here on the waterfront: One is topped by the winged lion, a traditional emblem of St. Mark that became by extension the symbol of Venice itself; the other bears aloft a statue of St. Theodore (the first patron saint of Venice) and his dragon.

❹ Above the piazzetta rises the **Palazzo Ducale** (Doge's Palace), a Gothic-Renaissance fantasia of pink-and-white marble, a majestic expression of the prosperity and power attained by Venice during its most glorious period. Its top-heavy design (the dense upper floors rest on the graceful ground-floor colonnade) has always confounded architectural purists, who insist that proper architecture be set out the other way around. The palace was not only the residence of the doge but also the parliament house, home of the law courts, and a prison. Venice's government, set up sometime in the 7th century as a participatory democracy, provided for an elected ruler, the doge, to serve for life, but in practice he was simply a figurehead. Power really rested with the Great Council, originally an elected body but, from the 13th century on, an aristocratic stronghold, with members inheriting their seats from their noble ancestors. Laws were passed by the Senate, a group of 200 elected from the Great Council (which could have as many as 1,700 members); and executive powers belonged to the College, a committee of 25 leaders. In the 14th century, the Council of Ten was formed to deal with emergency situations; this group's meetings were not open to the public, and the Council often proved more powerful than the Senate, though its members could only serve for limited terms before new members were elected.

A fortress for the doge existed on this spot in the early 9th century; the building you see today was a product of the 12th century, although, like the basilica next door, it was continually added to and transformed throughout the centuries. You enter the palace at the ornate Gothic **Porta della Carta** (Gate of the Paper, where official decrees were traditionally posted), which opens onto an immense courtyard. Ahead is the **Scala dei Giganti** (Stairway of the Giants), guarded by huge statues of Mars and Neptune sculpted by Sansovino. Ordinary mortals do not get to climb these stairs, however; after paying your admission fee, walk along the arcade to reach the central interior staircase. Its upper flight is called the **Scala d'Oro** (Golden Staircase), also designed by Sansovino, with its lavish gilded decoration. While it may seem odd that the government's main council rooms and reception halls should be so far upstairs, imagine how effectively foreign emissaries must have been intimidated by this arduous climb.

Visitors also must have been overwhelmed by the sumptuous decoration of these apartments, their walls and ceilings covered with works by Venice's greatest artists. Among the grand rooms you can visit are the **Anticollegio** (a waiting room outside the College's chamber), which features two fine paintings, Tintoretto's *Bacchus and Ariadne Crowned by Venus* and Veronese's *Rape of Europa;* the **Sala del Collegio** (College Chamber), its ceiling magnificently painted by Veronese; and the **Sala del Senato** (Senate Chamber), with Tintoretto's *Triumph of Venice* on the ceiling. The huge *Paradise* on the end wall of the **Great Council Hall** is by Jacopo Tintoretto (1518–94): It is a dark, dynamic masterpiece and is the world's largest oil painting (23 by 75 feet), a vast work commissioned for a vast hall. Don't miss the gorgeous ceiling, with Veronese's majestic *Apotheosis of Venice* filling one of the center panels. Step onto the balcony of the Great Council Hall for a view of St. Mark's Basin, its waters churning with the wakes of countless boats. Look at the frieze of portraits of the first 76 doges around the upper part of the walls. One portrait is missing: A black painted curtain near the left-hand corner of the wall opposite Tintoretto's painting marks the spot where the portrait of Doge Marin Falier should be. A Latin inscription bluntly explains that Falier was executed for treason in 1355. The republic never forgave him.

At the ticket office of the Doge's Palace you can book a guided tour (unfortunately, only given in Italian) of the palace's secret rooms; it takes you to the doge's private apartments, up into the attic and Piombi Prison, and through hidden passageways to the torture chambers, where prisoners were interrogated. The 18th-century writer and libertine Casanova, a native of Venice, was imprisoned here in 1755, having somehow offended someone in power (the official accusation was of being a Freemason); he made a daring escape 15 months later and fled to France, where he continued his career of intrigue and scandal. From the east wing of the Doge's Palace, the enclosed marble **Ponte dei Sospiri** (Bridge of Sighs) arches across a narrow canal to the cramped, gloomy cell blocks of the so-called New Prison. (The bridge was named for the sighs of those being led to lifelong imprisonment; through its windows prisoners got their last glimpse of the outside world.) *Piazzetta San Marco, tel. 041/522–4951. Admission: 8,000 lire. Open Apr.–Oct., daily 9–7; Nov.–Mar., daily 9–4. Secret Itineraries Tour (available in Italian only) daily 10 AM and noon; reserve at least a day ahead if possible. Cost: 5,000 lire.*

Walk back to the far end of Piazza San Marco, where a massive ❺ marble staircase in the Fabbrica Nuova leads to the **Museo Correr,** an interesting and varied collection of historical items and paintings by old masters, once the private collection of the aristocrat Teodoro Correr, who donated them to the city in 1830. Exhibits range from the absurdly high-soled shoes worn

by 16th-century Venetian ladies (who had to be supported by a
servant on each side in order to walk on these precarious
perches) to fine artworks by the talented Bellini family of Renaissance painters. *Piazza San Marco, Ala Napoleonica, tel.
041/522–5625. Admission: 5,000 lire. Open Apr.–Oct., Wed.–
Mon. 9–7; Nov.–Mar., 9–4.*

Tour 2: The Grand Canal

Catch Vaporetto Line 1 at the San Marco landing stage for a
leisurely cruise along the **Grand Canal,** Venice's main thoroughfare. This 2-mile ribbon of water loops through the city.
When the canal is busiest, usually in the morning, large and
small craft crisscross its waters, stirring up a maelstrom that
sets gondolas rocking and sends green waves slapping at the
seaweed-slippery foundations of palaces. The quietest and
most romantic time to ride in a gondola along the Grand Canal
is about an hour or so before sunset: This is an experience you
shouldn't miss. However, for an overall sightseeing tour of the
canal, you'll get a better, more extensive view from the
vaporetto—which is both higher in the water and much less expensive. Try to get one of the coveted seats in the prow for a
clear view.

The Grand Canal has an average depth of about 9 feet and varies from 40 to 76 yards in width. It winds like an inverted letter
S through Venice, from the San Marco landing to the landing at
the train station (Ferrovia), passing under three bridges and
between 200 palaces dating from the 14th century to the 18th
century, most of them in Venetian Gothic or Renaissance style.

❻ Starting from San Marco, look left for **Santa Maria della Salute,**
the huge, white, domed 17th-century Baroque church designed
by Longhena. On the same side is the low, white marble wall
marking the never-completed **Palazzo Venier dei Leoni,** well

❼ worth a visit (April through October) to view the **Peggy Guggenheim Collection,** a small but choice gallery of 20th-century
paintings and sculptures in the heiress's lavish former apartments. Guggenheim (1898–1979) used her wealth and social
connections to become a serious patron of art—she was once
married to the painter Max Ernst—and her holdings include
works by Picasso, Kandinsky, Ernst, Pollock, and Motherwell,
among others. *Entrance on Calle San Cristoforo, Dorsoduro.
Tel. 041/520–6288. Admission: 7,000 lire (free Sat. 6–9). Open
Sun., Mon., Wed.–Fri. 11–6; Sat. 11–9.*

Across the canal you can see the imposing terraced front of the
Gritti Palace Hotel, occupying the former Palazzo Pisani. English critic John Ruskin stayed here with his young wife, Effie,
in 1851, while working on his book *Stones of Venice.* **Palazzo
Corner,** otherwise known as Ca' Grande, is also on the right
bank, just past the Santa Maria del Giglio stop. A Renaissance
beauty designed by Sansovino, with classical details, it now
houses the Prefecture. **Palazzo Barbaro,** the 15th-century
Gothic villa on the right bank just before the Accademia
Bridge, is where Henry James lived while writing *The Aspern
Papers*; later he made it the setting for his novel *Wings of the
Dove.* The **Accademia Bridge** is one of only three bridges span-
ning the Grand Canal; until the first version of this bridge was
built here, in 1854, the Rialto was the only bridge across the
Grand Canal. The current plain wooden bridge, dating from

1934, leads on the left bank to the wonderful **Accademia Gallery,** a treasure house of Venetian painting (*see* Tour 4, *below*).

A few minutes farther on, on the left bank at the Ca' Rezzonico stop, is **Ca' Rezzonico,** a Baroque mansion begun by Longhena in the 1660s and completed by another architect, Giorgio Massari, in the 1740s. This was English poet Robert Browning's last home, where he died in 1889. Return here to visit the **Museo del Settecento Veneziano** (Museum of 18th-Century Venice). Pictures by the 18th-century Venetian painters Gianantonio Guardi and Pietro Longhi, and a fine series of frescoes by their younger contemporary Giandomenico Tiepolo at the back of the palace, really open a window onto that frivolous social era. *Fondamenta Rezzonico, Dorsoduro, tel. 041/522-4543. Admission: 5,000 lire. Open Apr.–Oct., Sat.–Thurs. 9–7; Nov.–Mar., 9–4.*

Just past Ca' Rezzonico, still on the left bank, are two identical 15th-century Gothic palaces designed by Bartolomeo Bon for the Giustinian family. In the second one, composer Richard Wagner lived in 1858–59 while writing his opera *Tristan und Isolde.* Next door is **Ca' Foscari,** where one of Venice's two disgraced doges, Francesco Foscari, lived in 1457, when he was deposed by the Council of Ten. Now part of the University of Venice, it is adorned with lovely marble columns, tracery, and a frieze.

Turn to the right bank, as you round the bend in the canal, to see the **Palazzi Mocenigo,** a series of four buildings, the two central ones unified behind a double neoclassical facade, decorated with lions' heads. Byron lived in one of these from 1816 to 1819, and it is where he began his satiric epic *Don Juan,* enjoyed several reckless love affairs, and eventually stole Countess Guiccioli from her husband. A couple of years later, he wrote historical dramas about the traitor doge Marin Falier and the two Foscari doges. Just past the next vaporetto stop, still on the right bank, stands **Palazzo Corner-Spinelli,** a richly decorated Renaissance palace with arched windows, probably designed by Mauro Coducci (1440–1504). On the right bank across from the next vaporetto stop, look at Renaissance architecture in full flower in the imposing white **Palazzo Grimani,** by Michele Sanmicheli (1484–1559); today the Court of Appeals sits here.

The canal narrows and boat traffic increases as you approach the **Rialto Bridge,** arched high across the canal. The windows in the arch belong to the shops inside; plan to return here on foot and walk across to admire fine views up and down the Grand Canal. This is a commercial hub of the city, with open-air vegetable, fruit, and fish markets on the left, and on the right, an upscale shopping district. Just beyond the bridge on the right is the 16th-century **Fondaco dei Tedeschi,** originally used by merchants from various Germanic states as warehouses and offices for the all-important trade with Venice. Now that the Giorgione frescoes that once covered its facade have gone, it's a rather austere-looking building; today it's the city's main post office.

The Ca' d'Oro landing on the right, just beyond the Rialto, identifies the lovely Venetian Gothic palace of **Ca' d'Oro,** adorned with marble traceries and ornaments that were once embellished with pure gold. Today it houses the **Franchetti**

Gallery, a fine collection of tapestries, sculptures, and paintings. *Calle della Ca' d'Oro, tel. 041/523-8790. Admission: 4,000 lire. Open Mon.-Sat. 9-2, Sun. 9-1.*

A little farther up from Ca' d'Oro, over on the left bank, is the grand, Baroque **Ca' Pesaro,** designed by Longhena. It's now home to two rather dull art collections, the **Galleria d'Arte Moderna** (Modern Art Gallery, containing mostly 19th- and some 20th-century works, although the intention is also to display the gallery's large collection of contemporary art when restoration has been completed) and **Museo Orientale** (Oriental Art Museum). *Galleria d'Arte Moderna: tel. 041/721172, admission 2,000 lire, open Apr.-Oct., Tues.-Sun. 9-7; Nov.-Mar., 9-4. Museo Orientale: tel. 041/524-1173, admission 4,000 lire, open Tues.-Sat. 9-2, Sun. 9-1.*

Not far beyond, on the left, another white church is adorned with Baroque statues; this is **San Stae,** and the landing here is a gateway to a part of Venice that most tourists never see, a neighborhood of narrow canals, airy squares, and good *trattorie.* Back on the right bank, the Renaissance **Palazzo Vendramin-Calergi** (1509), designed by Coducci in white stone with red marble medallions and an imposing carved frieze, was where Wagner died in 1883; it is now the winter home of the **Casino** (*see* Nightlife, *below*). Turn to the left bank to see the **Fondaco dei Turchi,** built in the Veneto-Byzantine style during the 12th and 13th centuries, but very heavy-handedly restored during the 19th century; it was the trade center for the Turks from 1621 to 1838. Under its portico, the traitorous doge Marin Falier was buried after his execution. The **Museo di Storia Naturale** (Natural History Museum) occupies the building now. *Tel. 041/524-0885. Admission: 3,000 lire. Open Tues.-Sat. 9-1:30, Sun. 9-1.*

Another vaporetto stop away is **San Marcuola,** on the right. This unfinished brick church is guarded by cats and pigeons, and it marks the edge of another district that is off the beaten track and well worth exploring: Cannaregio and the old Jewish ghetto.

Tour 3: To the Arsenal and Beyond

To explore the city's eastern districts and see some of its most beautiful churches, head out of Piazza San Marco under the clock tower into the **Mercerie,** one of Venice's busiest streets. It's actually a five-part series of streets (Merceria dell'Orologio, di San Zulian, del Capitello, di San Salvador, and 2 Aprile) leading more or less directly from Piazza San Marco to the Rialto bridge. At Campo San Zulian and the church of San Giuliano, turn right onto Calle Guerra and Calle delle Bande to reach the graceful, white marble church of **Santa Maria Formosa.** It's on a lively square with a few sidewalk cafés and a small vegetable market on weekday mornings. Follow Calle Borgoloco into Campo San Marina, where you'll turn right, cross the little canal, and take Calle Castelli to the church of **Santa Maria dei Miracoli.** Perfectly proportioned and sheathed in marble, it's an early Renaissance gem, decorated inside with exquisite marble reliefs. Notice how the architect, Pietro Lombardo, made the church look bigger with various optical illusions: varying the color of the exterior marble to create the effect of distance; using extra pilasters to make the building's canal side look longer; slightly offsetting the arcade windows to make the arches look deeper. The church was built during the 1480s to house an image of the Virgin that is said to perform miracles—look for this icon on the high altar.

Behind the church, bear right to Calle Larga Giacinto Gallina, which leads to **Campo Santi Giovanni e Paolo,** site of the massive Dominican church of **Santi Giovanni e Paolo,** or San Zanipolo, as it's known in the slurred Venetian dialect. The powerful equestrian **monument of Bartolomeo Colleoni** by Florentine sculptor Andrea del Verrocchio (1435–88) stands in the square. Colleoni had served Venice well as a *condottiere,* or mercenary commander (the Venetians preferred to pay others to fight for them on land and had the money to do it). When he died in 1475, he left his fortune to the city on the condition that a statue be erected in his honor "in the piazza before St. Mark's." The republic's shrewd administrators coveted Colleoni's ducats but had no intention of honoring anyone, no matter how valorous, with a statue in Piazza San Marco. So they commissioned the statue and put it up before the Scuola di San Marco, which is off to the side here and is the headquarters of a charitable confraternity that happened to have the right name, enabling them to collect the loot. San Zanipolo itself contains tombs of several doges, as well as a wealth of artworks. Don't miss the Rosary Chapel, off the left transept; with its Veronese ceiling paintings, it's a sumptuous study in decoration, built in the 16th century to commemorate the victory of Lepanto in western Greece in 1571, when Venice and a combined European fleet succeeded in destroying the Turkish navy.

Continue beyond Santi Giovanni e Paolo to another large church, **San Francesco della Vigna,** built by Sansovino in 1534. A pretty cloister opens out from the severely simple gray-and-white interior. Not many tourists find their way here, and local youngsters play ball in the square shadowed by the church's austere classical Palladian facade.

Go left as you leave the church to begin the 500-yard walk to the **Campo dell'Arsenale,** at the main entrance to the **Arsenal,** an immense dockyard founded in 1104 to build and equip the fleet of the Venetian republic and augmented continually through the 16th century. For a republic founded on sea might, having a huge state-of-the-art shipyard was of paramount importance, and this one was renowned for its skill and size. All subsequent dockyards were named after it (the name comes from the Arabic *d'arsina,* meaning "workshop"). No wonder it has such a grandiose entrance, with four stone lions from ancient Greece guarding the great Renaissance gateway.

The **Museo Navale** (Naval Museum) on nearby Campo San Biagio has four floors of full-scale boat models, from gondolas and doges' ceremonial boats to Chinese junks, as well as other smaller boats guaranteed to fascinate children—and boat lovers. *Campo San Biagio, Castello, tel. 041/520–0276. Admission: 1,000 lire. Open Mon.–Sat. 9–1.*

If you still have time and energy, go east to the island and church of **San Pietro di Castello.** Two footbridges lead to this island. The church served as Venice's cathedral for centuries; now it presides over a picturesque workaday neighborhood, and its tipsy bell tower leans over a grassy square.

About midway between the Arsenal and St. Mark's, on your way back from the eastern district, is the **Scuola di San Giorgio degli Schiavoni,** one of numerous *scuole* built during the time of the republic. These weren't schools, as the present-day Italian word would imply, but confraternities devoted to charitable works. Many scuole were decorated lavishly, both in the private chapels and in the meeting halls where work was discussed. The Scuola di San Giorgio degli Schiavoni features works by Vittore Carpaccio (ca. 1465–1525), a local artist who often filled his otherwise devotional paintings with acutely observed details of Venetian life. Study the exuberance of his *St. George* as he slays the dragon or the vivid colors and details in *The Funeral of St. Jerome* and *St. Augustine in His Study. Calle dei Furlani, tel. 041/522–8828. Admission: 4,000 lire. Open Tues.–Sat. 10–12:30 and 3:30–6, Sun. 11–12:30.*

Tour 4: The Western and Northern Districts

If churches, art, and outdoor sculpture, and further ramblings through the back streets and along the old canals of Venice continue to interest you, head out of Piazza San Marco under the arcades of the Fabbrica Nuova at the far end of the square. If you want to make a detour for an expensive drink at the fabled **Harry's Bar,** just turn left down Calle Vallaresso, behind the Hotel Luna Baglioni. Then head for **Campo Morosini,** which everyone calls by its old name, Campo San Stefano, in honor of the 14th-century church off to one side of the square; stop in to see the ship's-keel roof, a type found in several of Venice's older churches and the work of its master shipbuilders. **Café Paolin,** with tables occupying most of one end of the square, is reputed to have Venice's best ice cream. It's a pleasant place in which to sit and watch the passing parade.

Join the stream of pedestrians crossing the Grand Canal on the Accademia Bridge to the district called Dorsoduro (literally, "hard back") because of its strong clay foundation. The bridge leads you directly to the **Accademia Gallery,** Venice's most important picture gallery. It has an extraordinary collection of Venetian paintings, attractively displayed and well lit. Highlights include Giovanni Bellini's altarpiece from the church of San Giobbe (notice how he carried the church's architectural details right into the frame of the painting) and his moving *Madonna with St. Catherine and the Magdalen;* a fine *St. George* by Andrea Mantegna, Bellini's brother-in-law from Padua, who was much admired by later Venetian painters; the *Tempest,* by Giorgione (1477–1510); and Veronese's monumental canvas, *Feast in the House of Levi.* This last painting was commissioned as a Last Supper, but the Inquisition took issue with Veronese's inclusion of jesters and German soldiers in the painting. Veronese avoided the charge of profanity by changing the title, and the picture was then supposed to depict the bawdy, but still biblical, feast of Levi. This museum was built on what was originally the Scuola della Carità and the church of Santa Maria della Carità; the body of the church has been preserved in a large room that contains the surviving fragments of Giorgione's masterful frescoes from the facade of the Fondaco dei Tedeschi (*see* Tour 2, *above*). A room preserved from the Scuola holds on one wall its original masterpiece, Titian's *Presentation of the Virgin.* And don't miss the room containing various views of 15th- and 16th-century Venice by Giovanni

Bellini's brother Gentile: Study them to see how much the city has changed since then—and how much it looks the same. *Campo della Carità, tel. 041/522–2247. Admission: 8,000 lire. Open Mon.–Sat. 9–2, Sun. 9–1.*

Off Campo San Barnaba, on Fondamenta Gherardini, you'll see a floating fruit-and-vegetable market tied up in the canal. It's one of the few left in Venice. Continue toward Campo Santa Margherita, passing **Mondonovo,** one of Venice's best mask shops (*see* Shopping, *below*).

At **Campo Santa Margherita,** a busy neighborhood shopping square, stop in to see Giambattista Tiepolo's ceiling paintings in the **Scuola dei Carmini.** The paintings, now displayed on the second floor, were commissioned to honor the Carmelite order by depicting prominent Carmelites in conversation with saints and angels. Of the three great Venetian painters whose names start with T (Titian, Tintoretto, and Tiepolo), Tiepolo came last chronologically (he painted in the 18th century, while the others were 16th-century artists) and achieved the greatest international fame in his own time, though an underlying melancholy in his ethereal, brightly colored paintings betrays a man of sober piety. Tiepolo's vivid techniques transformed some unpromising religious themes into flamboyant displays of color and movement. Mirrors are available on the benches to make it easier to see the ceiling without getting a sore neck. *Campo dei Carmini, tel. 041/528–9420. Admission: 5,000 lire. Open Mon.–Sat. 9–noon and 3–6.*

Continue on to the **Frari,** an immense Gothic church of russet-colored brick, built in the 14th century for the Franciscans. In keeping with the austere principles of the Franciscan order, the Frari is quite stark inside, with much less ornamentation than is typically found in other Venetian churches. The relative absence of decoration gives a select feeling to the church paintings, such as Bellini's *Madonna and Four Saints* in the sacristy. The most striking is Titian's large *Assumption* above the main altar, showing his clever use of the design of the church interior to frame his painting. Worldly and polished, Titian was also a fashionable portrait painter, and the Virgin's rapturous rise to heaven here is charged with very real human emotion. The *Pesaro Madonna* above the first altar on the left nave near the main altar is also by Titian; his wife, who died shortly afterward in childbirth, posed for the figure of Mary. Both of these pictures demonstrate Titian's love of robust, brilliant color and dramatic composition. The Madonna was radical for its time because the main figure was not placed squarely in the center of the painting, but see how dynamic the picture is as a result. On the same side of the church, look at the spooky pyramid-shape monument to the sculptor Antonio Canova (1757–1822), containing his heart. Across the nave is a 19th-century neoclassical monument to Titian, executed by two of Canova's pupils. *Admission: 1,000 lire. Open Apr.–Oct., Mon.–Sat. 9–noon and 2:30–6, Sun. 3–6; Nov.–Mar., Mon.–Sat. 9:30–noon and 3–5:30, Sun. 3–5:30.*

Behind the Frari is the **Scuola di San Rocco,** filled with dark, dramatic canvases by Tintoretto. Born some 30 years after Titian, Jacopo Robusti—called Tintoretto because his father was a dyer—was more mystical and devout than the sophisticated Titian. Though his colors are equally brilliant, he carried Titian's love of motion and odd composition to almost surreal effects, in the same Mannerist vein as El Greco (who was at one time a pupil of Titian's). In 1564, Tintoretto beat other painters competing for the commission to decorate this building by submitting not a sketch but a finished work, which he additionally offered free of charge. The series of more than 50 paintings that he ultimately created took a total of 23 years to complete. These works, depicting Old and New Testament themes, were restored during the 1970s, and Tintoretto's inventive use of light has once more been revealed. *Campo San Rocco, tel. 041/523–4864. Admission: 6,000 lire. Open weekdays 10–1, weekends 10–4.*

The area around San Rocco is well off the normal tourist trail, with narrow alleys and streets winding alongside small canals to little squares, where posters advertising political parties and sports events seem to be the only signs of life. Head back **28** past the Frari to **Campo San Polo,** one of Venice's largest squares and a favorite playground for neighborhood children. From here you take Calle della Madonetta, Calle dell'Olio, Rugheta del Ravano, and Ruga Vecchia San Giovanni to the **Rialto** shopping district, where you can cross the Grand Canal for the shortcut back to San Marco. Alternatively, you can go north from Campo San Polo by way of Calle Bernardo, Calle dello Scaleter, Rio Terrà Parrucchetta, and Calle del Tintor to **29** **Campo San Giacomo dell'Orio,** where the 13th-century church of San Giacomo stands on a charming square that few tourists ever find. Here you're not far from the **San Stae** vaporetto landing, so you can take the boat back along the Grand Canal to the heart of the city.

Tour 5: Islands of the Lagoon

Conical bundles of piles, called *bricole,* mark the navigable channels to help boats negotiate the shallow waters of the Venetian lagoon, with its islands of Murano, Burano, and Torcello. These islands are famous for their handicrafts—notably glass and lace—but guided tours here usually involve high-pressure attempts to make you buy, with little time left for anything else. It's much cheaper and more adventurous to make your own way around the islands, using the good vaporetto connections. Services to and from Venice use the landing stage at Fondamenta Nuove, almost due north of St. Mark's. The most distant island, Torcello, is ideal for picnics but has no food stores. Buy provisions in Venice if you plan to picnic there.

If you're making your way on foot to Fondamenta Nuove, stop **30** at the church of the **Gesuiti,** which dominates the Campo dei Gesuiti. This 18th-century church is built in an extravagantly Baroque style; the classical arches and straight lines of the Renaissance have been abandoned in favor of flowing, twisting forms. The marble of the gray-and-white interior is used like brocade, carved into swags and drapes. Titian's *Martyrdom of St. Lawrence,* above the first altar on the left, is a dramatic example of the great artist's feel for light and movement.

From **Fondamenta Nuove** you have a choice of vaporetti. Line 5 goes to San Michele and Murano; Line 12, which you can join at Murano, skips Venice's cemetery-island of San Michele and goes to Murano, Burano, and Torcello.

Numbers in the margin correspond to points of interest on the Venetian Lagoon map.

③ It's only a five-minute ride to **San Michele,** Venice's cypress-clad cemetery island, with its pretty Renaissance church of **San Michele in Isola,** designed by Coducci in 1478, and Venice's **cemetery.** It is a moving experience to walk among the gravestones, with the sound of lapping water on all sides. The American poet Ezra Pound, the great Russian impresario and art critic Sergey Diaghilev, and the composer Igor Stravinsky are buried here.

③ Another five minutes on Line 5 takes you to **Murano,** which, like Venice, is made up of a number of smaller islands, linked by bridges. Murano is known exclusively for its glassworks, which you can visit to see how glass is made. Many of these line the **Fondamenta dei Vetrai,** the canalside walkway leading away from the Colonna landing stage. The houses along this walk are much more colorful—and a lot simpler—than their Venetian counterparts; traditionally, they were workmen's cottages. Just before the junction with Murano's Grand Canal—250 yards up from the landing stage—is the church of **San Pietro Martire.** This 16th-century reconstruction of an earlier Gothic church has two works by Venetian masters: the *Madonna and Child,* by Giovanni Bellini, and *St. Jerome,* by Veronese.

Cross the Ponte Vivarini and turn right onto **Fondamenta Cavour.** Follow the Fondamenta around the corner to the **Museo Vetrario** (Glass Museum), which has a collection of Venetian glass that ranges from priceless antique to only slightly less expensive modern. The museum gives you a good idea of the history of Murano's glassworks, which were moved here from Venice in the 13th century because they were a fire risk. It's useful, too, to get a clear idea of authentic Venetian styles and patterns if you're planning to make some purchases later. *Tel. 041/739586. Admission: 5,000 lire. Open Apr.–Oct., Thurs.–Tues. 9–7; Nov.–Mar., 9–4.*

③ Make your way back along the same route to the landing stage and take Line 12 to **Burano,** which is about 30 minutes from Murano. It's a small island fishing village with houses painted in cheerful colors and a raffishly raked bell tower on the main square, about 100 yards from the landing stage and clearly visible from there. Lace is to Burano what glass is to Murano, but be prepared to pay a lot for the real thing. Stalls line the way from the landing stage to **Piazza Galuppi,** the main square; the vendors, many of them fishermen's wives, are generally good-natured and unfamiliar with the techniques of the hard sell.

The **Consorzio Merletti di Burano** (Lace Museum) on Piazza Galuppi is the best place to learn the intricacies of the lace-making traditions of Burano. It is also useful for learning the nature of the skills involved in making the more expensive lace, in case you intend to buy some lace on your way back to the vaporetto. *Piazza Galuppi, tel. 041/730034. Admission: 5,000 lire. Open Tues.–Sat. 9–6, Sun. 10–4.*

③ Vaporetto Line 12 continues from the Burano landing stage to the sleepy green island of **Torcello,** about 10 minutes farther. This is where the first Venetians landed in their flight from the barbarians 1,500 years ago. Even after many settlers left to found the city of Venice on the island of Rivo Alto (Rialto), Torcello continued to grow and prosper, until its main source of

Venetian Lagoon

income, wool manufacturing, was priced out of the market-place. It's hard to believe now, looking at this almost deserted island, that during the 16th century it had 20,000 inhabitants and 10 churches.

A brick-paved lane leads up from the landing stage and follows the curve of the canal toward the center of the island. You'll pass **Locanda Cipriani,** an inn famous for its good food and the patronage of Ernest Hemingway, who often came to Torcello for the solitude. These days Locanda Cipriani is about the busi-est spot on the island, as well-heeled customers arrive on high-speed powerboats for lunch.

Just beyond is the grassy square that holds the only surviving monuments of the island's past splendor. The low church of **Santa Fosca,** on the right, dates from the 11th century. Next to it is the cathedral of Santa Maria Assunta, also built in the 11th century: The ornate Byzantine mosaics are testimony to the im-portance and wealth of an island that could attract the best art-ists and craftsmen of its day. The vast mosaic on the inside of the facade depicts the Last Judgment as artists of the 11th and 12th centuries imagined it: Figures writhe in vividly depicted contortions of pain. Facing it, as if in mitigation, is the calm mo-saic figure of the Madonna, alone in a field of gold above the staunch array of apostles.

The trip back from Torcello retraces the route from Venice. Boats leave approximately every hour, and the trip takes about 50 minutes.

Tour 6: San Giorgio Maggiore and the Giudecca

Numbers in the margin correspond to points of interest on the Venice map.

Looking out across the Basin of San Marco, you can see the island of San Giorgio Maggiore, separated by a small channel from the Giudecca. A tall brick campanile on that distant bank perfectly complements the Campanile of San Marco. Behind it looms the stately dome of one of Venice's greatest churches, San Giorgio Maggiore. To reach the island, take a Line 5 or 8 vaporetto from San Zaccaria, which is near San Marco. (Make sure you're going on the clockwise route, designated *circolare destra*.)

A church has been on this island since the late 8th century, with a Benedictine monastery added in the 10th century. The present church of **San Giorgio Maggiore** was begun in 1566 by the greatest architect of his time, Andrea Palladio, whose work is so evident throughout the Venetian hinterland (*see* Chapter 6). Two of Palladio's hallmarks are mathematical harmony and architectural elements borrowed from classical Rome, both of which are evident in this superbly proportioned neoclassical church of red brick and white marble. Inside the church is refreshingly airy and simply decorated. Two important late Tintoretto paintings hang on either side of the chancel: *The Last Supper* and *The Gathering of Manna*. Above the first altar on the right-hand side of the nave is an *Adoration of the Shepherds* by Jacopo Bassano (1517–1592), a painter from Bassano del Grappa on the mainland, who possessed considerable originality and was especially adept at portraying nature and country life. Take the elevator up the Campanile outside (admission 2,000 lire) for a fine view of Venice and its harbor. *Open daily 9–12:30 and 2–5.*

The monastery of San Giorgio Maggiore, where the conclave that elected Pope Pius VII took place in 1800, later a barracks for the occupying Austrians, now houses an artistic foundation and is usually closed to the public. Palladio designed the monastery's first cloister, and Longhena was the architect for the grand Baroque library.

Catch the Line 5 or 8 vaporetto (still *circolare destra*) to reach the island of **Giudecca**, a crescent cupped around the southern shore of Venice. The Giudecca has always been seen as a place apart. Its name is something of a mystery. According to some, it derives from the possible settlement of Jews on the island during the 14th century, and according to others it was so called because during the 9th century nobles condemned (*giudicato*) to exile were sent here. It became a pleasure garden for wealthy Venetians during the long and luxurious decline of the republic. Even today it has an atmosphere of its own, quite different from the heart of Venice. In one regard it is still the province of the wealthy, however: The exclusive **Cipriani** hotel lies secluded on its eastern tip.

The main attraction here is the church of **Il Redentore,** also by Palladio. Its tranquil, stately facade is actually a series of superimposed temple fronts, topped by a dome and a pair of slim, almost minaretlike bell towers. The interior, like San Giorgio Maggiore's, is perfectly proportioned and airy, in contrast to the dusky clutter of the Basilica di San Marco.

On the third Sunday of July, the feast of Il Redentore (the Redeemer) is celebrated with a pontoon bridge being built over the channel to the Giudecca, commemorating the doge's annual visit to this church to offer thanks for the end of a 16th-century plague. Traditionally, the Venetians take to the water in boats en masse, at midnight fireworks explode over the lagoon, and a good time is had by all.

Vaporetto Lines 5 or 8 will take you back in the other direction *(circolare sinistra)* to San Marco, or you can take Line 5 or 8 *(circolare destra)* or Line 9 from the Giudecca directly across the channel to the **Zattere,** the broad waterfront promenade on Dorsoduro, where there are several inexpensive restaurants and a casual neighborhood atmosphere.

Shopping

Shopping in Venice is part of the fun of exploring the city, and you're sure to find plenty of interesting shops and boutiques as you explore. It's always a good idea to mark on your map the location of a shop that interests you; otherwise you may not be able to find it again in mazelike Venice. Shops are usually open 9–12:30 or 1 and 3:30 or 4–7:30 and are closed Sunday and on Monday morning. However, many tourist-oriented shops are open all day, every day. Food shops are closed Wednesday, except during the Christmas period, when they remain open. Some shops close for both a summer and a winter vacation.

Shopping Districts The main shopping areas are the **Mercerie,** the succession of narrow and crowded streets winding from Piazza San Marco to the Rialto, and the area around Campo San Salvador, Calle del Teatro, Campo Manin, and Campo San Fantin. The **San Marco** area is full of shops and top-name boutiques, such as Missoni, Valentino, Fendi, and Versace.

Department Stores The only thing approximating a department store here is **Coin,** at the Rialto bridge, featuring men's and women's fashions. The **Standa** stores on Campo San Luca, Strada Nuova, and the Lido have a wide range of goods at moderate prices.

Food Markets The open-air fruit and vegetable market at **Rialto** is colorful and animated throughout the morning, when Venetian housewives come to pick over the day's offerings and haggle with vendors. The adjacent fish market offers a vivid lesson in ichthyology, presenting some species you've probably never seen (open mornings Tues.–Sat.). At the other end of Venice, in the Castello district, is **Via Garibaldi,** the scene of another lively food market on weekday mornings. The **Standa** stores on Strada Nuova and the Lido also have supermarket sections, and there are other supermarkets tucked away in the city: among them, **SUVE** on Salizzada San Lio, **Mega** on Campo Santa Margherita, and **FULL** at San Basilio, at the western end of the Zattere.

Specialty Stores
Glassware Glass, most of it made in Murano, is Venice's number-one product, and you'll be confronted by mind-boggling displays of traditional and contemporary glassware, often kitsch. Take your time and be selective. Should you buy glass in Venice's shops or in the showrooms of Murano's factories? You will probably find that prices are pretty much the same; showrooms in Venice that are outlets of Murano glassworks sell at the same prices as the factories. However, because of competition, shops in Venice

stocking wares from various glassworks may charge slightly lower prices.

In Murano, most of the glass factories have showrooms where glassware is sold. The **Domus** shop (Fondamenta dei Vetrai) has a selection of smaller objects and jewelry from the best glassworks.

Lace   Venice's top name is **Jesurum,** with a shop at Piazza San Marco 60 and a much larger establishment at Ponte Canonica, behind the Basilica di San Marco. Remember that much of the lace and embroidered linen sold in Venice and on Burano is made in China or Taiwan.

Masks   These are a tradition in Venice; they were worn everywhere during the lengthy Carnival season in the 18th century. Shops throughout the city sell masks of all types. Among the most interesting are **Mondonovo** (Rio Terrà Canal), **Cà Macana** (Calle delle Botteghe, near San Barnaba), and **Laboratorio Artigiano Maschere** (Barbaria delle Tole, near Santi Giovanni e Paolo).

Prints   An old print of Venice makes a distinctive gift or souvenir. There are several print shops on Salizzada San Moisè and on the streets as you continue toward Campo Santo Stefano. Hand-printed paper and desk accessories, memo pads, and address books abound at the well-known **Piazzesi** shop (Campiello della Feltrina, near Santa Maria del Giglio).

Dining

The general standard of Venetian restaurants has suffered from the onslaught of mass tourism. It is very difficult to eat well in Venice at moderate prices, but it *is* possible. Look for places whose name includes the words *pizzeria* or *pizzeria-trattoria;* they are generally less expensive than those called *ristorante.* Although seafood is a specialty here, the fact that the wholesale cost of fish is generally higher than meat is reflected in the prices, and you will find some fish dishes very expensive, especially those that are priced by weight (mainly baked or steamed fish). You can satisfy your yen for seafood by ordering seafood risotto or pasta with seafood, dishes that are generally more reasonably priced. (In order to eat within the price categories listed below, avoid ordering the most expensive items on the menu.) If you drink wine, which is considerably cheaper than beer, ask for *vino sfuso* (draft wine), available just about everywhere and usually of a better quality than the cheaper bottled wines.

Under the auspices of the restaurant association, most of the city's restaurants offer special tourist menus, moderately priced according to the level of the restaurant and generally representing good value. It's always a good idea to reserve your table or have your hotel *portiere* do it for you. Dining hours are short, starting at 12:30 or 1 for lunch and ending at 2:30–3, when restaurants close for the afternoon, opening up again to start serving at about 8 and closing again at 11 or midnight. Most close one day a week and are also likely to close without notice for vacation or renovation. Few have signs on the outside, so when the metal blinds are shut tight, you can't tell a closed restaurant from a closed TV-repair shop. This makes them hard to spot when exploring the city. You may not find a cover charge *(pane e coperto)*, but a service charge of 10%–15% will almost surely be on the check.

Venetian cuisine is based on seafood, with a few culinary excursions inland. Antipasto may take the form of a seafood salad, *prosciutto di San Daniele* (cured ham) from the mainland, or pickled vegetables. As a first course Venetians favor risotto, a creamy rice dish that may be cooked with vegetables or shellfish. Pasta, too, is good with seafood sauces; Venice is *not* the place to order spaghetti with tomato sauce. *Pasticcio di pesce* is pasta baked with fish, usually *baccalà* (dried cod). A classic first course is *pasta e fagioli* (thick bean soup with pasta). *Bigoli* is strictly a local pasta, made of whole wheat, usually served with a salty *acciughe* (anchovy) sauce. Polenta, made of cornmeal, is another pillar of regional cooking. It's often served as an accompaniment to *fegato alla veneziana* (liver with onion, Venetian style). Local seafood includes *granseola* (crab) and *seppie* or *seppioline* (cuttlefish).

The dessert specialty in Venice is *tiramisù* (a heavenly concoction of creamy mascarpone cheese, coffee, and chocolate with pound cake); the recipe originated on the mainland, but the Venetians have adopted it enthusiastically. Local wines are the dry white Tocai and Pinot from the Friuli region and bubbly white Prosecco, a naturally fermented sparkling white wine that is a shade less dry. The best Prosecco comes from the Valdobbiadene; Cartizze, which is similar, is considered superior by some but is expensive. Popular red wines include Merlot, Cabernet, Raboso, and Refosco. You can sample all of these and more in Venice's many traditional wineshops (called *bacari*), where wine is served by the glass and accompanied by *cicchetti* (assorted tidbits), often substantial enough for a light meal. There are also good sandwich bars, including **Snack Bar Carla** (San Marco 1535; closed Sun.), behind the post office off Piazza San Marco (the colorful sign outside says "Pietro Panizzolo"). The area around the Rialto market has a lot of these snack bars and wineshops. The best pastries in town can be found at **Rosa Salva,** on Merceria San Salvador near the Rialto bridge, **Marchini,** Calle dei Spezier 2769, just off Campo Santo Stefano, near the Accademia Bridge, and **Pitteri,** Strada Nuova 3844, the main thoroughfare in the Cannaregio district. **Cip Ciap,** a take-out pizza shop on Calle del Mondo Novo 5799, just off Campo Santa Maria Formosa, sells a variety of good wholesome pizza slices and pies.

Unless otherwise noted, reservations are not needed and dress is casual. Highly recommended restaurants are indicated by a star ★.

Under 45,000 lire

Capitan Uncino. On a pretty square where few tourists go, this tavern has good seafood and meat dishes and a very palatable house wine. Risotto or *taglierini al nero di seppie* (noodles flavored with cuttlefish ink) are among its local specialties. *Campo San Giacomo dell'Orio 1501, Santa Croce, tel. 041/721901. MC, V. Closed Wed. San Biasio or San Stae landing.*

★ **Da Gigio.** An attractive, friendly, family-run trattoria on the quayside of a canal just off Strada Nuova, Da Gigio is popular with Venetians and visiting Italians, who appreciate the affable service and excellently cooked, homemade pasta and the fish and meat dishes, as well as the good-quality draft wine. It is useful, too, for a cheaper, simpler meal at lunchtime, at tables in the barroom. *Fondamenta de la Chiesa 3628A, Cannaregio, tel. 041/528–5140. Reservations advised in the evening. Dress: casual. AE, DC, MC, V. Closed Sun. evening and Mon., also 2 weeks in mid-Jan. and 2 weeks in Aug. Ca' d'Oro landing.*

L'Incontro. This trattoria has a faithful clientele of Venetians and visitors, attracted by generous meat dishes, friendly waiters, and reasonable prices. Menu choices include juicy steaks, wild duck, boar, and (with advance notice) roast suckling pig. It is near San Barnaba and Campo Santa Margherita. *Rio Terrà Canal 3062/A, Dorsoduro, tel. 041/522–2404. Reservations advised. MC, V. Closed Mon. Ca' Rezzonico landing.*

Al Mascaron. A lively, often crowded *bacaro* (old-style Venetian wine bar), Al Mascaron, with its paper tablecloths and very informal atmosphere, is a regular stop for locals who like to drop in on their way home from work to gossip, drink, and eat tidbits at the bar. There are also delicious and generous seafood pasta dishes. *Calle Lunga Santa Maria Formosa 5225, Castello, tel. 041/522–5995. Reservations advised. Dress: casual. No credit cards. Closed Sun., also end Dec.–mid-Jan. and mid-Aug.–end Aug. Rialto or San Zaccaria landing.*

Metropole Buffet. Here at the Hotel Metropole's Buffet, in a charming and comfortable room overlooking the waterfront by the Pietà Church, you can eat a substantial and tasty lunch or dinner (for a fixed price of around 40,000 lire), helping yourself from a varied selection of starters, soups, pastas, hot and cold dishes, and desserts. The price even includes a highly drinkable Bianco di Custoza (a light white wine from the Veneto region) on draft. *Riva degli Schiavoni 4149, Castello, tel. 041/520–5044. Reservations advised. Dress: casual. AE, DC, MC, V. Open all year. San Zaccaria landing.*

Al Mondo Novo. With a wide range of seafood and meat dishes, this eatery is open late and has piano music until 11. Try the seafood antipasto or *frittura di pesce* (fried fish). Near Santa Maria Formosa, it was a tavern in the 18th century. *Salizzada San Lio 5409, Castello, tel. 041/520–0898. AE, V. Closed Wed. Rialto landing.*

Da Raffaele. Near Santa Maria del Giglio, this tavern has wood-beamed ceilings and serves classic Venetian specialties, such as *fegato alla veneziana* (liver with onions) and risotto with seafood. In warm weather tables are set outdoors, alongside a canal. *Fondamenta delle Ostreghe 2347, San Marco, tel. 041/523–2317. Reservations advised. AE, DC, MC, V. Closed Thurs. Santa Maria del Giglio landing.*

Under 35,000 lire

Alle Fonte. This Sicilian-run pizzeria-trattoria in a tiny square just off the waterfront, with tables outside in summer, offers a varied selection of good food at good prices as well as excellent homemade ice cream. *Calle va in Crosera 3820 (off Campo Bandiera e Moro), Castello, tel. 041/523–8698. AE, MC, V. Closed Wed. Arsenale landing.*

Alle Lanternine. Tasty pastas and pizza—*margherita* (with tomatoes and cheese) or *con funghi* (with mushrooms)—are the specialties here, but there are fish and meat dishes, too. In summer you can dine outdoors under an arbor. Alle Lanternine is near Santa Fosca. *Campiello della Chiesa 2134, Cannaregio,* *tel. 041/721–679. AE, DC, MC, V. Closed Thurs. San Marcuola or Ca' d'Oro landing.*

Paradiso Perduto. Very popular with young people, this informal wine bar serves various types of seafood, pasta, and pizza; it is one of the few late-night venues in Venice, and it features live music on Monday evening. *Fondamenta Misericordia 2540, Cannaregio, tel. 041/720581. No credit cards. Closed Tues. San Marcuola landing.*

San Trovaso. A good-value set menu (including main course, dessert, and wine), a wide choice of Venetian dishes and pizzas, and a good house wine make this a popular place. Wood paneling and wine racks along the walls add atmosphere. Grilled fish is a good choice here. *Fondamenta Priuli 1018, Dorsoduro, tel. 041/520–3703. AE, DC, MC, V. Closed Mon. Accademia landing.*

Under 25,000 lire

Boldrin. This friendly cafeteria-style eating place offers a good daily selection of pasta and such meat dishes as *vitello arrosto* (roast veal) and scaloppine (veal escallopes). It is near San Giovanni Crisostomo. *Salizzada San Canciano 5550, Cannaregio, tel. 041/523–7859. No credit cards. Open for lunch only. Closed Sun. Rialto landing.*

Leon Bianco. Near Campo Manin, this rosticceria has good daily specials such as *penne all'arrabbiata* (pasta with a spicy tomato sauce). You can eat at marble counters on the premises or take your food to go. *Salizzada San Luca 4153, San Marco, tel. 041/522–1180. No credit cards. Open Sun.–Fri. 8–8, Sat. 8–3. Sant'Angelo or Rialto landing.*

Al Ponte. By a bridge near Campo San Polo, this popular wine bar, a favorite with both locals and students, serves such tidbits as meatballs and fried potatoes all day until 8:30 PM, with meat and pasta main courses available at lunchtime. *Ponte San Polo 2742, San Polo, tel. 041/523–7238. No credit cards. Closed Sun. and 3 weeks in Aug. San Tomà or San Silvestro landing.*

Da Silvio. The large garden and reasonable prices here attract a lively young crowd. Service can be slow. *Calle San Pantalon 3748, Dorsoduro, tel. 041/520–5833. MC. Closed Sun. San Tomà landing.*

Sottoprova. The set menu here is a good value year-round, but come in the summer, when you can eat at tables outside. Sottoprova is off the beaten track, near the public gardens and San Pietro di Castello. *Via Garibaldi 1698, Castello, tel. 041/520–6493. AE, MC, V. Closed Tues. Arsenale Giardini landing.*

Al Tucano. A neighborhood trattoria conveniently close to St. Mark's, Tucano serves pizza as well as risotto and grilled fish. *Ruga Giuffa 4835, San Marco, tel. 041/520–0811. No credit cards. Closed Thurs. San Zaccaria landing.*

Vino Vino. The annex of the famous Antico Martini restaurant, this is a highly informal wine bar where you can sample an impressive assortment of Italian vintages and munch on a limited selection of dishes from the kitchens of its upscale big sister, next door. It's open nonstop 10 AM–11 PM. *Calle delle Veste 2007/a, near Campo San Fantin, tel. 041/523–7027. AE, DC, MC, V. Closed Tues. Santa Maria del Giglio or San Marco landing.*

Splurges

Cantinone Storico. On a quiet canal near Accademia, this attractive and sophisticated but friendly trattoria serves such expertly prepared specialties as *risotto terra mare* (with scampi and *porcini*, or boletus, mushrooms) and *tagliolini al granchio* (pasta with crab sauce). The fresh-fish main courses and meat dishes are just as tempting, and the house wines equally good. The set menu (around 30,000 lire) offers a wide choice and is excellent value. A full meal à la carte will cost about 60,000–70,000 lire. *Fondamenta Bragadin 660–661, Dorsoduro, tel. 041/523–9577. Reservations advised. AE, DC, MC, V. Closed Sun., last week in July–first week in Aug., and 3 weeks before Carnival. Accademia or Zattere landing.*

★ **Da Fiore.** Long a favorite with an appreciative Venetian clientele, this rather low-key, elegant restaurant has been discovered by discriminating tourists, so it's imperative to reserve for an excellent seafood dinner, which might include such specialties as *pasticcio di pesce* (an oven-baked fish and pasta dish), *rombo* (turbot), or *orata* (bream). *Calle del Scaleter 2202, tel. 041/721308. Reservations essential. Dress: smart casual. AE, DC, MC, V. Closed Sun., Mon., mid-Aug.–early Sept., Dec. 25–Jan. 15.*

The Arts and Nightlife

The Arts

You'll find a list of current and upcoming events in the "Guest in Venice" booklet, free in the higher-category hotels, or available from the Assessorato al Turismo at Ca' Giustinian (2nd floor), Calle del Ridotto (close to Piazza San Marco). Keep an eye out for posters announcing concerts and other events. Venice hosts important temporary exhibitions in the Doge's Palace, in Palazzo Grassi at San Samuele on the Grand Canal, and in other venues. The **Biennale**, a cultural institution, organizes many events throughout the year, including the film festival, beginning at the end of August. The big Biennale international art exhibition, held from the end of June to the end of September, switched to odd-numbered years in 1993.

Concerts There are regular concerts at the Pietà Church, with an emphasis on Vivaldi, and also at San Stae—though prices tend to be high and the quality of performance uneven. Concerts are also held, sometimes free, in other churches by visiting choirs and musicians. For information on these often short-notice events, inquire at the APT office, and watch for posters on walls and in restaurants and shops. The **Kele e Teo Agency** (San Marco 4930, tel. 041/520–8722) handles tickets for many musical events.

Opera and Ballet **Teatro La Fenice,** on Campo San Fantin, is one of Italy's oldest opera houses. The season runs all year, except August, with an opera in performance most months. Concerts, ballets, and other musical events are also held there. For programs and tickets, write Biglietteria, Teatro La Fenice, Campo San Fantin, 30121 Venice, or call 041/521–0161, fax 041/522–1768. Tickets for opera performances go on sale at the box office about one month in advance. The box office is open Monday–Saturday 9:30–12:30

and 4–6. If there is a performance on Sunday, the box office remains open, closing on Monday instead.

Nightlife

Piazza San Marco in fair weather, when the cafés stay open late, is a meeting place for visitors and Venetians, though young Venetians tend to gravitate toward Campo San Luca and Campo San Salvador and Bartolomeo, near Rialto. There is far more nightlife in Venice than meets the eye. The best up-to-date guide to live music venues, discos, and late bars is *"Notturno Veneziano"* ("Venetian Nightlife"), published by the Assessorato alla Gioventù, the municipal Youth Department (Corte Contarini 1529, 4th floor, near Piazza San Marco), and available free at APT information offices. At present the guide is only available in Italian, but with its useful maps and easy-to-follow notes it should be decipherable to any serious nighthawk.

Bars, Discos, and Nightclubs The top hotel bars stay open late if customers want to linger, while among the night spots, the most popular meeting places for young Venetians are **Ai Canottieri** (Fondamenta San Giobbe 690, Cannaregio, tel. 041/71548, live music Tues., closed Sun.) and **Paradiso Perduto** (Fondamenta Misericordia 2540, Cannaregio, tel. 041/720581), which serves good pizzas and other hot dishes, at low prices (live music Sun., closed Wed.).

Casino The city-operated gambling casino is open April–September in a modern building on the Lido (Lungomare Marconi 4, tel. 041/529–7111) and in the beautiful Palazzo Vendramin Calergi (same phone) on the Grand Canal during the other months. Both are open daily 3 PM–about 4:30 AM.

6 Excursions from Venice

Padua, Verona, Trento, and Bolzano

Beyond the Venetian lagoon, the mainland is a green plain swelling with gently rounded hills and studded with some of Italy's most interesting smaller art cities. All of them came under Venice's domination at one time or another, and her influence is evident in their art and architecture—the ubiquitous lion of St. Mark appears on public buildings throughout the region. Some of Italy's best wines come from this area, too. To the northeast rise the majestic Dolomites, with spectacular mountain scenery and Tyrolean atmosphere. Bordering Switzerland and Austria, the Dolomites region is largely bilingual (German-Italian), and local crafts and food reflect their Austrian origins.

Although conspicuously upscale hotels, shops, and restaurants cater to the affluent local society, you can find good value in plainer establishments throughout the area. Public transportation is relatively fast and efficient. Good rail and bus connections make it possible to cover the region fairly thoroughly on excursions from the main cities.

Padua (Padova in Italian) makes a good base for visiting Treviso and Vicenza, and for an excursion into the Dolomites. (It could also be a base for day trips to Venice, only 30 minutes away by train.) Your other base in the region could be Verona, a lively and beautiful city with some four-star attractions, including romantic settings associated with Shakespeare's ill-fated Romeo and Juliet and an ancient Roman arena that still packs in the crowds.

Essential Information

Lodging The area around Venice has been playing host to visitors for centuries, and the result is a range of comfortable accommodations at every price. Common sense should tell you that the slightly out-of-the-way small hotel will cost you less than its counterpart in a stylish Adriatic resort. Expect to pay more as you approach Venice, since many of the mainland towns absorb the overflow during the times when Venice becomes most crowded, such as Carnival (the two weeks preceding Lent) and throughout the summer.

Highly recommended lodgings are indicated by a star ★.

Dining In the main cities of the Veneto region, restaurants are in the middle to upper price ranges, but in smaller towns and in the countryside you can find some real bargains in good eating. Seafood is the specialty along the coast; inland the cuisine features delicate risotto, radicchio, and asparagus. Polenta, made of cornmeal, is a staple throughout the area; it is served with thick, rich sauces or grilled as an accompaniment to meat dishes. The best local wines are the whites Soave, Tocai, Prosecco, Riesling, and Pinot, and the reds Bardolino, Valpolicella, Merlot, Cabernet, and Pinot Nero. Grappa is the locally distilled acquavit that, like vodka, comes in both clear and flavored versions.

Unless otherwise noted, reservations are not needed and dress is casual. Highly recommended restaurants are indicated by a star ★.

Shopping Many of the goods normally associated with Venice are actually produced in the surrounding areas—which means that with a bit of diligence or luck you can pick up a bargain from the source. Mountain towns and villages—Bassano del Grappa is one—have the strongest handicraft tradition, and you can find a wide range of goods in artisans' shops on the side streets. The main towns on the coastal plain are often associated with one or two specialties, either because of traditional skills or because of ancient trading rights that set a pattern of importing specific items from other parts of the Mediterranean.

The Arts and Nightlife Two performing arts venues are the star attractions of this region: the **Arena di Verona,** an ancient Roman arena where a spectacular opera season is mounted from July through September; and the **Teatro Olimpico** in Vicenza, designed by Andrea Palladio, where classical drama is performed.

Guided Tours **American Express** offers an excursion by bus from Venice to the villas of the Veneto region and to Padua (about 75,000 lire). *Tours Apr.–Oct., Tues., Thurs., Sat., Sun.*

Highlights for First-time Visitors

Arena di Verona (Tour 3: Verona)
Asolo (Tour 1: Padua and Points North)
Bassano del Grappa (Tour 1: Padua and Points North)
Cappella degli Scrovegni (Tour 1: Padua and Points North)
Cappella di San Giovanni, Bolzano (Tour 4: The Dolomites)
Castello di Buonconsiglio, Trento (Tour 4: The Dolomites)
La Rotonda (Tour 2: Vicenza)
Teatro Olimpico (Tour 2: Vicenza)

Tour 1: Padua and Points North

Although today it is surrounded by unattractive modern business districts, Padua is one of the Veneto region's major art cities—a bustling city with a medieval nucleus, the seat of a famous university founded in 1222. From here, convenient rail and bus service leads to several interesting towns nestled among the hills just north of the coastal plain: Treviso, Marostica, Asolo, and Bassano del Grappa.

From Rome and Milan
By Train

By fast trains, Rome is about 4½ hours away from Padua (via Florence and Bologna), Milan about 2½ hours away (via Verona and Vicenza).

By Car

From Milan, take the A4 autostrada east from Milan; from Rome, take the A1 to Bologna, then the A13 northeast to Padua.

From Venice
By Train

The trip to Padua takes about 30 minutes by rail from Venice; trains run every 15–30 minutes.

By Bus

ATP buses leave Venice's Piazzale Roma for Padua every 30 minutes; the trip takes about 45 minutes and costs 4,500 lire.

By Car

Padua is 20 kilometers (12½ miles) west on the A4 autostrada from Mestre, the mainland town that is linked by causeway to Venice. The drive takes about 40 minutes.

Padua

Tourist information: Stazione Ferroviaria (train station), tel. 049/875–2077.

From the train station (the bus terminal is a five-minute walk from the train station, on Via Boschetto), you can take city bus No. 3, 8, or 18 (fare is 1,000 lire) to downtown Padua, or set off on foot straight down **Corso del Popolo**, which changes its name to Corso Garibaldi about 400 yards away, when it crosses the Bacchiglione River.

To the left just across the river is the **Cappella degli Scrovegni** (Scrovegni Chapel), built in the 13th century near the site of an ancient Roman arena. The chapel was erected by a wealthy Paduan, Enrico Scrovegni, in honor of his deceased father. Scrovegni called on Giotto to decorate its interior, a task that occupied the great artist and his helpers from 1303 to 1305. They created a magnificent fresco cycle, arranged in typical medieval comic-strip fashion, illustrating the lives of Mary and Christ. *Corso Garibaldi, tel. 049/875–1153. Admission: 5,000 lire includes admission to the Musco Civico degli Eremitani, tel. 049/875–2321 (see below). Both open Apr.–Sept., Tues.–Sun. 9–7; Oct.–Mar. 9–5:30.*

Turn left from the chapel entrance and cross the gardens that now occupy the area of the original Roman arena to reach Piazza Eremitani and the 13th-century church of the **Eremitani**. It contains some fragments of frescoes by Andrea Mantegna (1431–1506), the brilliant, locally born artist, some of whose masterpieces are in nearby Mantua: Most of these frescoes, however, were destroyed in the Allied bombing of 1944. The **Museo Civico** (Civic Museum) here has its quota of works by Ve-

202

SLOVENIA

Tolmin

Nova Gorica

Cividale

Gorizia

Gemona

Montfalcone

Isonzo

Miramare Castle

Trieste

Koper

Portoroz

Piran

Golfo di Trieste

Adriatic Sea

Udine

S13

S464

S463

Tagliamento

Tolmezzo

A23

S52bis

Meduna

Portogruaro

Caorle

Pordenone

A28

S251

Lido di Jesolo

Calalzo

S48

S353

Cortina d'Ampezzo

S51

Sella di Fadalto

Vittorio Veneto

Conegliano

Oderzo

Piave

Livenza

Belluno

S203

S550

Valdobbiadene

S53

S53

Treviso

A4

S14

Predazzo

S47

Feltre

Montebelluna

Maser

Castelfranco Veneto

S13

A27

Villa Pisani

Venice

Bolzano

A22

TO MERANO

S239

S43

S38

Asolo

Bassano del Grappa

Marostica

S248

S248

S307

S307

S245

S307

Praglia

Padua

A4 (E70)

Trento

Rovereto

Arsiero

Schio

S46

Valdagno

Vicenza

S11

S53

A4

S.Bonifacio

Adige

Verona
see detail map

netian masters. A small road leads diagonally left from the church back to Corso Garibaldi. About a quarter mile farther along Corso Garibaldi is the **Caffè Pedrocchi** (Piazzetta Pedrocchi), a monumental 19th-century neoclassical coffeehouse that looks like a cross between a museum and a stage set.

Just to the left, on a side street leading off the other side of the Corso, is the 16th-century **University** building. This is worth a visit to see the exquisite and perfectly proportioned anatomy theater and a hall harboring a lectern used by Galileo. *Via VIII Febbraio. Admission free. Guided visits only. Closed for restoration. May reopen in 1994.*

The **Municipio** (City Hall) faces the University from the Caffè Pedrocchi side of the Corso. Behind it are three adjacent historic squares that form the heart of the city and are constantly crisscrossed by students on bicycles. In the largest square, scene of the city's outdoor market in the morning, is the **Palazzo della Ragione** (also called **Il Salone**), which was built during the Middle Ages as the seat of Padua's parliament. Today its street-level arcades shelter shops and cafés. In the frescoed Great Hall on the upper level is an enormous wooden horse, a 15th-century replica of the bronze steed in Donatello's equestrian statue of Gattamelata (*see below*). The hall is often used for exhibitions, and on those occasions it is open to the public.

Take a look at the 15th- and 16th-century buildings on Piazza dei Signori and at the cathedral a few steps away. Then return to the University and take the second street east of the Corso—Via del Santo—south to the huge basilica of **Sant'Antonio,** one of Padua's major attractions. Standing in front of the church is Donatello's powerful statue of the *condottiere* (mercenary general) Gattamelata, which was cast in bronze—that alone was a monumental technical achievement—in about 1450 and was to have an enormous influence on the development of Italian Renaissance sculpture. A cluster of Byzantine domes and slender, minaretlike towers gives the church an Oriental look reminiscent of San Marco in Venice. The interior is sumptuous, too, with marble reliefs by Tullio Lombardo, the greatest in a talented family of marble carvers who decorated many churches in the area—among them Santa Maria dei Miracoli in Venice. The artistic highlights here, however, all bear Donatello's name; the 15th-century Florentine master did the remarkable series of bronze reliefs illustrating the life of Saint Anthony—whose feast day, June 13, brings pilgrims from all parts of Europe—as well as the bronze statues of the Madonna and saints on the high altar.

Take a left outside the museum and walk along Via Belludi to **Prato della Valle,** an unusual and attractive piazza laid out in 1775, with a wooded oval park at the center, surrounded by a canal. At the southeast end of this immense square is the church of **Santa Giustina,** with finely inlaid choir stalls and Veronese's colossal altarpiece, *The Martyrdom of St. Justine.*

Lodging
Under 115,00 lire

Al Cason. Conveniently located near the station and bus terminal, this hotel caters to businesspeople. *Via Fra Paolo Sarpi 40, tel. 049/662636, fax 049/875–4217. 48 rooms with bath or shower. AE, DC, MC, V.*

Sant'Antonio. Within walking distance of all the sights, this small hotel is located near the Scrovegni Chapel. Rooms are clean and functional, with no frills. *Via San Fermo 118, tel. 049/*

875–1393, fax 049/875–2508. 34 rooms, 26 with bath or shower. DC, MC, V.

Under 60,000 lire **Bellevue.** A family-run hotel with a homey atmosphere and attractive rooms, it is located on the main street between the basilica of Sant'Antonio and Prato della Valle. All double rooms have small private baths. *Via Belludi 11, tel. 049/875–5547. 12 rooms, 8 with bath. No credit cards.*

CTG Hostel. A large, well-run hostel with clean dormitories and bathrooms, it is located in a quiet neighborhood about 10 minutes from Prato della Valle on foot. Take city bus No. 3, 8, or 12 from the train station. Meals are available. *Via Aleardi 30, tel. 049/875–2219. 110 beds. No credit cards.*

Verdi. Handily located near the cathedral and Piazza delle Erbe, the Verdi is a family-run place with simple furnishings. Take city bus No. 6 from the station to Piazza Capitaniato. *Via Dondi dell'Orologio 7, tel. 049/875–5744. 18 rooms, none with bath. No credit cards.*

Dining **Al Fagiano.** Because of its location close to the basilica of
Under 30,000 Sant'Antonio, this popular trattoria attracts a lot of tourists. All the same, it has maintained a high standard of cooking, serving some local specialties and well-known Italian classics, such as *pasta e fagioli* (pasta and bean soup), roast *capretto* (kid), or a platter of *arrosti misti* (assorted roast meats). Under the same management is a budget-priced hotel upstairs. *Via Locatelli 45, tel. 049/652913. Reservations advised. MC, V. Closed Mon. and July.*

Snack Bar Gancino. Next to the cathedral, this café offers a range of sandwiches and snacks good enough to make a meal of. *Piazza Duomo 1, tel. 049/657–781. No credit cards. Closed Sun.*

Shopping Every morning except Sunday, open-air markets in the squares around the Palazzo della Ragione sell foodstuffs, clothing, books, and old prints. On Saturday afternoon there is a similar market in Piazza Barbato, at Ponte di Brenta; take bus No. 18 from the train station. On the third Sunday of the month, an antiques and flea market is held in the morning in Prato della Valle.

The Arts and Because of its large student population, Padua has a number of
Nightlife beer halls and pizzerias that stay open late, among them **Alexander** (Via San Francesco 38, tel. 049/652884) and **Du Demon Pub** (Corso Vittorio Emanuele 185, tel. 049/667513).

Treviso

From Padua, take the train to Mestre and change for the Venice–Udine line; the trip takes 45 minutes. Buses are more direct, though the trip takes about an hour; they depart every 30 minutes or so from Padua's Piazza Boschetti. Bus and train fare is about the same: 5,000 lire one-way. Tourist office: Via Toniolo 41, to the right off Piazza Borsa, tel. 0422/547632.

Treviso has arcaded streets, frescoed houses, and channeled streams that run through the center of town. An attractive city, it can be explored on foot in half a day; its restaurants are good places to stop for lunch. The most important church here is **San Nicolò**, on Via San Nicolò, a few blocks north and across the river from the train station. An impressive Gothic building with an interesting vaulted ceiling, San Nicolò has columns with frescoes of the saints by 14th-century artist Tommaso da Modena. But the best is the remarkable series of 40 portraits of Dominican friars by the same artist in the seminary next door. They are astoundingly realistic, considering that some were painted as early as 1352, and include one of the earliest known portraits of someone wearing spectacles. *Via San Nicolò. For admission, inquire at the custodian's desk at the seminary entrance.*

As you explore the town, you'll see lots of old houses with decorated facades, many of them built in the 15th century. Go left from the front of the seminary a quarter mile to the **Duomo** (Cathedral). Inside, on the altar of one of the chapels to the right, is an *Annunciation* by Titian. Running alongside the cathedral are Via Canova and Via Calmaggiore, lined with some well-preserved medieval buildings. Via Calmaggiore leads to **Piazza dei Signori**, the heart of medieval Treviso and still the town's social center, with outdoor cafés and some impressive public buildings facing it. One of these, the Palazzo dei Trecento, has a small alley leading behind it. Follow the alley for about 200 yards, to the **Pescheria** (Fish Market), on an island in one of the small rivers that flow through town.

Dining
Under 30,000 lire

All'Oca Bianca. On a little street off Via Calmaggiore, between the cathedral and Piazza della Signoria, this is a popular tavern with good-value pasta dishes and roast meats. *Vicolo della Torre 7, tel. 0422/541–850. No credit cards. Closed Wed.*

★ **Beccherie.** In a town known for good eating, this rustic inn is a favorite. It's in the heart of old Treviso, behind the main square. Wooden beams, copper utensils, and Venetian provincial decor set the tone inside, and there are tables outside for fair-weather dining under the portico. Specialties vary with the season. In winter, look for *crespelle al radicchio* (crepes with radicchio) and *faraona in salsa peverada* (guinea hen in a peppery sauce); spring brings risotto with spring vegetables, *stinco di vitello* (roast veal shin), and *pasticcio di melanzane* (eggplant casserole). *Piazza Ancilotto 10, tel. 0422/540871. Reservations advised. AE, DC, MC, V. Closed Thurs., Fri. lunch, and July 12–30.*

Asolo and Maser

Buses run more or less hourly from Treviso to Asolo; the trip takes 35–45 minutes and costs about 4,000 lire. Six buses a day make the 7-kilometer (4-mile) side trip from Asolo to the Villa Barbaro in nearby Maser; the trip takes 15 minutes and the fare is about 3,000 lire one-way. Asolo tourist office: Via Santa Caterina 258, tel. 0423/529046, fax 0423/524137.

The most romantic and charming of the towns in the vicinity is Asolo, 35 kilometers (22 miles) northwest of Treviso and 11 kilometers (7 miles) east of Bassano del Grappa. This hillside hamlet was the consolation prize of an exiled queen. At the end of the 15th century, Venetian-born Caterina Cornaro was sent here by Venice's doges to keep her from interfering with their administration of her former kingdom of Cyprus, which she had inherited. To soothe the pain of exile, she established a lively and brilliant court in Asolo. Over the centuries, Venetian aristocrats continued to build gracious villas on the hillside, and in the 19th century Asolo once again became the idyllic haunt of musicians, poets, and painters. In the center of town you can explore **Piazza Maggiore,** with its Renaissance palaces and turn-of-the-century cafés, and then continue uphill, past Caterina's ruined castle and some Gothic-style houses, to the **Roman fortress** that stands on the summit. Other walks will take you past the villas once inhabited by Robert Browning and the actress Eleanora Duse. Be warned that Asolo's dreamy Old World atmosphere disappears on holiday weekends, when the crowds pour in.

Northeast of Asolo, in Maser, is **Villa Barbaro,** a gracious Renaissance creation, the work of Palladio. The fully furnished villa is still inhabited by its owners, who make you slip heavy felt scuffs over your shoes to protect the highly polished floors. The elaborate stuccos and opulent frescoes by Paolo Veronese bring the 16th century to life. This Venetian villa is worth going out of your way to see. *Admission: 6,000 lire. Open Apr.– Sept., Tues., weekends 3–6; Oct.–Mar., Tues., weekends 2:30–5.*

Dining   **Hosteria Ca' Derton.** The location is an attraction here: Ca' Der-
Splurge   ton is right on the main square. It has a pleasant, old-fashioned ambience, with early photos of Asolo on the walls and bouquets of dried flowers on each table. The friendly proprietor takes pride in the homemade pasta and desserts, and in offering a good selection of both local and international dishes. *Piazza D'Annunzio 11, tel. 0423/952730. Reservations advised. AE, DC, MC, V. Closed Mon. evening and Tues., Feb. 15–28, and Aug. 17–31.*

Shopping   On the second Sunday of every month, there is an antiques market in the center of Asolo; get there early for any real bargains.

Bassano del Grappa

From Padua, frequent daily ATP buses run direct to Bassano del Grappa, taking about 70 minutes. From Treviso, ATP buses leave hourly for Bassano del Grappa; the ride takes about 60 minutes. Either way, fares are approximately 6,000 lire one-way. Train service from Padua is less direct and slower. Buses arrive at Viale delle Fosse, a five-minute walk from Bassano's Piazza della Libertà. Tourist office: Largo Corona d'Italia 35, off Viale delle Fosse near the bus terminal, tel. 0424/524351, fax 0424/26703.

In the foothills of the Alps, Bassano del Grappa is a beautifully located town directly above the swift-flowing waters of the Brenta River at the foot of the Mount Grappa massif (5,880 feet). Bassano's old streets are lined with low buildings sporting wooden balconies and eye-catching flowerpots. Bright ceramic wares produced here and in nearby Nove are displayed in shops along byways that curve uphill toward a centuries-old square, and, even higher, to a belvedere with a good view of Mount Grappa and the beginning of the Valsugana Valley.

Bassano's most famous landmark is the covered bridge that has spanned the Brenta since the 13th century. Rebuilt countless times (floods are frequent), the present-day bridge is a postwar reconstruction using Andrea Palladio's 16th-century design. The great architect astutely chose to use wood as his medium, knowing that it could be replaced quickly and cheaply. Almost as famous is the characteristic Nardini liquor shop at one end of the bridge; it's redolent of the grappa that has been distilled here for more than a century.

Lodging
Splurge
★

Belvedere. Totally renovated in 1985, this historic hotel has richly decorated public rooms with period furnishings and Oriental rugs. A fireplace, piano music in the lounge, and an excellent restaurant (tel. 0424/526602, closed Sun.) with a garden provide a very pleasant stay. The bedrooms are decorated in traditional Venetian or chic contemporary style. Doubles with bath cost about 190,000 lire, including breakfast. *Piazzale G. Giardino 14, tel. 0424/529845, fax 0424/529849. 91 rooms with bath or shower. Facilities: air-conditioning, color TV. AE, DC, MC, V.*

Dining
Under 30,000 lire

Ottone. This attractive tavern in the center of Bassano, off Piazza della Libertà, serves frankfurters (known as *wurstel* in these parts), goulash, pasta, and hearty club sandwiches. *Via Matteotti 50, tel. 0424/522206. MC, V. Closed Mon. evening, Tues., and first 3 weeks of Aug.*

Marostica

From Bassano, hourly buses run west to Marostica, about 7 kilometers (4 miles) away; the fare is about 2,000 lire.

Though there are no specific attractions here, a quick side trip to Marostica from Bassano del Grappa is a pleasant diversion for travelers with time to spare. A castle on the hillside overlooks the town, and the main square is paved in checkerboard fashion. In even-numbered years, on the second weekend in September, a game of chess is acted out here by people in medieval costume.

Tour 2: Vicenza

Frequent train service runs to Vicenza: Travel time is 30 minutes from Padua, an hour from Venice. Tourist offices: Piazza Duomo 5, tel. 0444/544122; Piazza Matteotti, next to the Teatro Olimpico, tel. 0444/320854.

Vicenza, 32 kilometers (20 miles) west of Padua by rail or autostrada, bears the distinctive signature of the 16th-century architect Andrea Palladio. The architect, whose name is the basis of the term "Palladian," gracefully incorporated elements of classical architecture—columns, porticoes, and domes—into a style that reflected the Renaissance celebration of order and harmony. His elegant villas and palaces were influential in propagating classical architecture in Europe, especially Britain, and later in America.

In the mid-16th century, Palladio was given the opportunity to rebuild much of Vicenza, which had suffered great damage during the bloody wars waged against Venice by the League of Cambrai, an alliance of the papacy, France, the Holy Roman Empire, and several neighboring city-states. He imposed upon the city a number of his grand Roman-style buildings—rather an overstatement, considering the town's status. With the Basilica, begun in 1549 in the very heart of Vicenza, he ensured his reputation and embarked on a series of lordly buildings, all of which proclaim the same rigorous classicism.

From the train or bus station, Viale Roma leads straight north
to Porta Castello, a gateway through a fragment of the old city
wall and the starting point of the broad main avenue of Vicenza,
Corso Palladio. Before strolling down the Corso, however, you
may want to turn right just past the gate, go one block south,
and turn left to see the Gothic **Duomo,** which contains a gleaming altarpiece by Lorenzo Veneziano, a 14th-century Venetian
painter.

Corso Palladio is a memorable avenue, lined with a succession
of imposing palaces and churches that run the gamut from Venetian Gothic to Baroque, including the striking **Palazzo del
Comune,** about halfway along. Make a side trip left down Contrà Porti for a look at other splendid palaces and, back on Corso
Palladio, stop into the church of **Santa Corona** to see the exceptionally fine *Baptism of Christ* (1500) by Giovanni Bellini,
above the altar on the left just in front of the transept. **Palazzo
Chiericati,** on a square at the end of the Corso, is an exquisite and unmistakable Palladian building. The palace houses
the **Museo Civico,** with a representative collection of Venetian paintings. *Piazza Matteotti, tel. 0444/321348. Admission:
5,000 lire, including admission to Teatro Olimpico* (see below).
Open Tues.–Sat. 9:30–noon and 2:30–5; Sun. 10–noon.

On the other side of the square is the **Teatro Olimpico,**
Palladio's last, and perhaps finest, work. Based closely on the
model of the ancient Roman theater, it represents an important
development in theater and stage design and is noteworthy for
its acoustics and the cunningly devised false perspective of a
classical street in the permanent backdrop. *Piazza Matteotti,
tel. 0444/323781. Admission: 5,000 lire. Open Mar. 16–Oct. 15,
Mon.–Sat. 9:30–12:30 and 3–5:30, Sun. 9:30–noon; Oct. 16–
Mar. 15, Mon.–Sat. 9:30–noon and 2–4:30, Sun. 9:30–noon.*

Retrace your steps along Corso Palladio and, halfway back,
turn left onto Contrà del Monte, which leads to the elongated
Piazza dei Signori, the heart of the city. This is the site of
Palladio's **Basilica,** a confusing name, since it is not a church but
a courthouse, the Palazzo della Ragione. An early Palladian
masterpiece, it was actually a medieval building that the architect modernized. And the skill with which he wedded the
graceful two-story exterior loggias to the existing Gothic
structure is remarkable. He also designed, but never completed, the **Loggia del Capitaniato,** opposite.

Two of the most interesting villas of the Veneto region are a little more than a mile from the center of Vicenza, on the Este
road to the southeast. You can walk to both, but it is easier to
take the No. 8 bus from Corso Palladio to the Via San Bastiano
bus stop. From the bus stop you gently climb a quarter mile until you reach **Villa Valmarana dei Nani,** an 18th-century country
house decorated with a series of marvelous frescoes by
Giambattista Tiepolo: These are fantastic visions of a mythological world. The guest house holds more frescoes, these by
Tiepolo's son, Giandomenico. *Via San Bastiano 8, tel. 0444/
321803. Admission: 5,000 lire. Open Mar.–Nov., Tues.–Sat.
2:30–5:30, with hours extended in the high season (May–Sept.)
Wed., Thurs., Sat., Sun. 10–noon, Tues.–Sat. 3–6.*

From Villa Valmarana, continue along Via San Bastiano (which
narrows to the size of a path) for a few hundred yards to **La
Rotonda,** the most famous Palladian villa of all. Serene and

symmetrical, it was the model for Jefferson's Monticello. Take the time to admire it from all sides, and you'll see that it was the inspiration not just for Monticello but for nearly every state capital in the United States. The interior is a disappointment, but that's not why you came here anyway. *Via della Rotonda 33, tel. 0444/321793. Admission: to grounds, 3,000 lire; to interior, 5,000 lire. Open Mar. 15–Oct. 15. Grounds open Tues.–Thurs. 10–noon and 3–6; interior open Wed. 10–noon and 3–6.*

Lodging
Under 115,000

Vicenza. In the heart of the city, off Piazza dei Signori, this clean little hotel is best in the winter, when the chatter from the café-restaurant across the square doesn't continue until the wee hours. *Stradella dei Nodari 5, tel. 0444/321512. 30 rooms, 20 with bath. MC, V.*

Do Mori. Near the Hotel Vicenza but quieter, the Do Mori is also brighter, with freshly renovated rooms, refurbished in 1992. *Contrà Do Rode 26, tel. 0444/321–886. 25 rooms, 17 with bath. No credit cards.*

Dining
Under 30,000 lire

Al Paradiso. This pizzeria-trattoria just off Piazza dei Signori is one of a pair (the other is **Vecchia Guardia**), right next door to each other and owned by two brothers. The setting is lovely, with tables outside in the summer. The pizzas and other dishes are both tasty and reasonably priced. *Via Pescherie Vecchie 5, tel. 0444/322320. Closed Mon.*

The Arts and Nightlife

Even if your Italian is dismal, it's probably worth attending a performance of classical drama (in Italian) in the **Teatro Olimpico** in Vicenza. Palladio's masterpiece was designed to be used, not just admired. For details, contact Teatro Olimpico (Vicenza, tel. 0444/323781).

Tour 3: Verona

This attractive city, on the banks of the fast-flowing Adige River, is, after Venice, the top attraction in the region and rivals other Italian art cities. It has considerable charm; classical and medieval monuments; a picturesque town center where bright geraniums bloom in window boxes; and a romantic reputation, thanks to Shakespeare's *Romeo and Juliet*, which is set here. It is one of Italy's most alluring cities, despite extensive industrialization and urban development in its newer sections. Inevitably, with its lively Venetian air, proximity to Lake Garda, and renowned summer opera season, it attracts hordes of tourists, especially vacationing Germans and Austrians, who drive through the Brenner Pass just to the north.

Verona grew to power and prosperity within the Roman Empire as a result of its key commercial and military position in northern Italy. After the fall of the Empire, the city continued to flourish under the guidance of such Barbarian kings as Theodoric, Alboin, Pepin, and Berenger I, reaching its cultural and artistic peak during the 13th and 14th centuries, under the Della Scala dynasty. (You'll see the *scala*, or ladder, emblem all over town.) In 1404, however, Verona traded its independence for security and placed itself under the control of Venice. (The other recurring architectural motif is the lion of Saint Mark, symbol of allegiance to Venice.) Verona remained under Venetian protection until 1797, when Napoleon invaded. In 1814 the entire Veneto region was won by the Austrians, and it was finally united with the rest of Italy in 1866.

On the main Milan–Venice and Bologna–Trento train lines,
Verona is easy to reach. It is only about a half hour from Vicenza by train, a half hour from Padua, and 1½ hours from Venice. Verona also has its own airport at Villafranca; it is
connected by air with other cities in Italy and Europe. Tourist
offices: Via Leoncino 61, tel. 045/592828; Piazza delle Erbe 38,
tel. 045/800–0065 (open Apr.–Sept.).

*Numbers in the margin correspond to points of interest on the
Verona map.*

The obvious place to start your visit is at **Piazza Brà,** the vast
❶ and airy square at the center of the city, where the **Arena di Verona** is located. (Piazza Brà is a longish 25-minute walk from the
train station; take bus No. 2 from the station.) Built by the Romans in the 1st century AD, it is one of the largest and best-preserved Roman amphitheaters anywhere. Only four arches
remain of the outer rings, but the main structure is so complete
that it takes little imagination to picture it as the site of the cruel deaths of countless gladiators, wild beasts, and Christians.
Today it hosts Verona's summer opera, famous for spectacular
productions and audiences of as many as 22,000 (25,000 in ancient times). An informal, picnicky spirit adds to the fun. The
best operas to see here are the big, splashy ones that demand
huge choruses, "Cinerama" sets, lots of color and movement,
and, if possible, camels, horses, and/or elephants. The music
can be excellent, and the acoustics are fine, too. If you go, be
sure to bring or rent a cushion—four hours on 2,000-year-old
marble can be an ordeal (*see* The Arts and Nightlife, *below*).
*Arena di Verona, tel. 045/800–3204. Admission: 6,000 lire; free
the first Sunday of the month. Open Tues.–Sun. 8–6:30;
Tues.–Sun. 8–1:30 during opera season in July and August.*

Via Mazzini, an old and fashionable thoroughfare, leads off Piazza Brà to **Piazza delle Erbe** (Vegetable Market Square), site
of the ancient Roman forum and today a colorful market in the
morning, when huge, rectangular umbrellas are raised to
shade the neat ranks of fruits and vegetables. Off Piazza delle
Erbe is **Piazza dei Signori,** enclosed on all sides by stately pub-
❷ lic buildings. The 12th-century **Palazzo della Ragione** has a
somber-looking courtyard, Gothic staircase, and medieval tow-
❸ er. Opposite is the graceful **Loggia del Consiglio,** built in the
12th century to house city council meetings. At the end of the
❹ square is the **Palazzo del Governo,** the medieval stronghold
from which the Della Scalas ruled Verona with an iron fist.

❺ Just off this end of the square are the **Arche Scaligere,** the magnificent Gothic tombs of the Della Scalas, behind a 14th-
century wrought-iron fence bearing the family's ladder emblem. The tomb over the door of the church is the resting place
of Cangrande I, protector of Dante and patron of the arts; the
equestrian statue is a copy of the one on view at the Castelvecchio Museum (*see below*). In the same neighborhood are the
❻ ❼ Gothic church of **Sant'Anastasia** and the Romanesque **Duomo**
(Cathedral). The square by Sant'Anastasia leads onto a shady
riverside walkway along the swift-flowing but shallow Adige,
which always has a refreshingly cool breeze blowing from it,
thanks to its origins in the Alpine glaciers.

❽ Cross the Adige at Ponte Nuovo to see the **Giusti Gardens,** laid
out on several levels around a 16th-century villa. There's a formal Italian garden, an 18th-century maze, and a fine view of the

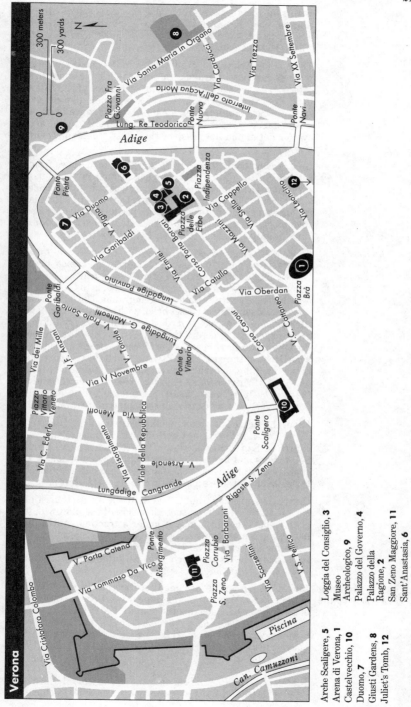

Verona

300 meters

300 yards

Adige

Piazza Fra Giovanni

Via Santa Maria in Organo

Via Carducci

Via Trezza

Via XX Settembre

Interrato dell'Acqua Morta

Lung. Re Teodorico

Ponte Nuovo

Ponte Navi

Ponte Pietra

Via Duomo

V. Pigna

Via Garibaldi

Via Emilei

Corso porta Borsari

Piazza delle Erbe

Piazza Indipendenza

Via Cappello

Via Stella

Via Mazzini

Via Leoncino

Via Catullo

Lungadige Panvinio

Lungadige G. Matteotti

V. Prato Santo

V. F. Anzani

Ponte Garibaldi

Via dei Mille

Via IV Novembre

V. Tonale

Ponte d. Vittoria

Via Menotti

Via Risorgimento

Viale della Repubblica

V. Arsenale

Piazza Vittorio Veneto

Via C. Ederle

Lungádige Cangrande

Ponte Scaligero

Rigaste S. Zeno

Ponte Risorgimento

V. Porta Catena

Via Tommaso Da Vico

Piazza S. Zeno

Piazza Corrubio

Via Barbarani

Via Scarsellini

V. S. Pellico

Via Cristoforo Colombo

Adige

Piscina

Can. Camuzzoni

Via Oberdan

Piazza Brà

Corso Cavour

V. C. Cattaneo

Arche Scaligere, **5**

Arena di Verona, **1**

Castelvecchio, **10**

Duomo, **7**

Giusti Gardens, **8**

Juliet's Tomb, **12**

Loggia del Consiglio, **3**

Museo Archeologico, **9**

Palazzo del Governo, **4**

Palazzo della Ragione, **2**

San Zeno Maggiore, **11**

Sant'Anastasia, **6**

city from the terrace, from which Johann von Goethe, the German poet and dramatist, drew inspiration. *Via Giardino Giusti, tel. 045/803–4029. Admission: 5,000 lire. Open daily Apr.–Oct. 8–8, Nov.–Mar. 8–sunset.*

The medieval church of Santa Maria in Organo is on the same road as the Giusti Gardens. Be sure to visit the choir and the refectory to see the inlaid-wood masterpieces of the 15th-century monk Fra Giovanni. A series of panels depicts varied scenes—local buildings, an idealized Renaissance town, wildlife, and fruit—that radiate a love of life and betray the artist's eye for detail and his grasp of the latest technique (perspective).

⑨ On the same bank of the river, there are good views from the terraces of the **Museo Archeologico,** located in an old monastery above the Roman Theater, which was built in the same era as the arena. The Roman Theater is in the museum grounds and is sometimes used for dramatic productions. *Rigaste del Redentore, tel. 045/800–0360. Admission: 5,000 lire; free on the first Sunday of the month. Open Tues.–Sun. 8–1:30.*

⑩ Cross the Adige on Ponte Pietra and head back to Sant' Anastasia to pick up Corso Sant'Anastasia, which becomes Corso Porta Borsari and then Corso Cavour, which is lined with attractive old buildings and palaces and leads to **Castelvecchio,** a 14th-century castle built for Cangrande II Della Scala. A crenellated building in russet brick with massive walls, towers, turrets, and a vast courtyard, it looks like a fairy-tale castle guarding a bridge across the Adige. Inside is the **Museo del Castelvecchio,** also known as the Museo Civico, which gives you a good look at the castle's vaulted halls and the treasures of Venetian painting and sculpture they contain. *Corso Cavour, tel. 045/594734. Admission: 5,000 lire; free on the first Sunday of the month. Open Tues.–Sun. 8–6:30; hours and admission cost may change when museum houses temporary exhibitions.*

⑪ From the castle it's a short walk upstream along Rigaste San Zeno and Via Barbarani to one of Italy's finest Romanesque churches, **San Zeno Maggiore.** It's set between two medieval bell towers and has a 13th-century rose window and a 12th-century portal. Inside, look for Mantegna's *Madonna* above the main altar; there's a peaceful cloister off the left nave.

⑫ Romantic souls may want to see what the astute tourist office says is **Juliet's Tomb,** on the other side of the old town; it's a pretty spot, though hardly a major attraction. Authentic or not, it is still popular with lovesick Italian teenagers, who leave notes for the tragic lover. *Via del Pontiere, tel. 045/800–0361. Admission: 5,000 lire; free on the first Sunday of the month. Open Tues.–Sun. 8–6:30.*

Lodging
Under 115,000 lire
Aurora. This is an old-fashioned hotel in a good position on Piazza delle Erbe, Verona's picturesque market square (ask for one of the 12 rooms overlooking the piazza). *Via Pelliciai 2, tel. 045/594717, fax 045/801–0806. 20 rooms, 15 with bath. MC, V.*
Cavour. Small and basic, this hotel is centrally located on a quiet byway between the Arena and Castelvecchio. *Vicolo Chiodo 4, tel. 045/590508. 17 rooms, most with shower. No credit cards.*
Torcolo. Just off Piazza Brà, near the Arena, this old-fashioned hotel is pleasant. Rooms are soberly furnished, and all have pri-

vate bathroom. *Vicolo Listone 3, tel. 045/800–7512, fax 045/
800–4058. 19 rooms with shower. No credit cards.*

Under 60,000 lire **Catullo.** Central, in the medieval district near the Arena, this is
a comfortable small hotel; some doubles have tiny balconies.
*Via Catullo 1, tel. 045/800–2786. 21 rooms, 3 with bath. No
credit cards.*

IYHF Hostel. Take bus No. 2 to Piazza Isolo, then walk to Via
Ponte Pignolo and follow the signs to this dormitory-style hos-
tel in a beautiful old villa with garden. It is one of the best in
Italy, with a *simpatico* staff and good food. Guests must leave
rooms during the day, and there's an 11 PM curfew. *Salita
Fontana del Ferro 15, tel 045/590360. 52 beds. No credit cards.*

Splurge **Giulietta e Romeo.** A value-for-the-money choice in the medieval part of Verona and very handy for sightseeing, this is a
simple but comfortable hotel with an irresistibly romantic
name. The hotel was renovated extensively in 1991. Doubles
with bath cost about 200,000 lire. *Vicolo Tre Marchetti 3, tel.
045/800–3554, fax 045/801–0862. 30 rooms with bath or shower.
AE, MC, V.*

Dining **Al Cacciatore.** One of Verona's historic *osterie*, or wineshops,
Under 30,000 lire this is near Piazza Isolo, across Ponte Nuovo from Piazza
Indipendenza, and it serves such hearty local dishes as roast
pork or risotto with seasonal vegetables. *Via Seminario 4, tel.
045/594291. No credit cards. Closed Sun.*

Alla Genovesa. In the heart of the medieval district, this large
trattoria has a good-value tourist menu. The kitchen produces
authentic local dishes and a homemade paté. *Strada Genovesa
5, tel. 045/541122. AE, DC, MC, V. Closed Wed.*

Vesuvio. Between Castelvecchio and San Zeno Maggiore, this
authentic Neapolitan pizzeria has tables on the riverbank in
summer and a lovely breezy view of the Adige. The same family
also has a branch on Corso Sant'Anastasia, just off Piazza delle
Erbe. *Via Rigaste 41, tel. 045/595634. MC, V. Closed Mon.*

Under 24,000 **McDonald's.** Very popular with young Veronese and their fami-
lies, this fast-food branch enjoys a prime location, just outside
Piazza Brà and the Roman Arena. *Corso Porta Nuova 14, near
Piazza Brà. No credit cards. Closed Thurs.*

Shopping Verona's **Piazza delle Erbe** market has a changing selection of
food, wines, clothing, some antiques, and even pets. It's open
daily.

The Arts and The spectacular summer opera season in the **Arena di Verona**
Nightlife runs from July through August, and the 22,000 in the audience
sit on the original stone terraces, which date from the time
when gladiators fought to the death. The opera stage is huge
and best suited to such grand operas as *Aida*, but the experience is memorable no matter what is being performed. *For tickets, contact Ente Lirico Arena di Verona, Piazza Brà 28, 37100
Verona, tel. 045/590109. The box office is at Arches 8–9 of the
Arena, tel. 045/590517 or 045/800–5151. Open weekdays 8:40–
12:20 and 3–5:50, Sat. 8:40–12:20. Tickets start at 20,000 lire.*

Tour 4: The Dolomites

Unlike other famous Alpine ranges, this vast, mountainous domain in northeast Italy has remained relatively undeveloped, despite its appeal as a winter-sports center. The landscape here can be breathtaking—snowcapped peaks glowing pink in the sunset, meadows studded with mountain wildflowers, castles perched high on sheer cliffs, secluded villages with Tyrolean-style woodcarving on the houses. The area's famous ski resorts—Cortina d'Ampezzo, Madonna di Campiglio, Val Gardena—can be quite pricey and hard to get to; for a more affordable taste of the Dolomites, make an excursion from Verona to the cities of Trento and Bolzano, with a side trip to the spa town of Merano.

Although the Dolomites overflow into the Lombardy region and the Veneto, most of the area falls into a region of Italy that has enjoyed special status since 1948—the Autonomous Region of Trentino-Alto Adige. The region's dual provinces are the Italian-speaking Trentino and the predominantly German-speaking Alto Adige, where culture, crafts, and food have an Austrian accent (until World War I, the area was Austria's South Tyrol). Also spoken in the area is Ladin, an offshoot of Latin still spoken by a small community that credits its survival to centuries of isolation in mountain fastnesses.

Trento

Trento is an hour from Verona by train. Tourist office: Via Alfieri 4, tel. 0461/983880.

Trento, capital of the autonomous Trentino province, is still Italian in atmosphere. Somehow this city has escaped the ravages of commercialization and retains its architectural charm, artistic attractions, and historic importance.

It was here, from 1545 to 1563, that the structure of the Catholic church was redefined, in the famous Council of Trent. This was the starting point of the Counter-Reformation, which brought half of Europe back to Catholicism. Until 1803, Trento itself was ruled by prince-bishops. You'll see the word *Consiglio* (Council) everywhere in Trento—in hotel, restaurant, and street names, and even on wine labels.

At its heart, Trento has a square—**Piazza del Duomo.** In the center is a Baroque fountain of Neptune; the massive, low, Romanesque **Duomo** forms the southern edge of the square. Before entering the cathedral, pause to savor the view of the mountaintops ranged majestically around the city and visible above the rooftops in every direction. The mountain weather can change within minutes, and you can never be sure of the same visibility when you reemerge from the cathedral.

Step inside to see the unusual arcaded stone stairways on either side of the austere nave. Ahead of you is the *baldacchino* (altar canopy), a clear copy of Bernini's masterpiece in St. Peter's in Rome. In a small chapel to the right is a mournful 15th-century Crucifixion, with Mary and the apostle John. This crucifix was a focal point of the Council of Trent: Each decree agreed on during the two decades of deliberations was solemnly read out in front of it. Outside, walk around the building to the back of the cathedral to see an exquisite display of 14th-century stonemasons' art, from the small porch to the intriguing knotted columns on the graceful apse.

The crenellated **Palazzo Pretorio,** which seems to be a wing of the cathedral, was built during the 13th century as the prudently fortified residence of the prince-bishops. Endowed with considerable power and autonomy, these clerics enjoyed a unique position in the medieval hierarchy. From the beginning of the 11th century, they wielded a twofold authority, administering civil and military affairs on behalf of the Holy Roman Emperor, and acting as the pope's representatives in ecclesiastical matters. At the same time, other parts of Italy were at war, with each side pledging its loyalty to one or the other power. This delicate balancing act continued for 800 years, ending when Austria secularized the principality in 1802.

The Palazzo Pretorio now houses the **Museo Diocesano Tridentino,** where you can see paintings showing the seating plan of the prelates during the Council of Trent; early 16th-century tapestries by Pieter van Aelst, the Belgian artist who carried out Raphael's designs for the Vatican tapestries; carved-wood altars and statues; and an 11th-century sacramentary, or book of services. These and other precious objects all come from the cathedral's treasury. *Piazza Duomo 18. Admission: 2,000 lire. Open mid-Feb.–mid-Nov., Mon.–Sat. 9:30–12:30 and 2:30–6.*

Return to Piazza del Duomo to reach **Via Cavour,** which leads off from the northwest side. About 100 yards down this narrow street is the Renaissance church of **Santa Maria Maggiore,** where many sessions of the Council of Trent were held. From here it's an easy 50-yard walk up the lane behind the church to **Via Belenzani,** famous for its Renaissance *palazzi,* whose frescoed façades add a colorful note to the street. Locals sometimes call this stretch of road Trento's outdoor gallery.

Turn right onto Via Manci and begin a pleasant 200-yard climb past souvenir shops and glassware outlets to the moated **Castello del Buonconsiglio** (Castle of Good Counsel). This huge castle was the stronghold of the prince-bishops; its position and size made it easier to defend than the Palazzo Pretorio. As you stand facing it, you can see the evolution of architectural styles, starting with the medieval fortifications of the Castelvecchio section on the far left, down to the more decorative Renaissance Magno Palazzo, built three centuries later in 1530. The castle now houses the **Museo Provinciale d'Arte** (Provincial Art Museum), where exhibits of art and archaeology are displayed in medieval halls or under Renaissance coffered ceilings. The 13th-century **Torre dell'Aquila** (Eagle's Tower) holds the highlight of the museum, a fresco cycle of the months of the year. It is full of charming and informatively detailed scenes of 15th-century life in both court and countryside. *Via B. Clesio 5. Admission: 4,000 lire. Open Tues.–Sun. 9–noon and 2–5.*

Walk along the front of the castle to the Castelvecchio end, on the left, and cross onto Piazza Raffaello Sanzio. The **Torre Verde** (Green Tower), part of Trento's 13th-century fortifications, stands here, alongside other fragments of the walls. From this square, Via Torre Verde leads back to the center of Trento: The road changes its name to **Via Torre Vanga** as it reaches the tower of that name, another 13th-century fortification, this time guarding the medieval bridge across the Adige, Ponte San Lorenzo.

From a cable-car station at the bridge, you can get a lift to **Belvedere di Sardagna,** a vantage point 1,200 feet above Trento.

Dining
Under 30,000 lire
★

Alla Mora. What was once an unpretentious trattoria is now an attractive restaurant with a touch of class and a luminous, airy courtyard for outdoor dining under market umbrellas. The menu offers something for all tastes, including such local specialties as *finferle con polenta* (wild mushrooms with polenta and local cheese) and a classic *pasta e fagioli* (pasta and bean soup); salad plates and seafood are also featured. *Via Roggia Grande 8, tel. 0461/984675. Reservations advised, especially for indoor dining. No credit cards. Closed Mon.*

Bolzano

On the same main train line as Trento, Bolzano is only 1¼ hours from Verona by train, 35 minutes from Trento. Service runs every hour. Tourist office: Piazza Walther 8, tel. 0471/ 970660; regional tourist office, Piazza Parrocchia 11, across from the cathedral, tel. 0471/993808.

North of Trento 52 kilometers (32 miles) along the Adige River, Bolzano (in German, Bozen) is the capital of Italy's autonomous province of Alto Adige, also known as South Tyrol. This quiet city at the confluence of the Isarco (Eisack) and Talvera rivers has retained a provincial appeal but contradicts its country image with commercial features acquired to cater to the needs of tourists. There are no high rises, but McDonald's can be seen—housed, of course, in a more archaic building.

A five-minute walk straight ahead on Viale Stazione from the train station will bring you to pedestrians-only **Piazza Walther,** named after the 12th-century German wandering minstrel Walther von der Vogelweide, whose songs lampooned the papacy and praised the Holy Roman Emperor. The square serves as an open-air living room where locals and tourists alike can be found at all hours sipping a drink (perhaps a glass of chilled Riesling) at the café tables.

At one corner of the square is the city's Gothic **Duomo** (Cathedral), built between the 12th and 14th centuries. Its lacy spire looks down on the mosaiclike tiles covering its pitched roof. Inside the church are 14th- and 15th-century frescoes and an intricately carved stone pulpit dating from 1514.

Via Posta leads from the other side of the square to **Piazza Domenicani,** with its 13th-century **Dominican church,** renowned as Bolzano's main repository for paintings, especially frescoes. In the adjoining **Cappella di San Giovanni,** you can see frescoes of the Giotto school, one of which is the *Triumph of Death* (ca. 1340). Despite its macabre title, this fresco shows the birth of a pre-Renaissance sense of depth and individuality.

From here the narrow Via Goethe leads to **Piazza delle Erbe,** where a bronze statue of Neptune presides over a bounteous fruit and vegetable market (Mon.–Sat. 8–1). The stalls spill over with colorful displays of local produce, bakeries and grocery stores showcase hot breads, pastries, cheeses, and delicatessen meats—a complete range of picnic supplies. Try the *speck* (smoked ham) and the Tyrolean-style apple strudel.

The market is at the beginning of Bolzano's main shopping street, **Via dei Portici** (Lauben), lined with long, narrow arcades. The shops specialize in Tyrolean handicrafts and clothing—lederhosen, loden goods, linen suits, and dirndls.

Via del Museo leads away from the market to the **Museo Civico,** which houses a rich collection of traditional costumes, wood carvings, and archaeological exhibits. The mixture of styles is a reflection of the region's cultural cross-fertilization. *Via del Museo 45. Admission: 2,000 lire. Open Tues.–Sat. 9–noon and 2:30–5:30, Sun. 10–1.*

Just across the road is **Ponte Talvera,** a bridge that extends across the Talvera River to the district of Gries. Cross over to visit the **Parrocchiale** (parish church) of Gries, with its elaborately carved, 15th-century wooden altar, and the Benedictine abbey and Baroque church of **Sant'Agostino.** The churches are about a half mile beyond the bridge, along Corso Libertà. Just beyond the parish church is the Passeggiata, a pathway that leads up to the **Guncina Hill,** where you get a panoramic view of Bolzano.

Recross the river and go immediately left, along the Lungotalvera Promenade, upstream to the 13th-century **Castel Mareccio** (Schloss Maretsch), nestled under the mountains and surrounded by vineyards. *Restaurant open to public; admission to castle by appointment only. Call 0471/976615 or contact the Bolzano tourist office.*

On the **Renon** (Ritten) plateau, just above Bolzano and reachable by the funicular to Soprabolzano, are the **Earth Pyramids,** a bizarre geological formation where erosion has left a forest of tall, thin, needlelike spires of rock, each topped with a boulder. *The Soprabolzano funicular leaves from Via Renon, about 300 yards to the left as you leave the Bolzano train station. At the top an electric train takes you to Collalbo, where you'll find the Earth Pyramids. Round-trip fare: about 14,000 lire.*

Dining
Under 30,000 lire

Batzenhausl. A medieval building in the center of town houses this crowded *stube* (Tyrolean-style drinking hall). It's a popular hangout for the local intellectual set, who hold long, animated conversations over glasses of local wine and tasty South Tyrolean specialties, such as *herrengröstl* (meat, potatoes, and herbs) and apple pancakes with ice cream. Try the fried Camembert. *Via Andreas Hofer 30, tel. 0471/976183. Reservations advised. No credit cards. Closed lunch, Tues., and 2 weeks in July.*

Cavallino Bianco/Weisses Roessl. This is another typical Tyrolean stube in the center of town, decorated with dark wood paneling, carved furniture, frescoes, and stuffed hunting trophies. A popular spot for local intellectuals and young people, it's also one of the few Bolzano restaurants that stay open until midnight. Waitresses in modified *trachten* (Tyrolean costume) serve such specialties as *kaseknoedel* (light cheese dumplings), *leberknoedel* (liver dumpling) soup, *wurstel* (frankfurters, or sausages), and *palaschinken* (sweet pancakelike crepes). *Via dei Bottai (Bindergasse) 6, tel. 0471/973267. No credit cards. Closed Sat. evening, Sun., and July.*

Merano

Merano is 40 minutes by train (hourly service) or bus (2 daily runs) from Bolzano. Tourist office: Via della Libertà 45, tel. 0473/35223.

Only 28 kilometers (17 miles) north of Bolzano, along the Adige Valley, is Merano (Meran), the second-largest town in the Alto Adige. Merano has been famous as a spa town for 150 years, known for its thermal waters, which, like those in many health spas, have natural radioactivity. It is also renowned for its "grape cure"—consisting of local grape juice, not wine. Sheltered by mountains, Merano has an unusually mild climate, with summer temperatures rarely exceeding 80° F and winters that usually stay above freezing, despite the skiing that is within easy reach. (Chair lifts and cable cars connect Merano with the high Alpine slopes of Avelengo and San Vigilio.)

Along the narrow streets of Merano's old town, houses sport little towers and huge wooden doors, and the pointed arches of the Gothic sit with surprising harmony next to neoclassical and Art Nouveau buildings. In the heart of the old town, **Piazza del Duomo,** is the 14th-century Gothic cathedral, with a crenellated facade and an ornate *campanile* (bell tower). The Cappella di **Santa Barbara,** just behind the cathedral, is an octagonal church containing a 15th-century *Pietà*.

Merano's main shopping street, the narrow, arcaded **Via dei Portici** (Lauben), runs west from the cathedral. A good place for souvenir shopping, it features most of the best regional products: wood carvings, Tyrolean-style clothes, embroidery, cheeses, salami, and fruit schnapps. Turn left when it ends, onto Via delle Corse, and head down to the Passirio River, about a quarter of a mile away. Cross the river via the Ponte del Teatro to reach the **Terme** (Municipal Baths), just on the other side. This huge complex is the nerve center of the spa facilities, although some hotels have their own. Technicians are trained to treat you with mud packs, massages, inhalation and sauna routines, or just with the thermal waters, which are said to be especially good for coronary and circulatory problems.

Dining
Under 24,000 lire

Dolomiten. This large beer cellar is just off Piazza del Duomo. Beyond the kitchen is a large dining room where customers share long wooden tables; in the summer you dine outdoors under a pergola. The menu offers such Tyrolean specialties as *canederli* (bread dumplings) served in broth or with speck, the local smoked prosciutto. Various types of *wurstel* are on the menu, as is polenta. *Via Haller 4, tel. 0473/36377. Reservations not necessary. MC, V. Closed Wed.*

Lodging
Splurge

Minerva. This turn-of-the-century hotel, built in 1909, is furnished in traditional period style. Set in a garden, it's about 10 minutes by foot from the town center, near several of the luxury hotels. Almost all rooms have balconies with views of the mountains. Full-board rates are about 110,000 per person; room only, including breakfast, is 85,000 lire per (double) room. *Via Cavour 95, tel. 0473/36712. 44 rooms with bath. Facilities: restaurant, pool. AE, DC. Closed Nov.–Mar. but reopens for 1 week Dec. 24–Jan. 1.*

7 The Italian Riviera

Including Genoa

The so-called Italian Riviera is the coastline of Italy's Liguria region, which consists of little more than this narrow coastal strip and an equally narrow mountainous backing made up of the sheltered seaview side of the Maritime Alps and the Ligurian Apennines. Stretching 349 kilometers (217 twisting miles) from the French border to Tuscany, Liguria actually has two Rivieras: the more built-up and slightly more expensive Riviera di Ponente (western Riviera) between France and Genoa, and the rockier, steeper Riviera di Levante (eastern Riviera) from Genoa eastward, which includes the most expensive spot on either Riviera, Portofino.

Every American schoolchild knows that Genoa, set in the heart of this rocky coast, is the birthplace of Christopher Columbus. That famous explorer was only one, and not the first or the last, in a long line of seafaring men whose activity centered in the ports of the two Rivieras of Italy.

Liguria is favored by a mild climate year-round; this, and the ease with which it can be reached from the rest of western Europe, has helped to make it one of the most popular regions in Italy for visitors. An impressive number of foreigners—British, American, French—have permanent residences here. For centuries, the region's charm has inspired poets and artists, many of whom came for a brief visit and stayed. Italians from inland cities flock to its beaches in summer or maintain their villas along its length, and some areas of the western coast have become especially popular with German and other European package-tour operators, almost swamping what were once attractive small seaside towns. The flavor of the area is cosmopolitan, a mellow blend of provincial and smart set, primitive and old-fashioned, and luxurious and up-to-date. The eye is caught, the attention held, by the contours of the coastline curving serpentinely in an arc from Ventimiglia to La Spezia; by the Ligurian Alps, plunging in sheer cliffs or sloping gradually to the sea; by the glamour and color of the resorts, the busy ports, the stately yachts against the skyline, and the grandiose view across the Gulf of Genoa from a hairpin curve on the highway.

As Italy's largest port, Genoa itself is a bustling city, with a proud history of trade and navigation that predates Columbus. Modern container ships unload at docks that centuries before served galleons and vessels bound for the spice routes. By the 3rd century BC, when the Romans conquered Liguria, Genoa was already an important trading station, which the Romans enhanced by building the Via Aurelia to link Rome with what is now France. The Middle Ages and the Renaissance saw the rise of Genoa as a great seaport, and the city—jumping-off place for the Crusades, commercial center of tremendous wealth and prestige, strategic bone of international contention—was of key importance to Europe. Thereafter, Genoa declined in rank as a sea power. Napoleon reduced all Liguria to an ineffective "family estate of the Bonapartes," as Tolstoy speaks of it in *War and Peace*. When the emperor was finally defeated at Waterloo, the region became part of Piedmont and reacquired its separate identity only after the unification of Italy.

People today come to Liguria less for its history and its art than for its mild climate, fine seafood, and coastal villages, many of which remain unspoiled. Tennis and *bocce* (Italian lawn bowling) are played all year, while during the summer the coast sees colorful flotillas of yachts and sailboats, often moored next to the boats of the hardworking local fishermen. The Mediterranean vegetation along the coast—myrtle, heather, broom, rosemary, and pine and olive trees—gives way to chestnut groves and terraced vineyards on the hills. Relaxed Liguria is the sort of place where knowing the difference between scrub pine and cypress means more than knowing your Rococo from your Renaissance.

It's easy to get around the Rivieras by public transportation— all the towns and cities on the coast are linked by train, there's good bus service to interesting inland towns, and boat service operates along the coast. It's possible to make Genoa a base for excursions to any of the destinations described in this chapter, but for those who want to explore the region in depth, we've described three separate tours: one for the city of Genoa, and then one for each of the two Rivieras. Travelers can find better beaches and a cleaner sea elsewhere; they come to the Italian Riviera for the scenery and the climate, for walks through medieval villages, and for a look at Genoa's fine museums.

Essential Information

Lodging Unfortunately, there are few hotel bargains along the Ligurian coast. Constant demand combines with a limited choice to create a high average price, at least in comparison with other Italian regions. Genoa, the largest city, has surprisingly few hotels, and these tend to be mainly expensive establishments geared toward the needs of business clients. Visitors prefer to stay in the towns and resorts along the coast, where there is a better range of accommodations. Here, though, you should try to have reservations, particularly during the peak summer period. The best bargains are in the less-visited inland areas: There are few hotels in this part of Liguria, but many of them are family-run and welcoming.

Highly recommended lodgings are indicated by a star ★.

Dining　Liguria makes the best of its coastal location by utilizing all sorts of seafood. Anchovies, sea bass, squid, and octopus are popular ingredients in the cuisine, which uses liberal amounts of olive oil and garlic. A famous Ligurian pasta sauce is *pesto*, made of pine nuts, garlic, oil, cheese, and a type of basil that grows only along the coastal hills. *Vitello* (veal) is the most popular meat and is often served stuffed, as in *cima*. You should also try the succulent *agnello* (lamb).

When not snacking on pizza sold by the slice or by weight, the Genoese and other Ligurians eat *focaccia*, a salty, pizzalike flat bread with various seasonings and fillings that goes well with a cool glass of wine. Local vineyards tend to produce mainly light and refreshing whites, such as Pigato, Vermentino Ligure, and Cinque Terre. Rossese and Dolceacqua are good reds. Desserts are less rich than those in other Italian regions, and the Ligurians often finish a meal with fresh fruit. Homemade *gelato* (ice cream) is another favorite.

Unless otherwise noted, reservations are not needed and dress is casual. Highly recommended restaurants are indicated by a star ★.

Boat Tours　Genoa is Italy's largest port and can be reached from the United States as well as other parts of Liguria and Italy (Sardinia, La Spezia, and Savona). Ships berth in the heart of Genoa, including cruise ships of the Genoa-based **Costa Cruise Line** (Via Gabriele D'Annunzio 2, tel. 010/54831) and ferries to various ports around the Mediterranean, operated by **Tirrenia Navigazione** (Stazione Marittima, tel. 010/258041).

A busy network of local services connects many of the resorts. For general information, contact **Servizio Marittimo del Tigullio** (Calata Zingari, Genoa, tel. 010/265712), which connects Genoa with most of the ports to the west and provides links to the east to Cinque Terre and Portovenere. Or contact **Camogli–San Fruttuoso Maritime Services** (Società Golfo Paradiso, Via Scalo 2, Camogli, tel. 0185/772091), which runs between Camogli and San Fruttuoso (on the Portofino promontory), as well as between Recco and Punta Chiappa, two other towns close to Camogli. Summer excursions link both ports with the Cinque Terre and Portovenere.

Shopping　Liguria is famous for its fine laces, its silver and gold filigree work, and its ceramics. Look also for bargains in velvet, macramé, olive wood, and marble. Genoa is the best spot to find all these specialties, but the coastal towns and villages along the two Ligurian Rivieras have bazaar-style markets in the central squares or along the harborfront. In these markets you can succeed with a bit of bargaining, and your chances improve if you're able to clinch your deal with a word or two in Italian.

Beaches　Along both Ligurian Rivieras, the beaches are protected by mountains, so the climate is mild and the foliage lush, but unfortunately, because of pollution, they are best used for sunbathing rather than swimming. The Riviera di Ponente, from Genoa west to the French border, has both sandy and pebbly beaches, with some quiet bays. **Alassio** has a long, sandy beach at the head of a bay. The villages of **Diano Marina** and **Pia** (near Finale Ligure) have fine sandy beaches with all the amenities of modern resorts. **Varazze** has a wide, sandy beach and many tall palm trees. **Arenzano,** 22 kilometers (14 miles) west of Genoa, is perhaps the last pleasant beach resort on the Riviera di Ponente before greater Genoa's industrial influence takes over. The beach is large and broad, endowed with nearly every sports facility.

The Riviera di Levante includes Genoa and the coast east as far as Portovenere. Beaches on this coast are rocky, with many spectacular cliffs near the sea. From Chiavari to Cavi di Lavagna, the coast becomes a bit gentler, with a few sandy areas. From Sestri Levante down to Portovenere, the coast is rugged; however, these areas are good for sailing.

The Arts and Nightlife Even Genoa, Liguria's largest city, cannot compare with Milan or Rome in the field of organized evening entertainment, but that isn't a problem because a lot of the fun of staying in Liguria is its informal and easygoing atmosphere. It's hard to imagine a more enjoyable activity than sipping local wine outside a café on a warm summer evening, knowing that your eardrums and wallet won't be damaged.

Highlights for First-time Visitors

Camogli (Tour 3: Riviera di Levante)
Cinque Terre (Tour 3: Riviera di Levante)
Giardino Hanbury (Tour 2: Riviera di Ponente)
Museo del Tesoro di San Lorenzo, Genoa (Tour 1: Genoa)
Palazzo Reale, Genoa (Tour 1: Genoa)
Portofino (Tour 3: Riviera di Levante)
Portovenere (Tour 3: Riviera di Levante)
San Remo (Tour 2: Riviera di Ponente)
Via Garibaldi, Genoa (Tour 1: Genoa)

Tour 1: Genoa

Visitors who come to Liguria for the sun and the sea generally avoid the busy, sprawling city of Genoa, which stretches 20 kilometers (12 miles) along the coast. Yet Genoa can offer a fascinating, rich, and colorful experience. Known as La Superba (The Proud), Genoa was from the 13th century a great maritime center that rivaled Venice and Pisa in power and splendor. Its bankers, merchants, and princes adorned the city with palaces and churches and amassed impressive collections of art. Genoa's lively medieval center is one of Europe's largest. While brimming with historical curiosities and buildings, Genoa is also a thoroughly modern city struggling with problems of traffic, noise and air pollution, and an increasing immigrant population. It is advanced in communications, electronics, and general commerce, and its port, Italy's largest, is being equipped to keep up with new technologies. The historic harbor area was given a face-lift in preparation for 1992 Columbus quincentennial celebrations and some of the fair installations have become a permanent part of the cityscape.

The Italian Riviera

KEY

‐‐‐‐ Ferry
+++++ Rail Lines

N →

0 _____ 10 miles
0 _____ 15 km

FRANCE

Dronero
Cuneo
Mondovì
Ormea
Calizzano
Alba
Acqui
Campo Ligure

S20
S28
S453
S28
A6
S29
S30
S334
A26
S35
A21
S226
S45
S536

RIVIERA DI PONENTE

Pigna
Dolceacqua
Mortola Inferiore
Ventimiglia
Bordighera
Ospedaletti
San Remo
Taggia
Imperia
Diano Marina
Cervo
Alassio
Albenga
Borghetto Santo Spirito
Finale Ligure
Noli
Savona
Albisola Marina
Varazze
Arenzano

A10
S1

Genoa
see detail map

A10
A12

RIVIERA DI LEVANTE

Nervi
Camogli
Portofino
Santa Margherita Ligure
Rapallo
Chiavari
Lavagna
Sestri Levante
Levanto
Cinque Terre
La Spezia
Portovenere
Lerici

S1
S225
S523

Golfo di Genova

TO CORSICA

TO CORSICA

TO CORSICA

TO BARCELONA AND BALEARIC ISLANDS

TO ELBA, SARDINIA, SICILY, AND NAPLES

From Rome and Frequent and fast train service connects Genoa with Milan (1½
Milan hours away) and Rome (five hours), stopping at **Stazione Prin-**
By Train **cipe,** one of Genoa's two main stations. (Trains from Rome may
stop briefly at the other, Stazione Brignole, before continuing
to Principe.)

By Bus The main station is at Piazza del Principe. The **Pesci** line (Piazza
della Vittoria 94r, Genoa, tel. 010/564936) operates services
from Genoa to all other parts of Italy, with frequent connections to Rome and Milan.

By Plane Genoa is one hour from Rome by air. **Cristoforo Colombo** International Airport, at Sestri Ponente (tel. 010/2411), only 6 kilometers (4 miles) from the center of Genoa, has regular flights to
all main European cities. Buses connect Cristoforo Colombo
with Genoa's air-transit terminal on Via Petrarca (tel. 010/
581318), off Piazza De Ferrari, stopping also at Piazza Acquaverde (Principe Station).

By Car Autostrada (highway) A12 south from Genoa links up with the
autostrada network for all southern destinations; Rome is a six-
hour drive from Genoa. The 150-kilometer (90-mile) trip north
to Milan on A7 takes two hours.

From Nice If Liguria is your first or only destination in Italy, you may
want to consider a flight into Nice, the nearest international
airport, just 2½ hours from Genoa across the border in France.

By Train Many trains from France, in particular the French Riviera,
pass along the Ligurian coast and stop at Genoa's **Stazione
Brignole** en route to all parts of Italy.

By Bus Buses operated by **SITA** (tel. 010/313851) link Genoa with the
French Riviera.

By Car Nice is 2½ hours west of Genoa on the A10 autostrada.

Guided Tours A three-hour city bus tour, with English-speaking guides, is
available, operated by Cioncoloni, Via Nizza 4, tel. 010/302142.
Buses leave the AMT (municipal bus system) office at Piazza
della Vittoria at 9 AM, also stopping to pick up passengers at
Piazza De Ferrari and Piazza Acquaverde. Tickets (about
30,000 lire) can be purchased on the bus, but seats should be
reserved in advance at Cioncoloni. For information, inquire at
the tourist booth at **Stazione Principe** (Piazza Acquaverde, tel.
010/262633).

You can also take a **boat tour** of the harbor in Genoa. The
hourlong tour includes a visit to the Lanterna, the breakwater
outside the harbor, the Bacino delle Grazie, and the Molo
Vecchio (Old Pier), and provides extensive views of the city. For
information, contact the **Cooperativa Batellieri** (Stazione
Marittima, Ponte dei Mille, Genoa, tel. 010/265712).

Genoa

*Tourist offices: main APT office, Via Roma 11, Piazza
Corvetto, tel. 010/581407; Stazione Principe, tel. 010/262633;
airport, tel. 010/241–5247.*

*Numbers in the margin correspond to points of interest on the
Genoa map.*

To get around the city, you can buy a 24-hour tourist ticket for
AMT city buses (for about 4,000 lire) at AMT booths at the

main stations; you have to show your passport. AMT bus No. 40 from Stazione Brignole and bus No. 41 from Stazione Principe take you to Piazza De Ferrari in the center of the city. If you arrive at Principe Station, you can walk down **Via Balbi,** which runs southeast from the train station toward the medieval town. On the right, at No. 10, is the **Palazzo Reale,** otherwise known as the **Palazzo Balbi Durazzo,** formerly the royal palace. The palace, which dates from the 17th century, contains paintings, sculptures, tapestries, and Oriental ceramics. The building was bought by the Royal House of Savoy in the early 19th century and has some magnificent rooms decorated in the lavish and frivolous Rococo style. The gallery of mirrors and the ballroom on the upper floor are particularly good examples. There are also works by Sir Anthony Van Dyck, who lived in Genoa for six years, from 1621, and painted many fine portraits of the Genoese nobility. *Tel. 010/247–0640. Admission: 4,000 lire. Open daily 9–1.*

② Opposite is the **Palazzo dell' Università,** built in the 1630s as a Jesuit college and the site of a university since 1803. Climb the stairway flanked by lions to visit the elegant courtyard, with its portico of double Doric columns.

A few minutes' walk along Via Balbi, in Piazza della Nunziata, is the 16th- to 17th-century church of the **Santissima Annunziata,** which has exuberantly frescoed vaults and is an excellent example of Genoese Baroque architecture.

Continue down Via Cairoli to **Via Garibaldi,** once known as the "Strada Nuova" (New Street). Genoa's leading patrician families built their residences here from 1554 onward to escape the cramped conditions of the medieval section of town; 13 palaces were built along the street in just 10 years. Via Garibaldi is one of the most impressive streets in Italy, and its palaces house some of the finest art collections in the country.

③ The 17th-century Baroque **Palazzo Rosso** (Red Palace), at No. 18, was one of the last palaces to be erected here. Named after the red stone used in its construction, it now contains, apart from a number of lavishly frescoed suites, works by Titian, Veronese, Caravaggio, and Rubens, as well as some fine portraits by Van Dyck. *Tel. 010/282641. Admission: 4,000 lire. Open Tues.–Sat. 9–7, Sun. 9–12:30.*

④ Opposite, at No. 10, is the **Palazzo Bianco.** Originally white, as its name suggests, the palace has become considerably darkened with age and grime. It has a fine art collection, with the Dutch and Flemish schools particularly well represented. *Tel. 010/291803. Admission: 4,000 lire. Open Tues.–Sat. 9–7, Sun. 9–12:30.*

⑤ The **Palazzo Tursi** (No. 9) is Genoa's town hall, built in the 16th century by the wealthy Nicolò Grimaldi. Also known as the Palazzo Municipale, it is made of pink stone quarried in the region. Visitors are welcome to view the richly decorated rooms and the famous Guarnerius violin that belonged to Paganini and is played once a year on Columbus Day (October 12). However, when the rooms are in use by Genoa's officials, as is often the case, they are closed to the public. *Tel. 010/20981. Admission free. Open Mon.–Sat.; call for hours.*

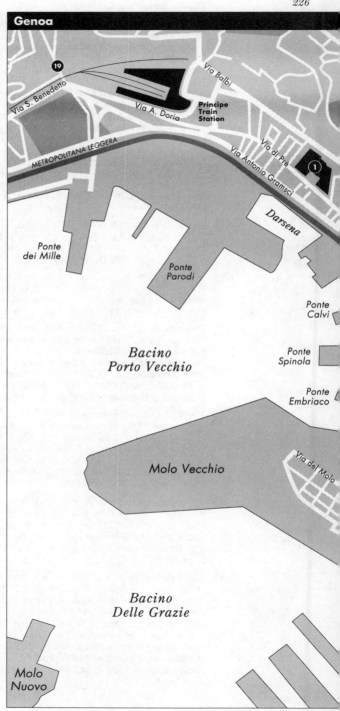

Genoa

19

Via S. Benedetto

Via A. Doria

Via Balbi

Principe Train Station

Via di Pre

Via Antonio Gramsci

METROPOLITANA LEGGERA

1

Darsena

Ponte dei Mille

Ponte Parodi

Ponte Calvi

Ponte Spinola

Ponte Embriaco

Bacino Porto Vecchio

Via del Molo

Molo Vecchio

Bacino Delle Grazie

Molo Nuovo

Most of the other palaces on Via Garibaldi can be visited only by applying to each building's *portiere* (concierge), but many have courtyards that are open to the public.

6 At the end of Via Garibaldi, on Piazza Portello, take the elevator to **Castelletto** for a good view of the old city. *Fare: 400 lire one-way. Continual service 6 AM–10:30 PM.*

Turn right at the end of Via Garibaldi onto the narrow streets that zigzag down into the **medieval city.** These winding, picturesque alleys—known as *caruggi*—contain many medieval buildings, some decorated with typically Ligurian black-and-white facades, that are on a more intimate scale than the grand, airy palaces of Via Garibaldi. The caruggi district is also the city's most disreputable. Don't go there after dark, or on holidays, when shops are closed and the alleys are deserted.

7 Make your way west toward the harbor and **San Siro,** Genoa's oldest church. Evidence of a church on the spot goes back to the 4th century, but the original edifice, which was Genoa's cathedral until the 9th century, was rebuilt during the 16th and 17th **8** centuries. Nearby, just off Via San Luca, is the **National Gallery,** housed in the richly adorned **Palazzo Spinola.** The collection contains, among other fine works, masterpieces by Luca Giordano (1634–1705) and Guido Reni (1575–1642). The *Ecce Homo,* by Antonello da Messina (1430–79), is a hauntingly beautiful painting and is also of historical interest because it was the Sicilian da Messina who first brought Flemish oil paints and techniques to Italy from his voyages in the Low Countries. *Piazza Pellicceria 1, tel. 010/294661. Admission: 4,000 lire. Open May–Sept., Tues–Sat. 9–7, Sun.–Mon. 9–1.*

9 Walk south down Via San Luca to Piazza Banchi to see the **Loggia dei Mercanti** (covered market). Then head back to the heart of the medieval quarter, to Via Soziglia, a street lined with shops selling handicrafts and tempting foods.

South of Piazza Soziglia is the quarter where wealthy Genoese built their homes during the 16th century. Prosperous guilds, such as the goldsmiths for whom Vico Indoratori and Via Orefici were named, also set up shop here. **Piazza San Matteo** is an excellently preserved medieval square, for 500 years the seat of the Doria family, who ruled Genoa and much of Liguria from the 16th to the 18th century and built fine palaces all over the city. The square is bounded by 13th- to 15th-century houses decorated with portals and loggias (open galleries). The black-**10** and-white church of **San Matteo** dates from the 12th century; its crypt contains the tomb of Andrea Doria, who framed a constitution for the city in 1529 and began his family's reign. Doria won his fame as an admiral, serving, in turn, the French and Spanish crowns but managing to maintain the independence of his native city.

Leaving Piazza San Matteo, continue down toward the cathedral of **San Lorenzo,** at the heart of medieval Genoa's political **11** and religious center. The cathedral is embellished inside and out with the contrasting black slate and white marble so common in Liguria. It was consecrated in 1118 to St. Lawrence, who passed through the city on his way to Rome during the 3rd century; the last campanile dates from the early 16th century. For hundreds of years the building was used for state as well as religious purposes: Civic elections, court rulings, and religious ceremonies and festivals all took place here. Note the lively

13th-century Gothic portal and the 15th- to 17th-century frescoes inside. The **Museo del Tesoro di San Lorenzo** (San Lorenzo Treasury Museum), located in the cathedral, contains some stunning medieval pieces. The art of goldsmiths and silversmiths, for which medieval Genoa was renowned, is particularly well represented here. *Admission: 2,000 lire. Open Tues.– Sat. 9:30–11:45 and 3–5:45.*

⑫ Across Piazza San Lorenzo is the **Palazzo Ducale,** built in the 16th century over a medieval hall, with a facade that was rebuilt in the late 18th century. The building has been restored and houses temporary exhibitions. Cross over the 19th-century thoroughfare of Via San Lorenzo, and head southwest into the old city center, where a settlement has existed since the 6th
⑬ century BC. **Santa Maria di Castello,** one of Genoa's greatest religious buildings, was an early Christian church. It was rebuilt in the 12th century and finally completed in 1513. You can visit the adjacent cloisters by special request (ask the sacristan) and see the fine artwork contained in the museum.

Take the little lane left from behind the church to reach the
⑭ 12th-century Romanesque church of **San Donato,** with its original portal and octagonal campanile. The 13th-century Gothic
⑮ church of **Sant'Agostino,** almost directly behind it, was damaged during World War II but still has a fine campanile and two well-preserved cloisters, which now house an excellent sculpture museum. *Piazza Sarzano 21, tel. 010/201661. Admission: 4,000 lire. Open Tues.–Sat. 9–7, Sun. 9–noon.*

At the southeastern end of the old city, the twin-towered, 12th-
⑯ century **Porta di Sant'Andrea,** or Porta Soprana, stands at the old gateway to the Roman road that led through Genoa. Nearby, in Piazza Dante, is the ruined ivy-covered house where
⑰ **Christopher Columbus** spent his childhood.

Taking Via Dante northwest, you'll hit **Piazza De Ferrari,** the center of modern Genoa. The World War II–ravaged opera
⑱ house, **Teatro Carlo Felice,** finally rebuilt, reopened in 1991, with a massive, much-criticized tower. It stands next to the **Academy of Fine Arts,** which contains a collection of Ligurian paintings from the 13th to the 19th century. The piazza, which also contains the Stock Exchange and part of the Ducal Palace, leads into Via XX Settembre, Genoa's chic modern shopping center. The spacious 19th-century urban layout of this part of town strongly contrasts with the narrow, crowded alleys of the medieval quarter, only a few minutes away.

A fitting end to a tour of Genoa could be a visit to the **harbor,** whose layout dates from Roman times. The Genoa inlet, the only one of its size along the Italian Riviera, was also used by the Phoenicians and Greeks as a harbor and a vantage point from which to penetrate inland to form settlements and to trade.

The **Lanterna,** a lighthouse more than 360 feet high, stands in the middle of the harbor. Built in 1544 at the height of Andrea Doria's career, it is one of Italy's oldest lighthouses and a traditional emblem of Genoa. A closer view of it, the Molo Vecchio (the historic dock, restored for 1992 events), and all of the harbor can be had from one of the informative harbor tours (*see* Guided Tours, *above*). The Bigo elevator ride left over from 1992 Columbus celebrations, provides a harbor view.

⑲ Dotted around the circumference of the city are a number of huge fortresses. Take the **Granarolo funicular,** actually a cog railway, up to one of the fortified gates in the 17th-century city walls. It takes 15 minutes to hoist you from Piazza del Principe, behind Stazione Principe on Piazza Acquaverde, to **Porta Granarolo,** 1,000 feet above, where you can get a good sense of the size of Genoa. *Fare: 400 lire. Leaves every ½-hour, on the ¼-hour, 6 AM–midnight.*

Lodging
Under 115,000 lire
Rio. Located by Ponte Calvi in the old harbor area, the sturdy, comfortable Rio was built during the 19th-century hotel boom. Marble floors and bright rooms give the hotel an airy feel, in refreshing contrast to the narrow streets that surround it. There is no restaurant, but a Continental breakfast is available. *Via al Ponte Calvi 5, tel. 010/290551, fax 010/290554. 47 rooms with shower. AE, DC, MC, V. Closed Jan.*

Under 60,000 lire
Mirella. Though small, this hotel is in a reassuringly well-kept building. Rooms are clean and ample. To reach it, walk down Via De Amicis from Stazione Brignole, turning right at the Hotel Astoria. *Via Gropallo 4, tel. 010/893722. 8 rooms, 3 with bath. No credit cards.*

Soana. On one of Genoa's elegant but noisy main streets, this is a clean hotel with simple furnishings; most rooms have private bathrooms, a big plus at these prices. Its central location near Piazza De Ferrari makes it convenient, too. *Via XX Settembre 23, tel. 010/562814. 16 rooms, 14 with bath. No credit cards.*

Youth Hostel. Opened in 1992, this hostel occupies a panoramic position about a half mile below the Righi funicular's upper terminal. (From Stazione Brignole, take the No. 40 bus to the end of the line.) There are four to eight beds per room, 210 beds in all, and some four-bed rooms for families have private baths. Bed and breakfast cost about 18,000 lire per person. The required AIG/IYHF card can be purchased on the spot for 30,000 lire. The hostel, which boasts a large terrace with a view of the city, opens at 5 PM and has a midnight curfew. There is a coffee bar on the premises; a cafeteria is planned for 1994. *Via Costanzi 120, tel. 010/242–2457. 210 beds, about 15 baths for dormitories. No credit cards.*

Splurge
★
Agnello d'Oro. The central location in Genoa's old quarter, about 100 yards from Stazione Principe, makes this modest hotel a good choice for travelers who want to be in the thick of things. The simple room furnishings have been improved by recent renovations, which include air-conditioning. Doubles with bath and breakfast cost 150,000 lire. *Vico delle Monachette 6, tel. 010/262084. 40 rooms, 37 with bath. Facilities: bar, terrace, restaurant (guests only; closed Oct.–Mar.). DC, MC, V.*

Dining
Under 30,000 lire
Trattoria Walter. This unpretentious, family-run restaurant is in the heart of the city, near Palazzo Spinola. The service is simple and straightforward, and the price is right for a good, inexpensive sampling of genuine Genoese specialties, including *trenette con pesto,* pasta with pesto sauce. *Via Colalanza 2, corner of Via San Luca, tel. 010/290524. No credit cards. Closed Sun. and Aug. 1–21.*

Under 24,000 lire
Colombo e Bruno. This down-to-earth trattoria popular with local workers is one of many similar establishments in the Borgo Incrociati district near Stazione Brignole. The setting is simple and the menu limited, but the food is good. You can't go

wrong with minestrone *alla genovese* (with pesto). *Borgo Incrociati 44/r, tel. 010/892-622. No credit cards. Closed Sun.*

Under 20,000 lire **Da Guglie.** The delectable display in the storefront window is a hint of what's inside: fried vegetables, focaccia, pasta, and minestrone. If you're in a hurry, you can pick up food to take out, too. Located near the cathedral, Da Guglie is open from 8 AM to 10 PM. *Via San Vincenzo 64/r, tel. 010/565765. No credit cards. Closed Sun. and Aug.*

Sa Pesta. Close to Da Guglie, this is the same type of typical Genoese eating place, with white-tile walls, marble-top tables, and a take-out counter. You can lunch on *farinata* (flatbread made of chick-pea flour) and *cima genovese* (stuffed breast of veal) for about 15,000 lire; in the evening, you will pay about 20,000 lire for a meal. Go before 7:30; they close early. *Via dei Giustiniani 16/r, tel. 010/208636. Reservations necessary. No credit cards. Closed Sat. evening, Sun., and Aug.*

Splurge **Trattoria La Buca.** Near Piazza De Ferrari, this trattoria has dark wood paneling and stained-glass windows. Although the menu features Tuscan food, including bean dishes, there are such local specialties as minestrone with pesto (vegetable soup with a spoonful of garlicky basil sauce) and *stufato* (stew). *Via Chiossone 5, tel. 010/294810. No credit cards. Closed Sun.*

The Arts The opera season (Oct.–May) of **Teatro Carlo Felice** (Via XXV Aprile, tel. 010/591697) attracts many lavish productions and occasionally sees the debut of a new work.

Festivals Europe's biggest boat show takes place here, as does the Euroflora flower show (held every five years—next in 1996). Classical dance and music are richly represented; Nervi Park, just outside the city, is the unique setting of an on-again-off-again ballet festival (*see* Tour 2, *below*). The annual Niccolò Paganini Violin Contest, internationally renowned, also takes place in Genoa.

Tour 2: The Riviera di Ponente

The Riviera di Ponente is a narrow coastal strip punctuated by rocky outcrops between wide bays and sandy coves. Another name for it is the Riviera dei Fiori (Riviera of Flowers), because flower cultivation is a major industry here. Ventimiglia and San Remo, at the western end of the Riviera di Ponente, make convenient touring bases; they can be inexpensive to stay in and have good transportation connections to the rest of this part of the Riviera.

Ventimiglia

Genoa–Ventimiglia trains run at least every hour and take about 2½ hours. Tourist office: Via Cavour 61, tel. 0184/351183; tourist information booth in train station.

Ventimiglia, about 9 kilometers (6 miles) from the French border, was once a pre-Roman settlement known as Albintimilium and contains some important archaeological remains, such as a 2nd-century AD amphitheater. A vital trade center for hundreds of years, it declined in prestige as Genoa grew and is now little more than a frontier town that lives on tourism and the cultivation of flowers. The town is divided in two by the Roia River. The **Città Vecchia** (Old City), on the western side, is what you'll see first: It is a well-preserved and typical medieval town. The 11th-century **Duomo** (Cathedral) has a Gothic portal dating from 1222. Walk up Via del Capo to the ancient walls, which offer fine views of the coast. S1 crosses the river into the new part of town, famous for its large flower market. Avoid Ventimiglia on Friday, a chaotic market day that draws crowds of bargain hunters from France.

Lodging
Under 85,000 lire

Sole Mare. On the seaward side of the Old City, on the beach promenade, this small hotel offers simply furnished rooms, many with a view of beach and sea. *Via Marconi 12, tel. 0184/ 351854. 28 rooms, 25 with bath or shower. AE, DC, MC, V. Closed Nov. 5–Dec. 20.*

Under 60,000 lire

Victoria. Near the train station, this small, family-run establishment is a friendly place. Some rooms are big enough for three beds. *Via Hanbury 5, tel. 0184/351231. 20 rooms, none with bath. No credit cards.*

Splurge
★

La Riserva. Just 3 miles west of Ventimiglia, but more than 1,100 feet above sea level, is the village of Castel d'Appio, where you'll find this innlike establishment. The staff is very helpful, providing, for example, regular lifts into town for those without cars. But there's no real need to leave La Riserva; apart from its excellent restaurant, it offers numerous activities and a lovely terrace for drinks or sunbathing. Full-board rates are a bargain. A double with breakfast costs about 150,000 lire, full board about 115,000 lire per person. Try for a room facing the sea. *Castel d'Appio, tel. 0184/229533, fax 0184/ 229712. 29 rooms with bath or shower. Facilities: restaurant, terrace bar, tennis, pool, garden, well-marked walks. AE, DC, MC, V. Closed Sept. 20–just before Easter (except Dec. 18– Jan. 6).*

Dining
Under 20,000 lire

Self-Service Suisse. This cafeteria on the train-station square offers fast and wholesome, if uninspired, food, including pastas and meat courses. *Piazza Cesare Battisti 34, tel. 0184/351128. No credit cards.*

Dolceacqua

The Riviera Trasporti bus company (Via Cavour 61, Ventimiglia, tel. 0184/351251) runs 11 daily buses (fewer on Sun.) to Dolceacqua. The trip takes 15 minutes and the fare is 1,800 lire.

A pleasant short excursion from Ventimiglia will take you away from the coast, up the Nervia River valley, to the lovely sounding medieval town of Dolceacqua (Sweetwater). Besides the town's ruined castle, there aren't many sights here, but it makes a charming place to wander around.

Mortola Inferiore

Riviera Trasporti buses run 8 to 10 times a day from Ventimiglia to Mortola Inferiore. The ride takes 15 minutes and costs 1,800 lire.

Just west of Ventimiglia, across the border from France, Mortola Inferiore is best known for the world-famous **Giardino**

Hanbury (Hanbury Garden), one of the largest botanical gardens in Italy. Planned and planted by a wealthy English merchant, Sir Thomas Hanbury, and his botanist brother, Daniel, in 1867, the gardens contain a variety of species from five continents—including many palms and succulents (plants of the cactus group). There are panoramic views of the sea from the gardens. *Giardino Hanbury, Mortola Inferiore, tel. 0184/39507. Admission: 9,000 lire. Open June–Sept., daily 9–6; Oct.–May, Thurs.–Tues. 10–4.*

On the ocean side of the road are the famous **Balzi Rossi** (Red Rocks), caves in the sheer rock, in which prehistoric man left traces of his life and magic rites. You can visit the caves and a small museum containing some of the objects found there. *Admission: 4,000 lire. Open July–Aug., Tues.–Sun. 9–1 and 2:30–6:30; Sept.–June, 9–1 and 2:30–6.*

Bordighera

From Ventimiglia, Riviera Trasporti buses take 15 minutes to reach Bordighera; the fare is 1,800 lire. Tourist office: Via Roberto 1, Palazzo del Parco, tel. 0184/262322.

Bordighera, just a few minutes east along the coast from Ventimiglia, is a famous winter resort dominating a broad promontory with lush vegetation. A large English colony, still very much in evidence, developed here in the second half of the 19th century, attracted by the mild climate. Bordighera is an elegant town with a fin de siècle atmosphere; expect to find people taking afternoon tea in the cafés, which also provide quick lunches. This garden spot was the first town in Europe to grow date palms, and its citizens still have the exclusive right to provide the Vatican with palm fronds for Easter celebrations. Walk along the **Lungomare Argentina,** the magnificent, mile-long seafront promenade, beginning at the western end of the town, for a good view westward to the French Côte d'Azur.

Dining **Le Chaudron.** The charming rustic interior of this centrally lo-
Splurge cated restaurant, with ancient Roman arches, makes it look as though it belongs across the French border in Provence. Ligurian seafood specialties predominate: Try the *branzino al sale grosso* (sea bass baked in a mold of sea salt) or *spaghetti con aragosta* (with tiny lobsters). Other specialties, such as the *coquilles St. Jacques* (scallops), reflect the French influence. A full meal here should run between 60,000 and 80,000 lire. *Piazza Bengasi 2, tel. 0184/263592. Reservations advised. AE, DC, MC, V. Closed Mon. and Feb. 1–15, July 1–15.*

San Remo

Buses leave every 15 minutes from Ventimiglia for San Remo; the trip takes 30 minutes and costs 2,000 lire. Tourist office: Corso Nuvoloni, tel. 0184/571571.

The largest and most elegant resort along the Riviera di Ponente, San Remo is also expensive and overly commercial, with none of the charm of the smaller Riviera towns. But it has a number of inexpensive hotels and good train and bus connections with other towns in this part of the Riviera. Renowned for its royal visitors, its famous casino (one of only four in Italy), and its romantic setting, San Remo still maintains some of the glamour of its heyday from the late 19th century to World War

II. Among the rich and famous who flocked to San Remo, drawn by the mild climate and pleasant countryside, were Alfred Nobel, who built a summer house here, and the Russian empress Maria Alexandrovna, wife of Czar Alexander II.

The old part of San Remo, **La Pigna** (meaning pine cone) is a warren of alleyways leading up to **Piazza Castello,** with a splendid view of the town. The Russian Orthodox church of **San Basilio,** with its onion domes, stands at one end of the **Corso dell'Imperatrice** and, like that imposing seafront promenade, is a legacy of the empress Maria.

The **San Remo Casino** is a sophisticated establishment reminiscent of the turn of the century. The view over the Ligurian coast is free, even if nothing else is. *Corso Inglese. Open daily 2 PM–2 AM.*

Lodging **Paradiso.** This small hotel is almost directly behind the Royal,
Splurge San Remo's most luxurious hotel, and it shares some of the advantages of its grander neighbor. A quiet, palm-fringed garden gives it an air of seclusion, which is a plus in this sometimes hectic city. The rooms are modern and bright, and many have a little terrace. The hotel restaurant has a good fixed-price menu. *Via Roccasterone 12, tel. 0184/571211, fax 0184/578176. 41 rooms with bath or shower. Facilities: restaurant, bar, garden. AE, DC, MC, V.*

Dining **Nuovo Piccolo Mondo.** This small, centrally located trattoria
Splurge has charm and a homey atmosphere—the old wooden chairs date back to the 1920s, when it opened. Family-run, it has a faithful clientele, so get there early to order Ligurian specialties such as *cima* (stuffed veal breast) and vegetable pies. *Via Piave 7, tel. 0184/509012. Reservations advised for lunch. No credit cards. Closed Sun., Wed. evening, and last 3 weeks in June.*

Tour 3: Riviera di Levante

Of the two Ligurian Rivieras, the Riviera di Levante is the wilder and more rugged. Here the hills drop sharply to the sea and are pierced by compact bays and inlets. Two peninsulas jut out from the Levante coastline. The first is the famous Portofino promontory, a rocky outcrop 40 million years old and covered with olive trees, pines, and cypresses. A network of nature and hiking trails crosses it, rewarding the energetic with sweeping views of the Ligurian coastline. Farther along the coast is the second peninsula, where the road goes inland, leaving the visitor to hike or take a train or boat to explore the Cinque Terre, five fishing villages clinging to cliff faces or perched on bluffs overlooking the sea. Good touring bases are Rapallo, at the edge of the Portofino promontory, and Levanto, which gives you access to the Cinque Terre.

Nervi

The No. 17 bus from Genoa (fare 1,000 lire) leaves every 30 minutes for Nervi and takes 30 minutes. Trains (1,800 lire) take 15 minutes and leave every 20 to 30 minutes.

Nervi, 10 kilometers (6 miles) east of Genoa, is an elegant turn-of-the-century resort. It's famous for the **Anita Garibaldi** promenade, with its splendid sea views, palm-lined roads, and 300 acres of parks rich in orange trees and exotics. In these grounds stand the Gropallo, Grimaldi, and Serra villas, the last of which contains the **Galleria d'Arte Moderna.** (Closed for restoration, it should reopen by 1994.) *Via Capolungo 3, tel. 010/ 372–6025. Admission: 4,000 lire. Open Tues.–Sat. 9–1:15 and 3–6, Sun. 9:15–12:45.*

Also worth seeing is the **Museo di Villa Luxoro.** It has 17th- and 18th-century Genoese furnishings, furniture, ceramics, and ornaments; Flemish and Genoese paintings and drawings; old silver and lace; and antique clocks. *Via Aurelia 29, tel. 010/ 372–2673. Admission: 4,000 lire. Open Tues.–Sat. 9–7, Sun. 9–12:30.*

The grounds of Villa Gropallo provide the setting for an **International Festival of Ballet** that is usually held throughout July.

Camogli

Take the MT Bus from Piazza della Vittoria in Genoa to Recco, where you must change to the Tigullio Line bus to Rapallo, which stops in Camogli. The trip takes about an hour and costs about 2,500 lire. The FS train from Genoa to La Spezia stops at Camogli; diretti trains take 30 minutes, locals about 45 minutes. The train fare is about 2,000 lire. Tourist office: Via XX Settembre 33/r, tel. 0185/770235.

Camogli, at the western edge of the large promontory and nature reserve known as the Portofino peninsula, is the first unspoiled port you'll reach, about 20 kilometers (12 miles) from Genoa. Camogli has always been a town of sailors, and by the 19th century this small village was leasing its ships throughout the continent. The festival of San Fortunato, held on the second Sunday of May each year, is noteworthy for the Sagra del Pesce, a public—and free—feast of freshly caught fish cooked in pans 12 feet wide. The village has multicolored houses, a huge 17th-century sea wall in the harbor, and the Dragone Castle, built onto the sheer rock face by the harbor. Within the castle is the impressive **Acquario del Tirreno,** with good displays of local marine life. The tanks are actually built into the ramparts. *Admission: 3,000 lire adults, 1,500 lire children under 10. Open May–Sept., daily 10–noon and 3–7; Oct.–Apr., daily 10–noon and 2–6.*

From Camogli you can reach, by foot or boat, the hamlets of **San Rocco, San Nicolò,** and **Punta Chiappa,** with their remarkable sea views. They lie along the western coast of the peninsula and are more natural and less fashionable than the towns facing south on the eastern coast. The small Romanesque church at San Nicolò was where sailors who survived dangerous voyages came to offer thanks.

Lodging
Splurge
★

Cenobio dei Dogi. Although this hilltop villa perched above the town was once the summer home of Genoa's doges (medieval elected rulers), it now has a modern appearance. The rooms have TV and air-conditioning, and the hotel facilities make it a compound that many visitors never wish to leave. Guests can relax in the colorful park gazing out on outstanding views of the Portofino peninsula, or they can enjoy numerous sporting activities. Although the rooms are not lavishly appointed, many have balconies with panoramic views. Prices are high, at about 260,000 lire. *Via Cuneo 34, tel. 0185/770041, fax 0185/772796.*

88 rooms with bath. Facilities: restaurant, bar, private beach, pool, tennis courts, park. AE, MC, V. Closed Jan. 7–Mar. 7.

Rapallo

From Genoa, take the train to Rapallo, a 30- to 45- minute ride. Tickets cost about 2,800 lire. From Camogli, a local train runs to Rapallo in 10 to 15 minutes and costs about 1,500 lire. The Tigullio bus from Recco to Camogli (see above) continues on to Rapallo; it takes about 15 minutes to reach Rapallo from Camogli. Tourist office: Via A. Diaz 9, tel. 0185/51282.

On the other side of the Portofino promontory from Camogli, at the peninsula's eastern base, lies Rapallo, once one of Europe's most fashionable resorts. The town passed its heyday before World War II and has suffered from the building boom brought on by tourism. Ezra Pound and D. H. Lawrence lived here, and many other writers, poets, and artists have been drawn to it. Today the town's natural harbor is filled with yachts. A single-span bridge on the eastern side of the bay is named after Hannibal, who is said to have passed through the area after crossing the Alps. Two ancient buildings are highlights in the center of town: The Cathedral of **Santi Gervasio e Protasio,** at the western end of Via Mazzini, was founded in the 6th century; across the road is the **Leper House of San Lorenzo,** which still retains parts of its original medieval frescoes on its exterior walls. While exploring the medieval part of town, you can browse for antique lace, for which Rapallo is famous. The **Museo Civico** has a collection of the handiwork. *Admission: 3,000 lire. Open Tues., Wed., Fri., Sat. 3–6, Thurs. 10–11:30.*

Lodging
Under 115,000 lire

Moderno e Reale. This converted 19th-century villa is surrounded by shady gardens, giving it a surprisingly quiet atmosphere, considering its central location near the port. The rooms are bright with colorful fabrics and modern pictures: Ask for one facing the sea. The train station is less than a quarter mile down Corso Matteotti. *Via Gramsci 6, tel. 0185/50601. 49 rooms, 38 rooms with bath or shower. Facilities: restaurant, bar, garden. DC, MC, V.*

Bel Soggiorno. Terraces overlooking a park and the sea make this turn-of-the-century mansion a pleasant choice. Rooms are simply furnished and fitted with modern baths, and many have good views. Old photos of Rapallo decorate the lobby. *Via Gramsci 10, tel. 0185/54527. 22 rooms with bath. No credit cards. Closed Nov.–Dec. 9.*

Under 85,000 lire

Giulio Cesare. Only a block from the sea, this old villalike building was totally renovated when it was transformed into a hotel. It offers comfortable rooms with modern furnishings and sea views. Many rooms have balconies. Traffic noise may be a problem because it's on the main road. Half board is required during high season (June–Sept.), at 90,000 lire per person. *Corso Colombo 62, tel. 0185/50685, fax 0185/60896. 33 rooms with bath. AE, MC, V. Closed Nov.–Dec. 20.*

Dining
Under 30,000 lire

Savoia. People-watching and pizzas are the attractions of this modern restaurant occupying a sunny position just off the beach. There's a good view of the promenade from nearly every table, and you can relax, knowing that the pizzas won't break the bank. Wash down your meal with a cool glass of Pigato. *Piazza IV Novembre 3, tel. 0185/247021. No credit cards. Closed Sun.*

Portofino

The Cooperativa Batellieri in Genoa (Ponte dei Mille, tel. 010/265712) has boat tours to Portofino for about 25,000 lire round-trip. From Rapallo you can take a bus to Santa Margherita Ligure (a 10-minute ride; buses leave every 20 minutes) and from there another short bus ride to Portofino. Getting to Portofino in the summer by bus can be a nightmare, however, given the traffic on the single narrow road. Portofino is only 8 kilometers (5 miles) from Rapallo, so you may want to hike there. Tourist office: Via Roma 35, tel. 0185/269–024.

Known as the Pearl of the Riviera, this enchanting fishing village is the refuge of some of Europe's wealthiest and most discerning pleasure-seekers. From the harbor, follow the signs for the climb to the **Castello di San Giorgio,** with its medieval relics and excellent views. *Admission: 3,000 lire. Open Apr.–Sept., Tues.–Sun. 10–6; Oct.–Mar., Tues.–Sun. 10–5.*

Across a small square is the church of **San Giorgio,** which is supposed to contain the saint's relics, brought back from the Holy Land by the Crusaders. Other excellent views can be seen from the lighthouse at **Punta del Capo,** a quarter of an hour's walk along a marked path from the village. The best vantage point over the entire peninsula and sea, however, is from **Monte di Portofino,** which looms 2,000 feet above the village and is worth the climb. If you are driving, take the road from Ruta (between Camogli and Rapallo) to Portofino Vetta; a few buses leave Camogli for Ruta and Portofino Vetta daily.

Take a picnic lunch to Punta del Capo or Monte di Portofino, and at other times buy food at a food store under the arcades. Resist the urge to sit down to eat or drink in Portofino because the establishments here cater to yachtsmen and will wreak havoc with your budget.

Santa Margherita Ligure

Take the train from Genoa to Santa Margherita Ligure; the ride takes about 40 minutes and costs about 3,200 lire. Buses run frequently between Rapallo and Santa Margherita, 10 minutes away, and between Santa Margherita and Portofino, a 10-minute ride under normal traffic conditions. Fares run about 1,800 lire. Tourist Office: Via 25 Aprile 2/b, tel. 0185/287485.

Santa Margherita Ligure is located on the eastern shore of the Portofino peninsula, roughly midway between Portofino at the tip and Rapallo at the base. Small and pretty, it is a quiet, upscale resort with accommodations for budget travelers as well. It has a palm-lined seaside promenade, a marina, the richly Rococo Basilica of Santa Margherita, and a busy Friday morning market on Via Palestro, next to the basilica. The town is as dull in the winter as it is lively in the summer, but it makes a good base for excursions to Portofino and other towns on the coast, by train, bus, or boat.

Lodging
Under 115,000 lire
★

Fasce. An extremely good value, this small, modern hotel is centrally located on one of the town's main streets, with views of the sea and the surrounding hills from its rooftop garden. The Italian owner and his English wife take a cordial interest in their guests' well-being and comfort. Rooms are attractively furnished and have satellite TV. *Via Bozzo 3, tel. 0185/286435, fax 0185/283580. 16 rooms with bath. Facilities: restaurant, parking. AE, DC, MC, V.*

Dining
Under 30,000 lire

Da Baicin. A very friendly family runs this bright trattoria, which has tables outside on the sidewalk affording a view of the seaside gardens in the center of Santa Margherita. The specialties of the house are *zuppa di pesce* (fish soup) and *pansotti alla salsa di noci* (delicate ravioli with creamy oil and walnut sauce). *Via Algeria 5, tel. 0185/286763. AE, DC, MC, V. Closed Mon. and Nov. 1–Dec. 15.*

Levanto

You can reach Levanto by train from Genoa in 35 minutes (fare 3,500 lire), from Rapallo in 10 minutes. Buses from Genoa (fare 2,800 lire) have to take a roundabout route and are much slower. Tourist office: Piazza Colombo 12, tel. 0187/808–125.

Gateway to the relatively inaccessible coastal area surrounding the Cinque Terre, Levanto is a secluded town with good beaches and a few graceful buildings that date from the 13th century. Many of the buildings are adorned with clever trompe l'oeil paintings that give the impression that real town folk are looking at you from their windows.

Lodging and
Dining
Under 115,000 lire
★

Stella Maris. Located in the center of Levanto and only a 10-minute walk from the beach, this is a real find. It takes up one floor of a 19th-century palazzo (the ground floor houses a palatial bank). Seven rooms are decorated with original frescoes and 19th-century furniture, and seven are modern; the couple who run the hotel have an infectious enthusiasm for the building's history and decoration. A half-board plan is required in summer, but that's no sacrifice because the home cooking features Ligurian seafood specialties; you can have your homemade ice cream in the sunny garden. *Via Marconi 4, tel. 0187/ 808258. 14 rooms with bath (showers). Facilities: restaurant, garden. No credit cards. Closed Nov.*

The Cinque Terre

The Cooperativa Batellieri in Genoa (Ponte dei Mille, tel. 010/ 265712) has boat tours to the Cinque Terre for about 32,000 lire round-trip. From Levanto, many visitors hike to the Cinque Terre villages; others take the small local train that runs hourly from Levanto to Riomaggiore, the southernmost point of the Cinque Terre, stopping at each station (fare 1,700). The complete run takes about 40 minutes. There is also a ferry from La Spezia that stops at each of the five towns on its 90-minute circuit.

Some of the best attractions near Levanto are within walking distance—but the walk can be a hike of up to five hours. Make sure you wear comfortable, sturdy shoes and carry a water bottle, since it can be very hot in the summer. Your goal is the group of almost inaccessible coastal villages known as the Cinque Terre, built against steep cliffs and reached by narrow roads that wind down from the hills; until about 50 years ago, they could be reached only by boat.

The first and largest is **Monterosso,** with a 12th-century church in the Ligurian style, lively markets, and small beaches. Next is **Vernazza,** a charming village of narrow streets, small squares and arcades, and the remains of forts dating from the Middle Ages. **Corniglia,** the middle village, is perched on a hillside amid vineyards; it offers excellent views of the entire coastal strip. The last two villages, **Manarola** and **Riomaggiore,** sit on tiny harbors hemmed in by sheer cliffs. It's an adventure to visit these five villages, and the reward for your exertion is a sense of tranquillity amid the dramatic coastal scenery.

Portovenere

To get to Portovenere, take the train from Genoa, Levanto, or Riomaggiore to La Spezia. The fare from Genoa to La Spezia is 5,700 lire; there are eight trains a day; the trip takes 90 minutes. From La Spezia, take either bus P for the 20-minute ride to Portovenere (fare 1,800 lire) or the 90-minute ferry (4,400 lire) from the landing at La Spezia's Passeggiata Morin, run by the Navigazione Golfo dei Poeti, tel. 0187/30387. Tourist office: Piazza Bastreri 1, tel. 0187/900–691.

Portovenere's small, colorful houses, some dating from the 12th century, were once all connected to the 12th- to 16th-century citadel, so that in times of attack the villagers could reach the safety of the battlements. The town has a strategic position at the end of a peninsula that extends southeast from the Cinque Terre and forms the western border of the Gulf of La Spezia. Lord Byron is said to have written *Childe Harold* here. The huge, strange grotto at the base of the sea-swept cliff is named after the poet, whose strength and courage were much admired after he swam across the gulf to the village of San Terenzo to visit his friend Shelley. Above the grotto, on a formidable solid mass of rock, is **San Pietro,** a 13th-century Gothic church built on the site of an ancient pagan shrine. With its black-and-white–striped exterior, it is a landmark recognizable from far out at sea.

Lodging
Under 115,000 lire

Locanda San Pietro. This good-value inn occupies a castle at the edge of the village and is five minutes from the beach. The rooms, decorated in Art Nouveau style, are quiet. Most have good views of the coastline around Portovenere. The restaurant features local cuisine and stresses seafood. *Portovenere, tel. 0187/900616. 31 rooms with bath or shower. Facilities: restaurant, bar. AE, MC. Closed Jan. 2–Mar. 14.*

Splurge
★

Royal Sporting. Appearances are deceptive at this modern hotel, which is located on the beach, about a 10-minute walk from the village. From the outside, the stone construction seems austere and unwelcoming, but the courtyards and interior are colorful and vibrant. There are fresh flowers and potted plants in the reception rooms and terraces, and the cool, airy rooms all have sea views. The sports facilities are among the best in the area. A double costs about 220,000, including breakfast. *Via dell'Olivo 345, tel. 0187/900326, fax 0187/529060. 62 rooms with bath. Facilities: restaurant, bar, pool, private beach, tennis court, gardens. AE, DC, MC, V. Closed Oct. 15–Apr. (open Easter week).*

Dining
Under 30,000

Da Iseo. Try to get one of the tables outside at this waterfront restaurant, which is decorated in the style of a local fishing hut, with nets and buoys along the walls. Seafood is the only choice: It's fresh and plentiful. Try the *zuppa di datteri* (Ligurian clam chowder), *spaghetti ai datteri* (with Ligurian clams), or the *fritto misto di frutti di mare* (mixed fried seafood). *Portovenere, tel. 0187/900610. Reservations advised in summer. AE, DC, MC. Closed Wed. and Jan.–Feb.*

L'Antica Osteria del Carrugio. Near the castle built to defend the coast from Pisan incursions, this is a tavern with maritime decor. The menu features seafood, which varies from day to day, depending on the catch. Specialties include trenette con pesto and focaccia. *Via Capellini 66, tel. 0187/900713. Closed Thurs. No credit cards.*

8 Piedmont/ Valle d'Aosta

From Turin to the Alps and Across the Po Plain

From the mountainous northwest corner of Italy to the broad Po plain spread at its feet (the name Piemonte, in Italian, means "foot of the mountains"), the Piedmont region and the autonomous Valle d'Aosta region just north of it offer a more Continental atmosphere than you'll find farther south in Italy, a look and spirit often akin to neighboring France and Switzerland. Piedmont's main city is Turin, a cosmopolitan center with a number of extraordinary museums and plenty of Old World charm, despite its large industrial areas. The Langhe district, near Alba, southeast of Turin, is a major wine-producing region, its hilly landscape blanketed with vineyards. The spectacular Valle d'Aosta boasts some of the highest mountains in Europe, with such famous (and pricey) ski resorts as Courmayeur and Breuil-Cervinia, although it is not impossible to find budget accommodations in the lesser known valleys. Efficient rail and bus networks make it possible to explore the region in a series of day trips from Turin, though the mountainous terrain makes for slow going on some routes.

Piedmont was originally inhabited by Celtic tribes who were absorbed by the Romans. As allies of Rome, the Celts held off Hannibal when he came down through the Alpine passes with his elephants but were eventually defeated, and their capital—Taurasia, the present Turin—was destroyed. The Romans rebuilt the city, giving its streets the grid pattern that survives today. Roman ruins can be found throughout both regions and are particularly abundant in the town of Aosta.

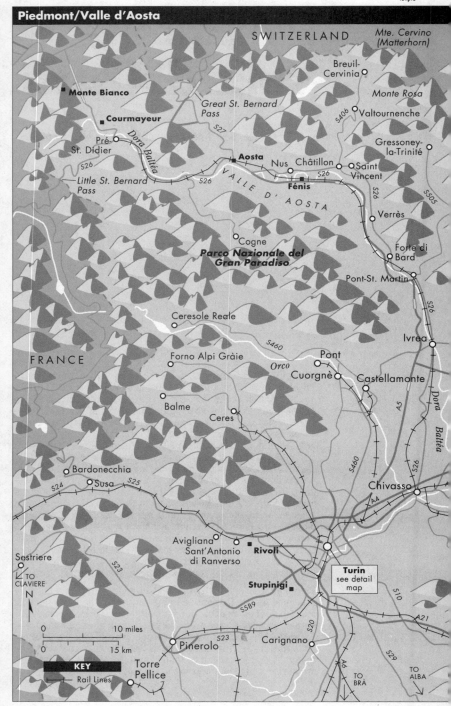

Piedmont/Valle d'Aosta

SWITZERLAND

Mte. Cervino
(Matterhorn)

Breuil-
Cervinia

Monte Rosa

■ Monte Bianco

Great St. Bernard
Pass

S27

Valtournenche

S406

Gressoney-
la-Trinité

■ Courmayeur

Pré-
St. Didier

Dora Baltéa

S26

Little St. Bernard
Pass

■ Aosta

Nus

Châtillon

Saint
Vincent

S26

S26

S405

VALLE D' AOSTA

■ Fénis

Verrès

Cogne

Parco Nazionale del
Gran Paradiso

Forte di
Bard

Pont-St. Martin

S26

FRANCE

Ceresole Reale

S460

Ivrea

Forno Alpi Gràie

Orco

Pont

Cuorgnè

Castellamonte

S26

Balme

Ceres

S460

A5

Dora Baltéa

Chivasso

Bardonecchia

S24

Susa

S25

A4

Turin
see detail
map

Avigliana
Sant'Antonio
di Ranverso

■ Rivoli

A5

S26

Sestriere

↙ TO
CLAVIERE

N ↑

Stupinigi ■

S10

A21

S23

0   10 miles
0   15 km

S589

S20

Pinerolo

S23

Carignano

A6

TO
ALBA

Torre
Pellice

TO
BRÀ

S29

KEY
━┼━ Rail Lines

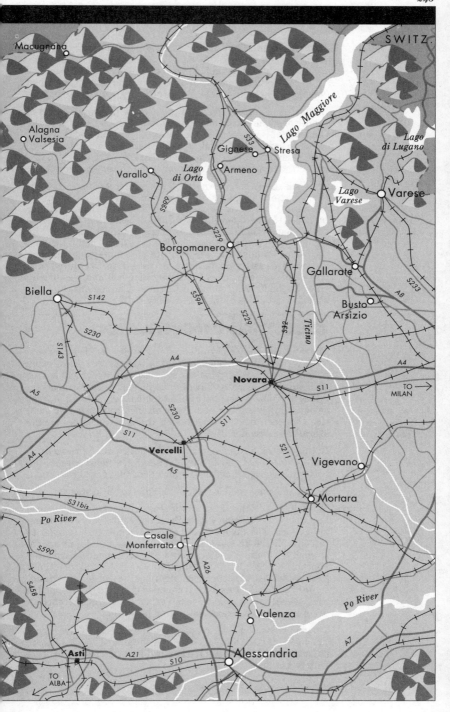

With the fall of the Roman Empire, Piedmont suffered the fate of the rest of Italy and was successively occupied and ravaged by barbarians from the east and the north. In the 11th century, a feudal French family named Savoy ruled Turin briefly; toward the end of the 13th century they returned to the area, where they would remain, almost continually, for 500 years. In 1798 the French republican armies invaded Italy, but when Napoleon's empire fell, the House of Savoy returned to power.

Beginning in 1848, Piedmont was one of the principal centers of the Risorgimento, the movement for Italian unity. In 1861 the Chamber of Deputies of Turin declared Italy a united kingdom. Rome became the capital in 1870, marking the end of Piedmont's importance in the political sphere. Nevertheless, the architectural splendors of Turin continue to draw travelers.

The Valle d'Aosta, to the north, is famous for its impressive fortified castles and splendid Alpine beauty. It was settled in the 3rd millennium BC by people from the Mediterranean and later by a Celtic tribe known as the Salassi, who eventually fell to the Romans. The Saracens were here in the 10th century; by the 12th century, the Savoy family had established itself, and the region's feudal nobles moved into the countryside, building the massive castles that still stand. Valle d'Aosta enjoyed relative autonomy as part of the Savoy kingdom and was briefly ruled by the French four separate times. The region is still officially bilingual, speaking both Italian and French.

Essential Information

Lodging There is a good variety of accommodations in Piedmont and Valle d'Aosta, but remember that outside of the cities, many people see the area as a two-season resort. Summer and winter occupancy rates are usually quite high, since skiers and mountaineers add to the competition for rooms then. When a hotel or chalet offers attractive half-board or off-season rates we mention that fact, because these deals can sometimes reduce the overall cost significantly.

In the mountain resorts, many of the hotels cater primarily to half- or full-board guests only, for stays of at least a week. It's better to take a package deal if you're coming for a ski vacation.

Highly recommended lodgings are indicated by a star ★.

Dining These two regions offer rustic specialties from farmhouse hearths or fine cuisine with a French accent—and everything in between. The favorite form of pasta is *agnolotti* (similar to ravioli), filled with meat, spinach, or cheese. Another regional specialty is *fonduta*—a local form of fondue, made with melted Fontina (a cheese from the Valle d'Aosta), eggs, and sometimes grated truffles. Another local dish is *cardi in bagna cauda*, made of edible thistles *(cardi)* chopped raw, and then dipped in a hot sauce *(bagna cauda*, meaning "hot bath") made from butter, oil, anchovies, cream, and shredded garlic.

Turin is known for delicate pastries and fine chocolates, especially *gianduiotti* (hazelnut-flavored chocolates). Valle d'Aosta is famous for a variety of schnappslike brandies made from fruit or herbs.

Piedmont is one of Italy's most important wine-producing regions. Most of the wines are full-bodied reds, such as Barolo, Nebbiolo, Freisa, Barbera, and Barbaresco. Asti Spumante, a sparkling wine, comes from the region, as does vermouth, which was developed in Piedmont by A. B. Carpano in 1786.

Unless otherwise noted, reservations are not needed and dress is casual. Highly recommended restaurants are indicated by a star ★.

Shopping Turin is the major city of Piedmont/Valle d'Aosta, and it has all the shopping that you would expect to find in a metropolis. Famous Cinzano and Martini & Rossi brand wines and vermouths are particular favorites, and salamis, cheeses, and delicious gianduiotti are also appreciated as gifts. Elsewhere in the region you'll find handicrafts, such as Borsalino hats from Alessandria and carved wooden objects from Aosta. You may also find good bargains in the antiques markets in many towns and villages.

Hiking and Climbing Devoted to skiing in the winter, the Alpine Valle d'Aosta region is excellent for hikers and mountain climbers in the summer. For information on hiking and climbing, contact the **Club Alpino Italiano** (Piazza Chanoux 8, Aosta, tel. 0165/40194, open Tues. and Fri. 8 PM–10 PM). For information on guides, contact the **Unione Valdostana Guide d'Alta Montagna** (Via Monte Emilius 13, Aosta, tel. 0165/34983).

The Arts and Nightlife Turin and, to a lesser extent, Aosta dominate the world of the arts in this northwest corner of Italy. Music is especially popular among the population as a whole, with entire towns and villages flocking enthusiastically to concerts, recitals, and special exhibitions. In the Valle d'Aosta, you can hear French folk songs in Alpine surroundings, while Piedmont itself (and especially Turin) is on the Genoa–Milan concert circuit. The best source of information about the arts is Turin's daily paper, *La Stampa*.

Turin is the major center for after-hours entertainment, although it has some competition from the swanky ski resorts of Courmayeur and Breuil-Cervinia. Elsewhere in Piedmont and Valle d'Aosta you'll find it best to limit yourself to sipping an after-dinner drink in a café on a busy city square or joining in the sometimes-boisterous songfests in the mountain hotel bars.

Highlights for First-time Visitors

Cloister of Sant'Orso, Aosta (Tour 2: The Valle d'Aosta)
Courmayeur (Tour 2: The Valle d'Aosta)
Fénis Castle (Tour 2: The Valle d'Aosta)
Mole Antonelliana, Turin (Tour 1: Turin and Its Outskirts)

Tour 1: Turin and Its Outskirts

Turin—in Italian, Torino—is roughly in the center of Piedmont–Valle d'Aosta; it is situated on the Po River, in the middle of the plain that marks the beginning of the Po Valley and stretches eastward all the way to the Adriatic. Apart from its role as northwest Italy's major industrial, cultural, and administrative hub, Turin is also a center of education, science, and the arts. Moreover, it has a reputation as Italy's main capital of black magic and the supernatural. This distinction is enhanced by the presence of Turin's most controversial, fascinating, and unsettling relic, the Sacra Sindone (Holy Shroud), still believed by many Catholics to be the cloth in which Christ's body was wrapped when he was taken down from the cross. The shroud, an ancient piece of linen more than four yards long and bearing the clear imprint of a human body, is rarely on view to the public. In 1988, after centuries of public debate about the cloth's authenticity, the Vatican agreed to have samples dated by scientists in the United States, Britain, and Italy. The tests showed the shroud to be a medieval fake, although how the human image became fused into it remains a mystery, and it continues to be revered as a holy relic.

From Rome and Milan
By Train

Turin is on the main Paris–Rome express line and is also connected with Milan, only 90 minutes away on the fast train. The fastest trains cover the 667-kilometer (400-mile) trip to Rome in about six hours, but most take about nine. Express train fares are about 16,000 lire from Milan, 54,000 from Rome.

By Bus

Two Turin-based lines, **SADEM** (Via della Repubblica 14, Grugliasco, Turin, tel. 011/301616) and **SAPAV** (Corso Torino 396, Pinerolo, Turin, tel. 011/794277), offer services along the autostrada network to Genoa, Milan, and more distant destinations in Italy. **SITA** buses, part of the nationwide system, also connect Turin with the rest of Italy. The main bus station is at the corner of Corso Inghilterra and Corso Vittorio Emanuele (tel. 011/442525). It takes two hours to travel by bus from Milan to Turin. There is no bus from Rome.

By Car

The A4 autostrada links Turin to Milan, a trip of 140 kilometers (87 miles). To reach Rome, a 595-kilometer (369-mile) journey, take the A21 east from Turin to Piacenza and get on the A1 south to Rome. The A6 heads south from Turin to the Ligurian coast and Genoa, 188 kilometers (117 miles) away.

By Plane

The region's only international airport, **Aeroporto di Caselle,** is 18 kilometers (11 miles) north of Turin. The airport is notoriously foggy in winter, and many flights are diverted to Genoa, on the coast, with bus connections provided to Turin. Buses from Caselle Airport to Turin arrive at the bus station on Corso Inghilterra in the center of the city.

Turin

Tourist offices: Porta Nuova train station, tel. 011/531327; Via Roma 222, just off Piazza San Carlo, tel. 011/535901.

Numbers in the margin correspond to points of interest on the Turin map.

Right in front of the train station is **Piazza Carlo Felice,** a landscaped park with fountain that marks the foot of Via Roma, one of the city's main thoroughfares. First opened in 1615, the porticoed Via Roma was largely rebuilt in the 1930s, during the time of Premier Benito Mussolini. Three streets up Via Roma ❶ ❷ from the train station, the churches of **San Carlo** and **Santa Cristina,** the latter with its ornate Baroque facade, flank the ❸ entrance to **Piazza San Carlo,** a stately, formal expanse considered by many to be the grandest square in Italy. In the center stands a statue of Duke Emanuele Filiberto of Savoy, victor, in

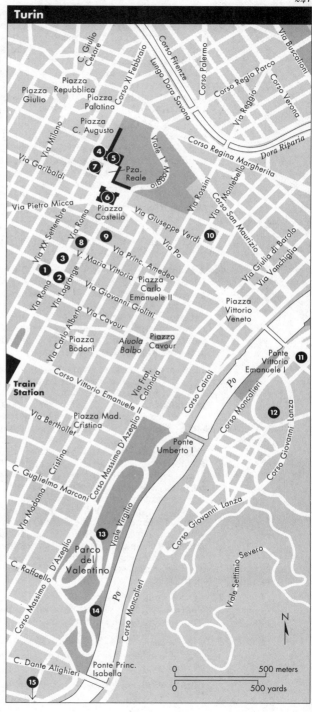

Turin

1557, of the battle of San Quintino, which heralded the peaceful resurgence of Turin under the Savoys, after years of bloody dynastic fighting. The fine bronze statue, erected in the 19th century, is one of Turin's symbols: The duke is returning his sword to its sheath at the end of the fight and is looking to the prosperous future of his family and the city. **Café San Carlo,** located under the arcades running alongside the square, is a historic coffeehouse where locals love to stop for coffee and pastry at tiny marble-topped tables under the huge crystal chandelier.

❹ Continue up Via Roma to the 15th-century **Duomo** (Cathedral), where the **Holy Shroud** is housed. The building, with its white marble facade and campanile (bell tower), stands in the heart of town on Piazza San Giovanni, adjacent to the Royal Palace. Inside, two monumental black marble staircases lead to the shadowy, black-marble-walled **Cappella della Sacra Sindone** (Chapel of the Holy Shroud), designed by the priest and architect Guarino Guarini (1604–83), a genius of the Baroque style who was official engineer and mathematician to the court of Duke Carlo Emanuele II of Savoy. Unfortunately, the chapel has been closed indefinitely for restoration and will probably remain closed through 1994.

❺ Adjoining the cathedral is the 17th-century **Palazzo Reale** (Royal Palace). The former Savoy royal residence, it is an imposing work of brick, stone, and marble that stands on the site of Turin's ancient Roman city gates. In contrast to its austere exterior, the palace's interior is characterized by luxurious, mostly Rococo decor, including tapestries, gilded ceilings, and sumptuous 17th- to 19th-century furniture. *Tel. 011/436–1455. Admission: 6,000 lire. Open Tues.–Sun. 9–2.*

❻ Pass through wrought-iron gates in the adjacent Piazza Castello to **Palazzo Madama,** named for the French queen Maria Cristina, who made it her home in the 17th century. The castle incorporates the remains of a Roman gate, as well as medieval and Renaissance additions. The architect Filippo Juvarra (1678–1736) designed the castle's elaborate Baroque facade in the early 18th century: He was intent on dispelling the idea that Italy's importance as a producer of contemporary art and architecture was in decline. Juvarra's bold use of the Baroque is also evident in the interior of the castle, where the huge marble staircase heralds his patron's wealth and prestige. The large assembly hall was the scene of the first Italian Senate meetings in the mid-19th century. Today the castle houses the **Museo Civico d'Arte Antica** (Civic Museum of Ancient Art), which has a rich collection of Gothic, Renaissance, and Rococo sculpture and paintings, as well as medieval illuminated manuscripts. This museum has been closed for some time for extensive restorations, and it is unlikely that it will actually reopen on the target date in 1994.

❼ In the same square is the church of **San Lorenzo,** built by Guarini from 1668 to 1680. Guarini was in his mid-60s when he began work on the church, but the sprightly collection of domes, columns, and florid Baroque features seems more the work of a younger architect cutting his teeth with a daring display of mathematical invention. The cupola and the vividly painted interior are standouts.

Baratti e Milano, located just to the east of Piazza Castello in the glass-roofed gallery between Via Lagrange and Via Po, is one of Turin's charming Old World cafés. It's famous for its chocolates, so you can indulge your sweet tooth here or buy some gianduiotti or candied chestnuts to take home to friends.

Retrace your steps two blocks down Via Roma to Guarini's **Palazzo dell'Accademia delle Scienze** (Palace of the Academy of Sciences). This large Baroque building, prefiguring the 18th century's preoccupation with logic and science, houses two of Turin's most famous museums. The **Museo Egizio** (Egyptian Museum) is considered by many to be one of the finest in scope outside Cairo. Its superb collection includes statues of pharaohs, mummies, and entire frescoes taken from royal tombs. Equally fascinating are the papyrus, art objects, and day-to-day utensils taken from the tombs of less noble ancient Egyptians. Look for the papyrus *Book of the Dead* and the 13th-century BC statue of Ramses II, which still glistens in its original colors. *Tel. 011/537581. Admission: 10,000 lire. Open Tues–Sun. 9–2.*

The **Galleria Sabauda,** in the same building, houses the collections of the house of Savoy. It is particularly rich in 16th- and 17th-century Dutch and Flemish paintings: Note Jan Van Eyck's *Saint Francis with Stigmata,* with the saint receiving the marks of Christ's wounds while a companion cringes beside him as if feeling it all himself. Other Dutch masterpieces include paintings by Anthony Van Dyck and Rembrandt. Simone del Pollaiuolo's *Tobias and the Angel* is showcased, and other Italian artists featured include Fra Angelico, Andrea Mantegna, and Paolo Veronese. *Tel. 011/547440. Admission: 6,000 lire. Open Tues.–Sun. 9–2.*

Diagonally across the square is another of Guarini's Baroque triumphs, the dark-red **Palazzo Carignano,** built from 1679 to 1685. This is one of Turin's and Italy's most historic buildings. Kings of Savoy Carlo Alberto (1798–1849) and Vittorio Emanuele II (1820–78) were born within its walls; Italy's first parliament met here from 1860 to 1865.

Take the little road behind the palazzo about 50 yards to Via Po, turn right, and take the fourth left (Via Montebello) to the striking **Mole Antonelliana.** You will probably have noticed this Turin landmark already: Its unusual square dome and thin, elaborate spire jut well above the city's rooftops. This odd structure, built between 1863 and 1897, was originally intended to be a synagogue, but costs escalated, and eventually it was bought by the city of Turin. In its time it was the tallest building in the world. There is an excellent view of the city, the plain surrounding it, and the Alps beyond from a terrace at the top of the dome. Take the elevator to the top. *Tel. 011/839–8314. Admission: 3,000 lire. Open Tues.–Sun. 9–7.*

Via Po leads to the large Piazza Vittorio Veneto, which slopes down to the Po River and the stone bridge, **Ponte Vittorio Emanuele.** Immediately across the bridge is the 19th-century church of **Gran Madre di Dio** (Great Mother of God), built in a neoclassical style based on the Pantheon in Rome. Turn right, along the Corso Moncalieri, to climb the Monte dei Cappuccini. At the top of this 150-foot hill are the church and convent of **Santa Maria del Monte,** which date from 1583. Don't be surprised if you find yourself in the middle of a wedding party: Local couples often come here to have their pictures taken.

Return to Corso Moncalieri and cross the next bridge downstream, Ponte Umberto I. Running along this cityside bank of the river is the **Parco del Valentino,** opened in 1856 and one of the most beautiful in Italy. The park has many pedestrian avenues, one of which, **Viale Virgilio,** goes right along the river

⑬ bank and leads to the **Castello del Valentino.** The design of this 17th-century castle, built more for appearance than for defense, is based on models of 16th-century French châteaux. The interior is particularly elaborate, with frescoed walls and rich decoration, but the real attraction of the castle is its riverside setting amid the greenery of the park. *Tel. 011/669–9372. Admission: 3,000 lire, free Fri. Open Tues.–Sat. 9–6, Sun. 10:30–6.*

Follow the riverside to the southern edge of the park, where

⑭ you'll find the **Borgo Medioevale** (Medieval Village), one of the most tranquil spots in Turin. The village, a faithful reproduction of medieval Piedmontese buildings, was created for the Turin Exposition of 1884. A visit here is like stepping back into the Middle Ages, with craftsmen's shops, houses, churches, and stores clustered along narrow streets and lanes. *Admission free. Open daily 8–8.*

No visit to car-manufacturing Turin would be complete with-

⑮ out a pilgrimage to the **Museo dell'Automobile** (Car Museum). Here you'll get an idea of the importance of FIAT—and automobiles, in general—to Turin's economy. A collection of antique cars dates from 1893, and displays show how the city has changed over the years as a result of its premier industry. *Corso Unità d'Italia, tel. 011/677666. Admission: 7,000 lire. Open Tues.–Sun. 10–6:30.*

Lodging **Piemontese.** In a fairly central location, not far from Porta
Under 115,000 lire Nuova Station and the main sights, this old building offers neat and simply furnished guest rooms. Rooms overlooking the street are noisy. *Via Berthollet 21, tel. 011/669–8101, fax 011/ 669–0571. 35 rooms, 28 with bath. AE, DC, MC, V.*

Under 85,000 lire **Smeraldo.** Located in a quiet residential area near the Automobile Museum, this very small hotel is modestly furnished. All rooms have private bathrooms, however, as well as telephones and radios. *Piazza Carducci 169/b, tel. 011/634577. 10 rooms with bath. AE, DC, MC, V.*

Under 60,000 lire **San Carlo.** Small and basic, the San Carlo is located right in the heart of things, on one of Turin's vast central squares, on the fourth floor of a 19th-century building. *Piazza San Carlo 197, tel. 011/553522. 13 rooms with shower. No credit cards.*

Splurge **Victoria.** Most of the rooms of this centrally located modern hotel are decorated in classic style with personalized touches. Room 316 has Indian motifs; 310, Old England; 206, Arabian; and so on. Some rooms have canopied beds, and 15 rooms on the top floor have terraces. A double room here goes for about 160,000 lire a night. *Via Nino Costa 4, tel. 011/561–1909, fax 011/561–1806. 65 rooms with bath. Facilities: bar, parking. AE, DC, MC, V.*

Dining **Amelia.** Family-run and efficient, this little trattoria is in the
Under 30,000 lire center of town, off Via Garibaldi. *Via dei Mercanti 6, tel. 011/ 518478. No credit cards. Closed Sat.*
Da Mauro. Try the Tuscan dishes in this lively, popular, family-run trattoria. Specialties include *cannelloni alla Mirella*

(stuffed rolls of noodle dough baked with mozzarella cheese), prosciutto and raw tomatoes, *castellana al prosciutto* (a thin cut of veal baked with Fontina cheese and prosciutto), and famous Florentine grilled beef. *Via Maria Vittoria 21, tel. 011/ 8397811. No credit cards. Closed Mon. and July.*

Porto di Savona. You have to look for this historic tavern under the arcades lining the square, where it was a stagecoach stop. Small dining rooms on the ground floor and upstairs have an old-fashioned air. At long wooden tables, customers dine on home-style Piedmontese cooking, including *pasticcio* (pasta casserole) with seasonal vegetables and *brasato* (beef braised in wine). *Piazza Vittorio Veneto 2, tel. 011/831453. Reservations advised. No credit cards. Closed Mon., Tues. lunch, and July.*

Under 24,000 lire **Il Blu.** Because of its central location near the air terminal and Piazza della Cittadella, Il Blu is filled with office workers and shoppers at lunchtime; it's more relaxed in the evening, when diners are at their leisure. The bunkerlike decor doesn't dim the appeal of enormous salads that are a meal in themselves. Good pastas and second courses are available, too. *Corso Siccardi 15/b, tel. 011/545550. AE, DC, V. Closed Sun. and Aug.*

Shopping Piazza San Carlo, Via Po, and Via Maria Vittoria are lined with antiques shops, some—but not all—specializing in 18th-century furniture and domestic items.

Go to the famous Balon Flea Market (Piazza Repubblica) on a Saturday morning for some excellent bargains in secondhand books and clothing and for stalls selling such local specialties as gianduiotti.

The Arts and Classical music concerts are held in the famous **Conservatorio**
Nightlife **Giuseppe Verdi** (Via Mazzini 11, tel. 011/810–4653) throughout the year, but mainly in the winter months. Sacred music and some modern religious pieces are performed in the **Duomo** on Sunday evening; these are usually advertised in the vestibule or in Turin's daily newspaper, *La Stampa.*

The **Teatro Regio,** one of Italy's leading opera houses, begins its season in December. You can buy tickets for most performances (premieres are sold out well in advance) at the box office facing Piazza Castello (tel. 011/881–5241).

Two good spots for unwinding to the rhythm of a disco beat are **Pick Up** (Via Barge 8) and **Patio** (Corso Moncalieri 346/14). Both are open late and cater to a mixed crowd of young Turinese, university students, and visitors.

Stupinigi

Bus No. 41, from Turin's Porta Nuova train station, goes to Stupinigi, the end of the line. The fare is 1,600 lire.

Just west of the city, the town of Stupinigi is worth visiting to see the **Palazzina di Caccia,** built by Juvarra in 1729 as a hunting lodge for the House of Savoy. It is more like a royal villa, with its many wings, landscaped gardens, and surrounding forests. This regal aspect was not lost on Napoleon, who lived here before claiming the crown of Italy. The castle interior is sumptuously decorated and today houses a collection of art and furniture in the appropriately named **Museo d'Arte e Ammo-**

biliamento. *Tel. 011/358–1220. Admission: 6,000 lire. Open Tues.–Sat. 9:30–5, Sun. 10–1 and 2–5.*

Rivoli

From downtown Turin, take tram No. 1 to Corso Francia, then switch to bus No. 36, which terminates at Rivoli. The fare is 1,600 lire.

During the Middle Ages, the Savoy court was based in this town, just 13 kilometers (8 miles) west of Turin. The 14th- to 15th-century **Casa del Conte Verde,** right in the center of town, is a good example of medieval architecture of the transitional period, when its defensive function was giving way to the decorative. The 18th-century Savoy castle, built in the Baroque style under the direction of Juvarra, now houses the **Museo d'Arte Moderna** (Modern Art Museum), which contains many examples of 20th-century Italian art. The Futurist movement is particularly well represented. *Tel. 011/958–1547. Admission: 8,000 lire. Open Tues.–Sun. 10–7.*

Tour 2: Valle d'Aosta

Valle d'Aosta is a scenic Alpine region, crossed by several major valleys and scores of tributary ones, most converging at or near Aosta, the region's capital. Besides a spectacular mountain backdrop, Aosta has great historical interest; it was colonized by the Romans, whose monuments have been well preserved, and nearby are some fine medieval churches and castles, including Fénis, the best-preserved fortress in this castle-studded area. An excursion to Aosta from Turin gives you a taste of the Valle d'Aosta's scenery en route.

If you enjoy hiking or skiing, you will want to spend more time in the mountains; head for the smaller towns, where prices are lower for everything from accommodations to lifts. Among them are Rhêmes–Notre Dame in the Rhêmes Valley, for which you take the bus from Aosta; or Antey-St-André, Torgnon, La Magdeleine, and Chamois, in the Cervino Valley, for which you can take a bus or a train to Chatillon and then local bus. In these towns, a *settimana bianca* (ski week) costs from 250,000 to 290,000 lire, depending on the season.

From Turin Express trains from Turin to Aosta take about two hours and
By Train cost about 10,500 lire.

By Bus **SAVDA** (Strada Ponte Suaz 6, Aosta, tel. 0141/361244) specializes in mountain service, providing frequent links between Aosta, Turin, and Courmayeur.

Aosta

Tourist office: Piazza Chanoux 8, tel. 0165/35655.

Aosta stands at the junction of two important trade routes from France to Italy—from the valleys of the Rhône and the Isère. Its significance as a trading post was recognized by the Romans, who built a garrison here in the 1st century BC. The present-day layout of streets in this small city, which is tucked away in the Alps more than 400 miles from Rome, is the clearest example of Roman street planning in Italy. Well-preserved Roman walls form a perfect rectangle around the center of Aosta, and the regular pattern of streets reflects its role as a military stronghold.

At the eastern entrance to town, in a square that commands a fine view over Aosta and the mountains, is the **Arco di Augusto** (Arch of Augustus), built in 25 BC to mark Rome's victory over the Celtic Salassi tribe. Across the square, and then a right turn off Via Sant'Anselmo, is the **Collegiata di Sant'Orso** (Collegiate Church of Saint Orso): the sort of church that has layers of history in its architecture. Originally there was a 6th-century chapel on this site, founded by the archdeacon Orso, a local saint. Most of this structure was destroyed or hidden when an 11th-century church was erected over it. This church, in turn, was encrusted with Gothic and later Baroque features, leaving the church a jigsaw puzzle of styles, but—surprisingly—not a chaotic jumble. The 11th-century features are almost un-touched in the crypt, and if you go up the stairs on the left from the main church, you can see the 11th-century frescoes (ask the sacristan for entrance). These frescoes, recently restored, de-pict the life of Christ and the apostles: Although only the tops are visible, you can see the expressions on the faces of the disci-ples. Take the doorway by the entrance to the crypt to see the crowning glory of Sant'Orso—the 12th-century **cloister.** Lo-cated alongside the church, it is enclosed by some 40 stone col-umns with masterfully carved capitals representing Old and New Testament subjects and scenes from the life of St. Orso.

Continue down Via Anselmo (named for St. Anselm, who was born in Aosta and later became archbishop of Canterbury in England) through the huge Roman **Porta Pretoria.** Turn right after this three-arched gateway to see the 72-foot-high ruin of the facade of the **Teatro Romano** (Roman Theater). Just ahead are the ruins of the 1st-century-BC amphitheater, which once held 20,000 spectators. Only 7 of its original 60 arches remain, and these are built onto the facade of the adjacent convent of **Santa Caterina.** The convent usually allows visitors in to see these arches (ask at the entrance).

About 100 yards west of the Roman theater (down Via Mon-signor de Sales) is Aosta's **Cathedral,** which dates from the 10th century, although all that remains from that period are the campaniles (bell towers). The decoration inside is mainly Goth-ic, but the principal attraction of the cathedral predates that era by 1,000 years: the carved ivory diptych (devotional work with two images) showing the Roman emperor Honorius and dating from AD 406. *For admission to the treasury, contact the sacristan at the Piccolo Seminario, 2 Piazza Giovanni XXIII (behind the cathedral).*

From Aosta you can take a cable car up to **Pila,** at an altitude of about 5,500 feet. For information on other excursions by cable car throughout the region, contact the **Società Valdostana Impianti a Fune** (Via Festaz 66, Aosta, tel. 0165/33327), or pick up the tourist office's invaluable timetable (*orario*) of bus, train, and cable-car services in the region.

Lodging
Under 115,000 lire

Cecchin. This attractive, family-run hotel is located across the Buthier River from the center of town, but it is within walking distance of the sights. It has only 10 rooms and a homey atmos-phere. There is a little garden. *Via Ponte Romano 27, tel. 0165/ 45262. 10 rooms with bath or shower. MC, V. Closed Oct. 15– Dec. 28.*

Rayon du Soleil. Saraillon, a residential district in the hills above Aosta, is the setting for this traditional redbrick mountain hotel set in a park. There are excellent views from the rooms, which are large, bright, and quiet. The hotel's interior is decorated in traditional dark wood. There are rooms suitable for disabled people. *Saraillon 16, tel. 0165/362247, fax 0165/ 236085. 45 rooms with bath. Facilities: garage, pool. AE, DC, MC, V. Closed Nov. 1–mid-Mar.*

Under 60,000 lire **Mancuso.** Railroad tracks separate this hotel from the center of Aosta, but it is within walking distance; go left on Via Carducci from the train station, and then take the underpass and turn left onto Via Voison. The hotel is quiet, run by an attentive family. Some rooms have little terraces, and all have private bath. The adjacent restaurant is good and inexpensive. *Via Voison 32, tel. 0165/34526. 12 rooms with bath. No credit cards.*

Dining **Praetoria.** Near the massive city gate of the same name, this is a
Under 30,000 lire small trattoria where you can order *fonduta* and *carbonada con polenta*, a rich beef stew served with cornmeal mush. *Via Sant'Anselmo 9, tel. 0165/44356. MC, V. Closed Thurs.*

Under 24,000 lire **La Brasserie du Commerce.** Small, lively, and informal, this restaurant is near Piazza Chanoux. On a sunny day try to get a table on the terrace. Typical valley dishes such as fonduta are on the menu, together with a wide range of vegetable dishes and salads. *Via de Tillier 10, tel. 0165/35613. No credit cards. Closed Sun.*

Splurge **Piemonte.** A small restaurant in the center of town, the Pie-
★ monte has a comfortable, rustic decor and offers *crespelle alla valdostana* (crepes with cheese) and *filetto alla provenzale* (beef fillet with porcini mushrooms). A full meal with wine costs about 45,000 lire. *Via Porta Pretoria 13, tel. 0165/40111. Reservations advised for lunch. MC, V. Closed Fri.*

Shopping One of the arcades in Piazza Chanoux houses a permanent crafts exhibition. Aosta and the surrounding countryside are famous for wood carvings and wrought-iron work, and this exhibition is a good place to pick up a bargain. Each year, on the last two days of January, the whole town turns out for the Sant'Orso Fair, when all sorts of handicrafts are on sale, including handmade lace from nearby Cogne, carved stonework, and brightly colored woolens.

The Arts and Each summer a series of concerts are held in different venues
Nightlife around the city. Organ recitals in July and August attract performers of world renown.

Fénis

Take a bus marked Fénis (tel. 0165/362287) from Aosta's Piazza Narbonne, near Piazza Chanoux in the center of town. The trip takes 30 minutes and costs 2,000 lire.

The many-turreted castle of Fénis was built in the mid-14th century by Aimone di Challant, another member of the prolific family that was related to the Savoys. This castle is the sort imagined by schoolchildren, with pointed turrets, portcullises, and spiral staircases. The 15th-century courtyard has a stairway leading to a loggia (open walkway) with wooden balconies. Inside you can see the medieval kitchen, with much of the original cooking equipment, and a collection of weapons in the armory. If you have time to visit only one castle in the Valle d'Aosta, this is it, though it may be partially closed for restoration. *Tel. 0165/764263. Admission: 4,000 lire. Open Mar.–Oct., Wed.–Mon. 9–6:30 (group tours every half hour); Nov.–Feb., Wed.–Mon. 9:30–noon and 2–5 (group tours every hour).*

Courmayeur and Monte Bianco

Courmayeur is an hour by bus from Aosta's Piazza Narbonne; the fare is 3,800 lire. Service is frequent, though buses are crowded, especially in winter. Trains from Turin go to Pré-Saint-Didier; a bus at the station there takes you to Courmayeur. Tourist office: Piazzale Monte Bianco, tel. 0165/842060.

Europe's tallest peak, Mont Blanc (Monte Bianco) looms over Courmayeur, an attractive mountain village set among thick pinewoods. Over the years it has become a favorite resort of moneyed vacationers, though travelers on a tighter budget can sample its scenic beauty on a day trip from Aosta.

The jet-set celebrities who flock here, particularly in winter, are following a tradition that dates from the late 17th century, when Courmayeur's natural springs first began to draw visitors. The scenic spectacle of the Alps gradually surpassed the springs as the biggest drawing point (the Alpine letters of the English poet Shelley were almost advertisements for the region), but the biggest change in the history of Courmayeur came in 1965, when the Mont Blanc tunnel opened. Now Courmayeur stands on one of the main routes from France into Italy, although the planners have managed to maintain some restrictions on wholesale development within the town.

The center of this elongated town is Piazzale Monte Bianco, where long-distance buses arrive and the tourist office is located. Since the only restaurants here are expensive, after a stroll around to get the flavor of the resort, you may want to buy some picnic provisions and then hike or take a lift up to the slopes. From Piazzale Monte Bianco, take a local bus to Entreves and **La Palud,** where the cable car *(funivia),* to Monte Bianco starts its breathtaking ascent. The cable car crosses into France, so have your passport ready. Remember, too, that the cable car depends on the weather, and that can mean being stuck on the French side, sometimes overnight: Have French money with you just in case. You'll ride up to the viewing platform at **Punta Helbronner** (over 11,000 feet), which is also the border post with France. Mont Blanc's attraction is not so much its shape (much less distinctive than the Matterhorn) as its expanse and the vistas from the top. The next stage, as you pass into French territory, is particularly impressive: You'll dangle above a huge glacial snow field (more than 2,000 feet below) and slowly make your way to the viewing station above **Chamonix.** From this point you'll be looking down into France, and if you change cable cars, you can make your way down to Chamonix itself. The return trip covers the same route, and the total time should be 90 minutes, although this is entirely dependent on the weather. *Funivie La Palud, tel. 0165/89925. Fare: 36,000 lire round-trip to Punta Helbronner; another 43,000 lire from Punta Helbronner to Chamonix.*

Lodging   **Cresta et Duc.** A bright, modern Alpine hotel in the center of
Splurge   town, the Cresta features plenty of wooden terraces, flowers,

and wooden furnishings. For relaxation there's a good restaurant, bar, billiards room, and lounges. The rooms are large and warm, and the hotel offers good full- and half-board rates. At 80,000–160,000 lire a night, it's a relative bargain for Courmayeur. *Via Circonvallazione 7, tel. 0165/842585, fax 0165/842591. 39 rooms (no singles) with bath. Facilities: restaurant, bar. AE, DC, MC, V. Closed end Apr.–end June, mid-Sept.–Dec. 20.*

Dining **Maison de Filippo.** Here you'll find country-style home cooking
Splurge in a character-filled mountain house furnished with antiques. Reserve in advance, for it's one of the most popular restaurants in the Valle d'Aosta. In summer, you can eat outside, surrounded by stunning views. There is a set menu only, featuring a daily selection of specialties, including a wide choice of antipasti and pasta dishes, such as *tortelloni alla valdostana* (ravioli baked with Fontina cheese and butter), agnolotti in various sauces, and *spaghetti affumicata* (with salami and bacon). The inn provides ample parking. The set menus run about 50,000 lire per person. *Entreves, tel. 0165/89968. Reservations required. V. Closed Tues., June 1–July 15, Nov.*

Parco Nazionale del Gran Paradiso

Take the train from Aosta to Pont St-Martin (about 4,200 lire) and then a local bus (2,300 lire) to Champorcher, near the Gran Paradiso National Park. You can also take a bus from Aosta to Cogne—a 50-minute trip that costs about 2,800 lire.

This huge park, once the domain of King Vittorio Emanuele II, was bequeathed to the nation after World War I. Gran Paradiso is one of Europe's most rugged and unspoiled wilderness areas, with wildlife and many plant species protected by law. Try to visit in May, when spring flowers are in bloom and most of the meadows are clear of snow. This is one of the few places in Europe where you can see the ibex (a mountain goat with horns up to three feet long) or the chamois (a small antelope whose soft skin nearly drove it to extinction). The village of **Cogne** is a good place to sample the peace and solitude of this vast park.

Tour 3: Asti

Heading southeast from Turin, you'll pass through the Monferrato, a hilly wooded area, rich in vineyards and truffles. Asti is one of the main cities of the Monferrato. It is known to Americans mainly because of its wines (there are excellent reds as well as the famous sparkling white spumante), but its strategic position on trade routes between Turin, Milan, and Genoa has given it a broad economic base. During the 12th century, Asti began to develop as a republic, at a time when other Italian cities were also flexing their economic and military muscles. It flourished during the following century, when the inhabitants began erecting lofty towers for its defense. Some of these towers remain, giving the city a medieval look.

From Porta Nuova station in Turin, frequent daily train service (fare 4,300 lire) runs to Asti, about 45 minutes away. Tourist office: Piazza Alfieri 34, tel. 0141/50357.

You can easily see the center of Asti on foot. From the train station, follow Corso Einaudi straight ahead, then bear right to

Piazza della Libertà. From there you'll enter the large triangular **Piazza Alfieri,** the heart of Asti. Head left for the Gothic church of **San Secondo.** San Secondo is the patron of Asti and of the city's favorite folklore event, the annual *palio,* a colorful, medieval-style race of horses and donkeys held on the third Sunday of September in the Campo del Palio, which you skirted on your way to Piazza Alfieri.

From the church of San Secondo, go left on Corso Vittorio Alfieri, a major east–west street. Originally built by ancient Romans, the Corso was known in medieval times as Contrada Maestra. It will lead you to Piazza Roma, where you'll see the **Torre Comentini,** one of Asti's 13th-century towers. After Piazza Roma, backtracking toward San Secondo, the third left off the Corso (Via Morelli) will take you to the tall, thin **Torre Troyana,** the best-preserved of the medieval towers. Torre Troyana is attached to Palazzo Troya, in Piazza Medici.

From the Torre Troyana, go left toward Piazza Catena and Via Natta to reach the **Duomo** (Cathedral). Asti's Duomo affords a striking lesson in the evolution of the Gothic style of architecture. The cathedral, built in the early 14th century, is decorated mainly in a Gothic style that emphasizes geometry and verticality: Pointed arches and narrow vaults are counterbalanced by the earlier, Romanesque attention to balance and symmetry. Then look at the porch, on the south side of the cathedral, facing the square. This addition, built in 1470, represents Gothic at its most florid and excessive.

Return to the Corso and turn right, walking for about two minutes until you see on your left the 18th-century church of Santa Caterina, which has incorporated another medieval tower, the **Torre Romana** (itself built on an ancient Roman base), as its bell tower.

From Asti you can take local buses to some of the interesting wine-producing towns in the vicinity, such as **Costigliole d'Asti, Canelli,** and the medieval town of **Alba.** Alba is also famous for its *tartufi bianchi* (white truffles), much rarer and more expensive than black ones and considered by connoisseurs to be the tastiest and most aromatic. They sell for at least $1,000 a pound wholesale. The highlight of Alba's truffle fair, in October, is the medieval Joust of the Hundred Towers.

Lodging **Rainero.** An older hotel in the center of Asti, near the station,
Under 115,000 lire Rainero has been under the same family management for three generations. It's been remodeled many times and is fitted with modern furnishings. There is no restaurant. *Via Cavour 85, tel. 0141/353866, fax 0141/353866. 49 rooms with bath. AE, DC, MC, V.*

Dining **Falcon Vecchio.** There's been a restaurant in this ancient house
Splurge in the historic center of Asti since the year 1670. Today, in intimate surroundings, the Falcon Vecchio serves rich local dishes that vary with the season. In fall and winter there are mushroom, truffle, and game dishes. Otherwise there's a big selection of antipasti; grilled vegetables; and mixed, boiled, or grilled meats *(bollito misto* or *arrosto misto).* A full meal with wine costs about 60,000. *Vicolo San Secondo 8, tel. 0141/593106. MC, V. Closed Sun. evening, Mon., and Aug.*

Festivals September is a month of fairs and celebrations in this famous wine city, and the Asti Competition in the middle of the month brings musicians, who perform in churches and halls in the city. For information, contact the tourist information office (Piazza Alfieri 34, tel. 0141/50357).

Tour 4: Vercelli

The Po River dominates the sweeping plain that runs east of Turin, punctuated by a handful of substantial cities. Vercelli is the rice capital of Italy and of Europe itself: Northern Italy's mainstay, risotto, owes its existence to the crop that was introduced to this fertile area during the late Middle Ages.

Some trains on both the Turin–Milan and Turin–Venice lines make a stop at Vercelli. The ride takes 50 minutes and costs about 5,700 lire. Tourist office: Viale Garibaldi 91, tel. 0161/ 64631.

Piazza Cavour is the heart of the medieval city and its former market square. It was to this small square that merchants across northern Italy came in the 15th century to buy bags of the novelty grain from the east—rice. Rising above the low rooftops around the square is the **Torre dell'Angelo** (Tower of the Angel), whose forbidding military appearance reflects its origin as a watchtower.

Vercelli has an unusual guided tour of the **Borsa Merci,** the rice exchange where the grain has been traded for centuries. Call first to check on tour times (Via Zumaglini 4, tel. 0161/5981).

Via Gioberti goes east from the square, leading to Via del Duomo, up on the left. Ahead of you is the campanile of the **Duomo** (Cathedral), which is at the end of the street, on Piazza D'Angennes. The building, mainly a late-16th-century construction on the site of what was a 5th-century church, contains tombs of several Savoy rulers in an octagonal chapel along the south (right) wall. The cathedral's *biblioteca* (library) contains the "Gospel of St. Eusebius," a 4th-century document, and the *Codex Vercellensis*, an 11th-century book of Anglo-Saxon poetry (ask in the cathedral if you can enter the library).

Cross Piazza Sant'Eusebio, which is directly in front of the cathedral, and follow Corso De Gasperi to the **Basilica di Sant'Andrea,** on the left. This Cistercian abbey church, built in the early 13th century with funds from another Abbey of St. Andrew (in England), witnessed the growing influence of northern Europe on Italy. Sant'Andrea is one of Italy's earliest examples of Gothic architecture, which spread from the north but ran out of steam before getting much farther south than the Po plain. The interior of the church is a soaring flight of Gothic imagination, with slender columns rising up to the ribbed vaults of the high ceiling. Tombs along the side aisle continue the preoccupation with stylized decoration and relief work. The gardens on the north (Corso De Gasperi side) of the basilica hold the remains of the abbey itself and some of the secondary buildings. It is only here that the unadulterated Gothic style is interrupted. The buildings surround a cloister in which you can see the pointed Gothic arches resting on the severe and more solid 12th-century Romanesque column bases.

Wander back to Piazza Camana through the **Città Vecchia,** a collection of narrow streets and alleys reached by taking Via Galileo (left from the basilica) and then making your way left into the narrow streets, using the Torre dell'Angelo in Piazza Cavour as your landmark. Many of the houses are five centuries old, and you can see partly hidden gardens and courtyards beyond the wrought-iron gates.

Dining **La Scala.** Close to the train station and the church of
Under 30,000 lire Sant'Andrea, this is a bright, popular place where you can dine inexpensively on pizza or risotto with seasonal vegetables. *Via Guala Bicheri 1, tel. 0161/66988. V. Closed Tues. V.*

Tour 5: Novara

Novara is the easternmost city in Piedmont, only about 10 kilometers (6 miles) west of the Ticino River, which forms the border with Lombardy. Milan is only 32 kilometers (20 miles) beyond the border, and over the centuries the opposing attractions of this neighboring giant and those of its regional capital, Turin, have made Novara a bit schizophrenic. During the Middle Ages, Novara's pivotal position between these two cities actually made it a battlefield. A major engagement took place as recently as 1849, when the Austrian forces from the east defeated the Piedmontese armies. Much of the present city dates from the late 19th and early 20th centuries, although there are interesting buildings from earlier periods scattered around Novara.

Most trains on the Turin–Milan line stop at Novara, a 50- to 60-minute trip from Turin. A second-class ticket on a rapid costs about 8,800 lire. Tourist office: Via Dominioni 4, tel. 0321/623398.

Novara's famous landmark, the tall, slender cupola of **San Gaudenzio,** was built between 1577 and 1690 and conforms to a Baroque design, with twisted columns and sumptuous statues. The main attraction for most people, though, is the cupola, which was built from 1840 to 1888 and soars to a height of just under 400 feet. This spire is visible from everywhere in the city and the surrounding countryside, and has become as much a symbol of Novara as the Mole Antonelliana is of Turin.

Take a left immediately after leaving the front door of San Gaudenzio and follow the small street south (against the flow of the one-way traffic). Soon you'll pass Corso Italia. Immediately to the left, after you've crossed this main street, is the **Broletto,** a cluster of well-preserved late-medieval buildings. Inside is the **Museo Civico,** which is full of Piedmontese military and social records from the Middle Ages through the 18th century. There are also some archaeological items going back to the Roman and early-Christian (4th–5th century) periods. *Tel. 0321/ 623021. Admission: 2,000 lire. Open Apr.–Sept., Tues.–Sun. 9–1 and 4–7; Oct.–Mar., Tues.–Sun. 9–noon and 3–5.*

Novara's **Duomo** is next to the Broletto. Its Romanesque origins are impossible to detect because major reconstruction in the past century left the building with an austere neoclassical appearance. You can delve into history more easily at the **Battistero** (Baptistery), which is just outside the entrance to the cathedral. This rotunda-shape building dates from the 5th century, although it was substantially enlarged during the 10th and 11th centuries. Recent restoration work has uncovered pre-Romanesque frescoes, over 1,000 years old, decorating the inside walls. Their flat, two-dimensional style reflects the influence of Byzantine icons, and their restored colors add a frightening feel to the depictions of scenes from the Apocalypse.

Lodging
Under 115,000 lire

Parmigiano. Located in the center of Novara, near the Broletto, this family-run hotel has clean rooms with modern furnishings in a centuries-old building with a renovated interior. A big plus is the in-house restaurant, where you can sample such local specialties as *paniscia*, a thick rice soup with beans and cabbage, and *casoeula*, a hearty stew with sausage, beef, and beans. *Via del Cattaneo 6, tel. 0321/23231. 40 rooms with bath or shower. Facilities: bar, restaurant. AE, DC, MC, V.*

Dining
Under 30,000 lire

Pizzeria A Marechiaro. It may seem strange to find such a characteristically Neapolitan pizzeria, complete with nautical decor, here on the Lombard plain, but this one has been satisfying homesick southern Italians since the 1950s. *Pizza margherita* (with mozzarella and tomatoes) and *spaghetti alle vongole* (with clam sauce) are always on the menu. *Via Fratelli Rosselli 11/a, tel. 0321/620237. Closed Wed. MC, V.*

9 Milan, Lombardy, and the Lakes

Milan's Malpensa airport is one of the country's two major international gateways (the other being Rome's Da Vinci airport), so the Lombardy region is a logical place to begin a visit to Italy. Progressive, highly industrialized, and economically dynamic, Lombardy exemplifies modern Italy at its sophisticated best. Its chief city, Milan, is Italy's industrial, banking, and commercial capital. While the plain of the Po River is heavily industrialized and inexorably flat, the region's great Renaissance cities—Bergamo, Brescia, Como, Mantua, and Pavia—preserve a wealth of artistic and historical sights. When you're ready for scenic beauty, head for lakes Garda, Como, and Maggiore, stretching like fingers toward the Alps. A well-organized and efficient transport system makes it possible to sample the major sights in a series of day excursions from Milan.

It can be a challenge to explore Lombardy, however, if you are traveling on a budget. Despite all its artistic and historical attractions, the area is geared to the businessman more than the tourist, and hence prices are at top levels, especially in Milan, Bergamo, Brescia, and the major lake resorts. Attractive budget accommodations are relatively few and far between, and in general you will find them inferior to comparably priced establishments in such tourist-conscious centers as Rome and Florence. Although you can manage to eat inexpensively, you may have to go out of your way to do so, or find the places where businesspeople go for a quick lunch or a snack.

Lombardy extends from the fringes of the Alps south through the vast Po plain. Strategically located, it has been an object of contention among various powers over the past 2,000 years, all of whom left their cultural mark. Explored by the Etruscans and settled by the Romans, it later came under control of the Germanic Lombard tribe—Longobardi in Italian—who gave the region its name. During the Middle Ages, powerful families such as the Viscontis, the Sforzas, and the Gonzagas made various Lombard cities their own little kingdoms. Charles V conquered the region in 1525, leading to 200 years of Spanish occupation, followed by a century of Austrian rule. When Napoleon swept over Europe, he made Milan the capital of Italy, a taste of glory the proud Lombards were loath to cede when Napoleon was finally routed. Lombards joined the 19th-century struggle against Hapsburg domination, which ended in the reestablishment of the Kingdom of Italy in 1861; in the 20th century, they led resistance to Mussolini and the German alliance. In the more recent past, Milan has established itself as a hot spot of fashion and design, a symbol of Italy's modern economic miracle.

Essential Information

Lodging Although Milan has fewer tourists than other large Italian cities, there is always competition for rooms, generated by the nearly year-round trade fairs and other business-related bookings. With so many business travelers to attract, most hotels strive for the upper end of the market, with high standards of comfort and correspondingly high prices. The listings below include the best of a small stock of lower-priced hotels; to avoid disappointment, reserve as far ahead as possible. Bear in mind that practically everything in Milan, including some hotels and most restaurants, closes in August.

Most of the famous lake resorts are quite expensive, with luxury hotels occupying beautiful old villas. A stroll around their well-landscaped grounds provides a taste of how the other half lives, but for overnight accommodations, head for the smaller towns around the lake, or, in the case of Lake Como, for the city of Como itself. Some resort hotels may offer lower rates outside the high season in July and August.

Highly recommended hotels are indicated by a star ★.

Dining Unlike most Italian regions, Lombardy exhibits a northern European preference for butter rather than oil as a cooking ingredient, which imparts a rich and distinctive flavor to the cuisine. Among the most popular specialties is *ossobuco alla milanese*, veal knuckle served with risotto (rice that has been cooked until almost all the liquid has evaporated and a creamy sauce remains). *Risotto milanese* uses chicken broth and has saffron added, which gives the dish a rich yellow color. The lakes are a good source of fish, particularly trout and pike.

Gorgonzola, a rich veined cheese, and *panettone*, a raised, fluffy fruitcake with raisins and candied fruit, both come from Milan and can be enjoyed throughout Lombardy. Although most of the wines in Lombardy are good accompaniments to the cuisine, try in particular to have the red Grumello or Sangue di Giuda (blood of Judas) wines or the light and delicious sparkling whites from the Franciacorta area.

Unless otherwise noted, reservations are not needed and dress is casual. Highly recommended restaurants are indicated by a star ★.

Shopping   Milan is the region's premier shopping city—in fact, it is one of the premier shopping cities in all of Europe—but it's no place for budget shoppers. Jewelers, antiques stores, and, above all, designer-fashion boutiques line the streets around Via Manzoni, Via Monte Napoleone, and Via della Spirga. Even away from Milan, in the lake resorts and the prosperous Lombard cities, luxury items fill the shop windows of the main streets. The region doesn't boast any particular local crafts or distinctive souvenir items either; for most travelers on a budget, window-shopping will probably replace actual retail transactions here.

The Arts and Nightlife   Milan is Lombardy's chief destination for culture and entertainment. The most famous venue is La Scala opera house, which offers classical concerts in October and November and a world-class opera season from early December through May. A night at La Scala can be the highlight of an opera buff's trip to Italy.

Highlights for First-Time Visitors

Accademia Carrara, Bergamo (Tour 2: Cities of the Plain).
Bellagio, Lake Como (Tour 3: Lake Garda).
Camera degli Sposi in the Palazzo Ducale, Mantua (Tour 2: Cities of the Plain).
Certosa, Pavia (Tour 2: Cities of the Plain).
Duomo (Tour 1: Milan).
Pinacoteca di Brera (Tour 1: Milan).
Santa Maria delle Grazie, the *Last Supper* (Tour 1: Milan).
Stresa (Tour 3: Lake Garda).

Tour 1: Milan

Milan's history as a capital city goes back at least 2,500 years. Its fortunes ever since, both as a great commercial trading center and as the object of regular conquest and occupation, are readily explained by its strategic position at the center of the Lombard plain. Directly south of the central passes across the Alps, Milan is bordered by three highly navigable rivers—the Po, the Ticino, and the Adda—which for centuries were the main arteries of an ingenious network of canals crisscrossing all Lombardy (and ultimately reaching most of northern Italy).

Virtually every invader in European history—Gaul, Roman, Goth, Longobard, and Frank—as well as every ruler of France, Spain, and Austria, has taken a turn at ruling the city and the region. Milan's glorious heyday of self-rule proved comparatively brief, from 1277 until 1500, when it was ruled by its two great family dynasties, the Visconti and subsequently the Sforza. These families were known, justly or not, for a peculiarly aristocratic mixture of refinement, classical learning, and cruelty, and much of the surviving grandeur of Gothic and Renaissance art and architecture is their doing. Be on the lookout in your wanderings for the Visconti family emblem—a viper, its jaws straining wide, devouring a child.

If you are wondering why so little seems to have survived from Milan's antiquity, the answer is simple—war. Three times in the city's history, partial or total destruction has followed conflict—in AD 539, 1157, and 1944.

From Overseas
By Plane
Milan has two principal airports. **Malpensa,** about 50 kilometers (31 miles) northwest of the city, handles all intercontinental traffic, and **Linate,** less than 10 kilometers (6 miles) east of the city, handles international and domestic traffic. For information for both airports, call 02/748-52200. Air Pullman buses run twice daily in the morning between Malpensa and Linate. The fare is 15,000 lire, and the ride takes 75 minutes.

A taxi stand is located directly outside the arrivals building doors at Malpensa. It will cost about 100,000 lire to get downtown. It's far cheaper to take the bus, which usually leaves every half hour between 8:15 AM and 11:15 PM. The cost is 10,000 lire, and it takes one hour to Milan's Milano Centrale (Central Station). Buy your ticket inside before embarking.

At Linate airport there is also a taxi stand directly in front of the arrivals building. Approximate fare to downtown is 20,000 lire, and the trip takes less than 20 minutes. Buses leave from Linate every 20 minutes for Milano Centrale. The trip takes about 20 minutes and costs 3,000 lire. You can also take ATM municipal bus No. 73 to Piazza San Babila (every 15 minutes 1,100 lire).

From Rome
By Train
Crack ETR 450 trains connect Rome and Milan, with departures in the morning and evening. The trip takes only four hours but costs about 140,000 lire one-way, including a mediocre breakfast or supper on a tray. An Intercity train costs 60,000 lire in second class; the trip takes about five hours from Rome. Trains arrive at **Milano Centrale** (tel. 02/675000), a bombastic, neo-Babylonian creation opened in 1931; it's located northeast of the historic center, about 5 kilometers (3 miles) from the Duomo and Galleria. Metro Line 3 links it with Piazza del Duomo.

By Bus
There is no bus service between Rome and Milan.

By Car
The drive from Rome to Milan on the A1 autostrada takes about six hours. Milan is surrounded by a ring road, the Tangenziale.

By Plane
From Rome's Da Vinci airport, the Alitalia shuttle flies to Milan's Linate airport, with departures every hour or even more frequently during peak hours. The trip takes less than an hour. Rome–Milan airfare is approximately 235,000 lire.

Getting Around Milan
By Public Transport
Milan has an excellent system of public transport, consisting of trolley cars, buses, and a subway system, the Metropolitana, which runs on three lines. Tickets for each must be purchased before you board and must be canceled by machines located at underground station entrances and mounted on poles inside trolleys and buses. Tickets cost 1,100 lire and can be purchased from news vendors, tobacconists, and machines at larger stops. Buy several at once—they remain valid until canceled.

By Car
Serious pollution is responsible for a rigorously enforced effort to ban all unnecessary traffic from the city's center. Cars lacking a special resident's permit will be stopped and ticketed. Parked cars may be towed. For taxi service, call 02/6767, 02/8585, or 02/8388. If age or infirmity entitle you to special dispensation and both taxis and other forms of cars with drivers

are unsuitable for your needs, ask your rental agency or hotel concierge for information about car permits for special cases.

By Bicycle As part of its campaign to ban cars from Milan's center, the city government has begun to set up a network of one-way bicycle-rental stations. At first rentals were free; now there is a small charge. Though the bicycles are clearly intended for residents who would otherwise use cars, current opinion is that tourists may use them, too (though individual proprietors of stands may arbitrarily decide to disagree, especially if you are unable to explain your rights in Italian). Look for yellow stands filled with yellow bicycles.

By Taxi Taxi fares seem expensive compared with those in American cities: A short downtown hop averages 8,000 lire. But drivers are honest here (to an extreme, compared with some cities).

Milan

Tourist offices: Stazione Centrale, tel. 02/669–0432; Via Marconi 1, off Piazza del Duomo, tel. 02/809662.

Numbers in the margin correspond to points of interest on the Milan map.

There's only one logical place to begin a walking tour of **Milan**—the **Duomo** (Cathedral), which has been fascinating and exasperating visitors and conquerors alike since it was begun by Galeazzo Visconti III, first duke of Milan, in 1386. Consecrated in 1577, and not wholly completed until 1897, it is the third-largest church in the world and the largest Gothic building in Italy.

Whether you concur with travel writer H. V. Morton, writing 25 years ago, that the cathedral is "one of the mightiest Gothic buildings ever created," or regard it as a spiny pastiche of centuries, there is no denying that for sheer size and complexity it is unequaled. Its capacity—though it is hard to imagine the church filled—is reckoned to be 40,000. Usually it is empty, a perfect sanctuary from the frenetic pace of life outside and the perfect place for solitary contemplation. The poet Shelley swore by it—claiming it was the only place to read Dante.

The building is adorned with 135 marble spires and 2,245 marble statues. The oldest part is the apse (the end of the cruciform opposite the portals). Its three colossal bays of curving and countercurved tracery, especially the bay adorning the exterior of the stained-glass windows, should not be missed.

Step inside and walk down the right aisle to the southern transept, to the tomb of Gian Giacomo Medici. The tomb owes something to Michelangelo but is generally considered its sculptor's (Leone Leoni's) masterpiece; it dates from the 1560s.

Directly ahead is the Duomo's most famous sculpture, the rather gruesome but anatomically instructive figure of St. Bartholomew, whose glorious martyrdom consisted of being flayed alive. It is usually said the saint stands "holding" his skin, but this is not quite accurate. It would appear more that he is luxuriating in it, much as a 1950s matron might show off a new fur stole.

As you enter the apse to admire those splendid windows, glance at the sacristy doors to the right and left of the altar.

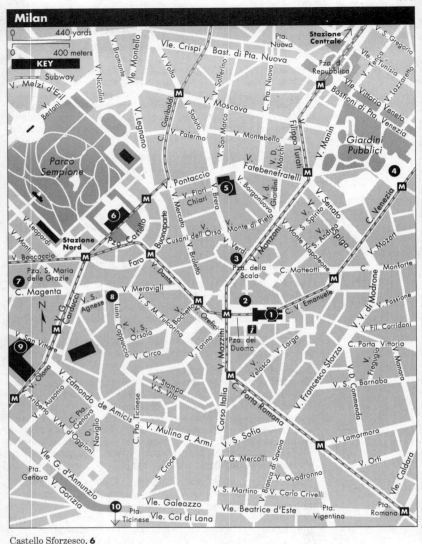

Milan

The lunette on the right dates from 1393; that on the left also dates from the 14th century.

Don't miss a visit to the Duomo's roof: Walk outside the left (north) transept to the stairs and elevator. Sad to say, late-20th-century air pollution has, on all but the rarest days, drastically reduced the view. But even in fog, the roof itself has a fairy-tale quality. As you stand among the forest of marble pinnacles, remember that virtually every inch of this gargantuan edifice, including the roof itself, is covered with precious white marble. *Admission: 3,000 lire for stairs, 5,000 lire for elevator.*

If you wish to learn more about the cathedral's history and see some of the treasures that have been removed from the exterior for safety, visit the **Duomo Museum.** *Museo del Duomo, Piazza del Duomo 14B, tel. 02/860358. Admission: 5,000 lire. Open Tues.–Sun. 9:30–12:30 and 3–6.*

The subterranean ruins of a 4th-century **baptistery** are located beneath the Duomo's piazza. Though opinion remains divided, it is widely believed that this may have been where Ambrose (Milan's first bishop and patron saint) baptized Augustine. *Battistero Paleocristiano. Access through the cathedral. Admission free. Open Tues.–Sun. 10–noon and 3–5.*

② The great glass-topped, barrel-vaulted tunnel just beyond the northern tip of the cathedral's facade is the **Galleria Vittorio Emanuele.** Anyone who has grown up on the periphery of a contemporary American city should recognize this spectacularly extravagant late-19th-century creation for what it is—one of the planet's earliest and most elegant shopping malls, rivaled perhaps only by G.U.M., off Red Square in Moscow, for sheer Belle Epoque splendor. Its architect, Giuseppe Mengoni, accidentally lost his footing and tumbled to his death on the floor of his own creation, just days before its opening.

Like its suburban American cousins, the Galleria fulfills a variety of social functions vastly more important than its ostensible commercial purpose. If you had only a half hour to spend in Milan, this would be the place to spend it. This is the city's heart, midway between the cathedral and La Scala opera house, and it is sometimes called *Il Salotto* (The Living Room). If you're a bit weary from your exploration of the Duomo, stop here to enjoy that most delightful of spectator sports—people-watching. Pull up a chair at one of the strategically situated tables that spill from the Galleria's bars and restaurants, and prepare to enjoy one of those monstrously surcharged coffees that are the modest price of a front-row seat at one of the best shows in Italy.

Like the cathedral, the Galleria is cruciform in shape. The space at the crossing, however, forms an octagon. If this is where you're standing, don't be afraid to look up and gawk. Even in poor weather, the great glass dome makes a splendid sight. And the mosaics, usually unnoticed, are a vastly underrated source of pleasure, even if they are not to be taken too seriously. They represent Europe, Asia, Africa, and America; those at the entrance arch are devoted to science, industry, art, and agriculture.

Books, clothing, food, wine, pens, jewelry, and myriad other goods are all for sale in the Galleria, and one of Milan's most correct and traditional restaurants, Savini, is located here.

There is, in addition, one of those curious Italian institutions, an *Albergo Diurno* (Daytime Hotel), where you can take an hour's nap or a bath, get a haircut or a pedicure, and have your suit pressed or a button replaced. Most of its patrons are Italian, but it is hard to think of a better oasis for a vacationer who's worn out from sightseeing.

Continue through the Galleria and head north into Piazza della Scala, home of the Teatro alla Scala, or **La Scala,** where Verdi's fame was established. It was completely renovated after its destruction by Allied bombs in 1943 and reopened at a performance led by Arturo Toscanini in 1946.

You need know nothing of opera to sense that, like Carnegie Hall, La Scala is something rather more than an auditorium. It looms as a symbol—both for the performer dreaming one day of singing here and for the buff who knows every note of *Rigoletto* by heart. For some, a visit to La Scala will be—even more than the Duomo—a solemn but pleasurable act of pilgrimage.

If you are lucky enough to be here during the opera season, which runs for approximately six months beginning each December, do whatever is necessary to attend—even if it requires perching among the rafters in one of the dread gallery seats. Hearing a Verdi or Puccini opera sung in Italian by Italians in Italy is a magical experience. For now, whet your appetite with a stroll through the theater's small museum, **Museo Teatrale alla Scala.** *Tel. 02/805-3418. Admission: 5,000 lire. Open year-round, Mon.-Sat. 9-noon and 2-6, plus May-Oct., Sun. 9:30-noon. Closed occasionally during rehearsals.*

At the northern end of Piazza della Scala, Via Manzoni leads straight into the heart of Milan's most luxurious shopping district, perhaps the most luxurious in all of Italy. Right here, in a few small streets laid out like a game of hopscotch—Via Monte Napoleone, Via Sant'Andrea, Via della Spiga—lie the shops of the great Italian designers, such as Armani, Versace, and Gianfranco Ferre. Don't expect affordable fashion—that has been relegated to the other side of the Duomo—but it costs nothing to stroll around and drink in the distinctive Milanese look and style. Milan's fortissimo is ready-to-wear, and twice a year, in March and October, the world's fashion elite descend upon the city for the famous ready-to-wear designer shows that invariably set next season's styles around the globe.

At the northern end of Via Manzoni you'll reach the **Giardini Pubblici,** a good park for young children. On the eastern side of the park, facing Corso Venezia, is the **Civico Museo di Storia Naturale,** with exhibits that appeal to animal and nature lovers. *Corso Venezia 55. Admission free. Open Tues.-Fri. 9:30-5:30, Sat., Sun. 9:30-7:30.*

From the southwestern corner of the park, follow Via Fatebenefratelli and then Via Pontaccio to Via Brera, where you'll find the **Pinacoteca di Brera,** on the right at No. 28. The picture collection here is star-studded, even by Italian standards. We suggest that you begin with the best, and leave the charming minor masterpieces for afterward. Ignore the 20th-century work displayed along the long entrance corridor and walk to the large, well-patrolled room (No. 22) with only two big paintings, both of which are behind glass.

It is hard to believe that Raphael painted the *Betrothal of the Virgin* when he was only 22, an age at which many of us are still struggling with the question of what to do with our lives. The other painting, Piero della Francesca's *Madonna with Saints and Angels*, is earlier but just as lovely, and much aided by its recent and skillful restoration and cleaning.

The gallery's best-known painting is probably the somber, beautiful, and moving *Dead Christ* by Mantegna, in Room 18. Though it is by far the smallest painting in the room, it dominates, with its sparse palette of gray and terra-cotta. Mantegna's shocking, almost surgical, precision in the rendering of Christ's wounds—the face propped up on a pillow, the day's growth of beard—tells of an all too human agony. It is one of the most quietly wondrous achievements of the Renaissance period, finding an unsuspected middle ground between the excesses of conventional gore and beauty in representing the Passion's saddest moment.

On your way out, pause a moment to view the fine paintings of Carlo Carrà (especially *La Musa Metafisica*, or *Metaphysical Muse*), suggesting Italy's confident and stylish response to the likes of Picasso and Max Ernst, and to the schools of Cubism and Surrealism. *Tel. 02/864–63501. Admission: 8,000 lire. Open Tues.–Sat. 9–5:30, Sun. 9–1.*

Take time to wander around the lively quarter surrounding the Pinacoteca di Brera. The narrow streets, lined by boutiques, crafts shops, cafés, restaurants, and music clubs, comprise what is often referred to as Milan's Greenwich Village. Longtime haunt of artists and musicians, it has a number of clubs and cafés that offer live music until late at night.

❻ The imposing **Castello Sforzesco** is a little more than two blocks west, along Via Pontaccio. For the serious student of Renaissance military engineering, it must be something of a travesty, so often has it been remodeled or rebuilt since it was begun in 1450 by the condottiere who founded the city's second dynastic family, Francesco Sforza, fourth duke of Milan. As for the rest of us, it's clearly everything a storybook castle ought to be. Huge, for one. It is also just across the road from what is claimed to be the best gelateria, or ice cream shop, in all northern Italy: **Viel** (Largo Cairoli) is at the right of the intersection in front of the Castello's southeast face.

Though today the word *mercenary* has a pejorative ring, during the Renaissance all Italy's great soldier-heroes were professionals hired by the cities and principalities they served. Of them—and there were thousands—Francesco Sforza is considered to have been one of the greatest and most honest. It is said that he could remember not only the names of his men but of their horses as well. It is with his era, and the building of the Castello, that we enter the enlightened age of the Renaissance.

Today the Castello houses municipal museums variously devoted to Egyptian and other antiquities, musical instruments, paintings, and sculpture. Highlights are the Salle delle Asse, a frescoed room still sometimes attributed to Leonardo da Vinci, and Michelangelo's unfinished *Rondanini Pietà*, believed to be his last work: an astounding achievement for a man nearly 90, but a sad memorial to genius at the end. *Piazza Castello. Tel. 02/6236, ext. 3947. Admission free. Open daily 9:30–5:30. Closed last Tues. of month.*

H.V. Morton noted that Milan might well be the only city on earth where you could give a taxi driver the title of a painting as your destination. If this appeals to you, flag one down and say, "*L'ultima Cena*, per favore," since this is how *The Last Supper* is known here. If not, walk a few blocks southwest of the Castello to the church and former Dominican monastery of **7** **Santa Maria delle Grazie**, on Corso Magenta. The famous work is in the **Cenacolo Vinciano**, which used to be the order's refectory.

The Last Supper has had an almost unbelievable history of bad luck and neglect—its near destruction in an American bombing raid in August 1943 was only the latest chapter in a series of misadventures, including, if one 19th-century source is to be believed, being whitewashed by the monks. Well-meant but disastrous attempts at restoration have done little to rectify the problem of the work's placement: It is situated on a wall that is unusually vulnerable to climatic dampness. Yet the artist chose to work slowly and patiently in oil pigments—which demand dry plaster—instead of proceeding hastily on wet plaster according to the conventional fresco technique. Aldous Huxley called it "the saddest work of art in the world." After years beneath a scaffold, with restorers patiently shifted from one square centimeter to another, Leonardo's famous masterpiece is still in a sad state, and studies in further methods to preserve this great fresco continue. However, it is nearer to its original glory than it has been at any time since the artist's death in 1519.

Despite Leonardo's carefully preserved preparatory sketches, in which the apostles are clearly labeled by name, there still remains some debate about a few identities in the final arrangement. But there can be no mistaking Judas, small and dark, his hand calmly reaching forward toward the bread, isolated from the terrible confusion that has taken the hearts of the others. One critic, Professor Frederick Hartt, offers an elegantly terse explanation for why the composition works: It combines "dramatic confusion" with "mathematical order." Certainly, the skillful and unobtrusive repetition of threes—in the windows, in the grouping of the figures, and in their placement—adds a mystical aspect to what at first seems simply the perfect observation of spontaneous human gesture. *Cenacolo Vinciano, tel. 02/498-7588. Admission: 6,000 lire. Open Tues.-Sun. 9-1:15, but hours may vary.*

Take at least a moment to visit Santa Maria delle Grazie itself. It's a handsome church, with a fine dome by Bramante, which was added along with a cloister at about the time Leonardo was commissioned to paint *The Last Supper*. If you're wondering how it was that two such giants came to be employed decorating and remodeling the refectory and church of a comparatively modest religious order, and not, say, the Duomo, the answer lies in the ambitious but largely unrealized plan to turn Santa Maria delle Grazie into a magnificent Sforza family mausoleum. Though Ludovico Il Moro Sforza, seventh duke of Milan, was but one generation away from the founding of the Sforza dynasty, he was its last ruler. Two years after Leonardo finished *The Last Supper*, Ludovico was defeated and imprisoned in a French dungeon for the remaining eight years of his life.

Go east on Corso Magenta, across Via Carducci, to visit the **8** city's **Museo Archeologico**. Housed in a former monastery, there are some enlightening relics from Milan's Roman past here, from everyday utensils and jewelry to several fine examples of mosaic pavement. *Corso Magenta 15. tel. 02/806598. Admission free. Open Wed.–Mon. 9:30–5:30.*

Next to the Museo Archeologico, Via Sant'Agnese leads to the church of **Sant'Ambrogio.** From there, take Via San Vittore to see the **Museo Nazionale della Scienza e della Tecnica,** which has models based on technical projects by Leonardo da Vinci and collections of locomotives, planes, and cars. *Via San Vittore 21, near Sant'Ambrogio, tel. 02/480-0040. Admission: 8,000 lire. Open Tues.–Sun. 9:30–4:50.*

If you have time, walk back to Via Carducci, which becomes Via Edmondo de Amicis, and follow it southeast until you can turn right onto Corso Porta Ticinese, which ends at the impressive early 19th-century arch of Porta Ticinese. Beyond lies the picturesque **Navigli district** in the southern part of the city. In medieval times a network of navigable canals, called *navigli*, crisscrossed Milan. Almost all have been covered over, except for two long canals, Naviglio Grande and Naviglio Pavese, and part of a third, Darsena. The canals are lined by quaint shops, art galleries, cafés, pubs, restaurants, and clubs. Much of Milan's nightlife is centered here, and the neighborhood has a romantic, bohemian atmosphere.

Lodging
Under 125,000 lire

Città Studi. Near the University and Piazzale Susa, this is a functionally furnished, modern hotel. Most rooms have private showers; the few without are an even better bargain. Take bus No. 61 from downtown. *Via Saldini 24, tel. 02/744666, fax 02/713122. 45 rooms, all with bath. AE, MC, V.*

London. A 10-minute walk from the Duomo, near the Cairoli Metro station, this clean hotel has large rooms, though the bathrooms are somewhat cramped. The friendly staff speaks English. *Via Rovello 3, tel. 02/720–2166, fax 02/805–7037. 29 rooms, 24 with bath. MC, V. Closed Dec. 23–Jan. 3 and Aug.*

La Pace. Located near the Loreto Metro station, La Pace has some furnishings with an attractive 19th-century look and a tiny garden. Bedrooms are in modern style. *Via Alfredo Catalani 69, tel. 02/261–9700, fax 02/261–12091. 20 rooms with bath. AE, DC, MC, V.*

San Francisco. Near the Piazzale Piola Metro station, this modern hotel has functional furnishings, with the added convenience of a TV and a telephone in the rooms. Family-run, it offers an inner garden. *Viale Lombardia 55, tel. 02/236–1009, fax 02/266–80377. 33 rooms, 31 with bath. AE, DC, MC, V.*

Under 100,000 lire

San Marco. A small, quiet hotel near the Loreto Metro station, it has clean bedrooms, a few without bath and therefore in this price category. It is a favorite with American students. *Via Piccinni 25, tel. 02/295–16414, fax 02/295–13243. 11 rooms, 7 with bath. MC, V.*

Under 65,000 lire

Arthur. Near the Stazione Centrale on a street where many 19th-century buildings have been converted to house small hotels of varying grades of acceptability, this hotel is one of the better establishments. It has large, clean rooms and faint touches of old-fashioned elegance at rock-bottom prices. *Via Lazzaretto 14, tel. 02/204–6294. 11 rooms, 7 with bath. No credit cards.*

Valley. Close to the Stazione Centrale and Metro lines, the Valley is clean and convenient. Guest rooms are basic; only three doubles with bath are available. Some of the staff speak English. *Via Superga 19, tel. 02/669–2777. 10 rooms, 8 with bath. No credit cards.*

Villa Mira. Near the Loreto Metro station, this family-run establishment is good value. All doubles have private bathrooms, and rooms are spotless though somewhat stark. *Via Sacchini 19, tel. 02/295–25618. 10 rooms, 8 with bath. No credit cards.*

Dining
Under 45,000 lire

La Capanna. A family-run trattoria with an upscale wine list, La Capanna is near the university and the Piazzale Piola Metro station. The menu offers classic Milanese dishes and such novelties as *spaghetti all'Attilio* (spaghetti with a creamy sauce of basil, garlic, and sausage), as well as seafood. The *torta di mele* is the Italian version of homemade apple pie. *Via Donatello 9, tel. 02/294–00884. Reservations advised. AE, DC, MC, V. Closed Mon. evening, Sat., and Aug.*

Dina e Pierino. This busy and friendly trattoria in the Brera district is decorated in early 1900s style. The menu features Tuscan cuisine. *Via Marsala 2, tel. 02/659–9488. Reservations advised. No credit cards. Closed Mon. and Aug.*

La Frittata. Near Sant'Ambrogio and the Porta Nuova Station, this small Tuscan restaurant and pizzeria stays open late. Take tram No. 8 from Cordusio. *Viale Papiniano 43, tel. 02/402643. AE, MC, V. Closed Tues. and Aug.*

Trattoria La Pesa. This popular eating place is a little out of the way, but Milanese consider it worth the trip. It is near the De Angeli Metro and bus No. 63 stops. The decor is straightforward trattoria style, and the menu features the specialties of Milan: *cotoletta* (breaded veal chop) and *osso buco* (braised veal shank). There is a room for nonsmokers and a bargain fixed-price lunch. *Via Fantoni 26, corner Via Rembrandt, tel. 02/403–5907. Reservations advised in the evening. AE, DC, MC, V. Closed Mon. evening and Sun.*

Under 35,000 lire

Abele. Open only in the evening, until late, this trattoria is simple and usually crowded. The specialties of the house are a selection of risottos and meal-size salads. It is located off Viale Monza, near Piazzale Loreto (Pasteur Metro station). *Via Temperanza 5, tel. 02/261–3855. Reservations advised. No credit cards. Closed Mon.*

La Bruschetta. You'll find this tiny, busy pizzeria off Corso Vittorio Emanuele, behind the Duomo; it is run by a partnership of Tuscans and Neapolitans. The wood stove is in full view, so you can see your pizza cooking in front of you, although there are plenty of nonpizza dishes available, too, such as *spaghetti alle cozze e vongole* (spaghetti with clam and mussel sauce). *Piazza Beccaria 12, tel. 02/802494. Reservations advised, but fast service means you never wait long. No credit cards. Closed Mon., Aug. 1–21, Dec. 24–28, Good Fri.–Easter Mon.*

Margherita. High-tech ambience, with pastel-colored neon tubing switched on high, characterizes this pizzeria near Piazza Castello and the Cairoli Metro station. *Via Giovanni sul Muro 5, tel. 02/805–3939. MC, V. Closed Sun.*

La Piazzetta. This busy lunch spot in the Brera district offers a salad bar and some hot dishes. *Via Solferino 25, tel. 02/659–1076. No credit cards. Closed Sun., Easter, and Aug.*

Taverna Moriggi. Near the stock exchange, it's a dusky, wood-paneled wine bar serving a fixed-price lunch for about 30,000 lire, or cold cuts and cheeses in the evening. *Via Moriggi 8, tel. 02/864–50880. No credit cards. Closed Sat. lunch and Sun.*

Under 25,000 lire **Grand'Italia.** Big and busy, it's crowded at lunchtime, when you can have pizza, *focaccia* (a pizza-like baked flat bread) with sandwich fillings, or a fixed-price lunch. The mood changes in the evening; although pizza is still available, a full meal can be costly. It's near the Moscova Metro station. *Via Palermo 5, tel. 02/877759. Closed Tues. and Sat. lunch.*

Magenta. Founded in 1908, Bar Magenta is a monument to Art Nouveau style and a swinging Milanese hangout. From late morning until 2 AM you can order thick, made-to-order sandwiches and light snacks. It's a lunchtime favorite of people in the fashion trade. *Via Carducci 13, at Corso Magenta, tel. 02/805–3808. No credit cards. Closed Mon.*

Panino Giusto. Some consider the sandwiches here to be the best in Milan. Try the Madeira, made with paté, creamy caprino cheese, and port wine. *Corso Garibaldi 125; tel. 02/655–4728. No credit cards. Closed Sun.*

Peck. A Milanese institution, this is a gourmet *rosticceria* (a sort of traditional fast-food place), with an array of luscious things to take out or eat on the spot. The location is handy for sightseers, near Piazza del Duomo. *Via Cantù 3, tel. 02/869–3017. AE, DC, MC, V. Closed Sun. and Mon.*

San Tomaso. An old beer hall in the Brera district, the San Tomaso has cafeteria-style lunch with made-to-order salads, cheese platters, and cold cuts. Very busy at lunchtime, it's quieter for supper. *Via San Tomaso 5, tel. 02/874510. Reservations advised in evening. No credit cards. Closed Sat. lunch and Sun.*

Spaghetteria. Near the Brera gallery, this restaurant is open only in the evening. The menu offers an amazing variety of pasta dishes: Order *assaggini* to taste several different types for one low price. *Via Solferino 3, tel. 02/872735. AE, MC, V. Closed Mon.*

Splurge
★ **Boeucc.** This restaurant (pronounced "birch") is Milan's oldest. It is located in the same square as novelist Alessandro Manzoni's house, not far from La Scala. Subtly lit, with cream-color fluted columns, chandeliers, thick carpets, and a garden for warm-weather dining, it has come a long way from the time when it was simply a cellar tavern, or "hole" (*boeucc* is old Milanese for hole). It serves Milanese food and a wide range of other dishes, including *penne al branzino e zucchine* (pasta with sea bass and zucchini sauce) and *gelato di castagne con zabaglione caldo* (chestnut ice cream with hot zabaglione). A full meal with wine costs about 85,000 lire. *Piazza Belgioioso 2, tel. 02/760–202224. Reservations required. Jacket advised. AE. Closed Sat., Sun. lunch, Aug., and Dec. 24–28.*

Shopping An Armani or Ferre ensemble can set you back several thousand dollars, but similar Italian taste and styling can be found at more affordable prices at **Fiorucci** (in the Galleria Passarella), **Benetton,** and **Emporio Armani,** or the department stores **La Rinascente** (in Piazza del Duomo) and **Coin** (Piazza Loreto). In between are covetable but sensible Italian fashion buys at shops like **Biffi, Komlas, Gemelli,** and **Max Mara.**

Canny Milanese regularly make the rounds of the dozens of factory outlets and discount stores in the city, often finding designer labels at 30%–70% off. Stock changes daily, and credit cards are not always accepted. Some of the better-known discount stores for men's and women's fashions (and in some cases, shoes) are **Il Salvagente** (Via Fratelli Bronzetti 16, tel. 02/761–

10328), **Leuce** (Via Panizzi 6, tel. 02/489–50907), **St. Laurent-Rive Gauche** (Piazza Sant'Erasmo 3, tel. 02/655–7795), **Stockhouse** (Via Alunno 10, tel. 02/403–6748), **Niki** (Via Fontana 19, tel. 02/551–81284), and **Floretta Coen** (Via San Calogero 3, tel. 02/839–7708). You can find designer shoes at whopping discounts at the outdoor market at **Piazzale Martini** on Wednesday morning and Saturday.

Shops are usually open 9–1 (closed Mon. morning) and 4–7:30; many are closed in August. Here are other possibilities:

Brera is an area with many unique shops. Walk along Via Brera, Via Solferino, Corso Garibaldi, and Via Paolo Sarpi.

Corso Buenos Aires is a wide avenue with a variety of shops, several offering moderately priced items.

Corso Vittorio Emanuele has clothing, leather goods, and shoe shops, some with items at reasonable prices.

Street markets on Saturday and Tuesday at **Viale Papiniano** (Metro: Sant'Agostino) and **Via Fauché** (Metro: Garibaldi) offer foodstuffs and a vast array of other goods sold at open-air stalls. Bargaining is no longer the custom; prices should be clearly marked. On Saturday, the **Senigallia** fair on Via Calatafimi (take bus No. 65) has old and new items. For old coins or stamps there is a specialized market on **Via Armorari,** near Piazza Cordusio (Metro: Cordusio). The best antiques markets are held on the last Sunday of each month along the **Navigli** and on the third Saturday of each month on **Via Fiori Chiari,** near Via Brera.

The Arts and Nightlife

Opera

The season at Milan's famous **La Scala** opera house runs from December 7 (St. Ambrose Day) through May. Seats are sold out well in advance. For information on schedules and the (unlikely) possibility of box-office tickets, contact Teatro alla Scala (Piazza della Scala, tel. 02/807041). To book tickets in advance, go to the entrance at Via Filodrammatici 2, or call 02/720–003744; if available, SRO tickets are sold before performances at the Museo della Scala entrance, to the left of the main entrance. From abroad you can book in advance by mail or fax (02/887–9297) or at CIT or other travel agencies (at agencies, no more than 10 days before performance). Consult the weekly *Viva Milano* for listings. Tickets start at 20,000 lire (standing room 10,000 lire) and go up to 200,000 lire. La Scala also presents a two-month season of classical concerts in October and November.

Theater

Milan's **Piccolo Teatro** (Via Rovello 2, tel. 02/877663) and **Teatro Manzoni** (Via Manzoni 40, tel. 02/790543) are noted for their excellent productions, but you'll need to speak Italian in order to appreciate them.

Jazz

Le Scimmie (Via Ascanio Sforza 49, tel. 02/894–02874) is a good spot for cool jazz in a relaxed atmosphere.

Discos

Lizard (Largo La Foppa, tel. 02/659–0890, closed Mon.) is trendy, loud, and expensive—a formula that doesn't deter the young Milanese crowd.

Contatto (Corso Sempione 76, tel. 02/331–4904, open daily midnight–dawn) and **After Dark** (Via Certosa 134, Milan, tel. 02/305585, closed Tues.) are gay clubs/discos for men only.

Bars **Gershwin's** (Via Corrado il Salico 10, tel. 02/849–7722) is a relaxed piano bar, where Cole Porter and Noel Coward, along with the bar's namesake, figure in the repertoire.

El Brellin (Vicolo Lavandai at the corner of Alzaia Naviglio Grande, tel. 02/5810–1351, closed Sun.) is one of the many bars in the Navigli district.

Tour 2: Cities of the Plain

This tour takes in some of the great Lombard cities of the Po River plain south of Milan—Pavia, most celebrated for its extravagant Certosa, or charterhouse; Bergamo, home of the Accademia Carrara, one of Italy's major art museums; Brescia, once part of the Venetian empire; and melancholy Mantua, home for almost 300 years of the fantastically wealthy Gonzaga dynasty. Each town is easily reached directly from Milan.

From Milan Intercity bus service is provided by such companies as SIA, **By Bus** SAL, and Autostradale; it is neither faster, cheaper, nor more convenient than train service. Most buses leave from Piazza Castello. For bus information, call **Autostradale** (tel. 02/801161) or **Zani Viaggi** (tel. 02/867131).

Pavia

To visit the town of Pavia itself, take the 30-minute train ride (fare 3,200 lire) from Milan on the main line to Genoa; from Pavia, a bus to the Certosa (fare 1,800 lire) leaves from Piazza Piave, in front of the train station. If you only want to visit the Certosa, take a direct bus from Piazza Castello in Milan (the trip takes about 45 minutes and costs 4,000 lire). Tourist office: Via Fabio Filzi 2, near the train station, tel. 0382/22156.

Located at the confluence of the Ticino and Po rivers, about 38 kilometers (24 miles) south of Milan, Pavia was once Milan's chief local rival. The city dates at least from the Roman era and was the capital of the Lombard kings for two centuries (572–774). Pavia subsequently came to be known as "the city of a hundred towers" (of which only a handful have survived). Its prestigious **university** was founded in 1361 on the site of a 10th-century law school but has claims dating from antiquity. The 14th-century **Castello Visconteo** (Piazza Castello) now houses the local **Museo Civico** (Civic Museum), which has an interesting archaeological collection and a picture gallery featuring works by Correggio (admission 5,000 lire, open Tues.–Sun. 9–1:30). Go right from the castle entrance and turn right, off Via Matteotti, to visit the tomb of Christianity's most celebrated convert, St. Augustine, housed in a Gothic marble ark on the high altar of the Romanesque church of **San Pietro in Ciel d'Oro.**

The main reason for stopping in Pavia, however, is to see the **Certosa** (the Carthusian monastery), 8 kilometers (5 miles) north of the city center. Its facade is stupendous, anticipating by several hundred years, with much the same relish as the Duomo in Milan, the delightful first commandment of Victorian architecture: Always decorate the decoration.

The Certosa's extravagant grandeur was due, in part, to the plan to have it house the tombs of the family of the first duke of Milan, Galeazzo Visconti III (he died during a plague, at age 49, in 1402). And extravagant it was—almost unimaginably so

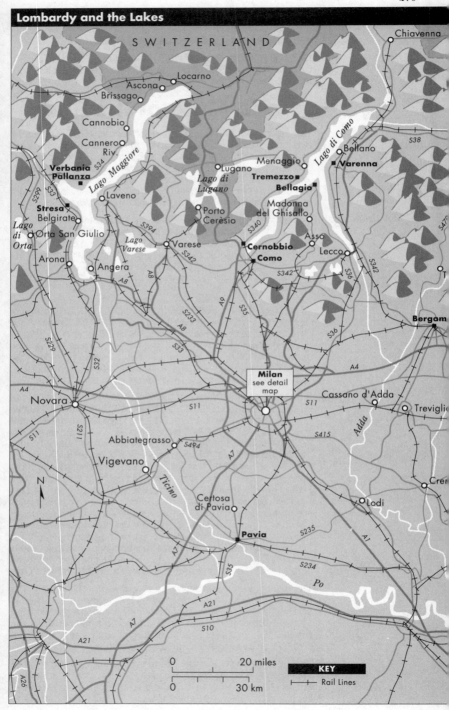

SWITZERLAND

Chiavenna

Locarno

Ascona

Brissago

Cannobio

Cannero Riv.

Lago Maggiore

Lugano

Lago di Lugano

Menaggio

Lago di Como

Bellano

Varenna

Verbania Pallanza

Tremezzo

Bellagio

S34

S33

S629

Stresa

Belgirate

Laveno

Porto Cerèsio

Madonna del Ghisallo

Lago di Orta

Orta San Giulio

Lago Varese

Varese

Cernobbio

Como

Asso

Lecco

S340

S38

S47

Arona

Angera

S394

S342

S342

S36

S342

A8

A8

A9

S35

S36

S233

Bergam

S229

S32

A8

S33

A4

A4

Novara

S11

Milan
see detail map

Cassano d'Adda

S11

Treviglio

S211

Abbiategrasso

S494

A7

Adda

S415

Vigevano

Ticino

Certosa di Pavia

S235

Lodi

Cren

Orta San Giulio

Pavia

S35

S234

A1

A21

Po

A7

A21

S10

A26

N

0 — 20 miles

0 — 30 km

KEY
┼─┼ Rail Lines

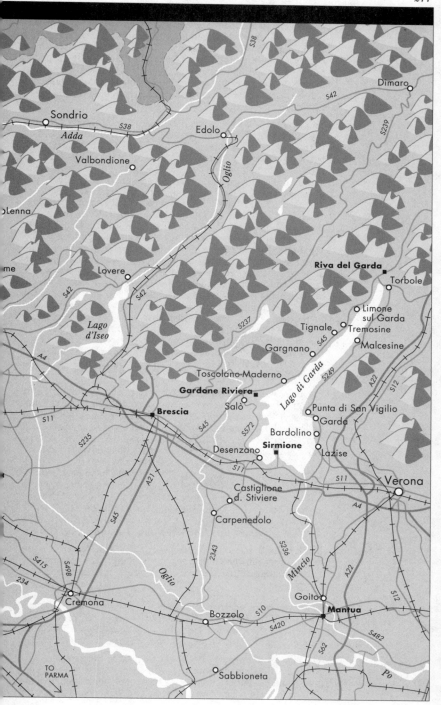

in an age before modern roads and transport. Only the very best marble was used in construction, transported, undoubtedly by barge, from the legendary quarries of Carrara, roughly 240 kilometers (150 miles) away. Though the ground plan may be Gothic—a cruciform in a series of squares—the gorgeous fabric that rises above it is triumphantly Renaissance. On the facade, in the lower frieze, are medallions of Roman emperors and Eastern monarchs; above them are low reliefs of the life of Christ, as well as that of Galeazzo Visconti III.

The first duke was the only Visconti to be interred here, and then only some 75 years after his death, in a tomb designed by Gian Cristoforo Romano. Look for it in the right transept. In the left transept is a tomb of greater human appeal—that of a rather stern middle-aged man and a beautiful young woman. The man is Ludovico il Moro Sforza, seventh duke of Milan, who commissioned Leonardo da Vinci to paint *The Last Supper*. The woman is his wife, one of the most celebrated women of her day, Beatrice d'Este, the embodiment of brains, culture, birth, and beauty. Married when he was 40 and she was 16, they had enjoyed six happy years of marriage when she died suddenly, giving birth to a stillborn child. Ludovico commissioned the sculptor Cristoforo Solari to design a joint tomb for the high altar of Santa Maria delle Grazie in Milan. Originally much larger, the tomb occupied the honored place in Santa Maria delle Grazie for some years as planned. Then, for reasons that are still mysterious, the Dominican monks, who seemed to care no more for their former patron than they did for their faded Leonardo fresco, sold the tomb to their Carthusian brothers to the south. Sadly, part of the tomb, and its remains, were lost. *Certosa, tel. 0382/925613. Admission free, donation requested. Open Sept.–Apr., Tues.–Sun. 9–11:30 and 2:30–4:30; May–Aug. 9–11:30 and 2:30–5:30.*

Dining **Locanda Vecchia Pavia.** Located next to the Duomo in Pavia
Splurge proper, this attractive restaurant decorated in the Art Nou-
★ veau style caters to sophisticated tastes. (If your appetite and budget call for simpler fare, try the well-stocked snack bars on Via Cavour or the Bar Vittoria, Strada Nuova 8). At the Vecchia Pavia you will find creative versions of traditional regional cuisine—including the local specialty, *rane* (frogs) in risotto or on a spit. *Casoncelli* (stuffed pasta) and *costoletta di vitello alla milanese* (breaded veal chop) are done with style, as are more imaginative seafood dishes. A full dinner with wine costs about 85,000 lire. *Via Cardinale Riboldi 2, tel. 0382/304132. Reservations required. Jacket advised. AE, DC, MC, V. Closed Mon., at lunch on Wed., Jan. 1–9, and Aug.*

Festivals During the first half of September, Pavia's **Settembre Pavese** festival presents street processions, displays, and concerts.

Bergamo

Frequent train service from Milan takes an hour and costs 5,000 lire. Tourist office: Viale Papa Giovanni XXIII 106, near the train station in the lower city, tel. 035/242226; in the upper city, at Vicolo Aquila Nera, off Via Colleoni, tel. 035/232730.

The old city of Bergamo lies at the foot of the Bergamese Alps. Actually, Bergamo is two cities—Bergamo Bassa (Lower Bergamo) and Bergamo Alta (Upper Bergamo), connected by a funicular railway. The train station and bus terminal are in

Bergamo Bassa; take bus No. 1 from the train station to the funicular on Viale Vittorio Emanuele, which runs every 15 minutes between the lower and upper parts of the city. High up on the hillside, walled in by the ruins of ancient Venetian fortifications, surmounted by a fortress, is Bergamo Alta. The principal monuments here—the 12th-century **Palazzo della Ragione,** the massive **Torre del Comune,** the **Duomo,** the church of **Santa Maria Maggiore** (containing the tomb of the 19th-century composer Gaetano Donizetti, who was born in Bergamo), the **Colleoni Chapel,** and the **baptistery**—are in or near the Piazza Vecchia. The dome and the sanctuary of the Colleoni Chapel are resplendent with Tiepolo's frescoes of the life of St. John the Baptist, added in the 18th century. The chapel was built in 1476, in the ornate but delicate Lombard Renaissance style, as a funeral monument for Bartolomeo Colleoni, a *condottiere,* or mercenary commander, who served Venice. *Admission free. Open daily 9–noon and 3–6.*

Take the funicular back down to Bergamo Bassa to see the **Accademia Carrara.** (If you want to go on foot, walk down Via Porta Dipinta to Porta Sant'Agostino, then down the steep, stairlike Via Noca to Piazza Carrara.) The Accademia Carrara is one of Italy's greatest and most important art collections. Many of the Venetian masters are represented—Mantegna, Carpaccio, Tiepolo, Guardi, Canaletto—and there are some magnificent Bellinis and Botticellis as well. *Piazza Carrara, tel. 035/399426. Admission 3,000 lire. Sun. free. Open Wed.– Mon. 9:30–12:15 and 2:30–5:15.*

Lodging **Agnello d'Oro.** A gem on a small piazzetta in the heart of Berga-
Under 115,000 lire mo Alta, Agnello d'Oro is a tall, narrow inn where everything
★ seems to be on a reassuringly human scale. The rooms are done in different colors and have lots of old prints on the walls, and many have small balconies with good views of the rest of the upper town. The lively restaurant is small but popular. *Via Gombito 22, tel. 035/249883, fax 035/235612. 20 rooms with bath or shower. Facilities: restaurant (closed Mon. and mid-Jan.– mid-Feb. AE, DC, MC, V.*

Arli. A commercial hotel off the main square in the lower town, this is a reliable choice for an overnight stay. *Largo Porta Nuova 12, tel. 035/222104, fax 035/223–9732. 48 rooms with bath. AE, V.*

Under 60,000 lire **Sant'Antonio.** Centrally located near the station, the Sant'Antonio is basic but clean. It attracts a regular clientele of workers and students from the province. *Via Paleocapa 1, tel. 035/ 210284. 34 rooms, 14 with bath. No credit cards.*

Dining **Casa Mia.** If you are coming from the train station, turn left at
Under 24,000 lire Porta Nuova and then left again at the end of Via Zambonate. This traditional and hospitable *osteria,* or wineshop, is a favorite with blue-collar workers and artisans who work in this part of town. *Cotoletta alla milanese* (breaded veal cutlet) and *coniglio* (rabbit) in various sauces are the specialties. Either reserve for lunch or arrive after 1 PM, when the crowd thins out. The menu of the day costs about 16,000 lire, including the good house wine. *Via San Bernardino 20/a, tel. 035/220–676. Closed Sun. No credit cards.*

Festivals Bergamo's **International Piano Festival,** held in Teatro Donizetti (Piazza Matteotti, tel. 035/249631), attracts world-class musicians in July and August.

Brescia

The Milan–Verona train line passes through Brescia. Some IC trains make the stop. The trip takes 45 minutes on the IC, an hour on the express. The fare is about 7,000 lire. Società Autostradale (tel. 02/801161) buses leave from Milan's Piazza Castello and go directly to the train station in Brescia. Fare is 8,000 lire. Tourist office: Corso Zanardelli 34, near the cathedral, tel. 030/43418.

Strategically located between Milan and Venice, Brescia was founded by the Romans; during the Middle Ages, it was alternately ruled by the neighboring overlords, the Visconti of Milan and the Scaligeri of Verona, then for nearly four centuries (1426–1797) was part of Venice's mainland territories.

The ruins of the **Capitolino,** a Capitoline Temple built by the emperor Vespasian in AD 73, testify to Brescia's Roman origin. Outstanding among the sculptures in the adjoining **Museo Romano** is the famed 1st-century bronze *Winged Victory. Via dei Musei, tel. 030/46031. Admission: 2,000 lire. Open Tues.–Sun. 9–12:30 and 2–5.*

More relics are in the **Museum of Christian Art** (also Via dei Musei), including a remarkable collection of early-medieval pieces, but the museum is only open for temporary exhibitions. (Check with the tourist office.) Otherwise, to the southeast of the center, the **Pinacoteca Tosio-Martinengo** accommodates—besides the works of the Brescia School—pictures by Raphael, Tintoretto, Tiepolo, and Clouet. *Piazza Moretto, tel. 030/ 59120. Admission: 2,000 lire. Open Tues.–Sun. 9–12:30 and 2–5.*

A network of squares in the center of town contains much that is worth savoring. Palladio and Sansovino contributed to the splendid marble **Loggia,** the great Lombard-Venetian palace overlooking Piazza della Loggia. Another palazzo is topped by the 16th-century **Torre dell'Orologio** (Clock Tower), modeled on the campanile in Venice's Piazza San Marco. On Piazza del Duomo, the 17th-century Baroque **cathedral** sits beside the simple 12th-century stone **rotonda.** Among the churches worth visiting is the **Madonna del Carmine,** behind which a flight of stairs climbs to the ramparts of the Venetian **Castello,** high enough to give a panoramic view over the town and across the plain to the distant Alps.

Dining
Under 20,000 lire
Rosticceria Mameli. The take-out counter downstairs offers ready-made pastas and meat courses, as well as fried tidbits. In the upstairs restaurant, a full meal costs about 28,000 lire. *Corso Mameli 53, tel. 030/59502. MC, V. Closed Mon.*

The Arts and Nightlife
The **Teatro Grande** (tel. 030/59448) holds a series of classical music concerts from November to May.

Mantua

By train Mantua is about 2½ hours from Milan (fare is about 10,500 lire), 40 minutes from Verona (3,200 lire). It's an hour from Brescia by bus (fare 6,000 lire). Tourist office: Piazza Mantegna 6, tel. 0376/350681.

Mantua is a rather melancholy city, wrapped in mists from three so-called lakes formed by the widening of the Mincio River. Though a little off the beaten track, it is often crowded with tourists and children on class trips. Mantua is the birthplace of the Roman poet Virgil, but it is better known as the capital of the Gonzaga dynasty's court, a center of Renaissance learning and refinement. During their rule, the Gonzagas built a huge palace and commissioned many famous artists to decorate it, among them Andrea Mantegna (1431–1506).

The Gonzagas, like the Visconti and Sforza of Milan (with whom they intermarried), lived with the regal pomp and circumstance befitting one of Italy's richest family dynasties. Their reign, first as marquesses and later as dukes, was a long one—stretching from the first half of the 14th into the beginning of the 18th century.

Even if you've had enough of old palaces, you may still wish to visit Mantua. First, Virgil was born near here. Second, Mantegna (painter of the poignant *Dead Christ* in Milan's Brera) was the Gonzaga court painter for 50 years, and his best-known and only large surviving fresco cycle can be seen here. In addition, there are two fine churches by Leon Battista Alberti (1404–72): **Sant'Andrea** (1471, some sections earlier or later) and **San Sebastiano** (1461). Both (much like Mantegna's work here) proved highly influential and were widely emulated by lesser architectural lights later in the Renaissance.

From the train station, walk along Via Solferino, Via Fratelli Bandiera, and Via Verdi to get to Piazza Mantegna which, with Piazza delle Erbe and Piazza Sordello, forms the historic heart of the city. Our tour begins at the 500-room complex that centuries of Gonzagas thought of, somehow, as home. The fortress and castle of the **Palazzo Ducale** (Ducal Palace), located at the northeast end of Piazza Sordello, looks like a palace that took centuries to build. From a distance, the group of buildings dwarfs the old town skyline, and the effect is fascinating. Unfortunately, the palace interiors may be seen only on a rigorous guided tour conducted in Italian by the municipality. *Piazza Sordello, tel. 0376/320283. Admission: 10,000 lire. Open Mar.– Sept., Tues.–Sat. 9–1 and 2–5, Sun. and Mon. 9–1; Oct.–Feb., Tues.–Sat. 9–1 and 2–4, Sun. and Mon. 9–1.*

Begun during the 13th century by predecessors of the Gonzagas, then expanded and remodeled by the rulers of Mantua from the 14th through the 18th centuries, the palace complex contains several buildings, courtyards, and gardens. Highlights of the tour include the following:

The **Appartamento dei Nani** (Dwarfs' Apartments) were literally that, dwarf-collecting being one of the more amusing occupations of Renaissance princes. According to historians, the dwarfs were not mistreated but were considered something between members of the family and celebrity comics. The apartments were built both for the dwarfs' delight and for that of the court.

The **Appartamento del Paradiso** (Paradise) is usually praised for its view but is somewhat more interesting for its decorator and first resident, Isabella d'Este. Not only was she married at 16, rather like her younger sister Beatrice (the beautiful young woman of the tomb in the Certosa at Pavia), but she was apparently also Ludovico il Moro Sforza's first and original choice for a wife—until he learned that she was already affianced to a Gonzaga rival. Isabella, too, is regarded as one of the great patrons of the Renaissance. She survived her sister by more than 40 years, and the archives of her correspondence, totaling more than 2,000 letters, are regarded as some of the most valuable records of the era.

The high point of all 500 rooms, if not of the city, is the **Camera degli Sposi** (literally "Bridal Chamber" but actually an audience chamber). It was painted by Mantegna over a nine-year period, when he was at the height of his power, and finished when he was 44. Here Mantegna made a startling advance in painting by organizing the picture's plane of representation in a way that systematically mimics the experience of human vision. Even now, more than five centuries after the event, you can almost sense the excitement of a mature artist, fully aware of his painting's great importance, expressing his vision with a masterly, joyous confidence.

The most serious Mantegna fancier will want to visit his house, **Casa di Andrea Mantegna** (Via Acerbi 47, tel. 0376/360506, admission free), but otherwise it is not of great intrinsic interest. It is located diagonally across from the church of San Sebastiano, and you must phone to arrange a visit. It is occasionally open for temporary art exhibitions, too (daily 9–12:30, 3:30–6:30). The artist's tomb is located in the first chapel on the left in another church, **Sant'Andrea,** which itself is considered Mantua's most important Renaissance creation. *Piazza delle Erbe, south of Piazza Sordello. Open daily 8–12:30 and 3–7.*

Due south, just beyond the town walls, is the **Palazzo Te,** built for Isabella d'Este's son, Federico II Gonzaga, between 1525 and 1535. Reopened in 1989 after restoration, it is the singular Mannerist creation of artist/architect Giulio Romano, decorated with mythological trompe l'oeil frescoes that are not to every visitor's taste. Whatever its faults, the palace does not skimp on pictorial drama. *Viale Te, tel. 0376/323266. Admission: 5,000 lire. Open Tues.–Sun. 10–6.*

Dining
Under 30,000 lire

Due Cavallini. Look for this friendly trattoria off Corso Garibaldi, about halfway between the Palazzo Ducale and the Palazzo Te. Its Mantuan clientele enjoys such local dishes as *tortelli di zucca* (squash-filled ravioli) and *bollito misto* (boiled meats). Be sure to try the *torta sbrisolona* (a type of shortcake), a local specialty, for dessert. *Via Salnitro 5, tel. 0376/322084. Reservations advised. No credit cards. Closed Tues.*

Festivals

Every year on the feast of the Assumption (August 15), a contest of street artists, or *madonnari,* is held in Mantua. Some of the painters, who draw on the sidewalk, in chalk, can reproduce art masterpieces (mainly Madonnas, hence their name) in an amazingly short time.

Tour 3: Lake Garda

Of all the curious things to be noted about Lake Garda, one is its perennial attraction for writers. Even the 16th-century essayist Michel de Montaigne, whose 15 months of travel journals contain not a single other reference to nature, paused to admire the view down the lake from Torbole, which he called "boundless."

Lake Garda is 50 kilometers (31 miles) long, ranges from 1½ to 10 miles wide, and is as much as 346 meters (1,135 feet) deep.

The terrain is flat at the lake's southern base, mountainous at its northern tip. As a consequence, the standard descriptions of it vary from stormy inland sea to crystalline Nordic fjord. It is the biggest lake in the region and by most accounts the cleanest.

From Milan Desenzano del Garda, a hub for visiting the lake, is an hour by train from Milan; the cost is about 10,000 lire. If you're driving, Desenzano is just north of the A4 autostrada, about 115 kilometers (70 miles) east of Milan.

From Brescia Desenzano is 30 minutes by train from Brescia (fare 2,400 lire), and only about 25 kilometers (15 miles) east on the A4.

From Verona Desenzano is 30 minutes by train from Verona (*see* Chapter 6; the train fare is 3,200 lire), and 30 kilometers (19 miles) west along the A4.

Getting Around the Lake Take the ferries for short trips, getting on and off at will. For information, call **Gestione Navigazione Laghi,** Via L. Ariosto 21, Milan, tel. 02/481–2086. A typical fare from Desenzano to Riva del Garda is 12,000 lire. Schedules for both ferries and the more expensive hydrofoils are posted at landings around the lake.

Desenzano del Garda tourist office: Via Porto Vecchio, tel. 030/ 914–1510.

Sirmione

From Desenzano, buses (2,000 lire) run along the lakeshore to Sirmione, 30 minutes away; ferries (2,500 lire) take less time. Tourist office: Viale Marconi 2, tel. 030/916245.

Our tour begins at Sirmione, an enchanting town on the southwest shore. The ruins here, at the water's edge, are a reminder that Garda has been a holiday resort for the pleasure-seeking well-to-do since the height of the Roman era. The locals will almost certainly tell you that the so-called **Grotte di Catullo** (Grottoes of Catullus) were once the site of the villa of Catullus, one of the greatest pleasure-seeking poets of all time. Present archaeological wisdom, however, does not concur, and there is some consensus that this was the site of two villas of slightly different periods, dating from about the 1st century AD. But never mind—the view through the cypresses and olive trees is lovely, and even if Catullus didn't have a villa here, he is closely associated with the area and undoubtedly did have a villa somewhere nearby. *Open Tues.–Sun. 9–6.*

Rocca Scaligera, the castle, was built, along with almost all the other castles on the lake, by the Della Scala family. As hereditary rulers of Verona for more than a century before control of the city was seized by the Visconti in 1402, they counted Garda among their possessions. You may wish to go inside (particularly if you have children with you), since there is a lovely view of the lake from the tower. The old part of town, in the shadow of the fortress, is still medieval in appearance. Or you may want to go for a swim at the nearby beach before continuing on the brief clockwise circuit of Lake Garda's shore. *Admission: 6,000 lire. Open June–Sept., Tues.–Sat. 9–6; Oct.–May, Tues.–Sat. 9–1; year-round Sun. 9–1.*

Lodging **Hotel Sirmione.** Just inside the city walls, near the Castello, **Splurge** this charming hotel, which is also a spa, sits amid gardens and terraces beside the lake. The guest rooms are newly decorated, with comfortable Scandinavian slat beds. Some have superbly executed built-in white furniture, and many have balconies. The dining room overlooks the lake and garden, and there is outdoor dining in fine weather. Many of the guests have been coming for years, and there's a homelike feeling about the place and the attentiveness of its staff. Full and half board are offered. *Piazza Castello 19, tel. 030/916331, fax 030/916558. 76 rooms with bath. Facilities: restaurant, bar, meeting room, pool, landing stage, parking, spa treatments. AE, DC, MC, V.*

Dining
Under 30,000 lire

Osteria del Pescatore. The specialty of this simple and popular restaurant is lake fish. The restaurant is located in town, on the road that leads to the Grotte di Catullo, and has a rustic look. Try grilled trout with a bottle of local white wine. *Via Piana 20, tel. 030/916216. Reservations advised. DC, MC, V. Closed Jan. and Wed. Oct.–May.*

Gardone Riviera

Gardone Riviera is best reached from Brescia, about 45 minutes away by bus (3,800 lire). Tourist office: Corso Repubblica 35, to the left as you get off the boat, tel. 0365/20347.

Once fashionable, now delightfully faded, this turn-of-the-century resort on the west shore of Lake Garda is dotted with aristocratic villas that have been converted into hotels. It nestles among hills covered with olive groves and outlined in dark cypresses. During the summer, and to a lesser extent during the winter months, it attracts a host of German vacationers. Gardone Riviera was the home of the flamboyant Gabriele d'Annunzio (1863–1938), one of Italy's greatest modern poets. D'Annunzio's estate, the **Vittoriale,** is an elaborate memorial to himself, clogged with souvenirs of conquests in art, love, and war (of which the largest is a ship's prow in the garden), and complete with a mausoleum. *Admission: 7,000 lire, including guided tour. Open Tues.–Sun. 9–12:30 and 2–5:30.*

The Arts and Nightlife

Il Vittoriale has a series of concerts in its outdoor theater during July and August. For information, call 0365/20347.

Riva del Garda

The bus from Desenzano to Riva del Garda takes about 2 hours and costs 6,800 lire; the boat takes 4 hours and costs 14,800 lire; the hydrofoil takes 2 hours and costs 20,000 lire. Tourist office: Giardini di Porta Orientale 8, tel. 0464/554444.

Riva del Garda is large and prosperous, and if you're here in summer, you may want to stay overnight if the towns farther south seem too crowded. Many of the town's public buildings date from the 15th century, when it was a strategic outpost of the Venetian Republic. The heart of town, the lakeside **Piazza 3 Novembre,** is surrounded by medieval palazzi. The **Torre Apponale,** predating the Venetian period by three centuries, looms above these houses: Its crenellations recall its defensive purpose. Standing in the piazza and looking out onto the lake, you can understand Riva del Garda's importance as a windsurfing center. Mountain-air drafts ensure good breezes on even the sultriest of midsummer days.

Tour 4: Lake Como

When somebody next asks you where to spend a honeymoon, an eminently sensible thing to say would be "Lake Como," and leave it at that. Though summer crowds do their best to vanquish the lake's dreamy mystery and civilized, slightly faded, millionaire's-row gentility, they fail. Como remains a place of consummate partnership between the beauties of nature and those of humanity. Accordingly, our tour of the lake is of gardens and villas (of which a couple of the finest are now hotels). Like so many of Italy's most beautiful villa gardens, those of Como owe their beauty to the landscape architecture of two eras: the Renaissance Italian, with its taste for order, and the 19th-century English, with its fondness for illusions of natural wildness. The two are often framed by vast areas of the most picturesque farmland—notably olive groves, fruit trees, and vineyards.

Como is some 47 kilometers (30 miles) long, measured north to south, and its southern half is divided into two long legs, or branches; it is also Europe's deepest lake (almost 411 meters, or 1,350 feet). Virgil liked Como at least as much as Garda, calling it simply our "greatest" lake.

From Milan The city of Como, at the southern tip of the lake's western
By Train branch, is only 30 minutes from Milan. Trains run every hour or even more frequently, some of them departing from Milan's Stazione Nord. They arrive in Como at either of two stations: the FS station on the west, close to the lake and the historic center; and in the newer part of town, the FN (Ferrovia Nord Milano) station for frequent commuter trains. Fares run about 3,900 lire to the FS station, 4,200 lire to the FN station.

By Car From the Tangenziale, take the A8 autostrada northwest from Milan a few kilometers until the A9 forks off north toward Como; stay on A9 for another 26 kilometers (16 miles) to Como.

Como

Tourist offices: booth in the FS station; main office is at Piazza Cavour 16, near the ferry landing, tel. 031/274064.

The obvious jumping-off point for excursions on the lake is the lively, modern city of Como. Well known for its textile industries, Como has been a center of silk weaving since the 16th century, but of far more interest to the traveler are its handsome medieval and Renaissance buildings. The older part of town is a cluster of low buildings around the lovely **Duomo**, a surprisingly harmonious fusion of the Gothic and Renaissance styles. Ensconced in niches on the facade of the church are, incongruously, statues of two eminent pagans, Pliny the Elder and the Younger, who were conceded the honor as Como's most illustrious citizens. The adjacent **Broletto** served as the town hall during the Middle Ages, and the 11th-century church of **Sant'Abbondio** is another fine medieval building.

From Como, a funicular at the end of Lungo Lario Trieste (runs every half hour, round-trip fare 6,000 lire) takes you up to **Brunate** for a splendid view of the town and lake from a plateau more than 600 meters (2,000 feet) high.

From the landing stage at Como you can take ferries to the charming little towns along the lake, getting on and off as you please. Fares are from 1,800 lire to about 10,000 lire, depending on distance. Pick up a timetable and rate chart at the tourist office or ticket booth.

Lodging
Under 115,000 lire

Tre Re. Located only a block west of Piazza del Duomo, this clean, spacious, and welcoming hotel is just a few steps from the cathedral. While the exterior gives away the age of this 16th-century palazzo, the rooms inside are airy, comfortable, and modernized. The moderately priced restaurant, which shares an ample terrace with the hotel, is popular for Sunday lunch. *Via Boldoni 20, tel. 031/265374. 32 rooms, 29 with bath or shower. Facilities: restaurant (closed Mon. and Dec. 10–Jan. 9), bar, parking. MC, V. Closed Dec. 10–Jan. 15.*

Dining
Under 30,000 lire

Taverna Messicana. Although its name evokes Mexican food, you can get standard pasta dishes as well as pizzas—with inventive or classic combinations—in this informal restaurant. *Piazza Mazzini 6, tel. 031/262463. No credit cards. Closed Mon.*

Cernobbio

Heading north from Como, the ferry stops first at Cernobbio. From the old square at the center of town, all paths seem to lead to the **Grand Hotel Villa d'Este,** a legendary lakeside resort hotel. Prices here are well beyond even the splurge range, but you may call ahead and ask to see its famous grounds (031/511471).

Originally built for Cardinal Tolomeo Gallio (who began life humbly as a fisherman) over the course of approximately 45 years (it was completed in 1615), the Villa d'Este has had a colorful and somewhat checkered history, swinging wildly between extremes of grandeur and dereliction. Its tenants have included the Jesuits, two generals, a ballerina, the disgraced and estranged wife of a future king of England (Caroline of Brunswick and George IV, respectively), a family of ordinary Italian nobles, and, finally, a czarina of Russia. Its life as a private residence ended in 1873, when it was turned into the fashionable hotel it has remained ever since. The name is not, as you might imagine, derived from some connection with Lombardy's famous d'Este sisters, but from a distant ancestral tie of Caroline Brunswick, called Guelfo d'Este (whose name, for some reason, she evidently liked).

Though the gardens are not as grand as they are reputed to have been during the villa's best days as a private residence, and though they have suffered some modification to make room for tennis courts and swimming pools, they still possess an aura of stately, monumental dignity. The alley of cypresses is a fine example of a proudly repeated Italian garden theme. The fanciful pavilions, temples, miniature forts, and mock ruins provide afternoon's walk of quietly whimsical surprises.

Tremezzo

Continue up the western shore to Tremezzo. If you are lucky enough to visit in late spring or very early summer, you will find the **Villa Carlotta** a riotous blaze of color, with more than 14 acres of azaleas and dozens of varieties of rhododendrons in full bloom. The range is remarkable, particularly considering the difficulties of transporting delicate, exotic vegetation before the age of aircraft. Palms, banana trees, cactus, eucalyptus, a sequoia, orchids, and camellias are only the beginning of a list that includes more than 500 species. The villa itself, built between 1690 and 1743 for the luxury-loving Marquis Giorgio Clerici, is slightly newer than the Villa d'Este.

According to local lore, one motive for the Villa Carlotta's magnificence was a keeping-up-with-the-Joneses sort of rivalry between the marquis's ambitious, self-made son-in-law, who inherited the estate, and the son-in-law's archrival, who built *his* summer palace directly across the lake. Whenever either added to his villa and garden, it was tantamount to taunting the other in public. Eventually the son-in-law's insatiable taste for self-aggrandizement prevailed. The villa's last (and final) owners were Prussian royalty (including the "Carlotta" of the villa's name), and the property was confiscated during the First World War.

The villa's interior is worth a visit, particularly if you have a taste for Antonio Canova's most romantic sculptures. The best-known is his *Cupid and Psyche*, which depicts the lovers locked in an odd but graceful and passionate embrace, with the young god above and behind, his wings extended, while Psyche, her lips willing, waits for a kiss that will never come. *Tel. 0344/40405. Admission to villa and gardens: 6,000 lire adults, 2,500 lire children. Open Apr.–Sept., daily 9–6; Mar. 15–31 and Oct., daily 9–noon and 2–4:30.*

Bellagio

At the pleasant resort town of Menaggio, just north of Tremezzo, the ferry crosses the western branch of the lake to land on the central peninsula. Here you'll get off at Bellagio, sometimes called the prettiest town in Europe. After a stroll of its cobblestoned streets, visit the garden of the **Villa Melzi.** *Admission: 4,000 lire. Open Mar.–Oct., daily 9–12:30 and 2–4:30.*

Villa Serbelloni, a property of the Rockefeller Foundation, is another villa to visit for its celebrated gardens. *Admission: 5,000 lire (includes 90-min. guided tour). Gardens open mid-Apr.–mid-Oct., Tues.–Sun. Guided visits only, at 10:30 and 4.*

The **Grand Hotel Villa Serbelloni,** the luxury resort hotel at the tip of the peninsula, exudes an atmosphere of 19th-century luxury that has not so much faded as mellowed; ask to stroll around the grounds, or splurge on a drink or light lunch on the terrace.

Varenna

Another lovely trip is by ferry from Bellagio to Varenna. The principal sight here is the lovely garden of the **Villa Monastero,** which, as its name suggests, was a monastery before it became a villa. Now it's an international science center. *Admission: 4,000 lire. Open Apr.–Oct., daily 9–noon and 2–5.*

Tour 5: Lake Maggiore

The most beautiful and idyllic of the Italian lakes, Lake Maggiore has its less mountainous eastern shore in Lombardy, its higher western shore in Piedmont, and its northern tip in Switzerland. Never more than 5 kilometers (3 miles) wide, the lake is almost 50 kilometers (30 miles) long. The better-known resorts are on the Piedmontese shore, particularly Stresa, a well-established tourist town that is just the place to unwind and drift into a siesta, to be awakened only by a cool, late-afternoon lake breeze.

From Milan
By Train
Stresa is an hour from Milan by train on the Domodossola line; the fare is 6,500 lire.

By Car
The A8 autostrada runs northwest from Milan, about 46 kilometers (28 miles) to the southern tip of the lake; continue on S33 up the western shore to Stresa.

Stresa

Tourist office: Via Principe Tomaso 70, tel. 0323/30150.

Stresa is a small town with a lot going for it. While capitalizing on its central lakeside position, with good connections to the Borromean islands in the lake, it retains a relaxing atmosphere that can only be described as charming. Its period of development was about a century ago, and the architecture reflects a genteel, languorous attitude that blends in with the subtropical vegetation. Hemingway's *A Farewell to Arms* was partly set here. From the train station, take Via Carducci on the right and continue to Via Principe Tomaso, where you turn left toward the embarcadero. Stop at one of the two adjacent waterfront squares, Piazza Marconi or Piazza Matteotti. Have a drink or an ice cream in one of the several cafés in Piazza Marconi and watch the Borromean island steamers preparing to set off from the landing stage a few yards away.

Make your way from the shore toward Corso Umberto 1, the main road that runs the length of the lake. The buildings on each side of you are decorated in a playful fashion, with mock windows painted onto blank walls, sometimes with what appears to be nosy locals giving you the eye. Turn left, and just about 50 yards up on the right is the entrance to the gardens of **Villa Pallavicino**, a stately residence built on the hill rising from the lake. As you wander around the grounds, with their palms and semitropical shrubs, don't be surprised if you're followed by a peacock or even an ostrich: They're part of the zoological garden, and they are allowed to roam almost at will. From the top of the hill you can see the gentle hills of the lake's Lombardy shore and, closer and to the left, the jewellike Borromean islands. *Admission: 8,000 lire adults, 6,000 lire children 4–14. Open mid-Mar.–Oct. 30, daily 9–6.*

Boats for the **Borromean Islands** leave every few minutes from the landing stage by Piazza Matteotti: Just look for the signs for "Navigazione Lago Maggiore." Although you can hire a boatman to take you to the islands, it's cheaper and just as convenient to use the regular service. Make sure you buy a ticket that allows you to visit all the islands—Bella, Dei Pescatori, and Madre. An excursion ticket that includes all of them plus Verbania Pallanza (*see below*) costs 10,500 lire.

The islands take their name from the Borromeo family, which has owned them since the 12th century. **Isola Bella** is the most famous of the three, and the first that you'll visit. Its name is actually a shortened form of Isabella, wife of the 16th-century count Carlo III Borromeo, who built the palace and terraced gardens, where peacocks roam among scented shrubs, statues, and fountains, as a gift for her. Few wedding presents anywhere have been more romantic. Wander up the 10 terraces: The view of the lake from the top is splendid. Before Count Carlo began his project, the island was rocky and almost devoid of vegetation; the soil had to be transported from the mainland. Visit the **Palazzo** to see the rooms where famous guests—including Napoleon and Mussolini—stayed in 18th-century splendor. *Admission to garden and palazzo: 10,000 lire. Open Apr.–Oct., daily 9–noon, and 1:30–5:30.*

Stop for a while at the second island, tiny **Isola dei Pescatori** (Island of the Fishermen), which is less than 100 yards wide and only about a quarter of a mile long. Of the three islands, this is the one that has remained closest to the way they all were before the Borromeos began their building projects. Little lanes twist through the island, which is nothing more than a tiny fishing village, crowded with souvenir stands in high season.

Isola Madre (Mother Island) is the largest of the three and, like Isola Bella, has a large **botanical garden** (Orto Botanico). There's not much to the island except the garden, but even dedicated nongardeners will appreciate the profusion of exotic trees and shrubs running down to the shore in every direction. Two special times to visit are April (for the camellias) and May (when azaleas and rhododendrons are in bloom). *Admission: 10,000 lire. Open Apr.–Oct., daily 9–noon and 1:30–5:30.*

Lodging
Under 115,000 lire
Primavera. Thanks to its quiet but very central location near the lake and embarcadero, guests can enjoy the balconies that are a feature of many rooms. This family-run hotel has a fresh, bright look. Bedrooms are furnished in light walnut; a comfortable lounge and a small bar are located on street level. *Via Cavour 39, tel. 0323/31286, fax 0323/33458. 32 rooms with bath. AE, DC, MC, V.*

Dining and Lodging
Under 85,000 lire
Luina. This centrally located, family-run hotel offers simple, clean accommodations. The attached trattoria serves good food at moderate prices. *Via Garibaldi 21, Stresa, tel. 0323/30285. 3 rooms with bath, 4 rooms share 1 bath. AE, DC, MC, V. Closed Mar. 15–Nov. 30.*

Verbania Pallanza

Take the ferry across the Gulf of Pallanza to the town of Verbania Pallanza, where the 17th-century **Palazzo Dugnani** has a splendid collection of peasant costumes. The **Villa Taranto** has magnificent botanical gardens containing some 20,000 species. Created by an enthusiastic Scotsman, Captain Neil McEachern, these gardens rank among Europe's finest. *Via Vittorio Veneto, tel. 0323/556667. Admission: 8,000 lire. Open Apr.–Oct., daily 8:30–7:30.*

10 Emilia-Romagna

Bologna to Rimini Along the Via Emilia

Traveling down from Milan through Emilia-Romagna, you may well choose to trace the route of the Via Emilia, the ancient highway laid out by the Romans in 187 BC. Running straight from the central garrison town of Piacenza to the Adriatic port of Rimini, this was the central spine along which the primary towns of the region developed. The old Roman road still exists (S9), and a modern superhighway (A1 from Milan to Bologna and A14 from Bologna to Rimini) runs parallel to it, as does the railway line from Milan. Traveling from the north, you'll pass through the towns of Piacenza, Parma, and Modena before hitting the regional capital, Bologna; otherwise the best strategy may be to base yourself in Bologna and make excursions from there: This is the itinerary we have suggested.

It was after the fall of Rome that the region began its fragmentation. Romagna, centered in Ravenna, was ruled from Constantinople. Ravenna eventually became the capital of the empire in the West in the 5th century, passing to papal rule in the 8th century. The city today, however, is still filled with reminders of two centuries of Byzantine rule.

The other cities of the region, from the Middle Ages onward, became the fiefs of important noble families—the Este in Ferrara and Modena, the Pallavicini in Piacenza, the Bentivoglio in Bologna, and the Malatesta in Rimini. Today all these cities bear the marks of their noble patrons. When in the 16th century the papacy managed to exert its power over the entire region, some of these cities were divided among the families of

Emilia-Romagna

KEY

—+— Rail Lines

N

30 miles
45 km

Adriatic Sea

Chioggia

Adria

Rovigo

Adige

Po

Mantova

Cremona

Sant' Agata
Busseto

Roncole

Cortemaggiore

Piacenza

Salsomaggiore

Bore

Bardi

Bedonia

Villafranca
in Lunigiana

La Spezia

Ligurian Sea

TO CORSICA

Carrara

Massa

Casina

Ciano
d'Enza

S. Polo
d'Enza

Montechiarugolo

Torrechiara

Parma

Reggio

Carpi

San Martino
di Mugnano

Modena

Mirandola

Poggio
Rusco

Finale

Cento

Ferrara

Copparo

Codigoro

Roverete

Comacchio

*Valli di
Comacchio*

Reno

Argenta

Bologna
see detail
map

Dozza

Imola

Faenza

Forlì

Predappio

S. Benedetto
in Alpe

Bagno di Romagna

Roncobilaccio

Prato

Pistoia

Montecatini

S. Marcello Pist.

Abetone

Cesenatico

Cervia

Sant'Apollinare in Classe

Ravenna

Cesena

Savignano

Rimini

SAN
MARINO

Bagno di Romagna

the reigning popes—hence the stamp of the Farnese family on Parma, Piacenza, and Ferrara.

The region was one of the first to join the quest for a unified Italy in the 19th century, pledging itself to the king of Italy and the forces of Garibaldi in the 1840s. Loyalty to the crown did not last long, however. The Italian socialist movement was born in the region, and throughout Italy Emilia-Romagna has been known for rebellion and dissent. Benito Mussolini was born here, although, in keeping with the local political atmosphere, he was a firebrand socialist during the early part of his career. Despite being the birthplace of Il Duce, Emilia-Romagna did not take to fascism: It was in this region that the antifascist resistance was born, and during the war the region suffered terribly at the hands of the Fascists and the Nazis.

Despite a long history of bloodletting, turmoil, and rebellion, the arts—both decorative and culinary—have always flourished in Emilia-Romagna. The great families financed painters, sculptors, and writers (Dante found a haven in Ravenna after being expelled from his native Florence). In modern times, Emilia-Romagna has given to the arts such famous sons as painter Giorgio Morandi, author Giorgio Bassani (author of *The Garden of the Finzi-Continis*), filmmaker Federico Fellini, and tenor Luciano Pavarotti.

Essential Information

Lodging   Geared more toward business than tourism, Emilia-Romagna has no shortage of expensive lodgings, but budget choices are somewhat limited. As a rule, the smaller the town, the less choice there is, but you may even have problems in Bologna, the main city in the region, where single rooms in particular are at a premium throughout the year. Always phone ahead (or ask the tourist office to do so for you) to prevent being left without a roof over your head.

On the eastern coast, however, especially in Rimini, tourism is the main industry, and there are hundreds of hotels, grand ones with all sorts of luxury facilities and modest boarding houses with only a few rooms. Many offer full- or half-board plans—an economical alternative to eating in Rimini's many, but not particularly distinguished, restaurants. You should not go to Rimini during tourist season without confirmed hotel reservations: In July and August the city is filled to overflowing.

Highly recommended lodgings are indicated by a star ★.

Dining   Gourmets the world over would argue that Emilia-Romagna's greatest contribution to mankind has been gastronomic. Bologna is the acknowledged leading city of Italian cuisine. It is home to two of the most famous Italian delicacies—foods that, sadly, have been poorly treated outside their native city. What the world calls "baloney" the Bolognese call *mortadella*, a robust pork sausage spiced with whole peppercorns (if there aren't peppercorns in it, then it isn't mortadella), which bears no resemblance to the stuff sliced at the typical U.S. deli counter. The other famous dish is *spaghetti al ragù*, known to the world as *spaghetti alla bolognese*. The spaghetti with meat sauce dished around the world is a far cry from the real thing. In Bologna a *ragù* sauce is made with onions, carrots, minced pork and veal, butter, and fresh tomatoes, and is cooked for five or six hours in a special earthen pot. It is, in a word, exquisite.

Bologna is also the home of tortellini, lasagna, and *vitello alla bolognese,* a veal cutlet smothered with prosciutto and Parmesan cheese. The rest of the province has made substantial contributions to the kitchen. Parma is the home of Parma ham and the most famous of all Italian cheeses, Parmesan. Modena is the birthplace of *zampone* (stuffed pigs' feet, which tastes much better than it sounds) and *aceto balsamico,* the dark brown, fragrant herb vinegar that is now a must on the shelves of any self-respecting gourmet.

High gastronomic standards are not always reflected in Emilia-Romagna's prices: There are as many low-cost places to eat here as you'll find anywhere in Italy.

The best-known wine of the region is Lambrusco, a sparkling red that has some admirers and many detractors. Some praise it for its tartness; others condemn it for the same quality. A lesser-known wine is Vino del Bosco, also a sparkling red, which comes from the region around Ferrara.

Unless otherwise noted, reservations are not needed and dress is casual. Highly recommended restaurants are indicated by a star ★.

Beaches Though thousands still flock annually to the beaches of Emilia-Romagna's Adriatic coast resorts, there are good reasons to be wary. The River Po is one of Europe's most polluted rivers, accumulating emissions along its long route through Italy's industrial heartland before it empties into the sea. Chemicals, oil spillage, and even radioactive materials have been found in the river, and bathing in it has officially been banned. There is no such prohibition in the resorts south of the Po delta, such as Comachio, or the much more popular beach town of Rimini.

In addition, since the late 1980s vast slicks of unsightly algae have drifted south from the Venetian lagoons, combining with industrial effluents to form a gross, gelatinous mass that is distasteful to look at, let alone paddle in. The algae have abated during the past year or so, but it will take many more years of careful environmental control before the problem disappears completely. Local communities generally warn people if it is considered unsafe to swim. The summer hordes have certainly not lessened because of these problems, but you may decide that the sea is nice just to look at and leave it at that.

The Arts and Bologna and Parma are the chief cultural centers of the region;
Nightlife Bologna offers a number of classical music concerts throughout the year, while Parma is known for its fine opera.

Highlights for First-time Visitors

Castello Estense, Ferrara (Tour 3: Ferrara, Ravenna, and Rimini).
Farnese Theater and Palazzo della Pilotta, Parma (Tour 2: Modena, Parma, and Piacenza).
Mosaics in church of San Vitale, Ravenna (Tour 3: Ferrara, Ravenna, and Rimini).
Piazza del Duomo, Parma (Tour 2: Modena, Parma, and Piacenza).

Tempio Malatestiano, Rimini (Tour 3: Ferrara, Ravenna, and Rimini).
Tomb of Galla Placidia, Ravenna (Tour 3: Ferrara, Ravenna, and Rimini).

Tour 1: Bologna

Throughout its long history, first as an Etruscan city, then a Roman one, then as an independent city-state in the Middle Ages, Bologna has always been a power in the north of Italy. Throughout the centuries, the city acquired a number of nicknames: "Bologna the Learned," in honor of its ancient (the oldest in the world) university; "Bologna the Turreted," recalling the forest of medieval towers that once rose from the city center (two remarkable examples still exist); and "Bologna the Fat," a tribute to the preeminent position the city holds in the world of cuisine.

Wars, sackings, rebellions, and aerial bombing do not seem to have made much of an impression on the old center of the city: The narrow, cobblestone streets are still there, as are the ancient churches, the massive palaces, the medieval towers, and the famous arcades that line many of the main thoroughfares.

The streets are always bustling with students. The university was founded in the year 1050, and by the 13th century it already had more than 10,000 students. It was a center for the teaching of law and theology, and it was ahead of its time in that many of the professors were women. Today the university has one of the most prominent business schools in Italy and the finest faculty of medicine in the country. Marconi, the inventor of wireless telegraphy, first formulated his ground-breaking theories in the physics labs of the university.

From Rome
By Train

Intercity trains from Rome take 2½ hours to reach Bologna and cost 42,000 lire; it's almost four hours on an Espresso, with tickets for the latter costing about 30,000 lire. There are frequent fast trains (leaving every hour or two hours all day), though most of the Espresso trains leave after 5 PM (for rail information in Bologna call 051/246490; in Rome call 06/4775).

By Car

Bologna lies at the hub of a network of toll highways: The A1, A13, and A14 meet here. Rome lies 408 kilometers (255 miles) south of Bologna along the A1 autostrada.

By Plane

Bologna is an important business and convention center and is therefore served by air routes that link it with other Italian cities, as well as by direct flights to European capitals. Seven planes a day make the hour-long flight from Rome. The airport, Guglielmo Marconi, lies in the locality of Borgo Panigale, 7 kilometers (4 miles) from town. A bus service connects it with a downtown air terminal at the central railway station in Bologna proper. For air-traffic information call 051/311578.

From Milan
By Train

Nonstop Intercity trains from Milan whisk you to Bologna in 1¾ hours; if you travel Diretto, with stops in Piacenza and Parma, the journey takes 2 hours and 15 minutes. Espresso trains rarely stop at either of these towns. Ordinary tickets cost about 15,000 lire, and there are frequent departures throughout the day on all lines (for rail information in Bologna call 051/246490; in Milan call 02/67500).

By Bus Tuesday through Saturday, one bus daily leaves Milan at 7:30 AM, arriving in Bologna at 11:30 AM; tickets cost around 14,000 lire. Contact Zani Viaggi, Foro Buonaparte 76 (near Piazza Castello), Milan, tel. 02/864–64854. There is also a once-daily bus service connecting Milan's Malpensa airport with Bologna's airport; it leaves Malpensa's Alitalia offices at 10:30 AM (reverse trip leaves Bologna's airport at 8:30 AM) and takes 3½ hours. Tickets cost 25,000 lire. Arrive 30 minutes before departure. Buses arrive in Bologna at Piazza XX Settembre (tel. 051/248374 or 051/245400).

By Car Milan lies 218 kilometers (136 miles) northwest of Bologna on the A1 autostrada.

From Venice and Florence
By Train The main train route between Venice and Florence runs through Bologna. The journey from Venice to Bologna takes 1½–2 hours. The trip from Florence to Bologna takes a little more than one hour. Service is frequent.

By Bus There is no bus service to Bologna from either Venice or Florence.

Bologna

Tourist offices: Via Marconi 45, tel. 051/237413; Guglielmo Marconi airport, tel. 051/381732; railway station, tel. 051/246541; Piazza Maggiore 6, tel. 051/239660.

Numbers in the margin correspond to points of interest on the Bologna map.

From the train station on Piazza delle Medaglie d'Oro, or the nearby bus station (Piazza XX Settembre), it's a bit of a hike to the center of town, where Bologna's sights are concentrated. Take a city bus (tickets 1,300 lire, valid for one hour, available from kiosks and tobacconists) to Piazza Maggiore, the heart of the city. Grouped around Piazza Maggiore and the adjacent Piazza del Nettuno are the imposing Basilica di San Petronio, the huge Palazzo Comunale, the Palazzo del Podestà, the Palazzo di Re Enzo, and the fountain of Neptune. It is one of the best groupings of public buildings in the entire country.

1 The **Basilica di San Petronio** was started during the 14th century, and work was still in progress on this vast building some 300 years later. It is still not finished, as you will see: The facade is partially decorated and lacks most of the marble facing that the architects planned on several hundred years ago. The main doorway was carved by the great Sienese master of the Renaissance, Jacopo della Quercia. Above the center of the door is a Madonna and Child, flanked by saints Ambrose and Petronius, patrons of the city.

The interior of the basilica is huge and echoing: 432 feet long and 185 feet wide. It is so vast that it's sobering to note that originally the Bolognans had planned an even bigger church (you can still see the columns erected to support the larger church outside the east end) but decided on this "toned down" version in the interest of economy. The church museum contains models to show how the church would have looked. The most important artworks in the church are in the left aisle, frescoes by Giovanni di Modena, dating from the first years of the 1400s. In the right aisle, laid out in the pavement of the church, is a huge sundial, placed there in 1655, showing the

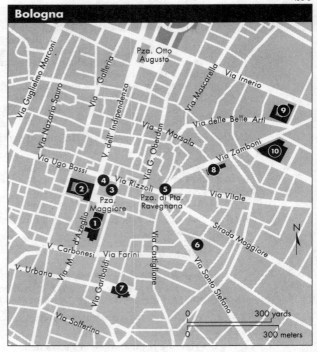

Bologna

time, date, and month. *Open daily 8–6. Museo di San Petronio
(inside church) open Mon., Wed., Fri.–Sun. 10–12:30.*

2 The **Palazzo Comunale,** on the right as you face the church, is a
mixture of styles and buildings, dating from the 13th to 15th
centuries. When Bologna was an independent commune, this
huge palace was the seat of government, a function it serves today. Over the door is a giant statue of Pope Gregory XIII, Bolo-
gna-born and most famous for his reorganization of the
calendar—a system still in use today.

The Palazzo Comunale contains a picture gallery, the Collezioni
Comunali d'Arte, which has paintings of the Middle Ages, as
well as some Renaissance works by Luca Signorelli and Tintoretto. The best reason to see the collection, however, is to view
the piazza from the upper stories of the palace. *Admission:
5,000 lire. Open Mon., Wed.–Sat. 9–2, Sun. 9–12:30.*

3 The **Palazzo del Podestà,** which faces the Duomo, was built in
1484, and attached to it is the soaring Torre dell'Arengo. The
bells in this tower have rung since 1453, whenever the city has
celebrated, mourned, or called its citizens to arms.

4 Next to the Palazzo del Podestà is the medieval **Palazzo di Re
Enzo,** the building in which King Enzo of Sardinia was imprisoned for 23 years (until his death in 1272). He had been unwise
enough to wage war on Bologna and was captured after the
fierce battle of Fossalta in 1249. The palace has other unhappy
associations: Common criminals received the last rites of the

church in the tiny chapel in the courtyard before being taken out to execution in Piazza Maggiore.

Next to the Palazzo di Re Enzo is the elaborate Baroque **fountain** by the sculptor Giambologna. Given Bologna's landlocked position, the choice of subject—the god of the sea, Neptune, and his attendant sirens and dolphins—seems rather odd. It was sculpted in 1566 and is known by the nickname Il Gigante (The Giant), which certainly fits.

The busy, chic Via Rizzoli runs from Piazza del Nettuno directly into the medieval section of the city, passing Piazza di Porta Ravegnana. Here are two of Bologna's famous towers: The taller, the **Torre degli Asinelli,** is 320 feet high and leans an alarming 7½ feet out of the perpendicular; the other tower, the Torre Garisenda, was shortened for safety during the 1500s. It is 165 feet high and tilts 10 feet. The Torre degli Asinelli can be climbed (500 steep stairs) and has a fine view of the city. *Admission: 3,000 lire. Open May–Sept., daily 9–6; Oct.–Apr., daily 9–5.*

The towers were built at the same time (1488) and are mentioned by Dante in the *Inferno.* They are the only two that remain of the more than 200 that once graced the city—every family of any importance had to have a tower as a symbol of its prestige and power.

From Piazza di Porta Ravegnana, turn right onto Via Santo Stefano. Four blocks along is the church of **Santo Stefano,** a remarkable building that is actually several churches contained in one building. The oldest, the church of Santi Vitale e Agricola, dates from the 8th century and contains a 14th-century nativity scene much loved by Bologna's children, who come at Christmas to pay their respects to the baby Jesus. The church of San Sepolcro (12th century) contains the courtyard of Pontius Pilate, so named for the basin in the center that's said to be the basin in which Pilate washed his hands after condemning Christ. *Open daily 9–noon and 3:30–6:30.*

There is also a museum here displaying various medieval religious works, where you can buy sundry items made by the monks, such as honey, shampoo, or jam. *Admission free. Open Mon.–Sat. 9–noon and 3:30–5:30, Sun. 9–1 and 3:30–5:30.*

Leaving the church, turn right onto Via Farini, then, a few blocks farther along, turn left onto Via Garibaldi. This leads you to the church of **San Domenico,** an interesting church that contains the tomb of St. Dominic, who died here in 1221. The tomb of the saint, called the Arca di San Domenico, is in the sixth chapel on the right. Many artists contributed to the decoration, notably Niccolò di Bari, who was so proud of his work here that he changed his name to Niccolò dell'Arca to commemorate it. The young Michelangelo carved the angel on the right. In the right transept of the church is a tablet marking the last resting place of the hapless King Enzo, whose prison you saw in Piazza Maggiore. In the square in front of San Domenico are two curious tombs raised above the ground on pillars, commemorating two famous 14th-century lawyers.

Returning to Piazza di Porta Ravegnana, turn up the busy Via Zamboni and stop a few blocks up on the right to see the church of **San Giacomo Maggiore.** Inside is the burial chamber of the Bentivoglio family, the leading family in Bologna in the Middle

Ages. The crypt is connected by underground passage to the Teatro Comunale, across the street—a rather odd feature until you realize that the family palazzo of the Bentivoglio used to stand on that spot. The most notable tomb is that of Antonio Bentivoglio, carved by Jacopo della Quercia in 1435. We can tell his profession—lecturer in law—from the group of students carved on the base, all listening intently to their professor. *Open daily 8–noon and 3:30–6.*

Continuing along Via Zamboni, you'll come to the principal art gallery of the city and one of the most important galleries in Italy, the **Pinacoteca Nazionale.** The collection here includes many works by the immortals of Italian painting, including Raphael's famous *Ecstasy of St. Cecilia.* There is also a beautiful multipaneled painting by Giotto and a Parmigianino *Madonna and Saints.* The centerpiece of the collection, however, are the many rooms devoted to the two greatest Bolognese painters, Guido Reni and Annibale Carracci, both masters of the late 16th century. Some of the most interesting paintings, from a historical point of view, are by Giuseppe Crespi, a Bolognese painter of the 18th century who avoided grand religious or historical themes, preferring instead to paint scenes of daily life in his native city. These small canvases give you an excellent idea of the boisterous, earthy life of old Bologna. *Via delle Belle Arti 56, tel. 051/243222. Admission: 6,000 lire. Open Tues.– Sat. 9–2, Sun. 9–1.*

The Pinacoteca Nazionale is on the edge of the **university** district, and it is worth a walk through the adjoining streets to get a sense of what an Italian university is like. There is no campus, as such, but a jumble of buildings, some dating as far back as the 15th century, with the bulk of them from the 17th and 18th centuries. This neighborhood, as in most college towns, has lots of bookshops, coffee shops, and cheap snack bars and restaurants; none is particularly distinguished, but all give a good idea of student life. Political slogans and sentiments are scrawled on walls all around the university and tend, for the most part, to be ferociously leftist.

Lodging **Accademia.** This small hotel is right in the middle of the university quarter, a comfortable base for exploring the area. The rooms are adequate, the staff friendly. *Via delle Belle Arti 6, tel. 051/263590 or 051/232318. 28 rooms, 24 with bath or shower. AE, DC, MC, V. Closed 2–3 weeks in Aug.*

Under 115,000 lire

Atlantic. Located between the train and bus stations and the center of town, this is a handy stop for travelers eager to dump their bags and recuperate after arrival in Bologna. Most of the modern, rather bland rooms have a telephone and TV, and the manager has a rudimentary knowledge of English, which can be useful. *Via Galliera 46, tel. 051/248488, fax 051/234591. 22 rooms, 11 with shower. Facilities: bar. MC, V.*

Under 85,000 lire **Apollo.** This cheap but comfortable hotel sits at the heart of the action, above a busy street-market a minute away from Piazza Maggiore. Rooms are functional and uncramped. There is nothing fancy here, but no squalor either. *Via Drapperie 5, tel. 051/ 223955. 8 rooms, 3 with bath or shower. No credit cards.*

Centrale. This is a good choice, in a small street off the main Via Ugo Bassi. Rooms are smartly furnished—some with a TV— though they offer little in the way of views. If possible, phone ahead to make a reservation. *Via della Zecca 2, tel. 051/225114. 20 rooms, 15 with shower. Facilities: bar, parking. MC, V.*

Under 60,000 lire **Ostello San Sisto.** This is the more picturesque of two official youth hostels within a few yards of each other on the outskirts of Bologna. The main disadvantage of both is their distance (6 kilometers or 3½ miles) from the town center. Bus No. 93 or 301 stops nearby, but the service ends at 8:15 PM on weekdays, 2:15 PM on Saturday; at other times catch No. 20/b from Via Indipendenza and walk a kilometer farther from the last stop. Once here, you will find a top-category hostel, smallish and relaxed but well-equipped with dining rooms and lounges. *Via Viadagola 14, tel. 051/519202. 60 beds. Facilities: meal service. No credit cards. Closed Dec. 20–Jan. 19.*

Splurge **Corona d'Oro.** Once a medieval printing house, this centrally
★ located hotel has been in business for more than a century. The public space is a delight, with a lyrical Art Nouveau decor, an atrium, and enough flowers for a wedding. The rooms are comfortable—all are air-conditioned and have color TV. *Via Oberdan 12, tel. 051/236456, fax 051/262679. 35 rooms with shower. Facilities: bar, conference room. AE, DC, MC, V. Closed Aug.*

Dining **Belle Arti.** With a brick ceiling and paneled walls, this is a
Under 30,000 lire cheerful spot for pizza cooked in the wood-fired oven or any of a tempting range of pasta dishes: Sample the *tagliatelle ai funghi porcini freschi* (with wild mushrooms)—pricier than the others but worth every lira. Fish and meat are available for the main course, as well as some original salad selections. *Via delle Belle Arti 14, tel. 051/225581. AE, DC, MC, V. Closed Wed.*

Da Carlo. Dining on the medieval terrace in summer is a treat in this attractive restaurant. Make sure to reserve a table outside. Specialties include delicate game, such as braised pigeon with artichokes. *Via Marchesana 6, tel. 051/233227. Reservations advised, especially in summer. MC, V. Closed Tues. and Jan. 1–20, Aug. 23–Sept. 3–4.*

Ruggero. Unless it's Thursday or Friday, when fish is the only option, meat is the thing to order at this unassuming trattoria next to the Hotel Due Torri. The *bollito misto* (mixed boiled meats) is tender and tasty, as are the roasts and the famous Bolognese mortadella. *Via degli Usberti 6, tel. 051/236–056. Reservations advised. AE, DC, MC, V. Closed Sat. lunch, Sun., and Aug.*

★ **Trattoria di Re Enzo.** For a break from Bolognese food, try this popular Neapolitan restaurant. Spaghetti with *datteri di mare* (razor clams) and tomato sauce can be a meal in itself. The best second course is grilled swordfish steak with a zesty pepper sauce. *Via Riva di Reno 79, tel. 051/234803. Reservations required. AE, DC, MC, V. Closed Sun. and Dec. 24–Jan. 2.*

Da Cesarina. Superbly located opposite the church complex of Santo Stefano, Cesarina specializes in country cooking, particularly game. The menu varies according to season, but if you see wild mushrooms (*funghi* or *porcini*), go for them. The atmosphere is cheerful and relaxed, and you can sit outside in summer. *Via Santo Stefano 19, tel. 051/232037. Reservations advised in summer. AE, DC, MC, V. Closed Mon. and Tues. lunch.*

Under 24,000 lire **Bertino.** Popularity has not spoiled this traditional neighborhood trattoria. Meals are simple but prepared with care: Try the *paglia e fieno* (yellow and green pasta) with sausage, or choose from the steaming tray of bollito misto. *Via delle Lame*

55, tel. 051/522230. AE, DC, MC, V. Closed Sun., Mon. evening, Dec. 25–Jan. 1, and Aug.

Rosteria Antico Brunetti. This old wood-paneled restaurant, founded in 1873, is very close to Piazza Maggiore and serves mainly pizzas to a mixed clientele. The specialty here is fish and seafood, which can go on your pizza or in your pasta. Dining is on two floors, but even then the restaurant fills quickly. *Via Caduti di Cefalonia 5, tel. 051/234441. AE, DC, MC, V. Closed Wed.*

Under 20,000 lire   **Matusel.** Bologna has long been renowned for its *hostarias*—down-to-earth wineshops—and this one, in the middle of the university district, upholds the tradition with honor. Bustling, noisy, and cheap, Matusel offers full meals with little ceremony but plenty of zip. *Via Bertoloni 2, tel. 051/231718. No credit cards. Closed Sun.*

Hostaria del San Carlino. With long wooden benches and tables on two levels, this hostaria has loads of atmosphere, its mainly young clientele occasionally adding to the conviviality by breaking into ad-lib musical accompaniment. As well as soups and good *panini* (sandwiches), there is an excellent selection of country dishes, especially Sardinian ones. Try the Sard *gnocchetti* (potato dumplings) or *agnolotti* (a kind of ravioli) for a first course—you may be satisfied enough to forego an entrée. This place stays open till late. *Via San Carlo 16, tel. 051/267496. No credit cards. Closed Sat. lunch and Sun.*

Splurge   **Da Cesari.** Wine made by the owner's family, such good pastas as *spaghetti alla chitarra* (with asparagus and prosciutto), and such entrées as duck with lemon and wild *radicchio* make this a fine treat, and not too expensive. Expect to pay around 40,000 lire a head for a full meal (more if you have fish). *Via De Carbonesi 8, tel. 051/237710. Reservations advised. AE, DC, MC, V. Closed Sun. and Aug.*

The Arts and Nightlife   Bologna hosts a wide selection of orchestral and chamber music concerts, as well as an acclaimed opera season. The 18th-century **Teatro Comunale** presents concerts by Italian and international orchestras throughout the year, but opera dominates the theater's winter season. All events sell out quickly, so be sure to reserve seats early (Largo Respighi 1, tel. 051/222999). The **Teatro dei Congressi** in the modern Fiera quarter is the usual venue for ballet and orchestral music (tel. 051/637–5165). Also check concert schedules for the **Sala Bossi** (Piazza Rossini 2, tel. 051/222997) and the **Sala Mozart** in the **Accademia Filarmonica,** the principal music school of the city (Via Guerazzi 13, tel. 051/235236).

A thriving university town, Bologna has much to offer in the way of cafés, birrerias, or beer halls, and aimless evening cruising. Start your evening off with a drink at **Osteria del Sole** (Vicolo dei Ranocchi, near Piazza Maggiore), a no-frills *enoteca* (wine bar) with a good selection of cheap local wines. If you fancy a hot crêpe on your ramblings, drop in at **Bombo Crep** (Via delle Moline 4). And if you want to end your evening at a disco, there are plenty to choose from: **Club Hobby One** (Via Mascarella 2) is usually lively, as is the **Sporting** (Galleria del Toro, off Via Ugo Bassi), which hosts a Latin-American evening every Thursday.

Tour 2: Modena, Parma, and Piacenza

Strung along the old Roman Via Emilia northwest of Bologna are three substantial modern cities with charming historic centers: Modena, Parma, and Piacenza. Modena, though an old town, is famous today for three very modern names: the high-performance cars Maserati and Ferrari, which are made here, and the opera star Luciano Pavarotti, who was born here. Parma was heavily damaged during World War II, but the central area around Piazza del Duomo survived intact, with cobbled, traffic-free streets that seem untouched by modern times. Piacenza, an important inland port since the earliest times, is surrounded today by ugly industrial suburbs (with a particularly unlovely oil and gas refinery), but these enclose a delightfully unspoiled medieval downtown.

From Bologna
By Train

Any Diretto trains bound for Milan visit these towns. The farthest of them, Piacenza, is only 90 minutes from Bologna, though it would be difficult to do justice to all three on one day trip.

Modena

Frequent trains (at least one departure every hour) connect Modena with Bologna in 25 minutes; tickets cost about 3,000 lire. Modena is also accessible on the local (and slow) Verona–Mantua–Bologna line. Tourist office: Via Scudari 30, tel. 059/222482.

The Via Emilia travels straight through the heart of Modena, running past its central Piazza Grande. The modern town that encircles the historic center is extensive. From the train station, it's a 10-minute walk to Piazza Grande along Corso Vittorio Emanuele.

While the old quarter is small, it is filled with an Old World atmosphere, narrow medieval streets, and pleasant piazzas. Begin your exploration at the **Duomo,** in the central Piazza Grande. The church is one of the finest examples of Romanesque architecture in the country and dates from the 12th century. Like the exterior of the Duomo in Parma, this one is decorated with medieval sculptures showing scenes from a mystery play based on the story of the Creation, as well as a realistic-looking scene of the sacking of a city by barbarian hordes, a reminder to the faithful to be ever vigilant in defense of the church. The bell tower is made of white marble and is known as *La Ghirlandina* (The Little Garland) because of the distinctive, garland-shape weather vane on its summit.

The interior of the church is very somber and is divided by an elaborately decorated gallery carved with scenes of the Passion of Christ. The carvings took 50 years to complete and are by an anonymous Modenese master of the 12th century. The tomb of the patron saint of Modena, San Geminiano, is in the crypt. *Open daily 8–6.*

The principal museum of the town is housed in the **Palazzo dei Musei,** a short walk from the Duomo (follow Via Emilia to Via di Sant'Agostino. The museum is in the piazza on the left). The collection was assembled in the mid-17th century by Francesco d'Este, duke of Modena, and the **Galleria Estense** is named in his honor. In the first room, there is a portrait bust of him by Bernini.

The duke was a man of many interests, as can be seen from his collections of objets d'art—ivories, coins, medals, and bronzes, as well as works of art dating from the Renaissance to the Baroque. There are works here by Correggio, as well as by masters from other parts of Italy, such as the Venetians Tintoretto and Veronese, the Bolognese Reni and the Carracci brothers, and the Neapolitan Salvator Rosa.

The gallery also houses the duke's **library,** a huge collection of illuminated books, of which the best known is the beautifully illustrated 15th-century *Bible of Borso d'Este.* A map, dated 1501, was one of the first in the world to show Columbus's discovery of America. *Admission: 4,000 lire. Open Tues.–Sat. 9–2, Sun. 9–1.*

In Piazza Roma (follow the curved Via Ramazzini away from the Palazzo dei Musei), you'll find the huge Baroque **palace** of the dukes of Modena, now a military academy. Once the province of the dukes only, it is still off-limits, except to flocks of cadets in elaborate uniforms. Behind the academy are Modena's large public gardens.

Lodging
Under 85,000 lire

La Torre. Modena's cheap hotels include some pretty murky choices; you could do much worse than La Torre, centrally located off the main Corso Canal Chiaro but undisturbed by traffic. It has polite service, basic, unfussy rooms, and the added advantage of being above an excellent restaurant. Book ahead if possible: This is a regular port of call for businesspeople. *Via Cervetta 5, tel. 059/222615, fax 059/216316. 26 rooms with bath or shower. Facilities: bar, garage. AE, DC, MC, V.*

Dining
Under 30,000 lire

Ristorante Pizzeria Santa Lucia. With plenty of tables in simple but hearty surroundings, the Santa Lucia packs in the customers in a town oddly lacking in good, low-priced eating places. But the lively clientele—mainly young—wouldn't come here if the food wasn't good, particularly the minestrone and abundant pasta dishes. The *ragù* here is as good as you'll find in Bologna. *Via Taglio 61, tel. 059/236078. Reservations advised on weekends and in summer. MC, V. Closed Mon.*

Splurge
★

Borso d'Este. One of the city's most highly regarded restaurants—particularly with the affluent youth—offers some delicious variations on old themes, such as ravioli stuffed with game and Parmesan. Other specialties include risotto *agli asparagi* and a mushroom tart with truffle sauce. *Piazza Roma 5, tel. 059/214114. Reservations required. AE, DC, MC, V. Closed Sat. lunch, Sun., and Aug.*

Parma

Hourly trains running between Bologna and Milan stop at Parma, halfway between Modena and Piacenza. Parma can also be reached on local lines from Brescia, Verona, and Mantua. Tourist office: Piazza Duomo 5, tel. 0521/234735.

Almost every major European power has had a hand in ruling Parma at one time or another. The Romans founded the city— it was little more than a garrison on the Via Emilia—and then a succession of feudal lords held sway here. In the 16th century came the ever-avaricious Farnese dukes, and then, in fast succession, the Spanish, French, and Austrians, with the Austrians taking over following the upheavals in central Europe after the fall of Napoleon. The French influence is strong. The great French novelist Stendhal lived in the city for several years and set his classic novel *The Charterhouse of Parma* here.

From the train station, walk straight ahead and turn left at the grand Piazza Pilotta to reach the historic center. **Piazza del Duomo**—site of the cathedral, the baptistery, the church of San Giovanni, and the palaces of the bishop and other notables—is the heart of the city, one of the most harmonious, tranquil city centers in Italy. Its focal point is the magnificent 12th-century **Duomo,** with two vigilant stone lions standing guard beside the main door. The arch of the entrance is decorated with figures representing the months of the year, a motif repeated inside the baptistery on the right-hand side of the square.

Some of the original 12th-century artwork still exists in the church, notably the *Descent from the Cross,* a carving in the right transept, by Benedetto Antelami (1150–1230), a sculptor and architect whose masterwork is this cathedral's baptistery (*see below*). You can still feel the emotion the artist wished to convey in the simple figures.

It is odd to turn from this austere work to the exuberant fresco in the dome, the *Assumption of the Virgin,* by the late-16th-century painter Antonio Correggio. The fresco was not well received when it was unveiled in 1530. "A mess of frogs' legs," the bishop of Parma is said to have called it. In contrast to the rather dark, somber interior of the cathedral, though, the beauty and light of the painting in the dome are a welcome relief. *Open daily 7:30–noon and 3–7.*

The **Baptistery,** standing to the side of the Duomo, is a solemn and simple Romanesque building outside and an uplifting Gothic building inside. The doors are richly decorated with figures, animals, and flowers, and the interior is adorned with figures carved by Antelami, showing the months and seasons. *Admission: 3,000 lire. Open daily 9–12:30 and 3–7.*

There are more paintings by Correggio in the nearby church of **San Giovanni Evangelista,** which has an elaborate Baroque facade and a Renaissance interior. Of the several works by Correggio in this church, it is his *St. John the Evangelist* (left transept) that is considered the finest. Also in this church (in the second and fourth chapels on the left) are works by Girolamo Parmigianino, a contemporary of Correggio and, as his name suggests, a native of Parma. *Open daily 6:30–noon and 3:30–8.*

Next door to the church, in the adjoining monastery, is a **pharmacy** where Benedictine monks used to mix herbal medicines. The 16th-century decorations still survive, while the potions (the people of Parma swore they would cure almost every ill) are, alas, gone—the pharmacy stopped production in 1881. *Admission: 3,000 lire. Open Tues.–Sun. 9–1.*

The **Galleria Nazionale** of Parma is the primary art gallery of the city, and it is housed in the vast and rather grim-looking **Palazzo della Pilotta,** on the banks of the river. The palace, built about 1600, is so big that from the air it is Parma's most recognizable sight—hence, the destruction done to it by Allied bombing in 1944. Much of the building has been restored, but not all. The palazzo takes its name from a sort of handball played within its precincts in the 17th century.

To enter the art museum, which is on the ground floor of the palace, you'll pass through the magnificent and elaborately Baroque **Teatro Farnese,** built in 1628 and based on Palladio's theater in the northern Italian town of Vicenza. Built entirely of wood, the theater was burned badly by the World War II bombs but has been faultlessly restored.

The art gallery itself is large and contains many examples of works by the two best-known painters of Parma—Correggio and Parmigianino. There are also works by Fra Angelico, Leonardo da Vinci, El Greco, and Il Bronzino. *Admission: 10,000 lire. Open Tues.–Sat. 9–2, Sun. 9–1.*

Near the Palazzo della Pilotta, on the Strada Garibaldi, is the **Camera del Correggio,** the former dining room of the abbess of the Convent of Saint Paul. It was extensively frescoed by Correggio, and, despite the religious character of the building, the decorations are entirely secular, with very worldly depictions of mythological scenes—the *Triumphs of the Goddess Diana,* the *Three Graces,* and the *Three Fates.* The building was closed for restoration in 1993, so check to make sure it is open again before setting out. *Admission free. Open Tues.–Sat. 9–2, Sun. 9–1.*

Near the central Piazza Garibaldi is **Madonna della Steccata,** a delightful 16th-century domed church famous for a wonderful fresco cycle by Parmigianino. The painter took so long to complete it that his exasperated patrons imprisoned him briefly for breach of contract before releasing him to complete the work. *Open daily 7:30–noon and 3–6:30.*

Lodging
Under 115,000 lire

Torino. A warm reception and pleasant surroundings are the best reasons for staying in this relaxed hotel. It's well run, comfortable, and located in a quiet pedestrian zone in the heart of town. *Via Mazza 7, tel. 0521/281046, fax 0521/230725. 33 rooms with bath or shower. Facilities: bar, air-conditioning, garage. AE, DC, MC, V. Closed Aug. 1–25 and Dec. 24–31.*

Under 85,000

Moderno. Close to the station, this is a functional stopover, with ample capacity and spacious, old-fashioned rooms. The hotel's somewhat bland character is compensated for by friendly service. *Via Cecchi 4, tel. 0521/772647. 46 rooms, 20 with bath or shower. Facilities: bar. No credit cards. Closed Aug. and Dec. 24–Jan. 3.*

Under 60,000 lire

Croce di Malta. This historic inn enjoys a wider fame as a restaurant (*see below*), but there are still several rooms available here, making this the best budget option in town. The premises once housed a convent, though little remains of it: Instead you get small, comfortable, well-converted rooms with pleasant views and unfailingly polite service. The wafts of cooking from downstairs every evening are a delicious distraction. *Borgo Palmia 8, tel. 0521/235643. 15 rooms, none with bath. Facilities: restaurant. AE, DC, MC, V.*

Dining
Under 30,000 lire

Croce di Malta. Once a convent, then an inn, this attractive restaurant with turn-of-the-century decor opened in 1984. It's in the heart of Parma, and the food is traditional local fare. The homemade pasta is light and delicate; try *tortelli* with squash filling or *tagliatelle* in any fashion. Second courses are well prepared and filling versions of classic veal and cheese dishes. *Borgo Palmia 8, tel. 0521/235643. Reservations advised. AE, DC, MC, V. Closed Sun.*

★ **Parma Rotta.** An old inn about 1.6 kilometers (1 mile) from downtown Parma, the Parma Rotta remains an informal neighborhood trattoria serving such hearty dishes as *pasta e fagioli* (bean-and-pasta soup), roast pork, and spit-roasted lamb. *Via Langhirano 158, tel. 0521/581323. Reservations advised on weekends. AE, DC, MC, V. Closed Sun. June–Sept., Mon. Oct.–May.*

Sant'Ambrogio. This is an informal restaurant in the center of town. Roast duck and turkey are the best bets, but try the *cotechino con crauti* (boiled pork sausage with pickled cabbage), too. *Vicolo Cinque Piaghe 1A, tel. 0521/234482. AE, DC, MC, V. Closed Mon.*

Splurge **La Greppia.** Here, at the best and most elegant restaurant in
★ the city, the risotto with porcini mushrooms is excellent, as are the pâté in Marsala wine, the *torta di melanzane* (eggplant pie), and the fried porcini mushrooms. *Via Garibaldi 39A, tel. 0521/233686. Reservations required. Jacket required. AE, DC, MC, V. Closed Thurs., Fri., July, and Dec. 24–Jan. 1.*

The Arts and Parma is the region's opera center, with performances held Oc-
Nightlife tober through March at the Teatro Regio (tel. 0521/218687) on Via Garibaldi. Opera here is taken just as seriously as in Milan, although tickets are a little easier to come by. Playwright Dario Fo helped found the **Teatro Stabile di Parma** (Viale Basetti 12, tel. 0521/208088), a theater whose productions still mix comedy and politics—though your understanding of the themes will be limited without a knowledge of Italian.

Piacenza

Trains from Bologna leave every hour or so for Piacenza, taking 90 minutes (tickets cost about 18,000 lire); Piacenza is about 50 minutes from Milan (tickets about 6,000 lire). Tourist office: Piazzetta Mercanti 10, tel. 0523/29324.

The heart of the city is **Piazza dei Cavalli** (Square of Horses), dominated by the massive Palazzo del Comune, a severe turreted and crenellated Gothic building of the 13th century. It was the seat of town government during those times when Piacenza was not under the iron fist of a ruling family. The equestrian statues from which Piazza dei Cavalli takes its name are images of members of the last and greatest of the rulers of Piacenza. The statue on the right is Ranuccio Farnese; on the left is his father, Alessandro Farnese. Alessandro was a beloved ruler, enlightened and fair; Ranuccio, his successor, was less successful. Both statues are the work of Francesco Mochi, a master sculptor of the Baroque period.

Walk out of the piazza on Via XX Settembre, which leads to Piacenza's impressive **cathedral,** a rather grim-looking building dating from the mid-12th century. Attached to the massive bell tower is a *gabbia* (iron cage), where evildoers were exposed naked to the scorn (and missiles) of the crowd in the marketplace below. The interior of the cathedral is an odd mixture of Gothic and Baroque. Fine medieval stonework decorates the pillars and the crypt, and there are extravagant frescoes by

17th-century artist Guercino in the dome of the cupola. *Open daily 7–noon and 4–7.*

The **Museo Civico,** the city-owned collection of Piacenzan art and antiquities, is housed in the vast Palazzo Farnese, which was started by the ruling family in 1558 but never completed. The museum was closed for many years for restoration and the reordering of the collection, but it is again open to the public. The highlight of this rather eclectic exhibit is the Etruscan Fegato di Piacenza, a bronze tablet in the shape of a *fegato* (liver), with the symbols of the gods of good and ill fortune marked on it. By comparing this master "liver" with one taken from the body of a freshly slaughtered sacrifice, the priests could predict the future. On a more humanistic note, the collection also contains a Botticelli, the *Madonna with St. John the Baptist,* and a series of Roman bronzes and mosaics. There are also carriages, arms and armor, and other paraphernalia owned by the Farnese, giving a good idea of the splendor of that powerful family. *Piazza Cittadella. Admission: 4,000 lire. Open Tues., Wed., Fri., 9–12:30, Thurs. 9–12:30 and 3:30–5:30, Sat. 9–12:30 and 3–6, Sun. 9:30–noon and 3:30–6:30.*

Lodging
Under 60,000 lire

Rangoni. This is the most comfortable of the city's budget hotels, just around the corner from the train station and five minutes' walk from the center. There's nothing fancy here, but it's serviceable enough and the lobby has an army of cats, apparently in permanent residence. *Piazzale Marconi 1, tel. 0523/21778. 12 rooms, 4 with shower. Facilities: bar, restaurant. No credit cards.*

Dining
Splurge
★

Antica Osteria del Teatro. Set on a lovely piazza in the center of town, this restaurant is generally held to be the best in Piacenza. Try the *tortelli* stuffed with ricotta, the roast duck, or the grilled sea bass. *Via Verdi 16, tel. 0523/23777. Reservations advised. AE, DC, MC, V. Closed Sun. eve., Mon., Aug. 1–25, and Jan. 1–25.*

Tour 3: Ferrara, Ravenna, and Rimini

This tour diverges from the Via Emilia northwards, for an easy excursion to the historic walled town of Ferrara. There's a university here, which means plenty of cheap spots for eating; cheap lodgings, on the other hand, are few and far between, and the available space as often as not is taken up by the resident student community. Still, Ferrara is a good base for excursions to Ravenna and Rimini, both easily reached from Ferrara by train. The rich mosaics of Ravenna are a compulsory stop on any itinerary in the area, worth a day at least. The seaside town of Rimini was the terminus of the Via Emilia, but today there are few remains of the Roman epoch in this popular Adriatic beach resort. If all you want is sand, sea, and all the paraphernalia of a tourist industry, you can skip the cultural attractions of Ferrara and Ravenna and go directly to Rimini from Bologna. Be aware, however, that in summer, particularly August, Rimini is extremely popular and hence crowded.

Ferrara

Trains leave Bologna for Ferrara at least every hour; Diretto service takes 30 minutes, Regionale 50 minutes (fare 4,000 lire). This is the Venice–Padua line, putting Ferrara within reach of Venice in less than 90 minutes. Call the Ferrara station (tel. 0532/770340) for information. Hourly buses from Bologna cost 5,700 lire and take an hour to reach Ferrara; contact ACFT (tel. 0532/49351) or ATC (tel. 051/248374) bus companies. Tourist office: Piazza Municipio 19, tel. 0532/209370 or 419269.

Ferrara is a city of turrets and towers, of a mighty castle protected by its deep moat, and historic palaces of great grandeur. Although the site has been inhabited since before Christ and was once the possession of Ravenna, the history of Ferrara begins in the 13th century, with the coming of the Este family. From 1259 until 1598 the city was ruled by the Este dukes, and in those 3½ centuries, the city was stamped indelibly with their mark.

It was during the Renaissance that the court of the Este came into full flower. In keeping with their time, the dukes could be politically ruthless—brother killed brother, son fought father—but they were avid scholars and enthusiastic patrons of the arts. Duke Niccolò III murdered his wife and her lover but was a cultivated man. The greatest of all the dukes, Ercole I, tried to poison his nephew, who laid claim to the duchy (and when that didn't work, he beheaded him), but it is to this pitiless man that Ferrara owes its great beauty. One of the most celebrated names in Italian history, Lucrezia Borgia, married into the Este family—and it seems that her infamous reputation is not at all deserved. She was beloved by the Ferrarese people and was mourned greatly when she died. She is buried in the church of Corpus Domini in the city.

Ferrara's train station is just outside the city wall, a 15-minute walk up the broad Viale Cavour to Piazza Castello and the town center. To save a walk, take bus No. 2 or 3 (fare 1,100 lire; buy tickets from tobacconists or newsagents). Long-distance buses arrive at a terminal 10 minutes' walk southwest of the center, on Corso Isonzo.

Naturally enough, the building that was the seat of Este power, the massive **Castello Estense,** in the center of the city in Piazza della Repubblica, dominates the town. It is a suitable symbol for the Este family: cold and menacing on the outside, lavishly decorated within. The public rooms are grand, but deep in the bowels of the fortress are chilling dungeons where enemies of the state were held in wretched conditions—a function these quarters served as recently as 1943, when antifascist prisoners were detained there.

The castle was begun in 1385, but work was going on as late as the 16th century. The Sala dei Giochi (the Games Room) is extravagantly decorated with walls painted to show pagan athletic scenes, and the Sala dell'Aurora to show the times of day. Oddly enough, the chapel on view is not Catholic but Protestant (one of the few to survive the Counter-Reformation), and was used by the Protestant Princess Renée of France, who married into the Este family in the 16th century. From the terraces of the castle—and from the hanging garden, reserved for the private use of the duchesses—are fine views of the town and the surrounding countryside. *Admission: 6,000 lire. Open Tues.–Sat. 9–1 and 2:30–6:30; Sun. 10–6.*

A few steps from the castle, along the Corso dei Martiri della Libertà, is the magnificent Gothic **Duomo,** with its facade of three tiers of arches and beautiful carvings above the central door. It was begun in 1135 and took more than a hundred years to complete. The interior does not live up to the expectations fostered by the facade. It was completely remodeled during the 17th century, and none of the original decoration remains in place. *Open daily 8–noon and 3–7.*

The treasures of the old interior are preserved in the **cathedral museum** above the church (entrance inside). Here are some of the lifelike carvings taken from one of the doors of the Duomo, dating from the 13th century and showing the months of the year. Also in the museum are a statue of the Madonna by the Sienese master Jacopo della Quercia and two masterpieces by the Ferrarese painter Cosimo Tura, an *Annunciation* and *St. George Slaying the Dragon. Admission free, but voluntary offerings taken. Open summer, Mon.–Sat. 10–noon and 3:30–6:30; winter, Mon.–Sat. 10–noon and 3–5.*

The area behind the Duomo, the southern part of the city stretching between the Corso della Giovecca and the ramparts above the river, is the oldest and most characteristic part of Ferrara. In this part of the old town, various members of the Este family built themselves pleasure palaces, the most famous of which is the **Palazzo Schifanoia** (*schifanoia* means carefree—literally, "fleeing boredom"). Begun in the 14th century, the palace was remodeled in 1466 and became the city's first Renaissance palazzo. The interior is lavishly decorated, particularly the Salone dei Mesi, with an extravagant series of frescoes showing the months of the year. The palace now houses the coins, statuary, and paintings of the **Museo Civico** (City Museum). *Via Scandiana 23. Admission: 2,500 lire, free 2nd Sun. and Mon. of each month. Open daily 9–7.*

Near the Palazzo Schifanoia, on Via XX Settembre, is the **Palazzo di Ludovico il Moro,** a magnificent 15th-century palace built for Ludovico Sforza, husband of Beatrice d'Este. The great, but unfinished, courtyard is the most interesting part of this luxurious palace, which also houses the region's **Museo Archeologico,** a repository of the relics of early man, the Etruscans, and Romans, found in the countryside surrounding the city. *Via XX Settembre 124.* Unfortunately the museum has been closed indefinitely.

In the same neighborhood, on Via Scienze, is the peaceful palace called the **Palazzo del Paradiso.** In the courtyard is the tomb of the great writer Ariosto, author of the most popular work of literature of the Renaissance, the poem "Orlando Furioso." The building now houses the city library. *Admission free. Open weekdays 9–7:30, Sat. 9–1.*

The Estes were great patrons of Ariosto, and he passed a good deal of his life in Ferrara. **Ariosto's house** lies in the northern part of the city, at Via Ariosto 67. The interior has been converted into an office building and is not open to the public.

Not far from the Palazzo del Paradiso, on Via Savonarola, is a charming 15th-century house, the **Casa Romei.** Downstairs there are rooms with 15th-century frescoes and several sculptures collected from churches that have been destroyed. *Via Savonarola 30. Admission: 4,000 lire. Open Tues.–Sun. 8:30–2.*

On the busy Corso della Giovecca is the **Palazzina di Marfisa d'Este,** an elegant 16th-century home that belonged to Marfisa d'Este, a great patron of the arts. The house has painted ceilings, fine 16th-century furniture, and a garden containing a grotto and an outdoor theater. *Corso della Giovecca 170. Admission: 2,000 lire, free 2nd Sun. and Mon. of each month. Open daily 9–12:30 and 2–5.*

From the castle, cross the Corso della Giovecca and walk up the wide Corso Ercole d'Este. At the corner of Corso Porta Mare is the **Palazzo dei Diamanti** (the Palace of Diamonds), so called for the 12,600 blocks of diamond-shaped stone that stud the facade. The palace was built during the 15th and 16th centuries and today contains an extensive art gallery devoted primarily to the painters of Ferrara. *Corso Ercole d'Este 21. Admission: 6,000 lire. Open Tues.–Sat. 9–2, Sun. 9–1.*

Lodging
Under 85,000 lire
★

San Paolo. Recently transposed from the heart of Ferrara's medieval quarter to a calmer location on the perimeter of the old city, the San Paolo comes recommended by the tourist office and travelers alike. It is still not an excessive distance from the action (10 minutes on foot to the Castello—hardly a sacrifice in a town so amenable for strolling), and guests can still hear the chiming of the Duomo's bells on a Sunday. The hotel's atmosphere is casual and sociable, the rooms bright and modern. Book early to avoid disappointment. *Via Baluardi 9, tel. 0532/762040, fax 0532/762040. 20 rooms, 16 with shower. No credit cards.*

Under 60,000 lire

Alfonsa. Tucked away behind Piazza Castello, this is a very convenient base from which to explore the city: clean and friendly without any extras. The manager will pin you down for hours of conversation, given half a chance. Rooms are viewless but functional. *Via Padiglioni 5, tel. 0532/205726. 19 rooms, 3 with bath. No credit cards.*

Dining
Under 30,000 lire

Pizzeria Ariostea. As pizzerias go, this one offers a smart locale, with trim, modern decor and a predominantly well-to-do young-professional clientele. Dishes are well prepared, not just pizzas but full meals: Sample the *pizza capricciosa,* overflowing with cheese and prosciutto, or the bollito misto. If you stick to the pizza menu, you can keep your bill under 18,000 lire. *Piazza Ariostea, tel. 0532/761660. AE, DC, MC, V. Closed Thurs.*

Under 24,000 lire

Bierfilz. A birreria on two levels, this is a favorite haunt of Ferrara's student population. Most come to drink the variety of draft beers, but you can also eat such snacks as panini, pasta, and fries. The dim lighting, wooden benches, and music all help to create a lively subterranean ambience. *Piazza Sacrati 32, tel. 0532/209725. No credit cards. Closed Wed.*

Ravenna

Local trains leave Ferrara every one or two hours for Ravenna, an hour and 10 minutes away. Tickets cost 6,000 lire. If you're coming directly from Bologna, change at Ferrara or at Castel Bolognese (on the Bologna–Rimini line). Six ATC buses daily from Bologna (tel. 051/248374) take two hours to Ravenna and cost 8,000 lire. Tourist office: Via Salara 8, tel. 0544/35404.

Easily negotiable on foot, Ravenna is a stately old city still living on the dreams of its faded glory. The high point in its long history was 1,500 years ago, when it became the capital of the Roman Empire, but by then the empire had begun its irreversible decline. The city was taken by the barbarian Ostrogoths during the 5th century; then, during the 6th, it was conquered by the Byzantines, who ruled it from Constantinople.

Because Ravenna spent much of its history looking to the East, its greatest art treasures show much Byzantine influence: Above all, Ravenna is a city of mosaics, the finest in Western art. A single 7,000-lire ticket will admit you to six of Ravenna's most important monuments: the Tomb of Galla Placida, the church of San Vitale, the Neonian Baptistery, and the church of Sant'Apollinare Nuovo, all described below, as well as the church of Spirito Santo and the Museo Arcivescovile e Cappella Sant'Andrea.

From the train station, follow Viale Farini to Piazza del Popolo, which adjoins Piazza XX Settembre. From there, signs will direct you up Via Cavour and Via San Vitale to the **Tomb of Galla Placidia** and the church of **San Vitale,** which have the best-known and most elaborate mosaics in the city. The little tomb and the great church stand side by side, but the tomb predates the church by at least a hundred years. Galla Placidia was the sister of the last emperor of Rome, Honorius, the man who moved the imperial capital to Ravenna in AD 402. She is said to have been beautiful and strong-willed, taking an active part in the governing of the crumbling empire. She was also one of the most active Christians of her day, endowing churches and supporting priests and their congregations throughout the realm. This tomb, built for her during the mid-5th century, is her monument. Outside, the tomb is a rather uninspired building of red brick; within, however, the color and clarity of the mosaics that decorate the ceiling are startling. The deep blue and gold catch the light and seem to glitter. The central dome has symbols of Christ and the evangelists, and above the door is a depiction of the Good Shepherd. The apostles, in groups of two (there are only eight of them, for some reason), ring the inner part of the dome. Notice the small doves at their feet, drinking from the water of faith. In the tiny transepts are some delightful pairs of deer (which represent souls), drinking from the fountain of resurrection. There are three sarcophagi in the tomb, and, it is thought, none of them contains the remains of Galla Placidia. She died in Rome in AD 450, and there is no record of her body having been transported back to the place where she wished to lie.

The mosaics of the Galla Placidia tomb are simple works that have not yet received the full impact of Byzantine influence. Quite the opposite is the case of the mosaics in the church of San Vitale, next door. The church was built in AD 547, after the Byzantines conquered the city, and it is decorated in an exclusively Byzantine style. In the area behind the altar are the most famous works in the church. These show accurate portraits of the emperor of the East, Justinian, attended by his court, and the bishop of Ravenna, Maximian. Facing him, across the chancel, is the emperor's wife, Theodora, with her entourage, holding a chalice containing the communion wine. From the elaborate headdresses and heavy cloaks of the emperor and empress, you can get a marvelous sense of the grandeur of the imperial court.

On the ceiling above the royal couple, ruling over all, is a mosaic of Christ the King. With him is the saint for whom the church is named, Vitale, and the founder of the church, Bishop Ecclesio, who holds a model of the building. *Tomb of Galla Placidia and church of San Vitale. Via San Vitale off Via Salara, near Piazza del Popolo. Admission: 3,000 lire (ticket valid for both). Open summer, daily 8:30–7; winter, daily 9–4:30.*

Next to the church is the **Museo Nazionale** of Ravenna, housed in a former monastery. The collection contains artifacts of ancient Rome, Byzantine fabrics and carvings, and other pieces of early Christian art. *Admission: 6,000 lire. Open Tues.–Sun. 8:30–1:30.*

To reach another great mosaic site, the **Neonian Baptistery,** return to Piazza del Popolo and walk along Via Battistero, toward Piazza John F. Kennedy. The Baptistery, next door to the 18th-century cathedral, is a few blocks along on the left. In keeping with the purpose of the building, the great mosaic in the dome shows the baptism of Christ, and beneath that scene are the apostles. The lowest band of mosaics contains Christian symbols, the Throne of God and the Cross. *Admission: 3,000 lire (ticket also valid for Museo Arcivescovile e Cappella Sant'Andrea). Open daily 9:30–4:30.*

A few blocks away, on Via Ricci, and next door to the large church of St. Francis, is a small neoclassical building containing the **tomb of Dante.** Exiled from his native Florence, the great poet, author of the *Divine Comedy*, died here in 1321. The Florentines have been trying to reclaim their famous son for hundreds of years, but the Ravennans refuse to give him up, arguing that Florence did not welcome Dante in life, so it doesn't deserve him in death. The site contains a small museum. *Admission: 3,000 lire; free on Sun. and holidays. Open Tues.–Sun. 9–noon.*

From the tomb of Dante, walk up Via Guaccimanni toward the busy Via Roma. At the intersection of the two streets, slightly to the left, is the last great mosaic site in the city proper, the church of **Sant'Apollinare Nuovo.** Since the left side of the church was reserved for women, it is only fitting that the mosaic decoration on that side is a scene of 22 virgins offering crowns to the Virgin Mary. On the right wall are 26 men carrying the crowns of martyrdom. They are approaching Christ, who is surrounded by angels. The mosaics in Sant'Apollinare Nuovo date from the early 6th century and are slightly older than the works in San Vitale. *Admission: 3,000 lire (ticket also valid for the church of Spirito Santo). Open May–Sept., daily 9:30–5:30; Oct.–Apr., daily 9:30–4:30.*

Lodging
Under 60,000 lire

Al Guaciglio. Walk straight out of the station and take the first turning on the right to find this small hotel. Rooms are neat and the atmosphere relaxed and friendly. Ravenna's center is just five minutes away. *Via Brancaleone 42, tel. 0544/39403. 16 rooms, 9 with shower. Facilities: restaurant, bar. MC, V.*

Dining
Under 24,000 lire

Ristorante Scai. Roast meat and game are what this restaurant does best, and a changing menu provides diners with pasta stuffed with roe deer, as well as main courses of venison, duck, pigs' feet, or rabbit. Budget-conscious carnivores can take advantage of the 20,000-lire tourist menu. *Piazza Baracca 22 (close to the church of San Vitale, at the end of Corso Cavour), tel. 0544/22520. AE, DC, MC, V. Closed Mon.*

Under 20,000 lire   **Ca de Ven.** A vaulted wine cellar in the heart of the old city, the Ca de Ven is a wonderful place for a hearty lunch or dinner. You sit at long tables with the other diners and feast on platters of delicious cold cuts; *piadine* (flat Romagna bread); and cold, heady white wine. If you're here in chilly weather, try the wholesome *pasta e fagioli* (pasta-and-bean soup). *Via C. Ricci 24, tel. 0544/30163. MC, V. Closed Mon.*

Rimini

From Ravenna, local trains leaving every one or two hours take an hour to reach Rimini (tickets 4,000 lire). From Bologna, fast trains on the Ancona–Bari line take about 75 minutes. Tourist offices: Piazzale Cesare Battisti, railway station, tel. 0541/51480; Piazzale Indipendenza, waterfront, tel. 0541/51101.

Rimini is the principal summer resort on the Adriatic Coast and one of the most popular holiday destinations in Italy. Every summer, beginning in June, the city is flooded with vacationers, not just from Italy but from France, Austria, Germany, Scandinavia, and Great Britain as well. The city is given over almost exclusively to tourism, with hundreds of hotels, grand and modest, and restaurants catering to virtually every national palate: You are just as likely to find a German *bierkeller* or an English tea shop as you are an Italian restaurant. The waterfront is lined with beach clubs that rent a patch of sand, a deck chair, and an umbrella by the day, week, month, or the entire season. Hotels along the beachfront have staked out their own private turf, so the chance of swimming (or even seeing the sea close up) without paying for the privilege is slim.

In the off-season, Rimini, in common with resorts the world over, is a ghost town. Some hotels and restaurants are open, but the majority are closed tight, hibernating until the return of the free-spending tourists. Summers are so crowded here that it is most unwise to go to Rimini without confirmed hotel reservations. For those who like sun by day, disco by night, and hordes of frolicking teenagers, Rimini is the town. Those who prefer more sedate vacations are advised to stay away.

The new town has just about swallowed the old, but there are signs here and there that tell of Rimini's long and turbulent history. Rimini stands at the junction of two great Roman consular roads: the Via Emilia and the Via Flaminia. In addition, in Roman times, it was an important port, making it a strategic and commercial center. From the 13th century onward, the city was controlled by the Malatesta family, an unpredictable group, capable of grand gestures and savage deeds. The famous lovers in Dante's *Inferno*, Paolo and Francesca, were Malatestas. Paolo was the brother of Gianciotto Malatesta; Francesca, Gianciotto's wife. Gianciotto murdered them both for having betrayed him. Sigismondo Malatesta, lord of the city in the middle of the 15th century, was a learned man of great wit and culture. He also banished his first wife, strangled his second, and poisoned his third. He lived with his beautiful mistress, Isotta, until her death. He was so grief-stricken that he raised a magnificent monument in her honor, the **Tempio Malatestiano.** It is the principal sight in the town.

Rimini's train station is midway between the sea and the historic center, a 10-minute walk either way. The oldest building in the city is the **Arco d'Augusto,** in Piazzale Giulio Cesare. It was erected in 27 BC, making it the oldest Roman arch in existence, and it marks the meeting of the Via Emilia and the Via Flaminia. From there, walk along Corso Augusto to Piazza Tre Martiri (where, legend says, the mule carrying St. Anthony suddenly stopped and knelt in honor of the Holy Sacrament that was being carried past at the time) and turn right onto Via Quattro Novembre. One block up, also on the right side, is Sigismondo's memorial to his great love, Isotta, the Tempio Malatestiano.

Despite the irregular—from the Catholic church's point of view—nature of Sigismondo's relationship with Isotta, the Tempio is today the **cathedral** of Rimini. The building was in fact originally a Franciscan church before Sigismondo took it over to make it into a monument to his beloved. The facade is a beautiful piece of Renaissance architecture by Leon Battista Alberti. It is in the shape of a Roman triumphal arch and is considered to be one of Alberti's masterpieces.

The interior is light and spacious and contains the tombs of both the lovers. The intertwined I, for Isotta, and the S, for Sigismondo, are dotted about everywhere and look rather like "$" signs. The carvings of elephants and roses recall the coat of arms of the Malatesta family. Sigismondo's tomb, on the right of the entrance door, is some distance from Isotta's in the second chapel. (Her tomb is on the left wall of the chapel; the original inscription in marble had a pagan twist and was covered with another in bronze.) On the right, in what is now the Tempio's book and gift shop, is a wonderful but badly damaged fresco by Piero della Francesca showing Sigismondo paying homage to his patron saint. Above the main altar of the church is a crucifix attributed to Giotto. *Open daily 7–noon and 3:30–7.*

Lodging
Under 85,000 lire

Annarita. Set back in a leafy, residential road leading off the main Viale Vespucci, this is a small but comfortable place frequented by a regular clientele: Availability may consequently be limited. Guests are expected to pay full board during the summer season. Facilities are rudimentary and rooms are basic, but the main benefits here are its closeness to the beach promenade and the convenient price. *Viale Misurata 24, tel. 0541/391044. Facilities: restaurant, bar, parking. No credit cards.*

Under 60,000 lire

Camping Italia. High season (August), when hotel vacancies are scarce in Rimini, is a good time to join the canvas brigade at this well-located campsite. If you don't have a tent, bungalows may be available, though this is less likely in the holiday season. Italian campsites can be crowded, rowdy affairs in midsummer—you are often squeezed up against your neighbors and drawn into their orbit, like it or not, though you can usually repitch your tent elsewhere. This is the most central of the campsites—not on the beach (none are), but just across the road from the Marina at Rivabella. Take bus No. 13 from the town center, a five-minute ride. *Via Toscanelli 112, tel. 0541/*

732882. Facilities: restaurant, bar, discotheque. No credit cards.

Splurge   **Club House Hotel.** Ultramodern and right on the sea, the Club House is a good hotel for summer vacations and is one of the few open during the off-season. All rooms have balconies, minibar, and color TV. Full-board rates (which are compulsory in summer) run between 130,000 and 200,000 lire per night for a double room. *Viale Vespucci 52, tel. 0541/391460, fax 0541/391442. 28 rooms with bath. Facilities: restaurant, bar, private beach, parking. AE, DC, MC, V.*

Dining   **La Bicocca.** This popular trattoria is a good place for an intro-
Under 30,000 lire   duction to the cuisine of Romagna. There are tasty pastas in
★   various seafood sauces, cheeses and local salamis, and excellent regional wines—all served in a cheerful atmosphere. *Vicolo Santa Chiara 105, tel. 0541/781148. Reservations advised. AE, DC. Closed Wed.*

★   **Zio.** Nothing but seafood is served here, and all of it is good value for the money. The *insalata frutti di mare* is an all-encompassing seafood antipasto; *tortellini alle vongole* (stuffed pasta in a white clam sauce), fish cannelloni, and simple grilled sole are also recommended. *Vicolo Santa Chiara 18, tel. 0541/786160. Reservations advised. DC, MC, V. Closed Wed. and July.*

Under 20,000 lire   **Rock Island.** Formerly a seafood restaurant, now a busy pub and *panineria* (snack and sandwich shop), the Rock Island is at the end of a pier right on the sea. You can eat and drink here, and take part in Rimini's raucous nightlife. Steamy, loud, and full of young people, it's not for the fainthearted. *Molo di Levante, tel. 0541/50178. No credit cards. Closed weekdays in winter.*

Faenza

Trains running between Bologna and Rimini include a stop at Faenza, halfway between the two (45 minutes from each).

On your way back to Bologna from Rimini, you may want to stop off at Faenza, a town that has been producing ceramics since the 12th century—its faience pottery is known the world over. In the central **Piazza del Popolo** are dozens of shops selling the town's product. Faenza is also home to the **Museo delle Ceramiche,** one of the largest ceramics museums in the world, covering the potter's art in all phases of history and in all parts of the world. *Viale Baccarini. Admission: 8,000 lire. Open Apr.–Oct., Tues.–Sat. 9–7, Sun. 9:30–1; Nov.–Mar., Tues.–Sat. 9:30–2.*

11 Umbria and the Marches

Perugia, Assisi, Urbino, Spoleto, and Orvieto

The two regions of Umbria and the Marches are undeservedly neglected on many tourist itineraries. Though they are centrally located in the Italian peninsula, between Florence and Rome, they are off Italy's main road and railway arteries and are thus often passed by. Yet Umbria is the green heart of Italy, a region of steep, austere hills, deep valleys, and fast-flowing rivers that has somehow escaped the unplanned industrial expansion that afflicts much of central Italy. Such important medieval towns as Perugia, Assisi, and Urbino nestle here, delightful cities that can still be experienced whole rather than as a series of museums and churches, forced marches through 2,000 years of Western culture. Virtually all the small towns in the region boast a castle, church, or museum worth a stop.

The earliest inhabitants of Umbria, the Umbri, were thought by the Romans to be the most ancient inhabitants of Italy. Little is known about them, since with the coming of Etruscan culture the tribe fled into the mountains in the eastern portion of the region. The Etruscans, who founded some of the great cities of Umbria, were in turn supplanted by the Romans. Unlike Tuscany and other regions of central Italy, Umbria had few powerful medieval families to exert control over the cities in the Middle Ages—proximity to Rome ensured that Umbria would always be more or less under papal domination.

The relative political stability of the region did not mean that Umbria was left in peace. Located in the center of the country, it has for much of its history been a battlefield, where armies

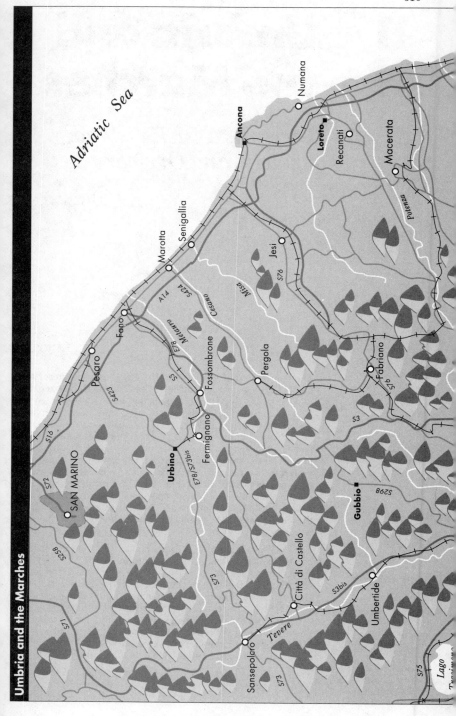

Umbria and the Marches

Adriatic Sea

Numana

Ancona

Loreto

Recanati

Macerata

Potenza

Senigallia

Marotta

Jesi

S76

Misa

Cesano

A14

S424

Metauro

E78

Fano

Pesaro

S3

Fossombrone

Pergola

Fabriano

S76

S223

S3

S16

SAN MARINO

S72

Fermignano

Urbino

E78/S73bis

S298

Gubbio

S258

Città di Castello

S73

S3bis

Umbertide

Tevere

S73bis

Sansepolcro

S73

S75

Lago
Trasimeno

S71

from north and south clashed. Hannibal destroyed a Roman army on the shores of Lake Trasimeno, and the full and bloody course of the interminable Guelph-Ghibelline conflict of the Middle Ages was played out in Umbria. In spite of—or perhaps because of—this bloodshed, Umbria has produced more than its share of Christian saints. The most famous is St. Francis, the decidedly unmartial saint whose life shaped the church and the history of his time. His great shrine at Assisi is visited by hundreds of thousands of pilgrims each year.

East of Umbria, the Marches—or Marche, in Italian—stretch between the hills of the southern Apennines down to the Adriatic Sea. It is a scenic region of mountains and valleys, with great turreted castles standing on high peaks, defending passes and roads—silent testament to the region's warring past. The Marches have passed through numerous hands. First the Romans supplanted the native civilizations; then Charlemagne supplanted the Romans (and gave the region its name: It was divided into "Marks," or provinces, under the rule of the Holy Roman Emperor); then began the seemingly neverending struggle between popes and local lords. Cesare Borgia succeeded in wresting control of the Marches from the local suzerains, annexing the region to the papacy of his father, Alexander VI.

Despite all this martial tussling, it was in the lonely mountain town of Urbino that the Renaissance came into its fullest flower; that small town became a haven of culture and learning that rivaled the greater, richer, and more powerful city of Florence, and even Rome itself.

Umbria's main city of Perugia makes a sensible base for touring by bus and train throughout Umbria. A visit to the Marches, on the eastern coast, involves a separate tour.

Essential Information

Lodging   Every place mentioned in the tours of Umbria and the Marches has some form of lodging, though the choice is not always great. Hotels can fill quickly, especially in the summer, so phone ahead and reserve as early as you can. The largest cities in the region—Perugia and Ancona—have the widest selection, and you are almost guaranteed a room here in your preferred price category; Assisi, at the other extreme, is often crammed with both tourists and pilgrims, and space is in demand at any season.

Highly recommended lodgings are indicated by a star ★.

Dining   Umbria is mountainous, and the cuisine of the region is typical of mountain people everywhere. The food is hearty and straightforward, with a stick-to-the-ribs quality that sees hardworking farmers and artisans through a long day's work and helps them make the steep climb home at night. Italians are generally thought not to eat much meat, but this is untrue of Italy in general and of Umbria in particular. Novelist Anthony Burgess once observed that a beefsteak in Italy is never *"una bistecca,"* but always *"una bella bistecca"*—a beautiful steak—and a simple steak in Umbria is almost always bella.

The region has made several important contributions to Italian cuisine. Particularly prized are black truffles from the area around Spoleto (signs warning against unlicensed truffle hunting are posted at the base of the grand Ponte delle Torri) and from the hills around the tiny town of Norcia. Norcia, in fact, exports truffles to France and hosts a truffle festival every year in November. Many regional dishes are given a grating of truffle before serving. The local pasta specialty—thick, handmade spaghetti called *ciriole* or *strengozzi*—is good *al tartufo*, with a dressing of excellent local olive oil and truffles.

In addition, Norcia's pork products—especially sausages, *salami*, and *arista* (pork chine)—are so famous that pork butchers throughout Italy are called *norcini*, no matter where they hail from, and pork butcher shops are called *norcinerie*.

In the Marches, fish in various forms is the thing to look for. One of the characteristic dishes in Ancona is *brodetto*, a rich fish chowder containing as many as nine types of Adriatic saltwater fish. Ascoli Piceno, inland, is famous for two dishes: *olive ascolane* (stuffed olives rolled in batter and deep-fried) and *vincisgrassi* (a local version of lasagne, with pieces of liver and béchamel sauce, far richer than you're likely to find elsewhere in Italy). Ascoli Piceno is also the home of the licorice-flavored liqueur *anisette*.

Unless otherwise noted, reservations are not needed and dress is casual. Even in the most upscale restaurants a tie is unnecessary, provided your general appearance is reasonably smart. Highly recommended restaurants are indicated by a star ★.

Shopping Pottery and wine are the two most famous Umbrian exports. Perugia is known for its chocolates. Gubbio, Perugia, Assisi, and Deruta are good places to shop for ceramics; the wine trade is concentrated in Orvieto.

Hiking Magnificent scenery makes Umbria fine hiking and mountaineering country. The area around Spoleto is particularly good, and the tourist office for the town will supply itineraries of walks and climbs to suit all ages and levels of ability.

Festivals The **Festival of Two Worlds** in Spoleto (mid-June–mid-July) features leading names in all branches of the arts—particularly music, opera, and theater—and draws thousands of visitors from all over the world. Tickets for all performances should be ordered in advance from the festival's box office (Via del Duomo 7, tel. 0743/220321). Information is available year-round from the festival's Rome office (Via Beccaria 18, tel. 06/321–0288).

Umbria's annual **jazz festival** attracts devotees from all over Europe to pay homage to some of the leading lights of the jazz world. Spread over 10 days in July in theaters and open-air venues throughout the region, this is an opportunity to listen to good music in often entrancing surroundings. For more information, write to the organizers at Casella Postale 228, 06100 Perugia, tel. 075/62432, or Perugia's tourist office (Piazza IV Novembre 3, tel. 075/572–3327). Between February and May, other jazz events take place as part of the **Teverearte** festival in the towns of Gubbio, Umbertide, Todi, Città di Castello, Sansepolcro, and Perugia. More information can be obtained from the festival's press office (Box 65, Ponte Felcino, Perugia, tel. 075/589–9891).

Highlights for First-time Visitors

Basilica of St. Francis, Assisi (Tour 2: Around Umbria).
Collegio del Cambio, Perugia (Tour 1: Perugia).
Duomo, Orvieto (Tour 2: Around Umbria).
Duomo, Spoleto (Tour 2: Around Umbria).
Ducal Palace, Urbino (Tour 3: The Marches).
Fontana Maggiore and Palazzo dei Priori, Perugia (Tour 1: Perugia).
House of the Virgin Mary, Loreto (Tour 3: The Marches).
Palazzo dei Consoli, Gubbio (Tour 1: Perugia).
Piazza del Popolo, Ascoli Piceno (Tour 3: The Marches).

Tour 1: Perugia

Perugia, the largest and richest of Umbria's cities, is an old and elegant place of great charm. Despite a rather grim crust of modern suburbs, Perugia's location on a series of hills high above the suburban plain has ensured that the medieval city remains almost completely intact. Perugia is the best-preserved hill town of its size, and few other places in Italy illustrate better the concept of the self-contained city-state that so shaped the course of Italian history.

As well as being a major attraction in its own right, Perugia is the transport hub of the region, and makes the most convenient base for exploring Umbria's other towns and villages.

From Rome and Florence By Train Diretto trains on the main Rome–Bologna–Milan line (6 trains a day from Rome, 10 from Florence) stop at Terontola–Cortona, where you can change to a train for Perugia (departures every hour or two). Total travel time from Rome is roughly three hours, and tickets cost around 17,000 lire; from Florence, 2½ to 3½ hours, with tickets costing 12,000 lire. From Rome, passengers can also take a train bound for Ancona and change at Foligno (nine departures daily, around 2½ hours' journey time, tickets cost about 15,000 lire).

By Bus The Sulga line (tel. 075/74641) runs three buses daily (two on Sunday) from Rome's Fiumicino airport and from Piazza Esedra in the city, one bus a day (5 PM) from Florence's bus station on Via della Stazione. The trip is two hours from Florence, and tickets cost around 15,000 lire. From Rome the trip is 2½ hours. Tickets cost 17,000–20,000 lire.

By Car The A1 autostrada, the principal north–south highway linking Florence and Rome, runs through the western edge of Umbria, passing through Orvieto. Coming south from Florence, exit the A1 at Valdichiana and get on S75bis, a route that takes you around Lake Trasimeno to Perugia. Coming north from Rome, exit the A1 at Orte and get on S204; just before Terni, turn onto S3bis and follow it north to Perugia.

By Plane Perugia has a small airport, Sant'Egidio, 12 kilometers (7½ miles) east of the city. Planes fly in from Milan only, with a journey time of about 80 minutes; tickets cost 218,000 lire.

Perugia

Tourist offices: Perugia's provincial tourist office, Via Mazzini 21, tel. 075/25341; city tourist office, Piazza IV Novembre 3, tel. 075/572-3327.

If you arrive in Perugia by train, you'll have to take a bus (No. 26, 27, 28, 29, 32, or 36) from the train station, which is in the unlovely suburbs, to **Piazza d'Italia,** the heart of the old town. Buy a ticket (1,000 lire) at the kiosk or in a machine and punch it on board. Long-distance buses arrive in the main bus station on Piazza dei Partigiani; from there, take an escalator to the historic city center, which is on a steep incline. The escalator penetrates the city's old walls and excavated Roman foundations without disturbing it's medieval flavor—a fascinating ride.

The nerve center of the city is the broad, stately **Corso Vannucci,** a pedestrian street that runs from Piazza d'Italia to Piazza IV Novembre. As evening falls, Corso Vannucci is filled with Perugians out for their evening *passeggiata,* a pleasant predinner stroll that may include a pause for an aperitif at one of the many bars that line the street.

Corso Vannucci runs into Piazza IV Novembre, a pretty, sunny square dominated by the **Duomo** (Cathedral of San Lorenzo); the medieval **Palazzo dei Priori,** or seat of government; and the **Fontana Maggiore,** a fountain by Giovanni and Nicola Pisano that dates from the 13th century.

The **Duomo** is a large and rather plain building dating from the Middle Ages but with many additions from the 15th and 16th centuries. The interior is vast and echoing, with little in the way of decoration. There are some elaborately carved choir stalls, executed by Giovanni Battista Bastone in 1520. The great relic of the church—the wedding ring of the Virgin Mary that the Perugians stole from the nearby town of Chiusi—is kept in a chapel in the left aisle. The ring is the size of a large bangle and is kept under lock (15 locks, actually) and key every day of the year except July 30, when it is open to view. *Duomo. Open daily 8–1 and 4–7:30.*

In the adjoining **Museum of the Duomo** there is a large array of precious objects associated with as the cathedral, including vestments, vessels, manuscripts, and gold work, as well as one outstanding piece of artwork, an early masterpiece by Luca Signorelli, the altarpiece showing the Madonna with St. John the Baptist, St. Onophrius, and St. Lawrence (1484). *Admission: 2,000 lire. Open Wed.–Fri. 9–noon, Sat. 9–noon and 3:30–5:30, Sun. 3:30–5:30.*

The **Palazzo dei Priori** faces the Duomo across the piazza. It is an imposing building, begun in the 13th century, with an unusual staircase that fans out into the square. The facade is decorated with symbols of Perugia's pride and past power: The griffin is the symbol of the city; the lion denotes Perugia's allegiance to the Guelph (or papal) cause; and both figures support the heavy chains of the gates of Siena, which fell to Perugian forces in 1358.

Attached to the Palazzo dei Priori, but entered from Corso Vannucci, is the **Collegio del Cambio,** a series of elaborate rooms that housed the meeting hall and chapel of the guild of bankers and money changers. The walls were frescoed from 1496 to 1500 by the most important Perugian painter of the Renaissance, Pietro Vannucci, better known as Perugino. The decorative subjects include common religious themes, such as the Nativity and the Transfiguration (on the end walls), but also figures intended to inspire the businessmen who congregated here. On the left wall are female figures representing the virtues, and beneath them the heroes and sages of antiquity. On the right wall are the Prophets and Sibyls—said to have been painted in part by Perugino's most famous pupil, Raphael, whose hand, the experts say, is most apparent in the figure of Fortitude. On one of the pilasters is a remarkably honest self-portrait of Perugino surmounted by a Latin inscription and contained in a *faux* frame. *Admission: 2,000 lire. Open Nov.– Feb., Tues.–Sat. 8–2, Sun. 9–12:30; Mar.–Oct., Tues.–Sat. 9– 12:30 and 2:30–5:30, Sun. 9–12:30.*

About a 10-minute walk south of the center along Corso Cavour leads to the **Archaeological Museum of Umbria,** which contains an excellent collection of Etruscan artifacts from throughout the region. Perugia was a flourishing Etruscan site long before it fell under Roman domination in 40 BC. (Other than this collection, little remains of Perugia's mysterious ancestors, although the Gate of Augustus, in Piazza Fortebraccio, the northern entrance to the city, is of Etruscan origin.) *Piazza Giordano Bruno. Admission: 4,000 lire. Open Mon.–Sat. 9–1:30 and 3–7, Sun. 9–1.*

Lodging
Under 115,000 lire

Palace Hotel Bellavista. The rooms in this hotel are decorated in splendid Belle Epoque grandeur, and many have views over the hills. The hotel's entrance is unimpressive, but the public rooms are palatial. Weekly rates are available. *Piazza d'Italia 12, tel. 075/572–0741, fax 075/572–9092. 70 rooms with bath or shower. Facilities: conference facilities, bar, breakfast room. AE, DC, MC, V.*

Priori. On a steep alley leading off the main Corso Vannucci, this is an unpretentious but elegant hotel that manages to be modern without sacrificing its identity. Rooms are spacious and cheerful, and there is a panoramic terrace where breakfast (included in the price) is served in summer. *Via Vermiglioli 3, tel. 075/572–3378, fax 075/572–3213. 50 rooms, 46 with bath or shower. Facilities: bar, garage. No credit cards.*

Under 85,000 lire

Eden. Newly refurbished and modernized, this third-story lodging now offers smart, well-equipped rooms, tastefully decorated in pastel colors, each with TV and telephone. The central location makes this a popular choice, so space may be limited in summer. *Via Caporali 9, tel. 075/572–8102. 15 rooms with shower. Facilities: bar. No credit cards.*

Under 60,000 lire

Ostello della Gioventù. IYH membership isn't required to stay at this unofficial youth hostel. It has an ultraconvenient location, just behind the cathedral, which is unusual for this type of accommodation. In other respects it is more conventional: Guests sleep in single-sex dormitories of five or six bunks per room and must vacate the premises between 9:30 AM and 4 PM. There is a dining area and television room but no kitchen. Many of the lodgers are students at Perugia's foreigners' university. Prices are low, at 14,000 per person per night. *Via Bontempi 13, tel. 075/22880. 40 beds. No credit cards.*

Dining
Under 30,000 lire

Il Falchetto. Here you'll find exceptional food at reasonable prices—making this Perugia's best restaurant bargain. The service is smart but relaxed, and the two dining rooms are medieval, with the kitchen and chef on view. The house specialty is *falchetti* (homemade gnocchi with spinach and ricotta cheese). *Via Bartolo 20, tel. 075/573–1675. Reservations advised. AE, DC, MC, V. Closed Mon.*

L'Escargot. The tone here is rather stiff and formal, but the dishes are reasonably priced and the quality good. Dining is on two levels, and it can get crowded. Sample the rich and creamy *maccheroni con funghi* (pasta with mushrooms), and leave room for a good selection of desserts. *Via Campo Battaglia 10, tel. 075/65851. AE, DC, MC, V. Closed Tues.*

Under 24,000 lire **Dal Mi Cocco.** If you can get a table, this popular restaurant is a must for anyone with a sense of adventure. The menu is in virtually incomprehensible dialect, though the waiters, who reveal humor and soft hearts beneath their gruff exteriors, are polished interpreters. With a menu that changes daily, what's offered on any particular night is limited, though the many regular customers can enjoy an ever-changing tour through Umbria's culinary diversity. Prices are good: A fixed-price, three-course meal costs 20,000 lire. *Arrosto misto* (mixed roast meats) is usually available, and always recommended. *Corso Garibaldi 12, tel. 075/62511. Reservations advised. No credit cards. Closed Mon.*

Shopping Perugia is a well-to-do town, and expensive designer boutiques line Corso Vannucci. The best and most typical thing to buy in Perugia, though, is some of the famous and delicious Perugina chocolate, especially the round chocolate-and-nut-filled *Baci* (kisses), wrapped in silver paper with enclosed fortunes.

For a more motley selection of knickknacks, Perugia holds an open-air antiques fair on the last weekend of every month, in the area behind the cathedral. Browse among the stalls to find, alongside more expensive objects, some original souvenirs: old postcards, books, war memorabilia, maps, faded photos, and more.

Tour 2: Around Umbria

From Perugia there are a number of easy day trips to make to various Umbrian towns and villages, most notably Gubbio, Spoleto, Assisi, and Orvieto, all of which have somehow survived into the 20th century with their medieval charm intact. Traveling to these towns by bus or train through rugged, mountainous terrain and lovely swathes of forested valleys, you can appreciate Umbria's unspoiled landscape to the fullest. Should you choose to linger in any of these historic hill towns, we have suggested some lodgings in each.

Torgiano

There are nine daily bus departures (Monday through Saturday) from Perugia's bus station on Piazza dei Partigiani. The trip to Torgiano takes 20 minutes and tickets cost 3,200 lire.

Wine lovers are certain to want to visit Torgiano, 15 kilometers (9 miles) southeast of Perugia. It is home to the famous Lungarotti winery, best known for delicious Rubesco Lungarotti, San Giorgio, and Chardonnay. The town is also home to the fascinating **Wine Museum,** which has a large collection of ancient wine vessels, presses, documents, and tools that tell the story of viticulture in Umbria and beyond. The museum traces the history of wine in all its uses—for drinking at the table, as medicine, and in mythology. *Corso Vittorio Emanuele 11. Admission: 3,000 lire. Open Apr.–Sept., daily 9–noon and 3–8; Oct.–Mar., daily 9–1 and 3–6.*

Gubbio

Ten buses a day leave Perugia for Gubbio; the trip takes 70 minutes and costs 6,200 lire. Tourist office: Piazza Oderisi 6, tel. 075/922–0693.

Forty kilometers (25 miles) northeast of Perugia, Gubbio is otherworldly, a small jewel of a medieval town tucked away in this mountainous corner of Umbria. Even at the height of summer, the cool serenity and silence of Gubbio's streets remain intact. The town is perched on the slopes of Mount Ingino, and the streets are dramatically steep.

Gubbio's relatively isolated position has kept it free of hordes of high-season visitors, but even during the busiest times of year the city lives up to its Italian nickname, The City of Silence.

From the central Piazza dei Quaranta Martiri (named for 40 hostages murdered by the Nazis in 1944), walk up the main street of the town, Via della Repubblica (a steep climb), to Piazza della Signoria. This square is dominated by the magnificent **Palazzo dei Consoli,** a medieval building designed and built by a local architect known as Gattapone—a man still much admired by today's residents (every other hotel, restaurant, and bar has been named after him).

While the Palazzo dei Consoli is impressive, it is the piazza itself that is most striking. When approached from the thicket of medieval streets, the wide and majestic square is an eye-opener. The piazza juts out from the hillside like an enormous terrace, giving wonderful views of the town and surrounding countryside.

The Palazzo dei Consoli houses a small **museum,** famous chiefly for the Tavole Eugubine, bronze tablets written in an ancient Umbrian language. Also in the museum are the *ceri,* three 16-foot-high poles crowned with statues of saints Ubaldo, George, and Anthony. These heavy pillars are the focal point of the best-known event in Gubbio, the Festival of the Candles ("Ceri"), held every May 15. On that day, teams of Gubbio's young men, dressed in medieval costumes and carrying the ceri, race up the steep slopes of Mount Ingino to the Monastery of St. Ubaldo, high above the town. This festival, enacted faithfully every year since 1151, is a picturesque, if strenuous, way of thanking the patron saints of the town for their assistance in a miraculous Gubbian victory over a league of 11 other towns. *Admission: 4,000 lire. Open Apr.–Sept., daily 9–12:30 and 3:30–6; Oct.–Mar., Tues.–Fri. 10–1 and 3–5; Sat. and Sun. 9–1 and 3–5; closed Mon.*

The **Duomo** and the **Palazzo Ducale** face each other across a narrow street on the highest tier of the town. The Duomo dates from the 13th century, with some Baroque additions—in particular, a lavishly decorated bishop's chapel. *Duomo. Open daily 9–5.*

The Palazzo Ducale is a scaled-down copy of the Palazzo Ducale in Urbino (Gubbio was once the possession of that city's ruling family, the Montefeltro). Gubbio's palazzo contains a small museum and a fine courtyard. There are magnificent views from some of the public rooms. *Palazzo Ducale. Admission: 4,000 lire. Open daily 9–2.*

Lodging
Under 115,000 lire

Hotel Bosone. Occupying the old central Palazzo Raffaelli, the Hotel Bosone has many rooms decorated with frescoes from the former palace. *Via XX Settembre 22 tel. 075/922–0688, fax 075/922–0552. 30 rooms with bath. Facilities: restaurant, bar. AE, DC, MC, V.*

Under 85,000 lire

Hotel Gattapone. Right in the center of town is this hotel with wonderful views of the sea of rooftops. It is casual and family-run, with good-size, modern, comfortable rooms. *Via Ansidei 6, tel. 075/927–2489, fax 075/927–1269. 13 rooms with bath. AE, DC, MC, V. Closed Jan.*

Dining
Under 30,000 lire

Fornace di Mastro Giorgio. This atmospheric restaurant is located in the medieval workshop of a famous master potter, one of Gubbio's most famous sons. The food is lighter than the typical Umbrian fare, with the occasional southern dish, such as *tiella barese* (a mixture of rice, mussels, and potatoes). *Via Mastro Giorgio 2, tel. 075/927–5740. Reservations advised in summer. AE, DC, MC, V. Closed Sun. evening and Mon.*

Grotta dell'Angelo. This rustic trattoria is in the lower part of the old town, near the main square and tourist information office. The menu features simple local specialties, including *capocollo* (a type of salami), *strengozzi* (homemade pasta), and *lasagna tartufata* (lasagna made with truffles). There are a few tables for outdoor dining. There are also some inexpensive guest rooms available here, good value at 70,000 lire. *Via Gioia 47, tel. 075/927–1747. Reservations advised. AE, DC, MC, V. Closed Tues. and Jan. 7–Feb. 7.*

Taverna del Lupo. It's one of the best restaurants in the city, as well as one of the largest. Taverna del Lupo seats 200 people and can get a bit hectic during the high season. Lasagna made in the Gubbian fashion, with ham and truffles, is the best pasta. You'll also find excellent desserts and an extensive wine cellar here. *Via Ansidei 21, tel. 075/927–4368. Reservations advised in high season. AE, DC, MC, V. Closed Mon. (except July–Aug.) and Jan.*

Shopping

The red glazes of Gubbio **pottery** have been famous since medieval times. The secret of the original glaze died with its inventor some 500 years ago, but there are contemporary potters who produce a fair facsimile.

Assisi

From Perugia, 10 buses a day (fare 4,200 lire) make the hour-long drive to Assisi. The train trip (fare 2,500 lire) takes 25 minutes; local buses (fare 1,000 lire) run every half hour from the station, 5 kilometers (3 miles) from the town. Tourist office: Piazza del Comune 12, tel. 075/812534.

The first sight of Assisi is memorable. The hill on which Assisi sits rises dramatically from the flat plain, and the town is dominated at the top of the mount by a medieval castle; on the lower slopes of the hill is the massive Basilica of San Francesco, rising majestically on graceful arched supports.

Except in the depths of the off-season, Assisi, the most famous and most visited city in Umbria, is always thronged with sightseers and pilgrims. Somehow, though, despite the press of visitors, there is an unspoiled quality to the city—although that charm can be taxed to the limit during major feasts of the church, such as Christmas or Easter, or on the feast of the patron saint himself (October 4). But if you come to Assisi on a weekday or in the low season, you are sure to see this charming rose-colored town at its best.

St. Francis was born here in 1181, the son of a well-to-do merchant. He had, by his own account, a riotous youth but forsook the pleasures of the flesh quite early, adopting a life of austerity. His mystical approach to poverty, asceticism, and the beauty of man and nature struck a responsive chord in the medieval mind, and he quickly attracted a vast number of followers. He was a humble and unassuming man, and his compassion and humility brought him great love and veneration in his own lifetime. Without actively seeking power, as did many clerics of his day, he amassed great influence and political power, changing the history of the Catholic church. He was the first person to receive the stigmata (wounds in his hands, feet, and side corresponding to the torments of Christ on the cross), injuries that caused him great pain and suffering, which he bore with characteristic patience. Nonetheless, St. Francis welcomed the coming of "Sister Death," in 1226. Today the Franciscans are the largest of all the Catholic orders. And among the mass of clergy at Assisi, you can identify the saint's followers by their simple, coarse brown habits bound by belts of knotted rope.

The **Basilica of San Francesco,** at the western end of the old town, is one of Italy's foremost monuments and was begun shortly after the saint's death. What St. Francis would have made of a church of such size, wealth, and grandeur—the opposite of all he preached and believed—is hard to imagine. His coffin, unearthed from its secret hiding place in 1818, is on display in the crypt below the lower church and is a place of piety. The basilica is not one church, but two huge structures built one over the other. The lower church is dim and full of candle-lit shadows, while the upper is a bright and airy place. Both are magnificently decorated artistic treasure houses, however, especially the upper church, where a fresco cycle by Giotto is a milestone in the history of Western art.

Visit the lower church first. The first chapel on the left of the nave was decorated by the Sienese master Simone Martini. Frescoed from 1322 to 1326, the paintings show the life of St. Martin—the sharing of his cloak with the poor man, the saint's knighthood, and his death.

There is some dispute about the paintings in the third chapel on the right. Experts have argued for years as to their authorship, with many saying that they were done by Giotto. The paintings depict the life of St. Mary Magdalen. There is a similar dispute about the works above the high altar—some say they are by Giotto; others claim them for an anonymous pupil. They depict the marriage of St. Francis to poverty, chastity, and obedience.

In the right transept are frescoes by Cimabue, a Madonna and Saints, one of them St. Francis himself. In the left transept are some of the best-known works of the Sienese painter Pietro Lorenzetti. They depict the Madonna with saints John and Francis, a Crucifixion, and a Descent from the Cross.

It is quite a contrast to climb the steps next to the altar and emerge into the bright sunlight and airy grace of the double-arched Renaissance cloister called the Cloister of the Dead. A door to the right leads to the treasury of the church and contains relics of St. Francis and other holy objects associated with the order.

The upper church is dominated by Giotto's 28 frescoes, each portraying incidents in the life of St. Francis. Although the artist was only in his twenties when he painted this cycle, the frescoes show that Giotto was the pivotal artist in the development of Western painting, breaking away from the stiff, unnatural styles of earlier generations and moving toward a realism and grace that reached its peak during the Renaissance. The paintings are viewed left to right, starting in the transept. The most beloved of all the scenes is probably that of *St. Francis Preaching to the Birds,* a touching painting that seems to sum up the gentle spirit of the saint. It stands in marked contrast to the scene of the dream of Innocent III. The pope dreams of a humble monk who will steady the church. Sure enough, in the panel next to the sleeping pope, you see a strong Francis supporting a church that seems to be on the verge of tumbling down. *Upper and lower churches. Open summer, Mon.–Sat. 6 AM–7 PM, Sun. 6 AM–7:30 PM; winter, Mon.–Sat. 6:30–noon and 2–6, Sun. 6:30 AM–7 PM.*

Follow Via San Francesco from the basilica up the hill to the central square of the town, Piazza del Comune. The **Temple of Minerva,** on the left, is made up of bits and pieces of a Roman temple that dates from the time of Augustus. It has been converted into a church. *Open daily 7–noon and 4–7.*

Follow Corso Mazzini out of the square, heading toward the church of **Santa Chiara.** This 13th-century church is dedicated to St. Clare, one of the earliest and most fervent of St. Francis's followers and the founder of the order of the Poor Ladies, or Poor Clares, in imitation of the Franciscans. The church contains the body of the saint, and in the chapel of the Crucifix (on the right) is the cross that spoke to St. Francis and led him to a life of piety. A member of St. Clare's order is stationed before the cross and is heavily veiled in perpetual adoration of the image. *Open daily 8–1 and 4–7.*

Walk past the church of Santa Chiara, along Via Borgo Aretino and out through the walls of the gate called the **Porta Nuova.** From there, approximately 1 kilometer (⅔ mile) farther on, you will reach the church of **San Damiano.** It was here that the crucifix spoke to St. Francis, saying, "Vade, Francisce, et repara domum meam" ("Go, Francis, and repair my house"). It was also in this church, pleasantly situated in an olive grove, that St. Francis brought St. Clare into the religious life. The church became the first home of her order, and it and its convent, simple and austere, give a far better idea of St. Francis and his movement than does the great basilica. *Open daily 8–12:30 and 2–6.*

Also on the outskirts of the town, on the plain near the train station, is the church of **Santa Maria degli Angeli.** It is a Baroque building constructed over the **Porziuncola,** a little chapel restored by St. Francis. The shrine is much venerated because it was here, in the Transito chapel, then a humble cell, that St. Francis died. *Open daily 9–1 and 4–7.*

Lodging
Under 115,000 lire
★

Hotel Umbra. A 16th-century town house is home to this hotel, which is located in a tranquil part of the city, an area closed to traffic, near Piazza del Comune. The rooms are arranged as small apartments, with tiny living rooms and terraces. *Via* *degli Archi 6, tel. 075/812240. 27 rooms with bath or shower. Facilities: restaurant (closed Tues.), bar. AE, DC, MC, V. Closed mid-Jan.–mid-Mar.*

Ostello della Pace. A stout medieval building houses this youth hostel, one of two in the area, situated about 500 yards outside the city walls, or a 15-minute walk from the center. Despite the old stone exterior, the hostel is new, opened in 1992, though the modern fittings do not compromise its old character. Family rooms are available, and temporary membership cards can be obtained from the reception desk. *Via Valecchi, tel. 075/ 816767. 60 beds. Facilities: bar, restaurant, garden, parking. No credit cards. Open all year.*

Splurge **Hotel Subasio.** This hotel, close to the Basilica of St. Francis, has counted Marlene Dietrich and Charlie Chaplin among its guests. It is housed in a converted monastery and has plenty of atmosphere. Some of the rooms remain a little monastic, but the views, comfortable old-fashioned sitting rooms, flowered terraces, and a lovely garden more than make up for the simplicity. Ask for a room with a view of the valley. *Via Frate Elia 2, tel. 075/812206, fax 075/816691. 61 rooms with bath. Facilities: restaurant, bar, baby-sitting, conference and group reception rooms, garden. AE, DC, MC, V.*

Dining **Buca di San Francesco.** This central restaurant is Assisi's busi-
Under 30,000 lire est and most popular. The setting is lovely no matter what the season. In summer you dine outside in a cool green garden; in winter, in the cozy cellars of the restaurant. The food is first-rate, and the *filetto al rubesco* (fillet steak cooked in a hearty red wine) is the specialty of the house. *Via Brizi 1, tel. 075/ 812204. Reservations advised in high season (June–Sept.). AE, DC, MC, V. Closed Mon. and July.*

La Fortezza. Parts of the walls of this modern restaurant were built by the Romans. The service is personable and the kitchen reliable. A particular standout is *coniglio in salsa di asparagi* (rabbit in asparagus sauce). La Fortezza also has seven simple but clean guest rooms available. *Vicolo della Fortezza 19b, tel. 075/812418. Reservations advised in high season. AE, DC, MC, V. Closed Thurs. (except Aug.–Sept.) and Feb.*

La Stalla. Just outside the town proper, this one-time stable has been turned into a simple and rustic restaurant. In summer, lunch and dinner are served outside under a delightful trellis shaded with vines and flowers. In keeping with the decor, the food is hearty country cooking. *Via Eremo delle Carceri 8, tel. 075/812317. No credit cards. Closed Mon.*

Spoleto

Twelve trains daily head from Perugia; you must change at Foligno to reach Spoleto (about an hour's journey in total). The train station is a 15-minute walk from Spoleto's center, but there are frequent local buses (fare: 1,000 lire). One bus a day goes direct from Perugia to Spoleto, a 90-minute journey that costs 8,700 lire. The bus leaves at 2 PM and belongs to the Spoletina line (tel. 0743/221991). Tourist office: Piazza della Libertà 7, tel. 0743/49890 or 0743/220311.

Spoleto is an enchanting town perfectly situated in wooded countryside. "A little bit of heaven fallen to earth," it was once called, and it is not hard to understand the sentiment. "Quaint" may be an overused term, but it is the most appropriate word to

describe this city that is still enclosed by stout medieval walls.
The chief pleasure of Spoleto is that the city itself is the sight.
There is no long tramp through museums and churches in store
for you here; rather, you can enjoy the simple treat of walking
through the maze of twisting streets and up and down cobbled
stairways, enjoying the beauty of the town and its wonderful
peace and quiet.

Quiet, that is, except when Spoleto is hosting the Festival of
Two Worlds, an arts festival, held every year from mid-June to
mid-July. Then the sleepy town is swamped with visitors who
come to see world-class plays and operas, hear concerts, and
see extensive exhibitions of paintings and sculpture. Hotels in
the city and countryside are filled to overflowing, and the
streets are packed with visitors. It is unwise to arrive in
Spoleto during this period without confirmed hotel reservations. Furthermore, experiencing the town itself, rather than
the festival, is very difficult during these months. Those
who don't care for crowds are advised to stay away during the
festival.

Spoleto is dominated by a huge castle that was built from 1359
to 1363 by the Gubbio-born architect Gattapone. It was until
recently a high-security prison but is now undergoing restoration and is shortly due to open to the public. The castle was
built to protect the town's most famous monument, the massive
bridge known as the **Ponte delle Torri** (Bridge of the Towers),
built by Gattapone on Roman foundations. This massive structure stands 262 feet above the gorge it spans and was originally
built as an aqueduct. The bridge is open to pedestrians, and a
walk across it affords marvelous views—looking down to the
river below is the best way to appreciate the colossal dimensions of the bridge, whose central span is actually higher than
that of the dome of St. Peter's in Rome.

The bridge and castle stand at the highest point in the town.
From there you can head downhill to the **Duomo,** set in a lovely
square. The church facade is dourly Romanesque, but with the
pleasant light addition of a Renaissance loggia. The contrast
between the heavy medieval work and the graceful later embel-
lishment graphically demonstrates the difference, not only in
style but in philosophy, of the two eras. The earlier was strong
but ungiving; the later, human and open-minded.

From Piazza del Duomo make your way to Piazza del Mercato,
site of the old Roman forum and today the main square of the
old town. The square is lined with bars and delicatessens that
serve good pastries and coffee.

The **Arch of Drusus,** off the southern end of the square, was
built by the Senate of Spoleto to honor the Roman general
Drusus, son of the emperor Tiberius.

North of Piazza del Mercato, past the picturesque Via
Fontesecca, with its tempting shops selling local pottery and
other handicrafts, is the church of **Sant'Eufemia** (in the courtyard of the archbishop's palace), an ancient, austere church
built in the 11th century. Its most interesting feature is the gallery above the nave, where female worshipers were required to
sit—a holdover from the Eastern church—one of the few such
galleries in this part of Italy. *Open summer, daily 8–8, winter,
daily 8–6.*

At the southern end of Corso Mazzini is a small but well-preserved **Roman theater,** used in summer for performances of Spoleto's arts festival. The theater was the site of one of the town's most macabre incidents. During the Middle Ages, Spoleto took the side of the Holy Roman Emperor in the interminable struggle between Guelph (papal) and Ghibelline (imperial) factions over the question of who would control central and northern Italy. Four hundred of the pope's supporters were massacred in the theater, and their bodies were burned in an enormous pyre. It is not an episode of which Spoleto is proud, and, furthermore, the Guelphs were triumphant in the end. Spoleto was incorporated into the states of the church in 1354. *Open summer, Tues.–Sun. 9–1:30 and 3–6; winter, Tues.–Sun. 9–1 and 2:30–6. Closed holidays.*

Lodging
Under 85,000 lire

Dell'Angelo. Don't even bother to seek a room in this modest hotel during festival time—in fact, space at any time during the summer is at a premium in this popular small lodging. The center-of-town location is ideal, and the prices are among Spoleto's lowest. Rooms are small but clean; facilities are minimal, but there's a lively trattoria downstairs. *Via Arco di Druso 25, tel. 0743/222385. 7 rooms with shower. No credit cards.*

Splurge

Hotel Gattapone. The tiny four-star Hotel Gattapone is situated at the top of the old town, near the Ponte delle Torri, and has wonderful views of the ancient bridge and the wooded slopes of Monteluco. The rooms are well furnished and tastefully decorated. *Via del Ponte 6, tel. 0743/223447, fax 0743/223448. 13 rooms with bath. Facilities: bar, garden. AE, DC, MC, V.*

Dining
Under 30,000 lire

Trattoria Panciolle. In the heart of Spoleto's medieval quarter, this restaurant has one of the most romantic settings you could wish for. Dining outside in summer is a delight in a small piazza filled with lime trees. Specialties include *stringozzi* (homemade pasta) with mushroom sauce and *agnello scottadito* (grilled lamb chops). Seven guest rooms are also available here. *Via del Duomo 3, tel. 0743/45598. Reservations advised. AE, MC, V. Closed Wed.*

Nicolaus. Opened in 1993 just outside the 12th-century Porta Fuga city gate, this hotel specializes in Apulian cuisine, which means lots of fish and such pasta dishes as *orecchiette a rape* ("little ears" with broccoli). For a main course, try the delicious *cartocci di scampi,* shrimp cooked in the oven with a lemony sauce. Pizzas are also available. The atmosphere is semiformal, the tone bright and modern. *Via Cecili 24, tel. 0743/49259. MC, V. Closed Mon.*

Splurge

Il Tartufo. Halfway between the train station and the center of town, Spoleto's most famous restaurant has a smart, modern dining room on the second floor and a rustic dining room downstairs—both of which incorporate the ruins of a Roman villa. The traditional cooking is spiced up in summer to appeal to the cosmopolitan crowd attending (or performing in) the Festival of Two Worlds. As its name indicates, the restaurant specializes in dishes prepared with truffles, though there is a second menu from which you can choose items that do not contain this expensive delicacy. *Piazza Garibaldi 24 tel. 0743/40236. Reservations required during the festival and recommended at other times of the year. AE, DC, MC, V. Closed Wed. and mid-July–1st week in Aug.*

Orvieto

There are five train departures daily from Perugia to Orvieto: All involve a change at Terontola–Cortona, and two of them require an additional change at Chiusi. Total journey time is two to three hours, and the total fare is roughly 9,000 lire. There is one bus a day (Monday through Saturday) from Perugia, leaving Piazza dei Partigiani at 2 PM. The trip takes 2½ hours and tickets are 10,700 lire. Tourist office: Piazza Duomo 24, tel. 0763/41772.

Orvieto is one of Umbria's greatest cities. Its commanding, dramatic position on a great square rock is an amazing sight, dominating the countryside for miles in every direction. This natural fort was first settled by the Etruscans, but not even Orvieto's defenses could withstand the might of the Romans, who attacked, sacked, and destroyed the city in 283 BC. From that time, Orvieto has had close ties with Rome. It was solidly Guelph during the Middle Ages, and for several hundred years popes sought refuge in the city, at some times seeking protection from their enemies, at other times fleeing from the summer heat of Rome. Orvieto's position on its rock has meant that little new building has ever been done here, giving the town an almost perfect medieval character.

When you arrive in Orvieto, take the funicular and then the waiting minibus (total fare 1,300 lire) to reach the city's centerpiece jewel, the **Duomo,** set in the wide and airy Piazza del Duomo. The church, built to commemorate the Miracle of Bolsena, was started in 1290 and received the attention of some of the greatest architects and sculptors of the time. It was further embellished inside by great Renaissance artists. The facade is a prodigious work, covered with carvings and mosaics, the latter intricately ornamenting practically every pillar and post and also used in large representations of religious scenes (many of these were restored or redone during the 18th and 19th centuries). The bas-relief on the lower parts of the pillars were carved by Maitani, one of the original architects of the building, and show scenes from the Old Testament and some particularly gruesome renderings of the Last Judgment and Hell, as well as a more tranquil Paradise. (They have been covered with Plexiglass, following some vandalizing in the 1960s.)

The vast interior of the cathedral is famous chiefly for the frescoes in the Cappella Nuova (the last chapel on the right, nearest the high altar). The earliest works here are above the altar and are by Fra Angelico. They show Christ in Glory and the Prophets. The major works in the chapel, however, are by Luca Signorelli and show a very graphic Last Judgment. The walls seem to be filled with muscular, writhing figures, and most critics draw a direct connection between these figures and the later Last Judgment of Michelangelo, on the wall of the Sistine Chapel. Leonardo da Vinci, however, was less than impressed. He said that the figures, with their rippling muscles, reminded him of sacks "stuffed full of nuts."

Across the nave of the cathedral from the Cappella Nuova is the Cappella del Corporale. It houses the relics of the Miracle of Bolsena, the raison d'être for the Duomo. A priest in the nearby town of Bolsena suddenly found himself assailed by doubts about the transubstantiation—he could not bring himself to believe that the body of Christ was contained in the consecrated communion host. His doubts were put to rest, however, when a wafer he had just blessed suddenly started to drip blood. Drops of blood fell onto the linen covering the altar, and this cloth and the host itself are the principal relics of the miracle. They are contained in a sumptuous gold-and-enamel reliquary on the altar of this chapel and are displayed on the Feast of Corpus Christi and at Easter. *Duomo. Open daily 7–1 and 3–dusk.*

To the right of the Duomo is the medieval **Palazzo dei Papi**, once the summer residence of popes, which contains the Archaeological Museum. *Admission free. Open May–Oct., Mon.–Sat. 9–1:30 and 3–7, Sun. 9–1; Nov.–Apr., Mon.–Sat. 9–1:30 and 2:30–6, Sun. 9–1.*

Orvieto is known for its wines, particularly the whites. Some of the finest wines in Umbria are produced here (Signorelli, when painting the Duomo, asked that part of his contract be paid in wine), and the rock on which the town sits is honeycombed with caves used to ferment the Trebbiano grapes that are used in making Orvieto vintages. Taking a glass of wine, therefore, at the **wine cellar** at No. 2, Piazza del Duomo, is as much a cultural experience as a refreshment stop. You'll find a good selection of sandwiches and snacks there as well.

Lodging
Under 115,000 lire

Virgilio. The modest Hotel Virgilio is situated right in Piazza del Duomo, and the rooms with views of the cathedral are wonderful. The rooms are small but well furnished. *Piazza del Duomo 5, tel. 0763/41882. 13 rooms, 2 with bath, 11 with shower. Facilities: bar. No credit cards.*

Under 85,000 lire

Duomo. Conveniently located in a back street behind the cathedral, this low-key hotel is little frequented for much of the year, but it's often full in August. The rooms are discreetly furnished, some with good views, and the management is polite and conscientious. *Via Maurizio 7, tel. 0763/41887. 17 rooms, 9 with bath. Facilities: bar. No credit cards.*

Posta. Secluded, but just five minutes' walk from the center, this old-fashioned hotel has a somewhat musty air that suits the somber furnishings. Guest rooms are uncluttered, with stylish, comfortable furniture. *Via Signorelli 18, tel. 0763/41909. 20 rooms, 8 with bath. Facilities: bar, garden, garage. No credit cards.*

Dining
Under 30,000 lire
★

Maurizio. In the heart of Orvieto, just opposite the cathedral, this warm and welcoming restaurant gets its share of tourists and has a local clientele as well. The decor is unusual, with wood sculptures by Orvieto craftsman Michelangeli. The menu offers hearty soups and such homemade pastas as *tronchetti* (a pasta roll with spinach and ricotta filling). The *menu turistico* (fixed price) here is a good bargain. *Via del Duomo 78, tel. 0763/41114. Reservations advised in summer. MC, V. Closed Tues. and 3 weeks in Jan.*

Splurge
★

Le Grotte del Funaro. This restaurant has an extraordinary location, deep in a series of caves within the volcanic rock beneath Orvieto. Once you have negotiated the steep steps, typical Umbrian specialties, such as *tagliatelle al vino rosso* (noodles with red wine sauce) and grilled beef with truffles, await. Sample the fine Orvieto wines, either the whites or the lesser-known reds. The 30,000 lire fixed-price menu here is excellent value. *Via Ripa Serancia 41, tel. 0763/43276. Reservations advised. AE, MC, DC, V. Closed Mon. and 2 weeks in July.*

Shopping   Orvieto is a center of woodworking, particularly of fine inlays and veneers. The Corso Cavour has a number of artisan shops specializing in woodwork, the best-known being the studio of the Michelangeli family, which is crammed with a variety of imaginatively designed objects ranging in size from a giant *armadio* (wardrobe) to a simple wooden spoon.

Minor arts, such as embroidery and lace making, flourish in Orvieto as well. One of the town's best shops for lace (*merletto*) is Duranti, at Via del Duomo 10.

Excellent Orvieto wines are justly prized throughout Italy and in foreign countries. The whites are fruity, with a tart aftertaste, and are made from the region's Trebbiano grapes. Orvieto also produces its own version of the Tuscan dessert wine *vin santo*. It is darker than its Tuscan cousin and is aged five years before bottling.

Tour 3: The Marches

It must be admitted that traveling in the Marches is not as easy as traveling in Umbria or Tuscany. The best touring base is the principal city, Ancona, which is not in itself particularly interesting. Much more interesting are the towns of Urbino and Ascoli Piceno, to the north and south respectively, remote enough from Ancona that you would be hard-pressed to visit either of them without spending the night.

From Rome   Intercity trains take 3¼ hours to Ancona; it's closer to four
By Train   hours on an Espresso or Diretto. Standard fare is about 20,000 lire, more on Intercity trains.

By Car   Take the A24 from Rome across to the Adriatic coast, where you can pick up the Adriatica superhighway (A14) linking the Marches to Bologna and Venice.

From Perugia   Change onto the main Rome–Ancona line at Foligno. The trip
By Train   takes 2½–3½ hours and costs about 12,500 lire.

By Bus   There is no direct Perugia–Ancona bus service, but you can take a bus from Perugia to Civitanova Marche, 50 kilometers south of Ancona, from which there are frequent trains to Ancona but no buses. The Perugia–Civitanova Marche service is run by Contram (tel. 0733/230906); tickets cost 8,600 lire. There is one departure a day from Perugia at 2:15 PM, and the journey takes four hours.

By Car   The mountain routes between Umbria and the Marches are tortuous. Drivers are advised to get onto the S3 at Foligno, which intersects with the A14 on the coast at Fano.

Ancona

Tourist offices: Via Thaon de Revel 4, tel. 071/33249; railway station, Piazza Fratelli Rosselli, tel. 071/41703.

Ancona was probably once a lovely city. It is set on an elbow-shape bluff (hence its name: *Ankon* is Greek for "elbow") that juts out into the Adriatic. But Ancona was the object of serious aerial bombing during the Second World War—it was, and is, an important port city—and was reduced to rubble. The city has been rebuilt in the unfortunate postwar poured-concrete style, practical and inexpensive but certainly not pleasing. Although once in a while there are glimpses of old architecture, unless you are taking a ferry to Venice, there is little reason to visit the city except as a base.

To reach the center of town where the port and most of Ancona's hotels and restaurants are, take bus No. 1 from outside the train station. There are some cheap hotels directly outside the station, but if you are planning to base yourself here for more than a day, you may feel feel more comfortable in one of the hotels nearer the town center.

Lodging
Under 115,000 lire

Hotel Roma e Pace. The only two reasons to stay in this hotel are the location and the price. It is good value for the money and centrally located, but the rooms are ugly and cramped, and the service slapdash and uncaring. A historical note: In 1904 a Russian named Josef Dzhugashvili applied for a job here and was refused. He later found better-paying employment as supreme head of the Soviet Union under the name Stalin. *Via Leopardi 1, tel. 071/202007. 73 rooms with bath or shower. Facilities: restaurant, bar. AE, DC, MC, V.*

Under 85,000 lire

Viale. Bus No. 1 stops directly outside this modern hotel just up from Largo XIV Maggio. The rooms are boxy but comfortable enough, each with telephone, television, and radio; there is a small, shady garden, too. Booking ahead is advisable in the summer. *Viale della Vittoria 23, tel. 071/201861. 26 rooms with shower. Facilities: bar, garden. AE, DC, MC, V.*

Dining
Under 30,000 lire

Giardino. This modern, well-run trattoria is in the center of town, just off Piazza Diaz on the main Viale della Vittoria. There is plenty of room inside, but in summer you will probably prefer to sit outdoors. Fish is the best choice here: The menu will vary according to season, but if it's available, try *rombo con rucola*, turbot served in a spicy tomato sauce with a slightly bitter lettuce salad as accompaniment. You can have pizza here, too. *Via Fabio Filzi 2, tel. 071/207–4660. Closed Wed. AE, DC, MC, V.*

Splurge

La Moretta. This family-run trattoria is located on the central Piazza del Plebiscito. In summer there is dining outside in the square, which has a fine view of the Baroque church of San Domenico. Among the specialties of La Moretta are *tagliatelle in salsa di ostriche* (pasta in an oyster sauce) and the famous brodetto fish stew. *Piazza del Plebiscito 52, tel. 071/202317. Reservations advised. DC, MC, V. Closed Sun. and Aug. 10–15.*

Urbino

Take the frequent train service from Ancona to the coastal town of Pesaro (a 50-minute journey; fare: 4,300 lire) and catch a local bus (10 departures daily from outside the train station; fare: 3,500 lire) for the 50-minute trip to Urbino. Buses stop outside the walls in Borgo Mercatale, from which you can reach the town center by elevator or stairs. Tourist office: Piazza Rinascimento 1, tel. 0722/2613.

Urbino is a majestic city, sitting atop a steep hill, with a skyline of towers and domes. It is something of a surprise to come upon it—the location is remote—and it is even stranger to reflect that this quiet country town was once a center of learning and culture almost without rival in western Europe. The town looks much as it did in the glory days of the 15th century, a cluster of warm brick and pale stone buildings, all topped with russet-color tiled roofs. The focal point is the immense and beautiful Ducal Palace.

The tradition of learning in Urbino continues to this day. The city is the home of a small but prestigious Italian state university—one of the oldest in the world—and while school is in session, the streets are filled with hordes of noisy students. It is very much a college town, with the usual array of bookshops, record stores, bars, and coffeehouses. During the summer, the Italian student population is replaced by foreigners who come to study Italian language and arts at several private fine-arts academies.

Urbino's fame rests on the reputation of three of its native sons: Duke Federico da Montefeltro, the enlightened warrior-patron who built the Ducal Palace; Raphael, one of the most influential painters in history and an embodiment of the spirit of the Renaissance; and the architect Donato Bramante, who translated the philosophy of the Renaissance into buildings of grace and beauty. Why three of the greatest men of the age should have been born within a generation of one another in this remote town has never been explained. Oddly enough, there is little work by either Bramante or Raphael in the city, but the duke's influence can still be felt strongly, even now, some 500 years after his death.

The **Ducal Palace** holds the place of honor in the city, and in no other palace of its era are the principles of the Renaissance stated quite so clearly. If the Renaissance was, in ideal form, a celebration of the nobility of man and his works, of the light and purity of the soul, then there is no place in Italy, the birthplace of the Renaissance, where these tenets are better illustrated. From the moment you enter the peaceful courtyard, you know that you are in a place of grace and beauty, the harmony of the building reflecting the high ideals of the men who built it.

Today the palace houses the **National Museum of the Marches,** with a superb collection of paintings, sculpture, and other objets d'art, well arranged and properly lit. It would be hard to mention all the great works in this collection—some originally the possessions of the Montefeltro family, others brought to the museum from churches and palaces throughout the region—but there are a few that must be singled out. Of these, perhaps the most famous is Piero della Francesca's enigmatic work *The Flagellation of Christ.* Much has been written about this painting, and few experts agree on its meaning. Legend has it that the three figures in the foreground represent a murdered member of the Montefeltro family (the barefoot young man) and his two murderers. Others claim the painting is a heavily veiled criticism of certain parts of Christian Europe— the iconography is obscure and the history extremely complicated. All the experts agree, though, that the painting is one of Piero della Francesca's masterpieces. Piero himself thought so. It is one of the few works he signed (on the lowest step supporting Pilate's throne).

Other masterworks in the collection are Paolo Uccello's *Profanation of the Host,* Piero della Francesca's *Madonna of Senigallia,* and Titian's *Resurrection* and *The Last Supper.* Duke Federico's study is an astonishingly elaborate but tiny room decorated with inlaid wood, said to be the work of Botti-

celli. *Piazza Duca Federico, tel. 0722/2760. Admission: 8,000
lire. Open Apr.–Sept., Mon.–Sat. 9–7 and Sun. 9–1; Oct.–
Mar., Mon.–Sat. 9–2, Sun. 9–1.*

The **house of the painter Raphael** really is the house in which he
was born and in which he took his first steps in painting (under
the direction of his artist father). There is some debate about
the fresco of the Madonna that adorns the house. Some say it is
by Raphael, others attribute it to the father—with Raphael's
mother and the young painter himself standing in as models for
the Madonna and Child. Either way, it's an interesting picture.
*Via Raffaello. Admission: 4,000 lire. Open Apr.–Sept., Tues.–
Sat., 9–1 and 3–7, Sun. 9–1; Oct.–Mar., Tues.–Sat. 9–2, Sun.
9–1. Closed Mon.*

Lodging
Under 85,000 lire

Hotel San Giovanni. This hotel is located in the old town and is
housed in a renovated medieval building. The rooms are basic,
clean, and comfortable—with wonderful views from Nos. 24
and 25—and there is a handy restaurant/pizzeria below. *Via
Barocci 13, tel. 0722/2827. 33 rooms, 15 with shower. No credit
cards. Closed July and Christmas week.*

Dining
Under 30,000 lire

Agripan. This restaurant melds the best of Italian cuisine with
organic and vegetarian recipes. All the ingredients come from
a local farm where only chemical-free methods are used, and
several fixed-price menus offer a selection of whatever is available fresh. First courses are grains, fresh pasta, or delicious
vegetable soup—or all three. Apart from the vegetarian
dishes, there are such traditional local specialties as *zamponi*
(pigs' feet) and lamb. The wine list features good, organically
produced wines. Smoking is not permitted here. *Via del Leone
(below Piazza del Popolo), tel. 0722/327448. No credit cards.
Closed Wed.*

Loreto

*Trains run hourly from Ancona to Loreto, a 20-minute trip
that costs 2,500 lire. Loreto's station is linked to the town center
by frequent local buses (fare 800 lire). Tourist office: Via Solari
3, tel. 071/977139.*

The small inland hill town of Loreto is famous for one of the
best-loved shrines in the world, that of the **house of the Virgin
Mary.** The legend is that angels moved the house from Nazareth, where the Virgin was living at the time of the Annunciation, to this hilltop in 1295. The reason for this sudden and
divinely inspired move was that Nazareth had fallen into the
hands of Muslim invaders—not suitable landlords, the angelic
hosts felt. More recently, following archaeological excavations
made at the behest of the church, evidence has come to light
proving that the house did once stand elsewhere and was
brought to the hilltop by human means around the time the angels are said to have done the job.

The house itself consists of three rough stone walls contained
within an elaborate marble tabernacle; built around this centerpiece is the giant Basilica of the Holy House, which dominates the town. Millions of visitors come to the site every year
(particularly at Easter and on the Feast of the Holy House, December 10), and the little town of Loreto can become uncom-
fortably crowded with pilgrims. Many great Italian architects,
including Bramante, Sangallo, and Sansovino, contributed to

the design of the basilica. Inside are a great many mediocre 19th- and 20th-century paintings, but also some fine works by such Renaissance masters as Luca Signorelli and Melozzo da Forlì.

Nervous air travelers may take comfort in the fact that the Holy Virgin of Loreto is the patroness of air travelers and that Pope John Paul II has composed a prayer for a safe flight—available in the church in a half-dozen languages.

Ascoli Piceno

Take the frequent train from Ancona to the coastal town of San Benedetto del Tronto (70 minutes; fare: 6,500 lire), and change for the local railway to Ascoli Piceno (another 45 minutes; fare: 3,200 lire). Service on this local railway runs 12 times a day, but not on Sunday. Tourist office: Piazza del Popolo, tel. 0736/255250.

Ascoli Piceno is not a hill town. Rather, it sits in a valley, ringed by steep hills and cut by the fast-racing Tronto River. The town is almost unique in Italy, in that it seems to have its traffic problems—in the historic center, at any rate—pretty much under control; cars can drive *around* the picturesque part of the city, but driving *through* it is most difficult. This feature makes Ascoli Piceno one of the most pleasant large towns in the country for exploring on foot. True, there is traffic, but you are not constantly assaulted by jams, noise, and exhaust fumes the way you are elsewhere.

The heart of the town is the majestic **Piazza del Popolo,** dominated by the Gothic church of San Francesco and the Palazzo del Popolo, a 13th-century town hall that contains a graceful Renaissance courtyard. The square itself functions as the living room of the entire city. At dusk each evening the piazza is packed with people standing in small groups, exchanging news and gossip as if at a cocktail party.

There are several bars in Piazza del Popolo, but two are exceptional. One, **Merletti,** in the corner closest to the Palazzo del Popolo, is a perfectly preserved turn-of-the-century coffeehouse, with a creaky wood floor, marble-topped tables, an ornate bar, and a large selection of homemade pastries. Have a cup of coffee here and feel as if you've stepped back in time. The other bar, **Mix,** is a modern, trendy place with a wonderful array of sandwiches and pizzas, as well as a fine wine list. It's an excellent place for a light lunch or snack.

Lodging
Under 85,000 lire

Albergo Piceno. The modest Albergo Piceno is the only hotel in the historic center of the city. It offers clean, basic accommodations—no frills at all here—but the staff is helpful and courteous, and the location is perfect. *Via Minucia 10, tel. 0736/252553. 32 rooms, 18 with bath. No credit cards.*

Dining
Under 30,000 lire
★

Ristorante Tornasacco. In this attractive, family-run restaurant with rustic decor and vaulted brick ceilings, you can sample Ascoli's specialties, including *vincisgrassi* and *olive ascolane*, as well as *maccheroncini alla contadina* (a homemade pasta in a thick meat sauce). *Piazza del Popolo 36, tel. 0736/254151. AE, DC, MC, V. Closed Fri. and June 15–30.*

12 Campania

*Naples, Pompeii, and
the Amalfi Drive*

A two-hour train ride south of Rome, Campania will be for many the first taste of the Mezzogiorno, the Italian south. Place names such as Capri, Sorrento, Pompeii, and Paestum sing to the imagination of scenic beauty and historic treasures. For better or worse, however, the region also presents all the sights and flavors traditionally associated with the stereotype of Italy as seen from abroad. Nowhere is this more true than in the city of Naples, where chaos and poverty rub shoulders with imperial grandeur and private wealth.

From Naples, trains, buses, and boats will take you around the magnificent Gulf of Naples to Pompeii; past Capri and Ischia; along the rocky coast to Sorrento, Amalfi, and Salerno; and farther still, past the Cilento promontory to Sapri and the Calabria border. Inland lie the bleak fringes of the Apennines and the rolling countryside around Benevento.

On each side of Naples, the earth fumes and grumbles, reminding natives and visitors alike that all this beauty was born of cataclysm. Toward Sorrento, Vesuvius smolders sleepily over the ruins of Herculaneum and Pompeii, while north of Naples, beyond Posillipo, the craters of the Solfatara spew steaming gases. And nearby are the dark, deep waters of Lake Averno, legendary entrance to Hades.

With these reminders of death and destruction so close at hand, it's no wonder that the southerner in general, and the Neapolitan in particular, chooses to take no chances, plunging enthusiastically into the task of living each moment to its fullest.

Campania was probably settled by the ancient Phoenicians, Cretans, and Greeks. Traces of their presence here date from approximately 1000 BC, some 300 years before the legendary founding of Rome. Herculaneum is said to have been established by Hercules himself, and as excavation of this once-great city—Greek and later Roman—progresses, further light will be thrown on the history of the entire Campania region.

The origin of Naples, once called Parthenope and later Neapolis, presumably can be traced to what are now the ruins of Cumae nearby, which legend tells us was already in existence in 800 BC. Here, in a dark, vaulted chamber, the Cumaean Sybil rendered her oracles. Greek civilization flourished for hundreds of years all along this coastline, but there was nothing in the way of centralized government until centuries later, when the Roman Empire, uniting all Italy for the first time, surged southward and absorbed the Greek colonies with little opposition. The Romans were quick to appreciate the sybaritic possibilities of such a lovely land, and it was in this region that the wealthy of the empire built their palatial country residences.

Naples and Campania, with the rest of Italy, decayed with the Roman Empire and collapsed into the abyss of the Middle Ages. Naples itself regained some importance under the rule of the Angevins during the latter part of the 13th century and continued its progress during the 1440s under Aragón rule. The nobles who served under the Spanish viceroys during the 16th and 17th centuries, when their harsh rule made all Italy quail, enjoyed their pleasures, and taverns and gaming houses thrived, even as Spain milked the area with its taxes.

After a short-lived Austrian occupation, Naples became the capital of the kingdom of the Two Sicilies, which the Bourbon kings established in 1738. Their rule was generally benevolent, as far as Campania was concerned, and their support of the papal authority in Rome was an important factor in the development of the rest of Italy. Their rule was important artistically, too, for not only did it contribute greatly to the architectural beauty of the region, but it attracted great musicians, artists, and writers, who were only too willing to enjoy the easy life of court in such magnificent natural surroundings.

Finally, Giuseppe Garibaldi launched his famous expedition, and in 1860 Naples was united with the rest of Italy. Times were relatively tranquil thereafter—with tourists of one nation or another thronging to Capri, Sorrento, Amalfi, and, of course, Naples—until World War II. Allied bombings did considerable damage in Naples and the bay area. At the fall of the fascist government, the sorely tried Neapolitans rose up against Nazi occupation troops and in four days of street fighting drove them out of the city. A monument to the *scugnizzo* (the typical Neapolitan street urchin) celebrates the youngsters who participated in the battle.

The war ended. Artists, tourists, writers, and ordinary lovers of beauty began to flow again into the Campania region that one ancient writer called "most blest by the Gods, most beloved by man." As the years have gone by, some parts have gained increased attention from the smart visitors, while others have lost the cachet they had. The balance is maintained, with a steady trend toward more and more tourist development.

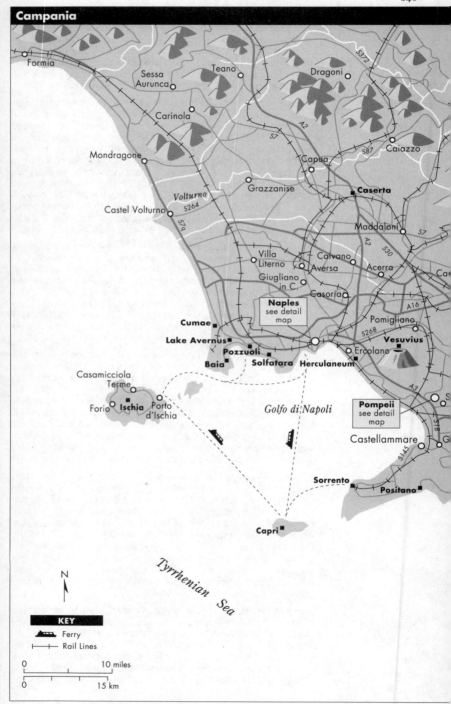

Campania

Formia

Sessa
Aurunca

Teano

Dragoni

S372

Carinola

A2

S7

Mondragone

Capua

S87

Caiazzo

Volturno   S264

Grazzanise

Caserta

Castel Volturno

S79

Maddaloni

S7

Villa
Literno

Calvano

S30

A2

Aversa

Acerra

Giugliano
in C.

Casoria

Naples
see detail
map

Cumae

Pomigliano

S268

Vesuvius

Lake Avernus

Pozzuoli

Ercolano

Baia

Solfatara

Herculaneum

A3

Casamicciola
Terme

Golfo di Napoli

Pompeii
see detail
map

Forio   **Ischia**   Porto
d'Ischia

Castellammare

S145

S18

Sorrento

Positano

Capri

Tyrrhenian Sea

N

KEY
🚢 Ferry
├──┼── Rail Lines

0 _____ 10 miles

0 _____ 15 km

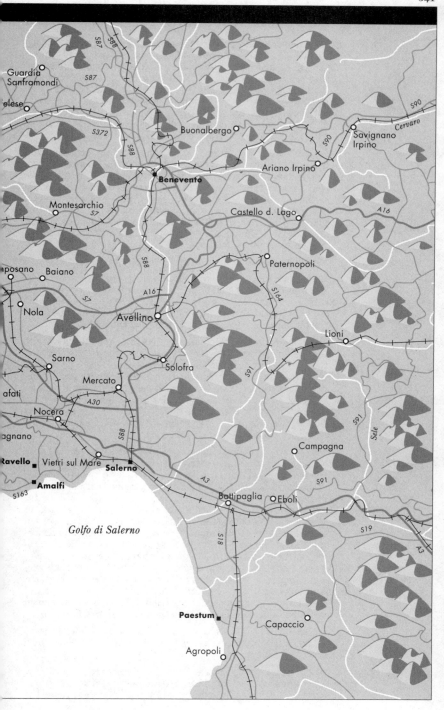

Golfo di Salerno

Essential Information

Lodging As befits a region where extremes of wealth and poverty meet, Campania offers a wide range of lodgings, including a good proportion of small, family-run ones. Travelers should be aware that prices and availability can change dramatically between the summer high season and the rest of the year. Naples itself naturally offers the widest choice, though most of its budget options are clustered around the station area in Piazza Garibaldi, which doubles as a red-light district after dark. Stick to the main roads and you should be safe enough.

For a more stress-free stay, opt for the outlying towns and villages of Sorrento, the Amalfi coast, or even the islands of Capri and Ischia. The latter have fewer possibilities for the cost-conscious tourist, and all of these places tend to fill up in high season, so book ahead. Out of season, prices are lower, but many resort properties shut down completely. Most of the places we list are always open, though, and outside the summer months, you should have no difficulty finding reasonably priced, comfortable lodgings.

Highly recommended lodgings are indicated by a star ★.

Dining Restaurant prices in the region are generally a little lower than those in Rome and northern Italy, though Capri restaurants can be very expensive. On the islands, Sorrento Peninsula, and Amalfi Coast, restaurants may be open daily during high season but may close for long periods during the winter.

Campania's cuisine is simple and relies heavily on the bounty of the region's fertile farmland. Its tomatoes are exported all over the world, but to try them here is a new experience. Even during the winter you can find tomato sauce made with small, sun-dried tomatoes plucked from bright-red strands that hang outdoors on kitchen balconies. Pasta is a staple here, and *spaghetti al pomodoro* or *al filetto di pomodoro* (both with simple tomato sauces) and *spaghetti alle vongole* (with clam sauce, either white or red) appear on most menus.

This is the homeland of pizza, served mainly in its simpler versions: *alla napoletana*, with anchovies; *alla margherita*, with tomato and mozzarella; *alla marinara*, with tomato, garlic, and oregano. Locally produced mozzarella is used in many dishes; one of the most gratifying on a hot day is *insalata caprese:* slices of mozzarella and ripe red tomato, garnished with basil. *Melanzane* (eggplant) and even zucchini are served *alla parmigiana* (fried and layered with tomato sauce and mozzarella). Meat may be served *alla pizzaiola*, cooked in a tomato-and-garlic sauce. Fish and seafood in general can be expensive, though fried calamari and *totani* (cuttlefish) are usually reasonably priced. Among the region's wines, Gragnano, Falerno, Lacrima Cristi, and Greco di Tufo are fine whites. Ischia and Ravello also produce good white wine. Campania's best-known reds are Aglianico, Taurasi, and the red version of Falerno.

Unless otherwise noted, reservations are not needed and dress is casual. Highly recommended restaurants are indicated by a star ★.

Shopping Naples sometimes seems like one vast street market, with various areas devoted to different crafts—watchmakers in one street, silversmiths in another, and so on. Tramping around the

Spaccanapoli area will take you past artisans' shops where items are made with a care and concentration that's rare in these automated times. The station zone running down to the port is the place to find more mundane items—not souvenir material but still fun to browse among. Don't be afraid to haggle, and keep your wits about you. The most innocent-looking old craftsman may be possessed of a shameless cunning—*furbizia*—that's bred in the bone.

Outside Naples there are plenty of fashionable boutiques on Capri and the Amalfi Coast, but the prices tend to be sky-high. Sorrento is the place to buy embroidered table linen and crocheted lace. Intarsia, a wood-inlay art, is a centuries-old tradition here, and shops offer everything from jewelry boxes to coffee tables with intarsia decorations. Towns all along the Amalfi Coast sell distinctive local pottery, with its sunny motifs and bright colors; stop off in Vietri sul Mare, near Salerno, to buy goods from local pottery workshops, including the Solimene and Pinto works.

Beaches The main problem with bathing in Campania is the Bay of Naples, which has a high level of pollution. The water is cleaner out on the isles of Ischia and Capri, though strips of sand here are hard to find—most of the shore is rock or gravel—and empty beaches are nonexistent in high season. The relatively unpopulated coast around Paestum is a good bet for sunbathing; otherwise, head north toward Formia.

The Arts and Nightlife Summer is the time when nightlife really takes off throughout Campania, and it's the best period for nightclubbing, hanging out in bars and birrerias, or going to rock and jazz concerts. Informal music festivals take place all summer long in Capri, Sorrento, Amalfi, and Ravello. Contact local tourist offices for details. In winter, Naples boasts some notable theater and opera productions.

If you just want to mingle with the crowds, every main piazza is lively until late in fair weather, especially in resort towns on the islands and on the Sorrento Peninsula. Capri's piazzetta is a classic example. Entertainment in the coastal resorts is mainly seasonal.

Highlights for First-time Visitors

Capodimonte (Tour 1: Naples and Its Bay).
Herculaneum (Tour 2: Herculaneum, Vesuvius, and Pompeii).
Mount Epomeo (Tour 4: Ischia and Capri).
Museo Archeologico (Tour 1: Naples and Its Bay).
Paestum's Temples (Tour 5: The Amalfi Drive: Sorrento to Salerno).
Pompeii (Tour 2: Herculaneum, Vesuvius, and Pompeii).
Positano (Tour 5: The Amalfi Drive: Sorrento to Salerno).
Ravello (Tour 5: The Amalfi Drive: Sorrento to Salerno).
Royal Palace (Tour 3: Caserta and Benevento).
Villa Jovis (Tour 4: Ischia and Capri).

Tour 1: Naples and Its Bay

Few fall in love with Naples at first sight, and many complain about its obvious flaws: decay and delinquency. But practically everyone who takes the time and trouble to discover its artistic riches and appreciate its vivacious atmosphere considers it worth the effort.

Why visit Naples at all? First, it's the most sensible base—particularly if you're traveling by public transportation—from which to explore Pompeii, Herculaneum, Vesuvius, and the Phlegrean Fields. Second, it's the home of the Museo Archeologico Nazionale (National Archaeological Museum), where the most important finds from Pompeii and Herculaneum are on display—everything from sculpture to carbonized fruit—and seeing them will add to the pleasure of your trip. Since the museum may be closed in the afternoon, depending on the time of year, spend the morning here and the afternoon visiting either the Phlegrean Fields or Herculaneum and Vesuvius. Spend the night back in Naples—perhaps at an opera or concert at the world-famous Teatro San Carlo—and the following morning, set out for Pompeii.

The Phlegrean Fields—the fields of fire—was the name once given to the entire region west of Naples, including the island of Ischia. The entire area floats freely on a mass of molten lava very close to the surface. The fires are still smoldering. Greek and Roman notions of the Underworld were not the blind imaginings of a primitive people; they were the creations of poets and writers who stood on this very ground—here in the Phlegrean Fields—and wrote down what they saw.

From Rome
By Train Frequent fast trains run from Rome's Termini Station, with tickets costing 15,400 lire. Intercity and Espresso trains take about two hours, Diretto trains nearly three hours, local trains much longer. All arrive at Naples' Stazione Centrale on Piazza Garibaldi.

By Car Italy's main north–south route, (A2, also known as the Autostrada del Sole), connects the capital with Naples and Campania. In good traffic the ride takes less than three hours.

By Plane **Capodichino Airport** (tel. 081/780–5763), 8 kilometers (5 miles) north of Naples, serves the Campania region. It handles domestic and international flights, including several flights daily between Naples and Rome (flight time: 45 minutes).

Getting Around Naples To minimize stress, stick to public transport and your own two feet. You can take the **subway** (Metropolitana) to distant destinations as far as Pozzuoli and Solfatara (be warned that the service stops at 11 PM). Use the **funicular** to avoid some weary uphill trudging, from Piazzas Amedeo and Montesanto, Via Toledo, and Via Mergellina. Neapolitan **buses** and **trams** are unpredictable and often crowded, but they can be useful, particularly traveling between the train station and the ferry and hydrofoil port (the No. 1 tram and Nos. 104 and 150 buses cover this route). Bus, subway, or funicular fares are all 1,000 lire; buy tickets from tobacconists or ticket kiosks before boarding, and punch them once you are inside. Alternatively, invest 2,500 lire in a ticket valid the entire day on all three means of transport. Punch the ticket on the first ride and display it to the driver on each subsequent ride.

Naples

*Tourist offices: Stazione Centrale, tel. 081/268779; Capodi-
chino Airport, tel. 081/780–5761; Piazza del Gesù, tel. 081/
552–3328; Piazza dei Martiri 58, tel. 081/405311.*

*Numbers in the margin correspond to points of interest on the
Naples map.*

To visit Naples, you need a good sense of humor and a firm grip
on your pocketbook and camera. Better still, leave all your valuables, including passport, in the hotel safe.

❶ A good place to start exploring is the **Castel Nuovo,** on Piazza
Municipio, facing the harbor. Also known as the Maschio
Angioino, this massive fortress was built by the Angevins (related to the French monarchy) in the 13th century and completely rebuilt by the Aragonese rulers (descendants of an
illegitimate branch of Spain's ruling line) who succeeded them.
The decorative marble triumphal arch that forms the entrance
was erected during the Renaissance in honor of King Alfonso I
of Aragón, and its rich bas-reliefs are credited to Francesco
Laurana. Set incongruously into the castle's heavy stone walls,
the arch is one of the finest works of its kind. Behind the castle,
which is not open to the public, is the **Molo Beverello,** the pier
from which boats and hydrofoils leave for Sorrento and the islands.

❷ On the next block is the **Teatro San Carlo,** a large 18th-century
theater redecorated in the white-and-gilt stucco of the neoclassical era. The theater was first built in 1737—40 years earlier
than Milan's La Scala—though it was destroyed by fire and rebuilt in 1816. You can visit the impressive interior as part of a
guided group, and casual visitors are sometimes allowed in during morning rehearsals.

Across the busy square is the imposing entrance to the glass-
roofed, turn-of-the-century **Galleria Umberto,** a shopping arcade where you can sit at one of several cafés and watch the vivacious Neapolitans as they go about their business.

❸ Next to the Teatro San Carlo is the huge **Palazzo Reale** (Royal
Palace). It dates from the early 1600s and was renovated by
successive rulers, including Napoleon's sister Caroline and her
ill-fated husband, Joachim Murat, who reigned briefly in Naples after the French emperor sent the Bourbons packing and
before they returned to reclaim their kingdom. Don't miss the
royal apartments, sumptuously furnished and full of precious
paintings, tapestries, porcelains, and other objets d'art. The
monumental marble staircase gives you an idea of the scale on
which Neapolitan rulers lived. *Piazza del Plebiscito, tel. 081/
413888. Admission: 6,000 lire. Open Apr.–Oct., Mon.–Sat. 9–
7:30; Nov.–Mar., Mon.–Sat. 9–2, Sun. 9–1.*

❹ **Piazza del Plebiscito,** the vast square next to the palace, was
laid out by order of Murat, whose architect was clearly inspired
by the colonnades of St. Peter's in Rome. The large church of
San Francesco di Paola in the middle of the colonnades was
added as a thanks offering for the Bourbon restoration by Ferdinand I, whose titles reflect the somewhat garbled history of
the kingdom of the Two Sicilies—made up of Naples (which included most of the southern Italian mainland) and Sicily itself.
They were united in the Middle Ages, then separated and unof-

Naples

346

Bacino del Piiier

Stazione Centrale
Pza. Garibaldi
Via Poerio
Via Cesare Rosaroll
Via Carbonara
Via P. Colletta
Corso Umberto I
Pza. del Mercato
Via Foria
Via Duomo
Via Vicaria Vecchia
Via Tribunali
Via S. Biagio
Via S. Biagio dei Librai
Pza. N. Amore
Via Nuova Marina
Via Foria
Pza. Cavour
Via E. Pessina
Piazza Dante
Via Toledo
Piazza del Gesù
Via Benedetto Croce
Via Monteoliveto
Corso Umberto I
Via A. Deperis
Via A. De Gaspari
Via A. Diaz
Via Toledo
Stazione Cumana
Via M.R. Imbriani
Via Salvator Rosa
Corso Vitt. Emanuele
FUNICOLARE DI MONTESANTO
Via Gracinio
Via Salvator Rosa
Piazza Leonardo
Via G. Orsi
Piazza Med.D'oro
Via Tino di Camaino
Via Giotto
Viale Michelangelo
Via G.L. Bernini
Via A. Scarlatti
Via Cimarosa
Villa Floridiana
Via Luca Giordano
VOMERO

6 7 8 9 10 11 12 13 14

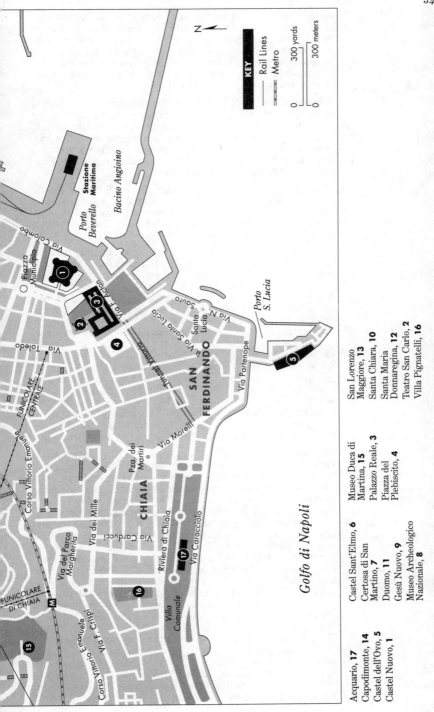

Golfo di Napoli

Acquario, **17**
Capodimonte, **14**
Castel dell'Ovo, **5**
Castel Nuovo, **1**

Castel Sant'Elmo, **6**
Certosa di San
Martino, **7**
Duomo, **11**
Gesù Nuovo, **9**
Museo Archeologico
Nazionale, **8**

Museo Duca di
Martina, **15**
Palazzo Reale, **3**
Piazza del
Plebiscito, **4**

San Lorenzo
Maggiore, **13**
Santa Chiara, **10**
Santa Maria
Donnaregina, **12**
Teatro San Carlo, **2**
Villa Pignatelli, **16**

KEY
Rail Lines
Metro

0   300 yards
0   300 meters

ficially reunited under the Spanish domination during the 16th and 17th centuries. In 1816, with Napoleon out of the way on St. Helena, Ferdinand IV of Naples, who also happened to be Ferdinand III of Sicily, officially merged the two kingdoms and proclaimed himself Ferdinand I of the kingdom of the Two Sicilies. His reactionary and repressive rule earned him a few more colorful titles among his rebellious subjects.

Follow Via Cesario Console along the waterfront to the port of Santa Lucia. At the end of a promontory you'll see the remains **❺** of **Castel dell'Ovo,** a 12th-century fortress built over the ruins of an ancient Roman villa. It commands a view of the entire harbor—proof, if you need it, that the Romans knew a premium location when they saw one. For the same reason, some of the city's top hotels share the same site.

Now take a deep breath, go back past Piazza del Plebiscito, and take Via Toledo (also known as Via Roma), one of the busiest commercial arteries in this perennially congested city. (Caflisch, at Via Toledo 25, is an historic café that now accommodates an Italian version of a fast-food counter.

Along the way, make a detour by way of the funicular from Pi-**❻** azza Montesanto up the Vomero Hill to **Castel Sant'Elmo,** a forbidding fortress built by the Spanish to dominate the port and the old city. The Spanish garrison was quartered in now-decaying tenements aligned in a tight-knit grid along incredibly narrow alleys; this notorious slum district is still known as the *Quartieri.* Follow Via Tito Angelini from the upper station **❼** of the funicular to the **Certosa di San Martino,** a Carthusian monastery restored in the 17th century in exuberant Neapolitan Baroque style. Inside, the Museo Nazionale di San Martino has an oddly eclectic collection of ships' models, antique *presepi* (Christmas crèches), and Neapolitan landscape paintings, but you're here mainly to see the splendidly decorated church and annexes, the pretty garden, and the view from the balcony off room 25. There's another fine view from the square in front of the Certosa. *Museo Nazionale di San Martino, tel. 081/578–1769. Admission: 6,000 lire. Open Tues.–Sat. 9–2, Sun. 9–1.*

As you resume your walk up Via Toledo, you'll pass a great variety of shops and plenty of coffee bars with plump, tempting pastries. Students from the nearby music conservatory hang out in **Piazza Dante,** the semicircular hub of an area rich in inexpensive trattorias and pizzerias. On the other side of Piazza Dante, Via Toledo becomes Via Pessina, which leads straight to **❽** the **Museo Archeologico Nazionale,** a major attraction for anyone interested in antiquity and for those planning to visit Pompeii or Herculaneum. The huge red building, a cavalry barracks during the 16th century, is dusty and unkempt, but it holds one of the world's great collections of Greek and Roman antiquities, including such extraordinary sculptures as the colossal *Farnese Bull,* an exquisite Aphrodite attributed to the 4th-century BC Greek sculptor Praxiteles, and an equestrian statue of the Roman emperor Nerva. Vividly colored mosaics and countless artistic and household objects from Pompeii and Herculaneum provide insight into the life and art of ancient Rome. The most recent addition to the treasures on display is an entire fresco sequence—more than 300 feet—discovered in 1765 in perfect condition at the Temple of Isis in Pompeii and now exhibited for the first time. Invest in an up-to-date printed museum guide, because exhibits are poorly labeled. *Piazza*

Museo, tel. 081/440166. Admission: 8,000 lire. Open May–Sept., Mon.–Sat. 9–7:30; Oct.–Apr., Mon.–Sat. 9–2, Sun. 9–1.

Retrace your steps to Via Toledo to explore the heart of the old city, where the arrow-straight Spaccanapoli, a street divided into tracts bearing several names, runs through (*spacca* means "cut through") from west to east, beginning with Via Scura just west of Via Toledo and ending with Via Vicaria Vecchia just east of Via del Duomo, retracing one of the main arteries of the Greek and later Roman settlement. The tourist information office at **Piazza del Gesù** (*see above*) can provide pamphlets with itineraries tracing the city's development in ancient, medieval, and modern times.

9 The oddly faceted stone facade of the church of **Gesù Nuovo** was designed as part of a palace, but plans were changed as construction progressed, and it became the front of an elaborately decorated Baroque church. Opposite is the monastery church **10** of **Santa Chiara,** a Neapolitan landmark and the subject of a famous old song. It was built during the 1300s in Provençal Gothic style and is best known for the quiet charm of its cloister garden, with columns and benches sheathed in 18th-century ceramic tiles painted with delicate floral motifs and vivid landscapes. The cloister is undergoing restoration, but some of the tiles are still visible; the entrance is off the courtyard at the left of the church. *Piazza Gesù Nuovo. Admission free. Open daily 8:30–12:30 and 4–6:30.*

The next section of Spaccanapoli, **Via Benedetto Croce,** was named in honor of the illustrious philosopher who was born here in 1866, in the building at No. 12. Continue past peeling palaces, dark workshops where artisans ply their trades, and many churches and street shrines. Where the street changes to **Via San Biagio dei Librai,** the shops stage a special fair of hand-carved crèche figures during the weeks before Christmas.

11 Turn left onto Via del Duomo to the **Duomo** (Cathedral). It was established during the 1200s, but the building you see was erected a century later and has since undergone radical changes, especially during the Baroque age. Inside the cathedral, 110 ancient columns salvaged from pagan buildings are set into the piers supporting the 350-year-old wooden ceiling. Off the left aisle you'll step down into the 4th-century church of Santa Restituta, which was incorporated into the cathedral; though it was redecorated during the late 1600s in the prevalent Baroque style, a few very old mosaics remain in the baptistery and in a chapel on the left. On the right aisle of the cathedral, in the chapel of San Gennaro (open 8–noon), are multicolored marble and frescoes honoring St. Januarius, miracle-working patron saint of Naples, whose altar and relics are encased in silver. Twice a year—on September 19, his feast day, and on the first Sunday in May, which commemorates the transference of his relics to Naples—his dried blood, contained in two sealed vials, is believed to liquefy during rites in his honor. These dates see the arrival of large numbers of devout Neapolitans offering up prayers in his memory.

About 100 yards ahead, on each side of the cathedral, are two of **12** the most interesting of the city's many churches, **Santa Maria 13 Donnaregina,** on Largo Donnaregina, to the north, and **San Lorenzo Maggiore,** to the southwest, on Via Tribunali. Both were built during the Middle Ages and decorated with 14th-century frescoes. Santa Maria Donnaregina has the towering Gothic funeral monument of Mary of Hungary, wife of Charles II of Anjou, who is said to have commissioned the frescoes in the church at a cost of 33 ounces of gold.

With San Lorenzo Maggiore on your left, walk down busy Via Tribunali to Porta Alba and Piazza Dante, at the junction with Via Toledo. Here you can catch a taxi or bus No. 109 to **Capodimonte,** the royal palace built by the Bourbons during the 18th century in a vast park that served as the royal hunting preserve and later as the site of the Capodimonte porcelain works that the family established. Allow plenty of time for the palace; it's packed with works of art, begining with the excellent collection of paintings in the Galleria Nazionale on the top floor. Included are works from the 13th to the 18th century, including many familiar masterpieces by Dutch and Spanish masters, as well as by the great Italians. At the coffee bar halfway through, be sure to climb the stairs to the roof terrace for a sweeping view of the bay. Then continue through halls hung with dramatic Mannerist works of the 17th and 18th centuries, among them some stunning paintings by Caravaggio (1573–1610), originally hung in the city's churches. Downstairs are 19th-century Italian paintings and the royal apartments, where numerous portraits provide a close-up of the unmistakable Bourbon features, a challenge to any court painter. You'll also find beautiful antique furniture, most of it on the splashy scale so dear to the Bourbons, and a staggering collection of porcelain and majolica from the various royal residences. *Parco di Capodimonte, tel. 081/744–1307. Admission: 8,000 lire. Open Tues.–Sat. 9–2, Sun. 9–1.*

Another museum with a view—and with more porcelain—sits at the top of the Chiaia funicular, which you can take from Via del Parco Margherita. The **Museo Duca di Martina** is set on the slopes of the Vomero Hill, in a park known as Villa Floridiana. It houses a fine collection of European and Oriental porcelain and other objets d'art in a neoclassical residence built during the early 19th century by King Ferdinand I for his wife; their portraits greet you as you enter. Enjoy the view from the terrace behind the museum. *Via Cimarosa 77, tel. 081/578–8418. Admission: 4,000 lire. Open Tues.–Sat. 9–2, Sun. 9–1.*

Near the lower station of the Chiaia funicular is another small, dignified museum in the park of **Villa Pignatelli.** The low-key exhibits are of limited interest to anyone who doesn't like 19th-century furniture, but there's a collection of antique coaches and carriages in a pavilion on the grounds that is worth a look. And a stroll in the park provides a pleasant respite from the noisy city streets. *Riviera di Chiaia 200, tel. 081/669675. Admission: 4,000 lire, park free. Open Tues.–Sat. 9–2, Sun. 9–1.*

For a change of pace, especially if you have children along, go to the **Acquario** (Aquarium) in the public gardens on Via Caracciolo. Founded by a German naturalist during the late 19th century, it's the oldest in Europe. About 200 species of fish and marine plants thrive in large tanks and undoubtedly fare better here than in the highly polluted waters of the Bay of Naples, their natural habitat. *Viale A. Dohrn, tel. 081/583–3111. Admission: 2,000 lire adults, 1,000 lire children. Open May–Sept., Tues.–Sat. 9–5, Sun. 9–6; Oct.–Apr., Tues.–Sat. 9–5, Sun. 9–2.*

Lodging
Under 115,000 lire

Ideal. It doesn't quite live up to its name, but the Ideal, a few steps from the train station, is nonetheless a useful hotel. The rooms are well equipped and the staff is professional and courteous. *Piazza Garibaldi 99, tel. 081/269237. 49 rooms, 30 with bath or shower. Facilities: bar. AE, MC, V.*

Tirreno. This hotel just off Piazza Garibaldi has recently been renovated and now provides a high standard of comfort. All the rooms have modern furnishings, a telephone, TV set, and minibar. *Via G. Pica 20, tel. 081/281750, fax 081/281750. 17 rooms with bath or shower. Facilities: bar. AE, MC, V.*

Under 85,000 lire

San Pietro. Just off Corso Umberto at the Piazza Garibaldi end, the San Pietro is rather gloomy, but comfortable, clean, and tidy enough. It's convenient both for the station and the boisterous market area of town. The rooms are old-fashioned, but the hotel's ample capacity ensures that you will almost always find space here. *Via San Pietro ad Aram 18, tel. 081/286040, fax 081/553–5914. 54 rooms, 20 with bath or shower. Facilities: bar. AE, DC, MC, V.*

Under 60,000 lire

Casanova. The cleanest and most amenable of the many budget hotels around the Piazza Garibaldi area, the Casanova is a popular choice—and consequently may not always have vacancies. The management is relaxed and friendly. Rooms are small and spartan but quiet—a big plus in Naples. The house dog, Zeus, already enjoys a certain fame among the traveling fraternity. *Via Venezia 2, tel. 081/268287, fax 081/554–3768. 16 rooms with bath, 4 share bath. AE, DC, MC, V.*

Ostello Mergellina. This youth hostel is a good choice for those who want a guaranteed standard of cleanliness at a minimum cost. It's in the highest category of the Italian YH rating system and is situated just behind Mergellina Station, thus handy to the hydrofoil port. The location is inconvenient for the city center, but by the same reckoning, it's well out of the chaos of downtown Naples. From Piazza Garibaldi, take the subway to Mergellina, or jump on a No. 150 or 152 bus, or on tram No. 1 or 2. Family rooms are available; single-sex dormitory rooms take a maximum of six people. The familiar hostel restrictions operate, including an 11:30 curfew. During July and August there's a three-day maximum stay. Non-YH members can take out a temporary membership for an additional 5,000 lire. *Salita della Grotta 3, tel. 081/761–2346, fax 081/551–3151. 200 beds. Facilities: restaurant. No credit cards.*

Dining
Under 30,000 lire

Ciro a Santa Brigida. Centrally located off Via Toledo near the Castel Nuovo, Ciro is a straightforward restaurant popular with business travelers, artists, and journalists who are more interested in food than in frills. In dining rooms on two levels, customers enjoy classic Neapolitan cuisine. Among the specialties: *sartù di riso* (rice casserole with meat and peas), and *scaloppe alla Ciro* (veal with prosciutto and mozzarella). There's pizza, too. *Via Santa Brigida 71, tel. 081/552–4072. Reservations advised. AE, DC, MC, V. Closed Sun. and Aug.*

Dante e Beatrice. A simple trattoria on central Piazza Dante, this popular spot features typical Neapolitan dishes in an unassuming setting. The menu may offer *pasta e fagioli* (very thick bean soup with pasta) and *maccheroni al ragù* (pasta with meat sauce). There is a good-value 25,000-lire tourist menu here. *Piazza Dante 44, tel. 081/549–9438. Reservations advised in the evening. No credit cards. Closed Wed. and Aug. 24–31.*

Bergantino. At lunchtime this brisk trattoria off Piazza Garibaldi is filled with businesspeople who appreciate the decent fare, smart decor, rapid service, and low prices. Pizzas are also available, and there is a 20,000-lire fixed-price menu at lunchtime. *Via Milano 16, tel. 081/553–9787. AE, MC, V. Closed Sun. and Aug. 10–20.*

Il Gobbetto. The walls in this small restaurant are covered with photographs of personalities in the acting world who have eaten here, an inescapable reminder of its close links with the Teatro San Carlo around the corner. As a result, the restaurant is often open late, humming with postperformance high spirits as the theatrical folk tuck into what is very acceptable fare. Try the *scaloppina al Gobbetto:* veal cutlets in a rich sauce of mozzarella, eggplant, tomato, and ham. *Via Sergente Maggiore 8 (off Via Toledo), tel. 081/411483. Reservations advised on weekends. AE, DC, MC, V. Closed Sun.*

Under 20,000 lire **Brandi's.** No one can come to Naples without sampling a pizza, and where better than here, where in 1889, the plain mozzarella and tomato pizza was invented and named in honor of Queen Margherita di Savoia. Although Brandi's offers a wide range of pizza toppings, it would be a shame not to try an authentic *pizza margherita,* to find out how it should be done. Popular with Neapolitans, Brandi's also offers a more expensive, three-course menu. *Salita Sant'Anna di Palazzo I (off Via Chiaia), tel. 081/416928. Reservations advised on weekends. No credit cards. Closed Mon.*

La Brace. If you are in the station area and fancy a cheaper and earthier lunch than can be had at Bergantino (*see above*), this is the place for you. Loud and busy, with a TV set blaring in the corner, La Brace is a superior fast-food joint, with a long menu that ranges from sophisticated seafood dishes to omelets. Prices are rock-bottom. *Via Silvio Spaventa 14, tel. 081/261260. No credit cards. Closed Sun.*

Pizzeria Trianon da Cirò. For those stranded at the Piazza Garibaldi end of Corso Umberto who don't feel like bucking the crowds at Brandi's, this makes an excellent second-best choice for pizzas. Though it lacks the other's historical resonance, it has a more cheery Neapolitan bustle, with marble tables and a blazing wood stove. The wide choice on the menu includes the house specialty, *pizza otto gusti* ("eight flavors"), a rich mix of cheeses and fresh vegetables. Beer and soft drinks are available (not wine). Smoking is not permitted. *Via Pietro Colletta 44, tel. 081/553–9426. No credit cards. Closed Sun. lunch.*

Splurge **La Sacrestia.** Popular with Neapolitans because of its location
★ and the quality of its food, La Sacrestia is set on the slopes of the Posillipo Hill, with marvelous views of the city and the bay. The specialties range from appetizing antipasti to *linguine con salsetta segreta* (pasta with a sauce of minutely chopped garden vegetables). Seafood has a place of honor on the menu, and there are interesting meat dishes as well. The setting, in a patrician villa, and the ambience are definitely upscale. *Via Orazio 116, tel. 081/761–1051. Reservations advised. AE, DC, MC, V. Closed Mon., Sun. in July, and Aug.*

The Arts Naples has a full opera season December to May at the **Teatro San Carlo** (Via San Carlo 93F, tel. 081/797–2331), one of Italy's top opera houses. For contemporary theater, the **Teatro Nuovo** (Via Montecalvario 16, tel. 081/406062) has new productions as well as film screenings. The **Teatro Bellini** (Via Conte di Ruvo, tel. 081/549–9688) is the place for rock and jazz events and light entertainment. Check the Naples newspaper *Il Mattino* for up-to-date information.

Nightlife Recommended bars in Naples include the sophisticated **Gabbiano** (Via Partenope 26, tel.081/411666), where there is often live music, or the **Chiatamoon Sax Café** (Via Chiatamone 18, tel. 081/422406). If nightclubbing is your scene, try **Rosolino** (Via Nazario Sauro 5–7, tel. 081/415873), which also has a quiet piano bar and a moderately priced restaurant.

Two discos to try are **Shaker** (Via Nazario Sauro 24, tel. 081/416775), which draws a mixed crowd of locals and guests from nearby hotels, and **Papillon** (Via Manzoni 207, tel. 081/769–0800), which caters to a young crowd.

Festivals A classical music festival, the **International Music Weeks,** takes place throughout May in Naples. Concerts are held at the **San Carlo,** the newly restored **Teatro Mercadante,** and in the neoclassic **Villa Pignatelli.** For information, contact the San Carlo box office (Via San Carlo 93F, tel. 081/797–2111).

The Solfatara and Pozzuoli

Bus No. 152 (fare 1,000 lire) from Piazza Garibaldi stops about 2 kilometers (1.3 miles) outside Pozzuoli, right outside the Solfatara; the route ends in Pozzuoli itself. You can also take the Cumana line train (also 1,500 lire) direct to Pozzuoli from Naples' Piazza Montesanto.

If you've never seen volcanic activity, don't miss the Solfatara, the sunken crater of a semiextinct volcano (it's quite safe if you stick to the path) whose only eruption was in 1198. Its sulfurous springs are said to be poisonous discharges from the wounds the Titans received in their war with Zeus before he hurled them down to hell.

The amphitheater at Pozzuoli (**Anfiteatro Flavio**) is slightly more than a mile farther west, on Via Domiziana, a short walk north from the town center, where the No. 152 bus stops. Explore the amphitheater's well-preserved underground passages and chambers, which give you a good sense of how wild animals were hoisted up into the arena for the spectacles staged there. It's the third-largest arena in Italy, after the Colosseum and Santa Maria Capua Vetere, and could accommodate 40,000 spectators, who were sometimes treated to mock naval battles when the arena was filled with water. *Admission: 4,000 lire. Open daily 9–two hours before sunset.*

You may want to make a short side trip to Pozzuoli's harbor and imagine St. Paul landing here in AD 61 en route to Rome. His own ship had been wrecked off Malta, and he was brought here on the *Castor and Pollux,* a grain ship from Alexandria that was carrying corn from Egypt to Italy only 18 years before the eruption at Vesuvius.

Lake Avernus

From Naples' Piazza Garibaldi, take a Sepsa line bus to Lucrino; it's a 20-minute walk from there to Lake Avernus. Alternatively, make the 5-kilometer (3-mile) walk from Baia (see below), which can be reached on the Cumana train line from Piazza Montesanto in Naples.

At Lake Avernus, you'll be standing at the very spot that the ancients considered to be the entrance to Hades. The best time to visit is at sunset or when the moon is rising. There's a restaurant on the west side, where you can dine on the terrace. Forested hills rise on three sides; the menacing cone of Monte Nuovo rises on the fourth. The smell of sulfur hangs over this sad, lonely landscape at the very gates of hell. No place evokes Homer, Virgil, and the cult of the Other World better than this silent, mysterious setting.

Baia

The Cumana line train from Naples' Piazza Montesanto runs direct to Baia; it takes about 40 minutes and costs 3,000 lire.

This ancient resort town may not mean much to you unless you have more than a passing interest in antiquity. Now largely under the sea, it was once the most fashionable resort area of the Roman Empire. Sulla, Pompey, Julius Caesar, Tiberius, Nero, Cicero all had holiday villas here. Petronius's *Satyricon* is a satire on the corruption and intrigue, the wonderful licentiousness, of Roman life at Baia. (Petronius was hired to arrange parties and entertainments for Nero, so he was in a position to know.) It was here at Baia that Emperor Claudius built a great villa for his wife, Messalina (who spent her nights indulging herself at public brothels); here that Agrippina poisoned her husband and was in turn murdered by her son, Nero; and here that Cleopatra was staying when Julius Caesar was murdered on the Ides of March. You can visit the excavations of the famous **baths.** *Via Fusaro 35, tel. 081/868-7592. Admission: 4,000 lire. Open daily 9–two hours before sunset.*

Cumae

From Naples, take the Circumflegrea train line from Piazza Montesanto to the modern town of Cumae (50–55 minutes, fare 3,000 lire); from Pozzuoli, take a local bus (the trip takes 15 minutes and costs 1,500 lire).

Cumae is perhaps the oldest Greek colony in Italy. During the 6th and 7th centuries BC, it overshadowed the Phlegrean Fields, including Naples. The **Sibyl's Cave** (Antro della Sibilla) is here—one of the most venerated sites in antiquity. During the 5th or 6th century BC, the Greeks hollowed the cave from the rock beneath the present ruins of Cumae's acropolis. Visitors walk through a dark, massive stone tunnel that opens into a vaulted chamber where the Sibyl rendered her oracles. Standing here, the sense of mystery, of communication with the invisible, is overwhelming. "This is the most romantic classical site in Italy," wrote H. V. Morton. "I would rather come here than to Pompeii."

Virgil wrote the epic *The Aeneid*, the story of the Trojan prince Aeneas's wanderings, partly to give Rome the historical legitimacy that Homer had given the Greeks. On his journey, Aeneas had to descend to the Underworld to speak to his father, and to find his way in, he needed the guidance of the Cumaean Sibyl.

Virgil did not dream up the Sibyl's cave or the entrance to Hades at Lake Avernus—he must have stood in both spots. When he wrote, *"Facilis descensus Averno"*—"The way to hell is easy"—it was because he knew the way. In Book VI of *The*

Aeneid, he described how Aeneas, arriving at Cumae, sought Apollo's throne (remains of the **Temple of Apollo** can still be seen) and "the deep hidden abode of the dread Sibyl,/An enormous cave. . . ." *Via Acropoli, tel. 081/854–3060. Admission: 4,000 lire. Open daily 9–two hours before sunset.*

The Sibyl was a prophetess, an old woman whom the ancients believed could communicate with the Other World. Two other famous ones were at Erythrae and Delphi. Foreign governments consulted the Sibyls before mounting campaigns. Wealthy aristocrats came to consult with their dead relatives. Businessmen came to get their dreams interpreted or to seek favorable omens before entering into financial agreements or setting off on journeys. Farmers came to remove curses on their cows. Love potions were a profitable source of revenue; women from Baia lined up for potions to slip into the wine of handsome charioteers who drove up and down the street in their gold-plated, four-horsepower chariots.

With the coming of the Olympian gods, the earlier gods of the soil were discredited or given new roles and names. Ancient rites, such as those surrounding the Cumaean Sibyl, were carried out in secret and known as the Mysteries. The Romans—like the Soviets—tried in vain to replace these Mysteries by deifying the state in the person of its rulers. Yet even the Caesars appealed to forces of the Other World. And until the 4th century AD, the Sibyl was consulted by the Christian bishop of Rome.

Tour 2: Herculaneum, Vesuvius, and Pompeii

Volcanic ash and mud preserved the Roman towns of Herculaneum and Pompeii almost exactly as they were on the day Mount Vesuvius erupted in AD 79, leaving them not just archaeological ruins but living testimonies of daily life in the ancient world. All three sites are close enough to Naples to be visited in one day (with no lingering, however), allowing you to return to your hotel in Naples that night.

Herculaneum

The Circumvesuviana line (tel. 081/779–2444) runs frequent service from Naples down the coast, south to Ercolano (Herculaneum), Pompeii, and on to Sorrento. Trains leave from the central station in Piazza Garibaldi. It takes 15 minutes to get to Ercolano; the fare is 1,700 lire.

Ten kilometers (6 miles) south of Naples are the ruins of Herculaneum, which lie more than 60 feet below the modern town of Ercolano. The ruins are set among the acres of greenhouses that make this area one of Europe's principal flower-growing centers. The entrance to the site is a short walk south from Circumvesuviana Station. Hercules himself is said to have founded the town, which became a famous weekend retreat for the Roman elite. It had about 5,000 inhabitants when it was destroyed; many of them were fishermen, craftsmen, and artists. A lucky few patricians (aristocrats) owned villas overlooking the sea. Herculaneum had been damaged by an earthquake in

AD 63, and repairs were still being made 16 years later, when the gigantic eruption of Vesuvius (which also destroyed Pompeii) sent a fiery cloud of gas and pumice hurtling onto the town, which was completely buried under a tide of volcanic mud. This semiliquid mass seeped into the crevices and niches of every building, covering household objects and enveloping textiles and wood—sealing all in a compact, airtight tomb.

Casual excavation—and haphazard looting—began during the 18th century, but systematic digs were not initiated until the 1920s. Now less than half of Herculaneum has been excavated; with present-day Ercolano and the unlovely Resina Quarter (famous among bargain hunters as the area's largest second-hand clothing market) sitting on top of the site, progress is limited. From the ramp leading down to Herculaneum's neatly laid-out streets and well-preserved edifices, you'll get a good overall view of the site, as well as an idea of the amount of rock that had to be removed to bring it to light.

You could easily get lost in the streets of Pompeii, but not here. Most important buildings can be seen in about two hours. If you feel closer to the past at Herculaneum than at Pompeii, it's in part because there are fewer hawkers here. Also, though Herculaneum had only one-fourth the population of Pompeii and has only been partially excavated, what has been found is generally better preserved. In some cases you can even see the original wooden beams, staircases, and furniture.

At the entrance, pick up a map showing the gridlike layout of the dig. Decorations are especially delicate in the **House of the Mosaic Atrium,** with a pavement in a black-and-white checkerboard pattern, and in the **House of Neptune and Amphitrite,** named for the subjects of a still-bright mosaic on the wall of the nymphaeum (a recessed grotto with a fountain). Annexed to the latter house is a remarkably preserved wineshop, where *amphorae* (vases) still rest on wooden shelves turned to black carbon by the extreme heat of the lava. And in the **House of the Wooden Partition,** one of the best-preserved of all, there is a carbonized wooden partition with three doors. In the **Baths,** where there were separate sections for men and women, you can see benches; basins; and the hot, warm, and cold rooms, embellished with mosaics. The **House of the Bicentenary** was a patrician residence with smaller rooms on the upper floor, which may have been rented out to artisan-tenants, who were probably Christians: They left an emblem of the cross embedded in the wall. The *palaestra* (gymnasium); the 2,500-seat theater; the sumptuously decorated suburban baths; and the House of the Stags, with an elegant garden open to the sea breezes, are all relics that evoke a lively and luxurious way of life.

Until a few years ago it was believed that most of Herculaneum's inhabitants had managed to escape by sea, since few skeletons were found in the city. Excavations at Porta Marina, the gate in the sea wall leading to the beach, have revealed instead that many perished there, a few steps from the only escape route open to them. *Corso Ercolano, tel. 081/739–0963. Admission: 8,000 lire; children under 12 free. Open daily 9–one hour before sunset; ticket office closes 2 hours before sunset.*

Vesuvius

From the Ercolano stop of the Circumvesuviana, it's a 30-minute ride via bus (at 10, noon, and 2) to the Seggovia station, the lower terminal of a defunct chair lift. The bus fare is 2,000 lire. Climb the path to the crater, about a 30-minute walk.

You can visit Vesuvius either before or after Herculaneum. If possible, save the volcano till after you've toured the buried city and learned to appreciate its awesome power. The most important factor is whether the summit is lost in mist—when it is, you'll be lucky to see your hand in front of your face. The volcano is visible from Naples, and everywhere else along the Bay of Naples; the best advice is, when you see the summit clearing—it tends to be clearer in the afternoon—head for it. The view then is magnificent, with the curve of the coast and the tiny white houses among the orange and lemon blossoms.

Reaching the crater takes some effort. Though there's talk of putting the chair lift back in working order, no one is optimistic about the possibility. From the square in front of the chair-lift station, you must climb the soft, slippery, cinder track on foot, and you must pay about 4,000 lire for compulsory guide service, though the guides don't do much more than tell you to stay away from the edge of the crater. If you're not in shape, you'll probably find the climb tiring. Wear nonskid shoes (not sandals).

Pompeii

Take the Circumvesuviana train (2,000 lire) 30 minutes from Naples to the Pompeii Scavi-Villa dei Misteri station, close to the main entrance at the Porta Marina. CIAT buses run directly from Rome to Pompeii; tickets cost 24,000 lire. Tourist office: Piazza Esedra, near the Porta Marina gate, tel. 081/861-0913.

Numbers in the margin correspond to points of interest on the Pompeii map.

Ancient Pompeii was much larger than Herculaneum; a busy commercial center with a population of 10,000–20,000, it covered about 160 acres on the seaward end of the fertile Sarno plain. In 80 BC the Roman General Sulla turned Pompeii into a Roman colony, where wealthy patricians came to escape the turmoil of city life and relax in the sun.

The town was laid out in a grid pattern, with two main intersecting streets. The wealthiest took an entire block for themselves; those who were less fortunate built a house and rented out the front rooms, facing the street, as shops. The facades of these houses were relatively plain and seldom hinted at the care and attention lavished on the private rooms within.

When a visitor entered, he passed the shops and entered an open area (atrium). In the back was a receiving room. Behind was another open area, called the peristyle, with rows of columns and perhaps a garden with a fountain. Only good friends ever saw this private part of the house, which was surrounded by the bedrooms and the dining area.

Pompeiian, houses were designed around an inner garden so that families could turn their backs on the world outside. Today we install picture windows that break down visual barriers between ourselves and our neighbors; the people in these Roman towns had few windows, preferring to get their light from the central courtyard—the light within. How pleasant it must have been to come home from the forum or the baths to one's own secluded kingdom, with no visual reminders of a life outside one's own.

Not that public life was so intolerable. There were wineshops on almost every corner, and frequent shows at the amphitheater. The public fountains and toilets were fed by huge cisterns, connected by lead pipes beneath the sidewalks. Since garbage and rainwater collected in the streets of Pompeii, the sidewalks were raised, and huge stepping-stones were placed at crossings so pedestrians could keep their feet dry. Herculaneum had better drainage, with an underground sewer that led to the sea.

The ratio of free men to slaves was about three to two. A small, prosperous family had two or three slaves. Since all manual labor was considered degrading, the slaves did all housework and cooking, including the cutting of meat, which the family ate with spoons or with their hands. Everyone loved grapes, and figs were popular, too. Venison, chicken, and pork were the main dishes. Oranges weren't known, but people ate quinces (a good source of vitamin C) to guard against scurvy. Bread was made from wheat and barley (rye and oats were unknown) and washed down with wine made from the grapes of the slopes of Vesuvius.

The government was considered a democracy, but women, children, gladiators, and Jews couldn't vote. They did, however, express their opinions on election day, as you'll see in campaign graffiti left on public walls.

Some 15,000 graffiti were found in Pompeii and Herculaneum. Many were political announcements—one person recommending another for office, for example, and spelling out his qualifications. Some were bills announcing upcoming events—a play at the theater, a fight among gladiators at the amphitheater. Others were public notices—that wine was on sale, that an apartment would be vacant on the Ides of March. A good many were personal. Here are a few:

At the Baths: "What is the use of having a Venus if she's made of marble?"

At a hotel: "I've wet my bed. My sin I bare. But why? you ask. No pot was anywhere."

At the entrance to the front lavatory at a private house: "May I always and everywhere be as potent with women as I was here."

In a back room at the Suburban Baths: "Apelles the waiter dined most pleasantly with Dexter the slave of the emperor, and they had a screw at the same time." (Did they do it with each other, or only at the same time? Homosexuality would not have been uncommon.)

To get the most out of Pompeii, buy a detailed printed guide and map, and allow plenty of time—at least three or four hours. You should have a pocketful of small change (500-lire coins) for tipping the guards who are on duty at the most important villas. They will unlock the gates for you, insist on explaining the attractions, show you some mild Pompeiian pornography if you ask for it, and expect a tip for their services. If you hire a guide, make sure he's registered and standing inside the gate. Agree beforehand on the length of the tour and the price (it should cost 50,000–60,000 lire). You can begin from either Porta Marina or the Ingresso Anfiteatro (entrance to the amphitheater), but you may have an easier time finding a guide at the Ingresso Anfiteatro. *Pompei Scavi, tel. 081/861–1051. Admission: 10,000 lire; children under 12 free. Open daily 9–one hour before sunset; ticket office closes 2 hours before sunset.*

The following route, starting from Porta Marina, will help you locate the most interesting sights:

❶ Enter through **Porta Marina**, so called because it faces the sea. It is near the **Pompeii Villa Misteri Circumvesuviana Station.**
❷ On your right is the **Antiquarium,** which contains casts of hu-
❸ ❹ man bodies and a dog. Past the **Temple of Venus** is the **Basilica,** the law court, and the economic center of the city. Such oblong buildings ending in a semicircular projection (apse) were the model for early Christian churches, which had a nave (central aisle) and two side aisles separated by rows of columns. Standing in the Basilica, you can recognize the continuity between Roman and Christian architecture.

❺ The Basilica opens onto the **Forum** (Foro), the public meeting place, surrounded by temples and public buildings. It was here that elections were held and speeches and official announcements made—a sort of Roman version of the mall or the village green. Turn left. At the far (northern) end of the forum is the
❻ **Temple of Jupiter** (Tempio di Giove). Walk around the right side of the temple, cross the street, and continue north on **Via del Foro** (Forum Street). There is a restaurant on your left.

The next cross street becomes **Via della Fortuna** to your right, and **Via delle Terme** to your left. Turn right onto **Via della For-
❼ tuna,** and on the left is the **House of the Faun** (Casa del Fauno), an impressively luxurious private house, with wonderful mosaics (originals in the National Archaeological Museum in Naples).

Retrace your steps along **Via della Fortuna** to **Via del Foro.** Cross the street. You're now on **Via delle Terme.** The first en-
❽ trance on the right is the **House of the Tragic Poet** (Casa del Poeta Tragico). This is a typical middle-class house from the last days of Pompeii. Above the door is a mosaic of a chained dog and the inscription *Cave canem,* "Beware of the dog." Continue west on Via delle Terme to the end. Turn right and bear
❾ left along Via Consolare. Pass through the beautiful **Porta Ercolano** (Gate of Herculaneum)—the main gate that led to Herculaneum and Naples.

Now outside Pompeii, walk down **Via dei Sepolcri** (Street of the Tombs), lined with tombs and cypresses. The road makes a
❿ sharp left. At the four-way crossing, turn right to the **Villa of the Mysteries** (Villa dei Misteri). This patrician's villa contains what some consider to be the greatest surviving group of paintings from the ancient world, telling the story of a young bride (Ariadne) being initiated into the mysteries of the cult of Dionysus. Bacchus (Dionysus), the god of wine, was popular in a town so devoted to the pleasures of the flesh. But he also represented the triumph of the irrational—of all those mysterious forces that no official state religion could fully suppress. The cult of Dionysus, like the cult of the Cumaean Sibyl, gave peo-

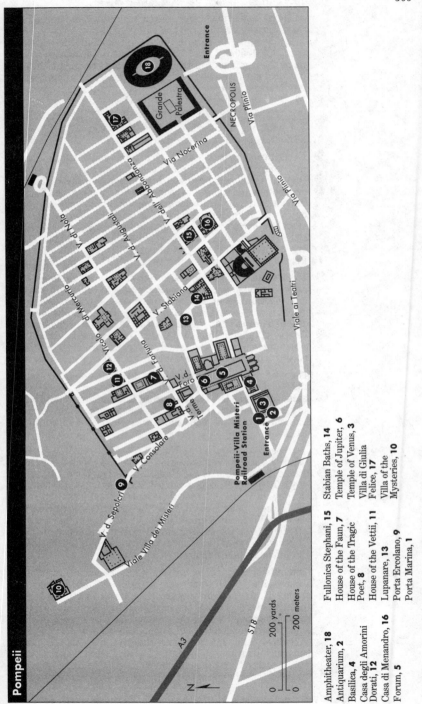

Pompeii

Amphitheater, **18**
Antiquarium, **2**
Basilica, **4**
Casa degli Amorini
Dorati, **12**
Casa di Menandro, **16**
Forum, **5**

Fullonica Stephani, **15**
House of the Faun, **7**
House of the Tragic
Poet, **8**
House of the Vettii, **11**
Lupanare, **13**
Porta Ercolano, **9**
Porta Marina, **1**

Stabian Baths, **14**
Temple of Jupiter, **6**
Temple of Venus, **3**
Villa di Giulia
Felice, **17**
Villa of the
Mysteries, **10**

0   200 yards
0   200 meters

ple a sense of control over fate, and in its focus on the Other World, helped pave the way for Christianity.

Return along **Via dei Sepolcri** to Pompeii. Retrace your steps down **Via Consolare,** which joins with **Vicolo di Narciso.** Make your first left onto **Vicolo di Mercurio.** Six blocks down is **Vicolo dei Vettii.** Around the corner, to the left, is the **House of the Vettii** (Casa dei Vetti). This is the best example of a rich middle-class merchant's house, faithfully restored.

Return, back around the corner, to **Vicolo di Mercurio.** Continue east one more block. You've now reached **Via Stabiana,** one of the two major intersecting streets of the town. Around the corner to the left is the **House of the Gilded Cupids** (Casa degli Amorini Dorati), an elegant, well-preserved home with original marble decorations in the garden.

From the door of the house, turn right down Via Stabiana, go three blocks, and turn right onto **Via Augustali.** Your first left will take you to the **Lupanare** (brothel) on **Vicolo del Lupanare.** On the walls are scenes of erotic games that clients could request. The beds have shoe marks left by visitors.

Continue south on Vicolo del Lupanare, turning left onto **Via dell'Abbondanza,** the town's other main street. On your left are the **Stabian Baths,** where people gathered in the evening to drown the burdens of the day. The baths were heated by underground furnaces. The heat circulated among the stone pillars supporting the floor, rose through flues in the walls, and escaped through chimneys. The water temperature could be set for cold, lukewarm, and hot. Bathers took a lukewarm bath to prepare for the hot room. A tepid bath came next, and then a plunge into cold water to tone up the skin. A vigorous massage with oil was followed by rest, reading, horseplay, and conversation.

Continue in the same direction, east on Via dell'Abbondanza (a left turn as you leave the baths). Two blocks down on your right is the **Fullonica Stephani,** a house converted into workshops for the cleaning of fabrics. All Roman citizens were required to wear togas in public, which weren't exactly easy to keep clean. It's not hard to imagine why there were more toga cleaners (fullers) in Pompeii than anything else, except perhaps bakers. The cloth was dunked in a tub full of water and chalk and stamped upon like so many grapes. Washed, the material was stretched across a wicker cage and exposed to sulfur fumes. The fuller carded it with a long brush, then placed it under a press. The harder the pressing, the whiter and brighter it became.

Go south, completely around the block. Behind the Fullonica Stephani is the entrance to the **Casa di Menandro,** a patrician's villa with many paintings and mosaics. Return to Via dell'Abbondanza. If you've had enough walking, turn left and go a few more blocks past the new restorations and then return to the Porta Marina, where your tour began. The recommended alternative is to turn right (east) on Via dell'Abbondanza to the **House of Julia Felix** (Villa di Giulia Felice), which has a large garden with a lovely portico. The wealthy lady who lived here ran a public bathhouse annex and rented out ground-floor rooms as shops.

18 Turn right past the villa and continue to the **Amphitheater** (Anfiteatro). The games here were between animals, between gladiators, and between animals and gladiators. There were also Olympic games and chariot races. The crowds rushed in as soon as the gates opened—women and slaves to the bleachers. When the emperor or some other important person was in attendance, exotic animals—lions and tigers, panthers, elephants, and rhinos—were released. At "half time," birds of prey were set against hares, or dogs against porcupines, the animals tied to opposite end of a rope so neither could escape. Most gladiators were slaves or prisoners, but a few were Germans or Syrians who enjoyed fighting. Teams of gladiators worked for impresarios, who hired them out to wealthy citizens, many of whom were running for office and hoping that the gory entertainment would buy them some votes. When a gladiator found himself at another's mercy, he extended a pleading hand to the president of the games. If the president turned his thumb up, the gladiator lived; if he turned his thumb down, the gladiator's throat was cut. The arena got pretty bloody after a night's entertainment and was sprinkled with red powder to camouflage the carnage. The victorious gladiator got money or a ribbon exempting him from further fights. If he was a slave, he was often set free. If the people of Pompeii had had trading cards, they would have collected portraits of gladiators; everyone had his favorite. Says one piece of graffiti: "Petronius Octavus fought thirty-four fights and then died, but Severus, a freedman, was victor in fifty-five fights and still lived; Nasica celebrates sixty victories." Pompeii had a gladiator school (Caserma dei Gladiatori), which you can visit on your way back to Porta Marina.

Return to Porta Marina, where your walk began, or exit through the Ingresso Anfiteatro and find a cab for the 1.6-kilometer (1-mile) trip back to Porta Marina.

The Arts One of the most impressive theater seasons is Pompeii's late-summer festival of the performing arts, known as the **Panatenee Pompeiane**. This series of classical plays takes place in July and August. For information, contact one of the three information offices: Naples (tel. 081/268779), Pompeii (tel. 081/863–1041), or Rome (tel. 06/488–3748).

Tour 3: Caserta and Benevento

A northward excursion from Naples takes you to Caserta, the Bourbons' version of Versailles, and to Benevento, where you'll view an almost perfectly preserved Roman arch. With the exception of some mountain scenery, there's not much else of interest on this route; Benevento was badly damaged by World War II bombings, and you will have to content yourself with picking out the medieval and even older relics that have survived in the oldest part of the city.

Caserta

Local trains leave Naples' Piazza Garibaldi station approximately every hour for Caserta (journey time 40 minutes, fare 3,200 lire). ACTP buses cost 2,400 lire, take about an hour, and leave every 30 minutes from Piazza Garibaldi (tel. 081/700–5091). Tourist office: Piazza Dante, tel. 0823/321137.

The royal palace at Caserta, known as the **Reggia,** shows how Bourbon royalty lived in the mid-18th century. Architect Luigi Vanvitelli devoted 20 years to its construction under Bourbon ruler Charles II, whose son, Charles III, moved in when it was completed in 1774. Both king and architect were inspired by Versailles, and the rectangular palace was conceived on a massive scale, with four interconnecting courtyards, 1,200 rooms, and a vast park. Though not as well maintained as its French counterpart, the main staircase is suitably grand, and the **royal apartments** are sumptuous. It was here, in what Eisenhower called "a castle near Naples," that the Allied High Command had its headquarters during World War II and here that German forces in Italy surrendered in April 1945. Most enjoyable are the gardens and parks, particularly the Cascades, where a life-size Diana and her maidens stand. The park is the Reggia's main attraction, with pools and fountains stretching for more than a mile, formal Italian gardens, and a delightful English garden. Some of the fountains are splendid and may be playing at full force now that the aqueduct built by the Bourbons has been repaired. If you don't like walking, a minibus makes a circuit of the grounds. *Piazza Carlo III. Admission: royal apartments, 6,000 lire; park, 4,000 lire; minibus, 1,500 lire. Royal apartments open Tues.–Sat. 9–1:30, Sun. 9–12:30; park Tues.–Sun., 9–one hour before sunset. Closed national holidays.*

Dining
Under 30,000 lire

La Castellana. In Caserta Vecchia, Caserta's medieval nucleus on the hillside overlooking the modern town, this tavern has atmosphere and hearty local specialties, such as *stringozzi alla castellana* (homemade pasta with a piquant tomato sauce served in individual casseroles) and *agnello alla castellana* (lamb sautéed in red wine). Dine inside or, in fair weather, under an arbor. *Via Torre 4, tel. 0823/371230. Reservations required on weekends. AE, DC, MC, V. Closed Thurs.*

Splurge

Antica Locanda Massa 1848. Near the Reggia, this large, informal restaurant is decorated in browns and white, in 19th-century, rustic style. In fair weather you'll eat alfresco under an arbor. The specialties are *linguine al cartoccio* (pasta steamed with fresh tomato and shellfish) and *gazzerielli alla borbone* (*gnocchi,* or potato dumplings, with cheese and truffle sauce). A full meal including wine will set you back 35,000–45,000 lire per person. *Via Mazzini 55, tel. 0823/321268. Reservations advised. AE, DC, MC, V. Closed Fri. and Aug. 5–20.*

Festivals

The festival **Settembre a Borgo,** with classical concerts, theatrical performances, and poetry readings, is held in the picturesque setting of Caserta Vecchia in September. For information, contact the Caserta tourist information office (tel. 0823/321137).

Benevento

By train, there are three morning departures, and then one every hour, from Napoli Centrale on the private Ferrovia Benevento–Napoli line: The journey takes about 80 minutes, and tickets cost 7,000 lire. There are also regular departures on the main line, though these take up to three hours and require a change at Caserta. The Ferrovia Benevento–Napoli line also runs a bus: six departures a day from Piazza Garibaldi, taking 90 minutes and costing 8,000 lire. Tourist office: Via Giustiniani 34, tel. 0824/314077.

Benevento became the capital of the Lombards, a northern tribe that invaded and settled what is now Lombardy, when they were ousted by Charlemagne during the 8th century. Tough and resourceful, the Lombards moved south and set up a new duchy in Benevento, later moving its seat south to Salerno, where they saw the potential of the fine natural harbor. Under papal rule during the 13th century, Benevento built a fine cathedral and endowed it with bronze doors that were a pinnacle of Romanesque art. The cathedral, doors, and a large part of the town were blasted by World War II bombs, so there's little left to see; fortunately, the majestic **Arch of Trajan** survived. To reach it, follow Viale Principe di Napoli from the station and take the first left after the river. The arch is a fine 2nd-century-AD work, decorated with reliefs exalting the accomplishments of Roman emperor Trajan, who sorted out Rome's finances, brought parts of the Middle East into the empire, and extended the Appian Way through Benevento to the Adriatic. From the arch, take Via Traiano and turn right onto Corso Garibaldi to get to the **Duomo** (Cathedral), which has been rebuilt, with the remaining panels of the original bronze doors in the chapter library. Via Carlo, behind the cathedral, leads to the ruins of a **Roman Theater,** with a seating capacity of 20,000. The theater is still in sufficiently good shape to host a summer opera and theater season. *Teatro Romano. Admission free. Open daily 9– one hour before sunset.*

Tour 4: Ischia and Capri

This pair of pleasure islands guards the entrance to the Bay of Naples. Capri, the smaller island to the south, is the more famous of the two and subsists almost entirely on the tourist trade. The mood is modish but somehow unspoiled: The summer set is made up of smart, wealthy types and college students, although you may never see the upper crust, as they spend their days baking in the sun in private villas.

Capri wows with its charm and beauty; Ischia takes time to cast its spell. An overnight stay is probably not long enough for the island to get into your blood. It does have its share of wine-growing villages beneath the lush volcanic slopes of Monte Epomeo, and unlike Capri, it enjoys a life of its own that survives when the tourists head home. But there are few signs of antiquity here, the architecture is unremarkable, the beaches are small and pebbly, there's little shopping beyond the high-trash gift shops that attract the German spa visitors, and most visitors are either German (off-season) or Italian (in-season). On the other hand, some of you will delight in discovering an island not yet overcome with tourists from the United States. The mistake you shouldn't make is expecting Ischia to be an unspoiled, undiscovered Capri. When Augustus gave the Neapolitans Ischia for Capri, he knew what he was doing.

Ischia

Ferries depart 8–10 times a day from Naples' Molo Beverello on the Caremar (tel. 081/551–3882) and Lauro (tel. 081/551–

3236) lines, the trip to Ischia takes about 1½ hours and costs about 6,700 lire. Hydrofoils leave hourly from Molo Beverello or Mergellina on the Lauro, Caremar, or SNAV (tel. 081/761–2348.) lines; they take 45 minutes and cost 12,800 lire. Note that Ischia is off limits to visitors' cars from May through September. Tourist offices: Via Iasolino, Porto Salvo, tel. 081/991146; Corso Vittoria Colonna 104, Porto d'Ischia, tel. 081/983066.

Ischia is volcanic in origin, and from its hidden reservoir of seething molten matter come the thermal springs said to cure whatever ails you. As early as 1580, a doctor named Iosolini published a book about the mineral wells at Ischia. "If your eyebrows fall off," he wrote, "go and try the baths at Piaggia Romano. Are you unhappy about your complexion? You will find the cure in the waters of Santa Maria del Popolo. Are you deaf? Then go to Bagno d'Ulmitello. If you know anyone who is getting bald, anyone who suffers from elephantiasis, or another whose wife yearns for a child, take the three of them immediately to the Bagno di Vitara; they will bless you."

Today the island is covered with thermal baths surrounded by tropical gardens—if you've never been to one before, don't miss the opportunity. Ischia also has some lovely hotel-resorts high in the mountains, offering therapeutic programs and rooms with breathtaking views of the sea. Should you want to plunk down in the sun for a few days and tune out the world, this is an ideal place in which to do just that.

Ischia Porto is the largest town on the island and the usual point of debarkation. It's no workaday port, however, but a pretty resort with plenty of hotels and low, flat-roofed houses arrayed on terraced hillsides above the water. Its narrow streets often become flights of steps that scale the hill, and its villas and gardens are framed by pines. If you're visiting Ischia for the day, your best bet is to recapture your youth at one of the mineral baths, and then indulge yourself at a harborfront restaurant.

Most of the hotels are along the beach in the part of town called **Ischia Ponte**, which gets its name from the bridge *(ponte)* built by Alfonso of Aragón in 1438 to link the picturesque castle on a small islet offshore with the town and port. For a while, the castle was the home of Vittoria Colonna, poetess and platonic soulmate of Michelangelo, with whom she carried on a lengthy correspondence, and granddaughter of Renaissance duke Federico da Montefeltro. If you choose to stay in Ischia Porto, you'll find a typical resort atmosphere; countless cafés, shops, and restaurants; and a half-mile stretch of fine sandy beach.

To explore more of the island, take advantage of the good bus service (tickets cost 1,200 lire and are valid for an hour).

One popular beach resort, just 5 kilometers (3 miles) west of Ischia Porto, is **Casamicciola.** Just west of that is the chic and upscale resort of **Lacco Ameno,** distinguished by a mushroom-shape rock offshore. Here, there are modern thermal baths where you can enjoy the benefits of Ischia's therapeutic waters, as well as luxury hotels such as the Regina Isabella, many with their own spa facilities.

The far western and southern coasts of the island are more rugged and attractive. The colorful port of **Forio,** at the extreme west, is an ideal stop for lunch or dinner. The sybaritic hot pools of the **Poseidon Gardens** spa establishment are on the Citara beach, south of Forio. You can sit like a Roman senator on a stone chair recessed in the rock and let the hot water cascade over you—all very campy, and fun. **Sant'Angelo,** on the southern coast, is a charming village; the road doesn't reach all the way into town, so it's free of traffic, and it's a five-minute boat ride from the beach of Maronti, at the foot of cliffs. The inland towns of **Serrara, Fontana,** and **Barano** are all located high above the sea; Fontana, most elevated of the three, is the base for excursions to the top of **Mount Epomeo,** the long-dormant volcano that dominates the island landscape. You can reach its 788-meter (2,585-foot) peak in about 1½ hours of relatively easy walking.

A good 35-kilometer (21-mile) road makes a circuit of the island; the ride takes most of a day at a leisurely pace, if you're stopping along the way to enjoy the views and perhaps have lunch. You can book a boat tour (30,000 lire) around the island at the booths in various ports along the coast; there's a one-hour stop at Sant'Angelo.

Lodging
Under 115,000 lire

Del Postiglione. An attractive pink Mediterranean-style edifice, this is smaller than it appears, with only 11 guest rooms. Its modest aura of luxury is created by marble floors, tropical plants adorning the outside, and generous balconies overlooking one of Ischia Porto's quiet back streets, a couple of minutes from the seafront. *Via Giacinto Gigante 19, tel. 081/991579, fax 081/991579. 11 rooms with bath or shower. Facilities: restaurant, bar, baby-sitting service. No credit cards.*

Parco Verde Terme. A three-star establishment surrounded by trees, with a modest lake and a swimming pool to boot, the Parco Verde's excellent facilities and low cost must be weighed against its distance from Ischia's port. It's a 20-minute walk from the action (though it's on a bus route), which undoubtedy explains its superb value. Prices drop below 80,000 lire for a double in winter, when you are guaranteed almost total privacy. Calm and courteous service help to make a sojourn here memorable. *Via Michele Mazzella 43, tel. 081/992282, fax 081/992773. 50 rooms with bath or shower. Facilities: restaurant, bar, swimming pool, garden, parking. No credit cards.*

Under 85,000 lire

Annabelle. Modern, elegantly furnished rooms make this hotel a good choice if you don't mind its slightly sequestered location—a good 10-minute walk from Ischia's port, though frequent buses stop just outside. Surrounding gardens heighten the sense of seclusion, making it a cool retreat in the midsummer sun. The Annabelle's standards of cleanliness and efficiency make this an excellent value, though off-season visitors will find it closed. *Via Variopinto 6, tel. 081/991890 or (toll-free) 1678/88083, fax 081/991890. 21 rooms with bath or shower. Facilities: restaurant. No credit cards.*

Under 60,000

Bristol. If you want to stay at Lacco Ameno and don't feel like splurging, you'll have to stay on the outskirts of town. About 300 yards from the sea, the Bristol is a well-equipped establishment with a swimming pool, a shady garden, and modern, clean furnishings. Despite its size it fills up quickly in the summer, so book ahead if possible; in winter this shouldn't be necessary. *Via Fundera 72, tel. 081/994566. 42 rooms with shower. Facilities: restaurant, bar, outdoor swimming pool. No credit cards.*

Capri

*Ferries depart six times a day (four in winter) from Naples'
Molo Beverello on the Caremar (tel. 081/551–3882) and
Navigazione Libera del Golfo (tel. 081/552–7209) lines; the trip
to Capri takes about 1½ hours and costs 7,300 lire. Hydrofoils
leave hourly from Molo Beverello or Mergellina on the
Caremar, Lauro (tel. 081/551–3236), Navigazione Libera, or
SNAV (tel. 081/761–2348) lines; they take 40 minutes and cost
around 13,500 lire. You can also take a ferry or hydrofoil from
Sorrento. Ferries cost 4,000–5,000 lire and take about an hour;
hydrofoils take 20 minutes and tickets cost 7,000–8,000 lire.
Note that from April 1 to October 31, no cars can be taken to the
island. Tourist offices: Marina Grande Pier, Capri port, tel.
081/837–0634; Piazza Umberto I, Capri town, tel. 081/
837–0686.*

The summer scene on Capri (accent on the first syllable) calls to
mind the stampeding of bulls through the narrow streets of
Pamplona: If you can visit in the spring or fall, do so. Yet even
the crowds are not enough to destroy Capri's very special
charm. The town is a Moorish opera set of shiny white houses,
tiny squares, and narrow medieval alleyways hung with flowers. You can take a bus or the funicular to reach the town, which
rests on top of rugged limestone cliffs hundreds of feet above
the sea.

The secret is for you to disappear while the day-trippers take
over—offering yourself to the sun at your hotel pool or exploring the hidden corners of the island. Even in the height of summer, you can enjoy a degree of privacy on one of the many paved
paths that wind around the island hundreds of feet above the
sea; if you're willing to walk, you can be as alone here as you've
ever wanted to be. Unlike the other islands in the Bay of Naples, Capri is not of volcanic origin but is an integral part of the
limestone chain of the Apennines, left above water when some
subterranean cataclysm sank its connecting link with the
mainland.

The Phoenicians were the earliest settlers of Capri. The
Greeks arrived during the 4th century BC and were followed by
the Romans, who made it their playground. Emperor Augustus vacationed here; Tiberius built 12 villas, scattered over the
island, and here he spent the later years of his life, refusing to
return to Rome even when he was near death. Capri was one of
the strongholds of the 15th-century pirate Barbarossa, who
first sacked it and then made a fortress of it. Moors and Greeks
had previously established their citadels on its heights, and pi-
rates from all corners of the world periodically raided it. In
1806 the British wanted to turn it into another Gibraltar and
were beginning to build fortifications when the French took it
away from them in 1808. However, the Roman influence has remained the strongest, reflecting a sybaritic way of life inherited from the Greek colonists on the mainland.

Capri has a reputation for being hideously expensive, and indeed some of its top-ranking hotels and restaurants are among
the most costly in Italy. But plenty of moderately priced hotels
and some inexpensive ones share the same fabulous views.
There are also moderately priced trattorias off the beaten tourist track.

Thousands of legends concerning the life and loves of mythological creatures, Roman emperors, Saracen invaders, and modern eccentrics combine to give Capri a voluptuous allure—sensuous and intoxicating—like the island's rare and delicious white wine. (Most of the wine passed off as "local" on Capri comes from the much more extensive vineyards of Ischia.) Certainly there are fewer pleasures more gratifying than gazing out at the sea from the quiet of a sun-dappled arbor while enjoying a glass of cold wine and flavorful *insalata caprese*, a minor work of art in itself, with smooth white mozzarella, fleshy red tomatoes, and bright-green basil.

All boats for Capri dock at **Marina Grande,** where you can board an excursion boat for the 90-minute tour to the **Blue Grotto.** If you're pressed for time, however, skip this sometimes frustrating and disappointing excursion. You board one boat to get to the grotto, then transfer to another, smaller one to get inside the grotto. If there's a backup of boats waiting to get in, you'll be given precious little time to enjoy the gorgeous color of the water and its silvery reflections. *Cost, including 4,000-lire admission to the grotto: about 16,900 lire. Open daily 9:30–two hours before sunset; departures less frequent in winter.*

As an alternative, take the approximately two-hour boat trip around the island—hassle-free and very enjoyable. These excursions start at Marina Grande and are run by the Grotta Azzurra company. The cost is 16,000 lire. Make either of these boat trips in the morning, when light and visibility are best.

There is a **tourist information office** on the pier where the boats from the mainland dock (another is in the main square in Capri town); ask for a brochure map *(piantina)* showing the many walks you can take to get the best views and escape the crowds. You may have to wait in line for the cog railway (3,000 lire round-trip) to the town of **Capri.** If it's not operating, there's bus service (1,000 lire) and taxis (about 4,000 lire). From the upper station, walk out into Piazza Umberto I, much better known as the *piazzetta*, the island's social center, *the* place to see and be seen, deliberately commercial and self-consciously picturesque at the same time. You can window-shop in expensive boutiques and browse in souvenir shops along Via Vittorio Emanuele, which leads south toward the many-domed **Certosa di San Giacomo.** The church and cloister of this much-restored monastery can be visited, and you should also pause long enough to enjoy the breathtaking view of Punta Tragara and the Faraglioni, three towering shoals, from the viewing stand at the edge of the cliff. *Via Certosa. Admission free. Open Tues.–Sun. 9–2.*

Beyond the monastery, Via Matteotti leads past bright shops and ice-cream stands to the **Giardini di Augusto** (Gardens of Augustus), a beautifully planted public garden with excellent views. From its terraces you can see the village of **Marina Piccola** below, where restaurants, cabanas, and swimming platforms huddle among the shoals. This is the best place on the island for swimming; you can reach it by bus or by following the steep and winding Via Krupp, actually a staircase cut into the rock, all the way down. (Friedrich Krupp, the German arms manufacturer, loved Capri and became one of the island's most generous benefactors.) Otherwise you swim off boats or take a hint from the family groups from Naples and Sorrento who swim off the unkempt but sandy beach at the end of Marina Grande past the cog railway station.

From the town of Capri, the 45-minute hike east to **Villa Jovis,** the grandest of the villas built by Tiberius, is strenuous but rewarding. Follow the signs for Villa Jovis, taking Via delle Botteghe from the piazzetta, then continuing along Via Croce and Via Tiberio. At the end of a lane that climbs the steep hill, with pretty views all the way, you'll come to the precipice over which the emperor reputedly disposed of the victims of his perverse attentions. From a natural terrace above, near a chapel, are spectacular views of the entire Bay of Naples and (on clear days) part of the Gulf of Salerno. Below are the ruins of Tiberius's palace. Allow 45 minutes each way for the walk alone. *Via Tiberio. Admission: 4,000 lire. Open daily 9–one hour before sunset.*

A shorter, more level walk along Via Tragara leads to a belvedere overlooking the Faraglioni; another takes you out of the town of Capri on Via Matermania to the so-called Natural Arch, an unusual rock formation near a natural grotto that the Romans transformed into a shrine. The 20-minute walk from the piazzetta along picturesque Via Madre Serafina and Via Castello to the belvedere at Punta Cannone gives you a panoramic view of the island.

You can take a bus from Marina Grande (1,500 lire) or a taxi (about 15,000 lire one-way; agree on the fare before starting out) up the tortuous road to **Anacapri,** the island's only other town. Here crowds are thickest around the square that is the starting point of the chair lift (5,500 lire) to the top of Mount Solaro. Elsewhere, Anacapri is quiet and appealing. Look for the church of **San Michele,** where a climb to the choir loft rewards one with a perspective of the magnificent 18th-century majolica tiled floor showing the Garden of Eden (open Apr.–Oct.). From Piazza della Vittoria, picturesque Via Capodimonte leads to **Villa San Michele,** the charming former home of Swedish scientist Axel Munthe and now a museum of his antiques and furniture. *Via Axel Munthe. Admission: 5,000 lire. Open Apr.–Sept., daily 9–6; Oct.–Mar., daily 10:30–3:30.*

Anacapri is also good for walks: Try the 40-minute walk (each way) to the Migliara belvedere and another walk of about an hour each way to the ruins of the Roman villa of Damecuta. If walking is not your idea of happiness, just join the other sybarites sitting in the piazzetta and remember that Augustus called Capri Apragopolis (City of Sweet Idleness) or, as the Italians would say, *dolce far niente* (pleasant idleness).

Lodging
Under 115,000 lire

Da Giorgio. A tiny, nondescript hostelry on the central Via Roma, this is the only choice in this price category that stays open all year. Rooms are somewhat cramped and sparsely furnished, though those facing the street enjoy a view of the sea far below. There are no single rooms available; the biggest asset is the inexpensive restaurant below. *Via Roma 31, tel. 081/ 837–0898. 9 rooms, 4 with shower. Facilities: bar, restaurant. No credit cards.*

Under 85,000 lire

Aida. Located a 10-minute walk from the center of town in a tiny lane that borders the Gardens of Augustus, the Aida offers a tranquil haven, well out of Capri's bustle and hard-sell and only 20 minutes away from the beach at Marina Piccola. The staff is sociable, and the guest rooms are spacious, comfortably furnished, and immaculately clean, looking onto a small garden. *Via Birago, tel. 081/837-0366. 14 rooms, 5 with bath. No credit cards. Closed Nov.-Apr.*

Stella Maris. The best budget choice for those who want to be at the heart of the action in Capri town, the Stella Maris lies right opposite the bus terminus. At the same time, the hotel enjoys a view over the sea from its upper-story, street-facing bedrooms, an added bonus if you don't mind a certain level of noise. Rooms are small and somewhat characterless, but clean enough: Don't expect to find much space here in high summer. *Via Roma 27, tel. 081/837-0452. 10 rooms, 4 with shower. Facilities: bar. No credit cards. Closed Nov.*

La Tosca. Pleasant and clean, the Tosca is situated on the same secluded back street as the Aida (*see above*). All the rooms are bright and airy in a shaded, garden setting, but choose one with an attached bathroom to enjoy the fine seaward views. Advance booking is advisable in high season. *Via Birago, tel. 081/837-0989. 12 rooms, 6 with bath. No credit cards. Closed Jan. and Feb.*

Under 60,000 **Girasole.** In a rustic setting outside Anacapri, the island's second town, this hotel is a reliable option if you can't get into the Villa Eva (*below*). As a second choice it's not quite top-notch, but it's the same setup: a rustic, family-run establishment with cooking facilities, about 20 minutes from the sea. Phone from Anacapri to be picked up. *Via Linciano 47, tel. 081/837-2351. 8 rooms with shower. No credit cards.*

★ **Villa Eva.** A couple of kilometers outside Anacapri, Villa Eva is well placed for both the beach and the Blue Grotto. Its large garden and country setting make it an ideal spot for families, and the friendly couple who run it welcome children. Each bedroom is refreshingly different, and much of the solid rustic furniture was built by the artist-proprietor. Unlike most of Capri's budget hotels, Villa Eva is open throughout the year— come in the winter and you can enjoy a welcoming log fire. Take the Blue Grotto bus from Anacapri, or phone ahead to be picked up. *Via La Fabbrica 8, Anacapri, tel. 081/837-2040. 18 rooms, 16 with bath. No credit cards.*

Splurge **Scalinatella.** The name means "little stairway," and that's how
★ this charming but modern small hotel is built, on terraces following the slope of the hill, overlooking the gardens, pool, and sea. The bedrooms are intimate, with alcoves and fresh, bright colors; the bathrooms feature Jacuzzis. The hotel has a small bar but no restaurant. Expect to pay up to 250,000 lire for a double. *Via Tragara 8, tel. 081/837-0633, fax 081/837-8291. 28 rooms with bath or shower. Facilities: bar, air-conditioning, pool, tennis court, garden. AE. Closed Nov.-Mar. 14.*

Dining **Da Gemma.** With its walls plastered with celebrity photos, this
Under 30,000 lire Capri town restaurant is split into two sections—one on a terrace with views overlooking the sea, the other enclosed, in a room that holds what is claimed to be the oldest oven on the island, in which pizzas and bread are cooked. *Gnocchi* are a house speciality, and you can order fish in all forms—though this can push the check right up. *Via Madre Serafina 6, tel. 081/837-7113. Reservations advised in summer. AE, DC, MC, V. Closed Mon.*

Verginiello. Completely overhauled in 1992, the Verginiello in Capri town offers a smart new decor, but it has resisted the temptation to push its prices through the roof. Climb down to it from Via Roma, and get there early to claim a seat by the window, so you can gaze down the steep drop to Marina Grande while dining on exquisite seafood dishes. The menu includes whatever fish is in season, though the lightly cooked calamari are available all through the year. The Verginiello also offers a range of pasta dishes and a pizza menu. *Via Lo Palazzo 25, tel. 081/837-0944. AE, DC, MC, V. Closed Fri.*

Splurge **La Capannina.** Known as one of Capri's best restaurants, La
★ Capannina is only a few steps from the busy social hub of the piazzetta. It has a vine-draped veranda for dining outdoors by candlelight in a garden setting. The specialties, aside from an authentic Capri wine with the house label, are homemade *ravioli alla caprese* (with a cheese filling, tomato sauce, and basil) and regional dishes. *Via delle Botteghe 14, tel. 081/837-0732. Reservations required in the evening. AE, MC, V. Closed Wed. (except Aug.) and Nov. 10–Mar. 15.*

Festivals Capri's **New Year's Eve** celebrations last all evening, with dancing and music culminating in a magnificent fireworks display. On **New Year's Day** there are celebrations all day, with marching bands, pageants, and all the vigorous revelry you would expect on this exuberant island.

Tour 5: The Amalfi Drive: Sorrento to Salerno

This is the most romantic drive in Italy. The road is gouged from the side of rocky cliffs plunging into the sea. Small boats lie in sandy coves like so many brightly colored fish. Erosion has contorted the rocks into mythological shapes and hollowed out fairy grottoes where the air is turquoise and the water an icy blue. White villages, dripping with flowers, nestle in coves or climb like vines up the steep, terraced hills. The road must have a thousand turns, each with a different view, on its dizzying 69-kilometer (43-mile) journey from Sorrento to Salerno.

To have your gaze free to take in these incredible views, bus service is highly recommended, at least between Sorrento and Salerno, the Amalfi Drive proper. The coastline between Naples and Castellammare, where road and railway turn off onto the Sorrento Peninsula, seems at times depressingly overbuilt and industrialized. After Castellammare, the scenery improves considerably as you near Sorrento (on the northern side of the peninsula), where russet cliffs rise perpendicularly from the sea. The really dramatic scenery, however, is on the other side (the southern, or Amalfi coast, side) of the peninsula, which is somewhat less overcome by tourists in summer, although you'd never guess that judging from the traffic along the Amalfi Drive itself.

There are several possible routes to take along the Amalfi coast. You can take a boat or train to Sorrento, as described below, and work your way back along the coast via local buses to Salerno, from which you can continue traveling south to Paestum, with its outstanding Greek temples. Or you can take the bus first to unglamorous Salerno and work your way back along the coast by bus to Sorrento, from which you may want to return to Naples by boat, enjoying the approach to the city by sea.

From Naples *By Train*	The Circumvesiviana train from Naples' Piazza Garibaldi station reaches Sorrento in an hour; tickets cost 3,900 lire. An hourly main-line train from Naples reaches Salerno in 45 minutes.
By Bus	SITA buses leave Naples every half hour (every two hours on weekends) from the terminus on Via Pisanelli, near Piazza Municipio (tel. 081/552–2176). They travel first to Salerno (an hour), where you must change buses; 10 buses a day run along the coast to Amalfi (70 minutes), Positano (another 50 minutes), and to Sorrento (another 50 minutes). Traveling this way, the total trip to Sorrento from Naples would take about four hours and cost 10,000 lire. There is, however, a direct bus from Capodichino airport to Sorrento, run twice a day by Curreri lines (tel. 081/801–5420) and taking just an hour.
By Boat	Hydrofoils to Sorrento depart six times daily from either Molo Beverello or Mergellina in Naples. The ride takes 45 minutes and costs 17,100 lire.
From Rome *By Bus*	CIAT (tel. 06/474–2801) operates direct buses from Rome to Sorrento (tickets cost 23,100 lire) and Amalfi (tickets cost 25,900 lire).

Sorrento

Until the mid-20th century, Sorrento was a small, genteel resort favored by central European princes, English aristocrats, and American literati. Now the town has grown and spread out along the crest of its famous cliffs, and apartments stand where citrus groves once bloomed. Tour groups arrive by the busload, and their ranks are swollen by Italian vacationers in the peak summer season. Like most resorts, Sorrento is best off-season, either in spring and early autumn, or in winter, when Campania's mild climate can make a stay anywhere along the coast pleasant. Another reason to avoid the peninsula during peak season is the heavy traffic on the single coast road, where cars and buses may be backed up for miles. Highlights of a visit to Sorrento include a stroll around town, with views of the Bay of Naples from the **Villa Comunale** or from the terrace behind the **Museo Correale.** The museum features a collection of decorative antiques, from ceramics to furniture to landscape paintings of the Neapolitan school. *Via Capasso. Admission: 5,000 lire; gardens only: 2,000 lire. Open Apr.–Sept., Mon., Wed.–Sat. 9:30–12:30 and 5–7, Sun. 9:30–12:30; Oct.–Mar., Mon., Wed.–Sat. 9–12:30 and 3–5, Sun. 9–12:30.*

Around Piazza Tasso are a number of shops selling embroidered goods and intarsia (wood-inlay) work. Along narrow Via San Cesareo, where the air is pungent with the perfumes of fruit and vegetable stands, there are more shops selling local and Italian handicrafts.

Explore the town's churches and narrow alleys, and follow Via Marina Grande, which turns into a pedestrian lane and stairway, to Sorrento's only real beach, where the fishermen pull up their boats. You can take a bus or walk a mile or so to Capo Sorrento, then follow the signs to the **Villa of Pollio Felice,** the scattered seaside remains of an ancient Roman villa, where you can swim off the rocks or simply admire the setting.

Lodging *Under 115,000 lire*	**Tirrenia.** Situated a 10-minute walk from Sorrento's center, the Tirrenia is old-fashioned in style and furnishings but still

enjoys a magnificent view from its restaurant and roof-top garden. Rooms are functional and lack character but are enhanced by balconies. *Via Capo 7, tel. 081/807–2264, fax 081/877–2100. Facilities: bar, restaurant. MC, V. Closed Nov.–Mar.*

Under 60,000 lire **Linda.** This and the Mara (*see below*) are the only budget accommodations open all year. Bland but clean, the Linda is located just above the bus and railway station. *Via degli Aranci 125, tel. 081/878–2916. 13 rooms, 10 with shower. No credit cards.*

Mara. Small and friendly, the Mara is close by the Correale Museum, in a modern block just up from the bus and train stations. The rooms (doubles only, some with balcony) are functional. *Via Rota 5, tel. 081/878–3665. 14 rooms, 10 with bath. Facilities: restaurant. No credit cards.*

Splurge **Bellevue Syrene.** A palatial villa in a garden overlooking the sea, the Bellevue has solid, old-fashioned comforts and plenty of charm, with Victorian nooks and alcoves, antique paintings, and worn Oriental rugs. The rooms are pleasant, with good views. *Piazza della Vittoria 5, tel. 081/878–1024, fax 081/878–3963. 50 rooms with bath. Facilities: restaurant, bar, garden, elevator to swimming area. AE, DC, MC, V.*

Dining **Antica Trattoria.** An Old World dining room inside and garden
Under 30,000 lire tables in fair weather make this a pleasant place for enjoying the local cooking. The atmosphere is homey and hospitable. The specialties are classic *spaghetti al pomodoro* (with fresh tomato sauce and basil) and *melanzane alla parmigiana* (eggplant). Two fixed-price menus are offered for 23,000 lire or 32,000 lire; à la carte is nearer 40,000 lire. *Via Giuliani 33, tel. 081/807–1082. Reservations advised for dinner. No credit cards. Closed Mon. and Jan. 10–Feb. 10.*

Parrucchiano. Centrally located and popular, this is one of Sorrento's oldest and best restaurants. You'll walk up a few steps to glassed-in veranda dining rooms filled, like greenhouses, with vines and plants. The menu offers classic local specialties, among them *panzerotti* (pastry shells filled with tomato and mozzarella) and *scaloppe alla sorrentina* (veal with tomato and mozzarella). *Corso Italia 71, tel. 081/8781321. Reservations advised weekends and in summer. MC, V. Closed Wed. (Nov.–May).*

Under 20,000 **Bussola Sud.** This modest trattoria/pizzeria has tables outside and a pleasant, relaxed atmosphere in summer, when the barbecue is often in use. At other times, the fare here is average: Stick to the basics—pizza and pasta—and you won't go wrong. There is also a *birreria* on the same premises, offering beer, snacks, and a gigantic satellite TV screen. *Piazza Antiche Mur, tel. 081/878–4290. No credit cards. Closed Tues. Oct.–May only.*

Shopping **Ferdinando Corciano,** in his shop on Via San Francesco, gives demonstrations of his intarsia work, producing decorative plaques with classic or contemporary motifs.

Nightlife You'll get a memorable view of the Bay of Naples from the terrace of the **Circolo dei Forestieri** (Via De Maio 35, Sorrento). Drinks are moderately priced, and there is live music in summer.

Festivals Each October sees the **International Cinema Convention** in Sorrento, which usually draws an elite collection of producers, directors, and stars in a less frantic atmosphere than that of the festival in Cannes. While much of the activity revolves around deal making, a number of previews are screened, and the town sees the festival as one last fling at the end of the summer season. For details, contact the Sorrento tourist office.

Positano

There is no train service to Positano, but the local bus takes 45 minutes from Sorrento (fare 2,500 lire). Tourist office: Via Marina, tel. 089/875067.

The most popular town along the Amalfi Drive, particularly among Americans, is Positano, a village of white, Moorish-type houses clinging dramatically to slopes around a small, sheltered bay. When John Steinbeck lived here in 1953, he wrote that it was difficult to consider tourism an industry because "there are not enough [tourists]." Alas, Positano has since been discovered. The artists came first, and, as happens wherever artists go, the wealthy followed and the artists fled. What Steinbeck wrote, however, still applies: "Positano bites deep. It is a dream place that isn't quite real when you are there and becomes beckoningly real after you have gone. Its houses climb a hill so steep it would be a cliff except that stairs are cut in it. I believe that whereas most house foundations are vertical, in Positano they are horizontal. The small curving bay of unbelievably blue and green water laps gently on a beach of small pebbles. There is only one narrow street and it does not come down to the water. Everything else is stairs, some of them as steep as ladders. You do not walk to visit a friend, you either climb or slide."

During the 10th century Positano was part of Amalfi's Maritime Republic, which rivaled Venice as an important mercantile power. Its heyday was in the 16th and 17th centuries, when its ships traded in the Near and Middle East, carrying spices, silks, and precious woods. The coming of the steamship during the mid-19th century led to the town's decline, and some three-fourths of the town's 8,000 citizens emigrated to America, mostly to New York. One major job of Positano's mayor has been to find space in the overcrowded cemetery for New York Positanesi who want to spend eternity here.

What had been reduced to a forgotten fishing village is now the number-one attraction on the coast, with hotels for every budget, charming restaurants, and dozens of boutiques. From here you can take hydrofoils to Capri during the summer, escorted bus rides to Ravello, and tours of the Emerald Grotto (*see below*).

Positano may not have a castle, but it does have another attraction that's bringing the town considerable wealth: stylish summer clothes. From January to March, buyers from all over the world come to Positano to buy the trend-setting handmade clothes that are sold in more than 200 boutiques. One-size loose-fitting cotton dresses; full skirts, plain or covered with lace—some in pastel colors with handprinted designs, others in bold block colors: bright oranges, pinks, and yellows. The choice is endless, and the prices—well, you're on vacation, and the same dresses would cost twice as much in New York or Rome.

No matter how much time you spend in Positano, make sure you have comfortable walking shoes—no heels, please!—and that your back and legs are strong enough to negotiate steps. If you're driving to Positano, be aware that parking space is almost impossible to find from Easter to September; book a hotel that offers parking, or, if you're just coming for the day, arrive early enough to get into a paid parking lot.

Lodging
Under 85,000 lire

Santa Caterina. There is more to this newly refurbished hotel than meets the eye: Rooms descend on three levels down the steep slope. The owners have made the most of the exquisite view over the town and seashore, which can be relished from each of the rooms as well as from generous balconies and terraces. On street level (the top floor), there is also an excellent fish restaurant, well patronized by the locals. It's quite a hike down to the beach—a good 15 minutes down the steps—but that's nothing new in Positano. *Via Pasitea 113, tel. 089/811513. 12 rooms, 6 with bath. Facilities: restaurant, bar. AE, DC, MC, V.*

Under 60,000 lire

Casa Guadagnano. Once you've found the Casa Guadagnano, buried within Positano's steep network of stairs and alleys, you'll appreciate its advantages: the view from its terrace restaurant and its proximity to the beach (five minutes down, longer on the way back up!). It's small, but the rooms are adequately furnished, some with a balcony, all with a view. *Via Fornillo 22, tel. 089/875042. 9 rooms, all with bath or shower. Facilities: restaurant. AE, DC, MC, V.*

Italia. This is a tiny place—more a private house, really—but the marvelous vista from its windows and balconies prevent it from feeling cramped. A large salon overgrown with plants and flowers frames the view. Guest rooms are small (doubles only). Signora Durso, who runs the Italia, tends the greenery with the same fussy concern she shows her guests, whom she has provided with a handy inside cooking area for their own use. *Via Pasitea 137, tel. 089/875024. 5 rooms with shower. No credit cards.*

Splurge

Palazzo Murat. The location is perfect—in the heart of town, near the beachside promenade, but set in a quiet, walled garden. The old wing is a historic palazzo with tall windows and wrought-iron balconies; the new wing is a whitewashed Mediterranean building with arches and terraces. You can relax in antique-accented lounges or in the charming vine-draped patio, and since there's no restaurant, you will avoid the half-board requirement applied in most hotels here in high season. Guests can expect to pay around 150,000 lire for a double room. *Via dei Mulini 23, tel. 089/875177, fax 089/811419. 28 rooms with bath and shower. Facilities: bar, garden. AE, DC, MC, V. Closed Nov. 5–Mar.*

Dining
Under 30,000 lire

Capurale. Among the popular restaurants on the beach promenade, this one just around the corner has the best food and the lowest prices. Tables are set under vines on a breezy sidewalk in the summer, upstairs and indoors in winter. *Spaghetti con melanzane* (with eggplant) and *crepes al formaggio* (cheese-filled crepes) are among the specialties. *Via Marina, tel. 089/875374. Reservations advised for outdoor tables and weekends off-season. No credit cards. Closed Nov. 3–Mar.*

Splurge

Buca di Bacco. After an aperitif at the town's most famous and fashionable café downstairs, you'll dine on a veranda overlooking the beach. The specialties include *spaghetti alle vongole* (with clam sauce) and *grigliata mista* (mixed grilled seafood). *Via Rampa Teglia 8, tel. 089/875699. Reservations advised in the evening. AE, DC, MC, V. Closed Nov. 6–Mar. 31.*

Nightlife **L'Africana** (Vettica Maggiore, Praiano). This is the premier nightclub on the Amalfi Coast, and it is built into a fantastic grotto above the sea. Praiano itself is only a couple of miles east of Positano on the coast road.

Amalfi

Hourly buses take 50 minutes to go from Positano to Amalfi (tickets 1,600 lire). Tourist office: Corso Roma 19, tel. 089/871107.

After Positano and Ravello, Amalfi is your third choice for a town to stay in along the drive. It would have to be a distant third, however, because of the congestion caused by tour buses, which make Amalfi the main stopping point on tourists' excursions. The town is romantically situated at the mouth of a deep gorge and has some good-quality hotels and restaurants. It's also a convenient base for excursions to Capri and the Emerald Grotto.

During the Middle Ages Amalfi was an independent maritime state—a little Republic of Venice—with a population of 50,000. The ship compass—trivia fans will be pleased to know—was invented here in 1302.

The main historical attraction is the **Duomo** (Cathedral of St. Andrew), which shows an interesting mix of Moorish and early-Gothic influences. The interior is a 10th-century Romanesque skeleton in an 18th-century Baroque dress. The transept (the transverse arms) and the choir are 13th-century. The handsome 12th-century campanile (bell tower) has identical Gothic domes at each corner. Don't miss the beautiful late-13th-century Moorish cloister, with its slender double columns. At least one critic has called the cathedral's facade the ugliest piece of serious architecture in Italy—decide for yourself. The same critic snickers at the tourists who fail to note the cathedral's greatest treasure, the 11th-century bronze doors from Constantinople.

If the sea is calm you can take a boat to the **Grotta Smeralda** (Emerald Grotto), a few kilometers back up the coast toward Positano. Boat tours leave from the Amalfi seafront approximately every two hours, according to demand; the charge is 10,000 lire per person. The grotto is named for its peculiar green light, casting an eerie emerald glow over impressive formations of stalagmites and stalactites, many of them underwater. *Admission: 4,000 lire. Open June–Sept., Mon.–Sat. 9–7; Oct.–May, Mon.–Sat. 10–4.*

The main street of Amalfi leads back through town from the cathedral to the mountains and passes a ceramic workshop and some water-driven paper mills where handcrafted paper is made and sold. Though it's not always open, there's a paper museum where you can see exactly how the mills work.

Lodging **Hotel Dei Cavalieri.** This terraced white Mediterranean-style
Under 115,000 lire hotel on the main road outside Amalfi has three villa annexes in grounds just across the road that extend all the way to a beach

below. The bedrooms are air-conditioned and functionally furnished, with splashy majolica tiled floors contributing a bright note throughout. An ample buffet breakfast is served, and though the half-board plan is mandatory during high season, you can dine either at the hotel or at several restaurants in Amalfi by special arrangement. Prices may shoot over the ceiling for this category in high season, however. *Via M. Comite 32, tel. 089/831333, fax 089/831354. 54 rooms with bath. Facilities: restaurant, bar, beach (via stairs), garage, minibus service into town. AE, DC, MC, V.*

Under 85,000 lire **Amalfi.** Up a flight of steps off the main Via Lorenzo d'Amalfi, this five-story hotel is one of the few inexpensive lodgings that is open all year. The best features are the garden—where there are also a couple of guest rooms hidden away (Nos. 315 and 316)—and the spacious rooftop terrace with broad views overlooking the town. As in most Amalfi hotels, you will be asked to take the half-board plan during the summer season, which will hike up the price. *Via dei Pastai 3, tel. 089/872440. 40 rooms with bath or shower. Facilities: bar, restaurant, garden, garage. MC, V.*

Splurge **Miramalfi.** A modern building perched above the sea, the Miramalfi has wonderful views, simple but attractive decor, terraces, a swimming pool, and a sunning/swimming area on the sea, as well as a quiet location just below the coast road, only a half mile from the center of town. Many rooms boast balconies with sea views. Expect to pay from 118,000 to 148,000 lire for a double. *Via Quasimodo 3, tel. 089/871588, fax 089/ 871588. 48 rooms with bath or shower. Facilities: restaurant, garden, parking. AE, DC, MC, V.*

Dining **La Caravella.** You'll find this welcoming establishment tucked
Under 30,000 lire away under some arches lining the coast road, next to the medi-
★ eval Arsenal, where Amalfi's mighty fleet once was provisioned. La Caravella has a nondescript entrance but a pleasant interior decorated in a medley of colors and paintings of old Amalfi. It's small and intimate; specialties include *scialatelli* (homemade pasta with shellfish sauce) and *pesce al limone* (fresh fish with lemon sauce). *Via M. Camera 12, tel. 089/ 871029. Reservations advised. AE, MC, V. Closed Tues. and Nov. 10–30.*

Ravello

From the seafront bus park in Amalfi, buses depart approximately every hour for the half-hour climb to Ravello. Tickets cost 1,500 lire. Tourist office: Piazza Duomo, tel. 089/857096.

Perched on a ridge high above Amalfi and the neighboring town of Atrani is Ravello, an enchanting village with stupendous views, quiet lanes, and two irresistibly romantic gardens—that of **Villa Rufolo,** where medieval ruins frame spectacular vistas, and **Villa Cimbrone,** a private estate open to the public with spectacular views of the entire Bay of Salerno.

Because Ravello is a long, steep drive from the sea, tour buses are discouraged, and crowds are less overwhelming than at Positano and Amalfi. By early afternoon, the day-trippers have departed, and the town becomes one of the most restful settings in the world. There's very little to do except walk through peaceful gardens, admire the view, and exist.

Lodging
Under 115,000 lire

Villa Amore. A 10-minute walk from the main Piazza Duomo, this hotel is family-run, tidy, and comfortable, with a garden and exhilarating views from most of its bedrooms. If you're looking for utter tranquillity, this is the place to find it, particularly at dusk, when the valley is tinged with a glorious purple light. Furnishings are modest but modern. Full board is available here and may be required in the summer. Reserve ahead. *Via Santa Chiara, tel. 089/857135. 15 bedrooms, 8 with bath. Facilities: restaurant, bar, garden. MC, V.*

Toro. A warm welcome is assured at this modest hotel just off Ravello's main square. Furnishing is simple but tasteful, though some of the rooms are on the small side: Ask for one with a view overlooking the hillside. In July and August guests must take the half-board plan. *Via Wagner 3, tel. 089/857211. 9 rooms with shower. Facilities: restaurant, bar, garden. AE, DC, MC, V. Closed Nov.–Mar.*

Splurge
★

Belvedere Caruso. Charmingly old-fashioned, spacious, and comfortable, this rambling villa hotel has plenty of character and a full share of Ravello's spectacular views from its terraces and balconied rooms. Relax in the garden belvedere with its memorable views. The restaurant is known for fine food and locally produced house wine. Guests can expect to pay around 150,000 lire for a double room. *Via Toro 52, tel. 089/857111, fax 089/857372. 26 rooms with bath or shower. Facilities: restaurant, garden. AE, DC, MC, V.*

Dining
Under 30,000 lire
★

Cumpa Cosimo. This family-run restaurant a few steps from the cathedral square offers a cordial welcome in three simple but attractive dining rooms. There's no view, but the food is excellent. Among the specialties are cheese crepes and roast lamb or kid. *Via Roma 44, tel. 089/857156. Reservations advised on weekends and summer evenings. AE, DC, MC, V. Closed Mon. (Nov.–Mar.).*

Salerno

Salerno is 70–90 minutes by bus from Amalfi (fare 2,400 lire), one hour from Naples (fare 4,300 lire). The train from Naples departs hourly and takes 45 minutes to one hour (fare 4,200 lire). Tourist office: Piazza Vittorio Veneto, tel. 089/231432.

Salerno, spread out along the bay, is a sad testimony to years of neglect and overdevelopment. An imposing Romanesque cathedral is the only site most tourists consider worth seeing here. Built in 1085 and remodeled during the 18th century, it has Byzantine doors (1099) from Constantinople and an outstanding 12th-century pulpit. In the new Diocesan Museum behind it is a collection of astounding medieval carved tablets (admission free). A few blocks away in the recently restored **monastery of San Benedetto,** a museum holds a handsome bronze head of Apollo fished out of the bay during the 1930s.

Paestum

Various lines operate buses from Salerno (Piazza Concordia, on the seafront 100 yards in front of the train station) to Paestum; the journey takes about an hour (fare 4,000 lire). Five local trains daily (two on Sunday) do the journey in 45 minutes, with tickets at 3,900 lire; the train station is about 50 yards from the ruins. Tourist office: Via Aquilia, tel. 0828/811016.

Some 50 kilometers (30 miles) down the coast from Salerno, near the undistinguished modern town of Capaccio, stands one of Italy's most majestic sights: the remarkably well-preserved Greek temples of Paestum. The ruins stand on the site of the ancient city of Poseidonia, founded by Greek colonists during the 7th century BC. When the Romans took over the colony in 273 BC and called it Paestum, they enlarged the settlement, adding an amphitheater and a forum. Much of the archaeological material found on the site is displayed in the **museum,** and several rooms are devoted to the unique tomb paintings discovered in the area, rare examples of Greek and pre-Roman pictorial art. Across the road from the museum, framed by ranks of roses and oleanders, is the **Temple of Poseidon** (or Neptune), a magnificent Doric edifice, with 36 fluted columns and an extraordinarily well-preserved entablature (area above the capitals). Not even Greece itself possesses such a fine monument of Hellenic architecture. On the left of the temple is the so-called **Basilica,** the earliest of Paestum's standing edifices; it dates from very early in the 6th century BC. The name is an 18th-century misnomer, for the structure was in fact a temple sacred to Hera, the wife of Zeus. Behind it an ancient road leads to the **Forum** of the Roman era and the single column of the **Temple of Peace.** Beyond is the **Temple of Ceres.** Try to see the ruins in the late afternoon, when the light enhances the deep gold of the stone and the air is sharp with the cries of the crows that nest high on the temples. *Admission: 8,000 lire for museum and temple area. Open Apr.–Sept., daily 9–1 and 3–7:30; Oct.–Mar., daily 9–1.*

Lodging and Dining
Under 85,000 lire

Martini. Directly across the road from the Porta della Giustizia and only a few steps from the temples, the Martini has 13 cottage-type rooms, each with minibar, in a garden setting and a pleasant restaurant serving local specialties and seafood. *Zona Archeologica, tel. 0828/811451, fax 0828/811600. 27 rooms with bath or shower. Facilities: restaurant reservations advised, beach ½ mile away. AE, DC, MC, V.*

13 Apulia

Bari, Brindisi, and the Gargano Peninsula

Except for a few seaside resorts popular with Italians, Apulia is way off most tourist routes. All that most tourists see of the region (called Puglia by the Italians—English-speakers are really using the Latin term) is the blur outside their car or train windows as they hurtle toward Bari or Brindisi for ferry connections to Greece.

That's a pity, because this ancient land, the heel and spur of Italy's boot, repays the effort it takes to explore. Graceful churches and stout Norman castles dot the Bari area; lovely examples of Baroque and Rococo architecture distinguish such towns as Lecce and Martina Franca. Hills and forests cover the Gargano promontory, and miles of stunning beaches stretch along the Gulf of Taranto. Your trip will take you through a sun-baked countryside where expanses of silvery olive trees and giant prickly-pear cacti fight their way through the rocky soil, as if in defiance of the relentless summer heat. Local buildings, too, do their best to dispel the effects of the sun: Whitewashed ports stand coolly over the turquoise Mediterranean, and the landscape is studded with strange dwellings, called *trulli*, which look like pointed igloos made of stone.

The trulli date from the Middle Ages, but Apulia had long before been inhabited, conquered, and visited by travelers. The Greeks and later the Romans were quick to recognize the importance of this strategic peninsula, and among the nations that later raided or colonized Apulia were the Normans, Moors, and Spaniards, each of whom left a mark. Some of the most impressive buildings are the Romanesque churches and the pow-

Apulia

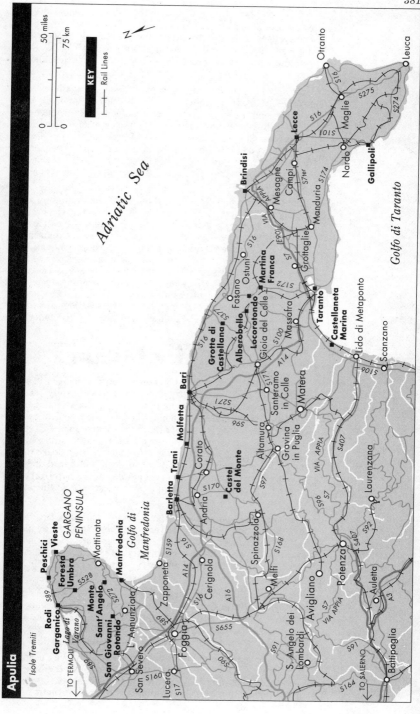

Isole Tremiti

Adriatic Sea

GARGANO PENINSULA

Golfo di Manfredonia

Golfo di Taranto

KEY
+—+— Rail Lines

0 — 50 miles
0 — 75 km

TO TERMOLI →

Rodi Garganico
Peschici
Vieste
Foresta Umbra
Mattinata
Lago di Varano
Monte Sant'Angelo
San Giovanni Rotondo
L'Annunziata
Manfredonia
San Severo
Lucera
Foggia
S. Angelo dei Lombardi
Zapponeta
Cerignola
Barletta
Trani
Andria
Corato
Molfetta
Castel del Monte
Spinazzola
Melfi
Avigliano
Potenza
Auletta
Battipaglia
Lourenzana
Bari
Grotte di Castellana
Alberobello
Locorotondo
Gioia del Colle
Santeramo in Colle
Altamura
Gravina in Puglia
Matera
Castellaneta Marina
Lido di Metaponto
Scanzano
Taranto
Massafra
Martina Franca
Fasano
Ostuni
Brindisi
Mesagne
Campi
Grottaglie
Manduria
Lecce
Otranto
Nardo
Gallipoli
Maglie
Leuca

TO SALERNO →

S89 S528 S272 S89 S160 S17 S90 S655 A16 S16 A14 S159 S170 S97 S168 S655 S91 S7 S407 S96 VIA APPIA A3 S92 S407 S96 S271 S96 A14 S100 S171 S7 S172 S271 S16 S16 S606 S7 VIA APPIA S7bis S174 S101 S16 S275 S274 S7ter VIA APPIA (E90) erful castles built by 13th-century Holy Roman Emperor Frederick II of Swabia (part of present-day Bavaria), king of Sicily and Jerusalem. One of the outstanding personalities of the Middle Ages, he was dubbed "Wonder of the World" for his wideranging interests in literature, science, mathematics, and nature.

Precisely because it is off the beaten track, Apulia is more affordable than many other regions of Italy. The cuisine is inexpensive and hearty, using local seafood and produce and picking the best from more than 2,000 years of foreign culinary influences. Shopping here consists of browsing through colorful street markets to buy local handicrafts. For the beaches and forests, travelers must rely on an irregular network of local bus routes, but all other places on these tours are conveniently reached by train.

Tour 1 covers Apulia's capital, Bari, and its surrounding area, mainly to the north. While Bari makes a useful touring base for the entire region, you may want to spend a night or two in such pretty seaside towns as Trani or Molfetta. Tour 2 explores farther north, to the Gargano promontory, where you can base yourself at Foggia, the inland provincial center, or any of a number of beach resorts. The last tour pushes south, taking in the trulli country (the region of dome-shape stone dwellings) and the larger cities of Brindisi, Taranto, and Lecce, as far as the fishing port of Gallipoli. Stop off just about anywhere along the coast between Gallipoli and Taranto for some fine swimming.

Essential Information

Lodging There has been a rapid development of tourist facilities in some areas of Apulia, particularly along the miles of sandy beaches on the Gargano spur, now one of the most popular summer resorts for Italians. Here, and elsewhere on the coast, big white Mediterranean-style beach hotels have sprung up one after the other. Most are similar in design, price, and quality. In the busy season, many cater only to guests paying full board (lodging plus three meals per day at the hotel) or half-board (lodging plus breakfast and one other meal per day at the hotel) on longer stays, and it is best to make your reservations through a travel agent.

Elsewhere in Apulia, particularly outside the big cities, hotel accommodations are still limited, and those that are available are generally modest—both in amenities and price—though this may be more than compensated for by friendly service. Some places, such as Bari during the annual Trade Fair in September, require reservations.

Many establishments, particularly the beach resorts, close during the winter months, so check for this also when choosing accommodations. And remember that in a region like this, which gets blazing hot in summer and bitter cold in winter, air-conditioning and central heating are important.

Don't ignore the camping possibilities along Apulia's coasts—by sacrificing a degree of comfort, you can have the beach at close hand for a minimal price. Many campsites have bungalow or trailer accommodations available for those without tents.

Bear in mind, however, that many of these establishments close during the winter months.

Highly recommended lodgings are indicated by a star ★.

Dining Anyone who likes to eat will love traveling in Apulia. Southern cuisine is hearty and healthy, based on homemade pastas and cheeses, fresh vegetables, seafood, and local olive oil. Open markets and delicatessens burst with local fruits, vegetables, pastries, sausages, smoked meats, and cheeses.

Here you will find dishes unavailable elsewhere in Italy, such as *'ncapriata*, also called *favi e fogghi* (a delicious puree of fava beans served as a first course with a side dish of bitter chicory or other cooked vegetables). *Focaccia barese* (stuffed pizza) makes a great snack or lunch.

Apulia's pasta specialties include *orecchiette* (small, flat, oval pieces of pasta), *troccoli* (homemade noodles cut with a special ridged rolling pin), and *strascenate* (rectangles of pasta with one rough side and one smooth side). Among the many typical sauces is *salsa alla Sangiovanniello* (made with olive oil, capers, anchovies, parsley, and hot peppers), from Brindisi.

Don't miss the dairy products, such as ricotta and buttery *burrata* cheese, and remember that Apulia has a wealth of excellent local wines, ranging from the strong white wine of Martina Franca to the sweet red Aleatico di Puglia, and the sweet white Moscato di Trani to the rich, dry red Castel del Monte.

Unless otherwise noted, reservations are not needed and dress is casual. Highly recommended restaurants are indicated by a star ★.

Shopping Apulia is rich in folk art, reflecting the influences of the many nations that have ruled the region throughout the centuries. Look for handmade goods, such as baskets, textiles, lace, carved-wood figures, pottery with traditional designs, and painted clay whistles. These are on sale in shops and open markets, where some bargaining can enter into the purchase.

Bicycling Apulia is the flattest of Italy's regions, well adapted to unstrenuous cycling. It's fun to see the hill towns and coastal villages on two wheels. You can rent bikes in most of the towns on our tours, but some of the recommended outlets are listed here.

Bari. *G.S. De Benedictus* (Via Nitti 23, tel. 080/344345).
Gioia del Colle. *G.S. Gioauto Renault* (Via Vittorio Emanuele, tel. 080/830417).
Manfredonia. *G.S. Cicli Castriotta* (Viale Beccarini 7, tel. 0884/23424).

Beaches For the Italians and other tourists who return each summer, the sea is one of the major attractions of Apulia. The sandy beaches along the **Gargano Peninsula,** although no longer "undiscovered," offer safe swimming. The entire coastline between **Bari** and **Brindisi** is well served with beach facilities. In even the smallest villages, you'll find beaches where there are changing rooms and—important in the blazing Apulian sun—beach umbrellas.

Along the Golfo di Taranto, try **Castellaneta Marina** or **Marina di Ginosa,** west of Taranto. The beaches around **Gallipoli** are good as well; try Torre del Pizzo and Lido Conchiglia. All of these resorts have campsites as well as a range of hotel accommodations, though these may close during winter.

The Arts and Nightlife In keeping with the general atmosphere of Apulia, the arts take on a folk flavor, with processions on religious occasions more prevalent than performing arts in theaters or opera houses. Still, there are some good festivals and pageants to help broaden your experience of life in Italy's deep south. The best newspaper for listings is the daily *Gazzetta del Mezzogiorno*, which covers the entire region.

Apulia is one of Italy's most rural regions, and even the cities have a marked provincial air to them. This can be frustrating for someone who expects the glamour of nightclubs and discos of the sort Milan and Rome have to offer. On the other hand, in the cafés surrounding the squares of most towns, you can have a ringside seat for that most Mediterranean of pageants—the *passeggiata*. Local people of all ages dress in their most stylish clothing and stroll through the streets, starting around sunset. This is Italian life at its most relaxed and, at the same time, most structured. No one is in a hurry; there is an air of laughter and conviviality; but young people will defer to their elders, and poorer people to those—the town doctor, lawyer, or monsignor—they consider to be their social superiors. And it's yours for the price of a cold drink at a sidewalk café.

Highlights for First-time Visitors

Alberobello and the Trulli (Tour 3: The Trulli District and the Heel of the Boot).

Appian Way Terminus, Brindisi (Tour 3: The Trulli District and the Heel of the Boot).

Basilica di Santa Croce, Lecce (Tour 3: The Trulli District and the Heel of the Boot).

Castel del Monte (Tour 1: Around Bari).

Foresta Umbra (Tour 2: The Gargano Peninsula).

Monte Sant' Angelo (Tour 2: The Gargano Peninsula).

Museo Archeologico, Bari (Tour 1: Around Bari).

Museo Nazionale, Taranto (Tour 3: The Trulli District and the Heel of the Boot).

Tour 1: Around Bari

Bari is a big, hectic, rough-and-tumble port and a transit point for travelers catching ferries across the Adriatic to Greece. The historic center, however, which most ferry passengers never see, has some interesting medieval buildings, as do three of the surrounding towns—Molfetta, Trani, and Barletta.

From Rome and Naples *By Train* There are two fast Intercity trains a day from Roma Termini to Bari, taking just over five hours (tickets cost 51,000 lire), and three Espresso trains taking six to seven hours. Otherwise, take any Naples-bound train and change at Aversa or Caserta for Bari; the total journey takes about seven hours. Standard tickets cost around 37,000 lire. From Naples, take the train to Aversa and change for a train to Bari; the trip takes four to five hours, the fare around 24,000 lire.

By Bus Three buses a day leave Rome's Piazza della Repubblica for Bari, arriving about five hours later. The service is run by Autolinee Marozzi (tel. 080/521–0365) and costs 45,000 lire.

By Car From Rome, take the A24/25 east to Pescara and go south on the A14 autostrada to Bari. From Naples, take the A16 east to the A14. Bari is linked to Brindisi, Taranto, and Foggia by fast highways and superhighways. The more scenic coastal roads can be very slow in summer.

By Plane Alitalia flies regularly from other Italian cities to Bari and Brindisi. **Palese Airport** is 8 kilometers (5 miles) west of Bari; **Papola Casale Airport** is 5 kilometers (3 miles) north of Brindisi. Regular bus services connect both airports with the cities.

Bari

Tourist offices: Via Melo 253, tel. 080/524–2361; Corso Vittorio Emanuele 68, tel. 080/521–9951.

Bari's train station is on Piazza Aldo Moro (formerly Piazza Roma and still shown that way on some older maps); the tourist office is off the right side of the square, on Via Melo. Long-distance buses arrive either in this square or at Piazza Eroi del Mare, off Corso Cavour.

Most of the city is set out in a logical, 19th-century grid pattern, following the designs of Joachim Murat, Napoleon's brother-in-law and the king of the Two Sicilies. The heart of the modern town is Piazza della Libertà, but just beyond it, across Corso Vittorio Emanuele, is the *città vecchia* (old town), a maze of narrow, crooked streets on the promontory that juts out between Bari's old and new ports. From Piazza Aldo Moro, a 20-minute walk along Corso Cavour will take you to the old town.

Here, overlooking the sea and just off Via Venezia, is the **Basilica di San Nicola** (St. Nicholas), built in the 11th century to house the bones of St. Nicholas, who is better known to us as St. Nick, or Santa Claus. His remains are said to have been stolen by Bari sailors from Myra, in what is now Turkey. The basilica, a solid and powerful construction, was the only building to survive the otherwise wholesale destruction of Bari by the Normans in 1152.

Follow the narrow Strada del Carmine from behind the basilica to reach the **Cattedrale** (Cathedral), a century younger than the basilica. The seat of the local bishop, it was the scene of many significant political marriages among important families in the Middle Ages. Its solid architecture reflects the Romanesque style favored by the Normans of that period.

The huge **Castello** (Castle) looms behind the cathedral. The current building dates from the time of Holy Roman Emperor Frederick II, who rebuilt an existing Norman-Byzantine castle to his own exacting specifications. Designed more for powerful effect than for beauty, it looks out beyond the cathedral to the Porto Vecchio (Old Port), Bari's small harbor. Inside is an interesting collection of medieval Apulian art. *Admission: 4,000 lire. Open Mon.–Sat. 9–1 and 3–7.*

From the castle go south, crossing Piazza Massari and Piazza della Libertà to take Via Cairoli to the **Museo Archeologico.** Inside is a fine collection of Apulian artifacts, including jewelry and weapons, some dating from the 7th century BC, that will leave you with a better understanding of why Apulia has been an important crossroads for more than 2,500 years. *Piazza Um-*

*berto I, tel. 080/521–1559. Admission free. Open Mon.–Sat.
9–1.*

Lodging
Under 115,000 lire

Bristol. Recently given a bright new finish, this is a good choice in the center of Bari's modern section, halfway between the train station and the old town. One of the few Bari hotels not geared exclusively to traveling businesspeople, it has spacious, light, first- and second-story rooms with modern furnishings and lots of potted plants. Space is usually in demand here, and you cannot always count on a room; book in advance, or phone from the station to check availability. *Via Calefati 15, tel. 080/521–1503, fax 080/521–1503. 18 rooms with shower. AE, DC, MC. V.*

Under 60,000 lire

Ostello del Levante. Given Bari's chronic shortage of accommodations, this hostel is the best budget option in the area. The main disadvantage is its inconvenient location 8 kilometers (5 miles) north of the city center, but it is only a short bus ride (No. 1) away, and when you find it you may appreciate its tranquil setting in a modern structure with easy access to the sea. Temporary membership is issued at the desk if you are not already a member. *Via Nicola Massaro 33, tel. 080/552–0282, fax 080/552–0282. 90 beds. Facilities: restaurant, parking, beach. No credit cards. Closed Dec. 21–Jan. 14.*

Dining
Under 30,000 lire

Ristorante al Pescatore. This is one of Bari's best fish restaurants, located in the old town opposite the castle and just around the corner from the cathedral. The cooking is done outside, where (in summer) you can sit amid a cheerful clamor of quaffing and dining. Try the *cefalo* (mullet) if it is available, accompanied by crisp salad and a carafe of invigorating local wine. *Piazza Federico II di Svevia, tel. 080/523-7039. AE, DC, MC, V. Closed Mon.*

Splurge

Vecchia Bari. You don't need to blow a lot of money in this restaurant, one of Bari's best and a favorite with troops of young people out to enjoy themselves. You could get by with spending no more than 45,000 lire a head for a full meal, and you will leave thoroughly satisfied. Go for any of the regional specialties on the menu: the orecchiette is a good first course, served in a buttery sauce with mushrooms; for an entrée, try the *agnello in crosta* (lamb baked with potatoes and mushrooms). The antipasti are good, too. *Via Dante 47, tel. 080/521–6496. Reservations advised weekends. AE, DC, MC, V. Closed Fri.*

The Arts

Bari's **Teatro Petruzzelli,** one of the most respected in southern Italy, hosts regular performances of drama, opera, and ballet. Built in 1903, it stands on Corso Cavour (tel. 080/524–1761). See the daily *Gazzetta del Mezzogiorno* or the monthly magazine *Ecobari* (free from the tourist office) for listings.

Molfetta

Hourly local trains from Bari (fare 2,500 lire) take 25 minutes to reach Molfetta, 25 kilometers (16 miles) to the north.

In common with other towns along this coast, Molfetta has a bustling old port reminiscent of such Venetian ports as Dubrovnik, across the Adriatic Sea. The town has an unusual 12th-century cathedral with distinct Byzantine features, such as the pyramid-shape covers on the three main domes.

Festivals If you are in the area during Easter, don't miss Molfetta's color-ful processions on Good Friday and Easter Saturday.

Trani

Two stops (a 15-minute ride) farther up the coast from Molfetta, Trani is a 40-minute train ride from Bari (tickets cost 4,000 lire). Tourist offices: Via Cavour 140, tel. 0883/ 588830; kiosk in Piazza della Repubblica, tel. 0883/43295.

Trani, 18 kilometers (11 miles) north of Molfetta, is the small-est but liveliest and most attractive of the fishing ports on this coast. From the train station, aim straight up Via Cavour to-ward the central Piazza della Repubblica, beyond which lie the old city and the port. The old town has polished stone streets and buildings, medieval churches, and a harbor filled with fish-ing boats. The 11th-century **cathedral,** considered one of the finest in Apulia, is built on a spit of land jutting into the sea. Trani had a flourishing Jewish community in medieval times, and there is still a Via Sinagoga (Synagogue Street) in the old town. Two of the four synagogues that existed here still sur-vive, as the 13th-century churches of **Santa Anna,** where there is still a Hebrew inscription, and **Santa Maria Scolanova.**

Lodging
Under 85,000 lire
Trani. Simple, modern, and near the station, the Trani offers good-value accommodations and has a restaurant. *Corso Imbriani 137, tel. 0883/588010, fax 0883/587625. 51 rooms with bath. Facilities: restaurant. AE, DC, MC, V.*

Under 60,000 lire
Albergo Lucy. This is a plain, hospitable hotel on a quiet piazza just off the port and next to the public gardens, along the sea-front. It has spacious rooms with high ceilings and balconies, and its friendly management extends a particular welcome to families. *Piazza Plebiscito 11, tel. 0883/41022. 8 rooms with bath. No credit cards.*

Dining
Under 30,000 lire
★
Antica Cattedrale. Just in front of the cathedral, on a spit of land jutting out into the sea, the Antica Cattedrale has an an-tique flavor, with stonework, vaulted ceilings, and terra-cotta tiled floors. There are also tables outside. Regional specialties are presented imaginatively: Try the baked crepes (similar to cannelloni); risotto made with salmon, crab, and cream; lob-ster; or grilled fish. *Piazza Archivio 2, tel. 0883/586568. Reser-vations required for Sun. lunch and dinner on summer weekends. AE, DC, MC, V. Closed Mon. and Nov.*

Barletta

Barletta is the next station north from Trani; hourly local trains take 10 minutes from Trani (fare 1,900 lire), 50 minutes from Bari (fare 4,300 lire). Tourist office: Via Gabbiani 4, tel. 0883/31373.

Barletta pales in comparison with the other points on this tour, its major attraction being the **Colossus,** a bronze statue over 15 feet tall, thought to be of the Byzantine emperor Valentinian and dating from the 5th century AD. Part of Venice's booty af-ter the sack of Byzantium's capital, Constantinople, in the 1200s, the Colossus was abandoned on the beach near Barletta when the ship carrying it to Venice foundered in a storm. It stands next to the church of San Sepolcro on Corso Vittorio Emanuele.

Dining | **La Casaccia.** Located near the castle, this modest restaurant
Under 30,000 lire | serves home cooking and local dishes, such as homemade
orecchiette and *penne piccanti* (spicy macaroni). *Via Cavour
40, tel. 0883/533719. Reservations required. No credit cards.
Closed Mon.*

Splurge **Bacco.** Here is a place where you can dine in style. Elegantly
★ furnished and centrally located, the Bacco has silver cutlery,
crystal, and flowers and candles on each table; there is a piano
bar in the evening. It serves innovative regional dishes, such as
gamberi al basilico (shrimp with basil), *spigola ai frutti di
mare* (sea bass with shellfish), and *capretto murgiano ai funghi
cardoncelli* (goat with mushrooms). The check here can set you
back as much as 90,000 lire, but it's a fair price for one of
Apulia's most famous restaurants. *Via Sipontina 10, tel. 0883/
571000. Jacket and tie required. AE, DC, MC, V. Closed Dec.
27–Jan. 5, Aug., Sun. and Mon.*

Festivals The **Disfida a Barletta,** held on the last Sunday in August, is a
reenactment of an event of the same name, which took place in
1503. The *disfida* (challenge) was issued by 13 Italian officers to
13 French officers after one of the French insulted the Italians
by stating that Italy would always be under foreign domination. The Italians taught the rash Frenchman and his compatri-
ots a lesson. Every Italian child learns this story at school.

Castel del Monte

*The fortress of Castel del Monte lies 30 kilometers (19 miles)
inland, in a remote spot that is awkward to reach unless you
have a car. In summer there may be a private bus service from
Bari, but don't count on it. Otherwise, the best way is to take
local buses from Barletta or Trani to the market towns of
Andria or Corato (around 12 kilometers/8 miles distant; tickets cost about 3,000 lire) and get a taxi from there, which will
cost around 20,000 lire more.*

Castel del Monte is one of Apulia's most impressive and mysterious monuments. Built on an isolated hill in the first half of the
13th century by Frederick II, Castel del Monte is a huge, bare,
octagonal castle with eight towers: It can be seen for miles
around and commands a stunning view. Very little is known
about the structure, since virtually no records exist. It has
none of the usual defense features associated with medieval
castles, so it probably had little military significance. Some
theories suggest that it might have been built as a hunting
lodge or may have served as an astronomical observatory or a
stop for pilgrims on their quest for the Holy Grail. *Admission:
4,000 lire, children under 12 free. Open Mon.–Sat. 9–1 and
3–7, Sun. and holidays 9–1.*

Tour 2: The Gargano Peninsula

Up the coast from Bari lies the Gargano Peninsula, the spur of
Italy's boot, where the region's most attractive and popular
beaches are found. Until a few years ago, this rocky promontory of whitewashed coastal towns, wide, sandy beaches, and
craggy limestone cliffs topped by deep-green scrub pine was

practically unknown: Some parts of the interior are still well off the usual tourist track. The beach-resort business has boomed during the past decade, though, and beaches can become crowded in midsummer.

The inland cities of Foggia and San Severo are useful transportation hubs, but you will find little of real interest in either town; it's better to base yourself closer to the seacoast, at Manfredonia, Monte Sant'Angelo, Rodi Garganico, Peschici, or Vieste.

From Rome, Naples, and Bari By Train All trains traveling up and down this coast stop at Foggia, including trains from Rome (3½ hours on Intercity trains) and Naples (3½ hours on Espresso trains, with a change at Aversa or Caserta). Tickets from Naples cost around 15,000 lire. Trains from Bari leave every half hour and take 90 minutes to reach Foggia.

Passengers can also get off at San Severo, just north of Foggia, to change onto the local (private) Ferrovie del Gargano (FG) line (tel. 0884/707393), serving the north coast as far as Peschici. There are also two departures daily on this line direct from Bari, but it is a slow journey, taking 3½ hours to Rodi. Stations on the FG line are often some distance from the towns they serve, so opt for buses if there is a choice. Note that rail passes are not valid on Italy's private rail lines.

By Bus From Rome's Piazza Esedra, daily buses leave for the Gargano at 5 PM, stopping at San Severo, Rodi Garganico, and Peschici, arriving at Vieste at 11:30 PM. A ticket from Rome to Vieste costs 39,000 lire. Buy tickets from the travel agent Eurojet (Piazza della Repubblica 58, tel. 06/474–2801). From Foggia, five buses daily (one on Sunday) leave from Piazza della Stazione, taking 2¾ hours to reach Vieste, via Manfredonia and Mattinata; a ticket from Foggia to Vieste costs 8,000 lire. The main bus companies in the area are Ferrovie del Gargano (tel. 0884/707393), SITA (tel. 0881/673117), handling mainly the internal routes, and ATAF (tel. 0884/707393), covering the coast. You can visit all places in the Gargano using these services, though you will be constrained by sporadic timetables and reduced services on Sunday.

By Car The A14 Bologna–Bari autostrada skirts the Gargano promontory; exit at Foggia (coming from the south) or Poggio Imperiale (from the north).

Tourist offices: Via Emilio Perrone, Foggia (tel. 0881/23141); Corso Manfredi 26, Manfredonia (tel. 0884/21998); Piazza Kennedy, Vieste (tel. 0884/78806).

The Gargano Peninsula

Manfredonia, a resort town on the southern side of the Gargano, lies about 40 kilometers (25 miles) northeast of Foggia. Take the winding coastal road (S89) northeast from the resort through miles of silvery olive groves interspersed with almond trees and prickly-pear cacti. Along the way you'll come across many local craftsmen's stalls selling homemade preserves, baskets, and carved olive-wood bowls and utensils. **Vieste,** a large town about 50 kilometers (30 miles) around on the tip of the spur, is the Gargano's main commercial center. But continue on to the north-shore resorts of **Peschici** and **Rodi Garganico,** whitewashed towns squeezed between the hills and the sea. You may want to make these your base for spending a few days exploring the beaches and coast.

The interior of the peninsula holds a world of complete contrast to Gargano's sunny coast. Here stands the majestic **Foresta Umbra** (Shady Forest), a dense growth of beeches, maples, syc-amores, and oaks generally found in more northerly climates but thriving here because of the altitude—3,200 feet above sea level. Between the trees are occasional dramatic vistas opening out over the Gulf of Manfredonia. You can always see a fair bit of the forest through the window on the daily SITA bus running inland from Rodi Garganico to Manfredonia, but without your own car, you will be unable to see much of this dense woodland. You can explore some of it, however, from the village of Vico del Gargano, accessible by local bus from Peschici or Rodi Garganico. Otherwise, in summer a bus runs twice a day from Rodi Garganico to the Visitor Center in the heart of the for-est—a useful base for excursions.

The interior is also important because of two centers for reli-gious pilgrimage. Perched amid olive groves on the rugged, white, limestone cliffs overlooking the gulf is the town of **Monte Sant'Angelo** (take SITA buses from Vico del Gargano, Mattinata, or Manfredonia; fares run from 2,200 to 5,000 lire). Pilgrims have flocked here for nearly 1,500 years—among them, St. Francis of Assisi and the Crusaders setting off for the Holy Land from the then-flourishing port of Manfredonia. The town is centered on the **Sanctuary of San Michele,** built above the grotto where the archangel Michael is believed to have ap-peared before shepherds in the year 490. Walk down a long se-ries of steps to get to the grotto itself—on the walls you can see the hand tracings left by pilgrims as votive symbols. Steps lead left from the sanctuary down to the **Tomb of Rotari,** which is believed to have been a medieval baptistery, with some re-markable 12th-century reliefs. More steep steps lead up to the large ruined Norman castle, which dominates the town. Here you'll have the best chance to appreciate the intricate pattern of the streets and steps winding their way up the side of the valley. To the right, looking out from the castle, you can see the town's medieval quarter, the Rione Junno, a maze of little white houses squeezed into one corner of the narrow valley. To get there from the castle, take the steps down to Piazza Cappelletti and then turn right.

Most shops in the Junno sell a local specialty called **ostia piena** (filled host), a pastry made with candied almonds and wafers, similar to communion hosts. The best place to munch them is at the southern end of the Junno, by the Villa Comunale, where you can also savor the view of the Gulf of Manfredonia. Sunset is the best time for this treat.

About 25 kilometers (16 miles) west of Monte Sant'Angelo, along the winding S272 (30 minutes by frequent SITA bus ser-vice from Manfredonia), is the ancient village of **San Giovanni Rotondo,** a pilgrimage center that has grown up around the shrine and tomb of Padre Pio (1887–1968). The monk is revered for his pious life, for miraculous intercessions, and for having received the stigmata, the signs of Christ's wounds. The **Casa Sollievo della Sofferenza** (Foundation for the Mitigation of Suf-fering), supported through contributions from around the world, is a testament to the enduring appeal of this holy man.

Lodging
Under 115,000 lire

Gargano. This is a typical big white beach hotel, with rooms decorated in blue and white and endowed with terraces. The disco/bar keeps the atmosphere lively on summer evenings. *Viale Beccarini 2, Manfredonia, tel. 0884/27621, fax 0884/ 26021. 46 rooms with bath or shower. Facilities: restaurant, outdoor pool, garage. V.*

Mizar. Simple, comfortably furnished rooms with terraces look out over the sea in this large, Mediterranean-style hotel. Local seafood is the attraction in the hotel restaurant. *Via Ippocampo, Lido del Sole, Rodi Garganico, tel. 0884/97021, fax 0884/97022. 54 rooms with bath. Facilities: restaurant, private beach, solarium. AE, MC, V. Closed Oct.–May.*

Valle Clavia. Olive and pine trees surround this modern, functional hotel located near the beach. Ask for room 30, which has a view of the sea. Prices may rise above the ceiling for this category during the months of July and August. *Valle Clavia, Peschici, tel. 0884/964209. 51 rooms with bath. Facilities: restaurant, garden, tennis court. MC, V. Closed Oct.–May.*

Under 85,000 lire

Locanda al Castello. Centrally located in Peschici, this small and friendly hostelry provides bright, plain rooms and a restaurant with hearty home cooking. *Via Castello 47, Peschici, tel. 0884/964038. Facilities: restaurant. No credit cards.*

Under 60,000 lire

Asi. Good value for the price, this hotel has modern, comfortable rooms and efficient service. It's large, so it rarely runs short of space, but reserve ahead if you are arriving at the beginning of May, when Foggia hosts one of Italy's oldest agricultural fairs. *Via Monfalcone 1, Foggia, tel. 0881/23327. 94 rooms, 35 with bath. No credit cards.*

Bologna. Foggia is primarily a commercial hub, so it has a limited choice of tourist accommodations. Most of the lodgings lie between the train station and the center of town, including this unremarkable but useful hotel. Ignore the rather seedy exterior: The rooms are decent and clean, and the management is friendly. *Via Monfalcone 53, Foggia, tel. 0881/621341. 20 rooms, none with bath. No credit cards.*

Campeggio Mattinata. Camping is a strong option on the Gargano Peninsula—there are more campsites than hotels here, and though most get pretty full in midsummer, you will never be turned away. This one is more central than most, a stone's throw from the sea, efficiently run, and with good facilities. Bungalows and sometimes tents are available for rent on a weekly basis. *Mattinata, tel. 0884/4313. Facilities: restaurant, pizzeria, bar, shops. No credit cards. Closed Oct.–May.*

Rotary. This simple but welcoming modern hotel is set just outside town amid olive and almond groves. Each room has a terrace with a good view of the Gulf of Manfredonia. *Via per Pulsano, Monte Sant'Angelo, tel. 0884/62146. 24 rooms with bath. Facilities: restaurant, shower. MC, V. Closed Nov.*

Splurge
★

Pizzomunno. Probably the most luxurious resort on the Gargano, Pizzomunno is right on the beach and is surrounded by a large park. It is large, white, modern, well-equipped, and fully air-conditioned. The rooms are ample and comfortable, and they all have terraces. There is a moderate–expensive restaurant specializing in fish, and there are many opportunities to unwind or try your hand at something a little more active, such as tennis or archery. *Via Litoranea, Vieste, tel. 08884/ 708741, fax 0884/707325. 183 rooms with bath. Facilities: restaurant, swimming pool, private beach, movie theater, disco,* *handball and tennis courts, archery, water sports, fitness center, sauna, child care. AE, DC, MC, V. Closed Nov.–Mar.*

Shopping In **Monte Sant'Angelo,** local craftsmen make and sell wooden utensils, furniture, and wrought-iron goods. Shoemaker Domenico Palena displays his unique leather sculptures at his tiny shop in the Junno quarter.

Tour 3: The Trulli District and the Heel of the Boot

This tour explores the southern part of Apulia, from Bari as far as the fishing port of Gallipoli on the Gulf of Taranto. Inland between Bari and Taranto, the most distinguishing feature of the country you'll pass through are the curious, pointed, dome-shaped constructions called trulli, used as dwellings, shops, churches, and even hotels. Taranto, snuggled up under the heel of Italy's boot, is a large naval base and industrial center with some pleasant beaches and resort towns nearby. Across on the Adriatic side of the heel is Brindisi, the terminus of the Roman Empire's famous Appian Way. The tour continues inland to the lovely Baroque town of Lecce, then back to the Gulf of Taranto to visit the small port of Gallipoli.

Grotte di Castellana

From Bari's main train station, on Piazza Aldo Moro, hourly Ferrovie Sud-Est (FSE; tel. 080/558–3222) trains take just under an hour to reach Castellana Grotte; tickets cost 3,200 lire.

The main attraction here is a huge network of caves—the Grotte di Castellana, discovered in 1938—lying a couple of kilometers west of town (follow signs from the train station). You can take one- or two-hour guided tours through the grottoes, which are filled with fantastically shaped stalagmites and stalactites: The grottoes constitute the largest network of caves on the Italian mainland. *Admission: 5,000 lire. Open Apr.–Sept., daily 8:30–12:15 and 2:30–6; Oct.–Mar., daily 9–noon and 2–5.*

Dining **Taverna degli Artisti.** Located near the caves, this rustic
Under 24,000 lire tavern-style restaurant with a big garden specializes in local home cooking, such as roast lamb, homemade orecchiette, and dishes with fanciful names—including *cannelloni all'Ernesto*, *timballo fine del mondo* (end-of-the-world timbale), and *involtini al purgatorio* (purgatory roulades). *Via Vito Matarrese 27, tel. 080/896–8234. No credit cards. Closed Thurs. (Oct.–June) and Dec.*

Splurge **Al Parco Chiancafredda.** The refined ambience and cuisine of
★ this restaurant, which is set apart from the tourist haunts in the area, make it pricier than its neighbors. But the food and service are worth the extra cost: Try such regional dishes as *sformato di verdura* (a kind of vegetable stew) and *agnello alla castellanese* (local lamb). *Via Chiancafredda 12, tel. 080/896–8710. Reservations required. DC. Closed Tues. and Nov.*

Also on the FSE line, Alberobello is 40 minutes from Castellana Grotte (fare 2,400 lire), about 1½ hours from Bari (fare 5,000 lire). Tourist office: Corso Vittorio Emanuele 15, tel. 080/721916.

The small town of Alberobello lies at the heart of the trulli district and holds Apulia's greatest concentration of trulli. It has become commercialized, and most accommodations are expensive now, but it's worth a visit to get the full impact of the trulli.

The origins of the igloo-shape structures go back to the 13th century, and maybe further: The trulli are built of local limestone, without mortar, and with a hole in the top for smoke. Some are painted with mystical or religious symbols, some are isolated, and others are joined together with roofs on various levels. The trulli zone of Alberobello, where more than 1,000 trulli crowd together along steep, narrow streets, is a national monument. It is also one of the most popular tourist destinations in Apulia and a gold mine for people who enjoy shopping for souvenirs (*see* Shopping, *below*).

Lodging
Under 85,000 lire

Astoria. The undistinguished but comfortably modern Astoria is conveniently located near the train station and the trulli zone. Most rooms have big, private balconies, and there is a garden as well as a moderately priced restaurant serving local dishes, such as homemade orecchiette and fava-bean puree with chicory. *Viale Bari 11, tel. 080/932–3320, fax 080/721290. 47 rooms with bath or shower. Facilities: restaurant, garden, bar, parking. AE, DC, MC, V.*

Splurge

Dei Trulli. Trulli-style cottages in a pinewood near the trulli zone make this a pleasant hotel, decorated with rustic furnishings, including folk-art rugs. There is a modestly priced restaurant serving local specialties. *Via Cadore 28, tel. 080/932–3555, fax 080/932–3560. 33 rooms with bath. Facilities: outdoor pool, garden, minibars. AE, MC, V.*

Dining
Under 30,000 lire
★

Trullo d'Oro. This welcoming restaurant occupies five trulli houses and is decorated in the rustic style, with dark wood beams, whitewashed walls, and an open hearth. Local country cooking includes dishes that use horse meat as well as lamb and veal, vegetable and cheese antipasti, pasta dishes with crisp raw vegetables on the side, and almond pastries. Specialties include roast lamb with *lampasciuni* (a type of wild onion) and *spaghetti al trullo*, made with tomatoes, garlic, olive oil, *rughetta* (arugula, a bitter green), and four cheeses. *Via F. Cavallotti 29, tel. 080/721820. Reservations required. AE, DC, MC, V. Closed Mon.*

Under 24,000 lire

Pugliese. A simple, homey restaurant with bare white walls in the trulli zone, Pugliese serves local dishes and has outdoor tables. Try the orecchiette, with a sauce of cream, mushrooms, and *pecorino* (ewe's milk) cheese, or *pannette alla Pugliese*, which consists of peppers, ground meat, mushrooms, and fresh tomatoes. There is a good fixed-price menu here for 20,000 lire. À la carte is nearer 30,000 lire. *Via F. Gigante, tel. 080/721437. AE, DC, MC, V. Closed Mon. during winter.*

Splurge

Il Poeta Contadino. Proprietor Marco Leonardo serves "creative regional cooking" in this rustic-style restaurant. Set in the heart of the attractive trulli zone, it features an outdoor terrace and candlelit tables. Specialties to look for are fish platters and a house antipasto selection. *Via Indipendenza 21, tel. 080/721917. Reservations advised for lunch. AE, DC, MC, V. Closed Mon., Jan. 7–Feb. 14.*

Shopping **Rugs** and **fabrics** are the best bets here, but because of the town's popularity with tourists, there is also a good deal of shoddy material. In the trulli quarter you'll find small shops selling hand-painted **clay figurines.**

Locorotondo and Martina Franca

The FSE line continues south from Alberobello, 10 minutes to Locorotondo and another 10 minutes from there to Martina Franca. Tickets from Alberobello to either town cost 1,500 lire. Tourist office: Piazza Roma 37, Martina Franca, tel. 080/ 705702.

A short distance southeast of Alberobello, these attractive towns lie only 6 kilometers (4 miles) apart. If you plan to stay overnight, your best bet for hotels and restaurants is Martina Franca, but also get off the train in Locorotondo, an attractive hillside town in the Itria Valley. From the train station, there are normally buses waiting to run passengers up to the center of town. Climb up to the road above the town for an aerial view: The *rotondo* in the town's name refers to the unusual circular pattern of the houses here.

Martina Franca is a graceful town with a dazzling mixture of medieval and Baroque architecture in the light-colored local stone. Turn left out of the train station and walk up Viale della Libertà to Piazza Roma, the center of town, a 20-minute walk. Ornate balconies hang above the twisting, narrow streets, with little alleys leading off into the surrounding hills. Martina Franca was developed as a military stronghold during the 14th century, when a surrounding wall with 24 towers was built, but now all that remains of that are the four gates that had been the only entrances.

Lodging **Da Luigi.** Martina Franca has three hotels in the center, but all
Under 85,000 lire charge more than 160,000 lire for a room. The remoteness of this small hostelry outside town accounts for its low price, for in all other respects Da Luigi provides excellent value, with clean, pleasant rooms and a friendly management. To reach the hotel, walk about a kilometer along the Taranto Road, or take one of the hourly Taranto-bound buses from the station. *Via Taranto, tel. 080/901666. 15 rooms with shower. Facilities: restaurant, bar, garden, garage. MC, V.*

Dining **La Tavernetta.** This small, dimly lit restaurant with a vaulted
Under 30,000 lire ceiling in the old-town center serves good home cooking and local specialties, starting with a pottery bowl full of local olives to nibble with the excellent house wine. Specialties include fava bean puree with cooked chicory and orecchiette with a side dish of *cocomero* (a vegetable that looks like a miniature round watermelon but tastes like a cross between a cucumber and a honeydew melon). Main-dish specialties include huge portions of mixed grilled lamb, liver, and spicy local sausage. *Corso Vittorio Emanuele 30, tel. 080/706323. No credit cards. Closed Mon.*

Under 24,000 lire **San Martino.** Next to a park on the edge of the old town, this is a welcoming family-run establishment where you can eat outside in summer. The pasta dishes (orecchiette and ravioli) are excellent, as is the local lamb (*agnello*); or you may be satisfied with a pizza cooked in the wood-burning oven. There is a 20,000-lire fixed-price menu. *Villa Carmine, tel. 080/903521. No credit cards. Closed Tues.*

Festivals   Martina Franca hosts a **Festival of the Itria Valley** every July and August, attracting not only local singers and orchestras but also artists of renown from all over Europe.

Taranto

From Martina Franca, FSE trains take 40 minutes to reach Taranto. FSE also runs a bus service from Piazza Crispi, off Corso Italia in Martina Franca. Tickets on either cost around 4,000 lire. There is also regular train service direct to Taranto from Bari, running every hour or half hour. Four Intercity trains daily make the trip in about 90 minutes; others take 2 hours. The fare is 8,800 lire, plus a supplement for the fast trains. Tourist office: Corso Umberto 113, tel. 099/432392.

Taranto—the stress is on the first syllable—was an important port even in Roman times. It occupies an excellent position on one side of a broad bay, the Mare Grande. A narrow channel forms the entrance to a smaller, landlocked, bay, the Mare Piccolo. Taranto's archaeological museum is Apulia's best, but the city itself, a large industrial center, has little else to offer. The coast on either side, however, offers some sandy beaches and small resorts.

From the train station on Piazza Duca d'Aosta, Via Duca d'Aosta leads straight over the bridge to the central island containing Taranto's old town, what little remains of it. The 14th-century church of **San Domenico** at the end of the promontory is worth a visit. At Piazza Castello, another bridge connects the promontory to the main part of town, where Taranto's most important attraction is located: the **Museo Nazionale**, with its large collection of prehistoric, Greek, and Roman artifacts from the immediate vicinity. (If you want to skip this 20-minute walk, take bus No. 8 from the train station to Corso Umberto, where the Museo Nazionale and the tourist information office stand.)

Some of the prehistoric items from Apulian tombs date from before 1000 BC, but more plentiful are the examples of intricate craftsmanship in the Greek jewelry from around 500 BC. The museum is a memorable testament to the importance of this ancient port, which has always taken full advantage of its unique trading position at the end of the Italian peninsula. *Corso Umberto 41, tel. 099/432112. Admission: 6,000 lire. Open Mon.–Sat. 9–2, Sun. 9–1. Closed on national holidays.*

Lodging   **Bologna.** Just around the corner from Taranto's museum, this
Under 85,000 lire   centrally located hotel is popular with businesspeople. It's not exactly exploding with life, but the big, old-fashioned guest rooms are well cushioned from any intrusive noises, it is comfortable enough, and the rates make it a reasonable value. *Via Regina Margherita 4, tel. 099/452–6701. 39 rooms, 11 with bath or shower. No credit cards.*

Dining   **Ristorante Basile.** If you want a quick, economical meal during
Under 20,000 lire   your stay in Taranto, drop into this basic trattoria, where the prices are rock-bottom and the portions abundant. There's an

18,000-lire tourist menu, and pizzas are also available. *Via Pitagora 76, tel. 099/26240. No credit cards. Closed Sat.*

Castellaneta Marina

Two stops west of Taranto on local trains, Castellaneta Marina is a 25-minute ride from the city. Tickets cost 2,400 lire.

What there is of a town center at Castellaneta Marina lies a kilometer farther from the train station. But this is hardly a town at all but more of a summer resort consisting of a few campsites, hotels, restaurants, and a handful of shops. The reason they are here at all, of course, is the wide expanse of sandy beach. Except in summer, there is very little reason to visit.

Lodging
Under 115,000 lire
★

Villa Giusy. Modern amenities blend with an old-fashioned flavor in this little resort hotel in a pinewood only 300 yards from a wide, sandy beach. Most rooms have a balcony. There's an inexpensive restaurant serving local specialties, and the hotel offers reasonable full- and half-board rates. *Via Sputnik 4, tel. 843–0031. 24 rooms with bath. Facilities: restaurant, garden, outdoor pool, children's playground. MC, V.*

Brindisi

Twelve daily main-line trains cross the heel of Italy from Taranto to Brindisi; the trip takes just over an hour and costs 4,800 lire. Brindisi is 90 minutes from Bari on Espresso trains; tickets cost around 5,000 lire. Tourist office: Piazza Dionisi, tel. 0831/521944.

Most people think of Brindisi (the first syllable, like that of Taranto, is stressed) only in terms of its ferry port, which links Italy with Greece. Although this impression fails to give credit to the broader importance of the city (it has a population of nearly 100,000), it is a present-day reminder of the role Brindisi has always played as gateway to the eastern Mediterranean and beyond. The core of the city is at the head of a deep channel, which branches into two harbors with the city between them. The train station and bus terminus are in Piazza Crispi; ferries leave from the Stazione Marittima, a 20-minute walk from the station down Corso Umberto and Corso Garibaldi. Look for the steeple of the **Duomo** (Cathedral) to get your bearings, but go beyond it and down the steps to the water's edge. Just to the left, along Viale Regina Margherita, you'll see a tall **Roman column** and the base of another one beside it. These were built in the 2nd century AD and marked the end of the **Via Appia** (Appian Way), the Imperial Roman road from the capital to the important southern seaport. Brindisi has seen a constant flow of naval and mercantile traffic throughout the centuries, and in the Middle Ages was an important launching point for several Crusades to the Holy Lands.

Return to the Duomo to have a look at the mosaic floor in the apse; the floor dates from the 12th century, although much of the rest of the cathedral was rebuilt during the 18th century. From the front of the Duomo, take Via Tarantini away from the Roman columns; this leads to Via Castello, where, about 500 yards from the Duomo, you'll turn right onto Via della Libertà. Just ahead is **Castello Svevo,** another of the defense fortifications built by the illustrious Frederick II during the 13th century. It guards the larger of the two inner harbors, and from the far side (the harborfront side) you can look back on the Roman column and the jutting old section of the city.

Lodging
Under 60,000 lire

Europa. The unprepossessing entrance to this hotel in the center of town is discouraging, but once you climb the stairs to the reception area, that impression is already forgotten. Guest rooms are plain but clean, most with TV. Ask for a room at the front, overlooking the square. *Piazza Cairoli 5. tel. 0831/528546, fax 0831/528546. 14 rooms, 6 with bath. AE, MC, V.*

Dining
Under 20,000 lire

L'Angoletto. Brindisi's shipping agents are outnumbered only by the town's trattorias, which will do everything short of kidnapping to attract customers. Prices are consequently low, but most places sacrifice quality and atmosphere. This small pizzeria off Corso Garibaldi doesn't. It serves unpretentious fare—the usual pizza menu, plus good, cheap local wine. Eat outside in the summer. *Via Pergola 3, no telephone. No credit cards. Closed Tues.*

Festivals

The **City of Brindisi Festival** (July–September) is a citywide display of art and folklore.

Lecce

Hourly Espresso trains from Brindisi take about 40 minutes to reach Lecce. Tickets cost 3,200 lire. Tourist office: Piazza Sant'Oronzo, tel. 0832/304443.

Few travelers even consider the short detour south from Brindisi to Lecce, an omission that has probably done more than anything else to preserve this honey-colored Baroque town, the crowning jewel on the tour of Apulia. Walk straight out of the train station to enter Lecce's old city through the gate on Viale Gallipoli. Although Lecce was founded before the time of the ancient Greeks, it is almost always associated with the term Lecce Baroque. This is because of a citywide impulse in the 17th century to redo the town in the Baroque fashion. But this was Baroque with a difference. Though Baroque architecture is often heavy and monumental, here it took on a lighter, more fanciful tone. Just look at the **Basilica di Santa Croce,** with the **Palazzo della Prefettura** abutting it. Although every column, window, pediment, and balcony is given a curling Baroque touch—and then an extra one for good measure—the overall effect is lighthearted. This is partly because the scale of the buildings is unintimidating and partly because the local stone used is a glowing honey color: It couldn't look menacing if it tried.

Coming out of the basilica, turn left, and 100 yards later, you will reach **Piazza Sant'Oronzo,** in the middle of which is a Roman column of the same era and style as the one remaining in Brindisi. Next to the column is the **Roman amphitheater:** The shallow rows of seats suggest a small-scale version of the Roman Colosseum or Verona's Arena.

Lodging
Under 85,000 lire

Cappello. This popular choice, a 10-minute walk from the center, is conveniently located outside the old city walls and close by the train station (take the first road on the left out of the station and walk 100 yards). Rooms are cramped but comfortable, and most have a TV. *Via Montegrappa 4, tel. 0832/308881, fax 0832/301535. 34 rooms with shower. No credit cards.*

Splurge **Risorgimento.** An old-fashioned hotel in a converted palace in the heart of the Baroque old town, the Risorgimento combines historic charm and decor with modern comfort. There is a restaurant, cocktail lounge, and rooftop garden with a great view of the town. You will pay around 145,000 lire for a double here. *Via Augusto Imperatore, tel. 0832/242125, fax 0832/245571. 57 rooms with bath or shower. Facilities: restaurant, conference rooms, rooftop garden. AE, DC, MC, V.*

Dining **Carlo V.** This pizzeria in the heart of Lecce is part of a complex
Under 24,000 lire that also includes a tearoom, wineshop, and formal restaurant, all housed in an atmospheric old palace owned by one of Lecce's noble families. The pizzas are delicious: Try the house specialty, prepared with wild mushrooms, salami, and sausage. *Piazzetta Falconieri, tel. 0832/243509. AE,DC, MC, V. Closed Mon.*

Shopping **Wrought-iron work** is the local specialty, but you should also look for works in **papier-mâché** (particularly nativity scenes).

The Arts In July, the public gardens are used for productions of drama and, sometimes, opera. Lecce features a festival of Baroque music in September, when churches throughout the city serve as venues.

Gallipoli

Nine FSE trains a day run from Lecce to Gallipoli. The trip takes about an hour; tickets cost 4,300 lire. To return to Taranto, you must take the train back through Lecce and Brindisi; there is no service from Gallipoli to Taranto.

The modern section of town lies on the mainland; turn right on the main street at the end of the central square and cross a 17th-century bridge to the old town, crowded onto its own small island in the gulf. The Greeks called it Kallipolis, the Romans Anxa. Like the famous Turkish town of the same name on the Dardanelles, the Italian Gallipoli occupies a strategic location and was therefore attacked repeatedly throughout the centuries—by the Normans in 1071, the Venetians in 1484, the British in 1809. The historic quarter, a mesh of narrow alleys and squares, is guarded by a formidable Aragonese **castello,** a massive fortification that grew out of an earlier Byzantine fortress that you can still see at the southeast corner. Other sights in town include the Baroque **Duomo** and the church of **La Purissima,** with its stuccoed interior as elaborate as a wedding cake (note especially the tile floor).

From Gallipoli's train station, local buses leave on routes up and down the coast, stopping at some good beaches. Try the long **Baia Verde** a couple of kilometers to the south, or the villages of **Santa Caterina** and **Santa Maria al Bagno** to the north.

Lodging **Al Pescatore.** This Spanish-style, 17th-century palace has re-
Under 85,000 lire cently been converted into a hotel and restaurant, keeping the
★ old courtyard and preserving the antique tone of the place. Guest rooms are clean and spacious (half of them look out over the sea). This is the only lodging left in Gallipoli's old quarter, and its seafood restaurant is one of the town's best. *Riviera Cristoforo Colombo 39, tel. 0833/263656. 14 rooms with bath. Facilities: restaurant, bar. No credit cards.*

Splurge   **Le Sirenuse.** There is a private beach and pinewoods at this gleaming white Mediterranean-style beach-hotel complex. It is fully air-conditioned, with comfortable rooms whose terraces have good views of the coast. Expect to pay around 140,000 lire here. *At Baia Verde beach, tel. 0833/273851, fax 0833/22539. 125 rooms with bath. Facilities: tennis, pool, playground. AE, DC, MC, V. Closed Nov.–Mar.*

Dining   **Marechiaro.** You have to cross a little bridge to reach this sim-
Under 30,000 lire   ple portside restaurant, which is not far from the town's histor-
★   ic center. Decorated with wood paneling and flowers, it has terraces with panoramic views of the coast. Try the *zuppa di pesce in bianco* (fish stew made without tomatoes) or the linguine with seafood. *Lungomare Marconi, tel. 0833/266143. Reservations advised on weekends. AE, DC, MC, V. Closed Tues. Oct.–May.*

14 Sicily

It's a lengthy train ride from any of the major Italian cities to the Straits of Messina, the 2-mile stretch of water that divides Sicily from the rest of the country. Perhaps because of this remoteness, Sicily presents a different aspect of Italy, Italian but not Italian, with separate traditions, a unique culture, and an often impenetrable dialect. There is poverty here—the result of the island's descent from its erstwhile position at the center of Mediterranean life to a humbler, more peripheral role in the nation's forward march—but there is also an abundance of artistic wealth.

Good and often cheap accommodations exist, along with a wide range of dining possibilities at affordable prices, though the farther you venture from the coast, the less of either you will find. Similarly, transportation facilities are more limited inland, though you should have no trouble reaching the places we have described below using trains, buses, and boats. On the whole, travel along the coasts and between the main towns is easiest by train, while buses are best for the smaller towns and villages and for penetrating the hinterland. For the islands, use ferries or the faster (but more expensive) hydrofoils, but remember that these services are often drastically reduced outside the summer months.

Arriving in Sicily for the first time, you may be surprised to see so many people with blond hair and blue eyes and to learn that two of the most popular boys' names are Ruggero (Roger) and Guglielmo (William), but that is what Sicily is all about. For 2,000 years it has been an island where unexpected contrasts somehow come together peacefully. Lying in a strategic position between Europe and Africa, Sicily at one time hosted two of the most advanced and enlightened capitals of Europe—a Greek one in Siracusa and an Arab-Norman one in Palermo. (The Normans are responsible for the blond-haired Rogers and blue-eyed Williams.) Sicily was one of the great melting pots of the ancient world and home to every great civilization that existed in the Mediterranean: Greek and Roman; then Arab and Norman; and, finally, French, Spanish, and Italian. Something of all of these peoples was absorbed into Sicily's artistic heritage, a rich tapestry of art and architecture that includes massive Romanesque cathedrals, two of the best-preserved Greek temples in the world, Roman amphitheaters, and delightful Baroque palaces and churches.

Modern Sicily is still a land of surprising contrasts. The traditional graciousness and nobility of the Sicilian people exist side by side with the atrocities and destructive influences of the Mafia. Alongside some of the most exquisite architecture in the world have sprouted the shabby products of some of the worst speculation imaginable. In recent years the island, like much of the Mediterranean coast, has seen a boom in popular tourism and a surge in condominium development that has only begun to be checked. The chic boutiques producing lace and linen in jet-set resort towns like Taormina do not betray the poverty in which their wares are produced.

You do not have to be paranoid about safety in Sicily, but you do have to be careful: Do not flaunt your gold jewelry, and keep your handbag securely strapped across your chest. Leaving valuables visible in your car while you go sightseeing is, naturally, inviting trouble. Be careful; then enjoy the company of the Sicilians. You will find them to be friendly and often willing to go out of their way to help tourists.

We have outlined three tours, oriented from Sicily's biggest cities, Palermo and Catania. The first tour concentrates on Palermo, the island's capital; the second covers the western part of the island; and the third explores the eastern end. There is no point in any tour that cannot be reached easily from either Palermo or Catania, although you may not want to base yourself in either of these two crowded cities, which can be insufferably hot in high summer. We have mentioned numerous lodgings in smaller centers along the routes.

Essential Information

Lodging Accommodations in Sicily are unevenly scattered around the island, and not all price ranges are equally represented. Palermo has the widest choice of all, although many of the budget options leave something to be desired. Catania, on the other hand, is surprisingly limited; many travelers prefer to stay in Siracusa, 75 minutes to the south. There are enclaves of luxurious hotels in such elite resorts as Taormina and some of the Aeolian Islands; Cefalù and Agrigento have a good choice of more expensive lodgings but surprisingly little in the lower price categories. And accommodations on any of Sicily's outlying islands can be extremely hard to find in August—make sure you reserve well in advance if you want to stay overnight during this period.

Sicily

TO SARDINIA

TO TUNIS

TO SARDINIA

Ustica ■

TO LIVORNO, GENOA

TO NAPLES

Tyrrh

San Vito
lo Capo ○

*Golfo di
Castellammare*

Mondello ○

Palermo ■

S113

Monreale ■

Trapani ■ **Erice** ■

A19

Termini

Mt. S.
Calogero

A19

I.
Favignana

Segesta ■

Corleone ○

S121

Marsala ■

S188 *A29*

**To
Pantelleria**

Castelvetrano ○

S115

S115

Selinunte ■

S118

Sciacca ○

S189

Caltaniss

S640

Agrigento ■

S115

Licata ○

Mediterranean Sea

N

KEY

🚢 Ferry
├─┼─ Rail Lines

0 — 20 miles

0 — 30 km

TO LINOSA

TO LAMPEDUSA

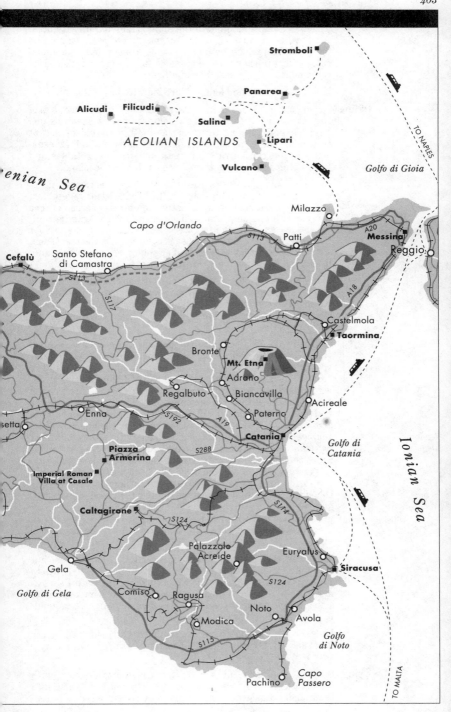

One good piece of news for budget travelers: Sicily does have excellent campsites on both the main island and its satellites. All have good washing facilities, most have restaurants and bars, and many have swimming pools, tennis courts, and discos. Collect information on these as well as other types of accommodation from local tourist offices.

Highly recommended lodgings are indicated by a star ★.

Dining   Eating out in Sicily can be quite affordable, though fish, one of the mainstays of the island's cuisine, is not as cheap as one might expect. Every town has at least a couple of decent trattorias where you can eat well and within your budget, especially if you concentrate on pasta and fresh vegetables and fruit—items that are in abundance on this fertile island.

Sicilian cooking reflects the different Mediterranean influences that have left their mark on the island. Fish, vegetables, and grains are used in imaginative combinations, sometimes served with Italian pastas and sometimes with Arab ingredients, such as *couscous* (steamed semolina). Sweet and sour tastes are deftly mingled, and each cook has a distinctive touch, so that *caponata* (an antipasto of eggplant, capers, olives, and, in eastern Sicily, peppers) is different at each restaurant.

Sicily has always been one of Italy's poorest areas, so meat is rarely seen on menus. When it *is* featured, it is usually prepared *alla brace* (charcoal-grilled) or in *falso magro* (a thin slice of meat rolled around sausage, onion, bacon, bits of egg, and cheese).

Seafood from Sicilian waters is the best and most varied in all Italy. *Tonno* (tuna) is a staple in many coastal areas, while *pesce spada* (swordfish) is equally common, if more expensive. Try *ricci* (sea urchins), which are a specialty of Mondello, near Palermo. Fish sauces for pasta are also noteworthy: *Pasta con le sarde* is made with fresh sardines, olive oil, anchovies, raisins, and pine nuts, and has the distinctive flavor of wild fennel. *Spaghetti alla Norma,* named for the heroine in the opera by local composer Vincenzo Bellini, has a sauce of tomatoes and fried eggplant. Desserts from Sicily are famous. *Cassata siciliana* is a rich combination of candied fruit, marzipan, and icing. *Gelato* (ice cream) is excellent and is usually homemade, sometimes in the form of *granita di limone,* a kind of lemon slush. Gooey cakes and very sweet desserts help raise the blood-sugar level, and the high priests of nouvelle cuisine would probably keel over if faced with a typical Sicilian dessert, such as chestnut ice cream covered with hot *zabaglione* (rich, foamy custard laced with Marsala).

The sweet dessert wine Marsala is Sicily's most famous, but there is a range of other local wines, from the dark red Faro to the sparkling dry Regaleali, which is excellent with fish. Almost every restaurant will have its own local wine available, considerably cheaper than the bottled variety and often equally good, if not better.

Unless otherwise noted, reservations are not needed and dress is casual. Highly recommended restaurants are indicated by a star ★.

Shopping   Sicily is one of the leaders in the Italian **ceramics** industry, with important factories at **Caltagirone,** in the interior, and **Santo Stefano di Camastra,** along the northern coast between Messina and Cefalù. Colorful Sicilian folk pottery can still be bought at bargain prices. Fratantoni, on Via Nazionale, in Santo Stefano di Camastra, has a wide selection and also some unusual pieces, such as gigantic ceramic heads—of Norman knights and Saracens—that can be used as planters. Branciforti in Caltagirone (Scala Santa Maria del Monte 3) produces elegant designs based on traditional motifs developed from the 10th to the 19th century. If you seek more modern designs, De Simone, whose Picasso-like faces on plates and pitchers are popular abroad, has an outlet at Via Messina Marina 633, and in Palermo at Piazza Leoni 2 and Via Stabile 133.

Place mats, tablecloths, napkins, and **clothing** decorated with fine petit point are good buys in **Cefalù, Taormina,** and **Erice,** but they are not cheap. Make sure that any linen you buy is produced in Sicily and not on another continent.

Hiking Sicily is a mountainous island, rugged and often desolate, qualities that favor striking out on foot to examine its natural beauties firsthand. A number of hostels (*rifugi*) have sprung up in areas where hotels are few and far between, especially in the Madonie range of mountains south of Cefalù, and on the slopes of the island's tallest peak, the famous volcano Mount Etna. Popular routes in these areas include walks from the base of Piano Battaglia (where there is a *rifugio*) to the high peaks of the Madonies and around the wooded slopes of Etna from Piano Provenzana, 15 kilometers (10 miles) above the town of Linguaglossa, near Taormina. Both of these places, incidentally, are Sicily's main skiing centers. For information on skiing and some detailed hiking itineraries, contact the tourist offices at Palermo (tel. 091/583847) and Catania (tel. 095/312124).

Hikers should bear in mind that though the mountains may provide respite from the suffocating heat of the summer, it can still get pretty hot and uncomfortable in mid-August, and water is often not in plentiful supply.

Beaches There is a surfeit of beaches in Sicily, but many of them are too rocky, too crowded, or too dirty to be enjoyed for long. Among the exceptions are **Mondello,** near Palermo, a popular sandy beach on a tiny peninsula jutting out into the Mediterranean; **Sant'Alessio** and **Santa Teresa,** north of Taormina (the beaches just below Taormina itself are disappointing); and **Capo San Vito,** on the northern coast, near Erice, a sandy beach on a promontory overlooking a bay in the Gulf of Castellammare.

Highlights for First-time Visitors

Cathedral in Piazza del Duomo, Siracusa (Tour 3:Eastern Sicily).
Cefalù (Tour 1: Palermo and Environs).
Imperial Roman Villa, Casale (Tour 3: Eastern Sicily).
Mt. Etna (Tour 3: Eastern Sicily).
National Archaeological Museum, Palermo (Tour 1: Palermo and Environs).
Palazzo dei Normanni, Palermo (Tour 1: Palermo and Environs).
Taormina (Tour 3: Eastern Sicily).
Valley of the Temples (Tour 2: Western Sicily).

Tour 1: Palermo and Environs

Once the intellectual capital of southern Europe, Palermo has always been at the crossroads of civilization. Favorably located on a crescent-shape bay at the foot of Monte Pellegrino, it has attracted almost every people and culture touching the Mediterranean world. To Palermo's credit, it has absorbed these diverse cultures into a unique personality that is at once Arab and Christian, Byzantine and Roman, Norman and Italian. The main tourist attractions are easily reached on foot, along three major streets: Corso Vittorio Emanuele, Via Maqueda, and Via Roma.

From Milan, Rome, and Naples
By Train
Direct express trains to Palermo originate in Milan and Rome. The Rome–Palermo journey takes at least 14 hours; a second-class ticket costs 63,300 lire (IC supplement is 21,800 lire). From Naples, expect to pay around 50,000 lire second-class for a ticket to Palermo, more on Intercity trains. At Villa San Giovanni, in Calabria, all trains are loaded onto a ferryboat to cross the strait to Messina. Trains pull in at the main Palermo station at the bottom of Via Roma (Piazza Giulio Cesare, tel. 091/616–1806).

By Bus
An early morning bus, run by **Segesta** (06/444–0370), leaves on Tuesday, Thursday, and Saturday at 7:45 AM from Rome's Piazza della Repubblica. Another company, **SAIS** (06/474–2801), leaves daily at 8 PM, also from Piazza della Repubblica. In both cases, the journey takes 13–14 hours; the fare is 65,000–70,000 lire. All out-of-town buses stop in the area around the train station—there is no separate bus terminal in Palermo.

By Boat
An overnight car ferry leaves nightly from Naples to Palermo. The price for a second-class cabin is about 70,000 lire (depending on the season). There is also weekly service from Cagliari, in Sardinia. For more information, telephone the **Tirrenia** line in Naples (tel. 081/720–1111) or Cagliari (tel. 070/666065).

Frequent car ferries, which also carry passengers, cross the Strait of Messina from Villa San Giovanni, in Calabria, to Messina in about 30 minutes (during the summer months, there can be considerable delays). Hydrofoils (*aliscafi*), which carry pasengers only, cross the strait in about 20 minutes. Ferries and hydrofoils arrive in Palermo at the Stazione Marittima (tel. 091/586830, summer only).

By Car
See car ferries under By Boat, *above.*

By Plane
Palermo can be reached by scheduled flights from Rome, Milan, or Naples and, during high season, by charter flights from London and other European cities. U.K. operators include **Citalia** (tel. 081/686–5533), **Italia nel Mondo** (tel. 071/828–9171), **Italflights** (tel. 071/405–6771), **Magic of Italy** (tel. 081/748–7575), and **Pilgrim Air** (tel. 081/748–1333).

Planes land at Punta Raisi airport (tel. 091/591275), 32 kilometers (20 miles) west of Palermo. An hourly coach service (last departure from the airport 11:50 PM, from Palermo 9:45 PM) connects the airport with the city center, stopping outside the Teatro Politeama in Piazza Castelnuovo and at the rail station.

Tickets are 4,500 lire. Taxis make the same journey, but charge an average of 50,000 lire per ride.

Getting Around Palermo City buses are useful for avoiding treks through traffic-filled streets, particularly between the rail station and the city center at Piazza Castelnuovo. Tickets, available from tobacconists and kiosks, cost 1,000 lire for one ride, or 3,000 lire for a ticket valid all day. Punch the tickets on boarding the bus (but only on the first ride you take with the all-day ticket, showing it to the driver on subsequent rides).

Palermo

Tourist offices: Piazza Castelnuovo 35, tel. 091/583847; Stazione Centrale, tel. 091/616–5914.

Palermo was first colonized by Phoenician traders in the 6th century BC, but it was their descendants, the Carthaginians, who built the important fortress here that caught the covetous eye of the Romans. After the First Punic War, the Romans took control of the city, in the 3rd century BC. After several invasions by the Vandals, Sicily was settled by Arabs, who made the country an emirate and made Palermo a showpiece capital that rivaled both Cordoba and Cairo in Oriental splendor. Nestled in the fertile Conca d'Oro (Golden Conch) plain; full of orange, lemon, and carob groves; and enclosed by limestone hills, Palermo became a magical world of palaces and mosques, minarets and palm trees.

It was such an attractive and sophisticated city that the Norman ruler Roger de Hauteville decided to conquer it and make it his capital (1061). The Norman occupation of Sicily resulted in the Golden Age of Palermo (from 1072 to 1194), a remarkable period of enlightenment and learning in which the arts flourished. The city of Palermo, which in the 11th century counted more than 300,000 inhabitants, became the center of the Norman court in all Europe and one of the most important ports of trade between East and West.

Eventually the Normans were replaced by the Swabian ruler Frederick II, the Holy Roman Emperor, and incorporated into the kingdom of the Two Sicilies. You will also see evidence in Palermo of the Baroque art and architecture of the Spanish viceroys, who came to power after the bloody Sicilian Vespers uprising of 1282, in which the French Angevin dynasty was overthrown. The Aragonese viceroys also brought the Inquisition to Palermo, which some historians believe helped foster the protective secret societies that eventually evolved into today's Mafia.

Corso Vittorio Emanuele is the main avenue leading west from the harbor, and most of the city's sights are on or near it. From the train station, walk north on Via Maqueda until it meets the Corso at Piazza Pretoria, and turn left, away from the harbor, to reach the Palazzo dei Normanni (Norman Royal Palace), now the seat of the Sicilian Parliament. The palace was unfortunately closed to the public for security reasons in 1992, but the **Cappella Palatina** (Palatine Chapel) inside, one of Italy's greatest art treasures, happily remains open. Built by Roger II in 1132, this is a dazzling example of the unique harmony of artistic elements that came together under the Normans. In it the skill of French and Sicilian masons was brought to bear on the decorative purity of Arab ornamentation and the splendor of Greek Byzantine mosaics. The interior is covered with glittering mosaics and capped by a splendid Arab honeycomb stalactite wooden ceiling. Biblical stories blend happily with scenes of Arab life—look for one showing a picnic in a harem—and Norman court pageantry. Stylized Moorish palm branches run along the walls below the mosaics and recall the battlements on Norman castles—each one a different mosaic composition.

Upstairs are the royal apartments, including the Sala di Ruggero (King Roger's Hall), decorated with medieval murals of hunting scenes. Unfortunately, these halls, which once hosted one of the most splendid courts in Europe, are also closed to the public. French, Latin, and Arabic were spoken here, and Arab astronomers and poets exchanged ideas with Latin and Greek scholars in what must have been one of the most unique marriages of culture in the Western world. *Cappella Palatina, Piazza Indipendenza. Admission free. Open weekdays 9–noon and 3–5, Sat. 9–noon, Sun. 9–10 and noon–1; closed during religious functions and wedding services.*

To the left of the front of Palazzo dei Normanni, along Via Benedettini, you'll see the five pink domes of the church of **San Giovanni degli Eremiti,** one of the most picturesque of Palermo's churches. The 12th-century church was built by the Normans on the sight of an earlier mosque—one of 200 that once stood in Palermo. The emirs ruled Palermo for almost two centuries and brought to it their passion for lush gardens and fountains. One is reminded of this while sitting in San Giovanni's delightful cloister of twin half columns, surrounded by palm trees, jasmine, oleander, and citrus trees. *Open Tues., Wed., Fri. 9–1 and 3–5; Mon., Thurs., Sat. 9–2; Sun. 9–1.*

Returning to Corso Vittorio Emanuele and going back toward Piazza Pretoria, on your left you will soon see the **Duomo,** a prime example of Palermitan eclecticism. Its turrets, towers, dome, and arches come together in the kind of meeting of diverse elements that King Roger, whose tomb is inside along with that of Frederick II, fostered during his reign. Be sure to walk outside and look at the back of the apse, which is gracefully decorated with interlacing Arab arches, inlaid with limestone and black volcanic tufa. *Open daily 9:30–noon and 4–5:30.*

Farther down the Corso is **Quattro Canti** (Four Corners), actually the intersection with Via Maqueda. Here four Baroque palaces from the Spanish rule meet at concave corners, each with its own fountain, Spanish ruler, patron saint, and representation of one of the four seasons.

Just to the right is Piazza Pretoria, with a lavishly decorated fountain, originally intended for a Florentine villa. The abundance of nude figures so shocked some Palermitans when it was unveiled in 1575 that it got the nickname "the fountain of shame." It is even more shameful at night, when it is illuminated.

If you cross to the far side of the fountain and continue to the right, you'll reach Piazza Bellini and the splendid Baroque church of **Santa Caterina** (1596). Its walls are covered in decorative 17th-century inlays of precious marble.

Across the piazza and up a staircase are two churches that form a delightful Norman complex. The orange-red domes belong to **San Cataldo** (1160), whose spare but intense interior, punctuated by antique Greek columns, retains much of its original medieval simplicity. The other church, with an elegant campanile, is the **Martorana**, which was erected in 1143 but had its interior altered considerably during the Baroque period. High along the western wall, however, is some of the oldest mosaic artwork of the Norman period. Near the entrance is an interesting mosaic of Roger being crowned by Christ. In it Roger is dressed in a bejeweled Byzantine stole, reflecting the Norman court's penchant for all things Byzantine. Archangels along the ceiling wear the same stole, wrapped around their shoulders and arms. Like the archangels, the Norman monarchs liked to think of themselves as emissaries from heaven, engaged in defending Christianity by ridding the island of infidel invaders. *La Martorana open Mon.–Sat. 8:30–1 and 3:30–7:30 (3:30–5:30 in winter), Sun. 8:30–1; to visit San Cataldo, ask the custodian of La Martorana.*

Heading toward the port, take Via Alloro to the **Palazzo Abatellis,** which houses the National Gallery of Sicily. Among its treasures is an Annunciation (1474) by Sicily's prominent Renaissance master, Antonello da Messina, and an arresting fresco by an unknown painter, titled *The Triumph of Death,* a macabre depiction of the plague years. *Via Alloro 4, tel. 091/616–4317. Admission: 2,000 lire. Open Mon.–Sat. 9–1:30; Tues., Thurs., and Fri. 3–6:30 (3–5 in winter); Sun. 9–12:30.*

Return to the Corso and go almost all the way to the water, turning right onto Via Butera to see the **International Museum of Marionettes,** with an impressive display of Sicilian and European puppets. The traditional Sicilian *pupi* (marionettes), with their glittering armor and fierce expressions, have become a symbol of Norman Sicily. Plots center on the chivalric legends of the troubadours, who, before the puppet theater, kept alive tales of Norman heroes in Sicily, such as Orlando Furioso and William the Bad. *Via Butera 1, tel. 091/328060. Admission: 2,000 lire. Open Mon.–Sat. 9–1; also Mon., Wed., and Fri. 4–7.*

Return to Corso Vittorio Emanuele and walk back toward Via Roma. Before you get there, you will come upon an outdoor market that spreads out into a maze of side streets around Piazza Domenico. This is the **Vucciria**—a dialect word that means "voices" or "hubbub." It's easy to see why. Hawkers everywhere deliver their unceasing chants from behind stands brimming with mounds of olives, blood oranges, wild fennel, and long-stemmed artichokes. One of them goes at the trunk of a swordfish with a cleaver, while across the way another holds up a giant squid or dangles an octopus. All the time, the din continues. It may be Palermo, but this is really the Casbah.

The **Vucciria** is full of stalls selling street food. Everything from *calzoni* (deep-fried meat- or cheese-filled pockets of dough) to *panelle* (chick-pea–flour fritters). If you want to try something typically Palermitan that is a bit adventurous but delicious, look for a stall with a big cast-iron pot selling *guasteddi* (fresh buns filled with thin strips of calf's spleen, ricotta cheese, and a delicious hot sauce).

Back on Via Roma, the **National Archaeological Museum** has a small but excellent collection. Especially interesting are the examples of prehistoric cave drawings and a marvelously reconstructed Doric frieze from the Greek Temple at Selinunte that gives you a good idea of the high level of artistic culture attained by the Greek colonists in Sicily some 2,500 years ago. *Piazza Olivella 4, tel. 091/587825. Admission: 2,000 lire. Open Mon.–Sat. 9–1:30 (9:30–2:30 June–Sept.), Sun. 9–12:30; also open Tues. and Fri. 3–6 (3:30–6:30 June–Sept.)*

Lodging
Under 115,000

Ponte. This hotel is frequented mainly by businesspeople who appreciate the relatively low rates, modern fittings, and central location, within easy walking distance of the port and the city center. The downside is the traffic noise outside, which you can avoid by asking for a room at the back—some with views overlooking the harbor. Rooms are functional but comfortable, each with TV, telephone, and minibar. *Via Francesco Crispi 99, tel. 091/583744, fax 091/581845. 137 rooms with bath or shower. Facilities: restaurant, bar. AE, DC, MC, V.*

Under 85,000

Principe del Belmonte. This is a tasteful choice on a relatively quiet street near Palermo's central Piazza Ruggero Settimo and not far from the port. It is family-run and friendly but has limited capacity: Phone first to be sure of a vacancy. *Via Principe di Belmonte 25, tel. 091/331065. 17 rooms, 14 with shower. Facilities: bar. AE, DC, MC, V.*

Under 60,000 lire

Cortese. The only reason this hotel is listed with Palermo's cheapies is its location—not remote, just rather hard to find. In fact, the Cortese is extremely central, signposted off Via Maqueda and Via dell'Università, close to Piazza Pretoria, and only a two-minute walk off the main road through ill-lit back streets. The furniture and fittings are modern and attractive, the decor bright, perhaps a conscious effort to dispel the gloom of the surrounding alleys. The hotel also offers access to a private beach outside Palermo. The price is a bargain—your only reservation might be the immediate neighborhood. *Via Scarparelli 16, tel. 091/331722, fax 091/331722. 27 rooms, 15 with shower. Facilities: restaurant, private beach. MC, V.*

Letizia. This unassuming hotel is on the second floor of a building on a side street off Via Vittorio Emanuele. Though small, its location means that it is not an obvious choice for tourists, so the chances of availability are good. Rooms are tidy and clean, some with stylish Baroque decoration (check No. 3), and good value. The management is relaxed and friendly. *Via Bottai 30, tel. 091/589110, fax 091/589110. 15 rooms, 6 with shower. No credit cards.*

Orientale. It is typical of Palermo that what would be a showpiece of period architecture anywhere else is here a forgotten, rather run-down hotel, its unprepossessing exterior giving no sign of the vestiges of splendor within. It's a pleasure every time you reenter the hotel, through its cobbled courtyard and up the stately, 18th-century stairway. The location is convenient for the train station, too. Don't expect the acme of comfort and loads of amenities, but the rooms are clean, well looked after by the elderly proprietor, and mostly spacious, not to say grand. Most impressive is No. 7, with its long balcony overlooking Via Maqueda. *Via Maqueda 26, tel. 091/616–5727. 21 rooms, 1 with shower. No credit cards.*

Petit. As the name implies, this is a tiny hotel, and in summer you'll be lucky to find a room here. If you do, you will be sleeping in a comfortable and friendly environment, well furnished though with minimal facilities. It's located on a pedestrian thoroughfare, which means no traffic noise, but the street has several bars and is popular with young Palermitans, so expect some after-hours rumpus—although it's pleasant enough when you're down in the bars yourself. The hotel is a convenient walk from the port and Piazza Castelnuovo, a bus ride from the rail station. *Via Principe Belmonte 84, tel. 091/323616. 6 rooms, 4 with shower. No credit cards.*

Splurge **Grande Albergo e delle Palme.** There is a faded charm about this *grande dame*, whose public rooms suggest the elegant life of Palermo society before the First World War, when tea dances and balls were held here. Guest rooms are uneven—some are charming period pieces stuffed with antiques and heavy fabrics, others are dark and cramped. There is an American-style cocktail bar and a rooftop terrace with good views of Palermo. The hotel has hosted Richard Wagner, who finished composing *Parsifal* here in 1882, and various leaders of the Mafia in the 1950s. Present-day guests pay around 240,000 lire for a double. *Via Roma 398, tel. 091/583933, fax 091/331545. 187 rooms with bath or shower. Facilities: restaurant, piano bar, rooftop terrace, garage. AE, DC, MC, V.*

Dining
Under 30,000 lire

Bellini. This is one of Palermo's best-known pizza restaurants, ever popular despite the somewhat offhanded service from waiters resembling extras in a gangster movie. The place trades briskly on its well-deserved reputation for good pizzas and pastas, and its unrivaled location in Piazza Bellini in premises once occupied by the theater of the same name. Get here early to bag a seat next to the window, from which you can look down on the churches of San Cataldo and La Martorana—or better still, eat alfresco in the square itself (summer only). *Piazza Bellini 6, tel. 091/616-5691. Reservations advised summer and weekends. AE, MC, V. Closed Wed.*

Strascinu. The specialty in this informal and busy restaurant is *pasta con le sarde*, the famous Arab-Sicilian blend of fresh sardines, wild fennel fronds, sultanas, and pine nuts. *Viale Regione Siciliana 2286, tel. 091/401292. Reservations advised. AE, DC. Closed Mon. and July 15–31.*

Under 24,000 lire

Il Mirto e la Rosa. This is Palermo's foremost vegetarian restaurant, though the classy decor puts it a world away from the vegetarian stereotype. Cool elegance is the keynote, with potted plants and Art Nouveau touches. Service is efficient, and the food is always at least interesting. The menu is split into cereals, including pasta and couscous, and proteins, including legumes and stuffed crepes. Salads are imaginatively prepared and side vegetables fresh and stylishly presented. There are three fixed-price menus under 18,000 lire (not available Saturday evening). *Via Principe Granatelli 30, tel. 091/324353. DC, MC, V. Closed Sun.*

Lo Sparviero. Just around the corner from Piazza Ungheria, this is part formal restaurant, part informal pizzeria/birreria, popular with the younger set. Wooden tables and benches, photos of movie icons on the walls, and rock music contribute toward the relaxed atmosphere. A traditional variety of pizzas emerge sizzling from the wood-fired oven; there are also some wonderful pasta and meat dishes. Spoil yourself with *spaghetti chitarra della casa*, with its sauce of radicchio, salmon, vodka, and cream, and wash it down with house wine or a selection of bottled or draft beers. *Via Sperlinga 23, tel. 091/331163. AE, MC, V. Closed Thurs.*

Under 20,000 lire **Antica Focacceria San Francesco.** On the square in front of the church of San Francesco, off Corso Vittorio Emanuele in the heart of Palermo, this is an institution, as you can see from the turn-of-the-century cabinets and fixtures of what is still a neighborhood bakery. But it also bakes and fries the snacks that locals love—and from which you can well make an inexpensive meal. Try *arancini* (rice croquettes) and *panelle* (chickpea fritters) or pizza right out of the oven. You can sit at marble-topped tables while you eat, or take food out if you wish. Beverages, including wine and beer, are available. *Via Paternostro 58, tel. 091/320264. No credit cards. Closed Mon.*

★ **Shangai.** There is nothing Chinese about this Palermo institution in the busy Vucciria market. It's on a terrace above the market (the source of all the ingredients): Look down and order your fish from the displays below, and it will be hoisted up in a wicker basket. The atmosphere is jovial and frantic, with lots of teasing and shouting. *Fritto misto* (literally "fried mix," but usually fish here) is always a good bet. *Vicolo Mezzani 34, tel. 091/589702. No credit cards. Closed Sun.*

Toto. A neighbor of the Shangai in the bustling Vucciria market, Toto is one of the plainest trattorias in town, serving fresh fish in a variety of ways, including *alla brace (grilled), fritto misto (fried)*, and in *zuppa di pesce (fish stew)*. Ask Toto to sing—he may even do magic tricks. At times this place makes even the Shangai look staid. *Via dei Coltellieri 5, no phone. No credit cards. Open lunch only. Closed Sun.*

Splurge **Charleston.** You'll feel pampered by the discreet service and el-
★ egant surroundings in this famous Palermo restaurant located on a quiet square in the heart of the city. Impeccably dressed waiters coast effortlessly through the high-ceilinged rooms, offering help with the extensive menu and wine list. Specialties run the gamut of Sicilian and international dishes, with an emphasis on seafood. Try the *spaghetti all'aragosta*, with its delicious lobster sauce, or the *pesce spada arrosto* (roast swordfish), but leave room for the sweet, rich house dessert, *torta Charleston*. The whole restaurant operation moves 8 kilometers (5 miles) north to a pavilion on the sea at Mondello from June 16 to September 25. *Charleston (Sept. 26–June 15), Piazza Ungheria 30, tel. 091/321366; Charleston le Terrazze (June 16–Sept. 25) Viale Regina Elena, Mondello, tel. 091/450171. Reservations required. Jacket and tie required. AE, DC, MC, V. Closed Sun.*

Shopping Behind Palermo's Duomo, on Via Papireto, is the **flea market,** a good place to hunt for antique marionettes of the Norman cavaliers or for brilliantly colored pieces of the *carretti siciliani* (Sicilian carts). This is also the antiques-store neighborhood, which spreads to the next street, Corso Amedeo.

The Arts and Palermo's **Teatro Biondo** (tel. 091/588755) is Sicily's foremost
Nightlife theater, featuring a winter season of plays from November to May. The stately **Teatro Politeama** (tel. 091/584334) is the venue for opera and ballet performances throughout the year. Summer is the best time to sample rock and jazz concerts in the open-air surroundings of the **Giardino Inglese,** off Via Libertà: Keep your eyes open for posters advertising these events. Palermo's well-established **Brass Group,** a jazz association, is

the best source of information for musical events of this kind (tel. 091/617–1274).

In summer, most of Palermo's nightlife shifts to its holiday satellite of **Mondello**, where a day on the beach is usually rounded off with some serious promenading, posing, and dancing in the resort's many discos.

Festivals From July 11 to 15, Palermo stages a **street fair** in honor of its patron saint, Santa Rosalia. There are fireworks displays in the evenings. **Epiphany** (Jan. 6) is celebrated with Byzantine rites and a procession of townspeople in local costume through the streets of Piana degli Albanesi, 24 kilometers (15 miles) south of Palermo. The village is named for the Albanian immigrants who first settled there, bringing with them the Byzantine Catholic rites. Buses to Piana degli Albanesi leave from Piazza Giulio Cesare (buy tickets, 3,000 lire, from Prestia & Commandè agency, Via Balsamo near the train station, tel. 091/580457).

Monreale

From Palermo, city bus No. 8 or 8/9 leave regularly from outside the train station, a 20-minute trip (tickets cost 1,000 lire). Tourist office: Piazza Duomo, tel. 091/656–4270.

Don't miss the splendid cathedral of Monreale, about 10 kilometers (6 miles) southwest of Palermo. It is lavishly decorated with mosaics depicting events from the Old and New Testaments—some 130 pictures, covering 6,000 square yards. (Bring 100-lire coins for illumination.) Be sure to see the rear exterior and the graceful Romanesque cloister to the left, laced with intricate arches, mosaic-inlaid twin columns, and capitals that represent one of the richest collections of Sicilian medieval sculpture. In a corner by the stylized palm tree fountain, look for a capital showing William II offering the cathedral to the Virgin. *Cathedral, tel. 091/640–4413. Open daily winter 8:30–12:30 and 3:30–6:30, summer 9–7. Cloister, tel. 091/640–4403. Admission: 2,000 lire. Open winter, Mon.–Sat. 9–1:30, Sun. 9–12:30; summer, Mon.–Sat. 9–12:30 and 4–7, Sun. 9–1.*

Dining **La Fattoria.** It's worth the 10-minute walk out of the bustle of
Under 30,000 lire Monreale to reach this rural restaurant on the outskirts of town, which specializes in fresh country produce from the surrounding fertile fields and orchards. A favorite with Palermitans on a Sunday it has plenty of space and a cheerful atmosphere. The house specialty is a pasta dish: *pennette caruso* (pasta with peas, meat, mozzarella, and cream, baked in the oven). The No. 9 bus stops just outside. *Via Circonvallazione 26, tel. 091/640–1134. Reservations advised on weekends. No credit cards.*

Cefalù

Frequent trains from Palermo make the 45-minute journey to Cefalù; the fare is 5,000 lire. You can also reach Cefalù by SAIS buses (tickets cost 6,100 lire), departing from Via Balsamo, near the Palermo train station (tel. 091/616–6027). Buses stop outside Cefalù's train station, south of the town center, 10 minutes on foot from the main Corso Ruggero. Tourist office: Corso Ruggero 77, tel. 0921/21050.

The popular summer resort of Cefalù, about 70 kilometers (42 miles) east of Palermo, along the coast, is a charming town built on a spur jutting out into the sea and dominated by a massive, 12th-century Romanesque **Duomo** that is one of the finest Norman cathedrals in Italy. King Roger began it in 1131 as a thanks offering for having been saved here from a shipwreck. Its mosaics rival those of Monreale. Both cathedrals are dominated by colossal mosaic figures of the Byzantine Pantocratic Christ, high in the bowl of their apses. The Monreale figure is an austere and powerful image, emphasizing the divinity of Christ, while the Cefalù Christ, softer and more compassionate, seems to stress his humanity. *Piazza del Duomo, tel. 0921/23454. Open daily 9–noon and 4–6 (summer, 3:30–8).*

Lodging
Under 115,000 lire

Le Calette. This seaside hotel is popular with Scandinavians and Germans, who know a good place to sunbathe when they see one. The modern hotel is surrounded by gardens on the three sides that don't face the sea, and guests can use the private beach. The rooms are bright and airy; those facing the sea escape the hot Sicilian sun. The Caldura district, where Le Calette is located, is a little more than a mile from the center of town—walkable, or you could catch a local bus. *Contrada Caldura, tel. 0921/24144, fax 0921/23688. 50 rooms with shower. Facilities: restaurant, bar, pool, private beach. AE, DC, MC, V. Closed Nov.–Apr.*

Under 60,000 lire

Locanda Cangelosi. The only budget option in town, this modest place is small and therefore may be all booked up during the busy summer season. The location is quiet and convenient: a 10-minute walk from the center of town and only one street away from the train station. Rooms are pleasant, some with comfy armchairs—unusual in Italy—and small balconies overlooking the street. *Via Umberto 26, tel. 0921/21591. 4 rooms with shared bath. No credit cards.*

Costa Ponente Camping. Cefalù's campsites are all located out of town; this one is the best. It's about 3 kilometers (2 miles) away—a viable walk, most of it along the beach, though there are buses from the train station. The facilities are first-class, the capacity almost unlimited, and there is a good beach nearby. It's only open in summer, but the Sanfilippo campsite next door is open year-round. *Contrada Ogliastrillo, tel. 0921/20085, fax 0921/23122. Facilities: restaurant, bar, outdoor pool, tennis courts. MC, V. Closed Oct.–Apr.*

Dining
Under 30,000 lire

Gabbiano. The name, meaning "seagull," is appropriate for a harborside restaurant decorated with a nautical theme and specializing in seafood. The house specialties are *involtini* (swordfish rolls) and *spaghetti alla marinara* (with a spicy sauce of tomatoes, garlic, and onions). *Via Lungomare Giardina 17, tel. 0921/21495. Reservations advised. AE, DC, MC, V. Closed Wed.*

Under 24,000 lire

Arkade Grill. This small trattoria off the main Corso Ruggero specializes in Tunisian cuisine, though there is an Italian menu, too. If you opt for the North African, you'll be rewarded by a rich, spicy minestrone-type soup and abundant portions of couscous, either fish or meat. *Via Vanni 9, tel. 0921/921950. Reservations not necessary. No credit cards. Closed Thurs.*

At least one hydrofoil daily and five ferries a week leave Palermo's Stazione Marittima for Ustica. The ferries take about 2½ hours; tickets cost around 15,000 lire. Hydrofoils take only 75 minutes and cost twice as much. Tourist office: Piazza Longo, tel. 091/844-9190.

Sixty kilometers (37 miles) north of Palermo, the island of Ustica is a tranquil refuge from the city's hubbub. If you cross over by the speedy hydrofoil, it's a manageable day trip; if you want to stay longer, check hotel availability before you leave (Palermo's tourist office will help)—it may be limited. There are no beaches here, but if you don't mind the jagged rocks (the entire island is of volcanic origin), the swimming is marvelous. In recent years Ustica (pronounced with the stress on the first syllable) has become an international center for scuba diving and snorkeling. Its rugged coast is dotted with grottoes that are washed by crystal-clear waters and filled with an incredible variety of interesting marine life. In July Ustica hosts an International Meeting of Marine Fishing that attracts sportsmen as well as marine biologists from all over the world.

Tour 2: Western Sicily

West of Palermo, the narrower end of this wedge-shape island is a rugged promontory reminiscent of the terrain in American westerns—and in fact, many "spaghetti westerns" were filmed here. The mix of Sicily's cultures is evident, from medieval Norman castles to some of the best classical Greek and Roman ruins in the world. All sites on this tour can be reached from Palermo by train or bus.

Trapani

Trapani is served by hourly buses from Palermo on the Tarantola line (tel. 0924/31020); tickets cost 11,000 lire, and the ride takes 90 minutes. Six daily trains make the trip from Palermo in 2¼ hours, and one train, leaving at 1 PM, makes it in 1 hour 50 minutes; the fare is 10,500 lire. Tourist offices: Piazza Saturno, tel. 0923/29000; Via Vito Sorba 15, tel. 0923/27273.

The modern town of Trapani (pronounced with the stress on the first syllable) is the departure point for trips to Segesta, Erice, to the Egadi Islands, and the island of Pantelleria, near the African coast. If you are familiar with North African couscous, Trapani is the place to try the Sicilian version, which is made with fish instead of meat. The result is a kind of fish stew with semolina, spiced with cinnamon, saffron, and black pepper.

Lodging
Under 85,000 lire

Nuovo Russo. This is a useful hotel in the heart of Trapani's old quarter, just off the main Corso and convenient to the port. Modern and efficiently run, there are no extras here, but the rooms are comfortable and the service personable. Be sure to book ahead during Easter, when hotels fill up quickly. *Via Tintori 4, tel. 0923/22166, fax 0923/26623. 35 rooms, 20 with shower. Facilities: bar, garage. No credit cards.*

Dining
Splurge
★

P & G. Couscous is a specialty of this small, popular restaurant on a quiet street between the train station and the Villa Margherita public gardens. The couscous features fish in summer and meat in winter. A mixed grill of meats in a zesty orange sauce will revive any appetite suffering from fish fatigue. Wash it all down with a bottle of Donnafugata, a good white from the Rallo vineyards at Marsala. You'll pay 35,000–40,000 lire for a full meal here. *Via Spalti 1, tel. 0923/547701. Reservations advised. AE, DC, MC, V. Closed Sun., Aug., and Dec. 25–Jan. 2.*

Segesta

A Tarantola bus from Trapani takes 30 minutes to Segesta; the fare is 7,000 lire round-trip. A minibus takes bus passengers from the car park to the temples. The morning train from Palermo to Trapani stops at the Segesta-Templo station; the trip takes 1¾ hours and costs 7,000 lire. It's a 20-minute walk uphill from the train station to the temple site.

About 85 kilometers (50 miles) southwest of Palermo is Segesta, where one of the most impressive Greek **temples** in the world is located—on the side of a windswept, barren hill overlooking a valley of wild fennel. Virtually intact, the temple is considered by some to be finer in its proportions and setting than any Doric temple left standing. The Greeks started the temple during the 5th century BC but never finished it. The walls and roof are missing, and the columns were never fluted. About a mile away, near the top of the hill, are the remains of a fine Greek theater, with impressive views, especially at sunset, of nearby Monte Erice and the sea.

Erice

Hourly buses make the ascent to Erice from Trapani. Round-trip tickets cost 4,500 lire for the 45-minute ride. Tourist office: Via Conte Pepoli 56, tel. 0923/869388.

Fourteen kilometers (9 miles) northeast of Trapani, and 2,450 feet up, Erice (pronounced with the stress on the first syllable) is an enchanting medieval mountaintop aerie of castles and palaces, fountains and cobblestone streets. Erice was the ancient Eryx and was dedicated to a fertility goddess whom the Phoenicians called Astarte; the Greeks, Aphrodite; and the Romans, Venus. According to Virgil, Aeneas built a temple to the goddess here, but it was destroyed when the Arabs took over and renamed the place Mohammed's Mountain. When the Normans arrived, they built a castle where today there is a public park with benches and belvederes, from which there are striking views of Trapani, the Egadi Islands, and, on a *very* clear day, Cape Bon and the Tunisian coast.

Lodging
Under 85,000 lire

Edelweiss. A reliable choice in the center of town, the Edelweiss is much in demand and you should always phone ahead to make sure of a room. The Christmas period, Easter, and the month of August are particularly busy times. Once in, though, you will find yourself amid amiable surroundings, tastefully furnished with an Old World accent. *Cortile P. Vincenzo, tel. 0923/869158, fax 0923/869158. 15 rooms with shower. Facilities: bar, restaurant, garage. AE, MC, V.*

Dining
Under 30,000 lire
★

La Taverna di Re Aceste. This popular restaurant is named for Acestus, the first king of Erice, and the house specialty, *cuscus Aceste* (a spicy, Arab-influenced semolina-and-seafood mixture), is in his honor, as are the murals along the walls. The chef also has a special pesto (pine-nut pasta sauce) dish made with wild herbs. Try the grilled fish, but ask the price, since you'll be paying by weight, not per order. Helpful waiters will guide you through the daily specials and the wine list; there's a three-course tourist menu for 28,000 lire. *Viale Conte Pepoli, tel. 0923/869084. Reservations advised. AE, DC, MC, V. Closed Wed. and Nov.*

Pantelleria

Ferry service from Trapani takes about five hours and costs around 30,000 lire one-way. Service is daily, except for Sundays in winter. Hydrofoils run three times a week and take 2½ hours; tickets cost about 45,000 lire. Ferry tickets are available from Siremar (tel. 0923/540515); hydrofoil tickets are available from Siremar and SNAV (tel. 0923/24014). For economical round-trip flights from Trapani's airport, contact Salvo Viaggi in Trapani (tel. 0923/27480). Tourist office: Via San Nicola, tel. 0923/911838.

Pantelleria, near the Tunisian coast, is one of Sicily's most evocative islands, although many find its starkness unappealing. Its volcanic formations, scant patches of forest, prehistoric tombs, and dramatic seascapes constitute an otherworldly landscape. From its grapes—the *zibibbo* (a strain of *moscato*) —the locals make an amber-color dessert wine and a strong, sweet wine called Tanit.

Marsala

Train service from Trapani runs frequently (10 trains a day) and takes roughly 30 minutes; the fare is 3,200 lire. AST buses leave Trapani's Piazza Malta seven times daily; the fare is 3,700 lire, and journey time is a little more than half an hour. Tourist office: Via Garibaldi 45, tel. 0923/714097.

Thirty kilometers (18 miles) south of Trapani, Marsala is a quiet seaside town that is world-famous for its rich-colored, sweet-tasting wine. In 1773 a British merchant named John Woodhouse happened upon Marsala and discovered that the wine there was as good as the port the British had long imported from Portugal. Two other wine merchants, Whitaker and Ingram, rushed in, and by 1800 Marsala was exporting its wine all over the British Empire.

Lodging
Under 115,000 lire
Stella d'Italia. Centrally located behind Piazza della Repubblica, this is a neat, rather nondescript hotel but well-equipped. It has the added advantage of a good restaurant. *Via Rapisardi 7, tel. 0923/953003. 51 rooms, 40 with bath or shower. Facilities: restaurant, bar, garage. AE, DC, MC, V.*

Selinunte

From Marsala, head for Castelveltrano, an 80-minute bus ride (five departures daily on the AST line, fare 4,500 lire) or a 50-minute train ride (fare 4,000 lire). From Palermo, it's a two-hour journey; there are five buses a day on the Salemi line (tel. 091/617–5411), leaving from Via Gregorio, near the train station, and tickets cost 8,500 lire. Once you get to Castelveltrano, frequent local buses (daily except Sunday, fare 2,000 lire) from the train station make the 20-minute trip to Selinunte.

Around the western promontory, on Sicily's south coast near the seedy town of Castelveltrano, an overwhelming array of ruined Greek temples is perched on a plateau overlooking the Mediterranean. Although it takes some effort to get here from Palermo, it's well worth the time for anyone interested in classical Greek civilization, because here stood one of the most superb colonies of ancient Greece.

The original complex held seven temples scattered over two sites separated by a harbor. Of the seven, only one—reconstructed in 1958—still stands. Founded in the 7th century BC, Selinunte became the rich and prosperous rival of Segesta, which in 409 BC turned to the Carthaginians for help. The Carthaginians sent an army commanded by Hannibal to raze the city. The temples were demolished, the city was laid flat, and 16,000 of Selinunte's inhabitants were slaughtered. The beautiful metopes preserved in Palermo's Archaeological Museum come from the frieze of Temple E here. There is also a small museum at the site that contains other excavated pieces. Selinunte is named after a local variety of wild celery that in spring still grows profusely among the ruined columns and overturned capitals. *Admission to site and museum: 2,000 lire. Open daily 9–one hour before sunset.*

Lodging
Under 60,000 lire

Ideal. You will only want to stay overnight in Castelvetrano if you have to, but if you do, this is the most convenient choice, close to the train station (go left out of the square and under the tracks). Facilities are minimal, and the rooms are modest, but the Ideal is clean enough and courteously staffed. *Via Partanna 26, tel. 0924/901454. 9 rooms without bath. No credit cards.*

Agrigento

There's frequent train and bus service from Palermo; the trip takes approximately 2½ hours. The bus costs 11,000 lire; the train, 10,000 lire. Trains arrive at Agrigento Centrale (don't get off at the remote Agrigento Bassa) in Piazza Marconi, just below the town's main thoroughfare, Via Atenea. Buses arrive at Piazza Fratelli Rosselli, at the back of the town. Local buses for the temples leave from Piazza Marconi every 30 minutes; take bus No. 8, 9, or 10, buying your ticket before boarding (fare: 900 lire). Tourist offices: Viale della Vittoria 255, tel. 0922/401352; Via Atenea 123, tel. 0922/20454.

About 100 kilometers (60 miles) east along the coast from Selinunte, Agrigento, or Akragas as the Greeks called it, was settled by the Greeks in 580 BC and grew wealthy through trade with Carthage, just across the Mediterranean. Despite attacks from the Carthaginians at the end of the 5th century BC, the city survived through the Roman era, the Middle Ages (when it came under Arab and Norman rule), and into the modern age, and structures from all these eras sit side by side today. The birthplace of both the ancient Greek philosopher Empedocles and the modern Italian playwright Luigi Pirandello, Agrigento is a study in contrasts, but its chief attraction, the Valley of the Temples, remains one of the most impressive classical sites in all of Italy.

Coming upon the **Valley of the Temples** for the first time is always a memorable moment—whether in the sunshine of spring, when they are surrounded by blossoming almond trees, or at night, when the temples are flood-lit. Even in winter, when the vegetation is limited to century plants *(agaves)* and gnarled gray olive trees, it is easy to understand why Pindar called Agrigento "the most beautiful city built by mortal men." Exiting from the highway, walk down from the parking lot on Via dei Templi and turn left. The first temple you encounter is the **Temple of Hercules**—eight pillars of the oldest temple in Agrigento, built during the 5th century BC. Up the hill is the **Temple of Concord,** one of the best-preserved Doric temples in the world and certainly the most impressive in Sicily. In the late afternoon, as the sun descends below the horizon, the temple's sandstone begins to change from honey-gold to pink russet, and the vertical lines of the fluted columns—probably once covered with brightly painted stucco—sharpen against the fading skyline. Follow the road that climbs around to the left, and you'll reach the **Temple of Juno,** which commands an exquisite view of the valley, especially at sunset. If you look carefully, you can see red fire marks on some of the columns—the result of the Carthaginian attack in 406 BC, which destroyed the city. Return to the parking lot in the Piazzale dei Templi (where there is a bar selling drinks and ice cream) and cross to the opposite side of the road, where the ruins continue. First is the **Temple of Jupiter,** the largest temple ever planned in Sicily. Though never completed, it was considered the eighth wonder of the world. The nearby sleeping giant is a copy of one of the 38 colossal Atlas figures, or telamones, that supported the temple's immense roof. The last temple is the much-photographed **Temple of Castor and Pollux,** whose four columns supporting part of an entablature have become a symbol of Agrigento, even though they were reconstructed in 1836, and probably from diverse buildings. At the end of Via dei Templi, where it turns left and becomes Via Petrarca, stands the **National Archaeological Museum,** which contains one of the original telamones, an impressive collection of Greek vases dating from the 7th century BC, and models of what the temples once looked like. *Tel. 0922/49726. Admission free. Open daily 9–1; also Tues., Thurs., and Sat. 4–7.*

On the opposite side of the road from the museum is the **Hellenistic and Roman Quarter,** which consists of four parallel streets, running north and south, that have been uncovered, along with the foundations of some houses from the Roman settlement (2nd century BC). Some of these streets still have their original mosaic pavements.

Lodging

Under 85,000 lire

Concordia. Centrally located off Via Atenea, the Concordia is a useful hotel, though it's often booked full—get here early, or better yet, phone ahead to reserve a room. Guest rooms are small and basic, but some (Nos. 32, 33, 40, 41, and 43) manage to squeeze in a modest view of the sea. Service is offhand; the staff is generally preoccupied with the constant turnover of guests. *Piazza San Francesco 11, tel. 0922/596266. 30 rooms with shower. Facilities: restaurant, bar. AE, MC, V.*

Under 60,000 lire

Bella Napoli. At the far end of Via Atenea, this hotel is little more than functional, but in a town with a chronic shortage of cheap accommodations, there is often space here when all other possibilities have been exhausted. The exterior lacks character, but the rooms are comfortable, and there's an added bonus of some exhilarating views from the roof. *Piazza Lena 6, tel. 0922/20435, fax 0922/20435. 46 rooms, 23 with shower. AE.*

Dining
Under 30,000 lire

Taverna Mosè. This restaurant is popular with sightseers from nearby temples, so it can get busy in the early evening, when it becomes too dark for temple exploring. The atmosphere is bustling, with waiters shouting orders at each other and at the kitchen. The house specialties are homemade sausages and grilled fish, and the wine list is comprehensive. *Contrada San Biagio, tel. 0922/26778. AE. Closed Mon.*

Vigneto. Unless you make reservations at this popular restaurant, it's best to arrive early to snag one of the tables on the terrace, which has a memorable view of the temples. The menu's daily specials reflect whatever is in season or freshest at the fish market. *Arrosti* (roast meats) are always a good bet. *Via Cavaleri Magazzeni 11, tel. 0922/414319. Reservations advised. AE, MC, V. Closed Tues. and Nov. 1–30.*

Under 20,000 lire

La Corte degli Sfizii. Despite the contrived (some would say kitsch) decor, this is not a bad restaurant, popular with locals and tourists alike. The *sfizii* (enticements) are portions of either fish or meat served as antipasti. If you are sticking to a tight budget, be content with the fixed-price menus (15,000–18,000 lire). Pizzas here are cooked in a wood stove; try the unconventional *pizza esotica* with tropical fruit, honey, and rum flambé. The fish is excellent, too. *Cortile Contarini (off Via Atenea), tel. 0922/595520. AE. Closed Wed.*

Festivals

On the first weekend in February, Agrigento hosts an Almond Blossom Festival, with international folk dances, a costumed parade, and the sale of marzipan and other sweets made from almonds.

Tour 3: Eastern Sicily

The hub of this tour is the sprawling city of Catania, on Sicily's eastern seaboard, site of Sicily's principal airport and a transportation junction. You will find it difficult to avoid Catania, uncongenial as it may be for visitors. Accommodations choices are limited, and the traffic is as bad as anywhere in Sicily, despite the pedestrians-only zones in the city center.

Catania does have several Baroque monuments, however, and it is a logical jumping-off point for some of Sicily's premier attractions: the classical treasures of Siracusa, the elite resort of Taormina, and the slopes of Mount Etna, whose vast presence glowers over Catania, as it does for miles around. Farther afield, you can pore over the mosaic marvels at Villa Casale, or bask in the tranquillity of the Aeolian Islands off the northeast coast. Except for the islands, reachable by ferry from Messina or Milazzo, trains are the most useful mode of transport for all destinations listed on this tour, though buses are a convenient standby.

From Rome and Naples
By Train

You can board trains direct for Catania from Rome and Naples. The journey takes about 10 hours from Rome, with second-class tickets at around 50,000 lire, more for Intercity trains.

By Bus

Two buses daily, at 7:45 AM and 8 PM, leave Rome's Piazza della Repubblica for Catania, run by the SAIS line (tel. 06/488–5924 or 06/474–2801). The trip takes more than 11 hours and costs around 60,000 lire.

By Boat

Frequent car ferries, which also carry passengers, cross the Strait of Messina from Villa San Giovanni, in Calabria, to Messina in about 30 minutes (during the summer months, there can be considerable delays). Fares are 22,000 lire for a medium-size car, 1,500 lire per passenger. Hydrofoils, which carry passengers only, cross the strait in about 20 minutes and cost 5,500 per person. Once a week Tirrenia line (tel. 081/720–1111 in Naples or tel. 0955/94003 in Reggio Calabria) ferries from Naples call in at Catania and Siracusa on their way to Malta; the line's three weekly ferries from Reggio Calabria to Malta also stop in Catania and Siracusa. Tickets range from 42,000 to 90,000 lire, depending on season and type of accommodation.

By Car   *See* car ferries under By Boat, *above.*

By Plane   Catania can be reached from Rome, Milan, or Naples, with direct charter flights arriving from London during the summer. Planes land at Fontanarossa airport, 5 kilometers (3 miles) south of Catania (tel. 095/341900). Local bus No. 24 runs from the airport to the city center roughly every 20 minutes (up to 10 PM), stopping in Piazza del Duomo; the trip takes 30 minutes and the fare is 1,000 lire. Expect to pay around 40,000 lire for a taxi.

From Palermo   Seven daily trains from Palermo make the trip to Catania in
By Train   3½–4 hours, stopping in Caltanissetta and Enna. The fare is 17,500 lire.

By Bus   SAIS (tel. 091/616–6028) buses for Catania leave every hour (until 8:30 PM) from Via Balsamo, near the Palermo train station, and take 2 hours and 40 minutes; the fare is 16,000 lire.

By Car   Highway A19 leads straight from Palermo to Catania, a distance of 200 kilometers (124 miles); driving time is about three hours. A19 is a toll-free highway.

Getting Around   Catania's city bus fare is 1,000 lire for one journey and 1,500 for
Catania   an unlimited-rides ticket valid for two hours; buy tickets before boarding.

Catania

Tourist offices: Largo Paisiello 5, tel. 095/312124; train station, tel. 095/531802; airport, tel. 095/341900.

The chief wonder of Sicily's second city, Catania, is that it is there at all. Its successive populations were deported by one Greek tyrant, sold into slavery by another, and driven out by the Carthaginians. Every time the city got back on its feet, it was struck by a new calamity: Plague decimated the population during the Middle Ages, a mile-wide stream of lava from Mt. Etna swallowed most of the city in 1663, and 25 years later a disastrous earthquake forced the Catanese to begin again. Today the city needs much renovation. Traffic flows in ever-increasing volume and adds to the smog from the industrial zone between Catania and Siracusa, but the views of Mt. Etna from Catania are superb. To Etna, Catania also owes a fertile surrounding plain and its site on nine successive layers of lava. Many of Catania's buildings are constructed from solidified lava, and the black lava stone has given the city a singular appearance. As a result, Catania is known as the city of lava and oranges.

Trains and most out-of-town buses pull in at Piazza Giovanni XXIII; the information kiosk inside the station can supply maps and accommodation lists. From the station, go straight down Corso Martiri della Libertà and Corso Sicilia to reach the central Via Etnea. Just northwest of here is Catania's public garden, the **Villa Bellini,** named after Catania's greatest native son: composer Vincenzo Bellini, whose operas have thrilled audiences since their premieres more than 150 years ago.

The Duomo, at the opposite end of Via Etnea, is a fine work by Vaccarini (1736), as is the obelisk-balancing elephant carved out of lava stone in the piazza in front. Bellini is buried inside the cathedral. Also inside is the sumptuous chapel of St. Agatha, Catania's patron saint, who is credited with having held off, more than once, the fiery flows of lava that threatened the city. During the festival of her feast day (Feb. 3–5) huge, 5-meter (17-foot), highly ornate, carved-wood *cannelore* (large bundles of candles) are paraded through the streets at night.

Bellini's home, now the **Bellini Museum,** in Piazza San Francesco, preserves memorabilia of the man and his work. *Piazza San Francesco 3. Admission free. Open Mon.–Sat. 9–1:30, Sun. 9–12:30.*

Lodging
Under 85,000 lire

Pensione Gresi. This fifth-floor hotel off Via Etnea appears entirely nondescript from outside, but there are hidden surprises within, in the shape of some lovely Baroque mouldings and ceiling decoration in most of the rooms. Chandeliers and painted putti enhance the effect, and many of the fixtures, too, are delightful relics of a bygone era—like the solid marble bathtub in room No. 1. If you're traveling solo and you like the idea of sleeping under putti, go for No. 9. Other facilities are minimal, though there are some good views over Via Etnea. Breakfast is somewhat overpriced at 7,000 lire. *Via Pacini 28, tel. 095/322709. 14 rooms, 6 with bath. No credit cards.*
Savona. This is Catania's best central choice, a stone's throw from Piazza del Duomo, efficiently run and—unusual for this city—well maintained. Guest rooms are spacious and comfortable, solidly furnished, and equipped with TV and telephones. Prices include breakfast. Parking will be a problem if you have a car.*Via Vittorio Emanuele 210, tel. 095/326982, fax 095/715–8169. 25 rooms, 15 with bath. Facilities: bar, breakfast room. No credit cards.*

Dining
Under 24,000 lire

U Ziu Turiddu. The fare here is excellent, but you have to work for it—there's no menu, and customers are largely left to look after themselves. The specialty is fish, displayed in the entrance fresh from the market: You make your selection, it is weighed, and it reappears minutes later, grilled or roasted. A mouth-watering choice of antipasti is laid out—again, you help yourself to as much as you want. Pasta is not available, but other dishes usually on hand are *zuppa di ceci* (chickpea soup) and *carciofi* (artichokes). The best advice if you don't speak Italian is to see what other people are eating and point to it. This trattoria has a regular clientele, and the ambience is casual and cheerful. *Via Musulmeli 50 (near Piazza Carlo Alberto), no telephone. No credit cards. Closed Sun. and Aug.*

Splurge
★

Costa Azzurra. This seafood restaurant is in the Ognina district, just north of the center and on the way to the Taormina road. Reserve a table on the veranda by the edge of the sea; there are good views of the harbor. The fritto misto can be ordered as an antipasto or a main course, and the pesce spada steak is a simple classic—served grilled with a large slice of lemon. Take bus No. 22 from Via Etnea, or No. 41 from the train station. *Via De Cristofaro 4, tel. 095/494920. Reservations advised. Jacket and tie required. AE, DC, MC, V. Closed Mon. and Aug.*

The Arts   **Teatro Bellini** (Piazza Bellini, tel. 095/312020) hosts an opera season from October to mid-June, attracting top singers and productions to the hometown of the great operatic composer.

Siracusa

Siracusa is a 90-minute train ride down the coast from Catania (frequent departures; fare 6,500 lire); otherwise take a SAIS (tel. 095/536168) or an AST (telephone tourist office 095/312124 for information) bus, departing hourly from near the train station (75 minutes, tickets 6,100 lire). Tourist offices: Via San Sebastiano 43, tel. 0931/461477; Via Maestranza 33, tel. 0931/464255; at entrance to Archaeological Park, tel. 0931/60510.

Sixty kilometers (36 miles) south of Catania, you can visit the first foothold of Greek civilization in Sicily, and some of the island's finest examples of Baroque art and architecture. Siracusa was founded in 734 BC by Greek colonists from Corinth and soon grew to rival, and even surpass, Athens in splendor and power. Siracusa became the largest, wealthiest city-state in Magna Grecia and the bulwark of Greek civilization. Although it suffered from tyrannical rule, such kings as Dionysius filled their courts during the 5th century BC with Greeks of the highest artistic stature—among them, Pindar, Aeschylus, and Archimedes. The Athenians did not welcome the rise of Siracusa and sent a fleet to destroy the rival city, but the natives outsmarted them in what was one of the greatest naval battles of ancient history (413 BC). Siracusa continued to prosper until it was conquered two centuries later by the Romans.

There are essentially two areas to be explored in Siracusa: the Archaeological Park, on the mainland (at the northern end of Corso Gelone), and the island of Ortygia, which juts out into the Ionian Sea (follow Corso Umberto southeast across the bridge). If your starting point is Piazzale Marconi, the square where out-of-town buses arrive, take Via Catania to reach Corso Gelone; Corso Umberto intersects the square. If you arrive by train, note that the station is only a short walk northwest of Piazzale Marconi.

The **Archaeological Park,** at the western edge of town, contains the ruins of a fine Roman amphitheater and the most complete Greek theater existing from antiquity. A comparison of these two structures reveals much about the differences between the Greek and Roman personalities. The Greek theater, in which the plays of Aeschylus premiered, was hewn out of the hillside rock in the 5th century BC. All the seats converge upon a single point—the stage—which had the natural scenery and the sky as its background. Drama as a kind of religious ritual was the intention here. In the Roman amphitheater, however, one of the largest of its kind around the 2nd century AD, the emphasis was on the spectacle of combative sports and the circus. The corridor where gladiators and beasts entered the ring is still intact, and the seats, some of which still bear the occupants' names, were hauled in and constructed on the site from huge slabs of limestone. A crowd-pleasing show, and not the elevation of men's minds, was the intention here. Climb to the top of the seating area in the Greek theater, which could accommodate 15,000, for a fine view. In May and June of even-numbered years, performances of Greek tragedies are held here. If the Archaeological Park is closed, go up Viale G. Rizzo from Viale Teracati, to the belvedere overlooking the ruins, which are floodlit at night.

Near the entrance to the park is the gigantic altar of Hieron, which was once used by the Greeks for sacrifices involving hundreds of animals at a time. Just beyond the ticket office, you will come upon a lush tropical garden full of palm and citrus trees. This is the Latomie del Paradiso, a series of quarries that served as prisons for the defeated Athenians, who were enslaved; the quarries once rang with the sound of their chisels and hammers. At one end is the Orecchio di Dionisio, with an ear-shaped entrance and unusual acoustics inside, as you'll discover if you clap your hands. The legend is that Dionysius used to listen in at the top of the quarry to hear what the slaves were plotting below. *Viale Augusto, tel. 0931/66206. Admission: 2,000 lire. Open Oct.–May, daily 9–4; June–Sept., daily 9–6.*

Not far from the Archaeological Park, off Viale Teocrito, are the **catacombs** of San Giovanni, one of the earliest-known Christian sites in the city. Inside the crypt of San Marciano is an altar where St. Paul preached on his way through Sicily to Rome. The frescoes in this small chapel are still bright and fresh, though some date from the 4th century AD. *Piazza San Giovanni. Admission: 2,000 lire. Open June–Sept., daily 10– noon and 3–6; Oct.–May, Thurs.–Tues. 10–noon.*

Continue walking east, toward the sea, along Viale Teocrito, and you'll soon come to the **papyrus studio** at No. 80, where you can see papyruses being prepared from reeds and then see the scrolls painted—an ancient tradition here. Siracusa, it seems, has the only climate outside the Nile Valley in which the papyrus plant—from which we get our word *paper*—thrives.

Nearby is the splendid **Archaeological Museum.** Its impressive collection is arranged by region around a central atrium and ranges from Neolithic pottery to fine Greek statues and vases. You will want to compare the Landolina Venus—a headless, stout goddess of love who rises out of the sea in measured modesty (she is a 1st-century Roman copy of the Greek original)— with the much earlier (300 BC) elegant Greek statue of Hercules in Section C. Of a completely different type is a marvelous fanged Gorgon, its tongue sticking out, that once adorned the cornice of the temple of Athena to ward off evildoers. The pieces are generally well lit, and there are also several interesting, instructive exhibits. One depicts the Temple of Apollo, the oldest Doric temple in Sicily, on the island of Ortygia. *Viale Teocrito, tel. 0931/464022. Admission: 2,000 lire. Open Tues.– Sat. 9–1, Sun. 9–12:30 (closed first and third Sun. of every month).*

Central Siracusa is a modern city, with Corso Gelone its main shopping street. At the street's southern end, Corso Umberto leads to the **Ortygia Island** bridge, which crosses a pretty harbor lined with fish restaurants. In the piazza on the other side of the bridge you'll find the ruins of the **Temple of Apollo** depicted in the Archaeological Museum. In fact, little of this noble Doric temple still remains today, except for some crumbled walls and shattered columns that survive along with a fragment (the window in the south wall) of a Norman church that was built much later on the same spot. Apart from this ancient Greek relic, Ortygia is composed almost entirely of warm, restrained Baroque buildings. This uniformity is the result of an earthquake in 1693 that necessitated major rebuilding at a time when the Baroque was very popular. Wander into the back streets—especially along Via della Maestranza or Via Veneto—and notice the bulbous wrought-iron balconies (said to have been invented to accommodate ladies' billowing skirts), the window-surrounds and cornices of buildings decorated with mermaids and gargoyles, and the stucco decoration on Palazzo Lantieri on Via Roma.

Ortygia has two main squares: Piazza Archimede and Piazza del Duomo. Piazza Archimede is easily recognized because of its Baroque fountain of fainting sea nymphs and dancing jets of water. The bars here are popular meeting places. **Piazza del Duomo,** one of the most beautiful piazzas in Italy, is a short walk away. The **Duomo** is an archive of island history, beginning with the bottom-most excavations that have unearthed remnants of Sicily's distant past, when the Siculi inhabitants worshiped their deities here. During the 5th century BC, the Greeks built a temple to Athena over it, and in the 7th century, Siracusa's first Christian cathedral was built on top of the Greek structure. The elegant columns of the original temple were incorporated into the present church and are clearly visible, embedded in the exterior wall along Via Minerva. The Greek columns were also used to dramatic advantage inside, where on one side they form chapels connected by elegant wrought-iron gates. The Baroque facade, added in 1700, displays a harmonious rhythm of concaves and convexes. The piazza in front is encircled by pink and white oleanders and surrounded by elegant buildings ornamented with filigree grillwork. In the right corner is the elegant **Palazzo Beneventano del Bosco,** with an impressive interior courtyard ending in a grand winding staircase. At the opposite end is the tiny Baroque church of **Santa Lucia alla Badia,** with an engaging wrought-iron balcony and pleasing facade. The feast of the city's patroness Santa Lucia (St. Lucy) is held on December 13, when a splendid silver statue of the saint is carried from the cathedral to the church on the site of her martyrdom, near the Catacombs of San Giovanni. A torchlight procession and band music accompany the bearers.

Walk down Via delle Vergini, behind the church, and turn onto Via Capodieci, where the **National Museum** is housed inside Palazzo Bellomo, a lovely Catalan-Gothic building with mullioned windows and an elegant exterior staircase. Among the select group of paintings and sculptures inside is a Santa Lucia by Caravaggio and a damaged but still brilliant Annunciation by Antonello da Messina. *Via Capodieci 14, tel. 0931/65343. Admission: 2,000 lire. Open Tues.–Sat. 9–1.*

Walk in the opposite direction, down Via Capodieci to the promenade along the harbor, and you'll come to the **Fountain of Arethusa,** a freshwater spring next to the sea. This anomaly is explained by a Greek legend that tells how the nymph Arethusa was changed into a fountain by the goddess Artemis (Diana) when she tried to escape the advances of the river god Alpheus. She fled from Greece, into the sea, with Alpheus in close pursuit, and emerged in Sicily at this spring. Supposedly even today, if you throw a cup into the river Alpheus in Greece, it will emerge here at this fountain, which at present is home to a few tired ducks and some dull-colored carp—but no cups. Steps lead to the tree-lined promenade along the harborfront, where you can buy a drink and watch the ships come in. Or you can walk out to the castle at the far end of the island, the **Castello Maniace,** now an army barracks but once a castle of Frederick II, from which there are fine views of the sea.

North of the city, on the highlands that overlook the sea, Dionysius created the fortress of **Euryalus** with the help of Archimedes, as protection against the Carthaginians. This astonishing boat-shape structure once covered 15,000 square yards. Its intricate maze of tunnels is fascinating, and the view from the heights is superb. To reach Euryalus, take bus No. 9, 10, or 11 from Ortygia or Corso Gelone, a 20-minute ride (fare 800 lire). *8 km (5 mi) northwest of Siracusa. Open 9–one hour before sunset.*

Lodging
Under 85,000 lire

Gran Bretagna. There are only two hotels on Siracusa's offshore island of Ortygia, and one of them is elite. This is the other, and in summer it will be difficult to find space here without a reservation. The location is ideal for sauntering around the old town. The hotel itself has nice touches—Art Nouveau decoration and liberal arrangements of potted plants—though the guest rooms tend to be cramped. Other negatives include an unforthcoming manager and the overpriced restaurant. *Via Savoia 21, tel. 0931/68765. 12 rooms, 3 with shower. Facilities: restaurant. AE, DC, MC, V.*

Under 60,000 lire

Ostello della Gioventù. This unofficial youth hostel (membership not required) is an excellent choice for anyone undaunted by the distance into town. It's located on the Epipolae ridge, close by the ancient fortress of Euryalus, with its wide views over the city and coastline. Buses are frequent (No. 9, 10, or 11 run from Ortygia or Corso Gelone, a 20-minute ride) and the hostel has a pleasant, laid-back atmosphere, with a terrace for relaxing and (sporadic) meal service. There is also an excellent pizzeria nearby. Unlike many hostels, this one has no regulations about vacating the premises during the daytime, but it does have typical hostel dormitory accommodations (average four to a room). *Via Epipoli 45, tel. 0931/711118. 40 beds. Facilities: bar, breakfast room, garden, parking. No credit cards.*

Dining
Under 30,000 lire

La Foglia. When the usual pizzas and pastas pall, this vegetarian restaurant can be something of a relief. All the ingredients are guaranteed fresh, and the soups are especially worth sampling; the only complaint is the rather meager portions. The atmosphere is quiet and homey, the decor arty, with occasional exhibitions of handicrafts or paintings by local artists. *Via Capodieci 39, tel. 0931/66233. AE, MC, V. Closed Tues.*

Pescomare. This fish restaurant is just down from Piazza del Duomo, housed in an atmospheric series of plant-filled courtyards—neither indoors nor wholly outdoors. The clientele is smart, the service polite, and the dishes exquisite. Menu choices depend on what the fishermen caught earlier in the day, but try the succulent giant clams if you want to treat yourself, and save space for a creamy rich zabaglione or any of the other good desserts. *Via Landolina 6, tel. 0931/21075. No credit cards. Closed Mon.*

Under 24,000 lire

Minerva. This trattoria is always crowded, no doubt largely because it's right opposite the Duomo on Ortygia island. The decor is simple and unpretentious; go for a table outside on the square if one is available (summer only). Try *maccheroni con ragù e ricotta*, pasta with a meat sauce lightly creamed with cheese. There are pizzas here, too. The tourist menu (18,000 lire) includes meat or fish. *Piazza del Duomo, tel. 0931/69404. Reservations advised in summer. Closed Mon. No credit cards.*

Il Giglio. In the nearby town of Noto, a gem of Baroque town planning just 40 minutes by bus or train from Siracusa, you will find this small trattoria in the center close to the cathedral. Make the trip for seafood dishes with a Spanish touch, prepared by Maria Luz Corruchaga and her husband, Corrado. Particularly recommended are *pasta al nero di seppia* (with cuttlefish) and *zuppa di vongole e cozze* (clam and mussel soup). *Piazza Municipio, tel. 0931/838640. Reservations advised weekends. No credit cards. Closed Sat. in winter.*

Splurge **Arlecchino.** A bustling, bohemian atmosphere pervades this restaurant, located midway between the archaeological zone and the Città Vecchia (Old Town). It's popular with artists and students, always a sign of good value. The Palermo-born proprietor serves specialties from his hometown, such as *risotto ai granchi* (with crab) and homemade cassata for dessert. Try for a table on the terrace. *Via dei Tolomei 5, tel. 0931/66386. AE, DC, MC, V. Closed Mon. and Aug.*

The Arts In May and June of even-numbered years, Siracusa's impressive **Teatro Greco** is the setting for performances of classical drama and comedy. For information, call 0931/67415.

Caltagirone

By AST bus, it's a 90-minute ride from Catania (seven buses a day, Mon.–Sat., from Via L. Sturzo 220, near the train station, tel. 095/531756). Bus tickets cost 7,400 lire. Ten trains a day make the two-hour trip; tickets cost 7,000 lire. Tourist office: Via Volta Libertini 3, tel. 0933/53809.

Seventy-six kilometers (48 miles) from Catania, Caltagirone is a charming Baroque town built over three hills. If you're arriving by bus for a day-trip, get off at the first stop to look around at the sights; if you're planning to spend the night here, however, stay on the bus until it reaches the new town, a kilometer farther on. The hotels and the train station are in the new town.

Caltagirone's status as a leader in the Sicilian ceramics industry is evident all around town—majolica balustrades, tile-decorated windowsills, and a monumental tile staircase of more than a hundred steps, each decorated with a different pattern. On the feast of San Giacomo (July 24), the staircase is illuminated with candles that form a tapestry design over the steps, the result of months of work preparing the 4,000 *coppi*, or cylinders of colored paper that hold oil lamps. At 9:30 PM on July 24, a squad of hundreds of boys springs into action to light the lamps, so that the staircase flares up all at once. There is an interesting **Ceramics Museum** in the public gardens, which were designed by Basile, the master of Sicilian Art Nouveau. The museum exhibits trace the craft from the earliest settlements, through the influential Arab period, to the present. *Museo Regionale della Ceramica, Giardino Pubblico, tel. 0933/21680. Open Mon.–Sat. 9:30–2, Sun. 9–1.*

Lodging
Under 85,000 lire

Donato. This is the best choice in Caltagirone, worth going out of your way for, which is exactly what you must do to reach it. It is in the new town, about a kilometer beyond the hospital. Once you arrive, you'll be happy about its remoteness, with sweeping views to the old town and restful rustic surroundings. The rooms are large and tasteful, and the attached restaurant is one of the best in town. *Via Porto Salvo 22b, tel. 0933/25684. 24 rooms with bath. Facilities: restaurant, bar, parking. AE, DC, MC, V.*

Piazza Armerina

From Caltagirone, buses to Piazza Armerina run four times a day on weekdays and once a day on Sunday and holidays; it's an hour's bus ride and costs 4,000 lire. From Catania, it takes 105 minutes by Etna Trasporti buses (fare 8,600 lire), which leave from Via D'Amico near the train station (tel. 095/532716, five daily departures Mon.–Sat., two on Sun.) Train options are more limited: From Catania, you go as far as Enna (6,500 lire) or Caltanissetta (8,800 lire), then change onto a bus (5,000 lire). This will take 3–4 hours plus waiting time. Tourist office: Via Cavour 15, tel. 0935/680201.

The tiny Baroque town of Piazza Armerina lies amid thick pine and eucalyptus woods to the northeast of Caltagirone. Its outstanding attraction, however, the Imperial Roman Villa, the exceptionally well-preserved and well-presented sumptuous country house of a Roman emperor, is about 6 kilometers (4 miles) southwest of the city, in Casale. A minibus runs six times daily between April and September, once daily (except Sunday) at 1:30 in winter, from outside the Hotel Selene on Via Gaeta, down from the bus terminal on Viale Generale Muscare; otherwise, it's a brisk hour's walk. Taxis charge about 40,000 lire to take you to the site, wait for an hour, and take you back—a good option for groups. The site is made up of four groups of buildings on different levels and is thought to have been a hunting lodge of the emperor Maximianus Heraclius (4th century AD). The excavations were not begun until 1950, and all the wall decorations and vaulting have been lost. However, some of the best mosaics of the Roman world cover 3,500 square meters under a shelter shaped to give an idea of the layout of the original buildings. The mosaics were probably made by Carthaginian artisans, because they are similar to those in the Tunis Bardo Museum. The entrance was through a triumphal arch that led into an atrium surrounded by a portico of columns. Through this, the *thermae*, or bathhouse, is reached. It is colorfully decorated with mosaic nymphs, a Neptune, and slaves massaging bathers. The Peristyle leads to the main villa, where in the Salone del Circo you look down on mosaics that illustrate Roman circus sports. Another apartment shows hunting scenes of tigers, elephants, and ostriches; the gym shows young girls exercising; the private apartments are covered with scenes from Greek and Roman mythology; and room No. 38 even has a touch of eroticism. *Tel. 0935/680036. Admission: 2,000 lire. Open daily 9–one hour before sunset.*

Dining
Under 24,000 lire

Centrale da Totò. In the center of Piazza Armerina, this reliable trattoria is often busy with sightseers and locals alike. The emphasis is on a family clientele rather than intimate or expense-account dining, and the portions reflect this *mangia, mangia* outlook. Try the *pappardelle alla Centrale*, a rich, filling pasta dish made with tomato sauce and fresh vegetables. *Via Mazzini 29, tel. 0935/680153. AE, DC, MC, V. Closed Mon.*

Festivals On August 13, the **Palio dei Normanni,** a medieval tournament with participants dressed in 14th-century costume, celebrates the city's prosperity under the Normans. The main event is a horse race.

Etna

Catania is the departure point for excursions around—but not always to the top of—Mt. Etna. Buses (fare 7,000 lire) leave from in front of the train station in early morning, or you can take the Circumetnea railroad around the volcano's base (12,000 lire round-trip).

Etna is one of the world's major active volcanoes, and the largest and highest in Europe. The cone of the crater rises to 2,801 meters (9,190 feet) above sea level. It has erupted nine times in the past three decades, most spectacularly in 1971 and 1983, when rivers of molten lava destroyed the two highest stations of the cable car that rises from the town of Sapienza. Travel in the vicinity of the crater depends at the moment on Etna's temperament, but you can walk up and down the enormous lava dunes and wander over its moonlike surface of dead craters. The rings of vegetation change markedly as you ascend, with vineyards and pine trees gradually giving way to broom and lichen.

Taormina

From Catania, frequent express trains (fare 4,000 lire) take 40 minutes to reach the seaside resort of Giardini-Naxos, from which hourly buses (fare 1,500 lire) make the ascent to Taormina. Alternatively, SAIS buses depart 12 times a day from Catania's train station (fare 5,000 lire), tel. 095/536168, and take about an hour and 40 minutes to Taormina. You'll arrive at Taormina's car park, a 10-minute walk from the center of town. Tourist offices: Largo Santa Caterina, Palazzo Corvaja, tel. 0942/23243; Corso Umberto 144, tel. 0942/23751.

Taormina's natural beauty is so great that even the considerable overdevelopment that the town has suffered in the past 50 years cannot spoil its grandeur. The view of the sea and Etna from its jagged, cactus-covered cliffs is as close to perfection as a panorama can get, especially on clear days, when the snow-capped volcano's white puffs of smoke are etched against the blue sky. Writers have extolled Taormina's beauty almost since its founding in the 6th century BC by Greeks from Naples. Goethe and D. H. Lawrence were among its enthusiasts. The Greeks put a high premium on finding impressive locations in which to stage their dramas, and Taormina's **Greek Theater** occupies one of the finest sites of any such theater. It was built during the 3rd century BC and rebuilt by the Romans during the 2nd century AD. Its acoustics are exceptional: Even today a stage whisper can be heard in the last rows. In summer, Taormina hosts an arts festival of music, cinema, and dance events, many of which are held in the Greek Theater. *Via Teatro Greco, tel. 0942/23220. Admission: 2,000 lire. Open daily 9–two hours before sunset.*

The main street in town is Corso Umberto, which is lined with smart boutiques and antiques shops. There are also the inevitable, and all too numerous, shops selling cheap pottery and jewelry made from Etna's black lava stone. Piazza 9 Aprile, along the Corso, commands wonderful views and is the perfect place to sit and have a cappuccino. The town's many 14th- and 15th-century palaces have been carefully preserved; especially beautiful is the **Palazzo Corvaja,** with characteristic black lava and white limestone inlays. (Today it houses the tourist office, open weekdays 8–2 and 2:30–7:30, Sat. 8–noon.) The medieval **Castello San Pancrazio** (admission free), enticingly perched on an adjoining cliff above the town, can be reached by footpath or car. If your passion for heights hasn't been exhausted, visit **Castelmola,** the tiny town above Taormina, where the Bar Turrisi makes its own refreshing almond wine—the perfect complement to the spectacular 360-degree panorama.

Lodging
Under 115,000 lire

Villa Fiorita. This converted private home near the Greek amphitheater has excellent views of the coast from nearly every room. The rooms vary in size and furnishings, but most are bright and colorful, with large windows that let in the sea breezes. Prices are reasonable for a hotel with a swimming pool and small garden. *Via Pirandello 39, tel. 0942/24122, fax 0942/625967. 24 rooms with bath or shower. Facilities: garden, pool, garage. AE, MC, V.*

Under 60,000 lire

Villa Liliana. On a rise on the edge of town, this small place has a pleasant rustic setting. It is run by a lovely lady (she calls herself "old") who is wilier than she makes herself out to be, but get on the right side of her and she'll look after you like her own. The rooms are basic, some with a good vista over the sea. The tangled garden provides welcome shade in the summer. *Via Dietro Cappuccini 4, tel. 0942/24373. 13 rooms, 3 with bath. Facilities: garden. No credit cards.*

Dining
Under 30,000 lire

Baccanale. Popular with tourists, this trattoria in the center of Taormina (near Via Croce) has a lively feel, with a veranda where you can sit overlooking the piazza. The decor is contrived but inoffensive, and the menu has all the regular items plus a few more: Try the grilled sardines, washed down with a carafe of house red. *Piazzetta Filea 3, tel. 0942/625390. No credit cards.*

★ **Il Faro.** Castelmola is a small village above Taormina, and as you dine in this family-run country restaurant, sitting under a grape arbor, you have an excellent view of the wild cliffs and sea. Meat dishes are recommended alla brace (grilled), particularly *pollo* (chicken) and *coniglio* (rabbit). Piera and Francesco, the owners, provide an antipasto of homegrown vegetables. Start your meal with *bruschetta all'ortolana* (country bread toasted with olive oil, topped with tomatoes and onions). *Via Rotabile, Contrada Petralia, tel. 0942/28193. Reservations advised. No credit cards. Closed Wed.*

Splurge

Giova Rosy Senior. One of Taormina's oldest restaurants, the Giova Rosy Senior is also known for its good-value menu and its central location, in the heart of Taormina. It faces the Palazzo Corvaja and the Teatro Comunale and is just a short walk from the Greek amphitheater. Try for an outside table. *The involtini di pesce spada* (stuffed swordfish rolls) are excellent. *Corso Umberto 38, tel. 0942/24411. Reservations required. AE, DC, MC, V. Closed Thurs. and Jan.–Feb.*

The Arts The churches and theaters of Taormina are the venues for a summer festival of **classical music,** held each year from May to September. For information, call 0942/23751.

Taormina's **Greek Theater** is the setting for regular theatrical performances from July to September. For information, call 0942/23220.

Taormina hosts an international **film festival** each July, also held in the grand setting of the Greek Theater. For information, call 0942/23220.

Messina

Messina is a 90-minute ride on fast trains (don't take locals) from Catania, 40 minutes from Taormina. The fare from Catania is 7,000 lire, from Taormina 4,000 lire. Frequent SAIS buses cover the same route in much the same time and cost 9,000 lire. Tourist office: Piazza Stazione, tel. 090/674236.

Although its main interest for travelers is as a ferry port Messina is attractive enough in its own right. The coast between Taormina and Messina, a stretch of about 50 kilometers (30 miles), is bordered by lush vegetation on one side and the sea on the other, and the seaside is dotted with inlets punctuated by gigantic, odd-shaped rocks. It was along this coast, legend says, that the giant Cyclopes hurled their boulders down on Ulysses and his terrified men as they fled to sea and on to their next adventure in Homer's *Odyssey.*

Messina's ancient history is a series of disasters, but the city nevertheless managed to develop a fine university and a thriving cultural environment. But at 5 o'clock in the morning on December 28, 1908, Messina changed from a flourishing metropolis of 120,000 to a heap of rubble, shaken to pieces by an earthquake that turned into a tidal wave and left 80,000 dead and the city almost completely leveled. As you approach the sickle-shape bay, from which ferries connect Sicily with the mainland, you'll see nothing to alert you to the relatively recent disaster, except that the 3,000-year-old city looks modern. The somewhat flat look is a precaution of seismic planning: Tall buildings are not permitted.

Arriving by either bus or train, you'll be right at Piazza della Repubblica, a five-minute walk from the port. Messina's **cathedral** has been entirely rebuilt (it was originally constructed by the Norman king Roger II in 1197, and the reconstruction has maintained much of the original plan, including a handsome crown of Norman battlements, an enormous oven apse, and a splendid wood-beam ceiling). The adjoining bell tower—of a much later date—is one of the city's principal attractions. It contains one of the largest and most complex mechanical clocks in the world, constructed in 1933 with a host of gilded automatons—a roaring lion, a crowing rooster, and numerous biblical figures—that go into action every day at the stroke of noon.

Messina is the birthplace of the great Renaissance painter Antonello da Messina, whose *Polyptych of the Rosary* (1473) can be seen along with two large Caravaggios in the **Regional Museum,** located along the sea in the northern outskirts of the city. Take city bus No. 8, 27, or 28 from the train station. *Viale della Libertà, tel. 090/358605. Admission: 2,000 lire. Open*

Mon.–Sat. 9–1:30 and 3–5:30 (closed Mon., Wed., and Fri. afternoons in winter), Sun. and holidays 9–12:30.

Lodging
Under 115,000 lire

Monza. Whether or not the hotel is named after Italy's top racing track, the noise outside suggests some connection. The rooms, however, are relatively well insulated, and the plush decor and professional service give a feeling of well-being and comfort. Close to the port and train station, and just off the central Piazza Cairoli, this is a useful hotel option. *Via San Martino 63, tel. 090/673755, fax 090/673755. 58 rooms, 48 with shower. AE, DC, MC, V.*

Under 60,000 lire

Roma. This cheap hotel enjoys a premium location in Piazza Duomo. Although the piazza is free of Messina's ubiquitous traffic, the hotel is not entirely noise-free: You may find yourself awakened by the chiming bells of the cathedral's famous bell tower. The rooms are basic and uninspiring, but they fill up early, so book ahead if you can. *Piazza Duomo 3, tel. 090/675566. 12 rooms without bath. No credit cards.*

Dining
Under 20,000 lire

Pippo Nunnari. If such a thing as a Sicilian deli exists, this is it—a favorite with lunchtime shoppers and workers behind Messina's central Piazza Cairoli. The food is fast, but the service can be slow: You must first obtain a ticket from the cashier, then elbow your way to the counter to attract the attention of the harrassed staff. Snacks here are delicious: Try an *arancino*, a deep-fried breaded rice ball filled with cheese (*bianco*) or meat (*rosso*); *mozzarella in carrozza* (a deep-fried bread pocket filled with cheese); or pizza covered with thin slices of potato and rosemary. The restaurant next door, of the same name and run by the same proprietor, is one of Messina's best, but pricey. *Via Ugo Bassi 157, tel. 090/293–8584. No credit cards. Open lunch only, closed Mon.*

Pizzeria del Capitano. There is always a crowd here awaiting takeaway pizzas, but you can sit down, too, and enjoy some of best pizzas in town at rock-bottom prices. There is nothing fancy on the menu, just a fairly traditional selection of pizzas cooked in a wood-fired oven, and a variety of ready-made snacks. Beer and soft drinks are available, but not wine. *Via dei Mille 88 (parallel to Piazza Cairoli), no telephone. No credit cards. Closed Mon.*

Festivals

Messina stages a **folklore parade** of huge traditional effigies called *Giganti*, each year on August 13 and 14.

The Aeolian Islands

Four hydrofoils daily (two in winter) make the 90-minute crossing to the main island of Lipari, leaving Messina's hydrofoil dock in Via Garibaldi (tel. 090/364044). Tickets cost 28,200 lire. Otherwise, go west along the coast to Milazzo to catch the cheaper Aeolian ferries (9,000 lire to Lipari). Hourly Giuntabus (tel. 090/673782) buses cost 5,500 lire and take 30 minutes to Milazzo, leaving from Via Terranova 8, near Messina's train station; hourly trains from Messina take 40 minutes to Milazzo and cost 3,200 lire. A comprehensive network of ferries and hydrofoils links Lipari with the other islands. Tourist office: Corso Vittorio Emanuele 202, Lipari, tel. 090/988–0095.

Just off Sicily's northeast coast lies an archipelago of seven beautiful islands of volcanic origin. The **Aeolian Islands** were

named after Aeolus, the Greek god of the winds, who is said to
keep all the earth's winds stuffed in a bag in his cave here. The
Aeolians are a fascinating world of grottoes and clear-water
caves carved by the waves through the centuries. They are ideal for snorkeling or scuba diving. All Sicily's islands are extremely popular in summer, and some of these seven, in
particular, can be unpleasantly overcrowded in July and August.

Lipari is the largest of the Aeolians and the one most developed
for tourism. Local buses circle the island and provide wonderful views. Take a bus ride away from Lipari town's distinctive
pastel-colored houses and into the fields of spiky agaves to
Acquacalda, at the northernmost tip of the island, where there
are interesting pumice and obsidian quarries. Or take a bus
west to San Calogero, where there are hot springs and mud
baths. Next to the port in Lipari town, on a plateau rising from
the island's red-lava base, are a 16th-century castle (site of a
youth hostel) and a 17th-century cathedral. Next door is the
Archaeological Museum, one of the best in Europe, with a collection of prehistoric finds—some dating as far back as 4,000
BC—from various sites in the archipelago. *Tel. 090/981–1031.*
Admission free. Open Mon.–Sat. 9–2, Sun. and holidays 9–1.

Vulcano, true to its name, has plenty of fumaroles sending up
jets of hot vapor, but the volcano here has long been dormant.
You can ascend to the crater (386 meters [1,274 feet] above sea
level) on muleback for a wonderful view or take boat rides into
the grottoes around the base. From Capo Grillo there is a view
of all the Aeolian.

Salina, the second-largest island, is also the most fertile—
which accounts for its good wine, the golden Malvasia. Excursions go up Mt. Fossa delle Felci, which rises to over 930 meters
(3,000 feet). It is also the highest of the islands, and the vineyards and fishing villages along its slopes add to its charm.

Panarea has some of the most dramatic scenery of the islands:
wild caves carved out of the rock and dazzling flora. The exceptionally clear water and the richness of the seabed here make
Panarea especially suitable for underwater exploration. There
is a small Bronze Age village at Capo Milazzese.

Stromboli consists entirely of the cone of an active volcano. The
view from the sea—especially at night, as an endless stream of
glowing red-hot lava flows into the water—is unforgettable.
Stromboli is in a constant state of mild dissatisfaction, and every now and then its anger flares up, so authorities insist that
you climb to the top (924 meters [3,050 feet] above sea level)
only with a guide. The climb takes about four hours.

Alicudi and **Filicudi** are just dots in the sea, but each has a hotel, and some local families put up guests. Filicudi is famous for
its unusual volcanic rock formations and the enchanting Grotto
del Bue Marino (Grotto of the Sea Ox). At Capo Graziano there
is a prehistoric village. Alicudi is the farthest outpost of the
Aeolians—it remains sparsely inhabited, wild, and at peace.

Italian Vocabulary

Words & Phrases

	English	*Italian*	*Pronunciation*
Basics	Yes/no	Sí/No	see/no
	Please	Per favore	pear fa-**vo**-ray
	Yes, please	Sí grazie	see **grah**-tsee-ay
	Thank you	Grazie	**grah**-tsee-ay
	You're welcome	Prego	**pray**-go
	Excuse me, sorry	Scusi	**skoo**-zee
	Sorry!	Mi spiace!	mee spee-**ah**-chay
	Good morning/ afternoon	Buon giorno	bwohn **jor**-no
	Goodevening	Buona sera	**bwoh**-na say-ra
	Goodbye	Arrivederci	a-ree-vah-**dare**-chee
	Mr.(Sir)	Signore	see-**nyo**-ray
	Mrs. (Ma'am)	Signora	see-**nyo**-ra
	Miss	Signorina	see-nyo-**ree**-na
	Pleased to meet you	Piacere	pee-ah-**chair**-ray
	How are you?	Come sta?	**ko**-may **sta**
	Very well, thanks	Bene, grazie	**ben**-ay **grah**-tsee-ay
	And you?	E lei?	ay **lay**-ee
	Hello (over the phone)	Pronto?	**proan**-to
Numbers	one	uno	**oo**-no
	two	due	**doo**-ay
	three	tre	tray
	four	quattro	**kwah**-tro
	five	cinque	**cheen**-kway
	six	sei	say
	seven	sette	**set**-ay
	eight	otto	**oh**-to
	nine	nove	**no**-vay
	ten	dieci	dee-**eh**-chee
	eleven	undici	**oon**-dee-chee
	twelve	dodici	**doe**-dee-chee
	thirteen	tredici	**tray**-dee-chee
	fourteen	quattordici	kwa-**tore**-dee-chee
	fifteen	quindici	**kwin**-dee-chee
	sixteen	sedici	**say**-dee-chee
	seventeen	diciassette	dee-cha-**set**-ay
	eighteen	diciotto	dee-**cho**-to
	nineteen	diciannove	dee-cha-**no**-vay
	twenty	venti	**vain**-tee
	twenty-one	ventuno	vain-**too**-no
	twenty-two	ventidue	vayn-tee-**doo**-ay
	thirty	trenta	**train**-ta
	forty	quaranta	kwa-**rahn**-ta
	fifty	cinquanta	cheen-**kwahn**-ta
	sixty	sessanta	seh-**sahn**-ta
	seventy	settanta	seh-**tahn**-ta
	eighty	ottanta	o-**tahn**-ta
	ninety	novanta	no-**vahn**-ta
	one hundred	cento	**chen**-to

| | ten thousand | diecimila | dee-eh-chee-**mee**-la |
| | one hundred thousand | centomila | chen-to-**mee**-la |

Colors	black	nero	**neh**-ro
	blue	azzurro	a-**tsu**-ro
	brown	marrone	mah-**ro**-nay
	green	verde	**vehr**-day
	pink	rosa	**ro**-za
	purple	porpora	**por**-por-a
	orange	arancio	a-**rahn**-cho
	red	rosso	**ros**-so
	white	bianco	bee-**ang**-ko
	yellow	giallo	**ja**-lo

Days of the week	Monday	lunedì	**loo**-neh-dee
	Tuesday	martedì	**mahr**-teh-dee
	Wednesday	mercoledì	**mare**-co-leh-dee
	Thursday	giovedì	**jo**-veh-dee
	Friday	venerdì	**ven**-air-dee
	Saturday	sabato	**sah**-ba-toe
	Sunday	domenica	doe-**men**-ee-ca

Months	January	gennaio	jeh-**nah**-yo
	February	febbraio	feh-**brah**-yo
	March	marzo	**mahr**-tso
	April	aprile	a-**pree**-lay
	May	maggio	**mah**-jo
	June	giugno	**joon**-yo
	July	luglio	**loo**-lee-o
	August	agosto	ah-**goo**-sto
	September	settembre	seh-**tem**-bray
	October	ottobre	o-**toe**-bray
	November	novembre	no-**vem**-bray
	December	dicembre	dee-**chem**-bray

Useful phrases	Do you speak English?	Parla inglese?	**par**-la een-**glay**-zay
	I don't speak Italian	Non parlo italiano	non **par**-lo ee-tal-**yah**-no
	I don't understand	Non capisco	non ka-**peess**-ko
	Can you please repeat?	Può ripetere?	pwo ree-**pet**-ay-ray
	I don't know	Non lo so	noan lo **so**
	I'm American/	Sono americano/a	**so**-no a-may-ree-**ka**-no/a
	British	Sono inglese	**so**-no een-**glay**-zay
	What's your name?	Come si chiama?	**ko**-may see kee-**ah**-ma
	My name is . . .	Mi chiamo . . .	mee kee-**ah**-mo
	What time is it?	Che ore sono?	kay **o**-ray **so**-no
	How?	Come?	**ko**-may
	When?	Quando?	**kwan**-doe

Yesterday/today/ tomorrow	Ieri/oggi/ domani	**yer**-ee/**o**-jee/ do-**mah**-nee
This morning/ afternoon	Stamattina/Oggi pomeriggio	sta-ma-**tee**-na/**o**-jee po-mer-**ee**-jo
Tonight	Stasera	sta-**ser**-a
What?	Che cosa?	kay **ko**-za
What is it?	Che cos'è?	kay ko-**zay**
Why?	Perché?	pear-**kay**
Who?	Chi?	kee
Where is . . . the bus stop?	Dov'è . . . la fermata dell'autobus?	doe-**veh** la fer-**ma**-ta del ow-toe-**booss**
the train station?	la stazione?	la sta-tsee-**oh**-nay
the subway station?	la metropolitana?	la may-tro-po-lee-**ta**-na
the terminal?	il terminal?	eel ter-mee-**nahl**
the post office?	l'ufficio postale?	loo-**fee**-cho po-**sta**-lay
the bank?	la banca?	la **bahn**-ka
the . . . hotel?	l'hotel . . . ?	lo-**tel**
the store?	il negozio?	ell nay-**go**-tsee-o
the cashier?	la cassa?	la **ka**-sa
the . . . museum?	il museo . . . ?	eel moo-**zay**-o
the hospital?	l'ospedale?	lo-spay-**dah**-lay
the first aid station?	il pronto soccorso?	eel **pron**-to so-**kor**-so
the elevator?	l'ascensore?	la-shen-**so**-ray
a telephone?	un telefono?	oon tay-**lay**-fo-no
Where are the rest rooms?	Dov'è il bagno?	doe-**vay** eel **bahn**-yo
Here/there Left/right	Qui/là A sinistra/a destra	kwee/la a see-**neess**-tra/ a **des**-tra
Straight ahead	Avanti dritto	a-**vahn**-tee **dree**-to
Is it near/far?	È vicino?/lontano?	ay vee-**chee**-no/ lon-**tah**-no
I'd like . . . a room	Vorrei . . . una camera	vo-**ray** **oo**-na **ka**-may-ra
the key	la chiave	la kee-**ah**-vay
a newspaper	un giornale	oon jor-**na**-lay
a stamp	un francobollo	oon frahn-ko-**bo**-lo
I'd like to buy . . .	Vorrei comprare . . .	vo-**ray** kom-**pra**-ray
a cigar	un sigaro	oon see-**ga**-ro
cigarettes	delle sigarette	day-lay see-ga-**ret**-ay
some matches	dei fiammiferi	day-ee fee-ah-**mee**-fer-ee
some soap	una saponetta	**oo**-na sa-po-**net**-a
a city plan	una pianta della città	**oo**-na **pyahn**-ta day-la chee-**ta**
a road map of . . .	una carta stradale di . . .	**oo**-na **cart**-a stra-**dah**-lay dee

a country map	una carta geografica	**oo**-na **cart**-a jay-o-**grah**-fee-ka
a magazine	una rivista	**oo**-na ree-**veess**-ta
envelopes	delle buste	**day**-lay **booss**-tay
writing paper	della carta da lettere	**day**-la **cart**-a da **let**-air-ay
a postcard	una cartolina	**oo**-na car-toe-**lee**-na
a guidebook	una guida turistica	**oo**-na **gwee**-da too-**reess**-tee-ka

How much is it?	Quanto costa?	**kwahn**-toe **coast**-a
It's expensive/cheap	È caro/economico	ay **car**-o/ay-ko-**no**-mee-ko
A little/a lot	Poco/tanto	**po**-ko/**tahn**-to
More/less	Più/meno	pee-**oo**/**may**-no
Enough/too (much)	Abbastanza/troppo	a-bas-**tahn**-sa/**tro**-po
I am sick	Sto male	sto **ma**-lay
Please call a doctor	Chiami un dottore	kee-**ah**-mee oon doe-**toe**-ray
Help!	Aiuto!	a-**yoo**-toe
Stop!	Alt!	ahlt
Fire!	Al fuoco!	ahl **fwo**-ko
Caution!/Look out!	Attenzione!	a-ten-**syon**-ay

Dining Out

A bottle of . . .	una bottiglia di . . .	**oo**-na bo-**tee**-lee-ah dee
A cup of . . .	Una tazza di . . .	**oo**-na **tah**-tsa dee
A glass of . . .	Un bicchiere di . . .	oon bee-key-**air**-ay dee
Ashtray	Il portacenere	eel por-ta-**chen**-ay-ray
Bill/check	Il conto	eel **cone**-toe
Bread	Il pane	eel **pa**-nay
Breakfast	La prima colazione	la **pree**-ma ko-la-**tsee**-oh-nay
Cheers!	Cin cin!	cheen cheen
Cocktail/aperitif	L'aperitivo	la-pay-ree-**tee**-vo
Dinner	La cena	la **chen**-a
Enjoy!	Buon appetito	bwone a-pay-**tee**-toe
Fixed-price menu	Menù a prezzo fisso	may-**noo** a **pret**-so **fee**-so
Fork	La forchetta	la for-**ket**-a
I am diabetic	Ho il diabete	o eel dee-a-**bay**-tay
I am on a diet	Sono a dieta	**so**-no a dee-**et**-a

I am vegetarian	Sono vegetariano/a	**so**-no vay-jay-ta-ree-**ah**-no/a
I cannot eat . . .	Non posso mangiare . . .	non **po**-so man-**ja**-ray
I'd like to order	Vorrei ordinare	vo-**ray** or-dee-**nah**-ray
I'd like . . .	Vorrei . . .	vo-**ray**
I'm hungry/thirsty	Ho fame/sete	o **fa**-may/**set**-ay
Is service included?	Il servizio è incluso?	eel ser-**vee**-tzee-o ay een-**kloo**-zo
It's good/bad	È buono/cattivo	ay **bwo**-no/ka-tee-vo
It's hot/cold	È caldo/freddo	ay **kahl**-doe/**fred**-o
Knife	Il coltello	eel kol-**tel**-o
Lunch	Il pranzo	eel **prahnt**-so
Menu	Il menù	eel may-**noo**
Napkin	Il tovagliolo	eel toe-va-lee-**oh**-lo
Please give me . . .	Mi dia . . .	mee **dee**-a
Salt	Il sale	eel **sah**-lay
Spoon	Il cucchiaio	eel koo-kee-**ah**-yo
Sugar	Lo zucchero	lo **tsoo**-ker-o
Waiter/Waitress	Cameriere/cameriera	ka-mare-**yer**-ay/ka-mare-**yer**-a
Wine list	La lista dei vini	la **lee**-sta **day**-ee **vee**-nee

Menu Guide

English	Italian
Set menu	Menù a prezzo fisso
Dish of the day	Piatto del giorno
Specialty of the house	Specialità della casa
Local specialties	Specialità locali
Extra charge	Extra . . .
In season	Di stagione
Cover charge/Service charge	Coperto/Servizio

Breakfast

Butter	Burro
Croissant	Cornetto
Eggs	Uova
Honey	Miele
Jam/Marmalade	Marmellata
Roll	Panino
Toast	Pane tostato

Starters

Assorted cold cuts	Affettati misti
Assorted seafood	Antipasto di pesce
Assorted appetizers	Antipasto misto
Toasted rounds of bread, fried or toasted in oil	Crostini/Crostoni
Diced-potato and vegetable salad with mayonnaise	Insalata russa
Eggplant parmigiana	Melanzane alla parmigiana
Fried mozzarella sandwich	Mozzarella in carrozza
Ham and melon	Prosciutto e melone
Cooked sausages and cured meats	Salumi cotti
Filled pastry shells	Vol-au-vents

Soups

"Angel hair," thin noodle soup	Capelli d'angelo
Cream of . . .	Crema di . . .
Pasta-and-bean soup	Pasta e fagioli
Egg-drop and parmesan cheese soup	Stracciatella

Pasta, Rice and Pizza

Filled pasta	Agnolotti/ravioli/tortellini
Potato dumplings	Gnocchi
Semolina dumplings	Gnocchi alla romana
Pasta	Pasta
with four cheeses	*ai quattro formaggi*
with basil/cheese/pine nuts/garlic sauce	*al pesto*
with tomato-based meat sauce	*al ragù*
with tomato sauce	*al sugo* or *al pomodoro*
with butter	*in bianco* or *al burro*
with egg, parmesan cheese, and pepper	*alla carbonara*
green (spinach-based) pasta	*verde*

Rice	Riso
Rice dish	Risotto
with mushrooms	*ai funghi*
with saffron	*alla milanese*
Noodles	Tagliatelle
Pizza	Pizza
Pizza with seafood, cheese, artichokes, and ham in four different sections	Pizza quattro stagioni
Pizza with tomato and mozzarella	Pizza margherita
Pizza with oil, garlic, and oregano	Pizza marinara

Fish and Seafood

Anchovies	Acciughe
Bass	Persico
Carp	Carpa
Clams	Vongole
Cod	Merluzzo
Crab	Granchio
Eel	Anguilla
Lobster	Aragosta
Mackerel	Sgombro
Mullet	Triglia
Mussels	Cozze
Octopus	Polpo
Oysters	Ostriche
Pike	Luccio
Prawns	Gamberoni
Salmon	Salmone
Shrimp	Scampi
Shrimps	Gamberetti
Sole	Sogliola
Squid	Calamari
Swordfish	Pescespada
Trout	Trota
Tuna	Tonno

Methods of Preparation

Baked	Al forno
Cold, with vinegar sauce	In carpione
Fish stew	Zuppa di pesce
Fried	Fritto
Grilled (usually charcoal)	Alla griglia
Seafood salad	In insalata
Smoked	Affumicato
Stuffed	Ripieno

Meat

Boar	Cinghiale
Brain	Cervella
Braised meat with wine	Brasato
Chop	Costoletta
Duck	Anatra
Lamb	Agnello
Baby lamb	Abbacchio
Liver	Fegato
Pheasant	Fagiano
Pork roast	Arista

Rabbit	*Coniglio*
Steak	Bistecca
Sliced raw steak with sauce	Carpaccio
Mixed boiled meat	Bollito misto

Methods of Preparation

Dipped in eggs and crumbs and fried	. . . alla milanese
Grilled	. . . ai ferri
Grilled (usually charcoal)	. . . alla griglia
Raw, with lemon/egg sauce	. . . alla tartara
Roasted	. . . arrosto
Very rare	. . . al sangue
Well done	. . . ben cotta
With ham and cheese	. . . alla valdostana
With Parmesan cheese and tomatoes	. . . alla parmigiana

Vegetables

Artichokes	Carciofi
Asparagus	Asparagi
Beans	Fagioli
Brussels sprouts	Cavolini di Bruxelles
Cabbage	Cavolo
Carrots	Carote
Cauliflower	Cavolfiore
Cucumber	Cetriolo
Eggplants	Melanzane
Green beans	Fagiolini
Leeks	Porri
Lentils	Lenticchie
Lettuce	Lattuga
Mushrooms	Funghi
Onions	Cipolle
Peas	Piselli
Peppers	Peperoni
Potatoes	Patate
Roasted potatoes	*Patate arroste*
Boiled potatoes	*Patate bollite*
Fried potatoes	*Patate fritte*
Small, roasted potatoes	*Patatine novelle*
Mashed potatoes	*Purè di patate*
Radishes	Rapanelli
Salad	Insalata
vegetable	*mista*
green	*verde*
Spinach	Spinaci
Tomatoes	Pomodori
Zucchini	Zucchine

Sauces, Herbs, and Spices

Basil	Basilico
Bay leaf	Lauro
Chervil	Cerfoglio
Dill	Aneto
Garlic	Aglio
Hot dip with anchovies (for vegetables)	Bagna cauda
Marjoram	Maggiorana

Mayonnaise	Maionese
Mustard	Mostarda *or* senape
Oil	Olio
Parsley-based sauce	Salsa verde
Pepper	Pepe
Rosemary	Rosmarino
Tartar sauce	Salsa tartara
Vinegar	Aceto
White sauce	Besciamella

Cheeses

Fresh:	Caprino fresco
	Mascarpone
	Mozzarella
	Ricotta
Mild:	Caciotta
	Caprino
	Fontina
	Grana
	Provola
	Provolone dolce
	Robiola
	Scamorza
Sharp:	Asiago
	Gorgonzola
	Groviera
	Pecorino
	Provolone piccante
	Taleggio
	Toma

Fruits and Nuts

Almonds	Mandorle
Apple	Mela
Apricot	Albicocca
Banana	Banana
Blackberries	More
Black currant	Ribes nero
Blueberries	Mirtilli
Cherries	Ciliege
Chestnuts	Castagne
Coconut	Noce di cocco
Dates	Datteri
Figs	Fichi
Green grapes	Uva bianca
Black grapes	Uva nera
Grapefruit	Pompelmo
Hazelnuts	Nocciole
Lemon	Limone
Melon	Melone
Nectarine	Nocepesca
Orange	Arancia
Pear	Pera
Peach	Pesca
Pineapple	Ananas
Plum	Prugna/Susina
Prune	Prugna secca
Raisins	Uva passa

Raspberries	Lamponi
Red currant	Ribes
Strawberries	Fragole
Tangerine	Mandarino
Walnuts	Noci
Watermelon	Anguria Cocomero
Dried fruit	Frutta secca
Fresh fruit	Frutta fresca
Fruit salad	Macedonia di frutta

Desserts

Custard-filled pastry, with candied fruit	Cannoli
Ricotta-filled pastry shells with sugar glaze	Cannoli alla siciliana
Ice cream with candied fruit	Cassata
Ricotta-filled cake with sugar glaze	Cassata siciliana
Chocolate	Cioccolato
Cup of ice cream	Coppa gelato
Caramel custard	Creme caramel
Pie	Crostata
Fruit pie	Crostata di frutta
Ice cream	Gelato
Flaked pastry	Millefoglie
Chestnuts and whipped cream cake	Montebianco
Whipped cream	Panna montata
Pastries	Paste
Sherbet	Sorbetto
Chocolate-coated ice cream	Tartufo
Fruit tart	Torta di frutta
Apple tart	Torta di mele
Ice-cream cake	Torta gelata
Vanilla	Vaniglia
Egg-based cream with sugar and Marsala wine	Zabaione
Ice-cream filled cake	Zuccotto

Alcoholic Drinks

On the rocks	Con ghiaccio
Straight	Liscio
With soda	Con seltz

Beer	Birra
light/dark	*chiara/scura*
Bitter cordial	Amaro
Brandy	Cognac
Cordial	Liquore
Aniseed cordial	Sambuca
Martini	Cocktail Martini
Port	Porto
Vermouth	Vermut/Martini
Wine	Vino
blush	*rosé*
dry	*secco*
full-bodied	*corposo*
light	*leggero*
red	*rosso*
sparkling	*spumante*

sweet	*dolce*
very dry	*brut*
white	*bianco*
Light wine	Vinello
Bottle	Bottiglia
Carafe	Caraffa
Flask	Fiasco

Nonalcoholic Drinks

Mineral water	Acqua minerale
carbonated	*gassata*
still	*non gassata*
Tap water	Acqua naturale
Tonic water	Acqua tonica
Coffee with steamed milk	Cappuccino
Espresso	Caffè espresso
with milk	*macchiato*
decaffeinated	*decaffeinato*
lighter espresso	*lungo*
with cordial	*corretto*
Fruit juice	Succo di frutta
Hot chocolate	Cioccolata calda
Lemonade	Limonata
Milk	Latte
Orangeade	Aranciata
Tea	Tè
with milk/lemon	*col latte/col limone*
iced	*freddo*

Index

Fodor's Travel Guides

Available at bookstores everywhere, or call 1–800–533–6478, 24 hours a day.

U.S. Guides

Alaska

Arizona

Boston

California

Cape Cod, Martha's Vineyard, Nantucket

The Carolinas & the Georgia Coast

Chicago

Colorado

Florida

Hawaii

Las Vegas, Reno, Tahoe

Los Angeles

Maine, Vermont, New Hampshire

Maui

Miami & the Keys

New England

New Orleans

New York City

Pacific North Coast

Philadelphia & the Pennsylvania Dutch Country

The Rockies

San Diego

San Francisco

Santa Fe, Taos, Albuquerque

Seattle & Vancouver

The South

The U.S. & British Virgin Islands

The Upper Great Lakes Region

USA

Vacations in New York State

Vacations on the Jersey Shore

Virginia & Maryland

Waikiki

Walt Disney World and the Orlando Area

Washington, D.C.

Foreign Guides

Acapulco, Ixtapa, Zihuatanejo

Australia & New Zealand

Austria

The Bahamas

Baja & Mexico's Pacific Coast Resorts

Barbados

Berlin

Bermuda

Brazil

Brittany & Normandy

Budapest

Canada

Cancun, Cozumel, Yucatan Peninsula

Caribbean

China

Costa Rica, Belize, Guatemala

The Czech Republic & Slovakia

Eastern Europe

Egypt

Euro Disney

Europe

Europe's Great Cities

Florence & Tuscany

France

Germany

Great Britain

Greece

The Himalayan Countries

Hong Kong

India

Ireland

Israel

Italy

Japan

Kenya & Tanzania

Korea

London

Madrid & Barcelona

Mexico

Montreal & Quebec City

Morocco

Moscow & St. Petersburg

The Netherlands, Belgium & Luxembourg

New Zealand

Norway

Nova Scotia, Prince Edward Island & New Brunswick

Paris

Portugal

Provence & the Riviera

Rome

Russia & the Baltic Countries

Scandinavia

Scotland

Singapore

South America

Southeast Asia

Spain

Sweden

Switzerland

Thailand

Tokyo

Toronto

Turkey

Vienna & the Danube Valley

Yugoslavia

WHEREVER
YOU TRAVEL,
_H_ELP IS NEVER
FAR AWAY.

From planning your trip to providing travel assistance along the way, American Express® Travel Service Offices* are always there to help.

Bari 80-521-0022
Florence 55-50981
Genoa 10-561-241
Milan 2-720-03694
Padua 49-666-133
Rome 6-67641
Sorrento 81-807-2363
Venice 41-520-0844
Verona 45-800-9040

SARDINIA
Cagliari 70-653-256
Olbia 789-24327

SICILY
Catania 95-376-933
Palermo 91-587-144
Taormina 942-625-255